The American Critical Archives is a series of reference books that provide representative selections of contemporary reviews of the main works of major American authors. Specifically, each volume contains both full reviews and excerpts from reviews that appeared in newspapers and weekly and monthly periodicals, generally within a few months of the publication of the work concerned. There is an introductory historical overview by the volume editor, as well as checklists of additional reviews located but not quoted.

This book represents the first comprehensive collection of contemporary reviews of the writing of Edith Wharton from the 1890s until her death in 1937. Many of the reviews are reprinted from hard-to-locate contemporary newspapers and periodicals. In addition, lists of other reviews, not presented here, are provided. These materials document the response of the reviewers to specific works and indicate the development of Wharton's reputation as a novelist, short-story writer, travel writer, and autobiographer.

AMERICAN CRITICAL ARCHIVES 2
Edith Wharton: The Contemporary Reviews

The American Critical Archives

GENERAL EDITOR: M. Thomas Inge, Randolph-Macon College

Edith Wharton

The Contemporary Reviews

Edited by

James W. Tuttleton
New York University

Kristin O. Lauer
Fordham University

Margaret P. Murray
Fordham University

CAMBRIDGE
UNIVERSITY PRESS

Published by the Press Syndicate of the University of Cambridge
The Pitt Building, Trumpington Street, Cambridge CB2 1RP
40 West 20th Street, New York, NY 10011–4211, USA
10 Stamford Road, Oakleigh, Victoria 3166, Australia

First published 1992

Printed in the United States of America

Library of Congress Cataloging-in-Publication Data
Edith Wharton: the contemporary reviews / edited by James W. Tuttleton,
Kristin O. Lauer, Margaret P. Murray.
p.   cm—(The American critical archives)
Includes index.
ISBN 0–521–38319–6 (hc)
1. Wharton, Edith, 1862–1937—Criticism and interpretation.
I. Tuttleton, James W.   II. Lauer, Kristin O.
III. Murray, Margaret P.   IV. Series.
PS3545.H16Z6456   1992
813'.52—dc20   91–43206
CIP
A catalog record for this book is available from the British Library

ISBN 0–521–38319–6   hardback

Contents

Series Editor's Preface

The American Critical Archives series documents a part of a writer's career that is usually difficult to examine, that is, the immediate response to each work as it was made public on the part of reviewers in contemporary newspapers and journals. Although it would not be feasible to reprint every review, each volume in the series reprints a selection of reviews designed to provide the reader with a proportionate sense of the critical response, whether it was positive, negative, or mixed. Checklists of other known reviews are also included to complete the documentary record and allow access for those who wish to do further reading and research.

The editor of each volume has provided an introduction that surveys the career of the author in the context of the contemporary critical response. Ideally, the introduction will inform the reader in brief of what is to be learned by a reading of the full volume. The reader then can go as deeply as necessary in terms of the kind of information desired—be it about a single work, a period in the author's life, or the author's entire career. The intent is to provide quick and easy access to the material for students, scholars, librarians, and general readers.

When completed, the American Critical Archives should constitute a comprehensive history of critical practice in America, and in some cases England, as the writers' careers were in progress. The volumes open a window on the patterns and forces that have shaped the history of American writing and the reputations of the writers. These are primary documents in the literary and cultural life of the nation.

M. THOMAS INGE

Introduction

If, as Irving Howe suggested in 1962, literary critics were still trying to refute the claim that Edith Wharton (1862–1937) was a rich, clever, narrow, dated, bleak, and minor Henry James, and if, as Gore Vidal has remarked, Edith Wharton has been denied her rightful place in American letters because of her sex, class, and residence abroad, the explanation may be found in some of Mrs. Wharton's earliest reviewers, who trivialized her work as that of a mere woman, sneered at the elite class that was her material, and dismissed her as out of touch with America. This is indeed paradoxical, since—from the very beginning of her career—Mrs. Wharton was simultaneously recognized as a writer of exceptional literary distinction. To examine reviews of the kind reprinted in this volume is to recognize how remarkable, even if she irritated them, nearly all of her reviewers understood her to be. The key words and phrases that stand out in these reviews are illuminating. She was praised for her "clarity," "delicacy," "distinction," "chaste and unerring discrimination," "polish," "grace," "skillful, finished writing," "command of good English," and "mastery of language." Reviewers found remarkable her "profundity of comprehension," "fine intuition," "profound and often startling insight into the deeper things of life," and the exceptional power with which she brought "subjective reality . . . into the field of vision." Hers was "conscientious workmanship" performed with the "ease of a skilled craftsman," with a "just sense of proportion." Her work was, in short, "serious art."

Readers and reviewers alike also praised Mrs. Wharton's fiction for its penetrating moral analysis, incisive social criticism, historical understanding, and aesthetic power. She had an avid popular readership, was extensively and usually favorably reviewed, made a substantial fortune from fiction royalties, won the Pulitzer Prize in 1920, had many of her works translated, and experienced several theatrical or film productions of her work in her lifetime. After her death, however, her critical reputation declined sharply. This phenomenon is not uncommon in the history of critical reputations; but in Mrs. Wharton's case the decline was so steep that Patricia Plant, in concluding her 1962 dissertation, "The Critical Reception of Edith Wharton's Fiction in America and England with an Annotated Enumerative Bibliography of Wharton Criticism from 1900 to 1961," felt obliged to do battle with a pervasive but simplistic view that Mrs. Wharton, born in the Genteel Era, was distinctly "old-fashioned" and would never regain the esteem with which most of her contemporaries had regarded her.

Fortunately, from the vantage point of the 1990s, Mrs. Wharton's star is again in the ascendant. But it is worthwhile to examine the early reviews of Mrs. Wharton's work because nearly all of the major issues that have preoccupied recent criticism are present, in some form or other, in the work of her reviewers between 1898 and 1938. Looking at the history of Wharton reviewing, it is possible to discover three phases in the reception of her work.

In the first phase, between 1899 and 1905—from *The Greater Inclination* up to *The House of Mirth*—Mrs. Wharton was sometimes praised but usually criticized as a writer in the school of Henry James. The response to her work in this early period—in the reviews of *The Touchstone* (1900), *Crucial Instances* (1901), *Sanctuary* (1903), and *The Descent of Man* (1904)—often depended on the reviewer's opinion of James himself. For better or worse, Mrs. Wharton broke in upon the literary scene at the very moment when James's achievements, especially those of the "major phase," were being hotly debated by critics in both England and America; they either liked or did not like the moral complexities and stylistic involutions of the "Master" in this mandarin phase. She was thus caught up in, and at times victimized by, a controversy not of her own making. In April 1899, in *Literary World*, for example, John Barry attacked Mrs. Wharton's style as reproducing some of Henry James's worst faults. On May 13, he commented that it had come to his attention that she disliked these comparisons with James, and therefore he had reason to hope that her subsequent work would "not be marred by a slavish adherence to the methods of a very questionable literary model." In August, the *Critic* reviewer went even farther, initiating a prejudice that would harm her for more than half a century. The reviewer accused her of "plagiarism, or unconscious adaptation. . . . Nor is the suggestion," he argued, "merely one of method." He found her dependence on James "in very substance, even in titular phrase." The idea that she was a minor James still recurs in Wharton criticism, a point of view usually expressed by those who have not read much of either author.

Even so, there was another side to this question of Jamesian influence. The reviewer of *The Touchstone* for the *Atlantic Monthly* observed in 1900 that she who "has sat at the feet of Henry James" and "unquestionably learned much from him . . . would now do well to rise from her deferential attitude. Better things than he can inspire are, we believe, within the scope of her still widening possibilities." Likewise, although the *Bookman* noted the Jamesian influence in saying that "she has caught his latest manner," its reviewer found that "she has improved upon his workmanship and therefore she deserves a wholly independent criticism." The London *Academy* was even more complimentary to Wharton, at James's expense. Although the reviewer found her subjects Jamesian, he added that "though she is subtle, she is much less subtle than Mr. James and—may we utter it?—possibly more articulate." The *Athenæum* found Madame de Treymes to be "a more subtle study than any of the characters in Mr. James's novel [*The American*]". This debate so tended to eclipse other aspects of her work that by 1904 the *Academy* reviewer of *The Descent of Man* pulled out of it entirely with this bit of self-congratulation: "[Let] the present reviewer account it to himself for righteousness that he has omitted all allusion to the particular King Charles's head of Mrs. Wharton's reviewers in general."

The entire question of Jamesian influence—or, to put it another way, of Mrs. Wharton's originality as a writer—thereafter became such a recurrent theme of Wharton criticism that it was difficult to see it in terms of a transient historical problem in the literary consciousness of the fin de siècle. But as these reviews will suggest, James himself was so controversial that the *literary* relationship between these two friends could hardly have been judged objectively. This situation is all the more remarkable because Mrs. Wharton, in fact, did not like James's novels of the "Major Phase" and told their Scribner editor, William Crary Brownell, that she could not read them.

The second phase of Wharton criticism in the early reviews runs from 1905, with her best-seller, *The House of Mirth*, until 1920, with her Pulitzer Prize–winning novel, *The Age of Innocence*. The mere publication of Mrs. Wharton's *Valley of Decision* (1902), with its historical setting of eighteenth-century Italy, ought to have made plain that she was no mere disciple of Henry James. But with *The House of Mirth* there could no longer be a question as to originality or discipleship to James. Here was a work of independent power and literary distinction, an episodic social chronicle written to quite different specifications of form and, in its irony and social satire, resembling in no manifest way the involutions of consciousness and style of *The Wings of the Dove* or *The Golden Bowl*. Lily Bart was said by the *Literary Digest* reviewer to surpass George Eliot's Gwendolyn Harleth (in *Daniel Deronda*); and for the *Outlook* reviewer, the novel marked "the transition in Mrs. Wharton's career from the region of cultivated tastes and skill to that of free, direct, individual creation." James MacArthur, in *Harper's Weekly*, noting the "sanity and truth" of her "relentless arraignment of the conditions which she portrays," found the novel "the most timely and terrible commentary on the heartless and cynical outcome of a state of things we see all about us at present that could be conceived. [It] appeals like an inspiration, and comes with the authority of one who is a seer."

This triumph was followed by other novels nearly as great as *The House of Mirth*, or perhaps even greater, according to a number of reviewers. This is the period when Edith Wharton became, in the critical literature, the first lady of American letters, owing to such achievements as *Madame de Treymes* (1907), *The Fruit of the Tree* (1907), *The Hermit and the Wild Woman* (1908), *Tales of Men and Ghosts* (1910), *Ethan Frome* (1911), *The Reef*

(1912), *The Custom of the Country* (1913), *Xingu* (1916), *Summer* (1917), *The Marne* (1918), and her Pulitzer Prize–winning novel, *The Age of Innocence* (1920).

During this second phase of her reception (1905–20), other themes, which would tend to dominate later Wharton criticism, emerged or became more strongly accented. One of these themes involves Mrs. Wharton's status as a female writer and her portrayals of female characters. A great deal of sexist bias is manifest in the reviewers' comments—some of them positive, some negative. On the positive side, Aline Gorren, in the *Critic*, called for female writers to write of women with authority and looked to Mrs. Wharton "primarily for the genius with which she will bring to the surface the underground movements of women's minds." Mrs. Wharton was also praised in the *Academy* for her "sympathetic delineation of her heroine's character [that of Lily Bart], her acute analysis of a woman's mind," and the London *Saturday Review* praised Mrs. Wharton's "masterly study of the modern American woman, . . . spoilt and selfish, and yet withal intensely lovable." The lovableness of the heroine—or, to put it somewhat differently, the ability of the reader to identify with her—seemed to be a criterion of the acceptance of some of her works. When Mrs. Wharton created Undine Spragg, Henry Boynton complained in the *Nation* that she was a caricature with "nothing to attach the deeper sympathies of the reader." And the *Spectator* complained that Charity Royall in *Summer* was hard to comprehend because there was no "emotional arousal." In fact, throughout her career, Mrs. Wharton was to incur the charge, here made in reference to *Xingu*, that there was "something inhuman in the detachment of her method" and that "she has a peculiar talent for the dissection of disillusioned, unhappy, uncomfortable or disagreeable natures."

These comments on Mrs. Wharton's heroines and on the degree of the writer's closeness to, or detachment from, them have an exceptional resonance in view of the feminist movement both in the early twentieth century and today. It is worth remembering that Edith Wharton came into her own at a time when feminist arguments were gathering force, when debates raged hotly over whether women belonged in the home or outside in the larger world, and when the suffragists were clamoring for women's right to vote, which finally came in 1920. Attitudes, both for and against women's potentialities and achievements, color some of Mrs. Wharton's reviews. As early as 1903, the *Independent* reviewer criticized Kate Orme as unrealistic because she lacked the kind of "tender, stupid womanly sanity" of "normal women [whose] very obtuseness is a sort of healing power. They do not condone what is wrong about them, because they do not know and cannot imagine it." From there the reviewer passed on to Mrs. Wharton herself, who was attacked as one of those female writers who "do not demonstrate the growth of principles and manly stamina so much as . . . a beautiful tender sentimentality peculiar to women, whether they are writers, mothers or missionaries." Another instance of a sexist slant, yet this time made in Mrs. Wharton's personal favor, contrasting her to other women, was the *Academy* reviewer's praise of her control of her imagination, as a "quality rare in women writers." H. G. Dwight, in *Putnam's Monthly*, rejoiced in 1908 that Edith Wharton was not one of the "golden geese" (typical American female novelists) and argued that when G. R. Carpenter complained that she had "defeminised" and "denationalised" herself (in his notorious *Bookman* attack on *Italian Backgrounds*), he was stating "her case more flatteringly" than he intended, for she did not belong among the lamentable American lady "apostles of culture." Harry Thurston Peck, in the *Commercial Advertiser*, praised her in 1899 as having "the fine intuition of a woman with the firmness and precision of a man," and even her friend Henry James, in a review collected in *Notes on Novelists* (1914), pointedly celebrated the way in which, in her fiction, "the masculine conclusion" so tended to "crown the feminine observation." Mrs. Wharton herself played into this ambiguous public discussion of the coexistence in her of masculine and feminine literary powers. "I conceive my subjects like a man," she told one of her correspondents, "that is, rather more architectonically & dramatically than most women—then execute them like a woman," so as to provide "the small incidental effects that women have always excelled in, the episodical characterization, I mean." Such was the prejudice against female writers, on the part of some reviewers, that she felt obliged to represent herself as possessing the powers of each sex.

During this second phase of her critical reception, reviewers also noticed, for better or worse, her birth and breeding and her attention, in the fiction, to class, convention, and social barriers. Very early in her career, in noting in *Literary World* that she was socially well connected in that city (her husband, Teddy, was of the well-to-do Boston Whartons), John Barry suggested that she might be able to write "studies of the leisure class such as Howells is asking for in *Literature*." And after the success of *The House of Mirth*, reviewers quickly tried to describe her subject as limited to society and manners. Although *Ethan Frome* was heralded as a great work of art, it was a puzzle to many reviewers who agreed with Katherine Mansfield that the manners and mores of Old New York "suit Mrs. Wharton's talent to a nicety." Carl Van Doren, in the *Nation*, called *The Age of Innocence* a "masterly achievement," for "she knows fashionable New York well in contrast to others who write about it." All of this is quite true, but Mrs. Wharton never appreciated reviewers or others who tried to circumscribe her imagination within one setting. When Henry James told Mrs. Wharton to avoid the Franco-American subject and advised her sister-in-law, Mary Cadwalader Jones, that Mrs. Wharton "*must* be tethered in native pastures, even if it reduce her to a back-yard in New York," the novelist replied with the New England settings of *The Fruit of the Tree*, *Ethan Frome*, and *Summer* and the

Franco-American settings of *Madame de Treymes* and *The Custom of the Country*.

But other reviewers were perturbed, on the ground of class bias, at this rich, well-born, highly cultivated novelist. Olivia Howard Dunbar of the *Critic* termed *The House of Mirth* a "fastidiously conducted literary raid," and the *Literary Digest* found "a certain unconscious condescension" in *The Fruit of the Tree*, arising from "the results of [Mrs. Wharton's] tradition and training." *Summer*, with its New England setting and culturally impoverished families, led Francis Hackett to accuse her in the *New Republic* of "going slumming among souls." Henry Boynton protested this charge, but admitted that Mrs. Wharton had "come perilously near being the idol of snobs." When it became clear in *French Ways and Their Meaning* (1919) that Mrs. Wharton had expatriated because she found America culturally and socially deficient, the indictment that she was an aristocrat with condescending attitudes toward the common people spilled over into a charge of virtual un-Americanism. In discussing that book, the *New Republic* reviewer remarked: "Some American snobs adopt England; others adopt France. . . . Can it be possible that America will survive this apologist and France this defender?"

Yet another charge against Mrs. Wharton arose in this second phase of her career, namely, that her works are bleak, disagreeable, and lacking in moral uplift. Trained in the tradition of Howellsian realism, yet averse to his claim that the writer ought to deal with the "smiling aspects of life, which are the more American," Mrs. Wharton offended a good many reviewers who sought in literature images of idealism, nobility, and heroism. Dunbar found *The House of Mirth* seriously lacking in contrasts, with "figures . . . all of one exceedingly unpleasant tone"; hence the book "cannot be accepted as a sober and comprehensive interpretation of life." The *Outlook* reviewer also objected to the "touch of futility [which] often lies on the people who move in Mrs. Wharton's novels; they are caught in a tangle which a little vigor of will would cut with a stroke." The *Spectator* criticized *The Hermit and the Wild Woman* (1908) for its lack of contrast, its unrelieved failure, disappointment, and disillusionment. It was not until the appearance of *Ethan Frome* in 1911, however, that this complaint came to overshadow other considerations. Most objections to the darkness of her work focused on the ending of the story. The London *Saturday Review* argued that she should have let Mattie and Ethan die, for the ending has "no motive we can discover." The reviewer also argued that "there are things too terrible in their failure to be told humanly by creature to creature." The *Bookman* likewise found it "hard to forgive the utter remorselessness" of the ending, citing "art for art's sake" as her only "justification." And although the *Nation* reviewer was positive in his assessment, he concluded of *Ethan Frome* that "it is to be hoped when Mrs. Wharton writes again she will bring her talent to bear on normal people and situations."

Some reviewers even equated her tragic endings with a lack of realism. Thus, the *Nation*, in reviewing *The Reef*, complained of the "blind alley" themes, from which there is no proper exit, dealing with problems of which "all possible solutions are equally unsatisfactory and undesirable"; and he claimed that Mrs. Wharton was "addicted" to them. Also speaking of *The Reef*, the *Sun* reviewer defined it as "a bitter, disheartening, sordid story and we could wish that Mrs. Wharton would look on brighter and nobler aspects of life." The New York *Times* reviewer compared her plots to "vivisection" of the characters as she "diabolically" arranged events to conspire against them. *Summer* was sometimes seen as "sordid" and "depressing," and Francis Hackett found Mrs. Wharton to be without redeeming humor, calling the landscape of *Xingu and Other Stories* "somewhat acid, cold and bleak." It is worth remembering that Mrs. Wharton was writing in an era when Stephen Crane, Frank Norris, Theodore Dreiser, and other figures in the history of American literary naturalism had made their mark—and had their defenders. But in the review media, a morally uplifting spirit seemed to be required. Even the English writer Katherine Mansfield asked, "Does Mrs. Wharton expect us to grow warm in a gallery where the temperature is so sparklingly cold?"

The third phase of Edith Wharton's critical reception was the period from 1920 to 1938. After the high-water mark of the 1921 Pulitzer Prize, Edith Wharton published eight completed novels, four novellas collected as *Old New York*, four collections of short fiction, a volume of ghost stories, a volume of poetry, an autobiography, and a book on the craft of fiction. (*The Buccaneers* appeared incomplete, posthumously, in 1938.) During this period there were, of course, many positive reviews. In 1922, Katherine Fullerton Gerould announced matter-of-factly in the *New York Times Book Review* that "there is no doubt that, soberly speaking, [Mrs. Wharton] is the best of living American novelists" and that *The Glimpses of the Moon* (1922) was her "masterpiece." Apropos of *A Son at the Front* (1923), William Lyon Phelps observed in the *Literary Digest International Book Review* that in that novel "there is nothing trivial; the subject has all the dignity of tragedy, and the style rises to the level of the theme. It must certainly rank high among our novelists' achievements." With respect to *Old New York* (1924), Lloyd Morris in The New York *Times* remarked that "The Old Maid" "affirms Mrs. Wharton's absolute command over the elements of her art, and again reveals that capacity to achieve flawless beauty which she has too often been content to deny." In 1925, Louise Maunsell Field, writing in the *Literary Digest International Book Review*, remarked: "That *The Mother's Recompense* is one of Mrs. Wharton's best novels, few will deny," and she went on to rate it above *The Age of Innocence* (because its tragedy "transcended" place and class). Likewise, Mary Shirley wrote in *Outlook*, "No recent novel of Mrs. Wharton's has impressed us so much [as *Hudson River Bracketed* (1929)]. It is beautifully written." And the *Times Literary Supplement* reviewer remarked that in *The Gods Arrive* "the social scenes are presented with her customary brilliance and finish." Mrs. Wharton, then, continued to command the respect of many of her reviewers.

Yet these were also the years of the disputed later novels, the years when critical attitudes and prejudices, some of which we have traced as far back as 1899, became solidified into a negative Wharton formula that survived into the 1970s. The great praise for her social satire was now translated into condemnation that she was old-fashioned, trapped in a lost era, out of touch with America, and too bitter to deal objectively with the postwar world. Many reviewers were still enthusiastic, but a disrespectful note came to be more and more in evidence. Never again were she and her reviewers to enjoy a community of interests that would give her the largely unalloyed positive critical attention she had earlier enjoyed. Each of the critical reservations that emerged in the earlier phases of her career became rigidified in this period. The reviews became formulaic, repeating old objections to the point of striking the dominant tone for half a century, and increasingly her artistry, psychological insight, grasp of character, and social criticism came under attack.

Oddly enough, during this last phase, Henry James's career began to be rehabilitated by the critics, and the comparisons of Mrs. Wharton's work with his resurfaced. Because of his recovered reputation, she was again cast into his shadow. Even Rebecca West used James, in her 1922 *New Statesman* review of *The Glimpses of the Moon*, to disparage Mrs. Wharton, saying that Mrs. Wharton wanted to "write books that are exactly like the books of Henry James," but since the subtle Jamesian method was not suited to explore Mrs. Wharton's environment or her subject—which West narrowed to the establishment of the American plutocracy—Mrs. Wharton had imitated James with a "deadly sterility." The novel was, according to West, a "dead thing." On the other hand, even if a Wharton work was praiseworthy, a reviewer might suggest that she owed her success to James. Frances Newman, in a 1926 commendation of *Here and Beyond*, in the *New York Evening Post Literary Review*, remarked on Mrs. Wharton's good fortune in having sat at James's feet, and asserted that *Madame de Treymes* and *The Age of Innocence* could not have been written if James had died in childhood.

By 1937, James had been reestablished as the "Master" and the arbiter of fictional standards. In reviewing the "near-masterpieces" in Edith Wharton's *Ghosts*, the Manchester *Guardian* asserted that James would have approved of them. But in discussing *The World Over* (1936), Katherine Simonds found in Mrs. Wharton's stories the "thinness of an echo" of James; they were "not true," while James's more universal tales remained true. And after *The Buccaneers* was published, Louise Bogan remarked in 1938 in the *Nation* that the novel was "dead at heart" since Henry James's concept of form had become in Mrs. Wharton's work mere plot. She argued that "Wharton's mildly ironic description of life in the great country houses" failed in comparison with

James's "true dissection." "We love," she contended, "the living people [of James] and merely watch the puppets [of Mrs. Wharton]."

With respect to her status as a female writer and her characterization of women, we find in the third phase a number of positive accounts of her heroines. Grace Frank in the *Saturday Review of Literature*, for example, called Judith Wheater of *The Children* (1928) an "altogether lovable child," one of Mrs. Wharton's "most unusual and delightful creations"; and Sherwin Lawrence Cook praised Judith as "a fine fighter and a happy spirit." But during this postwar period, in which the fiction was charged with a biting satire against Jazz Age and Depression-era follies, her characters were often called unconvincing or mere puppets. Clifton Fadiman argued in the New York *Evening Post* in 1928 that it was "impossible to believe in Mrs. Wharton's divorcees and precocious hotel children and ex-movie-star marchionesses," and the *Independent* reviewer criticized her satire as "shafts of implied indignation" that "pierce oaten dummies."

Moreover, a number of reviewers alleged again the inadequacy of her understanding of men characters. The female writer simply didn't understand men. Her men were sometimes felt to be mere "specimens"; Vance Weston, in *Hudson River Bracketed*, was called "only the husk of a character" by one reviewer; and V. S. Pritchett in the *Spectator* termed him "perhaps more of a problem than a man"; likewise, the *Independent* reviewer claimed that Mrs. Wharton could create nothing but a male type "uninteresting" to men. The reviewer of *Old New York* for the Springfield *Republican* asserted that a "few deft touches from a masculine hand would set him [Hayley Delane] right." Furthermore, the old theme of Mrs. Wharton's "masculine qualities" also extended into the postwar criticism. While a number of reviewers objected to yet another war novel in *A Son at the Front* (1923)—published five years after the armistice, when the topic seemed a dead issue—others were uneasy at the female writer's dealing with two central male figures, the young combatant and his father. It did not seem to matter that Mrs. Wharton had toured the front, seen combat firsthand, and written about it in *Fighting France: From Dunkerque to Belfort* (1915) and *The Marne* (1918). Warfare appeared to be a "man's subject."

One of the most striking aspects of her reception as a female writer, in this third phase, again related to her detachment from her characters, even her "coldness." References to the temperature of her work are evident from 1899 onward, but the growing dismay over Mrs. Wharton's biting postwar satires and an alleged "misanthropy" suggest that many reviewers continued to demand "sympathy" in the tone of a female author and a sympathetic treatment of character, especially female character. (In later years, Mrs. Wharton was to be charged with misogyny.) Yet, when Mrs. Wharton did reveal empathy with, or an understanding of, her heroines (e.g., Mrs. Clephane in *The Mother's Recompense* or Judith Wheater in *The Children*), she was condemned for "feminine" qualities, typically in the objection that she was writing merely women's magazine fiction, with happy endings for sympathetic heroines—in short, hackwork. On the other hand, in discussing Halo Tarrant in *The Gods Arrive* (1932), Louise Maunsell Field, in the *North American Review*, objected that Mrs. Wharton evaded every issue and that the only solution she could find to the love affair was to make Halo an honest woman in true eighteenth-century fashion. Isabel Paterson, in *New York Herald Tribune Books*, found Halo "a complete embodiment of the sentimental nineteenth century ideal of woman as the inspiration of genius, mistress and school mistress in one. If such a being ever existed, her function vanished with the passing of the century."

Those who applauded the later novels, in this third phase, often did so because they gave reviewers what they expected of Edith Wharton. For instance, the Springfield *Republican* praised *The Glimpses of the Moon* for its "vivid transcription of one phase of contemporary life," and the *Literary Digest* found that "no tract on the vanity of riches could be more forcible than the picture she has given of rich idlers who are a blot on their country." Carl Van Doren, in the *Nation*, found "her accustomed touches of social caricature" in the novel, and the London *Bookman* proclaimed that she could describe parasitic people better than any other author could. But in this third phase, what best characterized the negative reviews of Mrs. Wharton was her status as the grande dame of American letters who had moved to France, away from her natural material (New York society), and had become a Francophile who wrote biting satires about millionaires and the smart set, material deemed irrelevant to the experience of nearly all of her readers (especially in the Depression years). Mrs. Wharton's *age* came increasingly into question in the era of flaming youth, and she was spoken of frequently as an old-fashioned historian of manners whose retrospectives in works like *Old New York* lay outside contemporary culture and concerns. Certainly, Robert Morss Lovett's *Edith Wharton* (1925), in calling her old-fashioned and class-bound, did great damage to her reputation—at the price of an oversimplification of her diverse creative interests. This version of her history—as a cold, aloof, detached, cultured, hardly American cosmopolite—dominated criticism until the 1970s, when Mrs. Wharton's private papers became available and when R. W. B. Lewis wrote her definitive biography, with its stunning account of her passionate love affair with Morton Fullerton.

Yet, ironically, she was also both praised and condemned in these later years for a new mellowness after *The Age of Innocence*, critics pointing out a warmer, more sympathetic tone. But since it contradicted the fixed image of her coldness, many attributed it to materialistic concerns: She was writing for slick women's magazines merely to make money. If she abandoned the authorial detachment for which she had earlier been condemned, and wrote such pointedly moral novels about our social failings as *The Children, Twilight*

Sleep, and *The Glimpses of the Moon*, it was termed the sermonizing and carping of an old woman at war with the modern world. If she abandoned the dark, ironic, or tragic dénouements of her earlier fiction, which some critics had been condemning for years, and if she provided happier resolutions to the fiction, critics often termed her romantic, unrealistic, sentimental, or (again their favorite word) old-fashioned.

In typing Mrs. Wharton principally as a historian of manners of New York high society, many reviewers were consciously or unconsciously restricting her to the material they thought most interesting or acceptable—or to a social class they wished to attack. Henry Seidel Canby, in praising *Old New York* in the *Saturday Review of Literature*, remarked that "she should be urged to send her imagination home more often." But Dorothy Foster Gilman, reviewing *Twilight Sleep* (1927) in the Boston *Evening Transcript*, pinpoints the problem. Mrs. Wharton, she noted, was a "writer who steadfastly remained in the walk of life to which she has been called, by Deity and others. Having selected good society as the material from which her stories were to be fashioned," she has "told us with magnificent taste and fine reticence all we ought to know about well bred people at home and abroad." Gilman asserted that an "afternoon spent with Mrs. Wharton's literary creations," to many readers, was of "more value than a year devoted to the Vogue Book of Etiquette."

All of this is, no doubt, true (although it ignores works like *Ethan Frome* and *Summer*). But Gilman goes on to say that, in *Twilight Sleep*, Mrs. Wharton deserted her class with "disastrous effects," resulting in a "curious mist" obscuring not living characters but "puppets." The Jazz Age inanities, so scathingly satirized in some of her novels of the 1920s, led Edmund Wilson to remark in the *New Republic* that her residence abroad had made her novels "a little thin" and that her America was "shadowy" and "synthetic" because she had "lived so long abroad." Likewise, Louis Bromfield claimed in the *New York Evening Post Literary Review* that Wharton "neither understands nor wants to understand any save those who have titles or are in some way even vaguely part of old New York"—a comment that could have been made only by one who had not read *The Fruit of the Tree*, *Summer*, or "Bunner Sisters," among others. Perhaps the most typical of left-wing Depression-era complaints about her work was Newton Arvin's remark in 1934 in the *New Republic* that she would have "towered higher in American letters" if she could have overcome the obstacles of her class and her consequent vision of the world.

Comments like those of Bromfield and Arvin indicate how much some of the older reviewers had forgotten about Mrs. Wharton's career. And of course, some in the younger generation of reviewers never took the trouble to read her earlier works. Thus, the poet Louise Bogan could surprisingly assert in the *Nation* that, except in *Ethan Frome*, Mrs. Wharton "based her values not upon a free and rich feeling for life but on a feeling for decorum and pre-Wall

Street merchant respectability"—a remark that nullifies Lily Bart's yearning for the "Republic of the Spirit," Charity Royall's passion, Newland Archer's longing for freedom and love as represented by Ellen Olenska, Judith Wheater's love for her siblings, and Vance Weston's passion for the creative life. Edmund Wilson was truer to Mrs. Wharton's grand design when, in reviewing *The Buccaneers* for the *New Republic* in 1938, he singled out the heroine, Laura Testvalley, remarking the "peculiar appropriateness and felicity in the fact that Edith Wharton should have left as the last human symbol of her fiction this figure who embodies the revolutionary principle implicit in all her work."

Edith Wharton was indeed a revolutionary artist, though not precisely in the sense Edmund Wilson meant. She was revolutionary in that she did not hesitate to subject to moral and social criticism a number of the attitudes and unthinking habits of her fellow Americans both at home and abroad—the soul-deadening constraints of outmoded convention in the elite, the crass disrespect for tradition grotesquely visible in heartland America, the materialism that fueled the social machine and warped genuine human values, hedonism at all levels in the frenetic search for pleasure, cultural rootlessness in the provinces of America and in Jazz Age Europe, the obsession of American men with business and their leaving of "culture" to women, the failure of the education of the American woman for a life other than that of wife and mother, the impoverishment of the lives of married women once they had tied the knot (hence the failure of the family and its impact on children), the comparative absence of the aesthetic sense in America, and the low esteem in which Americans held their artists and intellectuals. In working out these themes, Mrs. Wharton exhibited a faithfulness to the actualities of life in her time that made her a forceful voice in the school of ironic and satiric realism, while her understanding of the social and psychological pressures that circumscribe our existence showed the darker implications of her scientific understanding. She was regarded by the modernist critics of the 1920s and 1930s as distinctly old-fashioned because she practiced and defended the realist novel while taking a dim view of the slice-of-life naturalism and stream-of-consciousness fluidity of some of her contemporaries.

In 1936, *Time* magazine summarized popular opinion in observing that "to the eyes of the younger generation, her polite and cultivated formality might well seem quaintly behind the times." But from our current perspective, both the literary naturalism and modernist experimentalism of that younger generation have now also receded into a past literary history where they stand on a plane no higher than that on which the realist novels of Howells, James, and Wharton stand. And if her novels seemed nostalgic to some of her younger contemporaries, her contemporaries' experimental novels now seem to us equally susceptible to nostalgia (if that is the feeling we wish to entertain for the literary production of the avant-garde writers of the 1920s and 1930s). Can we any longer rightly entertain a prejudice against the realist novel of the type she wrote on the ground that it is more old-fashioned than the experimental writing? It seems not. Since the realist novel has continued into our own time (in the triumphs of writers as diverse as Scott Fitzgerald, Ernest Hemingway, Saul Bellow, James Baldwin, John Cheever, Louis Auchincloss, John Updike, and Tom Wolfe), generational prejudice dissolves in the presence of the central aesthetic question: How well did Mrs. Wharton practice the art she elected to pursue?

As these reviews make plain, Mrs. Wharton was understood by her contemporary reviewers to be an exceptional artist, perhaps the best female novelist of her time, perhaps even the best American novelist. If this early estimate seems excessive, it is worth remembering that, in 1978, Gore Vidal remarked in "Of Writers and Class: In Praise of Edith Wharton" (*Atlantic Monthly*) that, to his mind, "Henry James and Edith Wharton are the two great American masters of the novel." This point of view, which has many adherents, suggests that the early reviewers' positive estimates have not been quite obliterated by the leftist resentment of her work in the 1930s, by the coming of subsequent writers, or by changing tastes in literary creation and criticism. Certainly, the emergence of an articulate feminism in the past twenty years has given Mrs. Wharton's exploration of what it means to be a woman—to be oneself as a woman, to be a woman in relation to men, and to be a woman in relation to society—a relevance more perennial than transient. There, of course, recur nowadays the old charges, for example, that of her coldness and detachment in dealing with her characters. (Janet Malcolm has bizarrely savaged Mrs. Wharton in "The Woman Who Hated Women" in the November 16, 1986 *New York Times Book Review*. Apparently to satirize women, and not men only, is, for Malcolm, to be misogynistic.) But the many new reprints of Mrs. Wharton's novels and stories, the development of new critical perspectives on her work in books and articles, and the many papers and panels at literary conferences suggest that readers today find that Edith Wharton still speaks to and about women in a compelling way. And of course, her achievement as a female writer stands as a model of what the feminine imagination can accomplish.

But setting aside these themes for the moment, we should note that Edith Wharton was also praised by her contemporaries—and is valued now—for those qualities that make her an artist of the first order: the aesthetic form of her greatest novels and stories in the irresistibility of their structure and plotting; her creation of memorable characters like Lily Bart, Ethan Frome, Charity Royall, and Newland Archer—characters who are alive with passions, feelings, and ideas that we can recognize as expressive of human nature in its rich variety; her convincing re-creation of the social worlds in which these characters move and interact; the profundity of her insight into human motivations and action; her astonishing grasp of ideas and of the appropriate dramatic forms in which they can be fictionally rendered; her insight into the operations of society itself and the limitations of social experience everywhere; her incisive wit; her sense of humor; her wickedly observant eye; her satirical gift in disposing of the vain and foolish. Among storytellers, she has few equals in America. And finally there is her style. A style inseparable from her themes and forms, it is far more than correct grammar or good English. It is compounded of her intelligence, her learning, her insight and understanding, but it is also compounded of a feeling for language and its possibilities that makes for felicity in the reading experience. Mrs. Wharton's earliest reviewers register these felicities in the pages that follow, as will most readers who turn to her fiction.

A Note on
the Selections

This volume offers a representative selection of reviews and excerpts from newspapers and other periodicals that is designed to provide an overview of the contemporaneous critical reception of the American novelist, poet, essayist, travel writer, literary critic, and short-story writer Edith Wharton (1862–1937).

The sources of these reviews and excerpts—since Mrs. Wharton was an expatriate living in France with a wide English readership—are American, French, and British newspapers and magazines of literary criticism and cultural commentary. The selections herein represent critical estimates of her individual books as each appeared, year by year. The only volume by Edith Wharton never to be reviewed, to our knowledge, was her first, *Verses*, privately published in Newport, Rhode Island, in 1878, when she was sixteen. In any case, by reading the reviews of her published work in chronological order, it is possible to form a trustworthy conception of the development of her reputation among her contemporaries.

Since Mrs. Wharton was a prolific and much reviewed author, not every review could, of course, be reprinted here. All of the known reviews that could not, for reasons of space, be included are listed after the reviews of each of her volumes. In some cases, reviews have been cut to eliminate repetitive plot summaries or digressions. In other cases, we have reprinted all of the known reviews of an individual book, and therefore no list of unreprinted reviews is appended. No claim as to the completeness of these lists is made, since long-forgotten items are still being turned up in many little-known (and even a few well-known but still unindexed) periodicals.

Each of the reprinted reviews has been selected for its cogency, persuasiveness, and importance in shaping Edith Wharton's reputation. It goes without saying, then, that major publications—like the *New York Times Book Review* or the *Times Literary Supplement*—are frequently represented. But in the case of controversial books with a "local" setting, such as *Ethan Frome* or *Summer*, an effort has been made to represent the regional reaction in less extensively circulated newspapers like the Springfield *Republican* or the Hartford

Courant. Wherever a critical argument has developed over a particular book, we have tried to give a fuller than ordinary sampling of opinion. We have also tried to give ampler space to the fictional works felt to be Mrs. Wharton's major achievements. Even so, Mrs. Wharton wrote in a variety of genres, each crucial instance of which merits coverage herein; and the exceptionally large oeuvre to be dealt with has required us to sacrifice some reviews of, for example, *The Age of Innocence* so that such lesser-known works as *The Decoration of Houses* and *Fighting France* could receive some attention. We have also tried to reprint notices by reviewers who were already or who later came to be important voices on the literary scene, for example, Louise Bogan, Henry Seidel Canby, E. M. Forster, Graham Greene, Henry James, Edwin Muir, J. Middleton Murry, Seán O'Faoláin, William Troy, Carl Van Doren, Rebecca West, and Edmund Wilson. Indeed, Mrs. Wharton was quite fortunate in the intellectual quality of most of her reviewers, whether anonymous or well known.

During the course of Edith Wharton's long and productive career, a few interviews with the author were published, and of course biographical accounts and essays in literary criticism were devoted to her with greater and greater regularity in her later lifetime. Although these had an effect on her reputation with her contemporaries, they have not been included in the present volume. Nor have we included posthumous reviews of Mrs. Wharton's *reprinted* works, of which, since her lifetime, there have been many. Finally, this collection does not reprint or list the many books and articles of biography and literary criticism that have appeared in great numbers since her death. A full list of them may be found in *Edith Wharton: An Annotated Secondary Bibliography* (New York: Garland, 1990), compiled by Kristin O. Lauer and Margaret P. Murray. Instead, in this volume, we have endeavored to supply a selection of contemporaneous reviews on which a just estimate of Mrs. Wharton's reputation, during her lifetime, may be formed.

Acknowledgments

The editors wish to thank the following newspapers, journals, and individuals for permission to reprint reviews: *America*, for "Reviews." *The Atlantic Monthly*, for "The Atlantic Bookshelf" and "The Bookshelf"; reprinted with the permission of *The Atlantic Monthly*. *The Catholic World*, for "French Ways and Their Meaning," "*Here and Beyond*," and "*The World Over*." Kraus Reprint, A Division of the Kraus Organization, Ltd., for "*The Glimpses of the Moon*." *The Nation*, for "An Elder America," "A Country without a Guidebook," "The American Spirit," "Cable and Fine Wire," "Fiction Briefs," "Short Stories by Novelists," "Flower of Manhattan," and "*The Decoration of Houses*." *The New Republic*, for "A Page of Fiction," "*A Son at the Front*," "*Old New York*," "New Novels by Old Hands," "Short Stories," "*Twilight Sleep*," "Recent Fiction," "Notes on Novels," "The Short Story Muddles On," "False Gods," "*The Age of Innocence*," and "The Revolutionary Governess." New York Post Corporation, for "Our America," "The Incidence of War," and "The Innocence of Age." *The New York Times*, for "As Mrs. Wharton Sees Us," "Mrs. Wharton's New House of Mirth," "Sons and Parents at the Front," "Mrs. Wharton Discusses the Art of Fiction," "Mrs. Wharton Brings *The House of Mirth* Up to Date," "Mrs. Wharton's Finely Fashioned Tales in *Here and Beyond*," "Mrs. Wharton's Latest Novel Has a Mellow Beauty...," "Six Months' Fiction," "Humor and Satire Enliven Mrs. Wharton's Novel...," "Mrs. Wharton Tilts at Society," "Mrs. Wharton Probes a Social Period...," "New Short Stories by Edith Wharton," "Mrs. Wharton Recalls an Era...," "Mrs. Wharton's New Stories...," "Edith Wharton's Unfinished Novel and Other Recent Fiction"; copyright © 1920, 1922, 1923, 1926, 1927, 1928, 1932, 1933, 1934 by the New York Times Company; reprinted by permission. *The New Yorker*, for "Dearest Edith"; reprinted by permission of *The New Yorker*. *North American Review*, for "New Books Revisited," "An Age of Innocence," and "The Modest Novelist." Omni Publications International, Ltd., for "Stories of Our Past," "*The World Over*," "The Life and Art of Edith Wharton," "Pathos Versus Tragedy," "Grave Tales," "Granules from an Hour-Glass," "Edith Wharton's Unfinished Novel," "Character Studies," "History of an Artist," "In the Willow Pattern," "Bittersweet," and "The New Books." *Publishers Weekly*, for "Were the Seventies Sinless?"; reprinted from the October 16, 1920, issue

THE DECORATION OF HOUSES

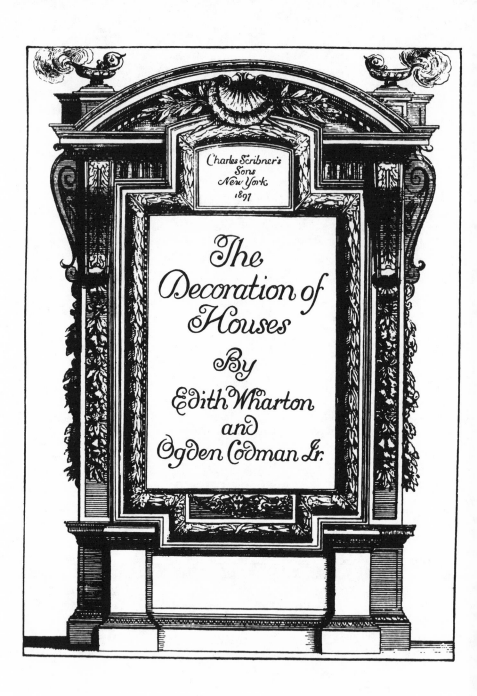

Charles Scribner's
Sons
New York
1897

The
Decoration of
Houses
By
Edith Wharton
and
Ogden Codman Jr.

Review of *The Decoration of Houses*, *Nation*, 65 (16 December 1897), 485

One opens a new book on decoration with a weary anticipation, remembering how much has been lately written on the subject for Americans, and to how little purpose; but now the whole style and practice of decoration has changed, and the teaching of the last generation has become obsolete. *The Decoration of Houses*, a handsome, interesting, and well-written book, not only is an example of the recent reversion to quasi-classic styles and methods, but signalizes the complete reaction that has thrown to the winds, even before the public discovered it, perhaps, the lately accepted doctrines of constructive virtue, sincerity, and the beauty of use. The authors take the new ground uncompromisingly, snap their fingers at sincerity, have no horror of shams, and stand simply on proportion, harmony of lines, and other architectural qualities. Any *"trompe l'œil* is permissible in decorative design," they say, "if it gives an impression of pleasure." To this have we already come; yet it seems not to have produced harmony between the outside and the inside of their volume.

The thread of their discussion is historical. Its fifty illustrations, taken from Italian, French, and English interiors, with a somewhat omnivorous appetite, are of various interest; but the book is the fruit of study, and of a larger knowledge of examples than has commonly been the case with its predecessors. It is aimed, not at professional readers, but at the public, whom it instructs with many intelligent criticisms and sensible directions, calling their attention to artistic aspects of decoration which have been neglected by writers of the last dispensation. It touches the root of present difficulty when it says in the preface, that "the vulgarity of current decoration has its source in the indifference of the wealthy to architectural fitness." But to the authors, architectural fitness means agreeable proportions and combination of lines and no more.

The temptation of the literature that we have left behind was that any ready-witted writer could discourse magisterially about decoration; and, inasmuch as his material was pure theory, it called for neither experience nor knowledge, nor yet for artistic or technical acquirement; in truth, after the beginning, the writers were mainly literary men and amateurs. Nevertheless there were valuable truths in their writings, and principles which, under due limitation, should have infused freshness, vitality, and manliness into decorative work. If these have been forgotten before they have borne their due fruit, the fruit may have been in the narrowness, vehemence, and want of technical enlightenment with which they were urged. But whether we are morally wise, or historically, the things we need for decorative work are taste and instinct for form—qualities which still wait their development among Americans. Till these are evolved, we must either intrust ourselves to professional hands, or be left to vibrate between the diets of dilettanti on the one hand and doctrinaires on the other.

"Hints for Home Decoration," *Critic*, 32 (8 January 1898), 20

Progress in ideas regarding the beauty and fitness of the ordering of house interiors is registered by the appearance of a book like this. Hitherto, such works have been of a general nature, covering much ground and teaching general elementary facts concerning the adornment of the home. Into the finer shades of house decoration it was not thought necessary or wise to go, because the public was not ready for it. There was still much education in such matters required before people should become knowing and fastidious enough to pick and choose among the abundant material gathered and still being gathered in the countries where specimens of old and modern decoration worthy of adaptation or direct imitation abound.

The salient feature of the present work is the effort of the authors to separate the decoration of palaces and grand houses from that of simpler residences and homes, thereby keeping always in the mind of the reader the needfulness of adapting decoration to the place where it is to remain. The great majority of people who may consult a book of the kind are not owners of palaces, but when they travel in Europe it is palaces for the most part which they examine and even if the palace contains apartments and suites arranged for the simple requirements of a family, the tourist rarely sees them, because they are not supposed to care for them, or because only the gala rooms and chambers are open to the public.

The illustrations, however, are largely drawn from just such magnificent places of temporary abode or festal use, so that to a person turning over the leaves of this book a false idea of its contents is conveyed. Not that the text ignores the decoration of splendid interiors. There is stuff here for the delectation and instruction of those who propose to build the most elaborate Newport palace-villa or the most modern of highly decorated hotels. But the authors thoroughly appreciate that the ordinary well-to-do person is not by way of decorating anything so costly, and have arranged their materials to suit him rather than the millionaire.

A note struck at the outset vibrates through the whole book, and it is a strong and true note. The decoration of an interior should harmonize with—nay, it should naturally be based upon—the architecture of the building. The discordance of decoration with architecture found so constantly nowadays is traced to the variety of styles demanded of the architect. "Before 1800 the decorator called upon to treat the interior of a house invariably found a suitable background prepared for his work, while much in the way of detail was intrusted to the workmen, who were trained in certain traditions, instead of being called upon to carry out in each new house the vagaries of a different designer." The leading part played by architecture in the proper decoration of an interior is emphasized; the authors go so far as to forbid the hanging of pictures tilted outward from the wall because these no longer take their true position as part of the architectural decoration of an interior, as they might if flat against the wall.

After a chapter on the "historical tradition," in which is noted the fact that the burgher of one generation lives more like the aristocrat of a previous generation than like his own predecessors, and that modern houses should look for precedents to the smaller apartments of palaces rather than the gala rooms, the subject of rooms in general is taken up. Here some pertinent remarks on fireplaces and furniture are introduced. The chapter on walls begins with the axiom, "Proportion is the good breeding of architecture"; that on doors considers the iniquity of sliding doors and portières. In the fifth chapter windows are considered and many sensible remarks are made concerning curtains, shades and shutters. The same may be said of the chapter on fireplaces. Ceiling and floor, hall and stairs, drawing-room, boudoir and morning-room are treated in three chapters. Gala rooms come next, followed by library and smoking-room. Dining-rooms, bedrooms, and school-room occupy three chapters and a concluding chapter is given to bric-à-brac. "Taste attaches but two conditions to the use of objects of art: that they shall be in scale with the rooms and that the room shall not be overcrowded with them." "Any work of art, regardless of its intrinsic merit, must justify its presence in a room by being more valuable than the space it occupies—more valuable, that is to say, to the general scheme of decoration."

These are a few principles laid down for the guidance of people striving to make their houses within not only comfortable but enduringly beautiful. Some of the æsthetic conclusions reached by the authors will seem too finely drawn; others are certainly too sweeping; but it is clear that much reading, much travel in Italy and France, and a good deal of independent thinking stand behind this pretty book. The illustrations are abundant, and while not intended as examples to imitate, reinforce the arguments in the text. They comprise simple pieces of furniture from different epochs as well as details of interiors in famous palaces in Italy and France. It depends very much on the kind of house to be decorated, whether a reader will get much direct aid and comfort from the book. Yet it is certain that no one can fail to learn a great deal from it and become, through reading it, more appreciative of what is worth noting in modern architecture as well as in the old buildings of Europe.

Edwin H. Blashfield, "House Decoration," *Book Buyer*, 16 (March 1898), 129–33

This book has come at an opportune moment. At the World's Fair it was proved beyond peradventure that when architect, sculptor, and painter work in harmony the result is good. Since then, terms hardly known before in America have become familiar: "mural painting," "architectural sculpture," "the allied arts," and on all sides one hears of the "Decorative Art movement."

Societies have been formed in behalf of the allied arts as applied to the treatment of great public monuments. Mrs. Wharton and Mr. Codman have in turn stepped forward as the protagonists of harmony in the treatment of that lesser but perhaps even more important monument, the private house, they show us the *room* as a part of the art evolution, that proportion governs here as elsewhere, that every part of the room or its furnishing, from the great chimney-piece to the smallest tabouret, is an enlisted soldier in the service of a general effect, that not a chair nor a table can be autonomous but rather that all must be disciplined. In sum, they show us that a room must not only relate to its own uses, but that all of its parts are interdependent and that it is in itself as much a composition as is any picture. To this wide field for the enunciation of principles, the balancing of relations, Mrs. Wharton and Mr. Codman have brought sincerity, enthusiasm, taste, technical knowledge, and clearness of presentation; once within the entrance hall of their house, they establish themselves firmly upon proportion as their guiding principle.

The lesson of their book is that, within this governed circle, invention, even inspiration at times, may find room for being, but that without it there is at once a disequilibrium which soon degenerates into chaos. Governing principles cannot be too plainly enunciated in a country which, like America, is in its aesthetically formative period. In a land which has art traditions, where the background is centuries old, the decorator working from a full mind may be pardoned many fantasies, the all-compelling sense of tradition will bring him back after he has had his fling; but in a new country, the man or woman who has just returned from Europe finds it hard to realize that the orderly confusion of the best houses there is the result of evolution, not of eccentricity. It ensues that in the new country barbarisms will abound, the result of an ignorant eclecticism which takes as readily from a decadent period as from one of upgrowth, from the Second Empire as from the *cinquecento*. Even when a good thing is chosen an untrained would-be decorator will often push it too far, and for the sake of his special effect will sacrifice the ensemble. Against all such procedure Mrs. Wharton and Mr. Codman set their faces resolutely. They lead us through the house from room to room; they remind us, and the modern householder has need of their reminder, that walls are meant to support something, that doors are for entrance and exit, that windows should give light and may be looked from, that fire-places may contain fire and should not be draped with silks nor even with woollens. They lead us by hall and stairs, and show us that a

place of passage differs in its requirements from a place of rest; they note "the mixed ancestry" of the modern drawing-room, half *bourgeois*, half *gala* in character (we all remember its caricature, "Boffin's Bower," where the husband's end of the room had a sanded floor and deal chairs, while that "highflyer at fashion," Mrs. Boffin, had gilding and upholstery at her end of the Bower). They take us through ball-room and gallery, and show us that the spacious magnificence of Italian state apartments was intended by their creators to relate not to the garish daylight which accompanies the modern tourist, but to torches and candles; and on their way through the music-room, they plead for more grace in the form of the piano, which has so suffered from "its elephantine supports" and the "weak curves of the lid." In the library they note the decorative value of books, and in the dining-room demand that light-colored walls shall help to light the whole room and thus to minimize the heat produced by artificial over-lighting; in the bed-room they denounce the upholstering into fixtures of stuff which should be movable and washable; last of all, in the nursery they find that the child who is to grow into the man or woman is well worthy to be influenced by an aesthetic environment.

Some readers may sigh that they cannot live up to such an ideal house as is here described, may say that in the economy of their aesthetic ordering they are forced by exiguity of space or by other considerations to run counter to some of the rules laid down by the authors; but the latter do not assert that the ideal is possible always or to all—their business is to enunciate principles and they do so emphatically and consistently. They would probably admit that their very consistency may sometimes, though rarely, force them to a conclusion unsuited to American conditions. Thus they say on page 41, in speaking of decorated walls, that many "artists who are wasting their energies on the production of indifferent landscapes and unsuccessful portraits might in the quite different field of decorative painting find the true expression of their talent."

Given adherence to the principles laid down by the authors, this is logical enough, for such adherence builds up a school on sound traditions. The mural-painter of Pompeii, the Renaissance painter of unimportant wall surfaces, might be a fourth-rate man, yet do yeoman service, for he was born of tradition and fostered upon principles, but in America to-day even the second-rate painter would, in ninety-nine cases out of a hundred, be the very one who knows and cares nothing about traditional principles in wall-painting. His "decorations" would be intolerable, and we may nowhere demand more severity of training than in the man whose work is to be mural, that is to say, immovable and constantly before our eyes. Probably no one would subscribe more readily to this dictum than would Mrs. Wharton and Mr. Codman, who, throughout their book, insist first and last upon limitations within certain lines, subjection to certain principles.

Every chapter of their book contains sentences potential in their corrective value, and the text is accompanied by many clearly printed reproductions in regard to which the authors are careful to remind us that if, as the advocates of severity rather than of luxury, they have seemed to take their examples from palaces and peculiarly pretentious buildings, they have chosen such because rooms which have been visited by the average tourist are, from their familiarity, more easily comprehended and therefore more elucidative than would be less well known interiors.

The book is a thoroughly welcome one and should be a very present help to the many who realize that the material environment of home life has a real influence, and who will be only too glad to find that this environment, if properly studied, can be understood, and that, although high art can be comprehended and great art possessed by few, any intelligent and well-to-do person may possess a good room or suite of rooms.

The authors address themselves to two classes, the moderately well-to-do and the wealthy. To the former they show that any well-proportioned room is a handsome room if not deformed by the application of bad detail, bad color, or the introduction of ugly furniture. In regard to the latter detail, furniture, etc., they further demonstrate that the greater cost of the good thing usually depends upon the fact that it is less commonly made than the bad thing, and show that once popularized it may become as cheap as its rival. In addressing themselves to the wealthy, the authors say quite truly that "every carefully studied detail examined by those who can afford to indulge their taste will in time find its way to the carpenter-built cottage," and that "once the right precedent is established it costs less to follow than to oppose it."

In fact, the effort of the authors is in the direction towards which every American architect, sculptor, painter, decorator, worthy of the name must tend if we would build up a national school of art; the direction which is pointed by "the sense of interrelation of parts, of unity of the whole . . ., the application of principles based on common sense and regulated by the laws of harmony and proportion."

7

Walter Berry, *The Decoration of Houses*, Bookman, 7 (April 1898), 161–3

It is said by Vasari that Brunelleschi's chief desire was to bring back good architecture, the good orders, in place of the barbarous style which had effaced them. This effacement of the good by the barbarous, and, following the barbarous, a revival of the good by a return to past forms, past ideals, are part of a law of ebb and flow everywhere visible in art. In every science the condition of progress is a continuous straining forward; in art and its allied branches this condition is often reversed: to advance may be to look backward. In analysing the latter proposition the first cause occurring in explanation is that of the loss, or at least the dulling, of the sense of simplicity. In the best Greek architecture, for instance, a small quantity of exquisite ornament is surrounded by plainness, making both doubly beautiful; in French Renaissance architecture, every surface is covered, leaving no spot on which the eye can rest, so that the whole becomes immoderate, confused, bewildering. This sense of the value of plainness is characteristic of every great age of art; in every period of decline exaggeration, pretentiousness, display, are dominant.

In no branch of art has a period of decline been more distinctly marked than in the decoration of houses during the last eighty years. The traditions of centuries, the ultimate tests of excellence—moderation, fitness, proportion—have become obscured, and what was once interior architecture has degenerated into mere upholstery. Indeed, so completely have these traditions been lost sight of, that for the last half century not a single work on house decoration as a branch of architecture has been published in England or in America.

It is to remedy this deficiency that *The Decoration of Houses* has been written, and the result is a work of large insight and appreciation, one that is certain to exert lasting influence in the revival of a subject generally misunderstood and mistreated.

The main theories which the book works out are simple, and may be summed up in a few words:

First. The true standpoint of interior decoration is that of *architectural proportion*, in contradistinction to the modern view, which is that of *superficial application of ornament*.

Second. Only a return to architectural principles, to the traditions and models of the past, can raise house decoration from incongruity and confusion to organic unity.

Third. Given the requirements of modern life, these models are chiefly to be found in buildings erected in Italy after the beginning of the sixteenth century, and especially in France and England after the full assimilation of the Italian influence.

Following the lines here indicated, the opening chapter, entitled "The Historical Tradition," after a brief outline of the stormy, unsettled conditions of mediæval life and the consequent impress of such conditions on both exterior and interior architecture, indicates the persistence of this feudal period, owing to the conflicts between the great nobles and the kings, both in France and in England. In Italy, however, social intercourse advanced more rapidly, and it is clearly shown that the rudimentary plan, the characteristic tendencies of our own house-planning, were developed from the mezzanine or intermediate story of the Italian Renaissance palace. Thus it may be said that Bramante is the father of the modern dwelling, but as the use of the mezzanine was not fully developed until the time of Peruzzi, the year 1500 represents an imaginary line drawn between mediæval and modern ways of living and house-planning.

Taking this as a starting-point, the process of development of house interiors is luminously traced: In Italy, from the "Massimi alle Colonne" to Palladio and to the decadence; in England, from the introduction of the Italian manner by Inigo Jones down to the Georgian models—those models which were afterward transported bodily to America and christened "colonial;" in France, throughout that long succession of artists, craftsmen, and artist-craftsmen who, from the ending of the Fronde almost to the present time, have ever remembered that the essence of a style lies not in its use of ornament, but in its handling of proportion, and of whom it may be said that whatever the hand found to do, that it did under the guidance of artistic fancy and feeling.

The broad lines being laid down, the fundamental principle—the importance of the right treatment of the component parts of an undecorated room—is fully developed. It was once thought that the effect of a room depended on the treatment of its wall-spaces and openings; now it is supposed to depend on curtains and portières, on furniture and bric-à-brac. In the best period of architecture, decoration was subordinate to architectural lines, and as the effect produced by a room depends mainly on the distribution of its openings, it becomes apparent that unless these and the surrounding wall-spaces are in right proportion there can be no harmony among the decorative processes. This factor, so fully dwelt upon by all the old decorators, from Vignola to Ware, has fallen into decay, and it is curious to note that in Eastlake's well-known *Hints on Household Taste* no mention whatever is made of doors, windows, and fireplaces.

The importance of the relations between proportion and decoration, between structure and ornament, having been strongly emphasised, each of the many rooms in a modern house is treated in turn, first from the evolutionary point of view, afterward from artistic and practical considerations. Not the least interesting part of the book is this tracing back the use of a room to its origin, showing that sometimes the present misuse is but a survival of older social conditions, or but the result of a misapprehension in regard to old customs through confusion of two essentially different types of rooms designed for essentially different phases of life.

From ball-rooms to nurseries, no part of the interior architecture of a house is omitted, the organic unities being always insisted on: the relation of a room as a whole to other rooms in the house, the relation of ornament to structure, the relation of furniture to ornament. Looking down the enfilade of the three great centuries, one is shown the incomparable ceilings of Mantegna, of Araldi, of Bérain; the perfect doors in the Ducal Palace of Mantua; the staircases of De Corny, the stair-rails of Jean Lamour and D'Ivry; the frescoes of Tiepolo and Le Riche; the carvings of Grinling Gibbons; the statues of Pajou; the mirrors of Mario dei Fiori. In these lucid pages and in the illustrations accompanying them, what rooms are held perfect, what models are in every sense worthy of admiration, all these, from a gala-room decorated by Giulio Romano to Cacialli's bath-room in the Pitti Palace, are made to demonstrate that, however splendid, however ornate, their effect is based on such harmony of line that their superficial ornament might be removed without loss to the composition.

It is for this reason that a return to the

9

traditions and models of the past is insisted on as the true way out of the labyrinth of incongruity wherein most modern decorators are helplessly wandering. The definite first conception—that decoration must harmonise with the structural limitation—a conception that held its own throughout every change of taste until the second quarter of the present century, has been effaced by a piling up of heterogeneous ornament, a multiplication of incongruous effects, much of which is held in admiration on account of its so-called originality. In art, "originality" is almost as fatal a term as "restoration." Ignorant of the traditions of old, unskilled in legitimate artistic requirements, the average decorator stands in firm belief that to bend to the acceptance of rules, which experience of centuries has established as the best, is to preclude the exercise of individual taste and to become subservient and servile, forgetting the admirable precept of the forgotten Isaac Ware, that while "it is mean in the undertaker of a great work to copy strictly, it is dangerous to give a loose to fancy *without a perfect knowledge how far a variation may be justified.*"

It is clearly in the attempt to help on toward this "perfect knowledge" that the present book has been written.

It is not proposed to discuss at length the various features of this work, or to go into detail regarding the many subjects there treated. The purpose of this review is to differentiate *The Decoration of Houses* from the many *Suggestions on Household Taste,* and the like, most of which have served only to aggravate the very defects which the present book is attempting to remedy. If the distinctive underlying principle—that the true expression of interior decoration rests not in superficial application of ornament, but in architectural proportion—has been plainly indicated, it is enough, and one need only add by way of summary the comprehensive words of the Conclusion: "The relation of proportion to decoration is like that of anatomy to sculpture: underneath are the everlasting laws."

Checklist of Additional Reviews

"*The Decoration of Houses,*" *Architect and Building News,* 22 January 1898, pp. 28–29.

THE GREATER INCLINATION

THE GREATER INCLINATION

BY EDITH WHARTON

CHARLES SCRIBNER'S
SONS, NEW YORK: 1899

John D. Barry, "New York Letter," *Literary World*, 1 April 1899, pp. 105–6

Another volume of short stories made of sterner stuff bears the rather far-fetched title of *The Greater Inclination*. I recall reading the first story, "The Muse's Tragedy," in *Scribner's Magazine* and being impressed by its fine quality and by its resemblance to the work of Mr. Henry James. The author, Miss Edith Wharton, has evidently studied Henry James very closely. In several of her stories in this volume she not only shows that she has been influenced by his method of developing a motive, but by his style as well. Some of his worst faults of style she reproduces with skill that after a time becomes very amusing, notably his trick of repeating words, which in James himself is at times exasperating, and his habit of spoiling the formation of his sentences by inserting parenthetical clauses. Surely, in the matter of style no living writer has fallen off so commentably as Henry James. After being one of the simplest and most luminous writers of English he has become one of the most dense and grotesque. His article on Du Maurier, one of the least complex of men, published about two years ago, if it lives at all, will live as one of the mysteries of our speech. Take, for example, the very first sentence in Miss Wharton's book; isn't this Henry James to the life? Even the names of the characters look like Henry James's names. "Danyers afterwards liked to fancy that he had recognized Mrs. Anerton at once; but that, of course, was absurd, since he had seen no portrait of her—she affected a strict anonymity, refusing even her photograph to the most privileged—and from Mrs. Memorall, whom he revered and cultivated as her friend, he had extracted but the one impressionist phrase: 'Oh, well, she's like one of those old prints where the lines have the value of color.'" Perhaps, however, it is a little unfair to accuse Mr. James of being capable of using such a phrase as "but the one." In other respects Miss Wharton's sentence is a marvel of—well, assimilation. Miss Wharton apparently does not believe in the principle that a writer should always begin his story or his article with a short phrase—a most admirable principle, by the way. At the start an author ought always to coax his reader to lure him on, and nothing alarms the average reader so much as a long sentence. That was a shrewd bit of advice given many years ago by Col. Thomas Wentworth Higginson to Miss Louisa Alcott, always to begin her stories with conversation. For most fiction readers there is no bait more alluring. In one story, "A Coward," which, sadly enough for my contention, is not quite up to the average merit of the book, Miss Wharton begins with conversation, striking a note that Mr. James frequently sounds, though he produces with it a finer, and far less consciously superior tone. "'My daughter Irene,' said Mrs. Carstyle (she made it rhyme with *tureen*), 'has had no social advantages; but if Mr. Carstyle had chosen'—(she paused significantly, and looked at the shabby sofa on the opposite side of the fireplace as though it had been Mr. Carstyle)." Now, as a matter of fact, most people pronounce Irene as if the name rhymed with *tureen*; so Miss Wharton's satire rather misses fire and becomes a rather feeble ridicule. It betrays, moreover, the superior attitude of mind toward character under discussion that is so offensive in many of our writers. However, this tone is noticeable only in "The Coward," which deals somewhat inadequately with a theme which Maupassant has handled in a masterly way. On the other hand, it contains at least one witty and luminous phrase worthy of Henry James himself. "Mrs. Carstyle was one of those women who make refinement vulgar." Could a certain well-known American type be more cleverly hit off than that? Mrs. Carstyle did not belong to New York either. After "The Muse's Tragedy," which for fineness is the best work in the book, "The Portrait" and "A Cup of Cold Water" are perhaps the most interesting. "A Cup of Cold Water" is built on the most romantic theme employed by the writer, but it is treated with vigor and simplicity, and with an insight into masculine character that is not often found in the fiction of women. "The Portrait" is in motive not remote from one of Henry James's greatest stories, "The Liar," and a capital motive it is; but under Miss Wharton's faltering treatment it loses much of its effectiveness. Miss Wharton has not as yet mastered her technique; but her book contains so much good material that it places her at once among the most promising of our more recent short-story writers.

John D. Barry, "New York Letter," *Literary World,* 13 May 1899, pp. 152–3

I am hearing a good deal of praise for *The Greater Inclination*, Mrs. Edith Wharton's collection of short stories brought out by the Scribners a few weeks ago, to which I have already referred. It is very generally regarded as one of the most promising books by a new writer of fiction published here in many years. It appears that Mrs. Wharton is more or less known in the social life here [Boston], which thus far has not produced many literary geniuses. She is said, by the way, not to relish the frequent references made by her readers to her indebtedness to Henry James, so her next book will probably not be marked by a slavish adherence to the methods of a very questionable literary model.

A writer like Mrs. Wharton ought to be able to give us some of those studies of our leisure class which Mr. Howells has lately been asking for in the pages of *Literature*. She surely could not have a more fruitful field; but, as Mr. Howells has pointed out, it is a field that invites the novelist rather than the short-story writer. However, now that Mrs. Wharton has tried her wings so successfully, there is no knowing how far they may carry her in future. The newspaper reports of the social proceedings in New York alone during the past few months have offered material for many a curious study of our changing conditions. "To become truly and deeply aristocratic," a foreign visitor sarcastically remarked to me not long ago, "there's nothing like a training in the principles of American democracy." It is only fair to say that at the moment he was chafing under the rude, but to me rather amusing, behavior at a theater of a group of people in a stage box who maintained under a fire of resentful glances and open remarks serenely magnificent and aristocratic unconsciousness of their surroundings.

F.J.G., "Mrs. Wharton and Her Use of the Epigram," *Book Buyer*, 18 (June 1899), 395–6

Some story-tellers with the gift for epigram leave the impression on one of using the smart sayings for beads on a string. The result may be ornamental, but no essential purpose is served. Others have the rare gift of weaving them into the texture of their prose, where they produce the same effect as a glowing touch of color in a piece of tapestry. But in this case it is impossible to consider the gleam apart from the complete scheme of color. It is to this latter class of artists, clearly, that Mrs. Wharton belongs. There are many flashes in the tales making up her volume, *The Greater Inclination*, which make one pause in sheer joy at the felicity of the touch. But you soon see that not one of these is put on without consideration of the total effect. In every instance you feel that the successful phrase, the happy aphorism, gives a clew to character, an aid to your knowledge of the temperament of the individual, such as is furnished by a gesture, or a trick of the eyes, when you try to form an estimate of a stranger met for the first time. Take a few examples from "The Muse's Tragedy": "She asked him the questions which are the wise woman's substitute for advice"; "You can't imagine the excuses a woman will invent for a man's not telling her that he loves her—pitiable arguments that she would see through at a glance if any other woman used them." These throw a backward and forward light on the narrative that can only be fully understood when the curious story is read. Take these in "A

Coward": "Miss Carstyle, the young man decided, was the kind of girl whose surroundings rub off on her"; "Nobody believes in a man who doesn't believe in himself, and Mr. Carstyle always seems to be winking at you through a slit in his professional manner." In a moment, the twinkling of an eye, you are able to place these two characters. Pages of description and repetition would not have served you so well.

There is the same skill in the matter of indirection in the general method of the stories. Each tale is mainly told between the lines. By a touch here and a touch there you are enabled to construct a prelude for yourself, and when you come to the last page you have no difficulty in carrying on the action to its remote possibilities, or to its inevitable subsequent proceedings. Mrs. Wharton makes you wonder again at the truth of the old axiom that, after all, there is nothing so eloquent as silence. And in spite of her reticence, nothing essential is taken for granted. You are never exasperated by anything lacking of what you would want to know.

It is hard to pick and choose where so much is excellent. But the excellences are varied. While "The Twilight of the God" will suggest to the reader a coming dramatist, it is safe to say that the courage and directness of "Souls Belated" will leave the most abiding impression on readers of the book. This story alone would stamp the writer as somebody to be reckoned with. And while there is a problem—and a big problem of the day—it is easy to see that Mrs. Wharton was only interested in the human elements of the situation. The grasp of the author may be best indicated by a passage in which the sensations of the woman are described at a critical point in the affair:

"In so large a charter of liberties as the mere act of leaving Tillotson seemed to confer, the mere question of divorce or no

15

divorce did not count. It was when she saw that she had left her husband, only to be with Gannett, that she perceived the significance of anything affecting their relations. Her husband, in casting her off, had virtually flung her at Gannett; it was thus that the world viewed it. The measure of alacrity with which Gannett would receive her would be the subject of curious speculation over afternoon tea-tables and in club rooms. She knew what would be said—she had heard so often of others! The recollection bathed her in misery. The men would probably back Gannett to 'do the decent thing'; but the ladies' eyebrows would emphasize the worthlessness of such enforced fidelity; and, after all, they would be right. She had put herself in a position where Gannett 'owed' her something; where, as a gentleman, he was bound to 'stand the damage.' The idea of accepting such compensation had never crossed her mind; the so-called rehabilitation of such a marriage had always seemed to her the only real disgrace."

The encounter of the American elopers and the English elopers at the fashionable Italian hotel, the new aspect convention and respectability take on, the longing to be above-board, the effort of the woman to leave the man and her weakening at the last moment, are told with great skill. As a study in temperament, nothing better has been done for a long time. And the small compass in which Mrs. Wharton succeeds in turning round is amazing.

In some of the stories, such as "The Portrait," "The Pelican" and "A Journey," her method is simpler. Yet it is where the difficulties are greatest that she succeeds in coming out of them most triumphantly.

Mary Tracy Earle, "Some New Short Stories," *Book Buyer*, 18 (June 1899), 399–401

All but one of the five writers whose recent books are here grouped together for convenience of comment, might have christened their collected stories by the title which Mrs. Wharton has chosen for hers, *The Greater Inclination*, for they deal with character, with its development through circumstance, the simple delineation of it, or the play of one personality upon another.

In *Tiverton Tales* Miss Alice Brown writes from an unstrained, warmly human and womanly point of view. . . .

The contrast between Mrs. Wharton's book and Miss Brown's is like one of those sharp contrasts in life which Mrs. Wharton uses so deftly, and although neither suffers by it, many a reader who in enthusiastic over one will find something uncongenial in the other. Mrs. Wharton writes of worldly people and commands a technique so perfect that once in a while the interest of the story is not quite vivid enough to sustain it. A great end is needed to keep the means from seeming formal in their freedom from blemish, and until the reader is stirred to interest in the people of the tale, he is likely to resent the nicety of expression and analysis which will delight him as soon as he begins to care, and sees that with the simplest material of incident Mrs. Wharton has done memorable work. It would be hard to find more original stories in their absolutely quiet way than "The Pelican" and "The Coward," while in "Souls Belated," Lydia's and Gannett's struggle with the problem of their life together after Lydia is divorced from her husband and free to marry Gannett is worked out so strongly, so entirely without appeal to sympathy, that after the necessary stating of the case in the beginning it has the intensity of a drama in actual life, overheard and needing no explanation. The courtesy of Mrs. Wharton's attitude toward her readers is noteworthy. She is an analyst, yet she only analyzes where to do so is the shortest way of stating the conditions, never to make the incidents or the conversations plain; if she can understand why her characters act and talk as they do, she takes it for granted that her readers can understand also, and she never "dots her i's" ostentatiously, even at the end of a story, and yet not an end is vague. "The Pelican" and "The Portrait" are told in the first person, with the assumption that the "person" is a man, but the work, strong, quiet, and dignified, does not need a signature to show that it is a woman's work after all, the work of a woman who, to use her own phrase, "reasons her emotions" and understands other women better than the keenest analyst among the men.

"The Rambler," Book Buyer, 18 (June 1899), 360

The photograph of Mrs. Edward Wharton, from Mr. Julian Story's painting, which forms the frontispiece to this number of The Book Buyer is Mrs. Wharton's most recent portrait and is considered by her friends to be the most satisfactory likeness she has had.

Mrs. Wharton's Book, The Greater In-

clination, which has met with a more cordial reception than a volume of short stories often finds, and which contains some of the most skilful and finished writing which has appeared in recent years, includes most of the work in fiction which she has accomplished, and is certainly a remarkable first book. Mrs. Wharton has no special literary creed to proclaim; she simply tries to tell a good story, when she gets one, as well and carefully as she can. She made some such reply, recently, to a question about her literary theories and aims. Her writing is her diversion, but as in many similar cases, the avocation possesses the worker so thoroughly that its elaboration in minutest detail becomes an essential part of the work. Mrs. Wharton's family, on both sides, are old New York people, and her home is here, though she has lived abroad for several years, and counts travel as one of the pleasantest incidents in life. Miss Mary Tracy Earle reviews her book appreciatively upon another page, and a correspondent writes at some length in praise of her use of epigram in the stories which give such confident promise for her future work.

Review of The Greater Inclination, New York Times Saturday Review, 24 June 1899, p. 408

Discernment of the ironical in human life is not rare, but authors having the quality are too frequently disposed to fancy their readers destitute of it, and to explain its existence until one wishes that they lived in a perfectly happy world where they would have neither the temptation nor the opportunity to write. Mrs. Wharton is not one of these. She exhibits misunderstood or wasted lives, self-deceivers, or unworshipped saints and if the reader does not perceive the quality of their fate he does not find it explained in a closing phrase or paragraph. In pursuit of this policy Mrs. Wharton strikingly resembles Mr. Mallock. In her conversational passages she is much like Mr. Henry James in the good days before all his characters confounded one another with epigrams. All the stories in the volume are good, and the little drama is worked out by a succession of the most delicate touches.

Harry Thurston Peck, "A New Writer Who Counts," *Bookman*, 9 (June 1899), 344–6

Amid the mass of vapid novels, ephemeral romances, and all the poor, thin, tawdry, slipshod writing that comes pouring from innumerable presses all over the country to discourage and disgust the student of contemporary literature, it is now and then vouchsafed, even to the most blasé of book reviewers, to find here and there something that reveals the stamp of true distinction and the form of serious art. We could count upon the fingers of one hand the books of the past year that any one would ever think of reading a second time or of referring to hereafter, and one of these rare exceptions to the general rule of mediocrity and dulness we have found in a volume of eight short stories by Mrs. Edith Wharton. Some of these stories had already appeared in the pages of a magazine [*Scribner's*] where,

apparently, they attracted no very marked attention, but the whole eight, with one exception, deserve in their collected form the most respectful consideration.

At the very outset it is necessary to set forth the undoubted fact that Mrs. Wharton, both in her choice of themes and in her treatment of them, has been influenced by the example of Mr. Henry James. At times one comes upon resemblances that are positively startling. Yet this is said in purely scientific spirit and with no intention whatsoever of regarding Mrs. Wharton as an imitator. The novels of Mr. James are to be divided into two distinct groups. In the first group will be found to lie his finer work, which reached its perfect evolution in those stories that have to do with what may be called international or cosmopolitan society. Of these novels we think that the greatest is *The American*, both because it combines all of Mr. James's delicate psychology with a really informing picture of a portion of society in France from which the casual foreigner is inexorably barred, and because it sounds a deeper and a truer note of passion than does any other book that he has written. Of late years, however, Mr. James has ceased to set before us the delicious bits of social contrast that made him quite unique, and has become an English writer pure and simple. There is not perceptible as yet any serious waning of his powers; and, indeed, his latest book, *The Two Magics*, contains one story that must be reckoned among the most remarkable of all the studies that he has ever made. Yet his themes have changed and with them his manner also. We said that he had become an English writer, but it would be more true to limit such a description of him still further, so as to view him simply as a literary Londoner, and as a Londoner who has narrowed his observation largely to the life and manners of a single set; for in his later books we cannot even in imagi-

18

nation wander far away from Hyde Park and the Row, from the men in frock coats with gardenias, and from the women whom they lightly love. We are always walking with Mr. James on Bond Street and Piccadilly, and there is a rather meretricious suggestion of the Burlington Arcade about some of the newest of his novels. Mr. James, indeed, has suffered just the least perceptible deterioration as moralist, in that he is becoming somewhat overfond of narrating in his interminable hinting way the disagreeable complications that arise perennially in the set which now appears to have become his special microcosm. This is all very well in itself; and no one can skirt the edges of a scandal more discreetly than can Mr. James; yet we sometimes feel that we could breathe a little more freely, and, in fact, could read his books with just a little more spontaneous pleasure, did he give us now and then a breath of the frosty, bracing air that blows, for instance, through the pages of *The Europeans*.

Now, it is obviously the later Henry James who has most deeply influenced the writer of *The Greater Inclination*, yet we cannot say that she has imitated him, because to our mind her stories, with the exception already noted, are superior in many ways to those of Mr. James's. She has caught his later manner, but she has improved upon his later workmanship, and therefore, she deserves a wholly independent criticism.

Of the stories in this book, three have to do exclusively with the sex-relation, and these are the strongest of the eight. One of the others, entitled "A Journey," is a study in nervous tension. Another, called "A Cup of Cold Water," is a powerful bit of emotional psychology. The last one in the book, "The Portrait," is slight in its workmanship, but ingenious in its theme. The fifth story, "A Coward," is the one failure to be noted, since it lacks

in some inexplicable way the sort of constructive coherence that ought to bind together the parts of even the very slightest work of fiction; for while a reader as a rule finds pleasure in the unexpected, the unexpected when once revealed ought to be quite in consonance with what has led up to it; and in "The Coward" this is not the case.

Mrs. Wharton's most amusing piece of work, as it is the one most strongly suggestive of Mr. James's lighter manner, is that which is called "The Pelican." It is a perfectly delicious study of the typical "lady lecturer," and is full of pure delight from the beginning to the end. "The Pelican" is one Mrs. Amyot, whose mother was the famous Irene Astarte Pratt, the author of a poem on the Fall of Man, and called by N.P. Willis "the female Milton of America." One of Mrs. Amyot's aunts had translated Euripides, and another was the dean of a girl's college. Mrs Amyot herself was very pretty, with features that were suggestive of "a cameo brooch divinity, humanised by a dimple." She had no sense of humour, and being obliged to make a living, she took to the popular exposition of Greek art and other things, and to acquiring a reputation for being "intellectual."

"The first time I saw her she was standing by the piano against a flippant background of Dresden china and photographs, telling a roomful of women, pre-occupied with their spring bonnets, all she thought she knew about Greek art." Her lectures were crowded, to the embarrassment of "a pale usher with an educated mispronunciation." When she lectured "she had an air of assuming that for her purpose the bull's-eye was everywhere, so that there was no need to be flustered in taking aim. . . . To the invaluable knack of not disturbing the association of ideas in her audience, she had the gift of what may be called a confidential manner, so that her fluent generalisations had the flavour of personal experience, of views sympathetically exchanged with her audience on the best way of knitting children's socks or of putting up preserves for the winter.... Mrs. Amyot's art was simply an extension of coquetry; she flirted with "her audience." Her auditors had no particular understanding of the subject of her discourse, but "it was a part of the whole duty of woman to be seen at her lectures;" for "she evidently represented a social obligation, like going to church, rather than any more personal interest." She had reams of testimonials from all sorts of persons, and the writer of the story says, "My only hope was that Mrs. Amyot might find one who would marry her in the defence of his convictions." Altogether the sketch is beautifully true to life and is spiced with continual epigram, while the story as a whole ends with a touch of the pathetic.

The longest, the strongest, and the most striking study in the book is that which tells of a couple who are travelling through Italy under circumstances that give a curious interest to the narrative of what befalls them. The man, one Gannett, is a popular novelist; his companion, Lydia, is a woman who has left her husband to make a new life for herself with Gannett. At the beginning of the story they are in a railway carriage alone together, and she has just received a copy of the decree which makes it possible for her to marry her companion. Both of them are uneasily conscious of a certain strangeness that has sprung up between them with the existence of this possibility. Gannett, with the natural instinct of a gentleman, at once falls to planning an immediate marriage; but through Lydia's mind run many thoughts, thoughts that she had had before, insistent, morbid thoughts.

She knew what would be said—she had heard it so often of others! The recollection bathed her in misery. The men would probably back Gannett to do "the decent thing"; but the ladies' eyebrows would emphasise the worthlessness of such enforced fidelity, and, after all, they would be right. She had put herself in a position where Gannett "owed" her something; where as a gentleman he was bound to "stand the damage." The idea of accepting such compensation had never crossed her mind; the so-called rehabilitation of such a marriage had always seemed to her the only real disgrace. What she dreaded was the necessity of having to explain herself; of having to combat his arguments, of calculating in spite of herself the exact measure of insistence with which he pressed them. She knew not whether she most shrank from his insisting too much or too little. In such a case the nicest sense of proportion might be at fault, and how easy to fall into the error of taking her resistance for a test of his sincerity! Whatever way she turned, an ironical implication confronted her.... Beneath all these preoccupations lurked the dread of what he was thinking. Her sensitiveness on this point was aggravated by another fear, as yet barely on the level of consciousness, the fear of unwillingly involving Gannett in the trammels of her dependence. To look upon him as an instrument of her liberation, to resist in herself the least tendency to a wifely taking possession of his future, had seemed to Lydia the only way of maintaining the dignity of their relation.... What was needful was the courage to recognise the moment when by some word or look their voluntary fellowship should be transformed into a bondage, the more wearing that it was based on none of those common obligations which make the most imperfect marriage in some sort a centre of gravity.

These thoughts come out in their conversation, which is fascinating in its play of motive and intense feeling. But it ends by the abrupt refusal of Lydia even to think of marriage, a decision which, manlike, he failed to understand.

> They had reached that memorable point in their heart history when for the first time the man seems obtuse and the woman irrational. It was the abundance of his intentions that consoled her for what they lacked in quality. After all, it would have been worse, incalculably worse, to have detected any over-readiness to understand her.

So far we have followed this narrative, the first part of which ends where we have left it. As to what ensues, we must refer the reader to the story itself. Taken as a whole, it is a most penetrating and almost painfully absorbing study of motive, and perhaps what strikes us most is the very subtle way in which at the end it seems to suggest (at least, we have so understood it) that there has begun to fall upon Gannett's mind the least shadow of distaste for the union that he had so long been vehemently urging.

In the way of fiction we have seen nothing this year that has impressed us so much as Mrs. Wharton's book. There is a finish, an assurance, and a tenacity of grasp about her work that show her to be already an accomplished literary artist; while, as we have said before, Mr. James himself has nothing to teach her in those half-elusive but exquisitely effective strokes that re-

veal in an instant a whole mental attitude or the hidden meaning of a profound emotion.

Review of *The Greater Inclination*, *Academy*, 57 (8 July 1899), 40

This book of short stories comes out of America, and it is good. It is very good. Mrs. Wharton is one of the few to grasp the obvious but much-neglected fact that the first business of a writer is to be able to write. Mrs. Wharton writes with the finished ease of the skilled craftsman, and with the feeling and distinction of an artist. Her imaginative talent is therefore absolutely at her disposal, a force which she can control perfectly and exploit to its fullest. Such a phenomenon is rare, especially among women writers.

She is clearly of the school of Mr. Henry James. Her subjects are chosen similarly to his—dramas of sentiment, of the soul; excursions into the obscure recesses of psychology. But there are exceptions, and it must be said that though she is subtle she is much less subtle than Mr. James, and—may we utter it?—possibly more articulate. She, at any rate, has divined that the expressiveness of language has its limits.

The story which pleased us best is "The Pelican," being the history of a lady-lecturer, a widow who began to earn a living "for the baby," and couldn't give it up, posing pathetically as a stressful sacrificial mother even when the baby was a rich financier with a wife and family.

Throughout this tale the phrasing is of the finest, the analysis unerring, the satire kindly keen, and the form without flaw.

What Mrs. Wharton lacks, and we feel the shortcoming to be grave, is a sense of the dramatic. Her themes are dramatic enough, but the drama seems to be decentralised, frittered away, instead of being gathered up (as surely the short story demands) into a single resounding stroke. This is so with "The Pelican," where the scene in which the "baby" makes his mother confess her duplicities distinctly does not show that effectiveness which is latent within it. "A Journey," again, suffers in the same way: the plight of the woman travelling with the husband whose death she must at all costs keep secret from the other occupants of the Pullman, is tremendous; but there is no *clou*, no adequate culmination. On the other hand, "Souls Belated" has a climax which is at once legitimate and striking.

The Greater Inclination may impress itself on neither the English nor the American public, but it is none the less distinguished and delightful; and if Mrs. Wharton continues to write up to the level of it, she cannot fail ultimately to make her mark.

Review of *The Greater Inclination*, *Saturday Review* [England], 88 (15 July 1899), 82

The Greater Inclination is a collection of seven short stories and a dialogue of a type with which certain American writers have made us familiar, and those that do not like the type need not trouble to read the book. Miss Wharton is subtle, introspective and sympathetic, with a delicacy of touch that rarely deserts her, though it does so occasionally. She has also a scholarly grace of style, a vividness of

phrase, and mastery of language that will commend her work to novel-readers who value such qualities, and who do not often find them in so high a degree.

William Morton Payne, "Recent Fiction," *Dial*, 27 (1 August 1899), 76–7

The note of distinction (as the French would understand it) is rarely met with in the English or American short story, but it may certainly be found upon almost every page of the book by Mrs. Edith Wharton, with which this hurried review must close. Under the collective title *The Greater Inclination*, which belongs to no one of the stories in particular, Mrs. Wharton has brought together eight pieces of delicate texture and artistic conception. Every one of them has the external shape and coloring of the world in which we mingle day by day, and every one of them is at heart a poignant spiritual tragedy. The veils that are spread over most lives by wont and custom conceal the inner workings from the eyes of all but a few; it is the privilege of the artist to penetrate their enveloping folds and scan the bare soul within. The present writer does not neglect the outward aspect of the lives which she depicts, but, as the conception becomes developed by touches so deft that we never think of the conscious artistic endeavor, the subjective reality is in each case brought by insensible degrees into the field of vision, until the gaze is at last focussed upon that alone, and the full triumph of the workmanship bursts upon us. This may sound like extravagant praise, but no conventional commendation would be adequate for such a book. Between these stories and those of the ordinary entertaining sort there is a great gulf fixed—there is all the difference between the pure gold of art and its pinchbeck imitations.

Review of *The Greater Inclination,* *Athenæum* [England], 3745 (5 August 1899), 189

Like many another clever analyst of human nature—and especially when, as apparently in this case, a first literary effort is being made—the author of these sketches takes a somewhat dreary view of her fellow-creatures. At the same time she has not succumbed to the temptation, so common at this end of the century to writers of her class, to dabble wholly in the mire. While it would be difficult to find anything more hopeless and cynical than the "Pelican," "A Journey," or even the "Muse's Tragedy," Miss Wharton is clearly a sufficiently keen observer to know in her heart, however much she may try to impress the contrary upon her readers, that humanity is not all dross. The gold shines through with great distinctness in "A Coward" and in "A Cup of Cold Water"; and, indeed, nowhere are her characters, though dreary enough in their motives and actions quite so comtemptible as they set out to be. "Souls Belated" is a particularly able bit of analysis, as showing the different effects of a common action upon a man's and a woman's point of view. The reader is, on the whole, left to decide for himself whether "the greater inclination" be towards honesty or the reverse, and he will probably decide in favour of the former. Miss Wharton has the further merit that, though presumably an American herself and writing of American men and women, she yet has a command of good English, and her nationality merely serves to add an alertness to her style which is usually lacking in this particular form of literature.

"Recent Fiction," *Critic,* 35 (August 1899), 746–8

Two hundred years ago things happened. Defoe, stringing together the fascinating series of events known as *Captain Singleton,* was the artist of an age that found its play in events rather than in experience. Anything that could happen was vastly more interesting than anyone to whom it could happen. That a man's feelings—and a woman's—were material for art had not entered into the heart of man to conceive. That the hero was awed, or terrified, or callous in the midst of shipwreck was a thing for casual mention; that winds blew and waves bellowed, masts snapped and leaks sprung were things of moment. It is a far cry from the time when things happened to this new day, wherein, Mr. James tells us, "It is an incident for a woman to stand up with her hand resting on a table and look out at you in a certain way,"—or, as he goes on to suggest, "if it be not an incident, I think it will be hard to say what it is." The distance from Defoe to Henry James must somehow be spanned if one is to appreciate the artistic quality of such work as *The Greater Inclination.*

It is not enough to say that these stories are realistic and that Henry James is their artistic sponsor. The reader is startled into a new appreciation of Mr. James and of

23

the realistic method in general. So much keenness of insight, so much cleverness of phrase were not born, one is inclined to believe, of a day. It is realism carried to the *nth* power. Every character feels and thinks and reflects and feels again. But nothing happens—unless it can be called happening for a young woman, alone in a room in a New York hotel, to be pointing a revolver at her head; or for a man with staring eyes and small pinched face to lie dead in his berth in the flying express. The revolver never goes off. The dead man tells no tales. But the interest holds. Each minutest detail is selected and related with the exactness that befits a tragedy. The outcome may be death, or the birth of a new soul. The method in either case is the same, in the daily newspaper as in the realistic novel, that of circumstantial and exact detail. That one sometimes fails to see the wood for the trees, or the story for the telling, is only a phase of realism. That the stories have sometimes the effect of having been related so minutely that there is neither room nor time for the end is perhaps only another phase of realism. But that the interest never flags is pure art.

The minor faults of realism lie on the surface, to be seen at a glance. Its power and virility are apprehended more slowly. If it has taken the artist two hundred years to discover that not in events, but in experience of events, lies material for art, it may surely be forgiven the common man that even now he sometimes fails to value justly the artistic and moral possibilities of the commonplace. To perceive clearly that "life, not the having lived, avails" is not merely an artistic experience. Its roots strike deep in intellectual and spiritual being. The generation that perceives that, rightly viewed, the joy or sorrow or apathy of the meanest soul outweighs fire and flood and murder and war and death has advanced far in sympathy, in civilization.

The artist that seeks to reveal this has chosen his rank. He is known by it. It is by the standards of such art that he must be judged and beside artists of this rank that he must be measured.

The stories in *The Greater Inclination* inevitably recall the work of Henry James. Nor is the suggestion merely one of method. In very substance, even in titular phrase, the author pays Mr. James the sincere flattery of imitation. What is "The Muse's Tragedy," but *The Tragic Muse* turned other end to; or "The Pelican," who lectures "for the sake of the baby," but a more clever and youthful "Greville Fane" and her ungrateful offspring? Doubtless when Miss Wharton sketched "The Portrait" she was unconscious of other model than Vard, the political rascal, or of other artist than Lillo, the psychic interpreter of character. But the reader is liable to be reminded—in more than shadowy fashion—of that remarkable story "The Liar," in which the sitter is likewise a scoundrel and the artist a man of psychic trend. The pointing out of plagiarism, or unconscious adaptation or imitation, is a task neither pleasant nor difficult nor lofty. It falls now and then, however, to the lot of the reviewer and becomes more imperative in proportion as the work considered is more clever.

It is Miss Wharton's cleverness that betrays her and assigns her to her place. It is her cleverness, indeed, that differentiates her from her master and from artists of like calibre. One questions whether the whole range of Mr. James's work would yield as many epigrams, as much striking phrase, as "The Pelican" alone could furnish. It is in the power to weld clever phrase into fibre, to subordinate epigram to end, that the author of "The Pelican" is lacking—the power of self-restraint. The soft harmonious haze of an autumn day is not hers, nor the quick stinging touch of twilight in winter, nor the waking of a

24

morning in spring. Spring, summer, and winter shall sooner lie down together some peaceful autumn day than the clever bits of writing in Miss Wharton's work efface themselves for the sake of anything so mild as style. In the meantime one may well be grateful for the cleverness and sparkle and interest. Whatever rank Miss Wharton shall ultimately choose to take, she has at least not fallen into the vulgar error of mistaking inanity for realism or the common fault of being able to see only with her eyes open.

Checklist of Additional Reviews

Harry Thurston Peck, "The Great Inclination," *Commercial Advertiser*, 102 (20 May 1899), 12.

Aline Gorren, "Studies in Souls," *Critic*, 37 (August 1900), 173–6.

THE TOUCHSTONE

(Published in England as *A Gift from the Grave*)

THE TOUCHSTONE
BY EDITH WHARTON
AUTHOR OF THE
GREATER INCLINATION

CHARLES SCRIBNER'S
SONS, NEW YORK: 1900

Harry Thurston Peck, *"The Touchstone," Bookman*, 11 (July 1900), 319–23

Mrs. Wharton's first book, *The Greater Inclination*, appeared last year at a time when the reading public was in the midst of a literary debauch which still unfortunately continues. Her artistic feeling, her deft, unerring touch, her profound and often startling insight into the deeper things of life, were revealed at the very moment when nose-rings and war-paint and barbaric gew-gaws were usurping the place which heretofore had been accorded to true literature. Hence, her book reminded us of an exquisite voice, trained to the most delicate and subtle modulations, but compelled to sing amidst the bray of horns and the frantic beating of a thousand tom-toms. Small wonder had the voice been drowned and had it never reached and charmed the ears that otherwise would have been opened to its harmonies. Yet, fortunately, *The Greater Inclination* was predestined to a happier fate. Discriminating persons felt at once its most unusual quality; and though its sales did not mount up into the hundreds of thousands, it won for its accomplished author a most enviable recognition, and it was not read merely to be cast aside and then forgotten like other "books of the day"; but it was treasured up as giving a sure and certain promise of still better and more fruitful effort in the future.

This promise has already been redeemed in the book before us, which marks, we think, a second stage in Mrs. Wharton's literary evolution. *The Touchstone* is not quite a novel, but represents that undefined and intermediate form of fiction which leads from the short story to the novel. It may be compared, in its extent and scope, with such of Henry James's works as are exemplified in "An International Episode," "The Impressions of a Cousin," and "Lady Barbarina"; and from a comparison with these it need in no way shrink.

Its theme may here be rather inadequately indicated. To give it with more fulness might rob the book of something of its interest by anticipating, and thus dulling, if ever so slightly, the expectant curiosity of the reader.

Glennard, the central figure of the story, is a man of the world, of no fortune, and in love with a young girl, one Alexa Trent, who, like himself, is poor. Could Glennard command a certain amount of ready money he could invest it in such a way as to secure a large return, and thus make possible to him a successful career. Without the money, he must not only let this opportunity go by, but he must give up his hope of marrying Alexa Trent; for she is about to be taken abroad by a wealthy aunt, who intends to remain in Europe for a number of years. Glennard, as he sits in his club one rainy evening, going over in mind the hardships and the humiliations of his position, and feeling to the last throb the pang of ambitious impotence, lets his eye wander over the columns of a London periodical, and finds there a published request for any letters written by the famous novelist, Margaret Aubyn, to be used by a gentleman engaged in writing her biography. The name of Margaret Aubyn stirs many sombre memories in Glennard's mind; for he had met her before she had become famous, and while he was on the threshold of early manhood. He had been, in a way, fascinated by her wonderful mental gifts; he had been proud that she had singled him out as her especial friend; and psychically, at least, he had almost loved her. In his love, however, or his liking, there was no element of the physical. She did not have within her the power to quicken his pulse, to stir ever so slightly the impulses of desire. . . . She on her side had, however, loved him deeply and passionately, and with a love that had endured throughout all the years of her lonely yet brilliant life. After she had made her home in England, and had learned that her love was given to a man who would never love her in return, she had found a curious comfort in making him the confidant of her inner life, and to him in her letters she had laid bare her very soul. . . .

To the very end she had written him so that sometimes it used to seem to him as though her letters came with every post. "He used to avoid looking in his letter-box when he came home to his rooms; but her writing seemed to spring out at him as he put his key in the door." It was the old tragic story of the love of a lifetime thrown at the feet of a man who did not care to take it up and cherish it. In the end, her marvellous self-surrender had even bored him. He had been

> . . . one who in the last years had requited her wonderful pages, her tragic outpourings of love, humility and pardon, with the scant phrases by which a man evades the vulgarest of sentimental importunities. He had been a brute in spite of himself; and sometimes, now that the remembrance of her face had faded, and only her voice and words remained with him, he chafed at his own inadequacy, his stupid inability to rise to the height of her passion. His egoism was not of a kind to mirror its complacency in the adventure. To have been loved by the most brilliant woman of her day, and to have been incapable of loving her, seemed to him, in looking

back, derisive evidence of his limitations; and his remorseful tenderness for her memory was complicated with a sense of irritation against her for having given him once for all the measure of his emotional capacity.

In Glennard, as he sits in his club, the printed request for any letters of Mrs. Aubyn suddenly starts an entirely new train of thought; and, going home to his rooms, he examines the packets which contain the hundreds of letters in which this famous woman had exposed to him all the happenings of her external life and all the overflowing thought and tenderness and emotion of the life which no one knew. The literary significance and, secondarily, the commercial value of these letters flash upon him in an instant. Might not they give him the means of gaining the foothold that he sought, and of winning at last the woman whom he loved? The thought frightens and yet fascinates. He consults a friend, to whom he confides the fact that he is the possessor of a quantity of letters written by the famous Mrs. Aubyn; and he invents a story to the effect that the letters had been bequeathed to him by a friend now dead, to whom they had been originally written. The friend, a worldly dilettante, urges their publication, as Glennard indeed had hoped he would do. It is plausibly argued by him that the letters of so famous a woman as Margaret Aubyn are not like the letters of a private person; that the world has a claim upon them; that they are an essential part of the century's literary history, and that in the publication of them there can be no dishonour, especially as both the writer and the man to whom they were written are now dead. Glennard takes the advice, and through this friend, Flamel, the letters find a publisher, and when published produce an immense and lasting sensation in the world of literature.

Meanwhile, Glennard has married Alexa Trent, he has prospered, and he sees before him the promise of a successful life. Then occurs the publication of the letters, and with their first appearance his happiness becomes embittered. His punishment has begun. Although no one except Flamel could possibly suspect him, the thought of what he had done lay heavily on his mind. . . .

He has to listen to innumerable comments upon the book, upon the woman who wrote the letters, upon the lack of fineness in the man who had allowed them to be published. He has to hear the whole theme made the subject of light jesting. He has to become profoundly conscious that his honour has been tainted and that the whole of his present life—its success, its prosperity, its outward happiness—is founded upon a betrayal and a lie. The last drop of bitterness is added when he finds that Barton Flamel is making love in a careless way to the woman for whose sake Glennard had sold himself to dishonour, and he becomes conscious that "he had sounded the depths of his humiliation, and that the lowest dregs of it, the very bottom slime, was the hateful necessity of having always, as long as the two men lived, to be civil to Barton Flamel." As the story proceeds further in its development, we find in Glennard's mind remorse becoming wholly morbid. His wife suspects at last. The two, with the consciousness of an unacknowledged secret blighting all their confidence in one another and keeping them apart, become estranged. Flamel grows serious in his love for Alexa Glennard. The situation is one of a strange psychological intensity. How Mrs. Wharton deals with it and what the outcome is must be discovered from the reading of her book.

That part of *The Touchstone* which seems to us the most irresistibly fascinating is the half-told, half-hinted story of the romance of Glennard and Margaret Aubyn—a second "Muse's Tragedy"—and its fascination largely comes from the fact that it *is* half hinted and half told. It is here that Mrs. Wharton shows her possession—for it is not an imitation—of the consummate art of which Henry James is such a master, and which is the art of not telling you too much, but of relieving the high lights by suggestive shadows, and by employing with effectiveness the piquancy and the poetry of the impalpable. There are a thousand little hints that stir the curiosity of the reader, that make him want to know, that compel him to guess, but that leave him after all his guessing still in doubt, precisely as he is left in doubt over so many of the mysteries which surround him in the walks of life itself, and from which the veil is never wholly drawn. How much did Glennard's interest in Mrs. Aubyn really mean in the days when they were together? Did he always feel the same physical recoil? What were the letters? And, above all, what were his answers to them? We feel as though we would give all the rest of the book for just a single one of her later missives, with one of his replies. The fancy plays about the subject and builds hypotheses with infinite and tantalising ingenuity, and still one is not gratified, but goes over the entire ground again and again, eternally inquiring and eternally disappointed.

The latter portion of the book is, on the whole, less satisfactory. The theme is really a very large one, and we somehow feel that the writer has not kept her subject well in hand, that it has escaped her now and then, and that she is herself conscious of the effort that she makes to grasp it and to keep it under her control. Especially unsatisfactory to us is the delineation of Alexa Glennard. She was a woman whose chief grace in Glennard's eyes was an inscrutable composure, an intelligent reserve, a serene inaction. She was of a "passionate justice." Her candour was the candour that is rare in woman. Her sense of honour was so keen that when she comes to know of what her husband has done—that he has sold the letters of another woman in order to win herself—she feels a most intense repulsion, and she becomes estranged from him, the man who has loved her so deeply, and whom she loves. She cannot bear to think that there should rest upon his life and hers the taint that comes from such an act as his. Yet it none the less appears that she accepts Flamel's devotion and makes him think at least that she returns it; and she gives as her excuse her wish to please and thus propitiate the only man who knows her husband's secret and who might use it to discredit him. Somehow, this does not quite convince; and among the unsolved mysteries of the book is that which centres in the question whether she did not really entertain a certain *tendresse* for Flamel, not only after she had guessed the truth, but long before her mind had been even stirred by a suspicion of it. Again, the later pages of the book push introspection to the verge of pure morbidity. There is even a touch of the hysterical suggested here and there; and, to be quite frank, we think that the Glennard of the last three chapters is too obviously the product of a feminine imagination. The conclusion is artistically telling, but perhaps a little too artistic to be quite harmonious with the realities of daily life.

No one can read a dozen pages of what Mrs. Wharton writes without being struck by her positive genius for finished phrase and telling epigram. In epigram, indeed, she is much superior to Mr. James; and some of her crisp and brilliant sentences deserve to become classic. We cannot refrain from quoting just a few of them.

There are times when the constancy of the woman one cannot marry is almost as trying as that of the woman one does not want to.

The young woman . . . combined with a kind of personal shyness an intellectual audacity that was like a deflected impulse of coquetry; one felt that if she had been prettier she would have had emotions instead of ideas.

Husbands who are notoriously inopportune may even die inopportunely.

No woman who does not dress well intuitively will ever do so by the light of reason.

. . . Genius is of small use to a woman who does not know how to do her hair.

Cleverness was useful in business; but in society it seemed to him as futile as the sham cascades formed by a stream that might have been used to drive a mill. He liked the collective point of view that goes with the civilised uniformity of dress-clothes.

Extremely subtle is the description of Glennard's nebulous "friendship" with Mrs. Aubyn as having "dragged on with halting renewals of sentiment, becoming more and more a banquet of empty dishes from which the covers were never removed." And this: "In the dissolution of sentimental partnerships it is seldom that both associates are able to withdraw their funds at the same time." But we must not rob the book of all its gems. Suffice it to say that Mrs. Wharton's novel is certain to give to the discriminating reader that rare delight which comes from the combination of remarkable intelligence, an extraordinary power of analysis, and a style that exemplifies precision, grace, lucidity, and above all, distinction.

Aline Gorren, "Studies in Souls," *Critic*, 37 (August 1900), 173–6

The literary revelation of the nature of women has chiefly hitherto been left to men. And it has been assumed that at the hands, at least, of the masters, the revelation has been complete. Men have maintained that it was complete. They have recognized in the women of Shakespeare and Balzac and Thackeray a play of emotion and action having all the shades of elusiveness of which their own observation of feminine psychology had given them experience. Nor has it been felt alone of the greatest that they understood the inconsequent sex. A number of minor novelists have achieved reputations on the strength of the same alleged penetration. "How well he understands women!" is a phrase that has helped many Bourgets to fame. I say, the same "alleged" penetration. For that the most impersonal and flexible psychologists ever succeed in entering *de cáp-a-pié* into the ken of the sex to which they do not belong should, upon the whole, always be considered open to doubt. There has never been any hesitancy in defining the limitations of women writers, even the most accomplished, in the interpretation of men. They have been freely accused of inability to create in fiction a man that was really a man. Well, some of the women created in the fiction of men are not really women. They are more apt to be real women than the

women writers' men are apt to be men; more apt precisely in proportion to the greater amount of genius funded in the accumulated store of masculine writing through the centuries. But, however, for that hypocrisy developed in women by the reasons that one knows, that secretiveness which makes them accept without disclaimer conventions regarding them which have been established by poets on one side and satirists on the other, one might have heard it oftener asserted that male psychological studies of feminine motives and sentiments have not invariably hit the mark.

If it be a question of complete revelations, it is safe to say that it is only from women themselves that they can be expected; just as the positively authoritative analysis of the masculine nature must be left to men. But the woman writer needs the rarer equipment for her task; it is, that is to say, a rarer thing—again, for all those known reasons—for her to possess the exact balance of qualities which will enable her to make her revelations dispassionately. In the author of *The Greater Inclination* this balance of qualities appears to exist in a remarkable degree. It strikes one that whoever has read quite understandingly four or five of the stories in that collection will always look thereafter, in anything that Mrs. Wharton may write, primarily for the genius with which she will bring to the surface the underground movements of women's minds. It is the worst feature of the twaddle that one hears about the soul of Woman, that to say this does not seem to confer any particular distinction. It has been noted that there are a great many novelists of the psychological school who make "divinations" of the nature of women a specialty. And a woman who "divines" her sex superlatively well is taken to be a subjective, an introspective, intense being, of the harp-like order, whose competency in this line of research is paid for by restrictions upon other points of her horizon. As a matter of fact, it is only by having many other points of her horizon open and free, so open and so free that they command wide sweeps of landscape, that the woman writer who writes about women will ever get the proper light upon her subject. Mrs. Wharton knows her own sex very well because she knows a great many other things very well. The casts which she takes of the involutions of the deep-down feelings of her sisters are quite marvelously faithful and lifelike; the liquid, before setting, has run into every crack and crevice. But how much one must have learned before one can know of what poses and moments—as really significant—to take a moulding!

The people the lining of whose souls Mrs. Whartons turns inside out are not New-Englanders That is, they are not rural New-Englanders. Some of them come from Boston and Cambridge; but, even then, they do not belong to the order of Mr. Howells's or Miss Mary Wilkins's New-Englanders. Their consciences are very conspicuous, to be sure; but it is not the familiar Covenanting conscience, warped by generations of bad air in shut-up homes under the New Hampshire snows, and harried by the peculiar nightmares bred of undigested apple-pie and transcendentalism. Mrs. Wharton's characters are taken from the order of freer and gentler spirits to whom the Almighty has given the great grace of larger opportunities. They are people "of the world." And they are mostly New-Yorkers. But Mrs. Wharton is a psychologist, and never departs from the psychological point of view, and these Americans "of the world" of hers, these New-Yorkers whom she puts on the scene, *have*, unmistakably, souls. Every thinking American must be grateful for this; and he must recognize that it is an achievement. It would not take much to make one go so far as to say that it is an almost unique achievement. The American soul, hitherto—so far, at least, as it could be got at for literary purposes—has clung to the atmosphere of the New England States with the pertinacity of a particular "control" hovering about a special medium at a spiritualist's séance. It appeared to be next to impossible to make it "materialize" anywhere else. The bodies of New-Yorkers, along with their clothes and some other externalities, were recognizable enough in certain of our novels. But inside there did not seem to be anything but vapor. Just what made those clubmen and Wall Street speculators, or journalists, or struggling lawyers, act in such or such a manner? After the first few steps of exploration within, one lost one's way in a fog. With the women it was no better; it was worse. The New York beauty-and-heiress has laughed and cried and been a good daughter and (supposedly) loved a man in many novels of New York life; and we have been good-natured, and have taken it all for granted. And, after we had laid the book aside, we have referred, mentally, to our explanatory formula: the formula that, the elements of the life of fashionable New-Yorkers being so largely drawn from alien sources, it was natural that they themselves should be *empruntés*, and therefore practically valueless as material to any true artist.

Such formulæ hold good until a true artist whose personal alchemy is different from that of other artists upsets them. His mind is a new focus of invention, and lights and influences radiate from it that bring out values and uses in what before had seemed to be rubbish. The worldly, or merely well-bred, Americans of Mrs. Wharton are not all front elevation; as one passes the façade and goes back into the perspectives with her the vapors sepa-

34

rate and mass themselves up, and, in the twilight, there is seen to be an interlacement of paths, and the masses have faintly distinguishable shapes. Mrs. Wharton takes the view that there *can* be something inside even when one spends one's summers at Newport;—which, after all, is credible. She makes it visible that one can be a female toady, sacrificing dignity and peace of mind to the keeping up of the pace and the appearances, dodging bills, and going out the back way to avoid dressmakers' emissaries, and yet be a woman passionately faithful to an ideal of heroism and of sacrifice to duty personified in a man:—"For years you were the tallest object on my horizon. I used to climb to the thought of you, as people who live in a flat country mount the church steeple for a view. It's wonderful how much I used to see from there! And the air was so strong and pure!" And there is no questioning the tragedy that overtakes that woman's life when, from the altered angle of vision of her riper experience, she discovers that the god has been no god at all through all those years, and that she nevermore can be made a little better just by the remembrance of him. Mrs. Wharton makes it visible that to have lived "in a commodious mansion in Fifth Avenue," with her mother-in-law "commanding the approaches from the second-story front windows," is not for a New York woman always to have been rendered proof against the troubles of the imagination. And the Mary Anerton of the "Muse's Tragedy," the emotional woman of *quarante ans*—and perhaps, also, of *cinquante*!—who is so true (so much truer, and so much more frequent, than the average woman would ever dare to reveal); the type of woman of whom Robert Louis Stevenson learned, in the latter part of his life, to know something, and of whom he spoke as representing a "desperate case of middle age";—this Mary Anerton is as moving and as superfluously lovable and charming as if she were not an American of the best American *monde*.

The Touchstone is a short novel, but its substance and method are only an extension of the substance and method of Mrs. Wharton's short stories. She does not handle crowds, nor the simultaneous development of many interrelated characters. She isolates one or two men and women, and studies them. The Glennard of the book is a dry and commonplace young man, who has never thought much about either his good or his bad qualities, and who does not know of what he is made. He commits a blackguardly act, and in the shame and horror of the self-exposure which ensues he sees himself so small, in his own eyes and in those of his wife, that he envelops her in the hatred that he pours upon himself. It is close to the life. The vapid, fatuous, vanity-sick sentimentality of his posthumous amorous coquetting with the memory of the woman whom he had despised in her lifetime is a master-stroke, and one of the strokes in Mrs. Wharton's work that stick in the memory. Alexa Trent fails, at first, to be quite realized (of course one speaks for one's self); but, toward the close, her figure detaches itself, and the image that she leaves is that of a woman whose love and faith have so flowered and twined about the moral uglinesses on which she would not dwell, at which she would not even look, that she has changed them at last into beauties. It is the feminine nature engaged in the "priest-like task of cold ablution round earth's human shores."

And Mrs. Wharton renders us the more conscious of the loveliness of the function that we feel that she does not make by any means the mistake of supposing that it is within every woman's capabilities to perform it.

"New Novels: *A Gift from the Grave*," *Athenæum* [England], 3799 (18 August 1900), 210

The publisher's pleasant little preface to this story explaining his choice of a title is too apologetic. Two or more names had been found, but each in turn was discovered to have been already appropriated. The author being for the time inaccessible, the publisher supplied *A Gift from the Grave*. To us it seems that no happier title could have been possible to convey the significance of this clever and delicately told tale. The substance of it produces an excellent, but decidedly painful situation of the kind that used to be called high psychological interest. It involves a question of moral conduct rather than one of merely good or bad taste. It is the publication (by the man to whom they were addressed) of the love letters of a dead woman celebrated in the world of literature. No one will doubt the heinousness of the offence, even though prompted by the strongest temptations—the desire of a moneyless man to secure the woman he loves. Yet the position, circumstances, and temperament of the man must have full consideration, for they are presented with remarkable subtlety and insight which, if not exactly sympathetic, is certainly comprehending. The nature of the writer and her attitude towards life, and especially towards her correspondent, are skillfully conveyed without her actual presence, or any of the letters themselves. The unconscious, innocent stabs inflicted by the man's wife and his friend, and construed by the victim into intentional attacks because of his own morbid, over-strained state, form a piece of agile verbal duelling. Certain touches remind one of a chapter in a book by Anstey, containing a sparring match between a man with a guilty conscience and his tormentor. There is some beauty in the later development of the story, where the wife displays a power of sympathy and affection of no mean degree. If the interest in the affair has begun to flag a little it is not because the expression of emotion is not adequate, nor the growth of the man's nobler nature uninspiring. *A Gift from the Grave*, like many other stories by American authors, is almost too polished. If it lack something, it is the grace of perfect simplicity and plain language.

"Recent American Fiction," *Atlantic Monthly*, 86 (September 1900), 418–19

Utterly dissimilar, in tone and intention, to the two novels already mentioned, is *The Touchstone*, by Edith Wharton, of which, however, there can hardly be higher praise than to say that it fully answers the expectations excited by a collection of short stories from the same hand published less than a year ago. The rather enigmatical title of that exceptionally refined *recueil*, *The Greater Inclination*, explained itself in the course of the book as a scientific metaphor. It meant the slight but conclusive deflection by incalculable circumstance of a trembling and all but equally hung balance of principle and motive. The sketches in question were all fragmentary; episodes or studies in a transient light, never the complete history of any one of the *dramatis personæ*. They were very clever, very subtle, very urbane;

quick, too, with the trained and polished wit of a woman of the world. But the author's extreme fastidiousness, her almost morbid fear of overlaying and overworking, prevented her from finishing anything. One or two of the stories ended, and ended effectively enough, in the middle of a sentence. The characters were all taken from the *milieu* of clubs and ballrooms; but within these conventional limits, the novelist found material for the most serious and searching psychological study. She is indeed no mean psychologist, and all the rare qualities of the earlier essays are seen to even heightened advantage in the new book. *The Touchstone* is a more sustained effort than any one of its predecessors, and it is well sustained. The analysis of the hero's mental struggle goes deeper; the ethical conclusion is more unhesitatingly drawn. The simple story need not be repeated here. It was plainly suggested in the first instance by the publication of the Browning Love Letters. If [Ellen Glasgow's] *The Voice of the People* is incredibly and almost amusingly innocent of extraneous literary influence, *The Touchstone* is replete with echoes, reflections, reminiscences from the lighter literature of many lands and languages. There is one distinguished contemporary writer, indeed, whose influence is too plain to be overlooked. Mrs. Wharton has sat at the feet of Henry James, and in the way of her art she has unquestionably learned much from him. But she would now do well to rise from her deferential attitude. Better things than he can inspire are, we believe, within the scope of her still widening possibilities.

The American city whose high life the author of *The Touchstone* has depicted without a trace of vulgarity (no common feat!) is New York; always with fond and respectful reminiscences of Philadelphia. Boston is but a byword there. Turning over our triad of novels yet once again,—

the Bostonian's Western tale, and the Southern tale, and the tale of what was once only the chief city of the Middle States but is now the metropolis of the Union,—we are freshly convinced that the Puritan vein and the transcendental vein are both worked out. Let us close the mouth of the echoing shaft, and heartily salute the young workers in less thoroughly explored and apparently richer mines. The life of the Northeastern states is too settled, circumscribed, and safe, it has been too long fat, and "set," and prosperous, to afford the best of dramatic material. If Spain had had will or the power to bombard the cities of the New England seaboard in the summer of 1898, we might have had some strong novels of New England life in the next generation. As it is, we must wait a little longer.

William Morton Payne, "Recent Fiction," *Dial*, 29 (1 September 1900), 126

Mrs. Edith Wharton's second book of fiction is not a collection of stories, like *The Greater Inclination*, but a single novel. Yet *The Touchstone*, although we must call it a novel, has really no more substance than one of the briefer sketches. It is the story of a single incident, and of its influence upon the lives of a man and his wife. It is a story that might easily have been told in fifty pages; the hundred additional pages that are given us merely serve to permit of a more detailed analysis of the situation created by a single thoughtless act. Yet we would not spare from the story a single page, for the writer's art is so exquisite that no one of her pages seems superfluous, or fails in its contribution to the deep impressiveness of her psychological study. If the book has a defect, that defect must be sought in the central conception, and not in the treatment. The hero has in his possession a great many letters, of the most intimate character, written to him by a woman who had loved him all her life, but whom he had been incapable of loving in return. That woman had become a famous writer, and after her death, anything that could throw light upon her personality was eagerly demanded by the public. The recipient of the letters, learning of this demand, and for lack of money unable to marry the woman he loves, actually sells this sacred correspondence to a publisher, suppressing his own name, and thereby removes the obstacle to his marriage. When he realizes what he has done he becomes remorseful, and Mrs. Wharton's purpose is to direct our attention to the workings of his conscience, to excite our sympathies for his sufferings. In this she is imperfectly successful, for it would tax the powers of the greatest novelist that ever lived to be entirely successful in such a task. The act in question is so despicable that no motive would seem adequate for its justification, no circumstances could be found more than palliating in the case of such an offense. Mrs. Wharton's treatment of this theme is all that we might desire, but it cannot give us a genuinely sympathetic interest in such a person as her hero. We cannot help feeling that he deserves even more than he suffers, and we remain suspicious of any moral regeneration that is brought about by means of his remorse. Yet it is the clear intention of the writer to have us accept this moral regeneration as a fact, and to forgive the offender as his own deceived wife forgives him in the end. In a word, the substance of this book is of a kind to repel rather than to attract; what does attract, and

even fascinate, is the delicacy of texture and the distinction of style which the work exhibits.

Review of *A Gift from the Grave,* Bookman [England], 18 (September 1900), 189

To meet with a book like this is a great refreshment to a reviewer. In writing fiction, Miss Wharton is doing the work to which she is called; there are proofs of it in every page. The situation is well conceived; and though it is connected with the literary world, it has a strong emotional interest. She has allowed herself just enough room to develop the situation adequately; none for subordinate matters, none for irrelevance. There may be an occasional hint of Meredithese, such as "She swept to him with a rescuing gesture." But, as a whole, the workmanship is excellent, very far above the average of what comes to us from America, fit expression for her sound and vigorous conception of character. Miss Wharton deals with that very ticklish theme, a man's rising on stepping-stones of his dead self to higher things. The thinking world is wont to be sad and sceptical in front of it, when the past self was a mean one. But the teller of this tale, though she takes the encouraging view, does not indulge in frivolous sentimentality. "The great renewals take effect as imperceptibly as the first workings of spring," she owns; and her faulty man has not reached saintship on the last page. By the way, the name is not the one chosen by the writer. Mr. Murray gives in a note his reasons for his choice.

Checklist of Additional Reviews

Ellen Burns Sherman, "Two Novels of the Psycho-Realistic School," *Book Buyer*, 20 (May 1900), 320–2.

CRUCIAL INSTANCES

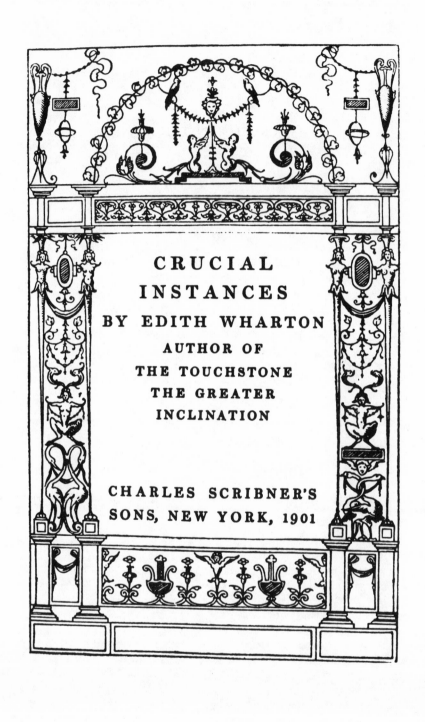

CRUCIAL
INSTANCES
BY EDITH WHARTON
AUTHOR OF
THE TOUCHSTONE
THE GREATER
INCLINATION

CHARLES SCRIBNER'S
SONS, NEW YORK, 1901

In this volume of short stories the writer works out her really difficult conceptions without the risk of inspiration. Her genius consists in a delicate perception of forms and color. She accepts the law of environment literally and invariably squeezes the right people out of a situation. They result from it and interpret it, in the same way that flowers show the sentimentality of the soil. "The Duchess at Prayer" is, perhaps, the most admirably written story of the series—an incident, by the way, which Balzac once developed somewhat differently. But even here the author shows the subconsciousness of a foreigner. She sees green bottle flies in the sunshine, and detects that ancient odor of crime which every true Italian takes for granted. The "fold on fold of blue mountains, clear as gauze against the sky," is only the rim over which her imagination gracefully fades. All within the valley is as bright and clearly defined as a conscientious artist can make it. Apparently her own national newness renders it impossible for Miss Wharton to see the "dust of centuries dark and deep" that must cover everything in Italy. She takes the tourist's point of view, and sees everything with startling vividness. Into those stories dealing with life subjectively she shows a mathematical accuracy. Every thought is a well defined line in the geometrical problem of life, and there are no tangents upon which the reader may rest from the toil of understanding. The proper appreciation of these stories will depend upon the reader's culture and mental endurance.

"Mrs. Wharton's
Nativity: The Clever and
Subtle Disciple of Henry
James a Native of the
American Metropolis,"
Munsey's Magazine, 25
(June 1901), 435–6

In view of the rarity of the native New York author, it is interesting to examine him, when discovered, as the product of the chief American city.

Probably Mrs. Edith Wharton is the most distinguished of the latter day crop of metropolitan authors. She was born in New York some thirty odd years ago, and she has written nothing for which her birthplace could have been the entire or even the chief inspiration.

She was educated mainly by tutors and governesses. She has been a great deal abroad, Italy in particular seeming almost a second home to her. She has been free from the ordinary failing of the rich woman who writes—that is, she has not used literature merely as an additional gem for a social coronet. No one who reads her admirable English, and who realizes the study and effort which admirable English entails, could believe that with Mrs. Wharton writing is a fad, secondary to the pursuits of a fashionable existence.

But distinctively of New York her stories are not. They are, socially, of Boston, or of London, or of that indistinctly bounded territory of rarified airs where the Henry James people dwell; or they are of Italy, with all its medieval dignity.

Some critic has said that Mrs. Wharton's weakness is in the depicting of masculine character. Her men are subtle and complex ladies wearing mustaches. This may lead one to wonder whether the fault is with Mrs. Wharton's power of characterization, or in the material that she has for study.

"Art and Life," *Academy*, 61 (27 July 1901), 75–6

Art, though in its cruder forms it seems to pervade life, is artificial and negligible. It is the embroidery on the coverlet that keeps us warm at night. We are happier with it, but we could be happy without it. A man may say that an appreciation of the classics alone makes life tolerable to him, but put him in an ice-house with Homer, and tell him that he may emerge only on condition of leaving Homer for ever behind, and he will leave Homer for ever behind. Life is, indeed, constantly and rudely reminding us that art is a mere game of make-believe, a diversion and a solace to be employed in the moments when life is a little less business-like than usual. We don't turn to *Adonais* while our friend is dying, but only when he is dead and there is nothing else to do. When life chooses to become intense, art is nowhere, neglected like a mistress in the wars, forgotten like a fable. The toothache will annihilate Beethoven's C Minor Symphony. Art is a very little thing, and only by borrowing some of the greatness of life can it become great. All the great works of art have simple, primitive, elemental themes, and achieve their greatness as much by their themes as by their execution. What shall be said, then, of the art which, avoiding the grand and permanent simplicities of life, turns for its theme to art itself, seeking to artificialise the artificial, to build a convention on a convention, to embroider the embroidery?

We have been led to this consideration, and to the somewhat facile pomposity of our title, by the perusal of a little book of admirable tales called *Crucial Instances* . . . by a novelist who truly deserves that often misapplied epithet "distinguished"— Edith Wharton. Mrs. Wharton persistently does her best work in writing about art, artists, and the other people who make of art their chief pre-occupation. And, though she not improbably is unaware of her limitation— since she gives prominence in this book to the conspicuous failures of it, her fine and rare talent is quite confined to that narrow circle of artificiality which is called art. Of the seven stories, two are about authors, two are about pictures, one is about a painter, and the remaining two alone—the first and the last—deal with sheer stark life. These latter are both concerned with adultery. One is a flat, painstaking recital of a nineteenth century Italian melodrama. The other is a mediæval legend closely resembling the most famous of all Balzac's short stories, told in a manner which would fain be Balzacian, but is not. Here we are sorrowfully compelled to listen to the strident shouting, over the bleak ways of life, of a voice which, in the close air of the studio, can be full of subtle significance and quiet impressiveness. We guess that the author means to strike us down by imaginative force, but all we are conscious of is a futile beating of the air with violent similes.

Cypresses that cut the sunshine *like* basalt shafts,

Maimed statues stretched their arms *like* rows of whining beggars,

A heavy door behind which the cold lurked *like* a knife,

A quibbling mouth that would have snapped at verbal errors *like* a lizard catching flies,

Lizards shot out of the cracked soil *like* flames,
White domes and roofs flashed *like* a smile.

Not thus, by the reiteration of *likes*, by the machinery of bizarre comparisons, is the tragic atmosphere to be created, but rather by simple and direct fervency of statement.

This done, he went on shipboard, and is now
A Seaman, a gray-headed Mariner.

There is tragedy, haunting and profound, got by the simple directness of Wordsworth's art, which suited the simple directness of his theme. But it is a proviso of Mrs. Wharton's gift that she cannot be direct. Her force curiously depends on its obliquity. She can only arrive at her destination by going somewhere else. She can only describe one thing by describing another. She is bound to talk the delicate and dulcet language of hints which Mr. Henry James and herself have perfected. And so she fails whenever her theme demands singleness, simplicity, naiveté. But when she leaves the few simple passions and desires of which real essential life is made, and comes to the unreal bewildering overlay of conventions which the leisured classes have constructed for themselves, and whose "complexity" they bewail, then she is at home; then she can be herself; then she can point at a truth with her elbow while looking the other way, convey a statement of fact while uttering the exact opposite, and generally achieve the highest virtuosity of fencing. One tale in this book, "The Recovery," is a little masterpiece; we say a little one. It is about an American citizen, who, by means of an instrument made for that purpose, daubed coloured pigments on oblong pieces of canvas in a particular way. He thought that no one had ever daubed with such skill as himself. But he had not been to Europe, where this craft of daubing had been carried on for hundreds of years. A female admirer arranged for a number of his oblong pieces of daubed canvas to be hung on the walls of a room in Paris, where people could see them. The American citizen also came to Paris. The exhibition of his canvases was not a failure, but he discovered, to his horror, that the European daubers had daubed in a different style from himself, and a better. For hours he was in despair, and then suddenly he resolved to learn the European method of daubing. And that is all. No question of love, hunger, pain, death; but merely this question of how to daub, which all the characters take seriously, as if it really mattered. And yet a masterpiece, though a little one. The extraordinary jargon of the inhabitants of that world where daubing is done, and when done is discussed, is rendered with a fidelity that will charm the initiate. "'He's too impossible!' cried Mrs. Davant, sweeping her at once into the central current of her grievance." . . .

What would the man who sowed the wheat that made the bread that these people ate make out of this intercommunication of souls? "H–ll and thunder—"? And yet *we* understand it, appreciate it; and we who can breathe the atmosphere of studios without inconvenience are apt to say that it is none the less clever, exact, truthful, subtle, because only a few persons can make head or tail of it. We can perceive, too, the fine satire of such a stroke as this in the delineation of the hero (What a hero!): "Keniston to his other claims to distinction added that of being hard to know. His friends always hastened to announce the fact to strangers— adding, after a pause of suspense, that they 'would see what they could do.' Visitors in whose favour he was induced to

45

make an exception were further warned that he never spoke unless he was interested, so that they mustn't mind if he remained silent." We can perceive the wonderfulness of the faculty disclosed in this truly brilliant *aperçu* of Paris: "Claudia ... turned aimlessly into the wide whirling brightness of the streets. . . ."

Take the story as a whole, take all the five stories, was the achievement worth achieving? We think so. There must be little art, as well as great art. But—and this is the moral we wish to inculcate—the little art is very little, very limited in its scope, its power, its appeal. The besetting danger of the time is, in art, to confuse the fine and subtle, the highly conventionalised, with the supreme elemental. No good quality can atone for the absence of the elemental. Art is not elemental—never will be nor can be. The moment it ceased to be an "attitude" towards life, it will cease to be art. And the artists of today are more and more prone to discuss themselves, to find their themes in their own artificial problems. The artists of the golden ages never did so. It is a sign of decadence, this preoccupation with the inessential. But we are as we are, planted here by a power beyond the ken of art. If the age be decadent, we can help it no more than an old man can help being old. To the decadent age, a decadent literature. Let us make it as excellent as we can, and enjoy it as bravely as we can. Let us especially not miss the distinction between fine and great. We who write have a sincere admiration for Mrs. Wharton's original and delicate talent; we have felt the temptation to give it all sorts of beautiful names; it suits us and our time; it is of the hour. But when we turn, for instance, to the poem whose last lines we have quoted above, we grow absurdly conscious of the instability of the whole Wharton fabric.

"Crucial Instances," *Athenæum* [England], 3850 (10 August 1901), 186

Subtlety and strenuousness are the most noticeable qualities in these pages, and they are characteristic of many American authors who are gifted with a fine dramatic instinct. The strenuousness has a tendency to predominate in the majority of her *Crucial Instances*; but there are one or two treated in a lighter vein which are at least as convincing as those confined exclusively to a tragic setting. "The Recovery," in which the artist discovers, after a brief sojourn in Paris, the inferiority of his own work, but rather rejoices in his awakening than suffers morbid regrets that he has been prepaid for work he no longer intends to do, is a clever study of the artistic temperament. "The Rembrandt" is, again, a happy combination of lightness and pathos in treatment. Amongst the more tragic instances "The Confessional" is a powerful piece of writing. The writer shows an intimate knowledge of Italy and the Italians, and has evidently made a careful study of some of the sombre pages in the history of that country.

"The Editor's Easy Chair," *Harper's Monthly Magazine* 103 (October 1901), 823–4

No one would now be be writing well if some one else had not been writing well before; and if Mrs. Edith Wharton writes so well as she does almost too much in the manner of Mr. Henry James, those who know her writing need not be assured that its likeness to that master's work is not a condition of its excellence. At her best, in those moments when the poetic impulse which is the heart of her endeavor fulfils itself in some lyrical picture singing to the eye, she writes as wholly upon her own authority as any one can after so many thousand years of writing. The reader can make our dim meaning clearer to himself by turning to the opening passage of that study of mediæval Italy called "The Duchess at Prayer," which opens Mrs. Wharton's latest book, *Crucial Instances*. "From the loggia, with its vanishing frescoes, I looked down an avenue barred by a ladder of cypress shadows to the ducal escutcheon and mutilated vases of the gate. *Flat noon* lay on the gardens, on fountains, porticoes, and grottoes. Below the terrace, *where a chrome-colored lichen had sheeted the balustrade as with fine laminæ of gold*, vineyards stooped to the rich valley clasped in hills. The lower slopes were strewn with white villages like stars spangling a summer dusk; and beyond these, fold on fold of blue mountain, clear as gauze against the sky." This is such very Italy that one who has truly known Italy could name the very moment and place of it all; and the phrases which we have italicized lest the reader should miss any implication of them are those effects of emotion by which the poet shares with the reader what she felt as well as what she thought in beholding the things.

A poet Mrs. Wharton is always, and not least a poet in her defeats. She fails as the poet often fails with such material as that of "The Duchess at Prayer," with the brute facts of the sin and the crime. The time and the place are wonderfully painted but the action is so weak that one finds one's self not much caring whether the statue of the praying duchess is placed over her hidden lover in the crypt or not. The action is compensatingly strong in the other Italian piece, "The Confessional," which closes the volume. This again is very Italy, not mediæval Italy, but revolutionary Italy, the Italy of day before yesterday, whose generous hopes have been blighted in the Italy of to-day. The translation of the drama to our land and hour, and to such a sordid scene and instant as an actual manufacturing town on Long Island, gives proof of the author's power upon reality which makes one doubt whether she was not baffled by the essential unreality of "The Duchess at Prayer." But, after all, she seems at her best in "The Recovery." The study of the painter overrated by home criticism and liberated to self-knowledge by a visit to Paris, where his intrinsic honesty gets the better of all the mistaken admiration of his worshippers and he begins anew, is of many precious psychological imports suggested with a constant and delicately sarcastic humor. Something of the same humor qualifies that charming sketch "The Rembrandt," but there it is a little sharper; in "The Angel at the Grave" it is felt rather as a pensive light on the pathetic event. It is this humor, in whatever force or phase it shows itself, which should enable the author to be solely herself. A poet may be unconsciously like some one else, even such a genuine poet as Mrs. Wharton, but a humorist cannot well reflect another method and another manner without knowing it.

THE VALLEY OF DECISION

THE VALLEY OF DECISION

A NOVEL

BY

EDITH WHARTON

VOLUME I

Multitudes, multitudes in the valley of decision

NEW YORK

CHARLES SCRIBNER'S SONS

MDCCCCII

Frederic Taber Cooper, "Mrs. Wharton's *The Valley of Decision*," *Bookman*, 15 (April 1902), 173–5

There is a type of artistic temperament that seems to find a sensuous satisfaction in vast canvases and themes of epic magnitude. And since, in a certain sense, the novelist has a far wider canvas than the artist upon which to paint his picture, he runs a proportionately greater chance of overestimating his strength. He is not limited by any single hour or day or year; he is not bounded by the visible horizon; he may cover a whole epoch in the history of an individual or a family or a nation; or he may concentrate himself upon a single crucial moment in the life of a man or a woman. The value of what he does depends not upon the breadth of the canvas, but upon the inherent truth of the perspective, the accuracy of the line and colour, the subtle and indefinable sense of proportion underlying the whole conception. Yet the temptation to strive for something big and broad and impressive, to paint humanity in the mass, to study not individual lives, but the complex development of a race has led astray more than one of our promising younger writers. It is the sort of task which demands a long apprenticeship. Kipling embodied in *Kim* the thoughtful deliberation of a dozen years. Zola was content to toil for more than twenty before he attempted to sum up the motley life of the French metropolis in a single volume, *Paris*. Tolstoy waited almost to the end of his career before trying to epitomise all Russia in his *Resurrection*, and even then, in spite of its acknowledged power, more than one critic questioned its right to the title of novel. Yet it is just this sort of colossal task that the author of *The Touchstone* serenely set for herself in *The Valley of Decision*; and the fact that the resulting novel is entitled to a modicum of honest and cordial praise is in itself a recognition of her versatility and her genius.

Mrs. Wharton was fortunate at the outset in her choice of a subject. She has attempted to sum up the life of Italy in the latter half of the eighteenth century, that crucial *settecento*, which has aptly been compared to the closing act of a tragedy. It was that period of fallacious calm following the war of the Austrian Succession, when beneath the surface all Italy was seething with undercurrents of discontent against the old established order of things; when "the little Italian courts were still dozing in fancied security under the wing of Bourbon and Hapsburg suzerains;" when clergy and nobles still clung tenaciously to their class privileges and united in their efforts to repress the spread of learning; when throngs of the ignorant and superstitious still crowded the highroads to the shrines of popular saints, and a small but growing number of enlightened spirits met in secret conclave to discuss forbidden new doctrines of philosophy and science. It is a vast subject, and one full of epic values—a subject which it is easy to imagine a Balzac or a Tolstoy treating in the bold, sweeping, impressionistic way that it demands. But it is not easy to imagine what an introspective writer, a Bourget, or a Henry James, could make of such a theme, and still less an avowed disciple of Mr. James, such as Mrs. Wharton has hitherto shown herself. That the resulting volume shows so much comparative excellence is a pleasant surprise. She has brought to her task a considerable amount of erudition. She is saturated to her finger-tips with the historical facts of the period—the motley and confusing tangle of petty dukedoms, the warring claims of Austria and of Spain. She has given us not merely a broad canvas but a moving panorama of the life of that restless time, presenting with a certain dramatic power the discontent of the masses; the petty intrigues of the Church and the aristocracy; the gilded uselessness of the typical fine lady with her *cavaliere servente*, her pet monkey and her parrot; the brutal ignorance of the peasantry; the disorders and license of the Bohemian world—all the various strata and substrata of the social life of the times. The book is less a novel than a sort of cultured *Sittengeschichte* of the epoch, as minute, as conscientious and as comprehensive as a chapter from Gibbon's *Rome*, yet lacking those little, vital, illuminating touches which help to make us see. Her most obvious fault seems to be her avoidance of the concrete and the specific. She delights in indulging in generalities. She leaves a mental impression of crowds and movement and the turmoil of hurrying, bustling human life; but when we search in our memory for further impressions, we find them misty and uncertain. The people, the scenes, the incidents, are often not necessarily Italian at all. She is seldom definite enough in her descriptions to be. Much of the time we miss even the sunshine, the blue sky, that redolence of warmth and colour and superficial gayety which is the very essence of Italy—which fills every page of Stendhal's *Chartreuse de Parme*, is woven into the woof and warp of *Romola*, and goes far toward redeeming even the tawdry sensationalism of such a writer as Ouida. There are times when one cannot help feeling that Mrs. Wharton has something in common with her hero, who, she tells us, "had lived through twelve Italian summers without sense of the sun-steeped quality of an atmosphere that even in shade gives each object a golden salience. He was conscious of it now only as it suggested fingering a missal stiff with gold leaf and edged with a swarming diversity of buds and insects." When she does pause to describe nature, it is usually from a purely æsthetic point of view, with the professional delight of an artist at a grouping of rocks, or trees, or hills which would make an effective picture—"a scene which Salvator might have painted;" or a bend in the road where "the roadside started into detail like the foreground of some minute Dutch painter." And it is characteristic that these descriptions are always of the briefest character. It is only when she becomes interested in some matter of æsthetic or philosophic interest that Mrs. Wharton becomes verbose. It is worth while to quote, even at some length, a characteristic passage of this latter type, for which such passages constitute a formidable proportion of the pages of these two volumes—pages which are apt to remain unread, if not uncut, by a large number of readers, both those who read frankly for amusement, and those who look upon the novel as a serious and important human document: "In the semi-Parisian capital, where French architects designed the king's pleasure-houses. . . ."

Considered in its aspect of a novel, a story of human interest, the shortcomings of *The Valley of Decision* are somewhat more intangible, yet none the less they make themselves felt. The characters are clearly and conscientiously drawn, the drama in which they play a part deals with vital questions of life and liberty and human happiness; and yet they leave us cold; they fail for the most part to touch the keynote of responsive sympathy. The explanation is somewhat hard to find; it lies, in part, at least, in the author's obvious willingness to subordinate her characters to the exposition of her main theme, the picture of Italy as a whole. With this end in view it must be granted that her plot is cleverly chosen. She has conceived a petty dukedom, Pianura, in the north of Italy, owing allegiance to Charles Ferdinand on the one hand, and attached by marriage to the house of Hapsburg on the other. The hero, Odo Valsecca, is of the Old Order, heir-presumptive to the throne of Pianura, and kept from the succession only by a sickly cousin and the latter's dying child. In his character Odo represents the conflicting tendencies of the times. He is in sympathy with the new ideas of progress and liberty, and has brief flashes of energy and enthusiasm. But they soon burn themselves out, for he is fundamentally lethargic and indifferent, inheriting the fatal taint of his house. The heroine, Fulvia Vivaldi, represents the new order. She is the daughter of a professor of philosophy, who pays by exile the penalty for his temerity in following up the forbidden learning. Under Fulvia's influence Odo becomes an enthusiastic disciple of the new philosophy, and he is on the point of sacrificing all his prospects and accompanying her to France, when the death of his cousin unexpectedly makes him Duke of Pianura. To both of them his duty is plain. He must accept the burden and devote his life to giving the people that liberty to which they are entitled. For Fulvia there are two alternatives. She may continue her way alone to Paris, or she may remain at Pianura in a capacity which she will not accept. "'The Regent's mistress?' she asked slowly. . . ."

So Odo returns alone to Pianura and in course of time marries his cousin's widow, of the House of Hapsburg, with whom he might eventually have been fairly happy. But three years later Fulvia changes her mind, comes back to him, and accepts the very conditions which she previously found such excellent reasons for refusing. No doubt, had Mrs. Wharton chosen, she might have given us a luminous picture of the mental transition through which her

heroine passed during these three years of self-inflicted exile. But she has not chosen to do so, and the result is an impression of inconsistency, a feeling that the Fulvia who went away and the Fulvia who returned are not one and the same person. Apparently, the only real necessity for her return was to pave the way for an effective and tragic ending. Fulvia spurs Odo on to give the people the liberal constitution for which they are not yet ready, and in the midst of the resulting riots receives in her heart the shot intended for her lover.

This, in hasty outline, is the plot of *The Valley of Decision*, and, frankly speaking, it is the least essential and least interesting aspect of the book. What really do count are her vivid pictures of life, the human interest of brief but crucial moments, her wonderful intuition in analysing complex emotions—in short, the same qualities which to a greater degree stamped the appearance of her earliest volume as a literary event. In taking up these volumes for a second time, one is apt to turn back to one of just a few brief scenes luminous with comprehension—such a passage as this, for instance, describing an incident in Odo's youth, when, as a boy of twelve, on his way to Turin, his lot fell in for a single night with a company of strolling players: "The pretty girl who had pillowed Odo's slumbers now knelt by his bed and laughingly drew on his stockings. . . . And all that day he scorched and froze with the thought that perhaps she had just been laughing at him."

Gertrude Hall, "One of the Unconquerable Army," *Book Buyer*, 24 (April 1902), 196–8

So sustained an effort on such a level compels admiration and a touch of wonder. I am reminded of the first skylark I heard and watched. Before it had nearly finished, I lifted my hand to my throat, sympathetically oppressed. Superfluously, I am sure. The copiousness of Mrs. Wharton's information, the effect of ease in handling it, and the long breath in recounting, suggest resources from which she can be trusted to draw, indefinitely unexhausted.

The scene of the story is Italy during the latter half of the eighteenth century. The most glittering, many-colored pageant of life imaginable passes on every page—to the point that at moments we fancy the object of the book to be a reflection of places, manners, a period, and feel a shade defrauded—to be presently wholly reassured.

Powdered gentlemen, rouged ladies, abbés, friars, French hair-dressers, Columbine and Scaramouch, chocolate, chairs, cards, masks, gilt coaches, *levers*, vapors, pet monkeys and turbaned blackamoors to mind them, apartments with stucco and mirrors, gardens with mossy statues and box-trees cut in shapes of peacocks—the atmosphere is that which goes with these, at the moment when a weariness of old forms and offences was dawning, and new ideals were expanding the hearts of men. We behold as if an edifice fantastically brilliant, trivial yet heavy, supported by haggard, bowed caryatids, with patient peasant-faces—and we see the palace begin to totter.

The episodes in the book unroll before us charmingly, interestingly, but yet "with scarcely a greater effect of reality than the episodes woven in some gayly tinted tapestry." But a tinted tapestry of what amenity, what felicity! At every turn pictures to which one would willingly go back, sure to be pleased afresh. Such is the remoteness, however, lent by this medium of art that every sort of immorality, turpitude, suffering, comes to us through it without shocking or moving.

The greatest effect of reality, on the other hand, belongs to the inner life of the hero. The book might have been called "Odo: His Sensations and Ideas." Indeed, the thoughtful, generous young Duke seems a descendant of Marius. Perhaps it is because his nature resembles that of the Epicurean that so do, vaguely, his fortunes. He finds his Flavian in Alfieri, in Fulvia his Cecilia, and, like that other, the great opportunity at the last of proving himself—of rising to the height of his ideal. When he stands before the angry populace, immovable and unafraid, feeling "a boyish satisfaction at his own steadiness of pulse and eye," we remember Marius, who, the moment after he had "taken upon himself all the heavy risk of another's position . . . possibly the danger of death, felt only satisfaction at the discovery of his possession of nerve." We remember him, too, at the reference to "deep springs of piety for inanimate things" in Odo; and again when Odo, at his foster-mother's reticence with regard to his former little companion, judges "that the girl must have died—of neglect, perhaps, or ill-usage—and that they feared to own it. His heart swelled, but not against them. They seemed to him no more accountable than cowed, hunger-driven animals." This Aurelian justice Marius would approve.

Pity, simple native pity for men, the wish to serve them, to lift, to relieve their sorrows is the mainspring of Odo's most characteristic actions and renunciations. It takes the outward form of trying to help them to liberty. Every effort of his in this, to all appearance, fails, and yet we feel in the end that his part has somehow been victory.

This persistent pity is touchingly symbolized. In the first pages of the book Odo is seen, a child—they call him the beggar-noble—gazing in a neglected chapel "at the vision of a pale haloed head floating against the dusky background of the chancel like a water-lily on its leaf. The face was that of the Saint of Assisi, a sunken, ravaged countenance, lit with an ecstasy of suffering that seemed not so much to reflect the anguish of the Christ, at whose feet the saint knelt, as the mute pain of all the poor, down-trodden folk on earth." In that suffering face the child finds a melancholy kinship. He is a little fellow who shrinks from any amusement associated with the frightening or hurting of animals.

Again, in the full flower of youth, after draughts of distracting life, he stands in the chapel. "Twilight held the place; but as he stood there the frescoes started out in the slant of sunrise, like dead faces floating to the surface of a river—dead faces, yes; plaintive spectres of his childish fears and longings, lost in the harsh daylight of experience. He had forgotten the very dreams they stood for: Lethe flowed between, and only one voice reached cross the torrent. It was that of Saint Francis, lover of the poor."

And at the end, after the ruin of all his designs and hopes, defeated in every worldly sense, a fugitive, he halts to revisit the old chapel. "The place laid its tranquillizing hush upon him and he knelt on the step beneath the altar. Something stirred in him as he knelt there—a prayer, yet not a prayer—a reaching out, obscure and inarticulate, toward all that had survived of his early hopes and faiths, a loosening of old founts of pity, a longing to be somehow, somewhere, reunited to his old belief in life.

"How long he knelt he knew not; but when he looked up, the chapel was full of a pale light, and in the first shaft of the sunrise the face of Saint Francis shone out on him. . . . He went forth into the daybreak, and rode away toward Piedmont," to lay his single sword again, unwearied, at the service of man, compassion and love for whom had persisted through every defeat and all ingratitude.

We are bewildered, with him, at the difficulties that arose on all sides to prevent his bringing to any fruits his most benevolent intentions. We are made to suspect once again that a man has no power—only seems to have it when he falls in with some Greater Intention than his own. "Nous ne savons pas ce qu'il faudrait savoir." "Nous ne faisons pas ce que nous voulons," we are forced to repeat. But the suspicion at the same time arises that the hero who, like this Odo, has, through all conflict and confusion unfalteringly striven for what is, according to his lights, the right, goes to form a stone in that temple which it is, perhaps, life's object to build.

A thought akin to this passes through Odo's mind as he listens to his learned love's oration—in academic cap and gown—upon Liberty. "The wall behind her was covered by an ancient fresco . . . representing the patron-scholars of the mediæval world, . . . Origen, Zeno, David, Lycurgus, Aristotle. . . . As he looked and listened, a weary sense of the reiterance of things came over him. For what were these ancient manipulators of ideas . . . but the forebears of the long line of theorists of whom Fulvia was the last inconscient mouth-piece? The new game was still

55

played with the old counters. . . . For generations, for centuries, man had fought on, crying for liberty, dreaming it was won, waking to find himself the slave of the new forces he had generated, burning and being burnt for the same beliefs under different guises, calling his instincts ideas, and his ideas revelations: destroying, rebuilding, falling, rising, mending broken weapons, championing extinct illusions, mistaking his failures for achievements, and planting his flag on the ramparts as they fell. And as the vision of this inveterate conflict rose before him, Odo saw that the beauty, the power, the immortality, dwelt not in the idea, but in the struggle for it."

"Yes." he muses on, "it was better, after all, to be one of that great, unconquerable army, though, like the Trojans fighting for a phantom Helen, they might be doing battle for the shadow of a shade; better to march in their ranks, endure with them, fight with them, fall with them, than to miss the great enveloping sense of brotherhood that turned defeat to victory."

The latter part of the book falls somewhat seriously upon the mood generated by the first. We feel we had been promised something different; we went on securely, despite the darkening sky. The bolt that strikes Fulvia finds us more unprepared than herself.

In the language of Pianura, let me say that this book of its Duke's fortunes is *simpatico—simpaticissimo*. It would be a genuine pleasure to watch the noble exile through the remainder of his career.

Hamilton Wright Mabie, "Mr. Mabie's Literary Talks," *Ladies' Home Journal*, 19 (May 1902), 17

The range of human experience and the wide differences of human conditions are brought very clearly into view if one turns from these records of contemporaneous experience in the New World to Mrs. Wharton's latest story *The Valley of Decision*. If Doctor [Booker T.] Washington [in *Up from Slavery*] and Mr. [Jacob] Riis [in *The Making of an American*] represent men of action using the pen for definite ends, Mrs. Wharton is the accomplished artist, to whom the art of writing is an end in itself.

She is a trained workman, with a passion for giving her work the touch of perfection. The artistic instinct which prompts her to refine, to polish, to give language not only precision, but that distinction which is partly a matter of skill and partly an endowment of spirit, directs her interest chiefly to old and ripe social forms, to ancient and highly organized societies.

In a number of recent short stories she has shown the charm of Italian life, and a rare skill in describing it. Her earlier work has led up by natural gradation to this long and striking piece of fiction. Her first book of short stories, *Crucial Instances*, made it clear that she cared chiefly for the subtle and perplexing problems of life and character, and that she had natural as well as trained skill in dealing with them. In her second book, *The Touchstone*, she worked out what is commonly called a psychological motive with insight, and with that delicate and sensitive art which is essentially a highly developed skill in suggestion, in bringing out clearly elusive shadings of mood and elusive states of feeling. *The Valley of Decision* is a natural growth of Mrs. Wharton's art; it is longer, stronger in many ways than anything she has done before. It is, at the same time, a study of temperament and of a society full of contrasts; the portrait of a high-minded man, capable of great sacrifices, whose career is arrested and his free development baffled by lack of clear decision, of the ability to choose between two courses of action when he sees clearly the difficulties in both courses; and the picture of a society polished, urbane, cultivated and elegant, and, at the same time, frivolous, heartless, corrupt and helpless in the face of the great Revolutionary movement which was filling all Europe with restlessness and which broke like a tempest in France at the close of the eighteenth century.

Mrs. Wharton deals with the secondary forces of life rather than with its decisive convictions; she is a student of moods rather than of the influence of action on character; she belongs therefore to the class of writers who deal with the subtleties of experience rather than with its decisive moments.

Review of *The Valley of Decision,* *Outlook*, 71 (24 May 1902), 209

The fiction of the season, like of many previous seasons here and abroad, has enriched literature with no masterpieces, but has put into our hands, in this country especially, some novels of high quality both in construction and style. The standard of literary workmanship among American writers has steadily advanced until it has passed the English and approached the French ideals of excellence of form and style. Mrs. Wharton's *Valley of Decision*, issued by Messrs. Charles Scribner's Sons, is a piece of expert literary craftsmanship. Mrs. Wharton has passed her apprenticeship and gained ease and individual force in the use of her materials. She has a sensitive imagination and was therefore responsive to the influence of the writers with whose methods and point of view she was in sympathy. Her earlier work shows traces of this influence. In *The Valley of Decision* there are suggestions of [Walter Pater's] "Marius the Epicurean" and of [Joseph Henry Shorthouse's] "John Inglesant," two stories which in theme and quality relate themselves inevitably to Mrs. Wharton's novel; but the story is a faithful reflection of its writer's mind and temperament. It deals with an Italian court on the eve of a revolution, and with a group of men and women who are typical as well as individual. The chief figures are sympathetically studied and are presented with subtle delicacy, with the nicest shadings, and with most searching insight. The story is not dramatic; it does not deal with the master passions in a masterly way; it is a carefully wrought study of a period and a temperament; an example of fine technique, a charmingly told story of deep and unusual interest.

H. W. Boynton, "Books New and Old," *Atlantic Monthly*, 89 (May 1902), 710–11

Sir Richard Calmady is the latest novel of a practiced novel-writer, while Mrs.

Wharton's *The Valley of Decision* is the first novel of a writer of matured power, whose product, remarkable in quality, has hitherto been small and entirely in the field of the short story. Yet the greater ease, as well as the greater unevenness of Lucas Malet's style, may be set down, not so much to the fact that she has written much, as to a radical difference in temperament and in aim. She is, one feels, comparatively unconscious of her manner of speech, so passionately absorbed is she in the problem which is to be solved, or, at least, to be presented in every possible light. Mrs. Wharton, on the other hand, is plainly concerned with her vehicle, and it is not at all probable that she will outgrow her concern; for her art is, for better or worse, a matter of greater moment to her than her audience is. Moreover, she is intellectually, rather than passionately, sympathetic with life, and the plane of action which most interests her is correspondingly remote from problems of temperament or pathology. The crises and the catastrophe of Odo Valsecca's life are upon the plane of the intellect and of the major morals.

Nothing better attests the consistency with which the author has held to this plane than her treatment of the sex relation, so all-important to a book like *Sir Richard Calmady*. What that relation was in eighteenth-century Italy might be gathered from this story alone. But the question is not up for discussion. It is therefore given no emphasis whatever; there were other conditions of the day, conditions of mind and of spirit, from which we are not to be distracted. The institution of the cicisbeo is mentioned without horror, and Odo's affairs of gallantry, according to the code of the time social rather than moral peccadillos, are recorded with the merest lifting of the brows. A Tito Melema would be not perhaps beyond Mrs. Wharton's powers, but contrary to her sense of fitness, since a pure art shrinks from the error of measuring one age by the foot rule of another.

The book has much to do with that twofold struggle between the spirit of scientific inquiry and the dogmatism of the church, and between the spirit of political freethinking and the conservatism of the people. But it is by no means a historical thesis in the garb of fiction. Pure and restrained as it is in method, free as it is from picturesqueness of phrase or obviously dramatic effect, its interest is a directly human interest. The new spirit of inquiry is made concrete in the person of Odo Valsecca, and the struggle is focused in the little duchy of Pianura, to which he falls heir. He is defeated on all sides; the woman he loves becomes the victim of the popular fury against himself; and he is driven into exile. So much might have happened, simply in the name of the cause for which he stands, to any simple, noble nature reared like his, swept into the whirlpool of contemporary speculation, and, like so many of the doomed followers of Voltaire and Rousseau, unable to see that special conditions, not abstract theory, determine the forms of thought and of government. But Odo Valsecca is not a mere type. Many of the lesser personages are of interest, but it is the personality of the young Duke himself which dominates the story. Though the writer's total theme is of extreme complexity, her narrative never ceases to concern itself with this central figure, and when we part with him the story is done. The perfection of that parting scene is unmarred by mere pathos, and to one who has followed and grown attached to the man, it is very real and moving.

"Before dawn the Duke left the palace. The high emotions of the night had ebbed. He saw himself now, in the ironic light of morning, as a fugitive too harmless to be worth pursuing. His enemies had let

58

him keep his sword because they had no cause to fear it. Alone he passed through the gardens of the palace, and out into the desert darkness of the streets. Skirting the wall of the Benedictine convent where Fulvia had lodged, he gained a street leading to the market-place. In the pallor of the waning night the ancient monuments of his race stood up mournful and deserted as a line of tombs. The city seemed a graveyard and he the ineffectual ghost of its dead past. . . . He reached the gates and gave the watchword. The gates were guarded, as he had been advised; but the captain of the watch let him pass without show of hesitation or curiosity. Though he had made no effort at disguise he went forth unrecognized, and the city closed her doors on him as carelessly as on any passing wanderer. . . . He tethered his horse to a gate-post, and walked across the rough cobble-stones to the chapel. . . . The place laid its tranquillizing hush on him, and he knelt on the step beneath the altar. Something stirred in him as he knelt there,—a prayer, yet not a prayer,—a reaching out, obscure and inarticulate, toward all that had survived of his early hopes and faiths, a loosening of old founts of pity, a longing to be somehow, somewhere reunited to his old belief in life.

"How long he knelt he knew not; but when he looked up the chapel was full of a pale light, and in the first shaft of the sunrise the face of St. Francis shone out on him. . . . He went forth into the daybreak and rode away toward Piedmont."

"The Columbian Reading Union," *Catholic World*, 75 (June 1902), 422–3

Readers are often bewildered by the claims of certain books as presented by the publishers. The following advertisement appeared in several New York dailies, with display type, on May I:

Edith Wharton's distinguished novel, *The Valley of Decision* (third edition).

Hamilton W. Mabie: "Rare and fine and full of distinction."

Margaret E. Sangster: "Lures from vista to vista with surpassing fascination."

Agnes Repplier: "A genuine *tour de force.*"

Jeannette L. Gilder: "Will give its author a high place among her fellow-craftsmen."

"Will undoubtedly become a classic."— *New York Sun.*

"The most splendid achievement of any American man or woman in fiction."— *Louisville Courier-Journal.*

"Stands out giant-like among its surroundings."—*Boston Evening Transcript.*

In two volumes, $2.00. Charles Scribner's Sons, New York.

Regarding this book, which seems to be so highly praised by the phrases quoted from well-known writers, including Agnes Repplier, a critical friend of The Columbian Reading Union writes as follows:

The Valley of Decision is the subtlest assault ever invented in English literature against the Catholic Church. The author had no intention of hurting higher education of women if conducted under pagan or anti-Catholic auspices. Her aim is to hurt the convents and the church. The book is of so squalid a nature that no refined woman would be willing to associate her name even with condemnation of it.

It will be remembered that the same Edith Wharton wrote an offensive poem on a Catholic saint, which was followed by an apology from the editor of the magazine in which it appeared.

Evidently the *Chicago Chronicle* has penetrated the mist surrounding the valley that haunted the imagination of Miss Wharton, until she put it in book form to obscure the vision of many readers. On the editorial page of the *Chronicle*, April 20, 1902, appeared the most satisfactory criticism that we have seen of this higher-education novel, which we gladly reproduce for the interests of historical truth:

The severest blow dealt against the higher education of women has been delivered by one of themselves, the author of *The Valley of Decision*, a somewhat tedious two-volume novel of the spurious "historical" variety.

It has been claimed by the opponents of equal education for men and women that whatever the intellectual results of the attempt, the moral result would be injurious to the family and society. It has been specifically urged that the tendency of the higher education would be to draw women more and more toward the laxer social standards of men, and to make women impatient of those restraints which until now have constituted the bulwarks of the home.

The Valley of Decision supports this theory. The heroine around whom the sympathy of the story is concentrated enjoys from early youth the advantages which other women, at least in the United States, must acquire, if at all, by long years of labor through primary and secondary schools into colleges and universities. A name of evil omen, whether in Roman history or in Ben Jonson's *Catiline*, Fulvia starts the heroine out on a path of aspira-

tion, independence, erudition, and ruin.

Her learning fails to develop moral or spiritual growth. In full womanhood, having had abundant experience enabling her to see the evils of society in the fullest glare of their malignity, Fulvia voluntarily accepts an unlawful and immoral social status from which all right-minded women instinctively recoil. She becomes the willing victim of a profligate weakling on a petty ducal throne, and feels neither shame nor remorse in her degradation.

The malign influence of such a novel upon the aspirations of American women for university privileges is made by the author the more certain and the more emphatic because the scene of the sinister fiction is laid in the country which was the first to open university doors to women. The poet Alfieri is dragged into the story to heighten the proportions of its all-pervading moral squalor. Sneering at the idea of a woman taking the degree of doctor of philosophy, the poet is made to say: "Oh, she's one of your prodigies of female learning, such as our topsy-turvy land produces; an incipient Laura Bassi or Gaetana Agnesi, to name the most distinguished of their tribe; though I believe that hitherto her father's good sense or her own has kept her from aspiring to academic honors. The beautiful Fulvia is a good daughter and devotes herself, I am told, to helping Vivaldi in his work, a far more becoming employment for one of her age and sex than defending Latin theses before a crew of ribald students."

But Fulvia's father was a sympathizer with his daughter's tastes, which he habitually promoted. To make the lesson of the moral failure of the higher education of women still more convincing, the author of *The Valley of Decision* reserves the bestowal of her final degree upon Fulvia until after the university and the whole town are familiar with her adoption of a shameless life and her open re-

60

jection of religious or conventional standards.

In Italy the universities were open to women soon after their foundation in the Middle Ages. At Bologna, which for centuries was one of the greatest universities in Europe, a number of women justly attained distinction as professors of the sciences, languages, and law. Laura Bassi was of a comparatively late time. So great was her reputation for learning, but also for virtue, that her doctorate was conferred under circumstances of civic and academic pomp. She married happily and became the mother of fourteen children.

Two sisters Agnesi were distinguished in Italian higher education. One, Maria Gaetana Agnesi, was an eminent professor and author in the exact sciences during the eighteenth century, and lived to be upward of eighty years of age. A younger sister was distinguished as a pianist and composer. Upon the entire array of the learned women of Italy whose careers have been historically noted there was never a breath of moral reproach.

The injury which *The Valley of Decision* inflicts upon the contemporary higher education of women is shrewdly designed in the contrast which this repulsive novel makes in its alienation of the higher education from religious and moral control.

The atmosphere which is created for the reader of *The Valley of Decision* is the most repulsive ever introduced into an American literary production. In the large company constituting the chief participants in a story projected along hackneyed guide-book information there is not from the first cover of the first volume to the last of the second one honest man or virtuous woman.

The moral squalor of *The Valley of Decision* is the more surprising because the scene is laid in the land which has given to literature and life the paramount group of ideal womanhood, Dante's Beatrice, Petrarch's Laura, Michael Angelo's Vitto-ria Colonna; and to Shakspere his two most engaging characters, blending in their mutual devotion of a noble womanhood erudition and chastity, Portia and Nerissa.

The womanhood of the United States may justly deplore that such a volume as *The Valley of Decision* should have its origin in the United States, in which the experiment of the higher education of women has thus far been courageously carried to an advancement which few of the universities have been able to withstand.

"*The Valley of Decision*," *Athenæum* [England], 3894 (14 June 1902), 748–9

To read the whole of *The Valley of Decision*—and it must be read all in all or not at all—needs determination. It is rather congested and heavy and laboured in manner, but it shows considerable thought and careful observation. After a time one gets broken in to the task and begins to feel that a few hundred pages more or less do not greatly signify. The exact and somewhat alarming number of the pages is six hundred and fifty. The story is divided into books, and this, perhaps, and the elaborate presentment and analysis of character and situation, and the detailed descriptions of scenes and ceremonies, add to the bulk. There is little to remind one of the author's previous success, *A Gift from the Grave*, unless it be the use of Latin derivatives and the constant avoidance of Saxon and monosyllabic words. Northern Italy is the scene of the story, and the time is late in the eighteenth century, when the great Revolution was setting in in France, and new ideas and ancient families were fleeing across the Alps from a distressful country. The author has expended time and trouble over her hero and other personages belonging to the ducal court of her story.

Frank Jewett Mather, Jr., "Literature," *Forum*, 34 (July 1902), 78–9

Good judges, with a rarely exampled unanimity, have exempted from the general dispraise of the current historical novels Mrs. Wharton's *The Valley of Decision*, as superior to its class. They might have gone further and said that it practically constitutes a class by itself; planning nothing less than to give a true portraiture of the Italian mind as it was just before the dawn of the struggle for independence. One can only praise the scheme which makes Prince Odo the inheritor of all the shackles of the past and the uncertain borrower of the hope which had spread from Jean Jacques through the slumbering nations. He is the type, or rather the personification, of the time in which he lives, the expression of all its aspirations as of its hesitancies. One may enjoy unreservedly the descriptive beauty of individual scenes. No eighteenth century vignette would have rendered more authentically or winsomely the enthusiast Fulvia and her philosophic parent as they first appear before the expectant prince. The book is learned to the core. Mrs. Wharton has wintered and summered her Jesuits, and has her Vulcanists, Neptunians, and Illuminati, at her fingers' tips; she knows her strolling players—and her Casanova, one may assume—like her pocket. But her book, which many are reading as an interesting historical study,

some way misses it as a novel. Her people are either refined away to mere symbols, like Prince Odo, or so vaguely characterized as to seem mere factors in Mrs. Wharton's historical demonstration. Red blood is only in Fulvia (occasionally) and in the Grand Duchess. Add to this that all the characters speak in just one distinguished literary tone—that of *Crucial Instances*—and the inventory of *The Valley of Decision* is sufficiently made.

Aline Gorren, "Mrs. Wharton's Philosophical Romance," *Critic*, 40 (July 1902), 541–3

When Mrs. Wharton wrote *The Valley of Decision*, she had in view a distinct purpose and in mind a definite model. The purpose was to make a study of the eighteenth century in Italy. The model which should fit the purpose was the philosophical romance, a *genre* which comparatively few have handled and which, naturally, appeals to few.

A picture of the disintegration of Italy in the eighteenth century is, localized, a picture of the disintegration of the old, caste-conception of society under the influence of the modern democratic spirit. The moment of crisis has been many times studied in France; that is, the moment of most salient crisis, for these changes proceed by a series of shocks and crises, beginning long before the summarizing attention apprehends them, and continuing long after the metamorphosis is supposed to have been consummated; and it is very proper to choose the French eighteenth century for this study. The germination of new ideas came to a visible explosion in France, after which things were really not so much the same in essence as they have elsewhere often had a trick of being after revolutions. The French mind has the abstracting quality that makes it approximately true to the consequences of its ideas. Moreover, the centralizing tendencies of France make it possible to see movements of thought lucidly there, in the ensemble. Italy knew fourteen hundred years of decentralization, and is not to this day an organic unit. The effort to give a total impression of the "stirring of unborn ideals" of intellectual and political freedom in the various Italian states of the latter half of the eighteenth century constituted a task of great complexity, demanding the subtlest insight, a judgement of the surest poise, large powers of discrimination in the play of confused factors, and human sympathies wide and warm.

There has been no book written in English for many years conceived in a higher spirit. The comparison with Walter Pater is inevitable. In French writing there is a nearer comparison, chronologically, with Anatole France, the word-tissue of whose books is as rare and lovely, and whose purpose (in his philosophical romances) is as much of the class of the things that endure. Mrs. Wharton knows the physical face of Italy as one knows that only which profoundly moves one. She takes Odo, her protagonist, through fields, by the side of marshes, along river-banks, washed in as Maurice Barrès washes on his page the scenery that is a background for his pale heroes. There is, in fact, very much of the feeling of Maurice Barrès in Mrs. Wharton's book. So much so that one wonders whether one should not prefer for it the designation of psychological—rather than philosophical—romance. That is what Maurice Barrès, in one of his prefaces, calls those

little works "Sous l'Oeil des Barbares," "Le Jardin de Bérénice," etc., which were not inconsiderably read in France a few years ago. His hero never does anything. But as he is caught in the tangle of the events of life those events act upon his plastic psychical self, and the vision that is given the reader of that action is the whole of the book. If there were reaction on his part we should have a "story," pages written more or less dramatically. As there is no reaction we have a passive picture,—a soul seen as one sees a lake that brightens or darkens, ripples or grows smooth again, as the hours pass over it and the seasons.

But Odo Valsecca is not so much a man to Mrs. Wharton, a dilettante descendant of an outworn feudal race, as a type, a representation of the prevailing mental condition of a people with a long, stupendous civilization behind it, and little power of renewal in the face of impending world-changes. Still less is Fulvia Vivaldi a woman, a personal study of a young *dottoressa*, a daughter of the time-honored learned section of the Italian middle-class. She too is a symbol. She symbolizes, in opposition to the hero, "the new standpoint from which . . . men were beginning to test the accepted forms of thought." She is the coming democracy, and the intransigent Genevan protest against the sensuous forms of faith;—and perhaps she does not quite escape a certain Genevan dryness and stiffness. After all, the book *is* probably to be called a philosophical romance, rather than a psychological one.

In any case, it is not to be called a novel. To call it so must appear to some persons to be a grave mistake. *The Valley of Decision* has much to gain by being placed definitely in the literary class to which it belongs; it has everything to lose by being classed in a *genus* none of whose essential marks and signs it possesses. Though there are many who will always

63

prove recalcitrant to the idea of the inevitable evolution of literary forms, it is certain that the evolution goes forward, unarrested. The novel has passed out of the reflective stage and perhaps even out of the analytical stage. That does not mean that fine novels will not still be written in which, padded around the synthetic projection of motive, passion, and personage, there will yet be both reflection and analysis. We may, however, count more and more on the synthesis, less and less on the analysis. It is hard to see how, for the present at least, the impulse everywhere at work to foreshorten and condense, can be set back. The novels that are truly in the spirit of the hour are conceived as long short-stories; and Mr. Brander Matthews has told us what the short-story is. It expresses us with extraordinary aptness, because, in spite of what we say to the contrary, this is not—it is no longer—a critical age. For good or evil, we have taken up the results of the critical-scientific work of five—four—three decades back, into our blood. Now we act upon them.

There are three reasons that may have withheld Mrs. Wharton from using intensely, dramatically, through the medium of two or three potent personifications, all the rich material whose details she has so thoroughly assimilated. She may have feared to seem to be writing a historical novel in the style of the last few years. Vivid and impassioned personification, the self-sustaining ardor of imagination that lets itself go without thinking of itself, may be increasingly difficult to her in the development of her reflective powers. There were features in her short stories that would have made one think otherwise. But where the taste is so fastidious, and the research of the right vehicle so exquisite, this is of course always the brooding danger. The third supposition is that life in the scenes, and at the time, chosen by her had a note of provinciality

that would have worked hemmingly on the effort to produce a strongly vitalized and rapidly moving piece of fiction.

As a matter of fact the eighteenth century was, in Italy, not a great century. Separate entities as they were at the time of the Renaissance, the Italian states yet lived then with a life that was cosmopolitan in the truest sense. And, torn apart as Italy was in the declining years of the Empire, there was then another great ideal abroad in the world, which, even as did the ideals of the Renaissance, animated scattered bodies of men everywhere with the same constructive thought. When we put down *Marius the Epicurean,* the book leaves us with the feeling of unity, solidarity. We have a total impression of the growing impetus of the great Christian idea. If Mrs. Wharton's romance does not hang together as closely as does Walter Pater's, if it seems more to fall out of its covers, the fault lies very much with the epoch of which it treats. All the old ideals were crumbling away in the Italy of the eighteenth century, but the new manifested themselves with no cohesion. The problem of the change from the religious-traditional and monarchical notions to the notions of man's right to govern his soul and his social status for himself presented itself otherwise to the Italian than to the Frenchman and the Englishman. There was never a Protestant question for him; there was no definite new vehicle in which the idea that high ethics need not necessarily be associated with the acceptance of ecclesiastically organized mediation between himself and Heaven could crystallize into shape. The temporal power of Rome might be felt in its oppression and its corruption; it was also felt in its beneficence. Political freedom, after the modern sense, came more slowly and painfully into existence for this cause. Those who wished, in the last half of the eighteenth century, for the dawning of the future could not draw effectually together, nor make themselves felt collectively. Economic reasons, reasons that it would be a long and subtle business to trace, prevented the fermentation of the age from rising absolutely from the soil in Italy. And where the new ideas are exclusively the property of the elect there can be nothing but dilettantism. It is precisely the lucidity with which Mrs. Wharton has seen all this, and the truth she has used in the presentation of every character, that have militated against the "driving power" of her beautiful piece of work. Provinciality is the result of a discrepancy between actual conditions and only half-understood or half-embraced aspirations received from the outside. There was, as I have said, a great deal of this provinciality in the Italy of Alfieri.

Mrs. Wharton shows us an Alfieri taken from the *vif*. His weakness, even his littleness, she has seen with all her characteristic justness of vision. The work, however, was immeasurably greater than the man in this case. And this, indeed, we should have liked to have been made to realize more forcibly. Here at least—and at last—was a very positive note where so much else was negative.

But the strong upward movement that culminated in the unification of Italy only came later. A novel of self-sacrificing action would have had to have been set in that later Italy of Mazzini, Garibaldi, Cavour. A novel, on the other hand, frankly pitched in the key of sensuousness might, amid such pictures of eighteenth-century Naples and Venice as Mrs Wharton has known how to draw, have been saturated with heady charm. Mrs. Wharton chose to take her own moment and method. Her charm is that of a refinement that has lost its illusions. She has all the understandings and all the charities; she has sometimes too all the cruelties of an on-look on life over which a merciful blindness never creeps. As a historical study, *The Valley of Decision* is as near to perfection as things human get to be. As a piece of fiction, it needed but to be a little more wrong to be a little more right. Prejudice may—and often does—give the spark of life and beauty, though prejudice is not beautiful in itself. And to be effectual —merely—is often to be beautiful also. And Mrs. Wharton knows this, for there is no manifestation of the beautiful to which her intuition does not reach.

SANCTUARY

SANCTUARY

BY

EDITH WHARTON

WITH ILLUSTRATIONS BY
WALTER APPLETON CLARK

CHARLES SCRIBNER'S SONS
NEW YORK : MDCCCCIII

"Sanctuary," Athenæum [England], 3971 (5 December 1903), 750

The familiar, though sufficiently tragic case of the mother who, having found marriage a failure, lives only to prevent her son from treading in his father's footsteps, is here, by Mrs. Wharton's original treatment, invested with unwonted interest and grace. None knows save his wife that the elder man has acted dishonourably in regard to a disputed inheritance, and with anguish she sees their son apparently on the point of yielding to a somewhat similar, but far more subtle temptation, in a question closely affecting his professional career. In the end, her influence, built up through years of devotion, triumphs over the hereditary moral taint, and leads him to renounce his hopes of worldly advancement, and the marriage on which his heart is set, rather than depart from the path of scrupulous rectitude. We cannot altogether refrain from a misgiving, founded on what we know of the young man's character, that he may hereafter have repented of this sacrifice; but the very fact of our being drawn into such a speculation proves that our interest has been aroused. The author's style has unusual vigour and distinction, and although the scene is laid in New York, there is a remarkable absence of those peculiarities of thought and speech which prejudice some English readers against a book.

"Edith Wharton's New Novel," Independent, 55 (10 December 1903), 2933–5

There was a time when writers of fiction were content with the narrative form. All our battle grounds were in the open, and the interest of the tale depended upon action, prowess, visible accomplishment. Only a few sages had discovered our psychic regions, and no one suspected their dramatic possibilities. But now the novelist with his colored crayon literary style and illuminating imagination has traveled thither, so that our romances, no less than our philosophies, are founded upon these deeper aspects of life. Poor human nature is being tested and tempted by every author in the country, some with a view to proving its evil possibilities, others with the nobler aim of rescuing a few virtues. Meanwhile the reader is amazed and edified at this demonstration of his heights and depths—is likely, indeed, to receive an overweening notion of his importance from the revelation. For, after all, life is not made up of "crucial instances," as Edith Wharton and other writers of her class would have us believe. And the things that challenge honor are usually more tangible than the subtleties with which she teases conscience.

Kate Orme, the heroine of her new novel, is a young girl, well bred, innocent and romantically sincere, who discovers in the man she is about to marry a flaw of character. Altho brought up in the midst of the usual social perversities of the rich and sensuous, nothing in imagination or experience has prepared her for this catastrophe, and like an outraged nun she retires, first to contemplate, then to adjust

69

her consciousness to this masculine fatality.

> "The pink shades had been lifted from the lamps and she saw him for the first time in an unmitigated glare. Such an exposure does not alter the features, but it lays an ugly emphasis on the most charming lines, pushes the smile into a grin, the curve of good nature to drooping slackness. And it was precisely into these flagging lines of extreme weakness that Denis's graceful contour flowed."

And with her faculties suddenly sharpened by this frightful perception she is suddenly awakened to a realization of the secret, well-bred vice in society about her. She had begun to perceive that the fair surface of life was honeycombed by a vast system of moral sewage. Every respectable household had its special arrangements for the disposal of family scandals; it was only among the reckless and improvident that such hygienic precautions were neglected.

Now it will be remembered that Mr. James Lane Allen's heroine in *The Mettle of the Pasture* had such an awakening from her maiden trance of innocence and happiness. But Mr. Allen is a man and was not disposed therefore to endow the injured woman with a morbid, prophetic subconsciousness, nor with that hysteria of moral pain which makes Kate Orme a feverish, tragic figure from beginning to ending. His heroine does not reason from her own sorrow that there is a universal social rottenness about her; and the reader has the comfortable conviction that if she recovers from the shock of that one glimpse into the dark pit of life, there is a tender, stupid womanly sanity in her which will insure peace and connubial confidence. And whatever the matrimonial tragedies

of life prove, or the science of such literary exponents of marital ethics as Mrs. Wharton suggests, these are really the normal women, and in the long run the most effect in the moral order of things. Their very obtuseness is a sort of healing power. They do not condone what is wrong about them, because they do not know and cannot imagine it. And their native aloofness is an eternal guaranty of morality in society.

But this is not Mrs. Wharton's point of view. She has by a purely intellectual process reached that point in psychic speculation which is esoteric to most people, and in the development of Kate Orme's character she forces the woman to face the agonizing contingencies of life. Having acknowledged that Denis is unworthy of her love, and having indeed conceived a contempt for him, her mind leaps to the contemplation of the future where she sees him married to another woman, who does not know of his dishonor.

> "And with this deception between them their child would be born: born to an inheritance of secret weakness, a vice of the moral fiber, as it might be born with some hidden physical taint which would destroy it before the cause could be detected. Well, what of it? Was she to hold herself responsible? ... Were not thousands of children born with some such unsuspected taint? ... Ah, but if here was one that she could have? What if she, who had had so exquisite a vision of wifehood, should reconstruct from its ruins this vision of protecting maternity—if her love for her lover should be, not lost, but transformed, enlarged, into this passion of charity for his race? ... "

70

Now this straining of the maternal instinct into prophecy is not character-istic of any maiden woman, but it is char-acteristic of Mrs. Wharton's psychic method for generating "crucial instances." This larger "sanctuary" of the feminine consciousness exists only in theory. What-ever may be said of men, the marrying woman only comes to love the race through the child she really has. That is the hypothesis of her maternal relation to the whole world; and it is a hypothesis which does not in the nature of things occur to the maiden mind. The "Sanctu-ary" that women like Kate Orme affords to tempted men is founded upon no such Quixotic notions of sacrifice, but it con-sists in their *telepathy* of goodness. There are many righteous women who never are sanctuary for any tried soul, because in them virtue is not vital. It is a form of moral selfishness which actually separates them from the needs of others. But Kate saves her son at the crucial moment from dishonor because for years he had been sheltered in the holiness of her love, and dominated by the sternness of her integ-rity. He was constrained to act honestly by the power of goodness that was rarely lodged in another. And to the discerning reader it is an open question whether the young man stood on his own legs or upon his mother's when the test came. And if he did not save himself, the maternal sanc-tuary is an ethical institution of question-able value.

On the whole, this is the kind of book a woman writes when she conceives her characters all walking upon moral mar-gins too narrow to be quite comfortable. And it does not demonstrate the growth of principles and manly stamina so much as it does a beautiful, tender sentimentality peculiar to women, whether they are writers, mothers or missionaries.

"Sanctuary," Nation, 77 (24 December 1903), 508

In the first part of the tale entitled *Sanctu-ary*, Mrs. Wharton describes a very inno-cent young girl receiving her first inti-mation of the existence of evil in a hith-erto beautiful world through her lover's confession of infamous conduct. The shock converts Miss Orme's love into loathing, and she resolves to abandon Mr. Peyton, but is deterred by a vision of his marrying some girl who would never know his secret and of a possible child "born to an inheri-tance of secret weakness, a vice of the moral fibre." This vision affects her so powerfully that she marries Peyton, her love for him having been enlarged into "this passion of charity for his race," and her whole being possessed by a "passion of spiritual motherhood that made her long to fling herself between the unborn child and its fate." The quasi-scientific treatment of such a fantastic notion does not clothe it with dignity, and the author fails to relate it to human experience.

The second part of the story is founded on common human nature, has much dramatic force, and so little necessary reference to the first part that, with some trifling alteration, it could stand alone. The relation between Mrs. Peyton and her son is well described, and the mother's conduct during the trying time of the son's exposure to a great temptation is wise enough to wipe out scores of mistakes and follies. Mrs. Wharton is much stronger in dramatic narrative and emotional scenes than in psychological analysis and scientific adventure, where the temptation to say something important leads her perilously near to nonsense. When one is discussing small affairs, there is at least an irritating

71

pretentiousness in such phrases as "the tolerance which allows for the inconscient element in all our judgments"; "caught in the inexorable continuity of life"; "reaching out for ultimate relations." This is the language of a text-book or a philosopher, not a simple story-teller with a particle of sense for style.

Frederic Taber Cooper, "Local Colour and Some Recent Novels," *Bookman* 18 (December 1903), 410–11.

There is no apparent straining after Local Colour in Mrs. Wharton's latest story, *Sanctuary.* Her stage setting is so quiet and unobtrusive that you do not stop to think about it, any more than she herself seems to have done. And yet, all the while you unconsciously take the locality for granted, because there is just one city in which her characters, and the things they say, and the things they do, all harmonise. It is usually safer not to try to interpret the symbolic meaning of Mrs. Wharton's stories or their titles, because there are so many different things that she may have meant, and at the same time there is the possibility that she may not have meant any one of those you have thought of. The facts of the plot, however, are unmistakable, and may be allowed to speak for themselves. In *Sanctuary*, she has added one more to the list of stories in which a young girl on the eve of marriage comes under the shadow of a man's past folly. In this case the man is not her betrothed husband, but his deceased brother. He has died in a Western mining town, and shortly afterwards the woman who took care of

him during his last illness appeared in New York, claiming to be his wife. But the family denied her claim, and the courts decided against her, chiefly on the testimony of the dead man's brother. And this would have been the end of the matter, if the woman had not seen fit to commit suicide, almost at the dead man's door. As a matter of fact, there had been a marriage, and the brother knew it, and deliberately bore false witness, in order to protect the family name and estate. Now, in real life if a young woman learned that the man she loved had been guilty of such a deed, and indirectly driven another woman to death, she would do one of two things. She would either put the man out of her life altogether, or she would discover that she loved him too well to do that, and instead would forgive him and weep over him and do her best to shield him. But Mrs. Wharton's heroine is not so much a flesh-and-blood young woman as she is a highly sensitised conscience. Her one thought is atonement and self-immolation. She wants to suffer with him. He must confess and be punished, go to prison if necessary for a few years, and she will wait patiently outside while his foul crimes are burned and purged away. But the man explains to her, with the care and succinctness that one uses towards a very small child, that such a course would be impracticable, and would bring sorrow upon many innocent persons, among them his mother and hers. And finally she is convinced, and while admitting to herself that she does not really love him, finds it consistent with her sense of duty to marry him. Here the story leaps a gulf of twenty-five years. The man has long been dead, but he has left a son, and that son and mother are inseparable. The young man is undergoing a crucial test. On the one hand are professional success, assured fame, the hand of the girl he loves, all at the cost of a dishonourable act—one in which there is no danger of detection. On the other are poverty, sorrow, and his mother's respect. She watches him day by day, in silence, wondering whether the old family taint is again going to crop out in the new generation; and day by day he fights against that silent influence. Had she spoken, implored, argued with him, he might have withstood her and added one more page of shame to the family record. But the brave, steadfast smile on the mother's face that he knows hides a breaking heart saves him in spite of himself. The connection between the earlier and the later portions of the story is slight, but some of the lessons that Mrs. Wharton meant to convey are obvious.

William Morton Payne, "Recent Fiction," *Dial*, 36 (16 February 1904), 118–19

Place aux dames! The most important books of fiction in our present selection are Mrs. Wharton's *Sanctuary* and Miss Glasgow's *The Deliverance*. Each of these novels is, in its own peculiar fashion, a masterpiece of conscientious workmanship, vivid in its portrayal of a half-tragic situation, and powerful in its appeal to our human sympathies. Aside from their common quality of successful performance, the two books stand far apart from one another. *Sanctuary* is no more than a novelette, hardly more than a short story, while *The Deliverance* is a full-grown work of fiction, spanning many years of suffering and unachieved purpose, and provided with a great multiplicity of incident and detail. But both are works of art in a highly satisfactory sense.

Mrs. Wharton's art is of subtler and more delicate quality than Miss Glasgow's. She presents us with a case of conscience, studied in two generations. A young woman learns, on the eve of her marriage, that the man she loves is endowed with a radical weakness of character, that he has sinned, and is unwilling to make open confession to the world and face the consequences of his dereliction. At first her whole high-strung nature revolts, and she casts him off. Second thought reverses her decision; she thinks of the moral weakness which must be the inheritance of the child of such a man; she decides that she will be the mother of that child, and devote her life to its strengthening against the sort of temptation to which the father had succumbed. This is the brief prologue to the story. The longer second part opens some score of years later, and the moral problem quickly presents itself. The father has long since died, and the son has grown to manhood. The father's sin had taken the form of a suppression of evidence the disclosure of which would have led to scandal and the loss of fortune. The son's temptation is to win a prize in his profession by appropriating the work of a dead friend, and passing it off as his own. The winning of the prize will mean to him both professional advancement and the love of the woman upon whom his heart is set. The ensuing conflict between his warring impulses is revealed to us only by hints and suggestions; it never comes to a dramatic issue, or even to direct discussion. The mother, trembling, stands aloof and awaits the outcome upon which depends the defeat or victory of a lifetime of consecration to a single aim. Words will not avail; the time has come when the man must save himself if he is to be saved at all. We approach the closing scene in breathless suspense; the situation is poignant to the extreme of endurance, and the relief is correspondingly great when the better nature of the young man triumphs, and he seeks the sanctuary of his mother's arms, seeing at last as by a lightning flash all that she has done for him, and all the larger implications of the struggle from which he has in the end emerged victorious. "I'm not worth the fight you've put up for me. But I want you to know that it's your doing—that if you had let go an instant I should have gone under—and that if I'd gone under I should never have come up again alive." These are the last words of this deeply moving book, and they linger long in the memory.

Aline Gorren, "The Influence of Personality," *Critic*, 44 (March 1904), 269–70

Mrs. Wharton has made, in *Sanctuary*, a contribution to the study of personal influence and psychical surroundings as used to deflect the logical development of inherited instincts and tendencies. Of course there is no such thing as a strictly logical development of inherited tendencies; of course the soul-problems in such situations as Mrs. Wharton has chosen to imagine are not to be worked out like demonstrable theorems: we are, as to heredity *versus* the environment, in an open field of conjecture where science burns, as yet, but a feeble rushlight among shadows. Faith is firmer here than science, however, and the stronger souls, whose love makes sanctuaries for the weaker, will continue sometimes to be justified of their works. Was the mother of Mrs. Wharton's tale justified of hers? Was the rescue of Dick Peyton from the peculiar temptation that beset him a

complete one? We cannot feel that it is so, nor that the end of the book is equal, in subtlety, in truth, or in surety of purpose, to the beginning.

In the first part Mrs. Wharton brings forward, indeed, a concept of great originality, and one that lifts the attention at once to a plane where very much is expected. It is thinkable that it might be asked whether young women like Kate, being disappointed in their lover's strength of character, often discover that their love has become transformed into a passion of pity, and a yearning desire of protection, for the child that may in the future be born of him, and that may lead, but for their influence, a life poisoned with the moral taint derived from the father. The answer is that this thing might very well happen with young women like Kate, but that Kates are rare. Given this girl as we feel her to be, and her marriage to the debonair Denis, with his insufficient sense of right and wrong, is not unnatural:

Now through the blur of sensations one image strangely persisted—the image of Denis's child. . . . The vision persisted—the vision of the child whose mother she was not to be. . . . Denis would marry some one else . . . he would marry a girl who knew nothing of his secret—he would marry a girl who trusted him and leaned on him, and with this deception between them their child would be born: born to an inheritance of secret weakness, a vice of the moral fibre, which would destroy it before the cause could be detected. . . . Well, and what of it? . . . Were not thousands of children born with some such unsuspected taint? Ah, but if here was one that she could save? What if she, who had so exquisite a vision of wifehood, should reconstruct from its ruins this vision of protecting maternity . . . of charity for her lover's race? If she might expiate his fault by becoming a refuge from its consequences? Before this strange extension of her love all the old limitations seemed to fall.

Is this "extension," after all, really very exceptional? Is it not, in some measure, what takes place in the life of very commonplace women, unconscious of soul, whose inchoate idealism, meeting deception in a commonplace mate, expends itself on the children? If one wished to psychologize rather far, might one not suppose, indeed, the maternal instincts to be, in fact, born of the deviated currents of sexual impulses,—necessarily deviated because of the relatively smaller average constancy of the male?

Be these things as they may, the mother of Mrs. Wharton's book is one of those exquisitely tempered products of the best moral and social influences in whom the elemental motives of action become transmuted into high ethical ideals. She marries the weak Denis Peyton, and thenceforward her life is a long, steady effort to envelop his son in the atmosphere of a sustaining but discreet love whose inbreathing may be to him a perpetually renewed safeguard against temptation. The young man's temptation is made to come in course of time, however, and very properly made to come on a higher plane than his father's. Dick is an architect, a lover of the refined life, anxious to excel in the accomplishing of beautiful things, but easily discouraged by failure. An opportunity presents itself to make a crucial test of his powers. While he is working on the plans with which he is to enter the competition for a great public building his friend Darrow, also an architect, falls ill and dies. Darrow is a man of talent, not very well treated by fortune,

who has always entertained for Dick, living easily in the sunshine of life, a romantic friendship. But would such a man's friendship lead him to bequeath his own plans for the competition to Dick with a request that his friend use them in lieu of those he was himself preparing? Does a man offer the chance for that sort of secret dishonor to his friend? Does he, if he believes his friend weak enough to succumb to the temptation, deliberately place the temptation in his way? Would he not rather shrink from making so easy the first step in what would, with Dick's character, be a career of progressive moral deterioration?

These sentimental sacrifices are not in the natural order with strong men, and Darrow was a strong man. These are the things that women do. And it is hard to regard with much interest the moral struggle of a man who does not know whether or not to pass a dead friend's drawings off as his own. Mrs. Wharton says of Dick's mother: "She had secured him against all ordinary forms of baseness; the vulnerable point lay higher, in that region of idealizing egotism which is the seat of life in such natures." But Dick's temptation seems gross enough, after all. He conquers, it is true. But, again, why should the dead Darrow's drawings have been simply destroyed? Why should they not have been sent, with his name attached, to the judges of the competition, and the glory, if such there was to be, have been posthumously his? Where the atmosphere of fiction is as fine and rare as in Mrs. Wharton's work these questions stand forth with a greater prominence than they might possess in the work of some others. She is of the order of those writers, indeed, with whom the saner vision is so native that it is always expected.

75

"Sanctuary—The Strength and Weakness of Edith Wharton's Latest Book," Munsey's Magazine, 31 (May 1904), 282

In *Sanctuary*, which is a study in psychology rather than a novel, Mrs. Edith Wharton treats, with her accustomed skill and power to charm, of a young man's hereditary weaknesses overcome by his mother's watchful devotion.

Kate Orme discovers in *Denis Peyton*, her fiancé, an unsuspected weakness of character, and an obliquity of moral vision, that fill her with dismay, and bring her almost to the point of breaking the engagement. Then there comes to her the feeling that *Denis*, if released, is likely to marry some one to whom he would not confess his failings as he has confessed them to her, and that with this deception between himself and his wife, their children would be born to an inheritance of moral weakness and lack of fiber. She resolves to save *Denis'* unborn progeny from this taint, and consents to the marriage.

The second part of the book finds *Mrs. Peyton*, now a widow, settled in New York with her son Dick, who, after a course at the Beaux Arts, has come home to practise his profession of architecture. Talented and successful as a student, his ability has met with no immediate recognition in New York, and his mother is waiting anxiously to see if he can stand the test of failure.

He has entered a competition for a design for a Museum of Sculpture, and feels that his future career depends upon the result. What also hangs upon it is his engagement to *Clemence Verney*, an ambitious young woman who has given him to understand that if he is successful she will marry him. A very talented friend of *Dick's*, *Darrow* by name, has also entered the competition, but dies suddenly a week before the entries are closed, leaving a letter for *Dick*, in which he tells him to use his plans if he can get any good out of them. *Dick* shows this letter to his mother, who thus becomes aware of the temptation to which he is exposed, for *Darrow's* plans are better than her son's.

The rest of the story is given over to the struggle in *Dick's* mind, and to a description of the intense feeling with which his mother awaits the result, wondering if her sacrifice, made years before, is to prove of no avail.

Mrs. Wharton treats the subject with her accustomed skill, though the lessening degree of humor in her recent books is to be regretted. Her deftness in characterization remains unchanged, and the cleverness of touch which with a few words places a personality clearly before the reader's eye is shown in her description of *Clemence Verney*, a girl of today, clever, ambitious, and as hard as she is brilliant.

Unfortunately, the incident upon which the development of the story depends is its one weak point. Self-sacrifice for the sake of the living commands our admiration; for the sake of the dead, our respect; but the sacrifice of the living is almost too Quixotic to stir the average reader's enthusiasm. Feeling as she did, *Kate Orme's* reasons for marrying *Denis Peyton* came perilously near absurdity.

76

THE DESCENT OF MAN AND OTHER STORIES

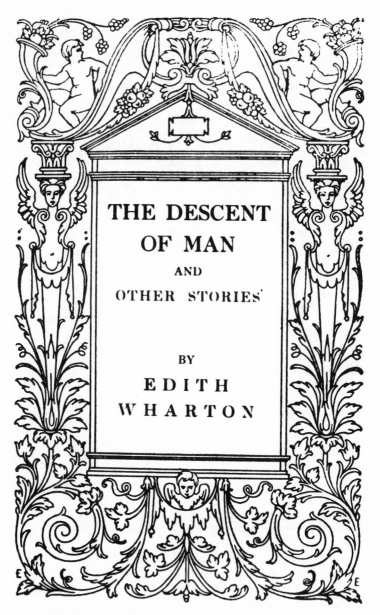

THE DESCENT OF MAN

AND

OTHER STORIES

BY

EDITH WHARTON

CHARLES SCRIBNER'S SONS, NEW YORK: 1904

Review of *The Descent of Man and Other Stories, Independent,* 56 (9 June 1904), 1334–5

There is, of course, such a thing as a purely artificial existence. And the illusion is so perfect that many people are born into it and die out of it without discovering that they have never really lived at all. This class may be illustrated by two singular extremes, the unfortunate rich and fashionable, whose sensibilities are more refined than their virtues or vices, and whose cares and woes are too splendid to deserve the sympathy of those who have real sorrows; the other is certain student types, whose thinking has led them away from realities into a region where right and wrong are so thinly shaded that one could never feel very good or very bad whatever his conduct might be. For all such types and conditions Edith Wharton is the best interpreter among American writers of fiction. The initial story in this new volume of short stories proves her genius along this line. The hero is a scientist. He despises the knavery of attempting to popularize knowledge by presenting it in sentimental forms, and to show his contempt he writes a pseudo scientific work which he expected to be taken as a burlesque upon the popular manner. But it is received more seriously and graciously by the public than anything he has ever done in earnest. He is amazed, mortified, but the money he gets from the fake is a bait which his hair-spun integrity cannot resist. He writes more books of the same kind because it pays. His "descent" consists in this small caper. But as he does not recognize any God, and his original morality consisted merely in a scholarly devotion to a standard of professional ethics, his descent is vulgar rather than tragic. "The Quicksand" is another geometrically accurate demonstration of the same idea from a different point of view. And the reader receives the impression that Mrs. Wharton has made a literary art of casuistry. Her characters have conscientious scruples that rarely deal with the real issues of life. And none of them have the will power to live up to their lights. Moral defeat is the sum total of every situation portrayed in this book. And no one except perhaps Mr. Henry James can present a revolting scene with more social delicacy. In the story "The Other Two" the heroine has three husbands, all so closely connected in business or otherwise that upon a certain occasion she serves tea to them around her own parlor fire. The very ease with which the incident passes is offensive; and the woman's tact suggests that she is like an old shoe, worn by so many that she has become disgustingly adjustable to all. But from first to last the elegance and delicacy of the language employed conceal the leprous truth as effectively as some decorative conversations will the license meant by the speakers. And nowhere, either in her ideas of virtue or vice, does she come into contact with normal life.

Rafford Pyke, "Two Novels of Cynicism," *Bookman,* 19 (July 1904), 512–15

A very unreasonable reviewer of Mrs. Wharton's latest book has expressed a feeling of disappointment after reading it. The book so closely resembles *The Greater Inclination,* both in its choice of themes and in its literary workmanship, as to cause this critic to exclaim, "Mrs. Wharton's measure as an author has now been definitely taken. It is obvious that nothing new is to be expected of her." We have characterised this reviewer as unreasonable, but he is no less ungrateful than unreasonable. He should rather have thanked Heaven that the sixth book of a contemporary American author shows all the strength, the fitness, and the distinction that made her first book so welcome to all who can appreciate these qualities.

The stories—one might also call them studies—which make up *The Descent of Man* are exquisitely done. Of their kind, none could be better. One lingers over each with a deep feeling of contentment at so rare a combination of perfect form and attractive content. Knowledge of the world, a sure psychology, and a well bred cynicism are here united. The cynicism is not a pose. It is not anything of which the writer herself is especially conscious. It merely represents an intellectual attitude, the result of wide experience and careful observation. Indeed, this cynicism is only that which life is pretty sure to teach us all, and it inheres in the conditions of civilised existence. Thus the story called "The Other Two" is simple enough and natural enough in its subject to pass with little comment; yet Mrs. Wharton has written it with so peculiar an understanding of its moral implications as to render it a bit of supremely artistic elucidation. Waythorn is the third husband of a woman who is gentle and affectionate, and against whom no one has a word to say, in spite of the fact that she has been twice divorced. She has a daughter, the offspring of her first marriage, and the child's illness makes it necessary for the first husband to visit Waythorn's home. An important business transaction brings Waythorn into a casual association with the second husband. In the beginning, the

necessity of meeting these two men, of having one of them in his house, and the likelihood of his wife's meeting them again, make Waythorn shudder and fill him with something like a physical repugnance. Moreover, the first husband, "a small, effaced-looking man," who "might have been a piano-tuner," and who blinks through a pair of gold-rimmed spectacles, leads Waythorn to wonder over the social evolution of the woman whom he has married. Her second husband, Varick, is a man of the world,—a gentleman in the conventional sense of the term.

"But this other man .... it was grotesquely uppermost in Waythorn's mind that Haskett had worn a made-up tie attached with an elastic. Why should that ridiculous detail symbolise the whole man? Waythorn was exasperated by his own paltriness, but the fact of the tie expanded, forced itself on him, became, as it were, the key to Alice's past. He could see her, as Mrs. Haskett, sitting in a 'front parlour' furnished in plush, with a pianola, and a copy of *Ben Hur* on the centre-table. He could see her going to the theatre with Haskett—or perhaps even to a 'church sociable' —she in a 'picture hat' and Haskett in a black frock-coat, a little creased, with the made-up tie on an elastic. On the way home they would stop and look at the illuminated shop-windows, lingering over the photographs of New York actresses. On Sunday afternoons Haskett would take her for a walk, pushing Lily ahead of them in a white enamelled perambulator, and Waythorn had a vision of the people they would stop and talk to."

It all gives Waythorn a sense of how

much there had been in the existence of his wife in which he had no share. And before long the impression is deepened when he thinks of her as having been for years the wife of Varick, a still different type of man. Yet, as he meets these men again and again, his early repugnance wears away. He insensibly becomes reconciled to the thought of them, and curiously at ease with them. It is a very subtle process of moral disintegration, in kind though not in degree the sort of moral decay which affects a *mari complaisant*. His wife is not embarrassed in the least; and though she seems so girlish and singularly soft and gentle as she sits beside him in her pale rose dress she is in reality only partly his and never can be really his alone.

"Waythorn had fancied that a woman can shed her past like a man. But now he saw that Alice was bound to hers both by the circumstances which forced her into continued relation with it and by the traces it had left on her nature. With grim irony, Waythorn compared himself to a member of a syndicate. He held so many shares in his wife's personality and his predecessors were his partners in the business. If there had been any element of passion in the transaction he would have felt less deteriorated by it. The fact that Alice took her change of husbands like a change of weather reduced the situation to mediocrity. . . . She was as easy as an old shoe— a shoe that too many feet had worn. Her elasticity was the result of tension in too many different directions. Alice Haskett—Alice Varick—Alice Waythorn—she had been each in turn, and had left hanging to each name a little of her privacy, a little of her personality, a little of the

inmost self where the unknown god abides."

And so at last we find the three men sitting together at Waythorn's fireside, with Alice smiling, propitiatory, graceful, and familiar, pouring tea for them; and Waythorn himself, now also pliable and familiar, taking the third cup with an easy laugh. This story is representative of all the others, and shows Mrs. Wharton to be a marvelously clever social vivisector. Perhaps the least successful thing in the whole book is a ghost-story entitled "The Lady's Maid's Bell," which is not sufficiently convincing to make one shudder; but the others are almost beyond praise. We shall not repeat the old remark about Mrs. Wharton's indebtedness to Henry James, except so far as to note that no young man outside the pages of these interesting and allied authors would ever think of addressing his mother casually as "My good woman."

Review of *The Descent of Man and Other Stories*, *Athenæum* [England], 4001 (2 July 1904), 13–14

Noblesse does not oblige one to read a volume of short stories straight through. But some people are misguided, and do so. It is a trial both to the stories and the reader. The mind, skipping as it were from pillar to post, is not at its surest. The stories, like, or it may be unlike, pictures in a gallery, suffer by their surroundings. The present volume is, as a whole, compounded of good motives. Several times we have been haunted by what is perhaps a mere fancy, that hints of Mr. Henry James are to be found here and there both in motive and manner. Yet Mrs. Wharton is an original writer. Her story called "A Gift from the Grave" proves it. Several of the motives belonging to these short stories are so good that we catch ourselves wishing that one or two of them could have been really satisfactorily developed by a master of the art of the short story. The tale which supplies the title to the volume has a good deal of cynical promise about it rather than real fulfilment. "The Other Two" is cleverly left for its dénouement to the reader's imagination. "The Reckoning" has an excellent idea well realized. "The Lady's Maid's Bell" is fantastic, and we do not quite know what to make of it. Perhaps, as it is based on the supernatural, that is a compliment. "Expiation," though not for the same reason, seems to us a little cryptic. The writing in all is much above the average.

"Mrs. Wharton's Short Stories," *Bookman* [England], 26 (July 1904), 140–1

If "The Descent of Man" is not the best story in the book to which it lends its name, it is one of the best, and is told with a dry humour and an irony such as few novelists in our days are endowed with. It tells of how Professor Linyard, having written and published certain learned scientific works for inconsiderable monetary rewards, breaks down in health and is sent away on a holiday. He goes chuckling over a secret design of occupying his enforced leisure in writing a skit on the "popular" scientific book. "In the most successful of these works, ancient

dogma and modern discovery were depicted in a close embrace under the lime-lights of a hazy transcendentalism; and the tableau never failed of its effect. Some of the books designed on this popular model had lately fallen into the Professor's hands, and they filled him with mingled rage and hilarity. The rage soon died: but he came to regard the mass of pseudo-literature as protecting the truth from desecration. But the hilarity remained and flowed into the form of his idea. And the idea—the divine incomparable idea—was simply that he should avenge his goddess by satirising her false interpreters." But when the book appears, the public read it seriously; nobody, not even the publisher, recognises the satire of it; and accepted as a supremely chatty and readable volume of everyday philosophic and pseudo-scientific gleanings, "The Vital Thing" booms and becomes the book of the season. It does for the Professor all that his really valuable work failed to do—it brings him large cheques and roaring popularity; he is interviewed and photographed, and besieged with profitable orders to write such compositions as "a series of 'Scientific Sermons' for the Round-the-Gas-Log column of *The Woman's World*." It is a great temptation; he has done enough of hard and ill-paid drudgery, and has a wife and family to consider; and after one or two backward yearnings toward the higher but unremunerative work he loves, the Professor succumbs and sets himself seriously to write another volume of the same meretricious but saleable order. The ironic pathos of the situation is not insisted upon, and the reader, like the Professor himself, is more impressed by the humour than the bitterness of it.

"Expiation" is another but widely different story of the literary life, though that same element of irony enters largely into it, as it does indeed, more or less, into all the stories, even into "The Lady's Maid's

Bell," a weird and mysterious narrative with a daylight ghost in it, and "The Letter," a finely dramatic episode of the Italian struggle for liberty.

But if we were to single out one story as the cleverest of the ten we should select, perhaps, "The Other Two." This is merely the record of Waythorn's marriage with a charming and lovable woman who had divorced two husbands. She has one child, a girl by her first husband, Mr. Haskett, and he is entitled under the divorce decree to see this child once a week. The child is ill, and it is the coming of Haskett to his house to see her on the day he and his wife return from their honeymoon, that begins to make Waythorn aware of certain delicate and painfully incongruous details that are inseparable from his new marital position. He shrinkingly keeps out of the way of this man, but next day, for they are all living in New York, he accidentally encounters his wife's second husband, Gus Varick, and is presently involved in intricate business relations with him, in spite of himself. Then he is unpleasantly shocked at meeting Haskett in his own house, when that meek, affectionate little man is there on his weekly visit to his daughter. By slow degrees, after much mental torment, Waythorn becomes reconciled to these and similar curiously humiliating sensations, habit forming "a protecting surface for his sensibilities." He grows more sympathetic and considerate towards Haskett than his wife is; comes to appreciate the good qualities of both these former husbands, and to doubt whether they were really the brutes his wife's divorcing of them had led the world to suppose. His increasing knowledge of them helps him to a more intimate comprehension of his wife's character. He began "to ask himself if it were not better to own a third of a wife who knew how to make a man happy than a whole one who had lacked opportunity to

acquire the art. . . . He even tried to trace the source of his obligations, to discriminate between the influences which had combined to produce his domestic happiness; he perceived that Haskett's commonness had made Alice worship good breeding, while Varick's liberal construction of the marriage bond had taught her to value the conjugal virtues; so that he was directly indebted to his predecessors for the devotion which made his life easy if not inspiring." The whole situation is intensely realised, and the subtle, elusive interplay of these four characters is a brilliant and masterly psychological study.

Mrs. Wharton is as rare an artist as Mr. Henry James; she has all his insight and subtlety of thought, and a simplicity and directness of expression that he lacks. America has not for long past sent us any stronger or more exquisitely finished fiction than the best of the stories in this book.

Review of *The Descent Of Man and Other Stories, Academy,* 67 (3 September 1904), 163

Wonderful mastery of her period as Mrs. Wharton displayed in *The Valley of Decision,* one was tempted to regard that work as by another author of the same name, and not as by the writer of *The Greater Inclination* and *Crucial Instances.* It is a bad impulse that inclines us to demand always from a particular author of the character with which we have first learned to associate him. Probably the results of Mrs. Wharton's excursion into eighteenth-century Italian life include, beside the acquirement by the world at large of a book such as we must go back to *John*

Inglesant to parallel, a widening and deepening of the author's insight into the human nature of her own time as a consequence of her study of the aspirations and motives of her dead and gone characters. It is, of course, the extraordinary directness with which Mrs. Wharton's probe goes to the spot under inspection, the deftness with which she is able to bring to the light of day what we had hidden even from ourselves, that account for the admiration with which we regard her short stories, for the delight with which we receive a third collection of them. And this admiration and delight dispose one to be uncritical. And yet it must be admitted that Mrs. Wharton is most successful when she is most fantastic, and that her skill consequently lies as much in the devising of hitherto unheard-of situations as in the artistry of words with which she conducts her creations through the maze in which she has set them. By the way, is Mrs. Wharton quite certain that Mrs. Fetherel, after complying with the final condition of her amazing pact with her uncle the bishop, and having for her part gained more from it than she had hoped, allowed herself to be surprised into a betrayal of her secret by a trifle of treachery which one would not imagine likely to affect her in the slightest? In two stories Mrs. Wharton has been beguiled by some mischievous sprite on to treacherous ground. "The Lady's Maid's Bell" and "A Venetian Night's Entertainment" are unworthy of a place in a volume containing "The Descent of Man," "Expiation," "The Quicksand," "The Reckoning" and "The Letter." And having committed this piece of fault-finding, let the present reviewer account it to himself for righteousness that he has omitted all allusion to the particular King Charles's head of Mrs. Wharton's reviewers in general, not from a wish to be singular, but from a sense of justice.

O. H. Dunbar, "The Descent of Man," Critic, 45 (August 1904), 187

Mrs. Wharton's Darwinian title refers, as one would expect, to the collapse of moral integrity in one of her short-story heroes,—if one may still apply this old-fashioned term to her leading characters—through a situation of Mrs. Wharton's characteristically ingenious devising. The fate of Professor Linyard, corrupted by the "big sale" of his too-satirical satire, forms one of those tragi-comedies which Mrs. Wharton handles with such consummate skill; but in being a shade too broad a burlesque upon contemporary "literary tendencies," the story falls somewhat below its author's admirable best. Several of the stories in this new volume, most of which have already appeared in magazines, are, however, of her very highest quality. "The Lady's Maid's Bell," in which a supremely good taste has throughout delicately avoided the too prolonged note, the too palpable effect, is that rare event of our day, an admirable ghost story. "The Dilettante" is an unusual idea, perfectly carried out. "The Mission of Jane" is a sardonic little comedy, one of the best Mrs. Wharton ever wrote. It happens also to be an example of the subtlety and variety of intention that Mrs. Wharton appears to bring to the writing of most of her stories. Part of the piquancy of its effect, indeed, may be due to the uncertainty in the reader's mind as to whether the writer is telling a good story, merely, or offering a "character-study," or deliciously satirizing the hackneyed forms that short stories are apt to take,—or all of these. The well-worn home-and-fireside motive of an estranged husband and wife brought together through the agency of a child, is just strongly enough suggested in this original story to increase one's delight in it. From any point of view, "Jane" is a masterpiece.

Mrs. Wharton's almost appalling capacity for penetration tempts her, almost invariably, to the study of a reaction, mental or moral. That is to say, she begins where most writers leave off. "The Quicksand" and "The Reckoning," even though one may hesitate to accept the close of the latter story, are of this order; and they bring also to mind that she brilliantly succeeds where other writers are likeliest to fail,—in supplying her story with a theme as well as a plot,—a theme, too, that is modern and pertinent. "The Quicksand," "The Other Two," and "Expiation" bear strongly on what are considered questions of the hour,—are indeed problem-stories; yet they are artistically inviolate because their author's concern with the problem has been purely a literary one. Mrs. Wharton is a finely interpretative artist with a just sense of proportion; an inveterate satirist who is yet incapable of extravagance or over-emphasis; and the possessor of a style excellently suited to her delicate purposes—a combination rare enough to make the publication of each of her books a happening of conspicuous importance.

Checklist of Additional Reviews

Reader Magazine, 4 (July 1904), 226.

ITALIAN VILLAS AND THEIR GARDENS

ITALIAN VILLAS

AND THEIR GARDENS

BY

EDITH WHARTON

ILLUSTRATED WITH PICTURES BY

MAXFIELD PARRISH

AND BY PHOTOGRAPHS

NEW YORK
THE CENTURY CO.
1904

"Italian Villas and Their Gardens," Nation, 79 (24 November 1904), 423

Mrs. Wharton has both the talent and the training needed for writing entertainingly and intelligently about her theme. To be alone a skilful artist with the pen is not enough. But add to this a discerning taste, a love for all things Italian, a rare appreciation of the highest form of garden art, and intimate knowledge of its finest examples, and we have an equipment that has given us one of the best of the many books upon the villas and gardens of Italy.

After a careful study of it one feels that Mrs. Wharton's words call up in an even truer fashion the intimate charm of the Villa Gamberaia or the sombre stateliness of the Villa d'Este than do the intensely personal, albeit highly poetic, illustrations of Maxfield Parrish. Her statements are the soberer and more measured of the two. They strike nearer the truth. His paintings clothe the form of the original in an always beautiful but sometimes overstrained scheme of color. And yet, from work of such great decorative charm, so touched with high imagination, it seems ungracious to withhold the fullest praise. In one way the comparison is scarcely fair, because the writer's thought suffers not at all in the change from manuscript to type, while the painter's (and especially the thought of such a colorist as Parrish) inevitably loses much in translation from canvas to color-print. Nor is this said in disparagement of the really admirable results of the three-plate process employed. The reproductions are the best of their kind, yet no mechanical process can render quite faithfully the full-tuned harmonies of Parrish's originals.

As the object of the book is not the description of the villa alone, but of its garden, and of the garden as it was at its best, before the influence of English taste had worked changes in most of the old villa gardens, the writer's choice of subjects is far more limited than one would at first suppose. Thus, in the neighborhood of Florence she finds but ten worthy of more than a mere mention, but these ten serve to fully illustrate all that was most characteristic in the Florentine villa. For Siena four examples suffice. Rome and its environs of course afford a field full of noble specimens of the art at its highest, while Genoa, Lombardy, and Venetia round out the finished whole.

The introductory essay upon the relation of the villa to its garden and of both to the landscape surrounding them is full of ideas which, even if they lay no claim to novelty, are eminently sane and just. . . .

As description forms so large a part of the book, it is to be regretted that plans, however meagre (mere thumbnail sketches would have served), have not been included among the illustrations. Without them, the descriptions, though well written, are sometimes hard to follow; with them, all would have been clear and simple. Those who have even a very considerable knowledge of the subject will find in the book description of places that have been but names to them, while those who know but little of the subject will find here an excellent introduction to it.

Anna Benneson McMahan, "Italian Country Houses," *Dial*, 37 (16 December 1904), 419–21

On first acquaintance the Italian villa does not, as a rule, appeal to the taste of the American. He is disappointed to find the house built up close to the highway instead of being approached by wide pathways and drives; in the garden, he misses the large flower-beds and expanses of green lawn to which he has been accustomed, he resents the primness and formality of outline, the pebbly walks, the artificial cut of trees and hedges, the absence of everything wild, the presence of arrangement everywhere. But, before very long, becoming accustomed to the Italian climate and to Italian ways of living, he begins to realize that both house and garden have a *rationale* of their own, that there is a logic behind all their forms and features, and that what at first had seemed senseless is really the product of high art combining, as all sound art must, logic and beauty into a harmonious whole.

The logic of the American garden is to furnish an agreeable outlook from the house windows or the street; the logic of the Italian garden is that it is a place to live in,— as a matter of fact it is lived in more than the house for months at a time. Therefore, the grounds are as carefully and conveniently planned as the house, with broad paths where two or more can walk abreast leading from one division to another; with shade for summer and sunny sheltered walks for winter easily accessible from the house; with terraces and formal gardens in the foreground from which lead ilex or laurel walks, clipped into shape in order to effect a transition between the straight lines of masonry and the untrimmed growth of the outlying woodland. Thus each step away from architecture brings a nearer approach to nature. Moreover, if the surrounding landscape be of the grand type, the artist has probably broadened and simplified his plan. Intricacy of detail, complicated groupings of terraces, fountains, labyrinths, and porticoes are found in sites where there is no great sweep of landscape attuning the eye to larger impressions. Where landscapes are the least grand, as in northern Italy, gardens are the most elaborate. The great pleasure-grounds overlooking the Roman Campagna, on the contrary, are laid out on severe and majestic lines; the parts are few, and the total effect is one of breadth and simplicity. And everywhere the climate of Italy combines with the artist to effect a gradual blending of nature and architecture by covering its bronze and stone and marble with an exquisite coloring of time, the *patina* which can neither be imitated nor acquired in any other land or in any other way. Even the unromantic site of the house on the high road is forgiven after one lives a while in an Italian villa and finds how thoroughly this secures to his private use the full extent of the grounds when no space has had to be sacrificed for the sake of a public approach to the house.

Such, then, are the typical excellencies of the old Italian garden: free circulation of sunlight and air about the house, abundance of water, easy access to dense shade, sheltered walks with different points of view, variety of effect produced by the skilful use of different levels, and, finally, breadth and simplicity of composition. Utility is at the foundation, but an artistic race can never content itself with mere utility, and æsthetic emotions are as necessary as breathing to the life of the Italian. The effect of passing from the

90

sunny fruitgarden to the dense grove, thence to the wide-reaching view, and again to the sheltered privacy of the pleached walk or the mossy coolness of the grotto,—all these were taken into account by the old artists who, centuries ago, studied the contrast of æsthetic emotions as keenly as they did the juxtaposition of dark cypress and pale lemon-tree, of deep shade and level sunlight. Moreover, their designs were based on a principle exactly the reverse of our own. Whereas the modern gardener's one idea of producing an effect of space is to annihilate boundaries, and to blend a vague whole with the landscape in general, the old garden-architect proceeded on the opposite principle, arguing that as a house containing a single huge room would be less interesting and less serviceable than one divided according to the varied requirements of its inmates, so also a garden which consists of merely one huge outdoor room is less interesting and less serviceable than one which has its logical divisions.

The American who stops long enough in Italy is sure, sooner or later, to come under the spell of the Italian villas and their gardens, and he who began by scoffing ends by praising. On some fair day, as he wanders under the umbrella pines of the Villa Borghese, or promenades the terraces of the Villa Medici, he yields to the garden-magic and ever after his bondage is complete.

But how shall he explain it? Who will understand him in his native land? *Why* does he like these stiff and ugly things that he exhibits in photograph? Analysis of impressions, especially of æsthetic impressions, is always a thankless task and requires genius of a peculiar kind.

Mrs. Edith Wharton, in writing of *Italian Villas and their Gardens*, and Mr. Maxfield Parrish by his pictures of them, have produced a book analytic enough to satisfy the most exacting mind and beautiful enough to content the most artistic taste. Mrs. Wharton is one who, having fallen under the ineffable spell of the Italian garden-magic, has found it "more potent, more enduring, more intoxicating to every sense than the most elaborate and glowing effects of modern horticulture," and she can also tell us why. She has analyzed the secret of the charm, and shows us that it is because the great object of all landscape gardening—the fusion of nature and art—has never been so successfully accomplished as in the treatment of the Italian country-house from the beginning of the sixteenth century to the end of the eighteenth. Indeed, next to sitting on a marble bench and watching the play of light and shade among the trees and statues of an Italian garden for oneself, is the pleasure of reading about it in this book. Who that has availed himself of the Wednesday afternoon privilege of rambling in the grounds of the Villa Medici at Rome, will not feel himself again transported there by Mrs. Wharton's description?

It is not necessary to be a student of garden-architecture to feel the spell of quiet and serenity which falls on one at the very gateway; but it is worth the student's while to try to analyze the elements of which the sensation is composed. Perhaps they will be found to resolve themselves into diversity, simplicity, fitness. The plan of the garden is simple, but its different parts are so contrasted as to produce, by the fewest means, a pleasant sense of variety without sacrifice of repose.... Emerging from the straight shady walks, with their effect of uniformity and repose, one comes on the flower-garden before the house, spreading to the sunshine its box-edged parterres adorned with fountains and statues. Here garden and house-front are harmonized by a strong predominance of architectural lines, and by the beautiful lateral loggia, with niches for statues, above which the upper ilex-wood rises. Tall hedges and trees there are none; for from the villa one looks across the garden at the wide sweep of the Campagna and the mountains; indeed, this is probably one of the first of the gardens which Gurlitt defines as "gardens to look out from" in contradistinction to the earlier sort, "gardens to look into." Mounting to the terrace, one comes to the third division of the garden, the wildwood with its irregular levels, through which a path leads to the mount, with a little temple on its summit. This is a rare feature in Italian grounds; in hilly Italy there was small need of creating the artificial hillocks so much esteemed in the old English gardens. In this case, however, the mount justifies its existence, for it affords a wonderful view over the other side of Rome and the Campagna.

In other chapters, we get similar sympathetic descriptions of the villas of Florence, of Siena, of Genoa, of Lombardy, Venetia, and other regions.

The cult of the Italian garden in America has hardly progressed further than an attempt to introduce Italian 'effects' by placing a marble bench here, a sun-dial there, and statues numerous. But it is not thus that we shall bring the old garden magic into our own garden patches. What will help us is to improve our opportunities for studying the old garden craft, which had for its aim to make a garden adapted to the uses for which it was to be put. Thus may we bring into our land-scape and our age not indeed the Italian garden itself, but the informing spirit which told those men of old that house, garden and landscape must each be planned with reference to the other and blended into one harmonious whole; which taught them how with simple materials and in a limited space they might give impressions of distance and sensations of the unexpected for which one now looks in vain outside of Italy.

The pictures, many of them in color, are of uncommon beauty and charm; while cover design and mechanical features throughout make the volume one of great distinction even at this time when publishers are vying with each other as never before in the elegance of their output.

"Pen and Pencil in Italy," *Critic*, 46 (February 1905), 166–8

This is a book which, from its title and its whole appearance, leads the reader to expect that in its pages Edith Wharton and Maxfield Parrish are to explain and portray the beauties of the villa gardens of Italy,—that both of these artists are to use their art in restoring these gardens to our mind's eye.

To speak of the pictures first, Mr. Parrish has performed his part of the task in a delightful and satisfactory way. He has put the best of his art into the subject, and he has succeeded in depicting the beauties of the Italian gardens as they have never been depicted before. His interest in architectural subjects, in color and form, has here found a field giving him ample scope. He has reproduced what he thought was beautiful,—the things that charmed him. The points of view selected have not always been most characteristic of the particular garden, but he has rather selected the point which offered the opportunity for the loveliest picture. In the Villa Lante, he shows us a cloud effect as it appears in a formal garden. In the theatre at La Palazzina, Siena, he has shown us the effect of brilliant sunlight on cypresses. In the Villa Corsini, we see how the façade of an Italian villa looks on a wintry day, with a light fall of snow. The reservoir of the Villa Falconiere gives us some cypresses against a clear sky, and the fact that these cypresses surround an architectural reservoir is left to our imagination. These pictures, however, are all interesting, and, in the main, Mr. Parrish has selected points of view which are characteristic of the most remarkable features of the individual villas. Although with a limited number of pictures it would be naturally impossible to illustrate so intricate a subject, the impression left on one's mind by this series of pictures is worthy of the subject,—the greatest praise we could bestow on the artist.

When, however, we turn from the illustrations to Mrs. Wharton's text, we are met by a distinct disappointment. The impression, the atmosphere, created by the illustrations, is not sustained in the text. The preface, entitled "Italian Garden-Magic" is, indeed, admirable. It is a short, precise, and most discriminating introduction to the subject of design in the Italian gardens; and of course even a popular book such as this must explain what, from the technical point of view, the Italian gardens were, and the sort of art which created them. But the preface includes all that such a book need contain of this technical explanation, and in passing to the body of the book we not unnaturally expected that Mrs. Wharton would in her way restore the gardens to us as Mr. Parrish has done in his way.

These gardens are not only consummate examples of landscape design, they are for us quite as much a historical memorial,—the remnant of another and highly interesting manner of living. The only way to make these gardens as vivid in a literary, as Mr. Parrish has made them in a pictorial sense, is to restore in some measure the lineaments of this way of living. Mr. Parrish has depicted the villas as they are to-day; but if they were created to-day, even supposing that contemporary architects were competent to create them, the form they would take would be widely different. They would be suited to the life of the people who were to occupy them. Inasmuch as the richest of American millionaires does not attach to his domestic life a horde of retainers, the houses would probably be smaller in size, and their grounds possibly less extensive in scale. The machinery of modern life is elaborate enough, but it is installed in the cellar and in the walls. The habits of modern life are simpler in some respects, but more complicated in others. All the conditions thus vaguely indicated, to say nothing of climate, would have a direct bearing upon the form which the architectural layout of a country place would take; and in order to revive in pictures and words a historic type of villa and landscape architecture, such as the Italian gardens, some description is necessary of the life of the people who occupied the villas. They were nearly all of them built and used by the Princes of the Church; and we cannot understand them, unless we know how these men lived and what sort of a pageant was rehearsed in the magnificent scenery of their houses and gardens. That Mrs. Wharton is admirably qualified to restore the pageant of the domestic life of Italian prelates of the seventeenth century, is sufficiently proved by her *Valley of Decision*, in which she performs, with delicate and resourceful art, a similar service for the

93

intellectual and social life of the eighteenth century; but if that book contained perhaps more history than fiction, her *Italian Villas* does not contain enough history to afford an appropriate and illuminating background to the accompanying pictures.

The body of the book is made up simply of historical and descriptive notes, dealing with the several villas. She tells us for whom they were built, and who built them, and when they were built. All this matter is excellent of its kind. Were it accompanied by full technical illustrations in close connection with the text, the book would constitute a useful guide to the student of Italian villa architecture, but this is not intended to be a guide-book. Mr. Parrish's pictures could not illustrate the details of such a text as this, and the text affords little assistance to the reader in completing the impression made by the pictures. There has been an attempt to supplement Mr. Parrish's pictures by the use of some photographs, but this was only a further mistake. It is an anachronism to use photographs in a book of which Mr. Parrish's illustrations are the pictorial feature, and the photographs themselves are insufficient for the purpose. The text must really remain unillustrated without the help of plans and sectional drawings.

If, however, the text and the illustrations of this book have been prepared from different points of view, there can be no doubt that Mr. Parrish's point of view is the more appropriate. When we look at his pictures, we get a feeling of pleasure and exhilaration, corresponding to the feeling which the gardens themselves give; and, as is natural under the circumstances, we wish in reading the book to sustain our pleasure and exhilaration. But Mrs. Wharton will not let us. "It is because," she says, in her preface, "in the modern revival of gardening so little attention has been paid to these first principles of the art, that the garden lover should not content himself with a vague enjoyment of old Italian gardens, but should try to extract from them principles which may be applied at home." Thus she prefers to make her book a book of instruction in the facts and principles of Italian garden design, rather than to assist Mr. Parrish in reviving the "vague enjoyment" which is the first impression produced by the gardens on every sensitive person. That such instruction is needed, we would not for a moment deny; but Mrs. Wharton should have seen the propriety of finding another time and place for her lesson.

Review of *Italian Villas and Their Gardens*, *International Studio*, 25 (April 1905), 179

The chief interest of this book consists in the coloured reproductions of drawings by Mr. Maxfield Parrish. These are of more than ordinary value, not only as pictures of the beautiful and stately old villas and gardens of Italy, but also for their own intrinsic merit as examples of decorative landscape work. Indeed, it is not too much to say that, judging from these illustrations, Mr. Parrish's landscape painting is of a very high order. Excellent as were his black-and-white drawings in *Golden Days* and *Mother Goose*, reviewed some time ago in these columns, it is evident that as a water-colour painter he is about to take an important position among the leading exponents of the art of our time. In addition to Mr. Parrish's drawings, a number of photographs help to illustrate the text, which is well written and contains much information concerning the villas and gardens selected for treatment.

ITALIAN BACKGROUNDS

ITALIAN BACKGROUNDS

BY

EDITH WHARTON

ILLUSTRATED BY E. C. PEIXOTTO

NEW YORK
CHARLES SCRIBNER'S SONS
MCMV

"Literature," *Independent*, 48 (8 June 1905), 1311–12

"*Italian Backgrounds*," *Nation*, 80 (22 June 1905), 508

Mrs. Wharton's title finds its explanation in the longest of these essays, wherein she calls attention to realistic bits of landscape, architecture or every day life, which the Italian artists were accustomed to paint in the background of the conventional religious figures.

"As with the study of Italian pictures, so it is with Italy herself. The country is divided, not into *partes tres*, but in two; a foreground and a background. The foreground is the property of the guide book and of its product, the mechanical sightseer; the background, that of the dawdler, the dreamer and the serious student of Italy."

It would seem impossible to get away from overdescribed places in Italy, but Mrs. Wharton is wonderfully successful at wandering in new by-paths and in discovering new shrines for the adoration of the artistic traveler. And even the streets, landscapes and pictures that are most familiar become again interesting as she describes their aspects under the varying conditions of weather, season, mood and circumstance. "Italian backgrounds" such as these she has already drawn in her novels, but they are interesting enough to form a book by themselves.

This collection of essays on Italian subjects is full of suggestive ideas on the point of view people take as to what they expect to find, and what they wish to see, in their travels. Mrs. Wharton has many unusual qualifications for writing on the art of Italy in its many phases, among others a brilliant style, historic research, and a catholicity of taste. She herself, to use her own classification of travellers, belongs "to those idlers who refused to measure art by time, and for whom Italy has a boundless horizon." The second category, "the happy few who remain more than three days," might well profit by her mediations as to how to employ their time and how to enjoy the "middle distance" which is their share; but, for the "hasty traveller" "for whom the foreground is asterisked," her experience cannot serve. He has neither time nor capacity for seeing; does he not hurry through the Vatican rooms as if flying from destiny, and wondering what he has come to see? It is quite true that Italy cannot be understood or enjoyed by a hasty survey of its art treasures and sites of interest; only long sojourn, the serious study of its history and art development can prepare one for seeing intelligently and understanding the *raison d'être* of the different epochs which have left their mark on all the great cities with such astonishing predominance. The baroque character of Rome, for instance that seventeenth-century "debased style," according to the guide-book, which Bernini, Borromeo, and Maderno evolved in architecture, and Guercino, the Caraccis and Claude Lorrain in painting, derived its inspiration directly from

97

Michelangelo's ceiling in the Sistina, and the Moses in San Pietro in Vincoli. It is the expression of ecclesiastical pomp and Spanish ceremonial blended with the desire for nature's lines and the feeling of space; and how wonderfully the seventeenth-century churches are in harmony with the ruins of old Rome, and how little there would remain of what Rome actually is, were we to eliminate the baroque and limit our admiration to its classic and medieval period. Styles are also very much subject to fashion. In Venice, where the "Byzantine Gothic" is the foreground, with a flavor of the early Renaissance, the eighteenth-century buildings were at one time considered the glory of the city, and St. Mark's was characterized as "barbarous Gothick." And it was this period which evolved Tiepolo, Canaletto, Guardi and Longhi, painters who in their respective work express so vividly the joyous, careless life of pleasure of their time.

The great point insisted on by our author is that we should understand how literature and art and nature and history are blended together and go to the making of each city; and that we find in the backgrounds of old masters of the fifteenth century the life that went on around the artist very truthfully depicted, while the foregrounds, with their holy families, saints, and donors, are merely conventional. We are warned against dividing ourselves into the two camps of Gothic and classical art; rather to keep our minds open to the appreciation and understanding of all that is good of whatsoever time.

In the chapter on "Picturesque Milan" we are given a very good description of the Portinari chapel behind the choir of Sant' Eustorgio; the mausoleum of Saint Peter Martyr, one of the most exquisite achievements of Italian art, and till quite recently very little visited and known. The combination of Michelozzo's design and reliefs with Vincenzo Foppa's painting is very remarkable in harmony of line and for pure iridescent color scales of pale red and blue overlapping each other like the feathers on the breast of a wood-pigeon. The terra-cotta frieze of angels dancing and swinging between them large bells of flowers and fruit is a theme of complete joyousness, quite unique in design. In the chapter on Milan, too, we get a good account of that pilgrimage church of the Madonna of Saronno, which all lovers of Luini and Gaudenzio Ferrari should visit, although these Luinis are rather in his latest manner, after he had fallen under Raphaelesque influence, while those of San Maurizio Maggiore are more characteristic of his peculiar charm.

Another excursion of great interest is our author's quest among the hills between Volterra and the Arno for the monastery containing a series of life-sized terra-cotta groups representing the scenes of the Passion, supposed to have been the work of a blind modeller of Gambazzi, an artist of the seventeenth century, named Gonnelli. These groups were found at San Vivaldo, a monastery which the Italian Government had restored to the Franciscan order, San Vivaldo having been a follower of the Poverello during the latter half of the thirteenth century. Mrs. Wharton had the satisfaction of establishing their attribution to an earlier epoch than that of Gonnelli, the close of the fifteenth or beginning of the sixteenth century, recognizing at once in them far greater artistic quality than they were supposed to have possessed.

"Pictures from Italy," Times Literary Supplement [England], 7 July 1905, p. 215

Mrs. Wharton's technical equipment as a writer may really be called faultless. She has an admirably lucid and classical style; she expresses herself with perfect simplicity, without superfluities or undue compressions; she has a keen instinct for the *mot propre*, and the most captious ear can hardly ever detect any trace of affectation in her use of language. It is extremely artificial writing, of course; there is no profuse, spontaneous flow; yet for all its chiselling and modelling and refinement there is no loss of vividness. Moreover, her sense of form and arrangement is unerring. Her short stories, from a purely technical point of view, occasionally rival the most pitiless of Guy de Maupassant's; and several of the group of Italian sketches which she now publishes have the same touch of finality. If the thing is to be done in this kind of way, it really cannot be done better. Here is no slackness, no uncertainty, no confused sentimentalism. Mrs. Wharton can give a lucid account of the most evanescent of impressions, she can reproduce intelligibly the tiniest thrill of pleasure. And then one of the greatest attractions of the book is that the reader can feel himself in such safe hands. He can trust implicitly in Mrs. Wharton's lightness of touch; there is no fear that any sweet holiday memory will be blurred for him by unsympathetic hands, or, worse still, by some piece of artificial sentiment. These delicate pictures from all parts of Italy, from the Bergamasque Alps, from the Campagna, from Syracuse, have the undoubted note of sincerity. It is pure enjoyment to see through such discriminating and observant eyes.

When Mrs. Wharton leaves the countryside and speaks of pictures and sculpture, she is apt to be less satisfactory. She is almost too impartial in her appreciation. It appears that she is so free from prejudice as to be able to admire the best work of every style and period. We feel this to be a little more than human, and it must be owned that we resent it. Of course, it is a pure gain in pleasure to be able to enjoy different kinds of excellence; but for all that an appreciation of art, without at least some streak of eclecticism, is almost bound to be slightly wanting in emotion. Mrs. Wharton seems to give equal affection to Carpaccio, to Luini, to Tiepolo; she even has a few kind words for Correggio. Yet surely no one of tender feeling can feel quite tenderly towards both a baroque façade and a piece of Veronese Gothic. Fortunately, in one of these essays Mrs. Wharton does give herself slightly away. In one place she yields without reserve to the fantastic Italian eighteenth century. Especially in a certain Venetian palace she positively revels in "the heavy baroque consoles and armchairs so familiar to students of Longhi's interiors, and of the charming prints in the first edition of Goldoni." Again, in another sketch she allows herself a few scornful words about the "transalpine points and pinnacles, which Ruskin taught a submissive generation of art-critics to regard as the typical expression of the Italian spirit." It is quite reassuring to find that Mrs. Wharton has, after all, a few prejudices like the rest of us. This prejudice in favour of the ridotto of San Moisè rather than the monuments of the Frari is the very latest of all the many that people have taken to Italy. It is a great deal more unreasonable than Ruskin's prejudice in favour of Gothic, but all the more does it betray that even Mrs. Wharton can on occasion be one-sided and unjust. This is very pleasant, because it comes just when it seemed that her impartiality might be due to a lack of warmth. It adds the attraction of personality to a very charming and cultivated book. . . .

G. R. Carpenter, "Mrs. Wharton's *Italian Backgrounds*," *Bookman*, 21 (August 1905), 609–10

Mrs. Wharton's rapidly but soundly established reputation as a writer lays upon the critic the duty of speedily informing the public of at least the contents and general character of a new work by her. This is a set of brief, highly polished sketches, partly of little frequented places, partly of well-known cities which she desires to present in new aspects. She tells of a midsummer descent from Splügen into the region about Brescia, of an extraordinary Sacred Way in the inaccessible hill-village of Cerveno, of sanctuaries in the Pennine Alps, of her virtual discovery in the terra-cotta groups at San Vivaldo of a "remarkable example of late *quattro-cento* art"; of Parma and Milan; of various March wanderings; and, in another key, of the ancient Christian solitaries, the last—odd fancy!—to behold the Pagan gods still lingering in the lost recesses of the Italian mountains.

But it is only in the final essay, on "Italian Backgrounds," that one gets a clew to the unity of the volume. The foregrounds of old Italian pictures, Mrs. Wharton says, were always conventional. Only in the figures and landscapes of the middle distance and the background was the artist free to express his individual sense of nature and contemporary life. The student of Italian painting must therefore, learn to reverse the perspective, and to see first and foremost what the painter revealed only incidentally. Similarly, Italy herself has her conventional foreground, her "monuments," and one must somehow "deconventionalise" these works of art by considering them chiefly "in relation to the life of which they are merely the ornamental façade." Then follow brief and learned but vivid sketches of life and art in seventeenth century Rome and eighteenth century Venice. We may, then, with propriety infer that the volume is to be understood as an attempt to formulate the elements of Italian life and scenery most essential to the appreciation of Italian art.

Deconventionalise! The idea is sound and the clumsy word sticks like a burr. Italy, more than any other country of Europe, needs to be deconventionalised, to be re-felt and re-stated. We have fixed our gaze so long on obvious "monuments" that we are virtually hypnotised by them, and lose all sense of their meaning and value. The phenomenon is common enough in other fields of thought. Recently I read a volume by a great philologian, whose attention had been so long concentrated on his hoard of hard-won facts that, miser-like, he had nothing to say about them. They were just facts. A powerful intellect had been so entranced by petty antiquarianism that it had lost its own individuality.

One suspects a touch of the same malady in Mrs. Wharton. She cannot deconventionalise Italy. It is personality that deconventionalises—witness the *Innocents Abroad*. How rudely and sanely that shattered, a generation ago, the cheap sentimentalism then current among sophisticated travellers. But Mrs. Wharton unwittingly has allowed herself to be hypnotised by Italian art. She has denationalised, defeminised herself. Her writing is not that of an American of today, not even of a woman, but merely of the art-antiquarian. She speaks scornfully of the casual traveller, but even her "unfortunate lady in spectacles, who looks like one of the Creator's rejected experiments, and carries a grey linen bag embroidered with forget-me-nots" may—who knows?—have seen Italy less conventionally than she. For, after all, it seems to me, Mrs. Wharton is merely following, in her polished essays, the familiar method of Symonds and Vernon Lee. Her style is extraordinarily good, but her thought is pedantic and inhuman. There is more freedom of vision in the Baedeker of our grandfathers' Vallery's quaint and sage *Voyages historiques, littéraires, et artistiques en Italie*.

Review of *Italian Backgrounds*, *Academy*, 69 (5 August 1905), 798–9

Inexhaustible are the charms of Italy as those of Cleopatra: "Age cannot wither her, nor custom stale Her infinite variety." Thousands of tourists invade her in spring and autumn from the north; nay, even in summer the infrequent Briton finds his path beset by ubiquitous *Tedeschi*; Italy is never out of season, for her climates are many and most of them are good when sought discreetly. Italian sun exhilarates the very English, and they take their pleasure with unwonted gaiety if the mosquito is merciful and the figs are ripe. Nor shall we blame them if they take it mutely; Coryat his "Crudities" will never rank as

a classic, nor can every Brown relate his adventures on the Italian lakes with an eloquence that shall thrill the breast of Jones and Robinson at Clapham. Brown is wise if he confines his literary efforts to marginalia on picture postcards destined to enrich the albums of the Brown family. To do him justice, his ambition rarely soars to higher flights; "mute and inglorious" is his motto, and Baedeker prompts his modest journal.

Some of Brown's fellow countrymen, nevertheless, are more ambitious, and many books are written, good, bad, and indifferent, about Italian travel. *Italian Backgrounds* is one of the good books, and Mrs. Wharton is far too well initiated to need any prompting by Baedeker:

> "One of the rarest and most delicate pleasures of the continental tourist," she writes, "is to circumvent the compiler of his guidebook.... The only refuge left from his [the compiler's] omniscience lies in approaching the places he describes by a route which he has not taken."

Mrs. Wharton's determination to attack San Vivaldo from the side of San Gimignano instead of Castel Fiorentino is of a piece with her sudden resolution, in a fit of discontent with Swiss stolidity, to descend from Splügen with its "aggressive salubrity and repose," its "landscape of a sanatorium prospectus," to Chiavenna and Tirano, Edolo and Lovere, all aglow with August heat. "The sun lay heavy on Iseo; and the railway journey thence to Brescia left in our brains a golden dazzle of heat." We suspect that the dazzle had really begun on the steamboat journey from Lovere, for the description of the Lago d'Iseo, so lovely and so little known, wanders off "under the spell of the Italian midsummer madness" into a dream of the eighteenth century with its comedy, its Tiepolo frescoes and its *carte du tendre*. Mrs. Wharton was haunted by a verse of Verlaine about "masques et bergamasques"; the poem in which it occurs has a fascination also for her reviewer, who copied it years ago for his private delectation from a volume which he does not possess; but at Iseo, in cooler weather, he did not find it run in his head, and he is not ashamed to confess that he owes to his sojourn at Sarnico the knowledge of three "systems" (the waiter's phrase) of eating strawberries. Not one of them has the remotest connection with cream . . . but he digresses.

Mrs. Wharton speaks briefly of the chief possessions of Brescia, the bronze Victory, the Martinengo Palace, the town-hall: "But in summer there is a strong temptation to sit and think of these things rather than to go and see them." That just and philosophic state of mind is not to be confused with laziness, nor is it attainable by sitting, for instance, at Splügen any more than at Clapham; at Brescia itself the novice cannot attain to it. It is the fruit of experience, the reward of him who returns with knowledge; nor can its full savour be tasted till the strong meat that Baedeker and his kind supply has been digested. The newly arrived must always waste his energy; it is unwise, therefore, to arrive when it is hot. Mrs. Wharton had been at Brescia before, and earned the right to listen to "a drone of intoning canons that freshened the air like the sound of a waterfall in a forest," and see the best of Romanino's Madonnas.

She and her companions had set out on this particular occasion to see the Bergamasque Alps.

"On the last day of the journey the most imperturbable member of the party, looking up from a prolonged study of the guide-book, announced that we had not seen the Bergamasque Alps at all. . . . It must be owned that at first the discovery was somewhat humiliating; but on reflection it left us overjoyed to think that we had still the Bergamasque Alps to visit."

Again a very pleasant frame of mind, but not so legitimate, perhaps, as the contemplative mood of Brescia.

Mrs. Wharton discourses in another chapter of the sanctuaries of the Pennine Alps, Oropa, Andorno Varallo, and all that she says of them awakens pleasant memories, but she can have no true intimacy with Orta if she can write "the wooded island of San Giuliano." The President of the Royal Academy made a similar slip, a few years ago, with regard to the name, but from no possible point of view can San Giulio's lovely island, with its massed buildings and few trees at either end, in garden or little piazza by the church, be painted or described as "wooded." "Isola Bella moored like a fantastic pleasure craft" is a happy phrase, but Isola di San Giulio far surpasses in beauty the baroque pleasaunce of the Borromei.

A chapter is given to Parma, and another to Milan, a city which much needs to be defended from the charge of monotony. The tourist who sees nothing but the Duomo, and misses San Maurizio Maggiore and Sant' Eustorgio is indeed to be pitied. Michelozzo's angel frieze in the Portinari Chapel is one of the great inventions of the world; one should sit beneath it while the divine office is chanted in the neighbouring church in such plainsong as one rarely hears in Italy. Mrs. Wharton appreciates, of course, Gaudenzio's glorious choir and orchestra of angels at Saronno; we wonder that she has no word for the solemn browns and blues of Borgognone's great apses in San

Simpliciano at Milan and the Certosa of Pavia.

"March in Italy" takes us to Syracuse, from Rome to Caprarola, and from Florence to Vallombrosa, and we are entertained with much good criticism (no easy thing or common) of scenery and weather. "Italian Backgrounds," the last essay in the book, deals largely with Venice in the eighteenth century, with Tiepolo and Longhi, the comedies of Goldoni and other literature which revives for us the life of their vanished age, and the baroque architecture, which, because it is so genuinely Italian, Mrs. Wharton vindicates from the scorn of purists. Her reaction from a too exclusive worship whether of Gothic or Renaissance architecture, leads her at times into a somewhat paradoxical admiration of the later style, but this is far better than blindness to any merit that it possesses. The book is written with genuine knowledge, with large and generous sympathy and in excellent English. The writer's knowledge of other languages is not quite so impeccable; we do not think that a priest can have been heard intoning "Mater admirabile" before the altar of the Black Virgin of Oropa. The drawings by E. C. Peixotto, with which the book is illustrated, are neat and decorative, but suffer from excessive reduction.

Walter Littlefield, "Italian Backgrounds and Views,"
New York Times Saturday Review, 9 September 1905, p. 588

Probably more than any other country, Italy is nowadays subjected to that process of mental tilling, that refinement of critical observation and expression of all that in her pertains to letters and the plastic arts which, according to its own new and strange terminology, is called "culture." And the persons who do the tilling and the observing and the expressing usually apply their superior talents to unfrequented and remote places and to objects which have hitherto eluded the toils of the academic investigator. Arthur Symons, Maurice Hewlett, Edward Hutton—to mention the most conspicuous among them—have sufficient that is common in belief, erudition, point of view, and style to give their thoughts and activities the dignity of a cult. They vie with each other in bringing to the surface bits of unsuspected and intimate information: in discerning secret and hidden meanings in literary and artistic monuments; in promoting the economy of the reader's attention and reaching for the superfluities of verbal condensation. And they sneer at the tourist and the guidebook.

So far this cult has sadly needed a liturgy and a priestess to formulate it. It has now gained both through its latest convert.

It was inevitable. The elusive yet none the less significant signs at the threshold of *Italian Backgrounds* marked Mrs. Wharton as a convert to the cult of Symons, Hewlett & Co., while the exceptional character of her literary gifts and the strong personality which manipulates them warned the reader to be on the outlook for a revelation. This revelation is to be found in the last chapter and reads as follows:

The foreground is the property of the guidebook and of its product, the mechanical sightseer; the background that of the dawdler, the dreamer, and serious student of Italy.

Many byways are trodden, many mysterious places and objects uncovered, many images and traditions smashed before the revelation may be perused and enjoyed. And the approach thereto presents many and varied obstacles for the uninitiated. Ruskin must be accepted as an untrustworthy mystic, Italian Gothic as a myth, Correggio as shrunken "to the limited immortality of the painter's painter," and "Bernini as the genius of the baroque movement." If these and things like them do not abash the reader from a further penetration of this Italian incognita, he may be assured of a certain amount of aesthetic glee in reading about it whether or not he is able to appreciate the extent of Italian indebtedness therein proclaimed. . . .

Italian Backgrounds should be translated into the language of the Peninsula so that the natives may learn, before Socialism, industry, and the practical sciences and professions entirely absorb them, how they have been humbugged by their own—by Marghieri, by Alinari, by Filippo Porena, and by dear old Cavacaselle. . . .

"*Italian Backgrounds*," *Spectator* [England], 95 (30 September 1905), 470–1

There is certainly a very wide difference between the traveller of to-day and the traveller of a century ago. Perhaps the difference lies not so much in the power of seeing and the power of feeling—we will not insult our grandfathers by any such conceited suggestion, for their knowledge of Italy, if not so wide as ours, was considerably deeper—as in the power of

expression, and in a certain way of laying bold on things by a new handle, or looking at them from what claims to be a completely personal, original point of view. We all, in fact, believe ourselves to be artists, impressionists. With us it is not even always the thing itself that has value; it is our own way of looking at it and talking about it. Perhaps we are a good deal more self-conscious than those old travellers were. We know how to use language and to make word-pictures, and this talent is so irresistible that the old kind of impression, which used sometimes to mean silence and humility in the presence of a masterpiece, has vanished out of the world altogether. Each beautiful thing becomes our own discovery. No one has ever seen it before, and the world must listen while we tell of it. Of course, in the hands of a true artist the result may be delightful. But in many cases it consists of a good deal of shallow chatter leavened with a small grain of original observation, and one becomes a little tired of the impressions, the sensations, the straining at some novelty of views and opinions of so many people who visit the immortal playground, Italy. Too often their writings suggest Italy as the weary victim of her admirers.

Mrs. Wharton knows Italy very well, and has given us a volume of really charming studies. They are not quite free, it is true, from the touch of self-consciousness, that air of infallibility and of saying things never said before, to which some of the above general remarks have referred, but they justify their existence by showing a real knowledge of art, a real love of Italy, and a clear sight of what makes her eternal beauty. By those who value the latest word in art, the exact taste of the moment, they will be found useful as well as enjoyable. They express in a very interesting way the modern turning towards the art of the seventeenth and eighteenth centuries. From toleration the modern art critic and patron steps quickly forward to admiration. Mrs. Wharton pleads very agreeably for Bernini's Rome and Tiepolo's Venice. She is perfectly right in her opposition to that narrow view of art which ceases to admire at the mid-Renaissance. She expresses what many an intelligent tourist has probably felt, in spite of his friends and his guide-book:—

"Goethe has long been held up to the derision of the enlightened student of art because he went to Assisi to see the Roman temple of Minerva, and omitted to visit the mediaeval church of Saint Francis; but how many modern sight-seers visit the church and omit the temple? And wherein lies their superior catholicity of taste? The fact is that, in this particular instance, foreground and background have changed places, and the modern tourist who neglects Minerva for Saint Francis is as narrowly bound by tradition as his eighteenth-century predecessor, with this difference, that whereas the latter knew nothing of mediaeval art and architecture, the modern tourist knows that the temple is there and deliberately turns his back on it."

Catholicity of taste, however, is a counsel of perfection, and will never be possessed by more than a few. The ordinary guide-book teacher will always teach the fashion and talk of the moment, be it Gothic, Renaissance, or baroque, and the ordinary tourist will listen and follow. Fortunate for us all if he contents himself with listening and does not begin to instruct in his turn.

Mrs. Wharton leads us away from the beaten track in several directions, and is a pleasant and intelligent guide. One of her prettiest studies is of "The Sanctuaries of the Pennine Alps." She does full justice to the wonderful beauty, richness, colour, and interest of that enchanting country where Switzerland melts into Italy. She visits the shrine of San Giovanni in the Val d'Andorno, and that of the famous Black Virgin of Oropa, near Biella, going on afterwards to Varallo and Orta to study their Sacred Ways. One cannot help wishing that it was not necessary to spoil the tone of the picture by sneering, ever so slightly, at these old devotions. No one would suspect a writer of modern enlightenment of believing in St. John's "posthumous thaumaturgy" or in the miracles of Our Lady of Oropa, "another 'find' of the indefatigable Saint Eusebius." But the true artist should see these things as they are without attempt at explanation, and, above all, without any touch of that patronage of the ancient and mysterious hardly worthy of a cultivated mind.

From an artist's point of view, the most interesting and valuable paper in Mrs. Wharton's book would probably be that called "A Tuscan Shrine." Here she seems to be justified in claiming the credit of a real discovery. Starting from Certaldo, in the Sienese country, where Boccaccio was born and died, she found an intelligent driver not a slave to hotels and guide-books, and drove by way of San Gimignano to San Vivaldo, an almost forgotten monastery among the hills between Volterra and the Arno. Here there was supposed to be a series of terra-cotta groups representing the scenes of the Passion, and having seen the wonderful work at Varallo—by the by, is Mr. Samuel Butler's striking book, *Ex Voto*, quite forgotten?—Mrs. Wharton was anxious to have the pleasure of comparing the two. These groups at San Vivaldo were supposed to be the work of Giovanni Gonnelli, a blind artist of the seventeenth century, and according to Florentine opinion were of very small merit. But all this was mere supposition, as no one, apparently, had ever seen them. Mrs. Wharton found them infinitely finer than she expected, and was convinced that, though possibly restored by the local artist Gonnelli, they were at least a hundred years earlier, and of the school of the Robbias. In fact, the "Presepio" at the Bargello, attributed to them, was removed from San Vivaldo some years ago. After ascertaining all the facts of the case by most careful examination, Mrs. Wharton had the San Vivaldo groups photographed by Signor Alinari, and the photographs appear to have convinced Professor Ridolfi (who had known them by hearsay as the work of Gonnelli) that they are in truth the work of Giovanni della Robbia or his school. This was a triumph in artistic criticism on which Mrs. Wharton may well pride herself. To rediscover for Italy one of Italy's real art treasures is an honour that falls to the lot of very few tourists of our day.

Before concluding our notice, we must give ourselves the pleasure of quoting a few lines of description of the Tuscan landscape, which show Mrs. Wharton's delicate talent of writing at its best. She is on the way to San Vivaldo:—

"The elements composing the foreground of such Tuscan scenes are almost always extremely simple— slopes trellised with vine and mulberry, under which the young wheat runs like green flame; stretches of ash-coloured olive orchard; and here and there a farm-house with projecting eaves and open loggia, guarded by its inevitable group of cypresses. These cypresses, with their velvety-textured spires of rusty black, acquire an extraordinary value against the neutral-tinted breadth of the landscape; distributed with the sparing hand with which a practised writer uses his exclamation-points, they seem to emphasise the more intimate meaning of the scene; calling the eye here to a shrine, there to a homestead, or testifying by their mere presence to the lost tradition of some barren knoll. But this significance of detail is one of the chief charms of the mid-Italian landscape."

Pale colouring, tender yet bright; beauty of line and meaning,—all this truly makes such a landscape "appear the crowning production of centuries of plastic expression."

A great deal of charming description is scattered through this volume. "March in Italy" is delightful; but on p. 135 why *Salamis*? Delightful too, in a different way, is "Sub Umbra Liliorum," an interesting impression of Parma, in which, however, rather less than justice is done to Correggio. The very pretty illustrations add much to the attractiveness of all these studies; their light and bright delicacy is in itself truly Italian.

Checklist of Additional Reviews

"Backgrounds of Italy," *New York Times Saturday Review*, 22 April 1905, p. 265.

Anna Benneson McMahan, "Italian By-Ways," *Dial*, 38 (16 May 1905), 352–3

"Book of the Week," *Outlook*, 80 (8 July 1905), 643.

"Wharton—Italian Backgrounds," *Critic*, 47 (September 1905), 287.

THE HOUSE OF MIRTH

THE HOUSE OF MIRTH

BY

EDITH WHARTON

WITH ILLUSTRATIONS BY A. B. WENZELL

NEW YORK
CHARLES SCRIBNER'S SONS
MDCCCCV

"Mrs. Wharton's Latest Novel,"
Independent, 59 (20 July 1905), 150–1

Mrs. Wharton's new novel is a story of society life, its refined ferocities, its sensual extravagances, its delicate immoralities and, above all, the tragedies which underlie its outward appearance of mirth and prosperity. Society, indeed, is the coming field in fiction for the author who knows how to reap his literary wheat from the tares that are sowed there. And we ought not to complain: These books are missionary efforts of a sensational kind, made in behalf of what is the most corrupt class of people in the world, if we are to take seriously the representations of writers like Mrs. Wharton and Robert Grant.

But there is one curious thing about the dogma upon which these stories are founded. It is that old-fashioned one, "the soul that sinneth it shall die." Now ministers have been obliged to abandon the rigors of this doctrine in the pulpit, or, at least to emphasize it less; but these novelists dramatize it with all the terrors of their imagination, and they demonstrate it by the life of every character in the story. Thus the men and women in this novel who go about showing their ghastly mirth give the impression of being "hair hung and breeze shaken," as the old preachers would say, over the ancient lake of fire and brimstone. This same class of writers find their ethics by what may be called the dredging process. Formerly we all got our morals and golden texts from the lives of saints and from the Holy Scriptures, whether we were writing or actually living them. But now it is the fashion to get them out of the cesspools of vice. The author who can portray the most sins in the best style is the most popular literary preacher now.

And, according to this standard, Mrs. Wharton should stand very high. She has selected a situation in that circle of society where conditions make for the destruction rather than the development of honor and virtue. The heroine, a capable, well poised woman, is inmeshed in it. And this is the tragedy—that a creature so morally sane should be subjected to a process sure to prove disintegrating. Her acting, her subterfuges, her pitiful treacheries are simply the threads of a common web which entangles with her every person in her set. She is surrounded by men and women whose esthetic sensibilities are so highly developed that they have become emasculated. Their pleasures are self-indulgences founded upon some social form of almost every vice. Meanwhile beauty is her own spirit's art of expression, just as religion might be a nun's. The need of money, the petty intrigues and delicately veiled temptations which follow, sully conscience and damage self-respect, even if they do not betray the woman to her moral death. And the whole picture is the more distressing than if the victim were a man, because the destroying of a woman means the passing of a finer spiritual nature. The thing must be accomplished with a frightful delicacy which is not so essential in the destruction of a man's character.

We all have the diathesis of iniquity in us, to be sure; but the question is how far right are these authors who prove that the development of the disease depends upon environment? And since it is such an excusing doctrine, it will be easy to inculcate. Then what will be the effect when these people accept it and resign themselves to being the inane creatures of circumstances? If Mrs. Wharton could write a story dramatizing a means of escape for her victims she would do a better business. As it is we would not be convinced even if the heroine marries for love instead of money. That depends upon the author's conception of what the sequel should be in order to make a good story. We know that in real life the woman could not hold out against such terrible odds. The trouble is our literary exponents have a spell cast over their imaginations. Their eyes are holden. And never since the old days in Greece, when men accepted fate with pagan cheerfulness, has fatalism been so emphasized as it is now, particularly in fiction. The difference is that we lack the pagan cheerfulness.

Some writers have a permanent literary style, others have merely a fleeting fashion of expression, which is not founded upon art and which is meant to appeal to the passing fancy of the public mind. Now some years ago, when Mrs. Wharton's stories first began to attract attention, it was claimed that she had that rare thing, distinction in literary style. And she still has a fine manner, but it is like the fine gowns of her heroines, a fashion of the times for interpreting decadent symptoms in human nature. What she says will not last, because it is simply the fashionable drawing of ephemeral types and still more ephemeral sentiments.

"A Notable Novel," *Outlook*, 81 (21 October 1905), 404–6

Mrs. Wharton's latest story, *The House of Mirth*, appears opportunely at the moment when some critics of the academic type are agreed that literature is an extinct force in American life, and that the noble art of fiction has degenerated into the profitable pastime of telling entertaining stories for frivolous-minded purchasers. It rises at once and with the effortless power of a true work of art into the region of clear instinct, open-minded intelligence, and dramatic feeling, in which novels of the first order are conceived and fashioned. It justifies itself as a piece of expert workmanship. It would be difficult to find a carelessly written sentence, an obscure phrase, a halting paragraph, in the text of the book. There are passages which might be omitted without loss to the dramatic completeness of the story, but the passages which could be condensed are few. The thoroughness of structure which binds the chapters by the logic of life not less firmly than by the order of events is sustained by a selective power in the use of words which suggests Flaubert's method without conveying any sense of labor. The story is the product of the most carefully calculated, the most skillfully handled, artistic values and effects; but the workmanship is the manner, not the substance, of the novel.

Behind a piece of work so happily combining spontaneity, divination, and scrupulous exactness of touch there always lies an apprenticeship; and in the light of this really notable achievement it is interesting to trace the stages by which a highly cultivated and witty woman has passed out of what may be called the academic stage into the region of creative art. There has been a note of prophecy in Mrs. Wharton's work from the beginning; the hint and sometimes the clear disclosure, in her earlier stories, of the novelist by the gift of God and the grace of nature, as well as by deliberate intention and exacting preparation. Such stories as "The Descent of Man," "The Reckoning," and *Sanctuary* predicted the deep human feeling, the decisive insight, the moral grasp, the dramatic energy, which lift *The*

House of Mirth to a very high plane of artistic achievement. There were other stories from the same hand which lacked this touch of divination, this breath of the higher life. They were admirably written, immensely clever, delightfully witty; but they were not deeply humanized; they lacked the impetus of the inevitable. *The Valley of Decision* was a work of a very high order of talent, but it lacked the impulse of genius; it never escaped from the delicately trained hand of its fashioner and fulfilled its own destiny in its own way. It was an elaborate and striking academic exercise; it was not a piece of original literature.

The House of Mirth marks the transition in Mrs. Wharton's career from the region of cultivated tastes and skill to that of free, direct, individual creation; she has often stood on the threshold of life; now she has entered into its tragic and mysterious secrets. To say that this story is far and away the best novel of society written by an American is to give it pre-eminence in a very small class; for the society novel, in the strict sense of the term, has never laid hold of the imagination of the writers of a country engrossed in settling the more pressing problems of life. There have been stories, like [Robert Grant's] "Unleavened Bread," which have dealt strongly with women shaped by new social conditions and unaccustomed social environments; but the attempts to draw pictures of society apart from deeper and more compelling interests have not been many, nor have they been successful. Mr. Warner's "Golden House" and "That Fortune" were the work of an accomplished writer, but not of a born novelist.

Mrs. Wharton knows at first hand the world she describes, and her story is free from those exaggerations, misplaced values, and happy-go-lucky descriptions of society life which make the great majority of so-called society novels cheap imita-

tions. *The House of Mirth* gains immensely by reason of its moderation, firm handling of the facts, discriminating emphasis, and freedom from didacticism. Mrs. Wharton has escaped the danger of setting up moral sign-posts on the road, and has given her novel a concentrated and tragic moral significance.

For *The House of Mirth* is deeply moralized because it is deeply humanized; it is impossible to touch life at first hand without saturating fiction with the moral element; for morality, as Mr. Morley says, is not *in* the nature of things; it *is* the nature of things. *Père Goriot, Madame Bovary, Anna Karénina, Vanity Fair, Adam Bede, The Scarlet Letter* must be counted great human documents, not because they set out to be text-books of character, but because they touched the very sources of life. From its title to its closing paragraph *The House of Mirth* is a judgment as searching, penetrating, relentless as life itself; and yet it never for a moment ceases to be a story of absorbing interest. No tract for the times could have been more scathing and opportune; but no novel of the hour is farther removed from the didactic mood and manner. The kind of society which it describes with merciless veracity has existed in every generation, and is to be found in every city. The story is laid in New York, but it has been told again and again of Rome, Paris, London, and it might be told of Boston, Chicago, New Orleans, San Francisco. Wherever men and women attempt to organize life for the sole purpose of pleasure, the terrible sag of society toward vulgarity and corruption inevitably shows itself. No fortunate conditions of birth and breeding can conceal the fact that a fast society is always a vulgar society. Human relations and intercourse can be kept sweet and wholesome only by generous aims and interests; without religion, art, literature, music, society

111

always degenerates. Summing up a scandal which involved a number of people prominent in English society a few years ago, the London *Spectator* said that the painful feature of the disclosures in the courts had not been that the people concerned were immoral, but that their amusements were so cheap, their interests so few and vapid, their life so insufferably stupid; and an old noblewoman of the highest standing, referring to the same scandal, asked: "Why do they call us the upper class? We seem to be the lowest class."

Some critics and readers will insist that Mrs. Wharton has described society as a whole. She has done nothing of the kind; she has made a firsthand study of a section of society which is always in evidence in every large community, and which is the inevitable result of leisure and wealth without cultivated tastes and generous aims. It is possible that the dramatic effect of the novel might have been heightened if a few men and women of a different and finer type had been introduced; for every one in the story is vulgar, heartless, uninteresting, or immoral. It is impossible to emphasize the physical side of life, cut off religious influences, break away from religious habits, give up the reading of books, make sport an occupation instead of a recreation, without fertilizing the soil out of which all manner of silliness, inanity, vulgarity, and immorality grow. The young woman, whatever her training and standing, who drinks cocktails, smokes, plays cards for money, and indulges in an occasional oath, may not go to the bad, but she cannot escape becoming coarse and vulgar. There may be some excuse for the newly rich women who lose their heads and imagine that fast society is good society; but the discouraging feature of the situation is the fact that of late years this set has been fed in Boston, New York, New Orleans, and other cities by those whose traditions ought to have committed them to refinement, dignity, sweetness, and high-mindedness.

It is too soon to say that *The House of Mirth* will take its place with the great works of fiction; it is not too soon to recognize its veracity, its power, its art. It is an invigorating piece of work from every point of view. Its popularity will deliver timorous writers and captious critics from the oft-exploded tradition that superiority limits the reading of a book and that uncompromising truth-telling is resented by all save a few choice spirits. Mrs. Wharton makes no concession to the optimistic mood which is supposed to dominate American readers, and no evasion of the inexorable logic of life. From the first chapter, trifling indiscretions, careless compromises, minor infidelities, begin to close round Lily Bart and bind her hand and foot until she becomes the victim of a series of circumstances none of which is really serious in itself, but which taken together forge an iron chain of fate. And to this achievement, which lies within the reach of the novelist of genius and of no other, Mrs. Wharton adds the equally great achievement of exposing the chief actor in her story to contamination at every turn, forcing compromise after compromise upon her, lowering her stage by stage in position and in her own self-respect, and yet preserving a core of integrity at the heart of her nature and sending her out of life with such compassion of comprehension that not a hand can be raised to hurl a stone. In the closing chapter Mrs. Wharton rises to a height not only far beyond the reach of her earlier work, but where only a few among her contemporaries can find place with her. A story of such integrity of insight and of workmanship is an achievement of high importance in American life.

"The House of Mirth," Spectator [England], 95 (28 October 1905), 657

Mrs. Wharton has recently and incontestably challenged comparison with the ablest of living American novelists, her volume of short stories, *The Descent of Man*, in particular revealing quite exceptional powers of insight and expression. Her reputation will certainly not suffer any decline by the publication of her new novel, in which she has given a finished and illuminating picture of the quest for pleasure as carried on by rich and "smart" New Yorkers of to-day. The obvious criticism of novels dealing with this subject-matter is that the *dramatis personæ*, as a rule, are so worthless or futile that it is impossible to feel any sympathy with them in their misfortunes. Mrs. Wharton, like a true artist, has realised that the society with which she is dealing, being highly sophisticated, can only be rendered really interesting by the introduction of a figure which has at least the possibilities of tragedy in it. This figure she has discovered in the highly complex, vivid, ill-starred heroine of her ironically named romance. Lily Bart is the orphan child of a New York merchant who was ruined by the selfish extravagance of his wife. Mrs. Bart, who died "of deep disgust" and mortification at her loss of fortune, looked eagerly to her daughter to win back her position by the weapon of her beauty, but did not live to see her ambition fulfilled. Thus at the opening of the story we find Lily, already a woman of twenty-nine, the victim to a great extent of antecedents and environment, suddenly confronted with the embarrassments of her position, at once that of a pensioner, a parasite, and an adventuress. . . .

The baleful influence of [the game of] "bridge," however, is only of episodic importance in this minute and painfully engrossing study of the career of a pleasure-seeker. The sacrifices of self-respect which Lily is driven to make in order to satisfy her thirst for luxury might well be supposed to alienate the reader, but in every phase of her devious career she never wholly forfeits sympathy, and in the end excites the liveliest compassion. With such antecedents and opportunities disaster was inevitable, but it is a disaster infinitely more tragic than the conventional unhappy ending of a lovely woman who stoops to folly. The relations between some of Lily's extravagant friends and their wives growing somewhat strained, the situation is saved by the sacrifice of the one honest woman of the set,—Lily herself. Perhaps Mrs. Wharton has shown too elaborate an ingenuity in contriving that every indiscretion, however venial, should ultimately recoil on her heroine with accumulated force, and the supreme humiliation of her failure to "range herself" by marrying the odious Mr. Rosedale is almost unbearably painful. Yet the story is so closely knit, so logically carried out, that one cannot but acquiesce in its inevitableness, and admire the skill with which Mrs. Wharton has contrived to reconcile her readers to a conclusion which at first seemed mercilessly inconclusive.

"A Review of the Important Books of the Year," Independent, 59 (16 November 1905), 1151

When we contemplate the year's fiction, there is much for which we should be thankful, not in the fiction, but in the people who read it. Few of them have been injured by it—not that the authors have preserved anything like a decalog attitude toward the issues of life, but most of us are sufficiently sophisticated by this time to overcome the suggestions of romantic writers in the conduct of real living. It is several years now since the young woman confessed that she "went wrong" because she read Swinburne's poetry and Balzac's novels. In fact, if there is anything in literary line upon line and precept upon precept, Mrs. Wharton's novel with the scenes laid in the Vanity Fair circles of New York life should detain many a belle in her downward course in that world of splendid shams and hollow mirth. The heroine, who was the most beautiful woman of the year in books, lies dead on the last page, but not before she had suffered her way up thru more shortcomings of nature and ambition than any other, and held out against greater odds of the world, the flesh and the devil. But it was a sort of blind, disabled survival of the good over the strong. And the sequel is in the form of a warning, not a hope. And, when we consider the damnation threats which surround us all from the cradle to the grave, that is the flaw in Mrs. Wharton's splendid sermon. People rise quicker to a hope. To offer a warning is like giving a stone when they ask for bread.

"New Novels," *Athenæum* [England], 4074 (24 November 1905), 718

To describe in a few words such a novel as Mrs. Wharton's is not easy. There is a great deal in it, and it differs from her others. Society as it is in New York and the various degrees of its "smartness" form the principal theme of the book, but it is particularly concerned with the fortunes of a beautiful girl suffering from want of dollars, the malady most difficult to cure in such a *milieu*. The girl is more attractive than her surroundings. Good work is shown in her characterization and in her external circumstances, and there is more in the picture of the mixed condition of her emotions and morals. Her unfortunate upbringing has given her small chance of rising above a circle where luxury and pleasure dominate, yet there are in her indestructible germs of nobler impulses. It is a pitiful story, told with restraint and insight and not a little subtlety.

"*The House of Mirth*, and Other Novels," *Nation*, 81 (30 November 1905), 447–8

At least two serious and authoritative writers have expressed a view of Mirth in memorable words. The Preacher, whose wisdom is enshrined in the Book of Ecclesiastes, was a man of moods; in a dreary moment he turned a gloomy eye on Mirth, and described her house as the house of fools. Milton, a less impetuous poet than the Preacher, and, we are inclined to think, a man of greater discernment, of more sedate habits, gazed genially at Mirth, hailing her as a "Goddess fair and free," begging her to "admit him of her crew." In great literature, therefore, the character of Mirth and of the habitués of her house remains undetermined, and (for most of us) to consider any subject that has been inconclusively discussed in great literature is to dwell forever in the shadow of doubt. Mrs. Wharton, who is a serious writer and is already hailed in some quarters as an authoritative one, appears to have escaped the blight of indecision. Perhaps, while meditating Mirth, she overlooked Milton, and could therefore the more easily, with a clear conscience and earnest conviction, range herself beside the Preacher. At all events she has written a long book in support of his dictum, a tale of American society, which assures us that the Preacher was a prophet, and that a bitter epigram may incorporate literal truth.

In order to do justice to Mrs. Wharton's book, a disposition to challenge her attitude towards her subject should be repressed. Having made up her mind, she seldom wavers or falters. Her weak moments are few. She is "thorough." The main prop of her argument is perspicaciously chosen. A woman, young, beautiful, and poor, whose only object in life is to make a great match (as American slang appropriately has it, "to marry rich"), is a pillar of strength for the purpose of delineating a society that has neither mind, morals, nor manners—a destitute society rolling in money. Many novelists have described the social career of this ill-fated young person, generally representing her as a victim of circumstance, herself possessing intrinsic virtues which either conquer superficial and accidental attributes or at least make a good enough showing to engage the reader's sympathy. Not in this lenient fashion has Mrs. Wharton seen and judged Miss Lily Bart. The image most constantly and consistently before her, most vividly presented, is not that of a naturally good girl, of an essentially nice girl, hurt, hardened, degraded by contact with a wicked world, but that of a girl born at the wicked world's level, who, failing to get a firm footing therein, is driven by bitter and repeated disappointment to take her leave by the agency of an over-dose of chloral. Miss Bart never willingly faces life beyond the precincts of the House of Mirth, but outstays her welcome there, resorting to ignominious shifts, pocketing rather deadly insults, until she is pushed out of doors and down, step by step, to the common highway.

Occasionally Mrs. Wharton's clear, severe vision wavers. She intimates that her Lily Bart is superior to her world, that she chafes in chains, and has intermittent attacks of soft and even sanctifying emotions. Mrs. Wharton is weakest when she is merciful. Miss Bart does seem to throw up her game at a critical moment and to let coveted prizes slip through her fingers; but such misfortunes strike us as unforeseen results of her folly or of an unexpected checkmate. There is no evidence of instinctive recoil from an intention recognized as ignoble. Even her final rejection of the monstrous conditions on fulfilment of which Mr. Rosedale has expressed a willingness to marry her, fails to establish any moral worth.

Blackmail is a resort of the infamous. A decent girl, one not necessarily clever or kind or well-bred, would have sent Mrs. Dorset's compromising letters back to her as soon as they fell into her hands. It is by the temptations that Miss Bart permitted to visit her that her character finally fails to commend itself for sympathetic judgment or compassion. "Dingy" is her favorite appellation for those who do not live in splendor on their own or other people's incomes. She had a mortal horror of dinginess, external dinginess, but lived and moved delightedly among souls of dinginess incomparable, beyond furbishing. The poor girl's inward eye was a feeble organ not susceptible of cultivation.

A hasty mental comparison between Miss Bart and famous heroines of society fiction, both English and French, suggests many points of resemblance, though in one respect she stands alone in dreary isolation. She has not a particle of genuine, fundamental, good human feeling, and has very little bad. Her assumed tender emotion for the cautious, not to say canny, Mr. Selden (a cold prig), never convinces any one, not even him. She cherishes no affectionate sentiments towards the mother who did her poor best for her, the aunt who supported her, the rich women who dressed her, or the poor friend who adored her. In no society could such a being exist except in that where the dismal and (to the reader) often tedious drama of her life goes on. The denizens of her *House of Mirth* are revolting. They eat and drink, expensively and often, but are never merry. They never think, and their talk is as the crackling of thorns. They break the seventh commandment without the excuse of passion, apparently playing with adultery and divorce (as they seem to play bridge for high stakes and drive motorcars) in order to assert privilege, to earn the absurd epithet, "smart." They have no ideas, no intellectual interests, neither wit nor humor nor tact nor grace.

If this is American society, the American House of Mirth, it is utterly unsuitable for conversion into literature. Literature demands all that such society has not—ideas, intellectual interests, sentiment, passion, humor, wit, tact, and grace; it can get along perfectly well without money, which is the only desire or possession of such society, its only claim for recognition even by the newspapers. A feeling for fair play obliges us to protest Mrs. Wharton's picture as a prejudiced one, yet it is not consciously unveracious. Though depressing, it is not wholly unprofitable. A perusal of Miss Bart's melancholy history will hardly incite those who are in society to pause and examine themselves, but it may cause those who are outside the ring to praise God for that he has been pleased to make them "dingy."

"Fiction: *The House of Mirth*," *Times Literary Supplement* [England], 1 December 1905, p. 421

One of the difficulties that never releases the habitual critic is the difficulty of preserving a fixed standard. It is easy to point out what appears to be good in a book, but very hard to keep it in its right relation to other good books. In other words the difficulty is not that you get your colours wrong, but that you get your "values" wrong. When you are offered a well-written and entertaining book, it seems not unjust to call it "very good"; but the trouble is that these words apply quite as well to *Hamlet* or to the *Iliad*. They also are very good. You discover that you have adopted a shifting standard, and that your values are falsified. Thus it is that when at rare intervals the critic is confronted with an exceptional book, he has a sudden desire to reconsider his position. The adequate words are there, only they have been already applied to other books, good of their kind, but on a lower plane, and no better words are left. Mrs. Wharton's new novel *The House of Mirth* . . . is such an exceptional book; and it is worth while insisting that our standard is, at any rate for the moment, a high one, before proceeding to praise it. A dozen other novels of the year are good; but this book is really good. Mrs. Wharton has shown again and again in her short stories that she possesses not only an extraordinary mastery over technique, but also the real spirit of comedy, watchful, sympathetic, and ironic too. She takes a more prolonged flight in this book, and with it marks the highest point she has yet reached. She brings all her humour and sureness of touch, and adds a sustained fire and beauty beyond anything she has written hitherto. The book is in the first place solidly founded upon a trenchant knowledge of the human spirit and its curious workings. There is not in the whole of it a single piece of conventional or secondhand characterization. Mrs. Wharton knows through and through the extremely modern types which she chooses. She registers to the last degree of delicacy the jumble of crudity and overcivilization which she finds in New York life of to-day. She describes coolly and patiently, without a touch of journalism or sentimentality, the interminable race after pleasure which that fierce little world, like many another, engages in till it unconsciously becomes more absorbed in the race than in its object. In the middle of this turmoil move the figures she selects: Selden, an extremely subtle discovery of the writer's, sympathetic and cultivated, slipping in and out of the society round him, a detached spectator, independent of what Mrs. Wharton calls the sumptuary side of life, who cannot help loving with his taste as well as his instinct, inevitably missing his opportunity when it arrives, as spectators of life will do; Rosedale, the Jew millionaire, who knows the place in society that he wants, knows exactly what it is worth his while to pay for it, and is prepared to pay it, who with all his meanness gets somehow to the heart of life, touches reality in a way in which the Seldens of the world, who are worse egotists than the Rosedales, will never do; and then, moving between the two, like a far more sophisticated Manon Lescaut, is Lily Bart, the central figure of the book, a portrait on which Mrs. Wharton has lavished all her skill and insight. She fights passionately to hold her precarious position in the House of Mirth, and, with all her advantages and all her efforts, is slowly

forced out of it. Now and then, for a moment, she half believes that it is not worth the trouble, and that Selden and the less complicated life that he represents has something curiously seductive to offer. And then at last, when she loves Selden, he fails her after all, and she has to face her catastrophe alone. It is hardly possible to praise too highly the way in which Mrs. Wharton has followed out this history, the truth she has put into it and the continuity she gives it, making this vacillating mind, among the crowd who know their own minds so well, shift and change without ever losing its identity. The whole book, indeed, is so good that it is worth while making a thankless effort to point out Mrs. Wharton's limitations in order to make sure that those difficult "values" have not been forgotten. What Mrs. Wharton appears to lack is in a word the creative gift at its fullest. She sees with certainty, and her hand is as sure as her eye. But with the richest imaginations something takes place beyond this. Detail may be rough and incorrect, but something entirely new has been conceived and embodied. That is what happens when fiction reaches its very highest point; and the *House of Mirth* may well be below this, and yet be what it is, an exceptional book.

James MacArthur, "Books and Bookmen," *Harper's Weekly*, 49 (2 December 1905), 1750

It is deeply significant surely of a growing literary taste in our country that the two most popular successes of the year in American fiction are works that depend as much upon an appreciation of artistic merit as upon the stirring human interest in the story. Both [Booth Tarkington's] *The Conquest of Canaan* and *The House of Mirth* make a dual demand upon intellectual and emotional sympathy. In their serial form one followed more closely the development of character and situation in the dramatic handling of the human conflict, but in book form one became more intensely alive to the aesthetic pleasure of the brilliant wit, the happy humor, the felicity of phrase, the salient characterization, the vivid descriptive power and luminous diction, in a word, the *distinction* which lifts these two books far above the mass of mediocre fiction (though much of the latter is of more than ordinary power and picturesque appeal), and stamps them not only as works of a higher order of imagination, but as having the authority and endowment of great literary art. And in both cases we can trace the springs of that artistic impulse to a chosen field of human study in American life, in the earliest works of the authors. No less in *The Greater Inclination* than in *The Gentleman from Indiana* do we see the special instinct and inquiry that have culminated in *The House of Mirth* and *The Conquest of Canaan*. In the books that lie between these may have been a wavering and wandering from the primal purpose which each by a natural aptitude and fitness was destined to fulfil, but there is evident now, as we look back from their latest achievement, a latent feeling after the one thing needful to the fruition of their genius, a steadfastness to their pursuit of the artistic ideal vouchsafed to them in the beginning. There are still others to whom we look for the elevation and sustenance of art in American letters, but for the moment our hopes and aspirations are centred on these two writers, and one is prone to look for a fairer superstructure to rise in the future upon the solid foundation of the present. Mean-

while, we have these two books for a present joy and pride in our literature.

No two novels could be more dissimilar in subject and method than these two books by Mr. Booth Tarkington and Mrs. Edith Wharton. In both there is the same artistic conscience at work, but they are widely separated by differences of temperament and that section of human society to which each has been called as a ministering agent of imaginative art. Mr. Tarkington is, first of all, a romanticist and a genial humorist. Mrs. Wharton is primarily a realist and a master of satire. The effect in Mr. Tarkington is that of a cheerful optimism; in Mrs. Wharton it tends to a salutary pessimism; both effects are the concomitant results of the present state of our democracy, where the higher ideals and spiritual needs of humanity are lowered and diverted from the channels of aspiration by the materialistic environment of social ambition, and the aesthetic craving for a comfortable complacency and elegance of life engendered by the sudden rise of the country to great wealth. The sanity and truth of Mrs. Wharton's relentless arraignment of the conditions which she portrays cannot be gainsaid; it is the most timely and terrible commentary on the heartless and cynical outcome of a state of things we see all about us at present that could be conceived. In its insight and penetration, its dramatic intensity and the shuddering disclosure of the hollow mockery and sordid tragedy of them that dwell in the House of Mirth, it appeals like an inspiration, and comes with the authority of one who is a seer. There is no preaching or moralizing, but beneath the sound of the crackling of thorns under a pot there rises an undercurrent of strong denunciation like the "Woe, woe unto you" of the prophets. Never was any society summoned to a sterner tribunal than in this book. There is no effort on Mrs. Wharton's part to subdue the somber shadow lurking on every page, yet that restraint which is hers by right of the artist rarely allows it to darken the gay and debonaire procession of mirth that goes heedlessly and lightly to its doom. It is there always, but only by suggestion, by inference, and the terror of the truth strikes home the more surely and swiftly for the eloquent silence of its appeal.

The pitiful pathos and tragic issue of Lily Bart's struggle, the low moral level of her pitiless, self-indulgent world, the utter lack of ideals, and at best the petrifying standards of worldly wisdom have led many to condemn *The House of Mirth* as depressing and degrading. For them, this is doubtless true, and if no smug complacency and cant go with their judgment, they may thank God for it. But the judgment of those who know whereof Mrs. Wharton writes compels respect and confidence, even if the realism of its art did not convince us of its truth. Depressing, even degrading, it may be, but not Mrs. Wharton is responsible for that, but the life which she has transferred through the potency of her imaginative insight to her pages. There is need as there is room in our fiction—the prevailing medium in literature today—for the warning from a joyless ineffectual existence that may well be the prelude to an invitation to rise to a higher plane of life. I am aware that this question of the absence of idealism in the book is being freely discussed. An eminent woman novelist recently wrote me: "It seems to me that she creates a very high ideal by her masterly presentation of the absence of all ideals. The recoil of dismay from that abyss to which she leads us throws us, somehow or other, into the Promised Land." It is the revulsion of feeling that calls a halt and leads us by the very instinct of spiritual self-preservation to a reorganization of our life forces, when we realize that "We have given our hearts away, a sordid boon!" It may seem as if one were unduly dwelling on the ethical import of the book, but in this case it is inevitable, for its ethical significance is inseparable from the human interest of the tale. The House of Mirth is but neighbor to the House of Mourning, and the human tragedy being enacted under cover of the fleeting dance of the hours conducted by the Comic Muse is "as terrible and beautiful and earnest as Life and Death!" For the rest—for Mrs. Wharton's remarkable and distinguished powers as a writer, nothing remains to be added to what has already been said. As a novelist she stands alone; there is none to compare her with, and her place is with the foremost exponents of cultivated American life in fiction.

It is little more than six years ago that I was privileged to hail *The Greater Inclination* in words that one remembers with self-gratification. As their significance bears as pertinently on her work to-day as it did then, I am tempted to recall one passage: "If we were to single out one book from those that have been published this season (1899) as exhibiting in the highest degree that rare creative power called literary genius, we should name *The Greater Inclination* by Edith Wharton. . . . Not only has Mrs. Wharton brought to these stories a remarkable power of insight and imagination, but the phase of life in America which she has chosen for treatment may be said to be altogether new in her hands. Her work is the more remarkable when we know that the process by which her results are reached have been gained largely through intuition and sympathy. One would almost imagine in reading these stories that the author must have suffered and gone deep into life in order to bring up from its depths such knowledge of the world as is disclosed in her pages. And yet this is far from being the case." Mrs. Wharton was born in New

119

York, and on both sides she comes of old New York stock, her mother being a Rhinelander. She has travelled a great deal, especially in Italy. Both Mrs. Wharton and her husband are passionately fond of animals, and have been for years the moving spirits in the Society for the Prevention of Cruelty to Animals in Rhode Island.

"The Abode of the Fool's Heart,"
Literary Digest, 31 (December 1905), 886

In whatever light Mrs. Wharton's *House of Mirth* may be regarded, it will win approval from all except the sentimentalists who demand the "happy ending." They will feel doubly aggrieved should they realize that it might have ended pleasantly without nullifying its strength. For surely, peace and happiness should have a "strength" as great as wretchedness and tragedy. But Mrs. Wharton, after deliberately creating the drastic atmosphere of the Furies, invisibly knotting black threads to enmesh their victim back of the soft bloom of Luxury's tapestry, may have felt it inartistic to turn on them, or, perhaps, may have lapsed into bondage to the pitiless force she had evoked. After spelling ruin as far as R, U, I, one must write "Joy" very emphatically to efface their effect.

The force and value of *The House of Mirth* lie in the pitiless psychological dissection of a beautiful young woman, Lily Bart, and of the forces and tendencies of "Society." The picture is not one to inspire admiration for our self-styled "best people," and the moral teaching of the book is at best negative. That such a girl should retain her simple bed-rock sense of the value of things and enough wholesome genuineness to hold the reader's sympathy in such surroundings and circumstances is, perhaps, something of a strain on the reader's sense of verity. None but the rigidly correct can help pitying her. Here is an exquisite, clever, well-bred girl, who is mistress of all the arts that make such a woman a success in society, yet finds herself, relatively, a pauper in it. For her income does not even enable her to "dress the part." She craves the luxuries of society—of New York society, which is a baser degree of aspiration—and to secure them has to "marry money," and to that, accordingly, Lily Bart deliberately bent herself. Deliberately, at least, when she had reached the ripe bloom of twenty-nine, and had been husband-hunting within the pale for a decade. It strikes an "outsider" as singular that she shouldn't have bagged her game before she reached a point where she had to "bolt" a disagreeable man to secure the money which meant the luxuries.

Lily certainly does things which accord poorly with her name. She decides to marry an enormously wealthy, negative little skinflint, and loses him. Then she sinks to considering "eligible" as a husband a most offensive and vulgar type of Jew, and even he gets away. She is a three months' guest on a yacht that she may divert the attentions of a husband from his wife and a man-guest cruising with them, who are "interested" in one another. She also goes twice to a bachelor's apartment unchaperoned, tho only for a sympathizing talk and a cigarette. This would appear to some as the kind of compromising step a girl of Lily Bart's stamp would have had the strength to deny herself. True, Mrs. Wharton represents her as of capricious turns, rebelling against the nauseating régime she has elected to. But a "creation" does not always ring true.

120

Miss Bart is a blend of Becky Sharp and Gwendolen Harleth. She is not as compellingly human as the one, nor as uninspiring as the other. Frankly, Mrs. Wharton has surpassed George Eliot in this theme. Not only is Lily Bart more congenial and better, as a human variation, than Gwendolen or Becky, but Mrs. Wharton's style is more plastic and seductive than that of Mrs. Lewes. It would be banale to allude to its suggestion of Henry James. But whatever else is to be said about it, *The House of Mirth*—ironic title— stands as Mrs. Wharton's most masterly achievement. This picture of the rank development of what are the dominant germs of New York Society and this strenuous study of one of its products and its victims is absorbingly interesting and makes its own appeal to human sympathy and pity. To approve it is a compliment the appreciative reader pays to his sense of literary perfection.

That this is one of the strongest pieces of writing that has appeared in this country for many a day is pretty nearly the unanimous verdict of the newspaper critics. "A finished and beautiful example of the modern novelist's art," declares the New York *Tribune* and the Providence *Journal* thinks it has the "essential quality of greatness." *The Christian Work* (New York) declares that "in tone, language, and dramatic force it stands unrivaled," and, in comparison with other recent books, *The World To-day*'s critic thinks it "is a giant among pigmies." "It is admirably done," remarks the Springfield *Republican*, but "whether it is the stuff of which great novels are made is another matter." *The House of Mirth*, according to the New York *Times*, "is a tragedy of our modern life, in which the relentlessness of what men used to call Fate and esteem, in their ignorance, a power beyond their control, is as vividly set forth as it ever was by Aeschylus or

Shakespeare." While the New York *Evening Post* and *The Sunny South* (Atlanta) think the work is admirably done, they add that they are disappointed in the story.

Olivia Howard Dunbar, "A Group of Novels," *Critic*, 47 (December 1905), 509–10

Anything like a fair estimate of Mrs. Wharton's novel is precluded, in most quarters, by the character of her material. A book understood to be a castigation, however indirect, of the "fast set" by a writer who can discuss social phases with authority, is practically certain of applause, and a large part of the interest popularly displayed in *The House of Mirth* is undoubtedly attributable to a mixture of curiosity and moral enthusiasm. Lily Bart, again, has been generally accepted as a type; and her story, therefore, becomes a social fable, rather than an individual tragedy, a "horrible warning," in so many chapters, to young women of sordid ambitions, love of luxury, and instability of character.

It may only be possible with time to discover how much, beyond an acute and spirited fable, the book really is. It is certainly not, as incautious admirers have already pronounced, a "great" novel. Nowhere does it attain the indescribably fine and radiant quality of the best of its author's short stories. That high-spirited zest in her performance, characteristic of Mrs. Wharton at her best, one misses here. But the greatest defect of the book is undoubtedly its lack of contrast. It has no high-lights. Its figures are all of one exceedingly unpleasant tone, the interplay of different types of character, one of the chief functions of the novelist, being excluded altogether. In short, the book is a little too much like a fastidiously conducted literary "raid" —which may result in displaying a garish group of frightened transgressors, but which cannot be accepted as a sober and comprehensive interpretation of life.

The last quality that one looks for in a first novel—*The Valley of Decision* is not, properly considered, a novel—is supreme constructive skill; yet this is perhaps the chief virtue of *The House of Mirth*. Mrs. Wharton presents her case with no false or uncertain strokes. Event follows event with exquisite reasonableness, and the final chapters, with their swift tragic impetus, are done not only with unwavering technical precision, but with grave, assured logic. As to the essential truth of the narrative, that is to say, there is not the faintest doubt in the world. Granted a Lily Bart, and a certain set of conditions, and her doom would be inevitable.

What one disturbedly wonders, however, in following the girl's unlovely history, is how much of it Mrs. Wharton has suppressed. Just as she insists upon Miss Bart's remarkable eyelashes because she feels responsibility to her as a heroine and a beauty, so we suspect there are various things about Lily which, because she is a heroine, we never learn at all. The reader is not allowed to know her with real intimacy, to get behind the scenes. One thinks of her, after all, as gloved, veiled, smiling, erectly on her guard.

Mrs. Wharton is not lacking in invention. It is the more surprising, therefore, that she should have permitted herself so old a device as that of the blackmailing charwoman who reclaimed the compromising letters most unnaturally cast by the punctilious Selden, half-torn, into the waste-basket. This entire episode is trump-

ery and melodramatic and weakens the plot.

As a promoter of discussion, *The House of Mirth* is incomparable. As a piece of artistic creation, it falls short of supreme excellence. As an indication that Mrs. Wharton can write a far better novel with material affording her greater latitude, this book will be held of value by the discerning.

E. E. Hale, Jr., "Mrs. Wharton's *The House of Mirth*," *Bookman*, 22 (December 1905), 364–6

The House of Mirth is the title which Mrs. Wharton has affixed to the most intense tragedy of recent years. A girl in New York society—a girl still, in spite of twenty-nine years, with all the vitality, spirit, charm that belong rightly to that title—begins to be very conscious that a time is near at hand when she must do something besides enjoy life as it comes. She is without parents, practically without money, and without any interests except the momentary occupations of the world she lives in. Naturally, marriage is the obvious thing, and two marriages are possible: one with money and one with a man. Not quite hard enough to pursue the first indomitably, she is not quite brave enough to abandon herself to the other. In a doubtful middle state, she allows herself to take only the step that seems necessary at the moment. The story shows inexorably what happened to her.

Why her fate should appear tragic save to herself may be a question. We have here no wreck of obvious possibilities and hopes, except of a meaner sort: Miss Lily Bart was not one of the stronger spirits of the world. She did not have the passions and interests of an artistic nature; she did not have the perceptions of intense vitality that go with a spiritual nature. Momentarily she was impressed by Selden's conception of the republic of the spirit as well as by the intrinsic power of Gerty Farish's young women's clubs. Still, she never saw clearly any better path while she slipped down the worse. She was, one might imagine, one of the useless ones of this world, and her fate, one might say, was no more tragic than the death of a butterfly; indeed, not so much so.

She did have, however, a very true and noble feeling, though blind enough, almost subconscious, without moral strength. Under favouring circumstances, with a different education and environment, she could have done great things. As it was, living in the limited world of New York, her possibilities went for nothing. But it is by this fine, distinguished temperament that the unhappy girl appeals to us more strongly than many of stronger mould. For it certainly is a tragedy when anything so rare and beautiful finds itself forced to mere denial of impossibilities. And it is Mrs. Wharton's great achievement, in a book where all is fine, that she makes us see and sympathise with the true distinction in a woman who on the surface has little else than beauty and charm.

The spectacle of this tragedy is presented upon a sordid stage. In spite of all the gold possessed by everybody but Miss Bart, it is not a brilliant world, and in spite of the cheerful name which Mrs. Wharton's irony attaches, it is not a cheerful one. Nobody except the heroine holds our interest or respect. Of Miss Bart's particular friends, Gus Trenor was a lout as well as a glutton, and his wife was a cold-hearted manager. George Dorset was a forlorn hypochondriac and his wife an implacable maniac. Rosedale had good things about him, but not enough to make him a pleasant friend. Mrs. Peniston was an insufferable example of brownstone-front respectability. And so on with the rest, all presented, of course, with the utmost happiness and sureness. Even the two good people are no real exceptions. Gertrude Farish was a good woman, worthy of respect and love. But Mrs. Wharton is so absorbed in her heroine's standpoint, or, rather, wishes us to be, that she has little but flouts for her. And as for Mr. Selden, it is chiefly by being informed of the fact that we know him to be that wondrous combination, an intelligent worldling.

There were once heard—may be heard to-day—complaints from such as dislike "such a combination of low-toned commonplaceness." Why should Mrs. Wharton "find it worth while continually to describe the belittling qualities and frailties of human nature instead of using her talent to give the world some uplifting picture of moral effort"? Why, indeed? Why is not comedy greater than tragedy? Why is not Prospero or Portia greater than Hamlet? That is certainly an interesting question, which we may properly refer to the æsthetic psychologist. Why, however, our complainant may continue, if one must be so deadly serious—why not relieve the scene a bit, if only for contrast? Is there no one interesting in the best society of New York? Perhaps there is, but perhaps, also, the Miss Barts do not know it. As for Lily, her heart has to be hardened, or, rather, her eyes have to be shut, lest she see, feel and be saved. It is a legitimate enough literary convention. You must combine these things so as to show the essentials: you cannot present the whole world.

There are books that do it: is not [Thackeray's] *The Newcomes* as tragic in

123

feeling and as severe in arraignment? Probably it is. Probably also, Mrs. Wharton is quite unable to keep her eye on her patient and her finger on her pulse and at the same time be charmed and delighted at the predominant joy and humour and beauty of human nature. Until she can do so, she should not be pronounced the greatest novelist of recent times. Pending her arrival at that modest eminence, we may be grateful that Mrs. Wharton accomplishes with apparent ease the most difficult part of her task.

For that she certainly does. Some time since it was said by a master of a very different kind of fiction that "it is one thing to remark and to dissect, with the most cutting logic, the complications of the human spirit; it is quite another to give them body and blood." Observation, analysis, logic: these processes, probably, Mrs. Wharton has employed rather more than Stevenson would have done. But whatever Mrs. Wharton may have done herself, these intellectual operations are not obvious in her book. "In anything fit to be called by the name of reading," continues the same authority, "the process should be absorbing and voluptuous; we should gloat over a book, be rapt clean out of ourselves, and rise from the perusal, our mind filled with the busiest kaleidoscopic dance of images, incapable of sleep or of continuous thought." That is a very exact description of a mental state that many will probably experience on reading The House of Mirth. It is not observation, analysis, logic; it is real humanity, if not the whole of it, and that is something likely to hold our interest and absorb our attention. After perhaps a slight repulsion at first, one is attracted to the unhappy butterfly, and follows her flutterings with a growing feeling, to which the last few pages come with a suave and necessary relief.

And after that, what then? one may ask. Suppose you are voluptuously absorbed, that your mind sees stars, that you cannot sleep? Is that all one can say? Is there no moral teaching? No problem? No message? No criticism of life? There is not, very fortunately, any one of these things. There is nothing that needs to be discussed or talked about, or answered. There is simply the impression of poignant tragedy, the pity and awe with which one becomes silent.

Alice Meynell, "The House of Mirth," Bookman [England], 29 (December 1905), 130–1

Mrs. Wharton is essentially a moralist, albeit with the whole modern resolve not to declare herself. A Gift from the Grave remains her highest, most complete, and most commanding work, because, in a memorable passage she set her sail to a natural wind. Moral passion swept through the world of that book—direct grief, emotion close to the fact of life, love, indignation, remorse, dishonour, and honour; all the storms of breasts complex, civilised, but incorrupt. In The House of Mirth we have to read of the fortunes of a woman full of desires and of self-love, but void of virtue, of passion, and of intellect; and round about her are only lovers of their own ease and supremacy; claimants to the right of a social contemptuousness towards other less fortunate egotists as the salt of life; and graspers of riches as its sweetness. To observe this horde without obvious irritation is a work demanding self-control, and Mrs. Wharton watches them from the sequestered bower of her fine art, taking wide views, keeping her own coun-

124

sel. It seems strange to say of a novelist who has filled five hundred pages with chosen words that she keeps her own counsel, but it is none the less obviously true of the writer of these five hundred remarkable pages. The keeping of her own counsel is one of the feats of her work. Is it indeed worth doing so well? Or rather, is not the other feat—that of the unlocking of a noble mind—worth doing? In much of her writing we were admitted to recognise her noble mind; we are reluctant to forego an intimacy that we valued. And when Mrs. Wharton goes about to keep her own counsel she does it, as she does everything, extraordinarily well.

Thackeray intended to keep his own counsel as a sentimentalist; but he did not do it well. He assigned the sentiment to certain characters—to women, to Laura Pendennis foremost—and pretended to be a moderately cynical man looking on with a smile; he took for himself, as it were, the part of Arthur Pendennis, whereas he was Laura at heart; and thus easily persuaded the duller readers in their multitude, during two generations, that he was of a cynical turn. But the author of *The House of Mirth* does not reveal herself, even dramatically. She is the greatest thing that a writer of fiction can be—a moralist; but there is no person in this story to bear the charge of the character.

And in this extremity of reserve lurks the one fault of art in the book—that is the indefiniteness of the "better part" which Selden has to offer to the self-loving and money-loving heroine. In the character of this young New York woman, about whom the whole history is written, we recognise two likenesses. She is partly Gwendolen Harleth and partly Hedda Gabler, yet with something modern in the place of Gwendolen's thirst after righteousness, and something intelligible in the place of Hedda's vice and Hedda's despair. Both resemblances therefore are slight. Now, in her slight likeness to Gwendolen Harleth she should have a kind of external conscience in the form of a man—a man at least esteemed, at least admirable. But the man in whom the role is just suggested, in *The House of Mirth*, is very little estimable. He has borne a part in the "cold obstruction" of the intrigues of man and woman in the world he lives in—a squalid past, we are compelled to see, because of the manner of woman who had been his random mistress. And the better art he shows the heroine, half-heartedly, as a way out of her pursuit of luxury, is vague. If it were definite we are sure it would be inadequate, and Mrs. Wharton ably leaves it in a little cloud. We choose, however, to pause where she passes, and to ask a closer question. All the answer we get is a tender of liberty, and obviously liberty is what the unfortunate egoist, the woman of the New York "world," needs urgently, and all but desperately; but in what liberty does the apostle of this vague apostolate himself abide? We see him in the beloved luxury in which all the persons of the book roll themselves with revolting joy. We cannot imagine Lawrence Selden following liberty into a hard, or a useful, or a wild, or a sacramental life. He sets open, or rather ajar, to the woman who inclines to love him, a door into a better world too dubious for faith, a better world open to nothing but a very justifiable suspicion; and where there is no definite place to go, or object in setting out, she does not go. She is less to blame than Mrs. Wharton.

We find her at the beginning poor, very lovely, member of the inner—the most contemptuous—social world of New York, in full pursuit of a millionaire. By the spite of her equals she misses her quarry; and the story that follows is the story of her failure to capture any other, until she dies, drifting consciously into the peril of an overdose of morphia. She

125

does some deeply dishonourable things on her way; plays a part in a yachting ménage to which the Elizabethans would give a plain name; is refused in marriage by an exceedingly vulgar Jew to whom she offers herself, having misunderstood his addresses, and yet sees him later as a friend; is betrayed and slandered before her world by one woman; helped with *molle* good nature by another, ruined by the general malice. Two good creatures—women—appear in the story: a little cousin given to good works, but the sequestered moralist makes her dowdy; a poor working-woman, but the sequestered moralist supplies her with a "fall" in her past.

It is the mode this year; next year, in a decade of years, it will not be the mode, so to hide a heart of emotion and of dignity. Meanwhile, it deprives us of the finest grace of Mrs. Wharton's genius—her imagery. When she wrote of moral passions and ideals, she used a splendid imagery. In *The House of Mirth* it is only towards the close, where tragedy darkens, and the writer permits herself to show she feels, that one or two admirable images prove to us how rich is the genius so long secluded.

William Morton Payne, "Recent Fiction," *Dial*, 40 (1 January 1906), 15–16

The House of Mirth appears to be the novel of the season in the sense that it is the novel that has occasioned the most discussion of a serious sort. It is a work which has enlisted the matured powers of a writer whose performance is always distinguished, and whose coupling of psychological insight with the gift of expression is probably not surpassed by any other woman novelist of our time. It is a story elaborated in every detail to a high degree of refinement, and evidently a product of the artistic conscience. Having paid this deserved tribute to its finer characteristics, we are bound to add that it is deficient in interest. The reason is not far to seek. There is no section of American society—or of society anywhere, for that matter—so absolutely devoid of appeal to the sympathies of normally-constituted intelligence as the vain and vulgar element that disports itself in our larger cities as the only society worth considering, this pretension being based upon wealth alone, with its natural accompaniment of self-seeking display and frivolity. A novelist of archangelical powers could not make interesting so sorry a phase of humanity as this, and because Mrs. Wharton has described for us this type and this alone, we turn her page impatiently, and look in vain for relief from their emptiness. What she can do with real material she has evidenced in *The Valley of Decision*, a book that we admire heartily enough to permit us the severity with which we are appraising the content, as distinguished from the form, of the present work. What justification may be offered for the book as a portrayal of any sort of human life is found in the plea of its satiric intent—of its character as an American *Vanity Fair*, —but this will not take us very far. The pungent wickedness of Becky Sharp gives her a reasonable excuse for being, but we cannot find in Lily Bart the positive qualities for either good or evil that make it worth while to follow her fortunes through five hundred and more pages of print. When she has come to the end of her tether, the moral of her story is embodied in an impressive paragraph:

> "It was no longer, however, from the vision of material poverty that

she turned with the greatest shrinking. She had a sense of deeper impoverishment—of an inner destitution compared to which outer conditions dwindled into insignificance. It was indeed miserable to be poor—to look forward to a shabby, anxious middle-age, leading by dreary degrees of economy and self-denial to gradual absorption in the dingy communal existence of the boarding-house. But there was something more miserable still—it was the clutch of solitude at her heart, the sense of being swept like a stray uprooted growth down the heedless current of the years. That was the feeling which possessed her now—the feeling of being something rootless and ephemeral, mere spin-drift of the whirling surface of existence, without anything to which the poor little tentacles of self could cling before the awful flood submerged them. And as she looked back she saw that there had never been a time when she had had any real relation to life. Her parents too had been rootless, blown hither and thither on every wind of fashion, without any personal existence to shelter them from its shifting gusts. She herself had grown up without any one spot of earth being dearer to her than another; there was no centre of early pieties, of grave endearing traditions, to which her heart could revert and from which it could draw strength for itself and tenderness for others."

This is so fine and true that it reconciles us in part to the complex of empty talk and petty intrigue and ignoble aim through which, as through a desert waste, we have toiled to reach it. But the question remains persistent whether it was worth while to describe at such length and with such infinite pains the career of any woman of whom it must be said in the end that she had never had any real relation to life. We are much inclined to doubt that it was worth while—for a writer of Mrs. Wharton's exceptional gifts.

Mary Moss, "Notes on New Novels," *Atlantic Monthly*, 97 (January 1906), 52–3

In *The House of Mirth*, to the contrary, Miss Bart's actions not only surprise you, but you are even ready to dispute Mrs. Wharton's knowledge of what her heroine really did do. Lily is a very complete study of the siren of a girl, too poor to keep up with the set in which she moves, who is unfortunately too radically snobbish to cut free from it. Her hold upon this society lies in beauty, elegance, adaptability, and willingness to amuse superfluous husbands (here again woman is the aggressor). Yet under this pliability, she is victim to a self-indulgence so boundless that, at last resort, it amounts to a fair imitation of principle. To be consistent, with her utterly sordid ideals, Lily should promptly knock herself down to the highest bidder. Yet at the very moment when the dull, eligible suitor has finally come to terms, Miss Bart must always see the sweetness of frisking off with a detrimental. She is too fastidious for the life she is leading, but unfit for any other available one. As a point of probability, would not Lily either have early succumbed or managed her way to better things? But when you find yourself discussing the truth of a novel, you are really paying it high tribute. Moreover, such inconsistencies are perhaps likely in a person whose conduct is guided entirely by taste, without a shadow of conviction. Lily is no more deliberately venal than she is deliberately decent. Certain surroundings and a comforting sense of being "in things" are necessary to her existence. A balloon may not scheme to get gas; it merely collapses without. On the whole, I believe that Mrs. Wharton knows the truth about Lily. She was as incapable of *meanness* as of any other form of economy. She only wanted a pretty gown, fresh flowers, a roll of dollars in her pocket for bridge, a pleasant companion, and all doors hospitably open to her. Simple, rational needs! That her income, though ample for a plainer life, was quite unequal to the pace of her friends naturally plunged her into trouble. As for the society in which poor Lily moves, Mrs. Wharton has no colors too black, no acid too biting, for its unredeemed odiousness and vulgarity. She shows its sensuality to be mere passionless curiosity; she displays its cautious balancing of affairs so that reputations are preserved, not lost, in the divorce courts; her people, with regard to the quality commonly known as virtue, resembling rich defaulters who are lucky enough through a technicality to miss a term in jail. The whole is brilliantly well conceived, brilliantly executed. Facets of light glitter before your eyes at the mere thought of it. No cheap sacrifice is made to the buying public's supposed craving for sweet pretty endings. There is but one lack. Read it with approval, with enjoyment. Put it down and go your way refreshed by a novel that held your attention unflaggingly to the end. That is exactly the crux! After finishing *Diana of the Crossways*, did you tranquilly proceed with the business of life? Did you not, at least, need—a dry handkerchief? Diana committed a far baser act than any of poor Lily's, yet we love her! Diana

betrayed a friend for money, yet we love her! For all its brilliancy, *The House of Mirth* has a certain shallowness; it is thin. At best, Lily can only inspire interest and curiosity. You see, you understand, and you ratify, but unfortunately, you do not greatly care. There is more pathos in what befell Miss Cather's wretched little degenerate Paul than in the pitiful fate of a beautiful girl like Lily Bart!

Indeed, after the somewhat arid glitter of *The House of Mirth*, you turn with a sense of comfortable repose to the seasoned solidity of the average English novel.

Alice May Boutell, "A Burst of Enthusiasm," *Critic*, 48 (January 1906), 87–8

It was with a sense of keen disappointment that one of The Critic's faithful readers, who had been looking forward to the December issue for a satisfying critique on *The House of Mirth*, laid down the number after reading the half page which alone was given to the consideration of that novel. It may be that to others beside Miss Dunbar Mrs. Wharton's last book is not a "great novel" but there are certainly those to whom it seems entitled to that rank. I, for one, must take issue with that statement as well as with others made in the criticism referred to. I cannot agree for instance that my interest in the book arose either from "curiosity" or "moral enthusiasm" or a mixture of both. There can be no question as to the supreme excellence of the book as a work of art; its technique, its style, are incomparable: but its chief charm does not after all lie in these. That, it seems to me, is the fact that, while reading it, one has the sense that one is living life, not reading about it, and isn't that the greatest possible test?

Are all "the figures" again, "of one exceedingly unpleasant tone"? Does Gerty Farish fall under that head or Selden or even Rosedale, one of the strongest as he is surely the frankest character in the book? As to the heroine, I find myself utterly at variance with the opinions of the critic. If I ever felt on terms of "real intimacy" with any one in a book it is with Lily Bart; as a matter of fact I feel better acquainted with her than with half of the real women I know. So far from thinking of her as "gloved, veiled, and on her guard," I live, with her, through all her little triumphs and failures, sympathize with her hurt pride, skilfully hid under a calm and smiling exterior, deplore her inconsistencies and changes of purpose, feel sorry for her faults and mistakes, for which she is honest enough to take the blame herself, and glory in her ultimate triumph. I use the word advisedly. Think to what depths she, with her inherited tendencies and in the midst of that artificial environment, might have fallen and how, after all, in every crisis of temptation, she did hold on to the best that was in her, sacrificing wealth, position, a life of ease—all that she had been taught to think of as of the most worth—so to do. Not one "unlovely thing" about or in her has been suppressed, never was author more honest with her readers than Mrs. Wharton has been in this regard; you see right into the heart, mind, and soul of this woman, and what do you read at the end? Not failure to my mind, but success, not as the world counts it to be sure, but success of the spirit. She keeps her true self, her noblest self, inviolate through all the petty ignominies as well as the great disasters that fall to her lot. To find her equal in fiction one must turn to George Eliot, Thomas Hardy, or George

Meredith; no other writers of English have done such justice to their women characters.

If the book as a whole may be regarded as a "castigation of the fast set," it is the most skilfully written sermon yet presented on this text. There is no lecturing, no cant, no tedious or cynical dissertation, on its morals or lack of morals. The picture simply is before you, you may look or you may pass it by. I would recommend a perusal of the book to all those on the lower rungs of the ladder whose greatest ambition is to achieve the top.

I cannot, in conclusion, refrain from voicing my admiration for the courage, no less than for the art of Mrs. Wharton's performance,—courage of a high order, for what she attempted demanded not only great skill but genius, for if she had failed not only her position in letters but in society would have been hazardous—but she has not failed.

"Novels: *The House of Mirth*,"

Saturday Review [England], 101 (17 February 1906), 209–10

Somewhat aweary though we are of the chronicles and exposures of what is vulgarly called "smart society" Miss Wharton's book, dealing as it does with these distasteful subjects, is still a noteworthy achievement. It is indeed a biting criticism of modern civilisation with its luxury worship and mean conventions. It is an appeal for our nobler illusions. The heroine of the novel, Lily Bart, is a masterly study of the modern American woman with her coldly corrupt nature and unhealthy charm. In her characterisation of Lily Bart the author exhibits an unerring instinct. She endows her with life and vitality and the reader follows every step in her chequered career with growing interest and excitement. Young, beautiful and fascinating, full of the joy of life, Lily Bart has been brought up among a "fast" set of people where every whim is gratified regardless of cost. The expense of keeping up the pace is too much for her scanty means and she finds herself at last deep in debt. Although innocent of intention of actual wrong she turns for assistance to a married man, the husband of one of her friends who promises to multiply her income by some mysterious investments on the Stock Exchange. She has a very rude awakening when she at last discovers that the wonderful "dividends" she has been obtaining have come out of his pocket, and that his interest in her affairs is by no means disinterested. Her discovery comes too late, after the man has hopelessly compromised her in the eyes of the world. Her friends and relatives "cut her" and she is left practically alone in the world except for one kind ugly woman friend who of course sticks to her through good report and ill—in the way ugly women have. It must not be supposed that Miss Wharton represents Lily Bart as a model of injured innocence. Quite the contrary. She is a thorough woman of the world, spoilt and selfish and yet withal intensely lovable. It is the striking art of Miss Wharton as a writer that keeps the reader's sympathy from first to last. She can evoke the emotions of pity, horror and love. In Lily Bart she has created a character that will haunt the imagination of the reader and live in his memory. The book is one of the few novels which can claim to rank as literature.

Mary K. Ford, "Two Studies in Luxury," *Critic*, 48 (March 1906), 249–50

In a recent article on "The Integrity of the American Character," ex-President Cleveland points out that what is most to be dreaded is such a deterioration in the moral fibre of a nation that there will be "nothing left to build repair upon." At the same time in an article on "The Decay of Self-Control," in one of the English monthlies, Dr. William Barry, the well-known Roman Catholic writer, is quoted as ascribing it, among other causes, to the multiplication of pleasures in life.

Through the far-reaching medium of fiction Mrs. Wharton has enforced this same lesson, and what she has done for American life in *The House of Mirth* Mr. Howard Sturgis, with as skilful a touch, has accomplished for the more significant society of London in his remarkably interesting novel, *Belchamber*.

It is rather striking that two such books should have appeared within six months of each other, for without being alike they have many points in common. Both describe life in the rich and self-indulgent society which many suppose to be the most desirable that either country has to offer. Each book traces the career of a young person brought up in the midst of great luxury—the one a man richly endowed by the accident of birth, the other a woman greatly gifted by nature—and both, alike victims of their environment, are left at the end of the story: the one, his hopes blighted, his aspirations crushed, with the rest of his life stretching drearily before him; the other, the more fortunate one, lying in her desolate room in a forlorn boarding-house, the peace of death upon her face.

No one can follow the fortunes of Lily Bart without realizing the deteriorating effect of a luxurious life upon the moral fibre of human beings; and the utterances of President Roosevelt upon the merits of a life of endeavor gain new force from Mrs. Wharton's brilliant social satire. Lily recognizes the best in people, and so far appreciates it that she refrains from many acts that others of her set consider permissible; but her standards are constantly being lowered, and she is continually skirting the edge of shady transactions so that finally, when by no fault of her own she finds herself in a very unpleasant predicament, she has really herself to thank for it. Her moral fibre has been so undermined by her self-indulgent way of life that she has neither the courage nor the decision to grasp the best when it is within reach. Even Selden, the nearest approach to a hero that the book contains, is infected by this same fatal vacillation, and only realizes when too late what he and Lily might have been to each other. The same indecision of character is the weakness of Sainty, the hero of *Belchamber*. He allows himself to become the prey of a scheming mother and her worthless daughter, and, in spite of the tremendous advantage of his wealth and position, and a strong desire to benefit his fellow-men, he never accomplishes anything. He and Lily are the victims of their surroundings, with this difference—Lily is a willing one, while Sainty makes a few ineffectual struggles before the waters of adverse circumstances close over him. As we read of these unfortunates we begin to understand those lines of Browning's which have provoked so much criticism from moralists:

Let a man contend to the uttermost
For his life's set prize, be what it will!
. . . . . .

And the sin I impute to each frustrate ghost
Was, the unlit lamp and the ungirt loin,
Though the end in sight was a crime, I say.

Both books are extremely well written, showing marked skill in the delineation of character. In their complete lack of any lovable character both books recall *Lady Rose's Daughter*. Most of the men and women described are hard and grasping if not distinctly vicious, and yet the variety shown is endless. It is discouraging to see how many kinds of objectionable people there are in the world.

That keen observer Mr. James Bryce, in his *American Commonwealth*, comments upon the pleasantness of social life in this country and considers that it arises in great measure from the absence of a caste system. He is undoubtedly right, but while this lack is a boon to our society it is a drawback to our fiction. The social inequalities of an aristocratic society add to a story a picturesque element which is entirely lacking in a democratic community and which gives the novel of English life an advantage to start with. Mrs. Wharton has as skilful a touch as Mr. Sturgis and is even wittier, but his superiority in constructive skill, joined to his advantage in *locale*, makes his book the more interesting of the two. As studies in contemporary manners they are matchless and of equal value.

To carry conviction to the minds of their readers, writers must speak with authority, and no one can read either of these books without feeling its veracity. There is no guesswork here, and the lesson that they teach is all the stronger from the fact that there is no preaching, no solemn arraignment of society; the characters speak for themselves, depicting in a most lifelike way the society which women strain every nerve to enter and for which

131

they are ready to sacrifice their happiness and that of their families. *The House of Mirth* contains nothing sadder than the glimpse we get of Lily's early home, her extravagant mother, her overworked father—a home of which her own miserable death is the legitimate outcome.

And what a lesson the book teaches! It is not for nothing that Mrs. Wharton has taken her title from the Book of Ecclesiastes, that cry of satiety that has come down the ages to us with its burden of "Vanity of vanities! all is vanity!"—a cry even more significant now than when it was uttered nearly three thousand years ago by the wisdom-sated monarch who in these words summed up his experience of life.

Checklist of Additional Reviews

"Recent Fiction and the Critics," *Current Literature*, 39 (1905), 689.

Academy, 69 (4 November 1905), 1155.

"To Lily Bart," *Reader*, 8 (July 1906), 181–4.

Thérèse Bentzon, "Le Monde où l'on s'amuse aux Etats-Unis," *Revue des Deux Mondes* [France], 1 November 1906, p. 200.

Henry Davray, "Lettres Anglaises," *Mercure de France*, 75 (1908), 182.

Lucien Maury, "Les Lettres: Mme. Edith Wharton," *Revue Politique et Littéraire* (*Revue Bleue*) [France], 46 (3 October 1908), 444–7.

Jean Lionnet, "Les Livres," *Revue Hebdomadaire* [France], 17 (10 October 1908), 253–6.

MADAME DE TREYMES

MADAME DE TREYMES

BY
EDITH WHARTON

WITH ILLUSTRATIONS

NEW YORK
CHARLES SCRIBNER'S SONS
1907

Hildegarde Hawthorne, "Mrs. Wharton's Heroines," *New York Times Saturday Review*, 9 March 1907, p. 137

Some one said at a dinner the other evening, "Never make a general statement about women, because at most you know a hundred or two, and the other millions probably don't in the least resemble any of your particular collection." But one may perhaps venture on a generalization of Mrs. Wharton's women, the women she is making familiar to us in one book after another; the women she has drawn with a fine point, decisively, yet with an extraordinary lack of sympathy. These women are creatures of the intellect, and the passions which disturb the current of their cold-flowing lives are of the mind, not of the heart. One suspects it is boredom which has thrown them into the arms of their lovers, when such a consummation occurs, rather than any overpowering emotion. It is never the madness of love which has swept them over barriers, good or evil, but an observing weariness, a smallness of soul which can discover in the legitimate acts of life neither their beauty nor their greatness. These women express not excess but emptiness. Having nothing within, they cannot become conscious of anything without. Their acts leave one unmoved. One does not care whether one of them dies in a garret or marries the rich Jew. It is immaterial whether another deserts her husband or sacrifices herself for her son. It doesn't matter to us, because we are instinctively assured that it doesn't matter to them. They would care very much if they were made to appear ridiculous or underbred; above all they do not want to lose caste, and appearance is the gigantic fetish of their lives, the great pseudo-fact which sways the currents of their white blood.

Mrs. Wharton writes with a deliberate art, a satisfying finish. To be sure, she is wholly devoid of humor, but humor as an asset in the world amid which her creations move would be absolutely undesirable. These people must take each other and be taken with the utmost seriousness. One wholehearted laugh would melt their icicle existences entirely away. Is it possible to conceive of one of the men even in this world of Wharton as overcome by a mad impulse of laughter, a realization of the huge joke? And the women!

No, one enters here in quietness, admiring the chiseled perfection of the archway, the careful poising of stone on stone, the measured proportions and balanced spaces. The acoustic properties of this theatre are excellent and we hear every whisper of the actors who play their carefully-thought-out parts with careful discretion. There will be no shrieks, no mess, no broken heads or hearts. Even if there is at times an appearance of these distressing relics of primitiveness, we know it is only an appearance. The dagger is at most driven into a saw-dust heart, the scream is modulated to accord with the orchestral accompaniment. The play being over we applaud, we rise, and we depart precisely as we entered.

Whether Mrs. Wharton could draw another type of men and women is neither here nor there. That there are a great many persons who move through just such a world as she depicts, and manage this big business of living just as she indicates is assuredly true. It all exists, and Mrs. Wharton is interested in its portrayal. She does it excellently if somewhat self-consciously, and we must needs be grateful, in a hurried age, for evidences of a love of perfection for its own sake.

In *Mme. de Treymes* Mrs. Wharton occupies herself with an American woman who is caught in the foreign maze and is endeavoring with the usual hushed elegance to escape from it. The husband is impossible, and enters only in a descriptive phrase or two. The French relatives, excepting only the sister-in-law, are the conventional French persons of the aristocracy of the Faubourg, the gates of which, Mrs. Wharton hints, are kept consummately closed against American ingression; even those few Americans who do slip in find but another barrier, as impenetrable as it is apparently transparent, between them and this almost ex-human world.

Mme. de Treymes, the sister-in-law in question, steps out fully before the footlights. She decidedly loses her Frenchness by the act—one cannot help contrasting her with Henry James's wonderful Frenchwoman in *The Ambassadors* a woman whose least breath is inspired with the air of her country, the very movements of whose mind conform to the construction of her mother tongue. Mme. de Treymes talks like an American woman; an American woman familiar with Paris, ça va, but American for all that. We do not clearly know whether her remarkable conversations are in French or English, though the weight of evidence tends to show that she speaks to the American hero in his own language. Her mastery of it is certainly astonishing, for not only the words but the manner of thought belong to his nationality rather than to hers. Albeit her sense of honor is more erratic than would be possible to any American woman of whom I know anything—general statements being inadmissible—she yet does not impress one as foreign. Mme. de Malrive, the real American, the American of the maze, is neither more nor less French

than she, certainly no more American. There are some relatives of the hero who are Baedekering through Europe, and they belong to the accepted American tourist type; they are somewhat out of the picture, however, for Mrs. Wharton loses interest in characters who do not represent her special attitude in life. They are objects on the horizon necessary for breaking the even line of monotony, but not existing for their own delight. Mrs. Wharton does not lose her felicity of phrase in describing these dwellers on the rim. There is a Mrs. Elmer Boykin, whose ineffectual personality she indicates by stating that "whatever had happened to her had merely added to the sum total of her inexperience." Mrs. Boykin is here as definitely presented to your perception as is, later on, one of those small gilt chairs "which always look surprised at being sat in." And you take quite as vivid an interest in the one as in the other.

The book is intended to present the contrast of the solidarity of the French family with the individual freedom maintaining in America. You get the impression of an ancestral hand working through the only partially alive entity of the old mother-head of the present group of Malrive, working to move this group according to certain laws, laws which brought it into being and which sustain it in its extraordinary existence. The members of this family move, as it were, in lockstep, and decayed bones are their jailers. The Americans coming into conflict with this condition find, as how can they help but find, that victory resides with death, that life yields once more, as it has always done, to the old Captain. The impression which survives with many of us that this victory is only apparent and that in the moment of seizing the flag death loses the citadel will scarcely suffice to console Mme. de Malrive for the useless sacrifice she is called upon to make, or

136

reconcile her lover to the ideals of the French aristocracy. But perhaps a woman who chooses for the father of her child the type of man so ably represented by M. de Malrive has no right to concern herself with life and sunshine. She has definitely turned her back on them to smile into the sombre eyes of disease and despair. Whoever writes her name in the witches' book is henceforth of their company and must ride with them through night. Bloody footsteps have a curious propensity for preceding as well as following the hapless traveler, and perhaps shadows are of all things hardest to shake off.

Mrs. Wharton puts very thoroughly before us the colorless twilight of this French background and its ghost-ruled inhabitants. She succeeds in painting her gray picture not so subtly that we forget her art, but exquisitely enough for us to recognize how fine that art is. The book is above all eminently well bred, and the members of Mrs. Wharton's audience are sure of not being disappointed in this last expression of her genius.

"Current Fiction," *Nation*, 84 (4 April 1907), 313

Mrs. Wharton's extraordinary mental adroitness and nicety of touch tempt one to think of her as a kind of delicate mechanism which may be counted upon to record with automatic minuteness certain lesser vibrations of the social ether. There is something a little inhuman in this infallible suavity and precision, these infinitesimal modulations within the prescribed and civil range. But this is as it should be with the chronicler of the sophisticated and the

well-bred. "Society" would be inhuman if it were perfect, if it were what it tries to be or tries to pretend to be; at the top of its breeding it actually achieves the appearance of inhumanity. But there is, we are told, a comfortable understanding that the appearance is sufficient. "Society," if we are to credit its chroniclers, gives with one hand while taking with the other, its morals being hardly less confessedly aboriginal than its manners are admittedly the very button on the cap of civilization. This compensatory *modus operandi* is observed with eager, if hardly magnanimous, interest by the dweller without the gates. What attraction has the Best Society to offer its public so moving as the spectacle of well-mannered misconduct in the sexual relation? What has it to offer a novelist or a dramatist so taking as the lure of its discreet variations upon the everlasting theme *à trois*? Mrs. Wharton is notably successful in rendering these variations, always with her negligent air of scorning the virtuosity with which nature and hard labor have equipped her. . . .

Unfortunately, it is her fate to interpret episodes and persons in the light of circumstance, instead of employing them to "individualize the universal." It was not hard to understand the failure of *The House of Mirth* as a play. Divested of the accessories with which the novelist's art had surrounded her, Lily Bart was seen to be an insignificant person, suggestive of a large class of insignificant persons, but quite failing to sum them up, to give them significance. It is hard to guess whether this would be true of the figure of Madame de Treymes. This much the reviewer must confess for himself: he began by questioning whether she was a credible Frenchwoman and ended by deciding that she is certainly a credible woman.

She is, according to Mrs. Wharton, the perfect flower of the French tradition. She

137

is surrounded by "an impalpable aura of grace"; her dress, like her manner, is distinguished by "quiet felicity." She is known to be involved in an intrigue with a nobleman, to pay whose gambling debts she has appropriated her brother's as well as her husband's money. Her brother, the disreputable marquis of tradition, has married an American girl, who now wishes to be freed from him so that she may marry an American. Madame de Treymes is asked to use her influence to gain the family consent to a divorce. She agrees on condition that the American make up the sum she has squandered on her lover. At this his sense of decency revolts, and he refuses. Presently she announces the consent of the family, professing shame for her proposal, and accepting the gratitude of the waiting pair. Eventually, after the granting of the divorce, it transpires that the family have from the first intended to consent to it. In outline, you say, it is a sufficiently sordid story, *Madame de Treymes* bearing a striking resemblance to the stage-worn adventuress of melodrama. Yet in Mrs. Wharton's portrait she is undeniably appealing. She is presented as a sacrifice upon the altar of French society and family convention. Her marriage is prescribed by family, her infidelity is practically sanctioned by her family, her duplicity in the present instance is dedicated to the welfare of the family. . . .

"Madame de Treymes," Athenæum [England], 4149 (4 May 1907), 535

Mrs. Wharton has selected a theme for her little novel or short story which reminds us strongly of that charming book *The American*. The scene is the same, and

the story hinges on the same conflict of ideals of race and class; but in this case the heroine, though wedded to a scion of the old nobility is, like the hero, an American by birth, and, moreover, not a widow. Her only hope of freedom lies in divorcing her unworthy husband—a measure likely to be opposed by his family, the situation being further complicated by the existence of a son and heir. The interest is centred less in the American Marquise herself than in her sister-in-law, Madame de Treymes, who, considered as a product of hereditary influences, seems a more subtle study than any of the characters in Mr. James's novel. The writing is distinguished by that blend of strength and grace which is characteristic of Mrs. Wharton, and we are not ill pleased with her sturdy faith in the superiority of the Anglo-Saxon and Protestant tradition.

"Madame de Treymes," Academy, 72 (11 May 1907), 465–6

Mrs. Wharton writes with wit and with distinction. All her work has quality; it bears the mark of a personality, and accordingly should be read. In *Madame de Treymes* she has found an excellent subject, which contains a fine effect in dramatic contrast. Fanny Frisbee is an American girl who has married a reprobate French marquis, and has been living in consequence for twelve years in Paris. The family into which she has married have the old Catholic traditions, and though she has obtained a separation from her husband, she does not sue for divorce, because she knows that the family will oppose it strongly, and she shrinks from scandal for her own sake and for the sake of her little boy. That is what John Durham discovers to be the position when the story opens. John Durham is a straightforward American gentleman with many of the traditions of George Washington. He has loved her as the American girl Fanny Frisbee, and loves her still as Madame de Malrive. He proposes to her immediately and is accepted on condition that he can obtain for her an undefended divorce. He finds that one of the family, her husband's sister, Madame de Treymes, is kindly disposed to Madame de Malrive. Through her agency he determines to work. He makes her acquaintance and a meeting is arranged in which to discuss the position. At this meeting Madame de Treymes behaves like an aristocratic sphinx. She tells him at once that the family are bitterly opposed to a divorce, and watches the effect of her words. They parley. Suddenly the mask falls from Madame de Treymes's face. She says that the man she loves must go away because of debts which he cannot meet. She will give Durham all the support of her great influence if he, rich American that he is, will write her a cheque. He refuses. Any subterfuge is against his upright nature. He will win his wife by fair means or none. He resigns himself to endurance. Naturally surprise overcomes him when he hears from this lady that Madame de Treymes has used her influence to such good purpose that the divorce will not be defended, and when he next meets Madame de Treymes she tells him that the pleasure of furthering the happiness of a man so noble as he, is its own reward. So the divorce proceeds; it is just on the verge of completion when he meets Madame de Treymes for the third time. She begins by triumphing over him. She has been successful in deceiving him. The family were no longer interested in the woman. They want the child. And the child they will inevitably get at the close

of the proceedings. But Madame de Treymes has reckoned without Durham's honesty, even as he has reckoned without her malign dishonesty. He will stop the proceedings immediately. Then she is touched by his bravery, and when she says that this is only a last lie he is touched by her kindness. "You poor good man," she says, and "you poor good woman," he answers, as he goes to carry out his own unhappiness. Now there is much that is admirable and subtle in the story and in its treatment. The different points of view of two types of character are set forth with great clearness. The story, however, loses its poignancy owing to the fact that these types are not individualised. The contrast between the old civilisation and the new civilisation is excellent and a good background from which the characters should stand out clearly. But they do not. We see John Durham and Madame de Treymes; we see an American, and we see a French woman of the old school. And in consequence we find our attention wandering to such impertinent questions as: Are all Americans so strait-laced?— are all French women so malignant and ingenious?—and of course the answer is that they are not; and the story loses the conviction which it would possess if the people were individuals and not emblematic of a nation's decadence or a nation's honesty.

Mary Moss,
"Mrs. Wharton's
Madame de Treymes,"
Bookman, 25 (May
1907), 303–4

Since such crude early attempts as Theodore Fay's preposterous *Norman Leslie* deserve scant consideration, Mr. Henry James may safely claim to have discovered the international episode as a motive for American fiction. In spite of many competitors, he has hitherto kept an easy supremacy in this field, with such masterpieces as *Daisy Miller, The American, The Princess Casamassima, The Ambassadors, The Golden Bowl,* not to mention a host of short stories. But among this brilliant company, Mrs. Wharton's *Madame de Treymes* must instantly take undisputed place. In fact, the author fairly challenges comparison by choosing a theme almost identical with that of *The American*—the clash between a spirited outsider and the intangible resistance of Old World traditions and standards. And to be frank, her latest story excels Mr. James's early one in the matter of probability. For my part I have never been quite satisfied that a man of Newman's imaginative force would not have broken through the network of obstacles, if only by not appreciating them, and have ended by carrying off the object of his homage.

Curiously enough, it is by an even greater subtlety than Mr. James's that Mrs. Wharton reaches a fine simplicity. Where he merely shows a picture of his American baffled by the Faubourg, Mrs. Wharton gives in addition the point at which the Faubourg miscalculates the rules governing our trans-Atlantic Code.

John Durham wished to marry Madame de Malrive, whom he had known in New York as Fanny Frisbee. This lady lives in Paris with the family of a husband from whom the French law has granted her a separation. A divorce is fully within her rights. It is a question of persuading the de Malrives not to test the case, so that the divorce may be awarded without trailing the scandal of a cause célèbre over the life of Fanny's young son. The story narrows down into a game played between John Durham and a French sister-in-law,

Christiane de Treymes. Having gone so far, a review must perforce stop, for fear of blemishing the reader's delight in following the series of infinitely delicate touches by which the contest for Fanny's freedom is unfolded.

At the very start, Mrs. Wharton succeeds in mastering the greatest technical difficulty in fiction, that of introducing her situation without confusion, and without a hint of clumsy retrospect. So few words are used—the whole is the fruit of such discreet elimination—that one short chapter puts you in full possession of every essential fact; yet nothing could be less marred by haste. Giving in simplest form the latest product of her own elaborate mental processes, Mrs. Wharton keeps that air of leisure proper to fiction which deals with states of mind rather than with bodily adventure.

From whatever point you look the story shows no flaw. The author brings out her three types of women with the utmost clearness. Durham's sisters, with their "handsome haphazard clothes," fresh from New York and not altogether unlike the Fanny Frisbee of old New York days—Fanny herself—"the same, but so mysteriously changed . . . with the mystery, the sense of unprobed depths of initiation which drew him to her as her freshness had never drawn him"—and above all Madame de Treymes, whose unfathomable completeness puts even Fanny's finish of mind and person in a slightly secondary place.

It is with this last creation of elegance and depravity that Durham must contend for his right to marry. The duel between these two runs through a series of astonishingly brilliant scenes. Mrs. Wharton falls into no cheap errors. Durham makes war with force, intelligence, and common sense; he is neither intimidated by the powers arrayed against him, nor does he underrate them. He commits none of the absurdities by which novel heroes are wont to create and sustain difficult situations. The real subtlety lies—where it belongs—in the situation itself, not in the ingenuity with which it is prolonged. Moreover, the fact that Mrs. Wharton lets the conclusion turn upon a fundamental moral issue gives a solidity to the whole story, placing it on a more durable ground than any sketch of contrasted nationalities, since it touches the permanent human questions of honour and duty. It is true that she touches these questions lightly, rather with brilliancy than with a heat, which would be alien to her own nature. She neither harrows you by describing Fanny in transports of despair, nor drags you through Madame de Treymes's equivocal pleasures. Her supreme skill lies in bringing you face to face with these women as they are after the past has moulded them. Gyp herself [the Comtesse de Mirabæu de Martel] could not more firmly convince you of the French woman's tragic perfidy, yet the detail is barely indicated. You only have the result in pure essence.

By sacrificing a possible long novel (for which *Madame de Treymes* contains ample material) through a miracle of condensation, in matter, in form, and by an unimpeachable distinction of style, Mrs. Wharton has written a short story which stands entirely above criticism.

Harry James Smith, "Some Recent Novels," *Atlantic Monthly*, 100 (July 1907), 131–2

Whether or not in her most recently published novelette Mrs. Wharton gives a just evaluation to the ideals of another race, there can be no two opinions of the story's literary merits. *Madame de Treymes* is marvelously well executed. At a time when American fiction seems more and more generally to be produced according to correspondence-school standards, it is an especial delight to contemplate the work of a master-craftsman, one who retains the older pride in the temper and delicacy of tools and to whom marketability is no test of excellence. Workmanship means so much after all. The acquisition of it is not to be whiffed up, like trench-water by a locomotive under full headway. Mrs. Wharton has put herself through a long and ardent apprenticeship, and her masters have been of the best, each in his sort.

It surely is not going too far to discover, in the present instance, an acknowledged indebtedness to the one from whom she has perhaps learned most. What Mr. Henry James has done more amply, with his careful distribution of light and his strange penumbral iridescences, Mrs. Wharton has successfully attempted on a restricted surface and through the more refractory medium of dry point. What we lose in repleteness and nuance we gain in focus, brilliancy, and definition. There is not a negligible sentence in Mrs. Wharton's story. With an ease which is the perfection of conscious art, with the conciseness of an Ibsen first act, the situation with all its essential antecedents is brought before us; and once established in its sharply-demarcated milieu, the story proceeds directly, neither dawdling nor hurrying, to its striking conclusion. The criticism of the intimate standards of another people is a bold undertaking. The Americans in *Madame de Treymes* we recognize as in their various ways representative, and—especially after Lily Bart's irresolute lover—it is gratifying to have for hero a man whom we may look upon as at once typical and worthy of respect. Americans of this type, as a French critic recently asserted, "chivalrous in their relations with all women, fraternally devoted in circumstances where other men would be merely gallant ... do exist: they even make up the majority;" and we like to meet them.

The accuracy of portraiture is of less importance to us in the case of Madame de Treymes herself, whose infinite variety, subterfuge, coquettishness, and pathos, all part of a preordained scheme, and in the final analysis possessed of a certain dignity, are manifestly an effort at interpretation from an alien point of view. Though one's instinctive feeling is that Mrs. Wharton must have done it right, French comment indicates that there is at least plenty of room for question. Madame Treymes *seems* actual enough; in the Faubourg that the author constructs for us she surely lives in flesh and blood; but Mrs. Wharton has a way of sharpening the boundaries of her action until the break between it and the unconsidered world outside is as sudden as between the edge of a chess-board and the table it lies on. One feels quite certain that, once the parts had been assigned, the game would have been played by the same moves and to the same conclusion that we find in this story.

Vernon Atwood, "The Hammock Novel, and Others," *Putnam's Monthly*, 2 (August 1907), 616–17

What ails the summer novel? Are we really less intelligent in summer than in winter? Is the summer reader too unexacting or the writer too indolent? Or is it, perhaps, that the canny publisher saves the sleaziest works of fiction for the season

when everybody is amiable because everybody is, more or less, out of doors?

Whatever the reason, this year's crop of facts seems to justify the light esteem in which summer fiction is held by the discerning. Even the novelists upon whom we have most relied will sometimes fail us in the spring. Mr. Henry James has not yet written a hammock novel, but short of Mr. James upon whom can we rely for an all-around-the-year conscientiousness in dealing with the consumer of fiction? ...

Perhaps most writers have this mysterious and unsatisfactory understudy among the multiplex personalities in their mental make-up, but at least there are yet no signs of one in Mrs. Wharton's intellectual constitution. And there is neither summer nor winter on the plane where her work is produced. *Madame de Treymes* is brief, indeed, but an absolutely flawless and satisfying piece of workmanship. It is one of those international episodes whose interest arises from certain fundamental differences between the French and the American temper of spirit.

Fanny de Malrive is a New York girl so unhappily married to a French marquis that even his family concede the impossibility of their life together, and countenance her when she leaves him and obtains the custody of her child. After some years of life devoted to this little son, John Durham, an old friend and neighbor, crosses her path, loves her and tries to exact a promise of marriage contingent upon a legal separation from her husband. Goodness, safety and peace, for which she longs inexpressibly after her married experiences in Paris, are embodied for her in John Durham, but she refuses to take any step forward toward freedom unless assured that her husband's family will not oppose her in any way: there must be no contest, no publicity, nothing which would enable her son to reproach her for seeking her own peace at the cost of aspersions upon the name to which he is born.

Durham turns for help to her sister-in-law, Madame de Treymes, who is willing to assist them with her influence if Durham will pay her lover's gambling debts—though she does not phrase the condition so badly. To Durham, happiness purchased at such a price would be tainted, and without explanation he abruptly declines her mediation. The fine point of the story depends upon the ultimate ability of the Frenchwoman to understand his motives and to admire them disinterestedly. That personal recklessness of conduct may well be united to absolute fineness of perception, insight and a generous enthusiasm for the subtler delicacies of feeling and behavior, is not an American idea. We are not in the habit of thinking these things after these ways, and the notion almost puts us to intellectual confusion. Such a union of qualities is, however, essentially Gallic and perfectly possible. Mrs. Wharton has etched the character of Madame de Treymes so finely and so strongly that it commands first belief and then sympathy. And this is a notable feat.

Scarcely less notable is the way in which she contrasts our American theory of the duty of the individual to be good and fine, and happy if he can, with the French idea of the importance and solidarity of the family. A few lines, and the whole thing, the characteristic attitude of two civilizations, is before you definitely. The author's detachment is perfect; she takes neither side but makes both very clear, and the intellectual pleasure which the reader experiences in consequence is something to be grateful for.

Checklist of Additional Reviews

"A Guide to the New Books," *Literary Digest*, 34 (20 April 1907), 640.

Spectator [England], 98 (11 May 1907), 764.

Olivia Howard Dunbar, "*Madame de Treymes*," *North American Review*, 185 (17 May 1907), 218–21.

"Recent Fiction and the Critics," *Current Literature*, 42 (June 1907), 693–4.

"A Review of the Season's Fiction: Various Localities," *Review of Reviews*, 35 (June 1907), 764–5.

"Comment on Current Books," *Outlook*, 86 (1 June 1907), 255.

"Literature," *Independent*, 62 (27 June 1907), 1528.

THE FRUIT OF THE TREE

THE FRUIT OF THE TREE

BY

EDITH WHARTON

WITH ILLUSTRATIONS BY ALONZO KIMBALL

NEW YORK
CHARLES SCRIBNER'S SONS
MDCCCCVII

"Current Fiction,"
Nation, 85 (17 October
1907), 352–3

Again Mrs. Wharton has done a difficult thing with ease and precision. With all the groping and stumbling of American novelists toward an interpretation of American life, it is a matter for thanksgiving that we have one who knows what she is about. With all her amenity and poise, her air of the disinterested observer, she is sure of her object and rarely fails to attain it. This book would seem at first to be a composite of three. Is it about the attitude of "the best society" toward common morality and justice; or the relation between employer and employed; or the duty of medical science to prolong life at the cost of hopeless suffering? Before the end one may perceive it to be a study of the selfishness induced in a strong man by preoccupation with his work, and in a strong woman by preoccupation with her happiness. Wisely, no doubt, Mrs. Wharton has embodied life, not lectured upon it, and it is unnecessary to reduce the interpretation to the last analysis in order to feel its meaning.

The amiable rottenness of "the best society" has been a favorite theme of Mrs. Wharton's; here it affords hardly more than a background for the principal scene. That is by no means the scene to which we are first introduced, and which holds our attention throughout the first book of the story. Book 1, by itself, seems to belong to a familiar type of current American fiction: the industrial novel. The Westmore Mills at Hanaford, a manufacturing town not far from New York, have within a generation launched upon the world, in the person of their young owner, Dick Westmore, a new devotee of leisure,

sport, and fashion. In due time he has married a beautiful society girl, Bessy Langhope, who has been brought up in the aroma, though not in the full pecuniary privilege, of the gay world. His death leaves her not heartbroken, though decently regretful, the heiress of his entire wealth. Presently she comes to Hanaford upon a virtuous but perfunctory errand of inspection; with the probability that she will merely pass through the mills in great lady fashion, shaking the dust of them from her feet with all possible expedition, and faring back to her own polite and luxurious world of Lynbrook and New York. Chance rescues her from the manipulation of the astute and plausible person whose unscrupulously successful management of the mills has piled a Pelion upon the Ossa of the Westmore income. The assistant manager, John Amherst, is a young man of good family (Mrs. Wharton could, perhaps, not be expected to put up with a hero who lacked that saving grace), with a bent for mechanics, a hunger for hard work, and strong opinions as to the rights of hard workers. She visits the mills with him, and learns from him of a peculiarly barbarous instance of the suffering imposed by unscrupulous management. She is moved by the visible instance, not by the principle involved; but this is not evident at the moment, and when at the end of the first book Amherst marries her, his faith in her seriousness is part of his love.

At this point the ordinary industrial novel might have been content to end, with a sound of wedding bells and popular plaudits; but here the social-sociological side-scene, like the social background, becomes mere setting for what, one supposes, would be called the psychological event. Amherst and his Bessy do not live happy ever after; the regeneration of the Westmore mills does not take place during the honeymoon. The man

147

discovers the woman to be selfish, shallow, emotional. She is surrounded by traditions, habits, and persons wherewith he has nothing in common. What interests one most, interests the other not at all; he does not care for her pleasures nor she for his work, especially when its development entails some personal sacrifice on her part. They virtually separate. The third person now assumes importance. Justine Brent is a trained nurse (of excellent family!), now a kind of companion to Bessy, and nurse to her little daughter by the first marriage. She is also a very good friend of Amherst's. Bessy is fatally injured as a direct result of disregarding Amherst's advice. Her life is deliberately, even desperately, prolonged by a young doctor who regards her as "a beautiful case," and is determined to score a hit. The other physicians, as well as Justine, believe that the torture is hopeless; and Justine, when she gets the chance, puts her out of her misery by an over-dose of morphine. In view of her own clear conscience and her knowledge of Amherst, she thinks that she has done the right thing, according to his lights as well as her own. Nevertheless, for negative reasons, she does not tell him, even after their eventual marriage, and the fact comes out horribly through the young doctor, now a morphia victim and blackmailer.

Then follows the really moving part of the tale; for Amherst, "like many men of emancipated thought, had remained subject to the old conventions of feeling." His reason assures him that Justine is guiltless and has done well; but he cannot bear the fact that she has technically killed Bessy. We shall betray nothing here of the further conduct of the story, except our conviction that, according to any enlightened view, it "turns out right." Persons who are content to dispose of such a novel as "unpleasant," are fain to make a silly affair of fiction.

"Novels and Tales," *Outlook*, 87 (23 November 1907), 621

Mrs. Wharton has a wholly different method, but she, too, invariably gives her reader the impression of thoroughbred competency in literary craftsmanship. She is always serious, though never heavy; she treats her art as if it were an achievement and not a dexterity; and she touches nothing to which she does not bring an insight, a knowledge, and a skill which set her apart from the host of easy producers of popular stories. One may dislike her work, but one cannot escape the charm of its quality, nor close his eyes to its deep if not always well-rounded truth. *The House of Mirth* was both interesting and profitable—a novel of genuine power; *The Fruit of the Tree* is not a bringer of joy, but it is penetrating in analysis, and evades none of the issues it raises. The industrial situation with which it deals is wholly subordinate to the questions of character it asks and does not always answer. Like the notable novel which preceded it, it lacks humor and contrast of character. The luxury and frivolity of a certain set of society people are almost too insistently driven home. A touch of futility often lies on the people who move in Mrs. Wharton's novels; they are caught in a tangle which a little vigor of will would cut with a stroke. The central figure in *The Fruit of the Tree*, however, does not bend, but he is swept bare of joy by a too rigorous fate.

Edward Clark Marsh, "Mrs. Wharton's *The Fruit of the Tree*," *Bookman*, 26 (November 1907), 273–5

It is one of the penalties of so striking a success as Mrs. Wharton achieved in *The House of Mirth* that for a long time to come all her work must endure the comparative judgment. The first question asked concerning *The Fruit of the Tree* will pertain neither to its proper merits nor its formal classification. "Is it as good as *The House of Mirth*?"—that is the query that must be met at the outset, unless it is anticipated by the no less pressing interrogation, "Will it be as popular as *The House of Mirth*?" The implied distinction must be maintained. Those shallow-pated readers who identify merit with popularity are not to be found in the intellectual circles to which Mrs. Wharton ministers. Rather is her most numerous following among those who forgive the popularity for the sake of the merit. But since the dual question is sure to be propounded, and the dilemma cannot be avoided by even the humblest commentator, I may at once lay a reckless hand on either horn by hazarding the opinion that *The Fruit of the Tree*, though a better book than its predecessor, is not likely to provoke an equal amount of that heated and emotional public discussion which is the true sign of popularity.

And so enough of the grocer's quantitative method of weighing genius. It is more gratifying to declare Mrs. Wharton's new book a novel that richly repays reading, without reference to intrusive comparisons. To the reader of much fiction of the day, and even more perhaps to the crafts-man, its craftsmanship must be a delight. It is not merely that the author knows how to write, though even this faculty, which ought to be taken for granted, is sufficiently rare. She knows also how to manage and develop a story. Her skill in this province of her art is all the more striking because her latest work is frankly disdainful of certain traditional precepts. It lacks unity. Its point of view is not single. It does not flow evenly, but leaps over years in a paragraph and halts for pages over a momentary incident. It takes in different groups of personages whose relations are shifting and varied, and the main interest is more than once transferred from one character to another.

These facts might well excite the academic person who reads by rule. But it should be remembered that Mrs. Wharton has established her right to ignore rules by first proving how faithfully she can observe them. The perfectly direct development of Lily Bart's career, though it was empty of the dramatic element, was structurally an almost faultless narrative. In *The Fruit of the Tree* the problem is, if not actually bigger, at least vastly more complex—or, rather, there are two or three distinct though related problems dealt with. It is not altogether discreditable to Mrs. Wharton that she has attempted a more difficult task, and the only valid test of her success or failure is the concrete one—the impression produced by an honest reading of the book. The truth is that the structure of the story is for the most part managed with admirable skill. The transitions are effected so easily that there is no jar, and the point of view throughout is large enough to allow for some variation without forcing a consciousness of the change. Only the shifting of attention from one to another of the principal characters, resulting in a lessening of the grip of the story, must be recorded as a positive fault. The stage is set in the beginning around the figure of John Amherst, at first a worker in the Westmore mills and eventually their virtual owner, and it is his relation to the mills that furnishes the semblance of a unifying interest. But the personal problem springing from this relationship falls into abeyance for a time as the character of his first wife emerges into the light, and it drops nearly out of sight before the more poignant demand of the situation which develops toward the end around the woman who becomes his second wife. Hers is the real drama, for which all that goes before is mere preparation. And the preparation goes back too far, is too thorough; the length of the approach dwarfs the edifice.

But I have dwelt too long on purely formal considerations. Mrs. Wharton's highly polished style and mastery of her craft imply at least that the stuff she has put into her book is worthy of some attention. But when one comes to examine the story itself and the ideas that lie back of it some very large questions obtrude themselves. Here the backward view with its comparison is inevitable again. No one who has followed this author's career attentively can have failed to note that *The House of Mirth* betrayed a decided change of front; and the terms in which this change is characterised are likely to involve one's view of the whole province of fiction. In her earlier work, and particularly in the best of it as contained in certain of her short stories, Mrs. Wharton showed herself the cultivator of a highly specialised field. The problems with which she dealt were subtle ones, and her characters were tinged with the morbid excess of sensibility which seems to us to belong to modern life. It was not for nothing that she was proclaimed the faithful disciple of Mr. Henry James. Perhaps the persistent attribution of this discipleship stung her to seek escape into a different field.

Whatever the reason, the marks of her former master's influence have almost wholly disappeared in her later work; for her recent book, *Madame de Treymes*, though reminiscent of Mr. James as to subject, is scarcely so as to treatment. In *The Fruit of the Tree* there is elaboration of plot, but little of the complexity that springs from the interaction of highly individualised characters. The persons of the drama are indeed somewhat conventionalised into the guise of "types," and the situation into which they are finally plunged provokes a reference to literature rather than to life. Ingeniously, plausibly as the climax is developed, it is possible to feel that it is a wonderfully clever invention, not an organic growth.

All this the contemner of popularity may explain by asserting that Mrs. Wharton's inspiration has dwindled as her technical mastery has increased. On the other hand, it may be declared that she has sought a universal note in the place of the limited appeal of her earlier work; and the advocate of this view can at least have the satisfaction of pointing triumphantly to the fact that she now has twenty readers where she formerly had one. For the reader who is honestly in doubt as between these two extremes of opinion there is no course open but to fall back on the heartiest praise of Mrs. Wharton's fine and exceptional gift, and the liveliest curiosity as to what pleasure it may still have in store for us.

"The Fruit of the Tree," *Independent*, 63 (12 December 1907), 1436–7

Mrs. Wharton is not only gifted, she is versatile. The two things are not always synonymous. Usually a genius is a genius because all his faculties point mightily in one direction, and he can do only one particular thing in his gifted manner. But Mrs. Wharton writes a number of different kinds of stories in an equally gifted manner. It is not long since she gave us *Madame de Treymes*, a volume in which the lives of several people were distilled into a kind of worldly-spirited vapor. Now comes *The Fruit of the Tree*, with the scenes laid among common American realities, and written out boldly, with no dim affectedness of phrasing which has alarmed some of us lest Mrs. Wharton should become a lady disciple of Henry James. By the fruit of the tree she means the consequences suffered by the leading characters from doing what they think is right, and this presents at once a problem which the moralists have always shirked— that the average human being may suffer more from meaning to do the right thing in a tight place than from doing wrong in any place. Whether this shirking is the result of cowardice or prudence it is impossible to say. We are still very primitive morally and retain childish notions of rewards quite out of keeping with the reward system of the slow eternities. But there is no cowardice or prudence in a novelist when it comes to dealing with the issues of life. Any one of them will seize upon our terrible uncertainties, make them certain and thus stagger us with our own fate made fictitious. So does Mrs. Wharton in this story. She grapples with a question which is sometimes whispered, looked by doctors and scientists from eye to eye, but which all have been too squeamish to answer. And she answers it with confident but inhuman courage—and in the name of an august compassion for all hopeless sufferers.

Naturally the scenes are laid in elegant drawing rooms adjacent to one of those sad industrial centers of the poor—naturally, because all the people in fiction these days are engaged in the terrible tragedy which is being fought out between the rich and the poor. The poor young assistant manager of the Westover Mills, who has theories for bettering conditions there among the operatives, marries the rich widow who owns the mills. He begins by attempting to spend his wife's income upon improvements for the workers. But with the passing of the honeymoon, she insists upon spending it in her own natural way, upon motor cars and squash courts. The consequent friction and ultimate separation of the two is inevitable. And the story would fail in interest if this were all, but Mrs. Wharton has apparently written thus far to give it the modern background, and to view it with the common life and adventurous ethical and intellectual spirit of the times. The real problem she presents and dramatizes is that of euthanasia.

Bessy Amherst, estranged wife and wilful heiress of the Westover Mills, is thrown from her horse and sustains an injury to her spine. She can never recover: a paralyzed, death-in-life existence is the best that could be hoped for. But it is even doubtful if she can be kept alive at all till her husband and father can reach her from distant countries. The surgeon fights for this. It is "a beautiful case." The unspeakable agonies of the sufferer restrained from death are not taken into account. The ambition of the surgeon is to win a reputation, a victory for science by prolonging life under conditions that forfeit life. Justine Brent, Bessy's devoted friend, herself a graduate nurse, sees the point, is horrified by the professional ambition to be gratified at such expense, and in a moment of fierce compassion for the agonized victim she administers sufficient morphia to rid both the pain and life in a moment.

She has no compunction for what she has done. But after her marriage to

Amherst herself some time later, the surgeon who had been thwarted of his ambition betrays her secret to her husband. And it is at this point that Mrs. Wharton contradicts human instinct in the action of her characters. According to her, the evil in practising euthanasia is not to the one who has been put mercifully out of pain into death, but it is to the one who does the practising. A nurse who has the courage to put her patient out of pain in such a manner and for the most humane of reasons becomes terrible and dangerous, because one cannot tell where she might draw the line next time between life and death. So in this story all who know of Justine's act conceive a still horror of her. She is obliged to fly and hide herself from this repulsion. Then suddenly, without any change in the facts as in the meaning of what she did for the tortured dying woman, she is restored to the warmth and tenderness of her family. It makes the story end cheerfully, but it is an absolutely false sequel to such an act. A woman who would put her patient out of pain in such a manner might kill her own baby if it had epilepsy, or her husband if he was hopelessly paralyzed. Whether wrong or not it is too dangerous to be permitted.

"New Novels: *The Fruit of the Tree*," *Athenæum* [England], 4181 (14 December 1907), 762

Mrs. Wharton's admirable method is in this novel applied to issues of wider human interest than those with which she usually deals. Her object at first appears to be that of placing in a strong light the contrast between the factory hand who makes money and the factory owner who spends it—a contrast which, on her showing, appears to be more painfully accentuated in America than here. But about midway through the story the centre of our attention is shifted to another problem, also essentially of our own day. We are asked, namely, to decide how far we can justify the modern passion for prolonging life when such prolongation is only a futile agony, especially if (as is by no means always the case) the sufferer prefers to die? The situation thus conceived is one of intense poignancy, and is treated with all the strength and artistic restraint which we expect from this author. The heroine, on whom, as a nurse, devolves the terrible burden of decision, is a strong, sympathetic figure; and all the other characters, except, perhaps, the impracticable philanthropist of a hero, are excellently studied and contrasted.

"Recent Fiction and the Critics," *Current Literature*, 43 (December 1907), 691–2

The fruit of Mrs. Wharton's tree grows not far away from her melancholy *House of Mirth*. We find in her latest novel the same cold precision, the same technical mastery, and the same lack of heart, the same hardness, which have made her unique among feminine writers of fiction. *The Fruit of the Tree* is indisputably an event of the year. Yet the opinion seems to prevail that its popular success will be less remarkable than that of its predecessor. Says Edward Clark Marsh in *The Bookman*:

"It is one of the penalties of so striking a success as Mrs. Wharton achieved in *The House of Mirth* that for a long time to come all her work must endure the comparative judgment. The first question asked concerning *The Fruit of the Tree* will pertain neither to its proper merits nor its formal classification. Is it as good as *The House of Mirth?*—that is the query that must be met at the outset, unless it is anticipated by the no less pressing interrogation, Will it be as popular as *The House of Mirth?* The implied distinction must be maintained. Those shallow-pated readers who identify merit with popularity are not to be found in the intellectual circles to which Mrs. Wharton ministers. Rather is her most numerous following among those who forgive the popularity for the sake of the merit. But since the dual question is sure to be propounded, and the dilemma cannot be avoided by even the humblest commentator, I may at once lay a reckless hand on either horn by hazarding the opinion that *The Fruit of the Tree*, tho a better book than its predecessor, is not likely to provoke an equal amount of that heated and emotional public discussion which is the true sign of popularity."

Jeanette Gilder (in the Chicago *Tribune*) likewise upholds this opinion. "As Charlotte Brontë will be best known as the author of *Jane Eyre*, so Mrs. Wharton will be best known as the author of *The House of Mirth*. *The Fruit of the Tree* is a good story, there are few writers of today who could equal it. Nevertheless it has not the elements of popularity that are found in *The House of Mirth*." Miss Gilder bases her contention partly on the fact that Mrs. Wharton's present book gives us less insight into the ways of the "smart set" than is given by her previous book, partly on the character of the heroine, who, while commanding our admiration from certain strong points in her character, fails to inspire us with the affectionate pity that we felt for the unfortunate Lily.

The Fruit of the Tree is even more complex than Mrs. Wharton's portrayal of high life. It would seem, says *The Evening Post*, at first to be a composite of three books. It takes up successively the attitude of "the best society" toward common morality and justice, the relation between employer and employed, and the problem involved in the question whether it is the duty of medical science to prolong life at the cost of hopeless suffering.

Mrs. Wharton enshrouds her characters with an atmosphere of fatality. When this is withdrawn, and without Mrs. Wharton's graces of style and unvaried by the effect of her philosophy, the plot of her story seems strangely crude and violent. The characters then, says the Boston *Transcript*, appear to be mere creatures of a novelist's will. John Amherst is an idealist without high executive ability. The overseer at the great Westmore Mills, he is convinced that the owners accumulate extortionate profits at the expense of their employees. He meets a beautiful young widow, owner of the works, and energetically battles for reforms, which even after gaining her hand, he is unable to bring about in the measure anticipated by him. She is absorbed in pleasure, he fondles plans of reform, and both are inwardly estranged from each other when the woman meets with an accident that hopelessly injures her spine. At this juncture, Justine Brent, who has appeared intermittently in previous chapters, a friend of the wife, begins to loom large in the story.

A trained nurse, she watches over the patient whose life is prolonged needlessly by the physician that he may test a theory in which she has no faith. Finally she is so obsessed with her friend's sufferings that she mercifully ends them by an overdose of morphine. There is no ulterior motive. Subsequently she marries Amherst, and when later a blackmailer subjects her to his demands, and her husband realizes that, technically at least, she has murdered his first wife, the problem begins. We leave them, in the words of one critic, in the end making believe to be happy in a deadly atmosphere of compromise. *The Evening Post*, on the other hand, states its conviction that according to the enlightened view the story turns out right.

The Times designates Mrs. Wharton's performance as "expert satire in frosty brilliance" and, while lavishing unstinted praise on the execution, deplores the lack of warmth, the human feeling, that we find, it says, in the novels of Mrs. Burnett. "The astonishing thing," it concludes, "is that we close the book with the feeling that, after all, the execution is superior to the idea; the story is better told than such a story deserves to be." To quote further:

> "We admire, but we are a little chilled; Mrs. Wharton sits at her desk like a disbodied intelligence, acute and critical and entirely unsympathetic; she is as detached as a scientific student viewing bacilli under a miscroscope. Her impersonality stings; her expert irony is not humane. Satire need not be always unkind; and if the world offers a spectacle ineffably amusing and contemptible, it is none the less ineffably pathetic. To turn back from

The Fruit of the Tree to *Vanity Fair* is to recall with a smile that Thackeray was once considered cynical; but it may also serve to remind us that, as mean and pitiful as we are, it is yet possible to treat our littleness great-heartedly."

When Mrs. Wharton first appeared as a novelist she was an ardent disciple of Henry James. Since then she has developed her own style, most fully perhaps in her two latest novels. Nevertheless most reviewers persist in labeling her as a disciple of our expatriated psychological novelist. One critic suggests that Mrs. Wharton's change of attitude in striking a more universal note than in her previous work is due largely to her irritation by this comparision. Whatever the reason, he remarks, her former master's influence has almost totally disappeared from her later work. A writer in the Chicago *Tribune*, which devoted two reviews to the book, observes that, save for Mr. James, no one writing to-day can so well describe those mysteries of the soul and intellect which are the product of highly developed civilization as Mrs. Wharton. She matches, we are told, her compeer in adroitness and exceeds him in lucidity.

Checklist of Additional Reviews

William Morton Payne, "Recent Fiction," *Dial*, 43 (16 November 1907), 317.
Literary Digest, 35 (14 December 1907), 920.

THE HERMIT AND THE WILD WOMAN AND OTHER STORIES

THE HERMIT
AND THE WILD WOMAN

AND OTHER STORIES

BY

EDITH WHARTON

NEW YORK
CHARLES SCRIBNER'S SONS
MCMVIII

"Short Stories by Mrs. Wharton: Volume Marked by Insight into Character, and Distinguished Style, Dealing with Situations of Moral Delicacy,"

New York Times Saturday Review, 3 October 1908, p. 541

In the difficult art of short-story writing Mrs. Wharton is extremely skillful. The public has not been invited to assist at her stumbling preliminary efforts, if such existed. She has always been able, so far as her general readers can say, to use her tools with the quiet ease of the practical workman, and, in addition to this effective craftsmanship, she has given proof of the deeper artistic impulse in her ability to rise to the level of her subject instead of molding her subject to fit her especial methods of execution. She is never more fortunate, that is, than when using as material for art one of the various human situations that involves extreme moral delicacy and a controlling emotion.

In the present volume her work is seen in several phases. The title story, "The Hermit and the Wild Woman," is in the form of an Italian legend and bears the mark of the author's familiarity with the history and literature, the art and faith of Italy. The other stories are of modern life and unequal in interest, although uniformly delightful in the felicity of their detail and the trained taste of their composition. "The Last Asset" abounds in acute observation of the little things that make up the sum of amusement for most of us, and is also a quite triumphant presentation on a small scale of contrasted masculine and feminine qualities, but the definition of the beginning is too great for the vagueness at the end. It is not a question of solving problems; the modern reader has learned by this time that he must do that for himself; but the method, the modeling, if we may borrow the word from another art, so crisp and precise at the opening, seems at the close to blur and fade, possibly because the type of the heroine has not been sufficiently realized—a type that has been attacked with more or less success by our greatest story tellers and has ranged from the primitive simplicity of a Little Nell to the complexity of a Maisie and a Nanda.

In "The Pretext," on the other hand, we have a bit of pattern weaving of considerable intricacy and of balanced and harmonious design. There are half a dozen possible answers to the suggested question, but the construction of the story is consistent and firm. The characters are clearly seen and produce upon us the effect they would produce in life. There is, perhaps, too obvious a denigration of the narrow setting—there have been pictures of narrower and colder aspects of our American scene that have managed to retain their local charm without the application on the part of their historian of a flattering coat of rose color; but the painter of human character is only rarely as competent a portraitist of places, and Mrs. Wharton is above all a delineator of character.

In "The Verdict" it is character as art tests and forms or betrays it; in the second story entitled "In Trust" it is character insidiously undermined and disintegrated by conflicting motives and influences; in "The Pot Boiler" it is character flouted by one of the most hateful ironies of fate—in every instance a distinguished style and a penetrating insight

157

makes the rude material into forms of expressive value.

"Comment on Current Books," Outlook, 90 (17 October 1908), 362

The reader of Mrs. Wharton's stories is always assured in advance of genuine, careful, and artistic workmanship, both in expression and in style; and the seven short stories which appear in the collection which takes its name from the first story, "The Hermit and the Wild Woman," are in these respects quite up to the standard of the author of *The House of Mirth*. They are not, however, either so novel in situation or so interesting as some of their predecessors. They deal with subtle problems, delicate situations, the nuances, so to speak, of conduct and temperament, for they are a little inclined to a certain form of preciosity from which Mrs. Wharton will do well to deliver herself. Her danger lies in that direction, and she is too keen an observer and too thoroughly trained an artist to forsake the vernacular for a dialect, or to pass from art into psychology.

"Short Stories," Athenæum [England], 4230 (21 November 1908), 644

In "The Hermit and the Wild Woman" ..., and at least two of the six accompanying tales, Mrs. Edith Wharton reaches her highest level. The title story—a study of mediaeval "religious" life—is a remarkable testimony to the broad-mindedness which, from a point of view essentially modern, can attain to a sympathic comprehension of the Ages of Faith. Among the remaining stories—all dealing more or less with the America of our own day—"The Last Asset" is distinguished by perfection of form and an irony which is never inhuman. It is a significant sign of the times that three of Mrs. Wharton's "modern instances" are taken from the artistic world. Of these "The Potboiler" is a charmingly humorous exposure of the fallacy that unpopularity necessarily implies greatness. The remaining pieces are perhaps less successful in satisfying the exacting requirements of the short story, but the workmanship is, as usual, careful and conscientious.

Review of *The Hermit and the Wild Woman*, Nation, 87 (26 November 1908), 525

That accomplished critic, H. D. Sedgwick, has asserted that Mrs. Wharton's most marked traits are her femininity and her cleverness. It must be said that her latest collection of short stories does not suggest an extension in the range of that cleverness. The initial tale, to be sure, is not what might have been expected—a hermit, say, in a Washington Square studio, with a wild woman tempting him across a tea-table somewhere in the upper regions of Fifth Avenue. This is the case of a real hermit in a wilderness, to whom comes, as if from nowhere, a wandering woman to be, not his temptress, but his helper and innocent solace till death parts

158

them: The trouble with the fable is that, after all, it is interesting rather than moving. One has the sense of its simply being another of Mrs. Wharton's amazingly skillful exercises. The succeeding tales indicate, perhaps, an increase of the tendency, first apparent in *The Fruit of the Tree*, to deal with some of the serious questions of modern social life in a larger sense of that term than has always interested her. But more striking than this is her growing preoccupation with the irony of things. One fancies these stories told with a faint smile and a slow shake of the head. Nothing "turns out right" in the romantic sense, and yet every dénouement is in accordance with some distinguishable and on the whole acceptable law. An aging and defeated man humbles his will and makes the only sacrifice which remains for him, to the woman who has ruined his life, for the sake of the pure and happy girl who is oddly enough the sound fruit of their wretchedly unsound union. Another man is balked in the fulfillment of his duty to a dead friend by a selfish woman, and makes the only atonement possible by giving up his life in another disinterested cause. A middle-aged woman, American and married, fancies a secret understanding between herself and a young Englishman. They part, but her inner life is transformed by her sense of virtual union with him. She is stripped bare of her illusion, and her last case is worse than her first. And so on: There is no lifting from minor to major, no relieving touch of cheerfulness. The stories are, of course, admirably told. . . .

"*The Hermit and the Wild Woman*," *Spectator* [England], 101 (28 November 1908), 886–7

Mrs. Wharton's indisputable talent perhaps reached its highwater mark in her previous collection of short stories, *The Descent of Man*. The merits which were then so conspicuous—subtlety, distinction of style, and the art of omission—reappear in the volume before us, but the impression created is hardly as strong. To begin with, we cannot think that she was altogether well advised in including in a set of ultra-modern stories the mediaeval quasi-allegory which gives its name to the book. Apart from that, the almost invariable recurrence of failure, disappointment, and disillusionment as the leading motives of each episode makes for depression as well as monotony. They are nearly all studies of the ironies, misunderstandings, and embarrassments of a sophisticated civilisation, and while lacking in the elemental quality of tragedy, they do not minister in any way to the gaiety of the reader. That, it may fairly be contended, is not necessarily the aim of the self-respecting artist; but the absence of contrast is a serious drawback. There are plenty of characters on the side of the angels, and they are by no means derided for their virtue; but, on the whole, the ignoble and selfish people have the best time, while the upright and honourable folk are rather of an ineffectual and self-effacing type. There is a touch of poignancy in most of these stories, but its edge is blunted by the anticipation of disaster which violates the law of suspense by eliminating the element of surprise, and by the invertebrate character of the victims of mischance. One of the cleverest and most painful sketches is that called "A Pretext." The wife of a singularly unprepossessing Professor in an American University town forestalls what she believes to be a declaration from an engaging young Englishman, and gives him his *congé*. She learns afterwards that he has broken off his engagement to an English girl owing to an attachment in America, and the report is confirmed by a visit from the young man's aunt, who comes all the way from England to appeal to his enchantress to release him. But on seeing the Professor's wife, who is no longer young or specially attractive, the aunt convinces her that it was impossible for her nephew to have been in love with her, and that he merely used her name as a pretext to conceal his attachment for another woman. Thus Mrs. Ransom—the Professor's wife—gains nothing from having "played the game" but a most mortifying humiliation, though the reader is left in the dark as to whether the aunt's interpretation was really the true one. Such ingenuity in the art of misery-making strikes us as superfluous, if not morbid, and there are traces of it in more than one of the other stories which compose the volume. An exception must, however, be readily made in favour of the last story, "The Best Man," an episode of modern American politics, in which the newly elected Governor of a State, threatened with a vindictive attack in the Press, takes the wind out of his enemies' sails by an act of heroic self-sacrifice. Rather than abandon a colleague with a doubtful past

whose co-operation is essential to the carrying out of an honest policy, he resolves—*splendidè verax*—to disclose a painful family secret. As he puts it:—"All I had to do was to say to myself: 'Go ahead, and do the best you can for the country.' The personal issue simply didn't exist. . . . Even if I don't gain my end it will be a good thing, for once, for the public to consider dispassionately how far a private calamity should be allowed to affect a career of public usefulness, and the next man who goes through what I'm undergoing may have cause to thank me if no one else does." Here Mrs. Wharton ascends to a higher plane, and bids us breathe an ampler air than is to be found in any of her other stories. The change is all the more welcome, since she gives us a fine picture of a really nobleminded American, whereas the impression derived from the other portraits of her compatriots is, if not hostile, at any rate by no means flattering to their strength of purpose or altitude of aim. No English writer could have ventured on so damaging a portrait of the American woman as that of Mrs. Newel in "The Last Asset" without incurring the charge of malice.

Checklist of Additional Reviews

Agnes Repplier, "A Sheaf of Autumn Fiction," *Outlook*, 90 (28 November 1908), 698, 702.

A MOTOR-FLIGHT THROUGH FRANCE

A MOTOR-FLIGHT
THROUGH FRANCE

BY

EDITH WHARTON

ILLUSTRATED

NEW YORK
CHARLES SCRIBNER'S SONS
1908

"Intimate France," *New York Times Saturday Review,* 31 October 1908, p. 637

"A Motor-Flight Through France," *Nation,* 87 (12 November 1908), 469

Those who have been charmed with Mrs. Wharton's novels will not be disappointed by her venture into the unfamiliar role of a travel writer. Hers is no guidebook, nor are her pages filled with automobile lore. The machine cuts the smallest figure, so that its insertion so prominently in the title becomes an intrusion. Mrs. Wharton accepts it as a mere incident, much as she might a locomotive or a carriage. It is a mere means of making acquaintance in the modern manner with scenes anciently accessible only by horse travel, and charmingly they are depicted. Fancy and insight and ancient lore are combined in characterizations of famous cathedrals, wayside inns, fortified churches, villages not on maps or time tables, and whatever else may be seen by an approach not unlike that through a side door or back stairs. The pictures are excellent, and the general make-up of the book is attractive. Not every one is fortunate enough to make such a journey, and only the fewest having made it are able to set down the itinerary in such fashion. But only fewer still can fail to share the enjoyment of having such company as Mrs. Wharton offers to those who would make her tour with her as cicerone. To those who have made the trip among the French cathedrals, or are thinking of such a tour, this book will be doubly delightful.

Mrs. Wharton's new book is brought out in a handsome, dignified form which suggests her *Italian Backgrounds,* but unfortunately, in the place of Peixotto's charming drawings, it is weighed down, both literally and metaphorically, with many stupid, obvious photographs on heavy glazed paper. Was Mrs. Wharton too indifferent to the outward form of her book to make any choice of illustrations? One suspects it, for something of the same indifference, the same formlessness is true of her own part in the work. The enormous overplus of material, the crude arrangement in three unrelated, unbalanced narratives, the absolutely abrupt ending, as of a letter of which the last page has been lost, all insistently suggest the pot-boiler. There's odds in pot-boilers, however, and no one but Mrs. Wharton could have written one like this. If she has neglected form in the mass, she never ceases to be the artist in detail. Never has her felicity of expression, her choice of the one right word, been more evident or more sure. The sentence we italicize in the following excellent sketch applies very neatly to the author's own style:

Save in the church itself, how frugally all the effects are produced—with how sober a use of greys and blacks, and pale high lights, as in some Van der Meer interior; yet how intense a suggestion of thrifty compact traditional life one gets from the low house-fronts, the barred gates, the glimpses of clean bare courts, the calm yet quick faces in the doorways. From these faces, again, one gets the same impression of *remarkable effects produced by the discreetest means.*

The more one appreciates Mrs. Wharton's rare powers of analysis and of imaginative reproduction, the more one wishes she had concentrated them upon one region and given us a picture of a French province as complete and unforgettable as that of Northern Italy in her *Valley of Decision.* In elaborating such a study she would have had time to record more of such shrewd and pleasant reflections as those which occur to her as she contemplates the nose of the sculptured Cardinal in Rouen Cathedral:

> We live in the day of little noses; that once stately feature, intrinsically feudal and aristocratic in character—the *maschio naso* extolled of Dante—has shrunk to democratic insignificance, like many another expression of individualism. And so one must look to the old painters and sculptors to see what a nose was meant to be—the prow of the face; the evidence of its owner's standing, of his relation to the world, and his inheritance from the past.

But the motor is waiting, and Mrs. Wharton and her reluctant readers must rush on. For motor-travel as means of seeing the country she makes an ingenious plea, but her own tale refutes her. Nowhere does she remain for more than the briefest of impressions, and again and again she is whisked past the very places she longs to see. And the reader, most of all, is left lamenting.

In recounting such tours as these, much space is naturally given to architecture,

and here Mrs. Wharton frankly and engagingly owns herself an amateur, pleading cleverly for "the kind of confused atavistic enjoyment that is made up of historical association, of a sense of mass and harmony, of the relation of the building to the sky above it, to the lights and shadows it creates about it—deeper than all, of a blind sense in the blood of its old racial power, the things it meant to far-off minds of which ours are the oft-dissolved and reconstituted fragments." Strong in her confidence in this "lesser yet legitimate order of appreciation," she does not hesitate to use the word "Gothic" in the good old "literary," unstructural sense—as in her description of Beauvais; indeed, one almost wonders that, being thus free from bondage to the precisians, she does not pause to worship the wonderful appealing "Gothic" of St. Ouen at Rouen, a Gothic just touched with coming decadence, a pathetic grace like that of Fletcher after Shakespeare, or that she fails to see in the grave front of Noyou, austerely bare, a kinship in spirit if not in structure to the grim Norman abbey-churches at Caen.

To sum up, one may say that this is a book to give keen pleasure to all who have themselves visited the scenes which Mrs. Wharton recalls so surely and charmingly, but that it is too wide in scope, too crowded with detail, too hasty in movement, to be very satisfactory to the untravelled.

164

"A Motor-Flight Through France,"
Spectator [England], 101 (5 December 1908), 947

Mrs. Wharton's originality of thought and distinction of style are here concerned with an inexhaustible subject: the beauty of romance of France. To this day one meets people who believe that the interior of France is ugly, flat, and unvaried, who have never so much as heard of many of the towns, churches, castles, abbeys, mentioned in this attractive book.

"The motor-car," says Mrs. Wharton, "has restored the romance of travel." The truth of this will be keenly enough felt by any one who can realise what the old posting days were, "the wonder, the adventure and the novelty" which waited on every hour of those old-time journeys, the freedom from bondage to ugly railway stations, the intimate acquaintance with the physical geography of a country, and with those little towns and villages "missed and yearned for from the windows of the train." Certainly no one can turn over these pages, with their delightful descriptions of places which for many of us might be in the interior of Africa, and their large number of interesting illustrations, without bowing down respectfully before the new and almost magic power of the automobile.

A glance at the contents of the book— Boulogne to Amiens, Rouen to Fontainebleau, Royat to Bourges, Paris to Poitiers, the Rhône to the Seine, &c., &c.—does not suggest anything like the treasures of novelty to be found within. Of course nothing is more true than that "we receive but what we give," and that the eye sees what it brings with it the faculty of seeing; and so it might be very possible to follow in Mrs. Wharton's footsteps without reaping her rich harvest of art, archeology, history, and the understanding of those natural features which explain the age-long changes in a country's life. But no one can read the book without having his eyes necessarily opened to much that is beautiful and new—newly discovered, for it is all old—old enough, after all, to baffle modern interpreters.

As to the merely technical study of these architectural wonders—which some hold to be the one right and necessary method— we are heartily with Mrs. Wharton when she defends her own way of looking at things,—

"the kind of confused atavistic enjoyment that is made up of historical association, of a sense of mass and harmony, of the relation of the building to the sky above it, to the lights and shadows it creates about it—deeper than all, of a blind sense in the blood of its old racial power, the things it meant to far-off minds of which ours are the oft-dissolved and reconstituted fragments."

"Familiarity with the past" of these ancient creations,—that is indeed the one way to understand the present.

"Fifty of the Year's Best Books,"
Literary Digest, 37 (12 December 1908), 911–12

It is not to be expected that Mrs. Wharton would write the ordinary book of travel—nor has she done so in the present volume. "The motor-car has restored the romance of travel," she declares; and to prove her contention she whirls her reader through the towns and picturesque country scenes of France on a motor-car that certainly leaves nothing to be desired by the traveler in the way of comfort and convenience. Mrs. Wharton dwells with delight on the freedom from the "ugliness and desolation created by the railway," as enjoyed by the motorist, and describes in her usual charming style the various objects of beauty and interest that flash by her car without being marred by intervening railroad yards, smoke, and general dulness. With no country is Mrs. Wharton more thoroughly familiar than with France, and her brilliant sketches of towns, castles, churches, men, and women, seen in passing, furnish excellent reading and lend to this book a piquancy not usually possest by others of its kind. For any one contemplating a motor trip through France it should serve, moreover, as an excellent guide.

"A Motor-Flight Through France,"
Review of Reviews, 38 (December 1908), 760

Never ending is the charm that rural and historic France has for the literary spirits of all nations. Two fascinating volumes of description on the charm of that France which is not Paris, written with a literary touch that makes them stand out from the great mass of books of European travel and. description, are Mary King Waddington's *Chateau and Country Life in France* . . . , and Mrs. Edith Wharton's *A Motor Flight Through France*. . . . Both volumes are illustrated,—Madame Waddington's from sketches and drawings, and Mrs. Wharton's largely from photographs. . . . Mrs. Wharton's text is found in her introductory sentence: "The motor car has restored the romance of travel." Her keenness of observation and delicate descriptive style never fail her.

Checklist of Additional Reviews

"Travel in Many Lands," *Independent*, 65 (19 November 1908), 1180.
"Books of Travel and Description," *Dial*, 41 (1 December 1908), 409.

ARTEMIS TO ACTÆON AND OTHER VERSE

ARTEMIS TO ACTÆON
AND OTHER VERSE

BY

EDITH WHARTON

NEW YORK
CHARLES SCRIBNER'S SONS
1909

"Recent Verse," *Spectator* [England], 103 (3 July 1909), 20

Mrs. Wharton, another novelist, has also turned to verse, and Artemis, too, is her inspiration. In form she is nearer classical standards, though she has none of the rich imaginative vigour of Mr. Hewlett. Her poetry, very beautiful and perfect in its way, makes its chief appeal to the intellect. "Artemis to Actæon" is a subtle re-reading of a legend which Mr. Hewlett interprets more simply. To Mrs. Wharton Actæon is the mortal who by his love and death gives the weary goddess a fresh immortality. So with the admirable monologue "Vesalius in Zante," where the philosophy of failure,

"The gods may give anew, but not restore,"

is expounded as Browning might have expounded it. In all the poems there is this plenitude of reasoning, creeds and ideals being shown against the background of some human life. The finest of the portraits seems to us to be "Margaret of Cortona," but as a lyric it would be difficult to overpraise the "Hunting-song" at the end of the volume. Mrs. Wharton is not easily quoted, for her work is closely interwoven, but these lines may give some conception of the vigour of her blank verse:—

"When Christ, the heavenly gardener,
Plucks flowers for Paradise (do I not
    know?),
He snaps the stem above the root, and
    presses
The ransomed soul between two
    convent walls,
A lifeless blossom in the Book of Life.
But when my lover gathered me, he
    lifted
Stem, root and all—ay, and the clinging
    mud—
And set me on his sill to spread and
    bloom
After the common way, take sun and
    rain,
And make a patch of brightness for the
    street."

"The New Books," *Review of Reviews*, 40 (July 1909), 123

"High seriousness" and "fine quality" have been said to be the chief characteristics of Edith Wharton's novels. These also apply to her recently issued collection of verse, entitled *Artemis to Actæon*—without, however, very much emotional appeal.

William Morton Payne, "Recent Poetry," *Dial*, 47 (16 August 1909), 101

The verse contained in Mrs. Wharton's *Artemis to Actæon* has the qualities to be expected from that accomplished writer. In her poems, perhaps more than in her stories, we find great refinement of feeling, subtlety of thought, and a diction that will bear close critical scrutiny. Intellectualized and spiritualized in a high degree, it provides the satisfaction that may always be got from intercourse with

169

a rich and serious mind. These very characteristics place it outside the category of poetry in the pure spontaneous sense; it is too sicklied o'er with the pale cast of thought, its artifice is too evident, its song (as far as it sings at all) does not well straight up from the heart. What we have said may be well enough illustrated by a passage from the titular poem, in which Artemis gives Actæon an elaborate explanation of the dulness of life upon Olympus, and of the reasons which prompted her to accept his worship and to slay him for his temerity. He has, she urges, no reason to complain,—

"For immortality is not to range
Unlimited through vast Olympian days,
Or sit in dull dominion over time;
But this—to drink fate's utmost at a
    draught,
Nor feel the wine grow stale upon the
    lip,
To scale the summit of some soaring
    moment,
Nor know the dulness of the long
    descent,
To snatch the crown of life and seal it
    up
Secure forever in the vaults of death."

There is more of vitality in the poem which comes a little later in the collection, taking the form of a dramatic monologue spoken by Vesalius when nearing the end of his days in exile. But even these words offer but a pale reflection of life itself. Mrs. Wharton's verse reveals only the grayer aspects of human existence, and has its being in the shadows.

"Age after age the fruit of knowledge
    falls
To ashes on men's lips;
Love fails, faith sickens, like a dying
    tree

Life sheds its dreams that no new spring
    recalls;
The longed-for ships
Come empty home or founder on the
    deep,
And eyes first lose their tears and then
    their sleep."

Thus opens the poem called "Non Dolet." The title makes a brave pretense, but its irony is too evident.

"New Books Reviewed," *North American Review*, 190 (November 1909), 702–3

Edith Wharton is a prose-writer *par excellence*, and while she reaches the lyric pitch in thought and substance there are moments when, fine craftsman that she is, diction and cadence halt and move in the measure of prose.

"Thou sawst me in the cloud, the wave,
    the bough,
The clod commoved with April."

The word "commoved" somehow translates us quickly into a realm of prose, as also does the false stress in the second line below:

"Yea, this we wait for, this renews us,
    this
Incarnates us, pale people of your
    dreams."

But just because she has so won the mastery of a prose style, she cannot give forth her full feeling about life without offering us poetry, for undoubtedly the substance of her thought dwells often in the realm of poetry.

The dramatic monologue of "Vesalius in Zante," reminiscent in form as it is of the great master of the dramatic monologue, is full of subtle psychology, fire and high thought, and its form is justified by such splendid lines as:

"They only, who reconquer day by day
The inch of ground they camped on
    overnight,
Have right of foothold on this crowded
    earth."

And again:

"But I so hugged the fleeting self of me,
So loved the lovely perishable hours,
So kissed myself to death upon their
    lips,
That on one pyre we perished in the
    end."

Best of all, Mrs. Wharton succeeds in the sonnet, that form which by its set laws and narrow compass offers a bridge between prose composition and poetry, and if one were to ask of whom she had most diligently studied the art of sonnet-making the answer, him who made "The House of Life" rises from such lines as:

"I heard her feet in irretrievable flight,"

"The touch of kisses that have missed
    my brow."

Most exquisite is the sextet from sonnet VIII:

"But other hearts a long, long road
    doth span,
From some far region of old works and
    wars,
And the weary armies of the thoughts
    of man
Have trampled it and furrowed it with
    scars,
And sometimes, husht, a sacred caravan
Moves over it alone, beneath the stars."

Mrs. Wharton is of the elect. She is one of those who accomplish whatever they set their hands to and she has innumerable facets of her soul. Having proved that she is among the finest writers of prose America has ever produced, she flashes another facet upon us, and we have a new poet and one we could not spare.

Checklist of Additional Reviews

"Books of Poems by Two Writers,"
    New York Times Saturday Review,
    14 (8 May 1909), 33.
Brian Hooker, "Some Springtime Verse,"
    Bookman, 29 (June 1909), 365–72.
Nation, 89 (15 July 1909), 55.
Athenæum [England], 4268 (14 August
    1909), 178.

TALES OF MEN AND GHOSTS

TALES OF
MEN AND GHOSTS

BY

EDITH WHARTON

NEW YORK
CHARLES SCRIBNER'S SONS
MCMX

"Tales of Men and Ghosts," Independent, 69 (17 November 1910), 1089

Mrs. Wharton's Tales of Men and Ghosts are of strangely unequal merit, the most ingenious of them, in the invention of its plot and the closeness of its relation to the possibilities of real life, being the first, "The Bolted Door," a gruesome fancy woven of crime and a denial of proffered atonement, prompted by weariness of life, because both law and medicine consider the confession a proof of insanity. There is a cramping of influence discernible in these pages.

"Current Fiction: Tales of Men and Ghosts," Nation, 91 (24 November 1910), 496

The enervating influence upon our popular story-writers of American magazine "policy" does not decrease with the seasons. One recalls the announcement, made something like a year ago, that Mrs. Wharton had been booked to write a series of ten or a dozen stories "about men." Here they are in the predestined number, capably turned out according to contract. They are ingenious and readable: so much the most doubtful forecaster must have been sure of. But their ingenuity is altogether too patent: they are too clearly trumped up out of the author's fancy; even the doubtful forecaster must have hoped for better things from the writer of The Valley of Decision and The House of Mirth. Her use of the short-story form is not to be complained of, since it is true that she is naturally an interpreter of the episode and the situation, rather than of action upon a large scale. Her latest essay in the novel, The Fruit of the Tree, resulted in a not very happy patching together of several distinct and obstinately detached episodes. But the book left one with an impression of earnest endeavor, if not of actually lofty achievement. Mrs. Wharton may have enjoyed the writing of these Tales of Men and Ghosts, but we venture to suppose that her enjoyment was upon the comparatively trivial plane of technical facility.

Not the least puzzling thing about this collection is its uncertainty of style. Two of the stories, "Afterward" and "The Letters," are (rather ineffectively) in her earlier manner—that Anglo-Gallic manner, with its nuances, its compunctions, its hiatuses; which reminds us of Bourget, when it does not go farther and fare worse by reminding us of Henry James. In The Valley of Decision this style seemed to have been so thoroughly assimilated by Mrs. Wharton, that one regarded her simply as one of the "psychological" school, as the cant was. Now one almost comes to doubt the spontaneity of that manner, with her. At all events, the rest of the stories here collected show hardly a trace of it. Their style is rather that alert and commonplace style of the magazine fiction of the day as turned out by an army of skillful practitioners.

Review of *Tales of Men and Ghosts*, *Anthenæum* [England], 4336 (3 December 1910), 700

The latter part of the title of Mrs. Edith Wharton's volume, *Tales of Men and Ghosts*, is not very felicitous. By ghosts most of us understand something different from the delicate subtle suggestion of an unseen world which haunts her pages, a world in which our subconscious selves continually move. The most genuine attempt at a material ghost appears in "Afterward," where the man whom Boyne has wronged, and who has attempted to commit suicide, comes after his death to fetch him. Here the skill of the writer is shown chiefly in the manner in which Boyne's wife sees the ghost through her husband's eyes, and gradually understands the situation. "The Bolted Door" is a curious and cynical study of a man who, having failed as a play-wright and being disgusted with life, tries to give himself up for a murder which he has actually committed, but only succeeds in being shut up in a lunatic asylum by his incredulous friends. There is great beauty of an elusive kind in "Daunt Diana"—in the attitude of Neave, a collector who is a mystic and a poet, towards the gem of his collection, which he buys twice over, ruining himself in the process, because he feels that the first time his Diana was won too easily.

Mrs. Wharton is, however, an artist who, in spite of her subtle gift for analysis, never forgets the power of pure human love, which, as she shows us in "Letters," has indeed the element of immortality.

"Tales of Men and Ghosts," *Bookman* [England], 40 (Spring Supplement 1911), 14

Miss Wharton's ten stories have more to do with men than with spirits; which is not unfortunate, for her ghosts are not very terrible creatures. One of them is a pair of eyes, which appear over the bed to a young American. "There they hang in the darkness, their swollen lids dropped across the little watery bulbs rolling loose in the orbits, and the puff of flesh making a muddy shadow underneath." Another is the wraith of a man whom an American business man has ruined in business; but this ghost has all its wits as well as all its limbs (if the expression is permissible) about it, and crosses the Atlantic in order to carry off the unscrupulous rival into limbo. The remaining tales are keen little studies of temperament, from the murderer who cannot get any one to believe his confession, to Lizzie West, who discovers after marriage that her husband has cheated her, and who refuses to let him learn her discovery. "The Legend" is a pretty satire upon literary cults; "Full Circle" also shows up the foibles of modern authors; and "The Debt," which is perhaps the most searching and ingenious of all, handles a nice problem of scientific ethics. It is in these studies of human nature that Miss Wharton excels. Her volume is three parts brilliant and always readable. Most of her characters have a comfortable way of inheriting fortunes at convenient moments in their careers, but this mannerism will not repel the large class of readers who like to see their heroes and heroines well provided for in things of this world.

176

Checklist of Additional Reviews

"A Guide to the New Books," *Literary Digest*, 41 (19 November 1910), 949.

ETHAN FROME

ETHAN FROME

BY

EDITH WHARTON

NEW YORK
CHARLES SCRIBNER'S SONS
MCMXI

"Three Lives in Supreme Torture: Mrs. Wharton's *Ethan Frome* a Cruel, Compelling, Haunting Story of New England," *New York Times Book Review*, 8 October 1911, p. 603

Mrs. Wharton prefers to present life in its unsmiling aspects, to look at it with the eye of the tragic poet, not with the deep sympathy, smiling tenderness, and affectionate tolerance of the greatest novelists. Thus she never shows life as it is, as the great novelists do, but as an aspect or view of life—the reflex of life on the writer if you will—which colors all things with some mastering mood of him or her.

The present grim tale of a bud of romance ice-bound and turned into a frozen horror in the frigid setting of a New England Winter landscape is conceived in the remorseless spirit of the Greek tragic muse. The rigidity of the bleak Puritan outlook on life does duty for the relentless Fates. It is a powerful and skillful performance and seems to recreate a life and an atmosphere essentially the same as that which breathes in the romances of Hawthorne. That atmosphere is, no doubt, the true emanation of the soul of New England—that New England, warped by the dour theology of the cruel and fanatic age that planted it, which was Hawthorne's own, and which now has retired to such frozen fastnesses as the lonely and starved village among the barren hills in which Mrs. Wharton places her story.

The story itself is one which will hardly bear even indication of what it is without an effect of marring it. It deals with a gaunt, tall farmer and his wife and another woman—a young girl, the wife's poor relation, who is, like them, an inmate of the desolate farmhouse perched bleakly in the midst of its barren acres. The man is one of those—found in all starved communities—who have been chained to the soil by the duty of caring for a family of stricken elders—a very incarnation of the tragedy of youth and strength wasted in the service of useless age. The wife is, as a wife, an accident. She is a whining slattern who hugs her imaginary ailments to her flat and barren breast and spends the scant substance wrung from the grudging northern earth upon quacks and patent nostrums. That, also, is a common type in starved and hopeless rural communities.

The girl is a pretty, gentle creature whose worldly efficiency has been tried and found wanting in the hard tasks of the shop girl in some busy little New England mill town, a human reed bruised in the wind. On the face of it it is a very sordid triangle. Actually, Mrs. Wharton has been able to invest the girl with such sweetness, such delicacy, such innocence, such child-likeness, to endow her with such simplicity and such wistfulness; the man himself is so utterly simple, so starved of joy; and both are so helpless in the toils of bitter circumstance that the effect is anything but sordid.

Moreover, the whole drama is enacted for the reader under the spell of a sure foreknowledge that tragedy is coming swift-footed to end the hardly more than glimpsed hope of happiness for the doomed pair who dwell apart in that house and watch for little comforts like faint candle beams beneath closed doors. A brief interlude of smiles and tears and shy glances and a mad moment of stolen kisses—and then the end. All that is crushed beneath the horror of a stretch of

181

long, ruined years. Retribution sits at the poor man's fireside in the shape of two haggard and witchlike figures—the gaunt wife and the wreck of the girl that was.

It is a cruel story. It is a compelling and haunting story. But it is a story which a bald telling, without the art which has thrown the crude material of the plot into due dramatic perspective and given it poetic atmosphere, could easily make absurd, or even revolting. The mere saying that Mrs. Wharton has brought about the catastrophe by sending two of her principal characters coasting down an icy hill and "smashing them up" for life—but not killing them—against a great tree near the bottom, conveys an impression of clumsiness and brutality which only the actual reading of the story will avail to dispel. Mrs. Wharton has, in fact, chosen to build of small, crude things and a rude and violent event a structure whose purpose is the infinite refinement of torture. All that is human and pitiful and tender in the tale—and there is much—is designed and contrived to sharpen the keen edge of that torture. And the victims lie stretched upon the rack for twenty years.

The author of *The House of Mirth*, which lacked much of being either a great novel or a true one, and which lacked also not a little of being a really convincing drama, in spite of the element of truth and the wide popular appeal which has caused it to stand forth in the public mind as Mrs. Wharton's most conspicuous achievement, has accomplished in this story something very much finer and stronger. There is in it much of the keen concentrated effectiveness which the author has more than once obtained in her short stories. If *Ethan Frome* is not a great novel—it is, indeed, hardly long enough to be called a novel at all, though it far oversteps short-story limits—it is, at least, an impressive tragedy.

There are writers who are both great novelists and great dramatists; that is, who reflect life with singular completeness and faithfulness at the same time that they give the overpowering impression of a shaping and designing destiny governing the fortunes of their leading personages and driving to an inevitable conclusion. Such a novelist, for instance, was George Meredith, from whom the modern makers of fiction borrow so much consciously and unconsciously. There are writers, again, who are merely novelists—who send their creatures to school, to life, not without smiles and tears and pangs to see them suffer. Such a novelist was Thackeray. And there are dramatists who do not write for the theatre and so pass as novelists. It seems to this reviewer that Mrs. Wharton belongs properly to the last classification and that *Ethan Frome* is the proof of it.

"Ethan Frome," Outlook, 99 (21 October 1911), 405

The rustic humor and unaffected kindness of Friendship Village are in broad contrast with the somber repression of mirth, the denial of normal human instincts, and the monotonous tone of gray which pervade Mrs. Wharton's short long story *Ethan Frome*. The background is an old, dilapidated farm-house framed by a bleak New England landscape, and the tragedy gains a penetrating pathos from the bareness of its surroundings and the sense of futility which issues from it; the incidents would be a mere group of fortuitous happenings, so insignificant that they would lack the dignity of a malicious fate, if it were not for the touch of patient loyalty with which Ethan Frome bears its dreary burden at the end. As a piece of artistic workmanship it would be hard to overstate the quality of this story; it is conceived and executed with a unity of insight, structural skill, and feeling for style which lies only within the reach of an artist who, like Guy de Maupassant, knows every resource of the art. It is to be hoped that when Mrs. Wharton writes again she will bring her great talent to bear on normal people and situations.

"Current Fiction: Ethan Frome," Nation, 93 (26 October 1911), 396–7

More than ten years ago Mrs. Wharton published a short story called "The Duchess at Prayer." Since that time we have cherished an estimate of her powers which no intermediate accession to her repertory has raised, nor even, to speak truth, quite justified. Practised, cosmopolitan, subtle, she has seemed, on the whole, to covet most earnestly the refinements of Henry James. In spite of her habit of a franker approach, her consistent rating of matter above manner, and the gravitation—we should hesitate to say transfer—of her interest from exotic to native themes; we might have been reasonably content to rank her as the greatest pupil of a little master, were it not for the appearance of Ethan Frome. This startling fulfillment recalls not only the promise of the early story, but its revelation of a more potent influence—the inspiriting example of a greater novelist to whom Mr. James's devoirs have been paid in the phrase, "The master of us all." Exactly how much the inception and execution of "The Duchess at Prayer" owed to Balzac's "La grande Bretèche" is beyond our present point,

which is, specifically, that the excellence of Mrs. Wharton's work in this case outstripped the charge of imitation, and allied her with that company of splendid talents whom neither magnificence nor the catastrophes of passion can abash.

There is certainly no imitative strain in Ethan Frome. The style is assured and entirely individual, the method direct and firm in its grasp upon substantial fact. Yet here is the companion-piece to the "Duchess," a variation upon the same theme of triumphant malice and tortured love, evoking the same emotions. And here as there the genius of a place presides, and the scene and the hour conspire to meet the racial temper. But there is this great difference: in the place of sumptuous memories, decaying under the sultry oppression of Italian noon, she was, at heart, a stranger; whereas she writes now of New England as one writes of home, plainly, and with a wealth of understanding and familiar allusion. Even the arrangement of the narrative is designed to fit the life described and its probabilities rather than to satisfy any precious scruples. A winter-bound stranger in an out-of-the-way Massachusetts hamlet recognizes in the limping figure of Ethan Frome the "ruin of a man," and apprehends some singular misfortunes behind his obvious plight. The sparse comment of a community respectful of privacies and little indulgent of curiosity yields but scanty information. Out of the native's penury come at length hours of enforced companionship, the daily rides to the station during which "Frome drove in silence, the reins loosely held in his left hand, his brown, seamed profile, under the helmet-like peak of the cap, relieved against the banks of snow."

"It was that night," explains the visitor, "that I found the clue to Ethan Frome, and began to put together this vision of his story." Such an approach could not be improved, forbearing, as it does, to

183

violate the seal of silence; nor could, we think, the conclusion of village confidences be spared, with its ultimate breaking down of reserve between the initiated, its natural cadence of secret curiosity, and its softening echo of unavailing human sympathy.

Surely, the melancholy spirit that haunts the remoter byways of rural New England has entered into this chronicle; over all its scenes breathe the benumbing and isolating rigors of her winters, a sense of invisible fetters, a consciousness of depleted resources, a reticence and self-contained endurance that even the houses know how to express, retired from the public way, or turned sideways to preserve a secluded entrance. Yet it is with a softly-breathed strain of native romance that the drama opens. As well try to transplant arbutus from its native habitat as to dissociate this exquisite burgeoning of passion from its homely circumstances and the inflexible trammels of a local speech meant for taciturnity rather than expression. Thriving on meagre opportunities and pleasures—the coasting, the picnic, the walk home from the "church sociable"—and on the sharing of frugal household cares, the love between the young farmer and the little dependent who inefficiently "helped" in his home, spread like a secret flowering too innocent and too fragrant to escape the wife's malicious eye. The brave and fragile figure of Mattie Silver is not an idealized one, although this is the type of New England girlhood whose modesty and touch of fairy grace have been the subject of much poetry.

The wife who stands for fate in this drama is a curious and repugnant figure. She introduces the same vein of close-mouthed malignity which darkens local history. The helpless fear and loathing she inspires in her husband is the essence of supernatural terror without its obsolete husk of ignorance. By showing this instance of a hypochondriac roused by jealousy out of a "sullen self-absorption" and transformed into a mysterious alien presence, an evil energy secreted from the long years of silent brooding, Mrs. Wharton touches on a very radical identity. We realize that the same gloating satisfaction that made the wife smile upon the parting lovers, had something to do with her capabilities as a nurse. Her pleasure at the sight of pain she had inflicted—was it, perchance, from such an evil spring that her strength was drawn for the long years of drudgery between two cripples?

No hero of fantastic legend was ever more literally hag-ridden than was Ethan Frome. The profound irony of his case is that it required his own goodness to complete her parasitic power over him. Without his innate honesty and his sense of duty he could have escaped her demands and her decrees, refused the money for her nostrums and "doctor books," followed the vision of a new free life "out West." In his submission to obligation and in his thwarted intellectual aspirations he typifies the remnant of an exceptional race whose spiritual inheritance has dwindled amid hard conditions until all distinction is forfeited except that of suffering; but which still indicates its quality, if only by its capacity for suffering.

The wonder is that the spectacle of so much pain can be made to yield so much beauty. And here the full range of Mrs. Wharton's imagination becomes apparent. There is possible, within the gamut of human experience, an exaltation of anguish which makes a solitude for itself, whose direct contemplation seals the impulse of speech and strikes cold upon the heart. Yet sometimes in reflection there is revealed, beneath the wringing torment, the lineaments of a wronged·and distorted loveliness. It is the piteous and intolerable conception which the Greeks expressed in the medusa head that Mrs. Wharton has dared to hold up to us anew, but the face she shows us is the face of our own people.

"Reviews of New Books," Hartford *Daily Courant*, 30 October 1911, p. 17

There is an artistic subtlety in the way Mrs. Wharton tells how she got the story of the isolated Fromes.

Mrs. Hale's "finer sensibility and a little more education" had enabled her to "judge with detachment" her neighbors in Starkfield. After all, it was not she, but Ethan himself in an hour of detachment who told the gruesome story to Mrs. Hale's lodger, Mrs. Hale furnishing the atmosphere or background—which Mrs. Wharton does not transcribe very well—in a "delicately shaded version of the Starkfield chronicle." In fact so far from this being a typical New England story it might have happened (although it probably did not happen) anywhere—"even in a community rich in pathological instances." It is not within the bounds of belief or sympathy, even in a novel, that a fairly well-to-do small farmer, of a cold and reserved nature, such as was Ethan Frome's until his "accident," should have manifested sentimentality for the cousin and help of his sickly or hypochondriac wife by "neglecting the mill that he might help her about the house and scrub the kitchen floor," or plan with her clumsy (and ineffectual) double suicide because the wife sent the girl away. The novel in spite of much admirable phrasing is not a study of life or character or locality. It is an unflinching tragedy of banalities, dyspepsia and spinal injury—purely physical.

"*Ethan Frome*," *Saturday Review* [England], 112 (18 November 1911), 650

Almost we are afraid to say that *Ethan Frome* is not a novel; for Mr. Wells is at this moment insisting that such criticism is as foolish as Mr. Trotter's contention that a dramatic exercise by Mr. Shaw is not a play. It is a novel in that it unfolds completely to our view the lives of its few people; but it is a short story in that the mood is throughout the same; and that the interest is from first to last fastened upon the one terrible incident of the story's climax. Also it is a short story because the story is short—it can be read easily at a sitting. For many reasons it is worth reading. The writing is singularly beautiful. It has passed through flame of the author's imagination. Yet, having read the story, we wish we had not read it. The error is in the end. There are things too terrible in their failure to be told humanly by creature to creature. Ethan Frome driving down with the girl he loved to death—here there is beauty and a defiance of the misery of circumstance which may sadden, but uplift, the reader. But these lovers could not die. They must live horribly on, mutilated and losing even the nobility of their passion in the wreck of their bodies. Had Mrs. Wharton allowed her creatures to die as they intended *Ethan Frome* would be high indeed among our shorter tales—high as [George Meredith's] *The Tale of Chloë*. She has marred her work with no motive we can discover. With Mrs. Wharton it could not have been the mere craving for the exaggerated terror which in art must always defeat itself. The end of

Ethan Frome is something at which we cover the eyes. We do not cover the eyes at the spectacle of a really great tragedy.

Frederic Taber Cooper, "Ethan Frome," Bookman, 34 (November 1911), 312

It is hard to forgive Mrs. Wharton for the utter remorselessness of her latest volume, *Ethan Frome*, for nowhere has she done anything more hopelessly, endlessly grey with blank despair. Ethan Frome is a man whose ambitions long ago burned themselves out. He early spent his vitality in the daily struggle of winning a bare sustenance from the grudging soil of a small New England farm. An invalid wife, whose imaginary ailments thrived on patent medicines, doubled his burden. And then, one day, a pretty young cousin, left destitute, came to live on the farm, and brought a breath of fragrance and gladness into the gloom. Neither Ethan nor the cousin meant to do wrong; it was simply one of those unconscious, inevitable attachments, almost primitive in its intensity. It never was even put into words, until the day when Ethan's wife, perhaps because of a smouldering jealousy, perhaps because the motive she gave was the true one, namely that the girl was shiftless and incompetent, sent her out into the world to shift for herself. It is while driving her over to the railway station that Ethan consents to the girl's wish that just once more he will take her coasting down a long hill that is a favourite coasting place throughout the neighbourhood. It is a long, steep, breathless rush, with a giant tree towering up near the foot, to be dexterously avoided at the last

moment. It is while he holds the girl close to him on the sled, that a ghastly temptation comes to Ethan and he voices it: How much easier, instead of letting her go away, to face unknown struggles, while he remained behind, eating his heart out with loneliness—how much easier merely to forget to steer! One shock of impact, and the end would come. And to this the girl consents. And neither of them foresees that not even the most carefully planned death is inevitable, and that fate is about to play upon them one of its grimmest tricks, and doom them to a lifelong punishment, she with a broken back, he with a warped and twisted frame, tied beyond escape to the slow starvation of the barren farm, and grudgingly watched over by the invalid wife, scarcely more alive than themselves. Art for art's sake is the one justification of a piece of work as perfect in technique as it is relentless in substance.

Review of Ethan Frome, Bookman [England], 41 (January 1912), 216

Mrs. Wharton has more than satisfied one's expectation, and her art has never been shown to greater advantage than in this story of Ethan Frome, the young Massachusetts farmer. It is a tragedy, almost unendurably poignant, but justified by its inevitableness. From his youth Fate dealt hardly with Ethan. His father died, leaving him a bleak unproductive farm, and a failing saw-mill. After a lingering illness, his mother also died. That was in the Fall; had it been in the Spring his future might have been different, but Ethan dared not face the winter alone in this "New England farmhouse that made the landscape lonelier." Then he took his first step toward the abyss: he asked Zeena, the tall, uncomely, raw-boned woman who had nursed his mother, to be his wife. From that time his life was a martyrdom, for Zeena soon showed her real character as a sickly, querulous neurotic. Then came the next stroke of Destiny. To save expense, for the poverty at the farm was grinding, Mattie Silver, the penniless young cousin of Zeena, was invited to live with them. As the girl served without pay her cousin suggested that on the rare occasions, when there was an entertainment in the village, Mattie should go to it, so that she should not feel too sharp a contrast between the life she had left and the isolation of the farm. On these occasions, Ethan, although at first he had inwardly demurred at the extra toil imposed on him, was accustomed to fetch home his wife's cousin. Soon he found himself wishing that the village might give all its nights to revelry. Gradually the wife's suspicions are aroused; a hired girl is employed, and Mattie must go. Poverty makes Ethan helpless; money might have saved two lives, if not three, but there is none. So the blow falls in the last act that is to consign the three to a living death. It is a beautiful, sad, but intensely human story, working out to its final conclusion with all the inevitability of a great Greek tragedy.

Checklist of Additional Reviews

"Half a Dozen Stories," Outlook, 99 (21 October 1911), 405.

"Feminine Literature," Independent, 71 (30 November 1911), 1204.

"Recent Fiction and the Critics," Current Literature, 52 (January 1912), 112–13.

C. Rachilde, "Sous la neige, par Edith Wharton," Mercure de France, 98 (1 July 1912), 123.

Lucien Maury, "Une Romancière américaine: Mme. E. Wharton," Revue Bleue [France], 2 (3 August 1912), 154–7.

J. G., "Sous la neige," Revue Critique Des Ideés et des Livres [France], 18 (10 August 1912), 380–1.

THE REEF

THE REEF

A NOVEL

BY

EDITH WHARTON

AUTHOR OF
"THE HOUSE OF MIRTH," "ETHAN FROME," ETC.

NEW YORK
D. APPLETON AND COMPANY
1912

"A New Novel by Mrs. Wharton,"
New York *Sun*,
23 November 1912, p. 8

In so far as the English of Edith Wharton's new story, *The Reef* . . . is concerned the promise of *Ethan Frome* is maintained; she has abandoned eccentricity and preciosity, she has dropped involved constructions and is content to write directly, trusting to the resources of her vocabulary for the necessary shading and coloring. The simplification of her style seems to carry with it a clearer exposition of the problems that trouble her, not that she sacrifices any subtlety of thought or moral distinction; she has simply learned that she must make herself understood by everybody, instead of leaving the initiated to guess her meaning. In this story she follows her usual practice of selecting a subject for the operating table and carefully dissecting it. There are more cheerful matters in life than she chooses to write about, but about tastes there is no use in disputing.

The story opens with a prelude that shows what Mrs. Wharton could do if she would take a less dismal view of life. A man of the world is thrown in with a young girl by accident and contrives to give her a thoroughly good time in Paris. They are both Americans; she is the eager minded, impulsive, innocent yet experienced young person, with no social connections, that writers of fiction like to let loose on Europe, and she has had a very hard life. He is sore over his treatment by a woman he wishes to marry. It is a pretty idyl so long as it lasts, but Mrs. Wharton chooses to give it a turn which shows that the man is no gentleman. To most readers, we imagine, this will be a shock.

With the story proper we come to the heroine, a society woman, who is the widow of an expatriated American and who lives on his French estate with her little daughter, her stepson and her mother-in-law, the widow of a French noble, and still more of an expatriate. The girl of the prelude is employed as governess of the child, so that the man who indulged in a passing adventure, and who is now the accepted lover of the heroine, finds himself in a fix when he is asked to give his opinion of the governess's character, and in a still worse one when he finds that the stepson intends to marry her. Mrs. Wharton shows much ingenuity in depicting his mental struggles, his efforts to escape without actual lying, his attempts to put an end to the situation and later in his specious pleas in explanation and extenuation of what he has done. She has made him commonplace, however, and all his twistings and evasions seem ignoble.

For the girl's tragedy we can feel more sympathy. She has found a place of rest after a long struggle, even the twist in her mind that would allow her to marry a boy she likes is comprehensible. When she discovers that it is the man she loves after all, she gives everything up and returns to the sordid life from which she hoped she had been rescued. It is clear that her side of the story has not been heard in full, but she and the man and the arbitrary and unpleasant situation are only brought in as the background and the relief for the figure of the heroine.

In spite of her motherhood and her widowhood she is an inexperienced girl who has never been allowed to step outside of the conventions. She has always repressed herself and has come to look on life as something unreal, but is constantly conscious that there is something she is missing. She knows she must change her

191

conventional ideas if she is to keep the man she loves, and the conflict in her soul is described with the utmost detail, from the moment of her first uneasiness that something is not quite right to the time when all that her lover has done is revealed to her, and she is forced to forgive him in spite of it. No finer study of psychology has Mrs. Wharton written: it is painful of course, for the woman is gentle and sweet, and all her suffering comes from another's guilt; more painful, perhaps, because with all excuses the man seems unworthy of her, but it is a true picture of one type of American woman, only uncommon because, in this case, the woman actually tries to see beyond herself.

There is plenty of satire on society and on some kinds of Americans who live away from their country; there are bright characterizations; there is much worldly wisdom. The one failure is the little girl; the author has made no effort to put life into her, which is perhaps as well because her presence is awkward in an intolerable situation. Yet it is a bitter, disheartening, sordid story and we could wish that Mrs. Wharton would look on brighter and nobler aspects of life.

H. I. Brock,
"Edith Wharton Positively Tortures Her Characters in Her New Novel," *New York Times Book Review*, 24 November 1912, p. 685

When Mrs. Wharton wrote *The House of Mirth*, and set all her woman readers talking about poor Lily Bart, there were those who asserted with some vehemence that she had used her even then notable technical skill and literary prestige to make the public swallow as a serious novel the identical stuff that vulgar yellow Sunday newspaper stories about rich society folks are made of. These carpers declared that Lily Bart, who failed so pathetically to qualify as a milliner after she had shilly-shallied away her chances of marrying either for love or for money, was not a whit better or truer than the stock heroine of melodrama, and they scolded Mrs. Wharton for taking Lily seriously and making her readers take her so.

Robert W. Chambers, who in those days had not abandoned his native method of the airy satirical for the richly gilt sensuous, made a very clever skit upon Mrs. Wharton's book—a skit which passed among a wider and less fastidious circle of readers for a novel almost as serious and quite as heart-searching as her own. It was, in fact, this skit (it was entitled "The Fighting Chance," and paralleled *The House of Mirth* incident for incident and character for character,) which started Chambers upon his downward career. It taught him that if he wrote burlesque with sufficient abandon the product was exactly what an enormous reading public wanted, and was prepared to accept as pure romance full of rich, damp sentiment.

As for Mrs. Wharton, humor has never been her strong point. She was, therefore, in no danger of falling into the dreadful habit of writing with her tongue in her cheek even without Mr. Chambers's warning example of what could be done with her own material. She has continued to be a perfectly serious novelist, and though she has been by no means uniformly successful in writing good novels, she finally achieved *Ethan Frome*. That grim and cruel tragedy was a marvelous example of her perfect skill with her method—

already partly illustrated in Lily Bart. The method—which is the method also of so eminent a practitioner of the novelist's art as Thomas Hardy—consists in its essence in taking a human being and subjecting him or her to a cumulative process of torture. The procedure is to hound him, to trap him, to afflict him with plagues, to pound him with disaster and pin-prick him with annoyance, to conspire with gods and men for his discomfort and his ruin, to play with him as a cat plays with a mouse, while the reader looks on at his shifts and writhings like a Roman gladiator or the Christian martyr thrown to the lions of the amphitheatre.

It is, of course, the primitive method of entertainment, and has all the best authority of antiquity behind it. Substitute the Sphinx for the house cat and the Fates and Furies and the offended gods for our modern, inexorable circumstances, and it is the method of Greek tragedy. There is no more effective means toward the purpose of keeping the reader stirred, interested, fascinated, appalled by what is going on.

In *Ethan Frome* it was a simple honest New England farmer who was selected for the victim. A little more rugged in appearance than most of his fellows, a little more starved, with a livelier natural capacity for what one has grown so weary of hearing called the "joy of living," but for which, nevertheless, one has no better name, he served as the subject of his creator's refined process of vivisection. In the present story it is a young woman— an American girl who is making a meagre living for herself in Europe—who provides the entertainment. Sophy Viner is the butterfly on the wheel. To be sure, Sophy is not really of the butterfly species. She has much sterner stuff in her than that. But she has desired ardently to play the butterfly—for once to flutter in the sun and be happy. She has her chance—and

she snatches it. The rest is paying for her fun. Sophy pays and so do others.

Naturally Mrs. Wharton is concerned with bringing out a situation—stating a social question—as well as with applying the rack and thumbscrew to Sophy and Sophy's rival and foil, a woman of that higher world to which Mrs. Wharton's heroines belong by a sort of birthright. What is a woman who is a widow of a man she never cared for to do? What is she to think when she discovers that the man who earliest touched her girlish fancy, who has continued to adore her at a distance while she was the wife of the other, who has come to woo her again with almost youthful ardor now that she is free, has in almost the crisis of that return had a little affair with a little governess in Paris? What is she to do and to think—especially when the little governess has since become her own daughter's governess, by pure chance, be it understood, and by no fault, connivance, or even knowledge of the man who is so distressingly a sinner?

The situation as it stands would appear to be trying enough. But Mrs. Wharton is not content to let it rest there. The affair in her mind lacks due complexity. The excuses for getting everybody concerned harrowed and hurt are not numerous enough. So she must have the widow's stepson in love with the little governess and the widow herself committed—before she knew the facts—to furthering the match between the two. There is now room for any number of situations and encounters rich in emotion and embarrassment to the persons of the drama and highly fever-inducing in the reader. Mrs. Wharton neglects none of the opportunities she has so artfully made for herself. There is no denying Mrs. Wharton's art. She is almost diabolically clever in arranging her conspiracies against the peace of mind of her characters, and against the

193

fatal disposition of the reader to throw books down without finishing them.

However, it is not by the story that she avails this time. The story is rather conspicuously a failure. Where she has made her mark here is in the creation of that vivid young creature Sophy Viner. Sophy is real; she lays hold of that in you which makes yourself real. Mrs. Wharton has sketched the girl lightly, very lightly, but very surely. There is that episode in Paris, a few short conversations, a glimpse or two into the past—and there is Sophy. Such a creation would amply excuse and redeem a much worse story than *The Reef*—a very bad title, by the way. Compton MacKenzie's Jenny in *Carnival* is able to stand beside Mrs. Wharton's Sophy without being cast into the shade of her vividness—but none of the other portraits of the modern young woman which the season's fiction supplies can do it.

The season's fiction is, nevertheless, full of such portraits. Even H. G. Wells's Ann Veronica, revived as Marjorie Pope, is dim beside Mrs. Wharton's young woman. To be sure, Mrs. Wharton has wisely confined her picture to one phase. Marjorie was vivid enough when she was changing cars at Tunbridge. "Marriage" faded her. A full life might have taken the color out of Sophy also; nay, must have done it. MacKenzie, we may remember, resorted to bloody and violent means to save Jenny. Nowhere is it truer than in fiction that those who would save their lives must lose them.

"Current Fiction," *Nation*, 95 (12 December 1912), 564

In his recent book on "Play-Making," Mr. William Archer has a chapter about "blind alley themes": themes from which there is no proper exit, problems of which "all possible solutions are equally unsatisfactory and undesirable." This does not mean simply that there is no way out through the door of stage convention, or that every conceivable exit is "unpleasant." It means, says Mr. Archer, that "there is no possible way out of them which is not worse than unpleasant: humiliating and distressing."

It is to the advantage of the dramatist that he must be on guard against such themes, that he must take care not to present life as a disheartening muddle. The novel, in its relatively fluid and indeterminate state, is as yet hardly conscious of this friendly inhibition. A novelist has, and ought to have, a freer hand than a playwright. It is his compensation for the want of that vivid and active contact with his audience which the playwright enjoys. But he may well bear in mind the caution addressed to dramatists by Mr. Archer: "The crimes of destiny there is some profit in contemplating; but its stupid vulgarities minister neither to profit nor delight."

Mrs. Wharton's chief failing is her addiction to themes of this type. The story of Lily Bart was not only disagreeable: it was depressing and humiliating. She was a victim of the stupid vulgarities of fate. The only way of releasing her from helpless and meaningless torment was the too easy way chosen by Mrs. Wharton, the way of death. It is not surprising that even the service of an expert playwright failed to make a successful play out of such material. Mrs. Wharton does not hesitate to make use of expedients which the stage is laughed at for tolerating. Lily's over-dose of chloral is one; an habitual employment of the "long arm of coincidence" is another. Miss Bart makes one visit to the rooms of Lawrence Selden, and is once lured to the house of Gus Trenor. Both times her departure is seen by acquaintances who happen to be passing the premises at the particular moment. The action of *The Reef* turns largely on a series of similar, carefully arranged contretemps.

But *The Reef*, even more clearly than *The House of Mirth*, is built upon a theme impossible of dramatic solution; and in this instance the novelist neither attempts a solution nor cuts the knot. The theme, stated baldly, is this: A still young man, on his way to belated tryst with the only woman he has ever wished to marry, gets a telegram that the meeting must be put off. No explanation is given, and he is about to turn back when chance throws him in contact with a pretty girl who seems to need his help. Both are alone and adrift, and the upshot is a ten days' amour in Paris. They part amicably. Some months later the original tryst is fulfilled, and the man finds installed in his true love's house, and about to marry her stepson, the girl of the Paris affair. This is intolerable: he makes a number of feeble attempts to get rid of the girl, but without avail. It is left for her to break her engagement with the stepson, because she loves the man, and clings to the memory of their brief relation—wants to "keep him all to herself." So she disappears—but not before the older woman has learned the whole truth. Then follow a series of scenes in which the man and the woman torture each other with extraordinary ingenuity. The woman is very modern—tense, quivering, always self-conscious, often hysterical. She decides to part with the man—and on the eve of parting gives herself to him so that she may for once "be to him all" that the hated girl had been. They do not part at the moment, there are a few more chapters of emotional backing and filling, and we leave them at that exercise—well content to leave them. It is clearly impossible that they should ever be happy together— or apart. The only figure which finds its

way, in a sense, out of the blind alley, is that of the girl—a figure at least braver and less forlorn than the rest. Stripped of the verbal felicities and subtleties, of the air of grave absorption in the human scene, of the elegances of social setting, which are Mrs. Wharton's familiar assets, the story is a paltry one, or nearly that.

"Uncharted," *Saturday Review* [England], 114 (21 December 1912), 773–4

In several well-remembered tales of youthful adventure there was a reef; we knew it as the point which the vessel must strike before a few members of the crew could land on the lonely island. To the sailors it had truly been hidden from sight, but to us it had a definite position which we could have marked on any chart. It would have been, in fact, the first thing to be set down on a map of our own making. Unfortunately, a study of Mrs. Wharton's novel gives no such sense of certainty, and in the end grave doubts are left as to the point at which the lives of certain of her characters struck the submerged rocks. To start with, she shows us one Darrow travelling to Paris, and in great dudgeon because his affair with Anna Leath is not going smoothly. On the way he meets Sophy Viner, a young woman who among several charms reckons those of being without money and, for all practical purposes, without friends. As her chief desire is to see life in a mild way and her outlook is not bounded by the convention, it follows in the most natural manner that they elect to stay at the same hotel while he acts as her guide and protector. Only when a wet day made it impossible for them to see any more of the sights of Paris did their relations depart from an unconventionally proper course. With Darrow's return to London the incident closed in an apparently tranquil manner. The couple make their next appearance at the house of Anna Leath, who is a widow with a step-son and a daughter, and to the latter of these Sophy has by some strange chance been appointed governess. Darrow in the meanwhile has made up his difference with Anna, whom he expects to marry shortly, and his dismay at finding her in company with the partner of his Paris adventure is considerable. Various questions of honour disturb his mind, but the final blow comes when Sophy's engagement to young Leath is announced, and, as neither of the transgressors feels capable of keeping up the deception for any length of time, a general confession follows, with results disastrous both to them and to the innocent parties.

The author has certainly shown considerable skill in presenting the mental states of the persons concerned, but the interest would be greater had they not reached their position by such haphazard means, for the tragedy upon which an open verdict must be returned is always unsatisfactory. In ancient Greece the way was always to lay the blame upon the gods; but with Shakespeare came the idea that sins are like birds which on their own wings come home to roost. Our quarrel with Mrs. Wharton is that though she gives us chapter after chapter of delightfully written prose, they contain no hint of her own theory of tragedy. Of course the whole imbroglio is started by yielding to temptation on a wet day in Paris, but neither materially nor mentally would either Darrow or Sophy have suffered for it had it not been for coincidences which we can only regard as amazing. Had the girl, for instance, obtained a post in any other family, or become engaged to any other nice boy, her career would have undoubtedly been highly successful, and there is not the smallest sign that her conscience would have troubled her or that her affection for her former lover would have ever played a part in her life except as a pleasant memory. Another treatment of the story might have shown that she came on the reef because she was wandering across France in a way dangerous to any young woman, but this would go no further towards explaining the unhappy chances which followed, and the author would therefore have done no better by adopting the modern economic theory of tragedy. In the end we are forced to think that the fates were excessively unkind and got in their blows with rare shrewdness, or, in other words, that a great deal of ingenuity has been expended on making a plot for the story. Of the author's masterly and merciless analysis of human temperaments we could say much, but the abnormal circumstances in which the characters are placed prevents the novel as a whole from making good a claim to serious consideration. Mrs. Wharton could do much better work than this, for she has style and understanding.

M. P. Willcocks, "A Tragedy of Four," *Bookman* [England], 43 (January 1913), 224–5

There are, they say, but five possible plots in the world: of these Mrs. Wharton has chosen in her latest novel perhaps the commonest of all. Yet this fact by no means detracts from the value of the story, for in her hands a *motif* taken from melodrama becomes a new thing. *The Reef* is at once a study in character contrast of the simplest kind and a revelation in spiritual tragedy of the subtlest. The subject is the contrast between apparent victory and actual defeat, for the woman who seemed to win is really the woman who lost, when laying her hand on substance she found but shadow. Incidentally, too, *The Reef* throws a searchlight on the basic difference between the way in which men and women view the ethics of love adventure.

George Darrow, on his way to Anna Leath, is irritated by a telegram putting off his visit without excuse. By the malice of that fate which waits on weak moments he falls in with Sophy Viner, one of the thousands of women who, with their backs to the wall, are fighting poverty with no weapon of education or professional training. Darrow gives the child what she has never had before—a good time, but emerges from the affair no longer an honourable man. He becomes so much the meaner while Sophy, shallow in brain but profound in instinct, learns from it a power of nobility and sacrifice which nothing else could have taught her. A year later, when his suit of Anna Leath is on the verge of success, he finds Sophy engaged to her stepson.

It is curious to note how Mrs. Wharton deals with a situation so full of irony as this. Where, for instance, Anatole France would have laid stress on the priggish hypocrisy of Darrow, the man who is actually shocked at seeing a woman contemplate the very course of action to which he has already committed himself, Mrs. Wharton is overcome with pity for the four people concerned: for the boy who adores a girl with no love to give him, for the woman so deceived, for the girl so perplexed and the man so harassed. The situation is grimly humorous, but Mrs. Wharton fails to see this apparently. Day after day these people skate over the thin ice of revelation till the facts leap to life

just because they are in the air, they cannot remain unknown. And although Sophy effaces herself, it is Anna who will always suffer, since between herself and Darrow at every simplest incident a mocking memory comes before her of the shadowy third. The final touch of satire is given when Darrow refuses to satisfy Anna's morbid curiosity, saying: "It would put something irremediable between us," when the something irremediable is already there to spoil their lives.

The colourlessness of Mrs. Wharton's style bleaches all comment from her pages: what remains therefore of satire is of the very stuff of the tale itself. Yet the work is unequal. Sophy and Anna live; never has the world-tossed wanderer, the smirched thing with a pure heart, been better done than in the former; never could a *grande dame* beating at the gates of life be more vivid than in the latter. But the lad Owen is a whirl of inexplicable hysteria; the man Darrow but an irritating enigma. Mrs. Wharton deals so delicately with these masculine nerves that their possessors remain but phantoms. Darrow would not have captured Anna, nor would he have held Sophy: he was not man enough to flutter the dovecotes in this fashion. It is, too, a defect in Mrs. Wharton's delicate cameo-work that her sentimental conflicts are so isolated from the workaday world. Her characters live in a vacuum. Darrow, for instance, is called a diplomat but actually he has no trade but that of philandering. To draw people so is to botanise without recognising the soil from which the plant grows.

Yet to carp thus is rather to gird at a style of novel-writing, for the works of the high-priest of this school, Mr. Henry James, exhibit exactly the same divorce between a drama and what must have been its inevitable setting, the buying and selling, the eating and drinking, all the activities of the market place, whether of

197

national or individual life. And if a good deal of the weird contrast of actuality is lost by this method of secluding a tragedy, at the same time it leaves more room for the subtle interplay of mind with mind which makes Mrs. Wharton's work so fascinating. We are here very near to the "psychic" drama of Maeterlinck, and within its strictly drawn boundaries *The Reef* is a very fine book.

Checklist of Additional Reviews

Régis Michaud, "Le Roman aux Etats-Unis," *Revue du Mois* [France], 15 (10 July 1913), 106–9.

THE CUSTOM OF THE COUNTRY

THE CUSTOM OF THE COUNTRY

BY

EDITH WHARTON

NEW YORK

CHARLES SCRIBNER'S SONS

MCMXIII

"The Custom of the Country," Nation, 96 (15 May 1913), 494

In her latest novel Mrs. Wharton is concerned with a type of American womanhood which might be described as one of the stock figures of the newer fiction, if it were not for the consideration that Mrs. Wharton's Undine Spragg is not a stock figure at all, but is very much alive. The fact that the spending American woman is always turning up in our literature must be taken as a sign that she is to be found in life. Robert Herrick is apparently of the opinion that there is no other kind of woman, if one is to judge from the way she haunts his books. His latest novel is concerned with very much the same type as Undine, allowing for geographical and minor social differences. The fierce determination to "get on" in society; the passion for enjoyment which is more correctly to be described as excitement; the utter lack of concern for the father or husband who finances the process of getting on; and the lack of interest in the sources from which the supporting male procures the sinews of war—these are familiar traits which do not grow stale through repetition. That men shall earn and women shall spend, without intruding upon each other's territory, is the custom of the country as Mrs. Wharton defines it. For the husband to confide his business troubles to his wife would be almost as odd as for the wife to make her husband a repository of her troubles with the dressmaker. It is a division of functions which we have apparently developed to an unrivalled state of perfection.

The custom of the country is, at first

sight, all the harder to explain when one considers that, as compared with the firmly established traditions of Europe, we are still a pioneer people. A generation ago we were a pioneer nation in a very real sense. The West, that region from which come the passionate pilgrims of "society" who make the Fifth Avenue shops very much what they are, was then coming under subjection to a race of hardworking Americans whose wives toiled quite as hard and spent quite as little as their husbands. The rigors of pioneer life fall more painfully upon the woman than upon the man. The unending household toil; the bearing of children, as children are born to-day in the new country of the Canadian West, where physicians are scarce and not particularly skilled; the rearing of children under conditions that would make the modern advocate of child-culture stand aghast, are part of the enormous task of motherhood in regions where man is still at close-grips with his environment. This was true of the pioneer in the Middle West, as it was true two centuries ago of New England, whose civilization was built up at an enormous expenditure of women's lives. Mere man, for all his natural arrogance, would be the last to deny the equal share taken by his women-folk in the conquest of a continent and the up-building of a nation.

If, after a generation, we find that there has been a marked change in the distribution of economic functions; if the daughters of the women who peopled and helped to take the West have assumed the exclusive function of spenders, leaving it to their brothers to carry on the business of wealth production, the reason is to be found in our rapid emergence from the pioneer stage. The function of distributing money is not altogether assumed by the American woman; it is conferred on her by the male as compensation for what she has suffered and achieved in the past.

201

The sense of protection, of chivalry—if one may use the term so hateful to the emancipated woman—has no opportunity to express itself when the struggle for existence is so bitter as to call for unremitting labor by every one in the family. When economic pressure relaxes it is natural that the women of the family should be the first to feel the relief. This sense of obligation for past services and past hardships may not be consciously present to the mind of the American man. He does not realize his motives so clearly as he does with regard to his children when he determines that they shall miss nothing of the good things of life which their parents had to go without. But unconsciously the same factor enters into his attitude to women. His son, after having his chance, is still to go on with the serious business of life. His daughter must simply have every chance with no questions asked.

That the American male has gone too far in the other direction is partly to be explained by the national temperament, partly by the very suddenness with which we have emerged from hardship into prosperity. If the climb had been more gradual the enjoyment of leisure might have been more evenly distributed. But it would be idle to overlook the inherent difference in faculty between men and women, and an equally apparent difference in adaptability. The aspirations for the softer, finer things of life are stronger in the female of the species. The advent of leisure gives more immediate freedom to feelings long repressed. If prosperity has produced women of the type of Undine Spragg, in her all selfish, unreasoning longing for enjoyment, it is also true that through the women of America such interest as we display in literature, in music, in art, makes itself largely manifest. Here is where their superior adaptability counts. Our men have been much slower in casting off the habits of a fuller life. To-day we are undoubtedly in the position of having placed woman on a pedestal and left her there lonely and rather dizzy.

"Critical Reviews of the Season's Latest Books," New York *Sun*, 18 October 1913, p. 8

The American society woman of today, with her puerile ambitions and her tenacity of purpose, is the subject of Edith Wharton's displeasure in *The Custom of the Country*. . . . She has been held up to scorn by a good many writers of fiction of late, both those who wish to preach and those who wish to depict or satirise the life of the society of wealth whose doings are chronicled in the newspapers. She provokes Mrs. Wharton into forgetting her art in the effort to be emphatic, and employing crude methods that are evidently as strange to her as to the readers of her books. These may well feel uncertain about the meaning of the title, whether it refers to the social conventions that stand in the way of her heroine or whether Mrs. Wharton applies it cynically to the American habit of letting women have their own way, and to the abuses of the divorce laws.

She has constructed an ideal monster, perfect in that at no time does she betray any human feeling, a model for other women who are pushing their way and a standard by which the people who are watching them may measure them. She has two valuable assets, her confidence in the power of her own beauty and the inflexible determination to have whatever she wants at once and at any cost, characteristics which to the male observer may

202

seem general to the sex, but which in this case are developed to an acute degree. She is ignorant; she is lacking in intelligence; she does not know enough to try to find out what the society she forces herself into is like or to acquire a superficial varnish of its manners; she is sexless, with no feeling for men, nor for her child, nor for her parents; she is recklessly extravagant with money, though she is not mercenary, but merely needs it to carry out her will, and to obtain it regards neither her own honor nor that of others[;] she is absolutely unmoral and has no sense of decency whether as regards the truth or the marriage relation, not to speak of the more delicate points in character or in the manners of respectable society. She manages to obtain her desire over and over again, only to discover, as many others have done, that what she really wants is something she has not got yet. In Mrs. Wharton's picture she never falters; the one hint of weakening is when she meets her male counterpart, who understands her, but she quickly and bravely gets over that. She is absolutely selfish, logical and repulsive.

To make a creature such as she is win her way in society calls for some dexterity, which Mrs. Wharton disdains to use. The minute details about New York ways in the old respectable set, in the boisterous world that the newspapers 'el' about, among those who aspire to enter it, cannot conceal the violence with which the heroine is plumped into society. Her intrusion into the Faubourg Saint Germain later is passed over with equal crudeness. The contrast between the husband's and the wife's impressions in the Italian honeymoon is a bit too tragic for humor or preciosity, and in the careful description of French family life the reader for the first time may feel some sympathy for the heroine and wonder why her husband married her at all. No detail of the vulgarity of the last alliance she enters into is passed over.

With a character such as Mrs. Wharton has drawn it is evident that we have to do with abstract types and not with live men and women; the reprehensible actions are so gross as hardly to need denunciation. For the other people are merely lay figures. It is interesting to see Mrs. Wharton emerge from her own sphere, but in this case there is a distinct loss of art, whatever effect her warning may have.

L.M.F., "Mrs. Wharton's Novel: *The Custom of the Country* a Book Which Will Excite Much Discussion," *New York Times Review of Books*, 19 October 1913, p. 557

"Why haven't we taught our women to take an interest in our work? Simply because we do not take enough interest in them. . . . It is normal for a man to work hard for a woman—what's abnormal is his not caring to tell her anything about it." So says one of the characters in Mrs. Wharton's new book, adding that "for an American to do such telling would be against the custom of the country"—a break in that system of unlimited, half-contemptuous indulgence, of lavishing one's fortune upon one's womenfolk, but withholding one's confidence, of which Undine Spragg is "a monstrously perfect result . . . the completest proof of its triumph."

If all this be true, then the more rapidly that system is changed the better, for Undine Spragg is the most repellent heroine we have encountered in many a long day—so "monstrous" that at times she seems scarcely human, yet so cleverly portrayed that she is always real. When we are introduced to her she is living in a hotel on the west side, whither she has induced her parents to remove from the house on West End Avenue they had bought on first coming to New York from Apex City some two years before. Already she has made tentative efforts at social advancement through Summers spent at various resorts. The account of those Summers when Undine acquired new standards, only to discover each time that they were subjects for ridicule to people a trifle higher up in the social scale, is the condensed history of many a "climber." But Undine had a determination to get what she wanted which was not easily to be balked; her father had made money—was, for Apex, a rich man—and both her parents considered that to gratify all her wishes was their only duty in life; therefore they obediently settled amid the gilded splendors of the Stentorian, where poor Mrs. Spragg's one companion was her masseuse. Undine, however, had a schoolfriend, Mabel Lipscomb, who promptly introduced her into her own "set." But these were not the people whom Undine, who had long and faithfully studied society columns of the Sunday papers, wanted to know. And it is when she is discontented, bitterly disappointed at her lack of social opportunities that there occurs the one incident in the book which seems strained to the requirements of the plot— she meets Ralph Marvell at a dance at the Stentorian. It is not merely because he is one of those old New Yorkers whose traditions centre about Washington Square that Marvell's coming to the Stentorian dance seems a trifle unnatural. Were he

represented as having the least taste for adventure, or unconventionality, or independence, his appearance there would be explicable enough. He is, however, an intensely conservative person, whose inherited ideas have weakened the fibre of his character rather than lent it even the brace of starch. His meeting with Undine once over, the rest follows naturally enough. Dazzled by his social position, she marries him despite his comparative poverty and speedily adapts herself to the society which had once seemed so hopelessly out of reach. But she is far from satisfied, and her attempts—usually successful—to get what she wants carry her through numerous episodes and several phases of social life.

The book resembles *The House of Mirth* in tone and atmosphere, but Undine Spragg is without any of Lily Bart's redeeming characteristics; she is merely greed personified—without conscience, heart, sense of honor, or sense of humor. She wants the best that can possibly be had in the way of luxury and position; scruples as to ways and means never enter her head. She is "respectable," and rather boasts of the fact, but when respectability seems to bar her from the fortune she desires she sacrifices it without an instant's hesitation or qualm. Her principal weakness lies in the lack of imagination, which makes it impossible for her to understand the aspect certain of her acts wear to other people, and this same deficiency renders her unable to calculate any save immediate consequences. Absence of imagination it is which brings her to the verge of social shipwreck, and her escape is due simply to a piece of good luck. Natural affection she has none; her parents' devotion she accepts as a matter of course, her child's birth she resents, and she is perfectly willing to resign the boy to his father's care until she discovers that she can use him as a means of extortion. Many men fall in love with her, for she is wonderfully beautiful, with a smile "like refracted sunlight," and sweet tempered so long as everything is going her way. They usually tire of her, however, because she has no intelligence; only an imitative faculty so strongly developed that soon she, who, when first invited to dine with Mrs. Fairford, came perilously near to writing her reply on the pigeon-blood note paper which "Boudoir Chat" had pronounced the latest thing, attained a social competence which obliged even Bowen to admire her skill in disposing of the companion she did not want. This imitative faculty sufficed for the entirely frivolous New York society in which she held a place during several years, but when she was transplanted to that of the Faubourg St. Germain it proved completely inadequate.

If Undine is repellent, it cannot be said that human nature as reflected in the pages of this novel is ever particularly attractive. The Marvells and Dagonets of Washington Square are mere ghosts of a narrow past, futile, bloodless, out of touch alike with the "Invaders" who have swarmed into and captured New York society, and with the people who are doing the real, worth-while work of the world. The possessors of certain aesthetic tastes and a fine sense of probity, but expert in "the vocabulary of evasion," shirkers to the very backbone, every one of them. The Van Degans and their kind, affiliated with those others by such bargain marriages as that of Clare, are materialists whose creed is eat, drink and be merry, whose religion is a frank worship of the Golden Calf. The French aristocrats are stronger through their sense of union, their ideal of "The Family." Raymond de Chelles, for all his limitations, wins a respect one cannot but deny Ralph Marvell. De Chelles had some power of the will; yet he, like Ralph, succumbs at last

before the brute force of money. Undine's father, Abner L. Spragg, is about the only really likable person in the book; his humorous tolerance of "a son-in-law who expected to be pensioned like a Grand Army veteran," his resistance to Elmer Moffatt, and his devotion to his wife and child make him an agreeable contrast to such men as Van Degan.

It is Elmer Moffatt, however, who next to Undine herself is the most impressive figure in this novel. Typical in many ways, he shows the human quality she lacks by his kindliness and his genuine love of beautiful things. There is something symbolic in his capture of the famous de Chelles tapestries. One feels the force of the man, even during his time of defeat. He has a bigness the other characters are nearly all without; his materialism, like his success, is on a huge scale. He sweeps much before him as he moves through the hothouse in which all the scenes of the story are laid.

To say that Mrs. Wharton has reproduced every faintest variation in the temperature of those hothouses with absolute exactness seems at this late day as unnecessary as is any reference to her flexible, perfectly finished style, of which each exquisite phrase is a separate delight. The atmosphere, the way in which every form, every flower grows she understands and describes with a quiet aloofness. But it is the hothouse, sometimes the forcing house, of which she tells in this latest novel; always the thermometer stands at fever heat, and fresh air is a thing unknown. One feels a strong desire to break the glass and let in a little wind and rain, even though they might destroy such delicate exotics as Mrs. Fairford.

The Custom of the Country is a book which will arouse some dissension and much discussion, for it is a criticism of certain phases of life which by their blatancy attract a great deal of attention. The theme of the spoilt, utterly selfish woman is of course no new one, but it has rarely been developed in a manner so skillful, so delicate, and so completely ruthless.

H[enry] W. B[oynton], "Mrs. Wharton's Manner," *Nation*, 97 (30 October 1913), 404–5

Mrs. Wharton's early successes as a writer of short stories were not the chance successes of a tyro. She had already served her apprenticeship, without making the public pay for the crude products of that trying phase of experience. She had learned what she wanted to do, and how to do it. She could take a situation or an episode involving two or three human figures, and wring the truth from it—the truth as she personally saw it. She could drive home her interpretation with witty phrase and epigram. She could make people "sit up," without the use of vulgar stimulants. If there was one quality which pleased her audience more than her brilliancy, it was her breeding. A final zest was given to the enjoyment of her style by the sense that it was gentlemanlike. That sense was misleading, of course, for she has always been strongly feminine; but it is possible for a voice a trifle deeper than common, a gesture somewhat more frank, to enhance the charm of femininity by its hint of contradiction.

But beneath the suavity and self-possession of her manner there has always been a restless spirit, and the time passed soon when the exercise of wit and adroitness could soothe it. She had, besides, the resource of the study, and the richest of art. Turning from the short story to the novel, she called them to her aid. She

ranged herself in that school of sophistication, of finesse, half-lights, and rich, dim accessories, which was then ascendant. She knew her Meredith, her James, her Howells, and the greater masters of France— Bourget, Stendhal, and the rest. She wished to address herself to no vulgar audience. The very titles of those earlier books, *The Greater Inclination, Crucial Instances, The Valley of Decision*, were a snub to the populace and a challenge to the fastidious. The populace does not deal in comparatives, *nuances*, reservations, compunctions.

There lies, however, between the reading masses and the small choir of the elect, a surprising body of persons, chiefly feminine, who aspire to sophistication and connoisseurship. The aspiration, as applied to literature, was more fashionable ten years ago than now, perhaps. Certainly a good many readers who aspired in that way were attracted to Mrs. Wharton's earlier novels. To wander through the pages of *The Valley of Decision*, for example, was to breathe an atmosphere of polite and erudite adventure, in lands where life had become a finished thing long before American crudity began. It was not a very good story as a story; but the charm of its style, of its leisurely winding along paths of old-world glamour, was indubitable. There was something else—the occurrence here and there of an episode vivid and telling, the work not of the gentleman and scholar and agreeable cicerone, under whose guidance we seemed, for the most part, to be quietly progressing, but of Mrs. Wharton, the story-teller.

Looking back, from this remove, we suspect that those episodes, so incidentally and even negligently vouchsafed, were the most genuine part of the book: the rest, a brilliant *tour de force*. Its very elegance, its languor, its abstentions from display of wit or from excess of any sort,

206

mark it as a feat. For Mrs. Wharton is not a gentleman or a reflective philosopher. She is a nervous, cultivated American woman, an extremely clever performer on one of the favorite instruments of the hour: a virtuoso, but in the popular sense of the word. And she has been too clever not to find her way instinctively to the larger audience which was ready for her.

With *The House of Mirth* she captured it. Here, almost in the flesh, was that society to which striving America looks up with delighted consternation. Here was a story of the "Four Hundred" written from the inside, a moving picture of high life. It could have been the work of no one but Mrs. Wharton, and yet was plainly the work of another than the Mrs. Wharton of "The Dilettante" or *The Valley of Decision*. Both her wit and her erudition were now under better control. She no longer sparkled for the sake of sparkling, or alluded for the sake of allusion. In fact, she must have had a pretty clear notion of the audience she was addressing and of its needs.

It was not an altogether different audience from her older one; but it was wider, more various. The novelist, like the playwright, must, if he expects to command a satisfactory hearing, appeal, in some sense, to the mass as an individual. What Mr. A. B. Walkley has said of the theatre audience applies, roughly to what may be called the magazine audience. The element of physical contact and contagion is lacking; but the constituency of the newsstands does somehow pull together as one man. "A crowd," Mr. Walkley says, "forms a new entity, with a mind and character of its own; it differs from the individuals composing it, just as our bodies are unlike the cells of which they are made up, or just as a chemical combination is unlike its separate ingredients."

Before *The House of Mirth* Mrs. Wharton had not set herself seriously to the task of captivating the magazine audience. She had tickled its ears with her clever wisps of satire and badinage. She had gone over its head entirely with *The Valley of Decision*, and the books on Italy which followed. Now, at one stroke, she succeeded in rousing it to excited attention with the *House of Mirth*. Not that Mrs. Wharton abased herself to the magazine manner. Her style was as finished and urbane as ever. But at last its refinement was felt to be in keeping with the theme. Here, in elegant black and white, were the superior beings to whom democracy had hitherto been able to award only the humbler tributes of the society column and *Town Topics*.

The tale of Lily Bart could have been justified only as lifted to the plane of tragedy. In Mrs. Wharton's hands, adroit as they are, it remained sordid and vulgar. Something might have been done with it in the way of uncompromising realism; so, at least, a negative force and meaning might have been given to it. But in attempting to employ the machinery of tragic romance, Mrs. Wharton attempted the impossible. Lily is not a tragic figure, but a feeble and paltry one. Such glamour as she has is the meretricious glamour of social position; and this is true of all her "set."

Perhaps Mrs. Wharton felt the irony of Lily's fame. No doubt she was annoyed by the persistent attempts to give a local habitation and a name to each of her imaginary figures of New York. That was her penalty for not having made them also imaginative. At all events, in *Madame de Treymes* she withdrew to a safer and sounder field. Here, as in *Sanctuary*, she challenged the closest comparison with Miss Anne Douglas Sedgwick (who, then irreproachable, has since gained popularity with *Tante*). A delicate study of old-world life on a comparatively small scale, *Madame de Treymes* went its quiet way.

But in *The Fruit of the Tree* Mrs. Wharton again made, to speak coarsely, a hit. It was not precisely the same kind of hit as that which she had scored in *The House of Mirth*. It lacked two elements of popular appeal which had counted in the earlier novel. It did not paint the society of our dreams—that of New York and environs—and it did not turn upon a problem of sex. But there was a problem—and it interested the public because it was a problem which everybody has attacked, however casually, and nobody has solved: is it right, under any circumstance, to put a human being "out of misery"? Unluckily, this is even less approachably a "well-made" novel than *The House of Mirth*. Its six hundred odd pages contain material for two distinct novels—or perhaps we should say for a dozen short stories. And, as in *The House of Mirth*, its material was presented with nothing more than cleverness—without the transforming touch of imagination.

In *The Custom of the Country*, we are told, Mrs. Wharton has returned to the field of *The House of Mirth*. We do not find this to be literally true. The heroine of this story is not a Lily Bart, but an Undine Spragg, of Apex City, Arizona [Indiana]. We find her in New York, to be sure, bent upon breaking in among the best people. In fact, when we meet her she has been there two years, with her attendant parents, and has not yet broken in. But she is on the eve of it. In a Bohemian circle to which she has penetrated, she meets a fashionable portrait-painter, Claud Walsingham Popple, and is much impressed with his fine presence and manners. Through him she meets, and is not impressed by, a real scion of the aristocracy, Ralph Marvell. He at once, without another excuse than her crude young beauty, falls in love with her; and as soon as she realizes that he is "the real thing," she succumbs.

Now, Undine Spragg is not a new type. We have met her recently in many novels—in Mr. Herrick's *One Woman's Life*, in Mr. Dreiser, in the recent *Joan Thursday* of Mr. Louis Joseph Vance; in fact, wherever among our novelists realism continues to rear its head. She is the daughter of the plain people, forging towards success and happiness in the fashionable sense of the term. The thing that is hard to pardon in her is that she appears a caricature instead of a refinement of that type. Undine Spragg is as hard, as vulgar, as calculating, as selfish as any professional daughter of pleasure could be. That she is physically cold does not prevent her being twice divorced in pursuit of the main chance, and finally falling back upon her first husband because he is not only a multimillionaire, but the only person who understands her. They are unmistakably a pair.

There is nothing to attach the deeper sympathies of the reader to this person or to any other in the book. Paul [Ralph] Marvell, who dies by his own hand, is well out of it, and that is all we feel; with his elegance and sensitiveness, he shows the futility that besets most of Mrs. Wharton's finer-grained male Americana. The Count de Trézac [de Chelles], who succeeds him, is of similar type, except for the fact that "the custom of the country," with him, makes the family of more importance than the wife, and so stiffens his backbone against her encroachments. Most of the other figures in the book are caricatured, from the masseuse and manicure artist, Mrs. Heeny, to the unspeakable Van Degen.

With all its amenity of manner, *The Custom of the Country* has a sharply satirical tone. The heroine is a mere monster of vulgarity; and Mrs. Wharton seems to feel a ruthless satisfaction in exposing her in all her enormity. The result is a defeat of what should have been the main purpose, to interest us in the Spragg. A caricature does not remain interesting to the length of six hundred pages. And there is no use trying to convey on paper the charm of a physical beauty which has no backing in mind or character. The mood of satire seems to be growing upon Mrs. Wharton, a dubious sign in a writer who has passed a certain age. It is hard to feel that, clever and effective and varied as her work has been, and is, she has ever yet veritably "found herself"—the self of assured power which seemed to exist potentially in her first books. Ten years ago, a stranger asking an American who was the most distinguished of our novelists would very likely have heard the name of Mrs. Wharton. It is not altogether due to the fact that other (potential) giants have arisen among us, that the answer would now hardly be the same.

"Fiction," Athenæum [England], 4490 (15 November 1913), 554

The modern American young woman, with her wondrous self-assurance, her arrogance towards the male creatures who support her, and her physical perfections, has often been portrayed in fiction; but it has been left to Mrs. Wharton to expound her whole significance. In The Custom of the Country we are introduced to a state of society as chaotic, crude, and purely imitative as that of Hayti or Liberia, but full of force, and held together by a curious patriotism. From this strange soil there rises like a flower Undine Spragg, whose history is the subject of the book.

The daughter of a leading citizen of Apex, Undine was engaged while yet a child to a young dentist of that city, and ran away about the same time with one Elmer Moffatt, an adventurer, whom she married and divorced in a fortnight. All this was no more detrimental to her maiden pride than water on a duck's back. She had quite forgotten the adventure by the time her parents, on a rise of fortune, moved to New York to a splendid suite in the Stentorian Hotel. She married into one of the best, old-fashioned New York families, not mentioning her previous marriage and divorce; but the real aristocracy of her new relatives soon disgusted her. Attracted by the vulgar splendour of some millionaires, she made decided overtures to one of them, forsook her child, divorced her husband, but for once miscalculated. The millionaire, for reasons of his own, declined to marry her, and she retired to Paris in a state of temporary disillusionment. Reviving presently, she married a French count, and in the course of time divorced him, when she finally joined hands with the same Elmer Moffatt—now a multi-millionaire—with whom she had eloped from Apex City in her teens.

It is, of course, a monstrous record from the sentimental standpoint. But Mrs. Wharton, by avoiding the least hint of sentiment, and laying stress upon the sequence of environment, upbringing, character, has made her heroine a natural and pathetic figure. She succeeds in winning for a cold and selfish character the kindly sympathy which comes of understanding—an achievement of which any novelist might well be proud. Undine Spragg is always striving for the best obtainable, as she conceives it; it is her misfortune that her aims are all material and egotistic. No sooner has she attained a social height than her mind's eye discerns another yet more radiant and desirable. This explains her strange inconstancy in the married state. She has no scruples, fails to see how any one on earth can justly blame her for discarding men who do not give her everything she wants with the readiness her father showed. For Abner E. Spragg, whose "private rule of conduct was as simple as his business morality was complicated," and whose lips were often "busy with a phantom toothpick," had served her will at home.

> "'Why haven't we taught our women to take an interest in our work?' [inquires a cynical observer in the book.] 'Simply because we don't take enough interest in *them*. ... The slaving is no argument against the indifference. To slave for women is part of the old American tradition; lots of people give their lives for dogmas they've ceased to believe in. Then again, in this country the passion for making money has preceded the knowing how to spend it, and the American man lavishes his fortune on his wife because he does not know what else to do with it. ... Where does the real life of most American men lie? In some woman's drawing-room or in their offices?'"

The passage is suggestive of a curious parallel between the freest of all women and Circassian pets.

When (on the last page of the book) Undine learnt that, as a woman who had been divorced, she could not hope to be Ambassadress in London,

> "she burst into an angry laugh, and the blood flamed up into her face. 'I never heard of anything so insulting!' she cried, as if the rule had been invented to humiliate her."

The cry rings truly of the spoilt *Circassian*.

Mrs. Wharton's latest work is no mere entertaining story. It is a courageous and at the same time sympathetic study of Americans.

"Novels," *Saturday Review* [England], 116 (22 November 1913), 658–9

Mrs. Wharton has assembled as many detestable people as it is possible to pack between the covers of a six-hundred-page novel. It is a sordid society into which we are introduced—a set of vulgar Americans, blatant and pushing, whose only standard of values is the dollar.

Undine, the daughter of Mr. and Mrs. Spragg, named after a patent hair-curler which had founded the fortune of the family, is the pivot on which the novel turns. She may be regarded as symbolic of a certain type of American woman whom Mrs. Wharton desires to hold up to scorn and reprobation. She has not a single redeeming moral feature. Cold, greedy, heartless, and wayward, without a soul and with no realisation of anything but the outward glitter and tinsel of life, she has only one passion, and that is for endless amusement. To achieve this everybody and everything must be sacrificed. She exploits her beauty to this end most successfully, and has a constant relay of husbands, whom she discards one by one without a pang as soon as they begin to be tiresome or to resist her craving for pleasure. Her first marriage, made entirely for position—her husband belonging to one of the "old families" ruling New York—turns out a failure as soon as she realises that "she had given herself to the exclusive and the dowdy when the future belonged to the showy and promiscuous;

that she was in the case of those who have cast in their lot with a fallen cause, or who have hired an opera box on the wrong night".

But even in the light of this experience her subsequent matrimonial adventures do not turn out successful. As the wife of the Marquis de Chelles she discovered the incompatibility of temperament between a Frenchman and an American woman. She failed to understand his reluctance to sell up his ancestral home, tapestries, and furniture to minister to her extravagance and to supply her with the luxuries that had become so necessary for her. "I understand", she cried, "that you care for all this old stuff more than you do for me, and that you'd rather see me miserable than touch one of your great-grandfather's armchairs".

So once more "the custom of the country"—the divorce court—is brought into play, and it would seem that Undine's idea of bliss had at last been realised when she finds herself the wife of one of her girlhood's lovers, Elmer Moffatt, then ineligible, but now a billionaire. And now for the first time she is forced to learn that divorce has its drawbacks. She wishes her husband to be Ambassador in England, but Elmer has to assure her "they won't have divorced ambassadresses". And she felt it was the one part in life she was really made for.

"I want", says one of the characters in the book, "to get a general view of the whole problem of American marriages". "If that's what you want", is the reply, "you must make haste! Most of them don't last long enough to be classified."

Mrs. Wharton's book gives us that general view of American marriages. It is a scathing exposure of the scandals of divorce and of the mean standards of a certain section of American society. Brilliantly written, it should be read as a parable.

Frederic Taber Cooper, "The Custom of the Country," Bookman 38 (December 1913), 416–17

Three husbands seem to be the customary allowance granted by novelists to the pushing, climbing, heartless type of American woman, who will sacrifice everything to her social ambitions and insatiable love of pleasure. Three husbands, it will be remembered, were given by Robert Grant to Selma White, the heroine of *Unleavened Bread*; three also by Winston Churchill to the heroine of *A Modern Chronicle*; and similarly, Mrs. Wharton is equally generous to Undine Spragg, the central figure of her latest volume, *The Custom of the Country*. It is a brilliantly cynical picture of feminine ruthlessness, and a fundamental inability to conceive of father, mother, friends and husbands having been created for any other purpose than to gratify every passing whim of this one beautiful and utterly spoiled young woman. Mrs. Wharton has painted Undine Spragg with an unsparing mercilessness that almost makes the reader wince. It is a splendid and memorable piece of work, a portrait to form a worthy contrast to the equally unforgettable one of Lily Bart. But there is little object in analysing in detail the separate episodes which make Miss Spragg successively Mrs. Ralph Marvell, the Marquise de Chelles, and Mrs. Elmer Moffatt. They are of a nature that cannot be adequately conveyed at second hand; it is not what happens that matters, it is the play of human motives and human limitations behind the happenings that makes this volume one of Mrs. Wharton's finest achievements. And the final touch of the closing paragraph is a perfect climax, a crowning touch of comprehension of monumental and perennial dissatisfaction. . . .

F. M. Colby, "The Book of the Month," *North American Review*, 199 (February 1914), 294–9

A Sunday paper that I have just now been reading quotes in an apologetic and rather startled manner a Frenchman's comment on international marriages. The Frenchman, in bitter words, lays all the blame or the failure of these matings on the American wives, who, he says, are cold, indifferent, impertinent, aggressive, lacking in grace, reserve, and modesty, incapable of self-sacrifice, having no interest in their husband's affairs, restless, and ever seeking the new, the extravagant, and the morbid. While in France marriage is, he declares, a union of two sympathetic persons, a union of two interests, in America, where every one harps on equality, the husband finds no reciprocity in the matter of personal liberty. So when an American girl captures some prince, duke, marquis, count, or baron, by methods resembling "red Indian stratagem," she expects of him flattery, indulgence, and freedom, but on her part recognizes no duties at all toward him. "She cannot adapt herself to the equality existing in European families, to the community of life and interests." Considering the ferocity of foreigners on this subject any time these past ten years, it seems odd to find the thing run in with the news of the day.

The Marquis de Chelles in Mrs. Wharton's new novel expresses this point of view less clumsily, when, turning angrily on his young American wife, he refuses to sell the ancestral tapestries:

"Ah, that's your answer—that's all you feel when you lay hands on things that are sacred to us!" He stopped a moment, and then let his voice break out with the volume she had felt to be gathering. "And you're all alike," he exclaimed, "every one of you. You come from a country we don't know, and can't imagine, a country you care for so little that before you've been a day in ours you've forgotten the very house you were born in—if it wasn't torn down before you knew it! You come among us speaking our language and not knowing what we mean; wanting the things we want, and not knowing why we want them; aping our weaknesses, exaggerating our follies, ignoring or ridiculing all we care about—you come from hotels as big as towns, and from towns as flimsy as paper, where the streets haven't time to be named, and the buildings are demolished before they're dry, and the people are as proud of changing as we are of holding to what we have—and we're fools enough to imagine that because you copy our ways and pick up our slang you understand anything about the things that make life decent and honorable for us!"

Who but a Sunday editor, undoubtedly the most easily startled of human beings, could feel the least surprise at this steady damnation of the American wife, whether by foreign observer or by native novelist? Take, for example, the British weekly magazines. Years ago they formed the habit of exposing her and they would no more dream of leaving off now than of omitting the article on "What the Birds Are Doing in Devonshire." Time and again they have burst out upon the American woman all at once, as when one Dr. Andrew McPnail, some three years ago, called her a Hanoverian rat, a San José scale, a noxious weed, a jade, a giantess, and a potato-bug, and was immediately copied approvingly by the other British magazines, and widely quoted on the Continent. He said she was sterile and would soon die out; also that she was a monstrous and unwholesome growth sure to overspread and kill the rest of the species; and in spite of the apparent conflict in the terms, everybody seemed pleased with the sentiment. Indeed, the very words "American wife" have become to many foreigners proverbial, and, it is said, they take the figure on Bedloes Island for a symbol of American woman hood—the colossus of some splendid divorcée who had neglected many husbands and got on in the world—instead of Liberty Enlightening it. As to our native fiction, its figure of the bad American wife, or woman in her social ascension, seems hardly less monumental and fixed.

Mrs. Wharton's Undine Spragg is a creature of great beauty and much natural ability, with a wonderful nose for social distinctions. Her life is, for the most part, a series of little upward movements out of the "wrong set" into the right one. As a child in the yellow "frame" cottage of Apex City she yearned for gentility, and she continued to yearn for it, even after the family was installed in the plush parlors of the Mealey House. At each stage she soon perceived that there was something better still beyond and she resolutely sought it, dragging her parents from third-rate to second-rate hotels, and rising from "buggy-rides" with a dentist's assistant to an affair with a riding-master who said he

was an exiled nobleman. She discovered that he was not, and profited from the lesson. She profited, indeed, from every social lesson, especially from one imparted to her by her mother's *masseuse*, the friendly Mrs. Heeny, who was an authority on New York's best society. "The wrong set," said Mrs. Heeny, "is like fly-paper; once you are in it you can pull and pull, but you'll never get out of it again." This was after Undine was fairly launched, in a private drawing-room of the Hotel Stentorian in New York, whither her parents, now prosperous, had brought her in order that she might have "her chance." The walls were hung with salmon-pink damask, and in the center of the room was a gilt table with an onyx top, bearing a palm in a gilt basket and a copy of *The Hound of the Baskervilles*. Here for the moment she was happy, but she soon saw that it was not "the thing."

The consummate reviewer would no doubt point out many striking analogies, and I wish my memory were not so bad. But I am sure that her pedigree runs back to Mrs. Potiphar, and that forebears may be found in the writings of Charles Dudley Warner and Mrs. Burton Harrison, and that she is related to Selma White, and to the heroine of *The Breadwinners*, and to the young woman that Mr. Robert Herrick published last spring, and to the young woman in Helen Huntington's *Marshlights*, published last autumn. Not to imply that she is a compilation, a thing of literary shreds and patches, for, on the contrary, she is uncommonly wellknit. I refer merely to the persistency of the type, the grip on our fiction of this same climbing woman, who rises from rag carpets to ormolu in the eighteen-sixties and from ingrain carpets to marble suites in 1913, and from ordinary becomes important, and from important becomes *chic*, and leaves behind her, oh! such a devastated trail of sad and outgrown things—red table-cloths, little homes with "Welcome" on the door-mat, flats without a bell-boy, flats with, *fiancés* in every stratum, beginning, of course, with the buggy-riding era, gas logs, good souls in linen dusters, the broken father, the friend who might have helped her, the sensitive child, and the financially ascending series of husbands. For it is graved on the tablets of literary destiny that she who with cold heart deserts the ranks where gum is chewed shall soon desert a husband in a fur-lined overcoat, and from that point on the cruel anabasis into best society is predeterminate, and she goes to the devil like clockwork. Now the gods and graces have been kind to Mrs. Wharton, who can always renovate a stale matter or see a familiar object with fresh eyes, but for the others there is the danger that in their treatment of this climbing woman they may fall into a sort of ritual. For her lines are hardening every year, and since minor fiction lives on itself in strange autophagy, she already seems an allegory bearing a moral lesson and nothing else, like Death or Satan in a mystery, or like some figure in a revel, which at the moment of entrance is grasped by the mind once and for all time—*adventavit asinus fortis et pulcherrimus*—and so an end to surprises and to all the fun of guessing.

By a stroke of fortune Undine Spragg was swept to the very summit of New York gentility through her marriage to Ralph Marvell, the flower of Washington Square aristocracy. There is an admirable description of the Marvells and their connections, who represent New York's waning *noblesse*:

Ralph sometimes called his mother and grandfather the Aborigines, and likened them to those vanishing denizens of the American continent doomed to rapid extinction with the advance of the invading race. He was fond of describing Washington Square as the "Reservation," and of prophesying that before long its inhabitants would be exhibited at ethnological shows, pathetically engaged in the exercise of their primitive industries.

Small, cautious, middle-class, had been the ideals of aboriginal New York; but it suddenly struck the young man that they were singularly coherent and respectable as contrasted with the chaos of indiscriminate appetites which made up its modern tendencies. He, too, had wanted to be "modern," had revolted, half-humorously, against the restrictions and exclusions of the old code; and it must have been by one of the ironic reversions of heredity that, at this precise point, he began to see what there was to be said on the other side—*his* side, as he felt it now to be.

Undine found these people "frumpy" and was soon absorbed in the brilliant "Van Degen set," which is described with many caustic touches. In dealing with these mental unfortunates Mrs. Wharton differentiates the types most cleverly while keeping the even tenor of her contempt.

It is wonderful how in a word or two she can call to the mind a type or extinguish a pretension or present a complete picture to the eye. Disagreeable persons are never condemned or brought obviously to ridicule by Mrs. Wharton. They are in a delicate phrase or two artistically snubbed. For example, the "lovely, aimless" Mrs. Beringer, who kept "a home for stray opinions and could never quite tell them apart"; Mr. Popple, the painter, whose portraits were "not pictures of Mrs. or Miss So-and-so, but simply of the impression Popple thinks he's made on them"; and "the Harvey Shallums, fresh

214

from Paris, and dragging in their wake a bewildered nobleman vaguely designated as 'the Count,' who offered cautious conversational openings, like an explorer trying beads on savages." To the extinguishment of the above-mentioned Mr. Popple she devotes more space.

Mr. Popple, like all great men, had at first had his ups and downs; but his reputation had been permanently established by the verdict of a wealthy patron who, returning from an excursion into other fields of portraiture, had given it as the final fruit of his experience that Popple was the only man who could "do pearls." To sitters for whom this was of the first consequence it was another of the artist's merits that he always subordinated art to elegance, in life as well as in his portraits. . . . Mr. Popple, in fact, held that the personality of the artist should at all times be dissembled behind that of the man. It was his opinion that the essence of good breeding lay in tossing off a picture as easily as you lit a cigarette. Ralph Marvell had once said of him that when he began a portrait he always turned back his cuffs and said, "Ladies and gentlemen, you can see there's absolutely nothing here." He was, moreover, as literary as he was artistic; possessing an unequaled acquaintance with contemporary fiction, and dipping even into the lighter type of memoirs, in which the old acquaintances of history are served up in the disguise of *A Royal Sorceress, or Passion in a Palace.* The mastery with which Mr. Popple discussed the novel of the day, especially in relation to the sensibilities of its hero and heroine, gave Undine a sense of intellectual activity which contrasted strikingly with Marvell's flippant estimate of such works. "Passion," the artist implied, would have been the dominant note of his life, had it not been held in check by a sentiment of exalted chivalry, and by the sense that a nature of such emotional intensity as his must always be "ridden on the curb."

Back and forth between Paris and New York, with an occasional visit to Dakota, when husbands must be dropped, Undine speeds ruthlessly along, driven by the few simple appetites with which the author has endowed her. Ralph, the Washington Square husband, commits suicide, being of that fragile and poetic mold which in fiction at least usually dies of wrong petticoat. De Chelles, the French aristocrat, is of tougher fiber, and survives. The third and final husband is the coarse-grained, self-made man, now become a great figure in the world of finance, whom in her girlhood she had secretly married. But it is ungrateful to telescope into a summary a book which so plainly owes its interest not to the ins and outs of circumstance or to the development of character, but to what Henry James calls the "social scene." It is astonishing that reviewers should be complaining that Mrs. Wharton is not "sympathetic" with the characters, that her revelations are "hard and cruel," that only the weaker sort of person described by her has any "heart," etc. She has written books in other moods. Why blame her for not being all things at once, and for not throwing in something at intervals to reassure us that, after all, human nature is a lovely thing? Surely it is permissible to survey a few groups of miscellaneous New-Yorkers in a spirit, say, of cool inquiry, without yearning to clasp a single member of them to one's bosom. It does not seem to me that this is cynicism. It seems rather a measure of mental hygiene. And I for one have found myself disliking almost everybody in the volume and yet reading with great pleasure every word of it—rather a grim pleasure, to be sure, and not so keen as that afforded by her work in other fields.

And I like this reduction of our showy social mess to its rather meager simplicities, and the picture of New York, not as a metropolis, but as a village gone into hypertrophy, with its trades-people turned wholesale and socially important, and furriers, tobacconists, jewelers, and carpetmen, all wonderfully swollen into newspaper notables, while some genuine Napoleon of green vegetables is unaccountably left out, and its queer, loud, unaccustomed gentilities, and its fearful anxieties of taste. I am told that many corner grocer under a magnifying-glass looks exactly like a great financier—just as a flea looks like a dinosaur seen through the microscope. In Mrs. Wharton's gentry of Manhattan we see the gentry of her Apex City, unchanged in texture, but, by accident of wealth, rather ridiculously distended.

Review of *The Custom of the Country*, *Bookman* [England], 45 (March 1914), 330

The heroine of this American tale is a much-married person. Undine Spragg finally weds a man to whom, as a girl, she had been married clandestinely, and from whom she had been separated forcibly by her parents. Then the second husband came on the scene. Marriage for him turns out to be a tragedy; he commits suicide, when Undine deserts him. A French nobleman is the lady's next husband, and finally, Mr. Moffatt, who is now a wealthy man. Mrs. Wharton's irony calls this rapid mating the custom of her country, but she is too fine an artist to exaggerate the point. One of the notable features in her novel is the artistic restraint she has shown, on two occasions. She depicts the troubles inflicted by this divorce custom upon the child, but the pathos is not over-drawn. Again, she draws with admirable skill the parents of Undine, people who have made money rapidly, and come to New York in order to let their daughter get into society; the description of Mrs. Spragg's loneliness in the New York hotel, of her pathetic isolation and helplessness, is one of the best things in the story. But it is written without over-colouring. Mrs. Wharton uses these scenes and situations in order to bring out the character of her heroine, and the characterisation is subtle, clever, and convincing. It is an unlovely plot. Mrs. Wharton does not conceal the inner misery of a woman who is inferior to all the men she marries, thanks to her greedy love of pleasure. But no moral is drawn. The story is left to tell its own warning. It is this which makes it effective. There is less bitterness than in *The House of Mirth*, though the situation is practically the same; but the subordination of the satire to the artistic construction of the tale is equally prominent. Hardly any of Mrs. Wharton's recent novels displays quite such unity and penetration as this incisive study of the modern American woman of fashion.

216

Henry James,
"The Younger Generation,"
Times Literary
Supplement [England],
2 April 1914, 157–8

The exception we speak of would be *The Custom of the Country*, in which, as in Mrs. Wharton's other fictions, we recognize the happy fact of an abuse of no one of the resources it enjoys at the expense of the others; the whole series offering as general an example of dialogue flowering and not weeding, illustrational and not itself starved of illustration, or starved of referability and association, which is the same thing, as meets the eye in any glance which leaves Mr. Wells at Mr. Wells's best-inspired hour out of our account. The truth is, however, that Mrs. Wharton is herself here out of our account, even as we have easily recognized Mr. Galsworthy and Mr. Maurice Hewlett to be; these three authors, with whatever differences between them, remaining essentially votaries of selection and intention and being embodiments thereby, in each case, of some state over and above that simple state of possession of much evidence, that confused conception of what the "slice" of life must consist of, which forms the text of our remarks.

Mrs. Wharton, *her* conception of the "slice" so clarified and cultivated, would herself of course form a text in quite another connexion, as Mr. Hewlett and Mr. Galsworthy would do each in his own, which we abstain from specifying; but there are two or three grounds on which the author of *Ethan Frome, The Valley of Decision* and *The House of Mirth*, whom we brush by with reluctance, would point the moral of the treasure of amusement

sitting in the lap of method with a felicity peculiarly her own. If one of these is that she, too, has clearly a saturation—which it would be ever so interesting to determine and appreciate—we have it from her not in the crude state but in the extract, the extract that makes all the difference for our sense of an artistic economy, the thing in the world surely on which our richest amusement most depends. If the extract, as would appear, is the result of an artistic economy, as the latter is its logical motive, so we find it associated in Mrs. Wharton with such appeals to our interest, for instance, as the fact that, absolutely sole among our students of this form, she suffers, she even encourages, her expression to flower into some sharp image or figure of her thought when that will make the thought more finely touch us. Her step, without straying, encounters the living analogy, which she gathers, in passing, without awkwardness of pause, and which the page then carries on its breast as a trophy plucked by a happy adventurous dash, a token of spirit and temper as well as a proof of vision. We note it as one of the *kinds* of proof of vision that most fail us in that comparative desert of the inselective where our imagination has itself to hunt out or call down (often among strange witnessed flounderings or sand-storms) such analogies as may mercifully, which is a little more vividly, "put" the thing.

Mrs. Wharton not only owes to her cultivated art of putting it the distinction enjoyed when some ideal of expression has the *whole* of the case, the case once made its concern, in charge, but might further act for us, were we to follow up her exhibition, as lighting not a little that question of tone, the author's own intrinsic, as to which we have just seen Mr. Conrad's late production rather tend to darken counsel. *The Custom of the Country* is an eminent instance of the sort of tonic value most opposed to that baffled relation between the subject-matter and its emergence which we find constituted by the circumvallations of "*Chance.*" Mrs. Wharton's reaction in presence of the aspects of life hitherto, it would seem, mainly exposed to her is for the most part the ironic; to which we gather these particular aspects to have so much ministered that were we to pursue the quest we might recognize in them precisely the saturation as to which we a moment ago reserved our judgment. *The Custom of the Country* is at any rate consistently, almost scientifically satiric, as indeed the satiric light was doubtless the only one in which the elements could at all be focussed together. But this happens directly to the profit of something that, as we read, becomes more and more one with the principle of authority at work; the light that gathers is a dry light, of great intensity, and the effect, if not rather the very essence, of its dryness is a particular fine asperity. The usual "creative" conditions and associations, as we have elsewhere languished among them, are, thanks to this, ever so sensibly altered; the general authoritative relation attested becomes clear; we move in an air purged at a stroke of the old sentimental and romantic values, the perversions with the maximum of waste of perversions, and we shall not here attempt to state what this makes for in the way of æsthetic refreshment and relief; the waste having kept us so dangling on the dark æsthetic abyss. A shade of asperity may be in such fashion a security against waste, and in the dearth of displayed securities we should welcome it on that ground alone. It helps at any rate to constitute for the talent manifest in *The Custom* a rare identity, so far should we have to go to seek another instance of the dry, or call it perhaps even the hard, intellectual touch in the soft, or call it perhaps even the humid, temperamental air; in other words of the masculine conclusion tending so to crown the feminine observation.

Checklist of Additional Reviews

Edwin Francis Edgett, "Edith Wharton's New Novel: An Extremely Conventional Portrayal of the Social Climber," Boston *Evening Transcript*, 18 October 1913, Part 3, p. 8.

"Customs of Two Countries," *Independent*, 76 (13 November 1913), 313.

"Five New Novels by Women," *Outlook*, 105 (15 November 1913), 571.

"The Hundred Best Books of the Year,"*New York Times Book Review*, 30 November 1913, p. 664.

"Mrs. Wharton's New Novel," *Nation and Athenæum* [England], 14 (December 1913), 446, 448.

FIGHTING FRANCE: FROM DUNKERQUE TO BELFORT

FIGHTING FRANCE

FROM DUNKERQUE TO BELFORT

BY

EDITH WHARTON

ILLUSTRATED

CHARLES SCRIBNER'S SONS
NEW YORK : MCMXV

"Mrs. Wharton and Kipling on the War: Famous Writers Tell of Their Experiences at the Front—Recent Books on the European Conflict," *New York Times Book Review*, 5 December 1915, p. 490

Mrs. Wharton's impressions of France in war time are imparted with her unfailing touch of literary distinction. Whether she is depicting the outward aspects of trench life, or the inmost soul of the people, she does it with that calm intelligence and habitual felicity of expression which have made her a peculiarly apt interpreter of the French temperament. She has visited the trenches all the way from the English Channel to the Swiss frontier, has heard the roar of the biggest German guns at Dixmude, and watched the French recapture a village in Argonne; but perhaps the most distinctive feature of her six chapters is her analysis of the spirit of the French Nation.

The author has been in France ever since the war began—chiefly in Paris, where she has organized sewing and lace-making enterprises to aid the sad army of refugee women. A visit to ruined Poperinghe, near Ypres, was made for the purpose of finding the designs for a certain kind of lace cushion made in an abandoned convent there. Everywhere she has been in close relations with French people of all classes. No other American has had better opportunities for looking deep into the national psychology.

Before the Germans struck the first blow the universal French attitude was indicated in the words, "We don't want war—mais il faut que cela finisse!" This eternal menace has got to stop! With that determination the French went to their task, and it has been the backbone of their calm valor ever since. But the "tone of France," as Mrs. Wharton calls it, has come through several phases. The first days of the war were full of a kind of unrealizing confidence; not boastful or fatuous, yet very different from the clear-headed tenacity into which it had developed a few months later. Self-restraint was the most notable characteristic of the people. The crowd that stood looking at the first captured German flag was silent, as if already realizing what it would cost to keep it and add others to it.

After six months of fighting, the French soldiers in the trenches, even the youngest, impressed the author as having a look of quiet authority. All their little oddities, meannesses, and vulgarities had been burnt away in a great flame of self-dedication. She speaks of this as a wonderful example of the rapidity with which a deep purpose can model the human countenance. It impressed her again in the Vosges Mountains. Men of widely different classes were not only on terms of the most democratic equality, but their mental and moral fraternity was complete. . . .

As the slow months have dragged by, bringing a calamity unheard of in human annals, the white glow of dedication throughout France has not waned, but has gradually deepened into exaltation, energy, the hot resolve to dominate the disaster. Mrs. Wharton does not deny that there have been faltering notes, mothers and widows for whom a single grave has turned the conflict into an idiot's tale. But there have not been enough of these to change the national tone. The vast majority hide their despair and seem to say of the great national effort: "Though it

221

slay me, yet I trust in it." This, says the author, is the finest triumph of France; that its myriad fiery currents flow from so many hearts made insensible by suffering, that so many dead hands feed its undying lamp.

Next to the wounded Mrs. Wharton found the "éclopés" the most depressing sight at the front. The "éclopés" are the unwounded but shattered, frost-bitten, deafened, and half-paralyzed wretches who are daily shipped back by thousands to recuperate from the effects of shell fire. After these the sight that affected her most deeply was that of humble homes, still warm with the intimacies of family life, reduced to a heap of bricks and twisted stovepipe. At Gerbéviller she met a former Mayor of the town on a pile of rubbish that had been his beautiful home. In Crévic only one house had been destroyed—that of General Lyauty, who in August had saved Morocco to France by his prompt and audacious action. The Germans had located his home in this obscure village of Lorraine, had gone straight to it, and burned it down after first making a separate bonfire of his papers, portraits, furniture, and family relics.

In the north, at Cassel, Mrs. Wharton felt the house rock under her five times to an accompaniment of sound which she compares to that of the simultaneous shutting of all the iron shop shutters in the world. It was the great German siege gun at Dixmude. The next day at Dunkirk she saw the results of that bombardment. Every house was shuttered and the streets were empty. At the foot of David's statue of Jean Bart, just where her motor had stood while she was taking tea in the hotel two days before, was a crater thirty feet across, made by one of the big shells.

Mrs. Wharton's war book, like her novels, is written in a style that makes one think of carved ivory. It contains thirteen good photographic illustrations.

Florence Finch Kelly, "Eye Witnesses of the War: *Fighting France*," *Bookman*, 42 (December 1915), 462–3

Like sunlight outside a stained glass window, Mrs. Wharton's absorbing book illuminates for her countrymen the figure of France at war. It is a book to be thankful for, a book that no one can afford to miss who wants to understand the full significance of the part that France is taking in the conflict. She remarks, near the end of a chapter containing the account of her visit along the firing-line in Northern France, that to leave the front was like coming down from the mountains. So one feels, upon closing her book, that it is like coming out of a great cathedral. And yet it is merely a simply told, realistic narrative of the things observed by a writer with the seeing eye in the daily life of the French people, both the civilians at home and the soldiers at the front.

The first chapter tells how Paris met the beginning of the war and the last one tells how all France is facing the present stage of the struggle. The intermediate sections describe the trips the author has taken to the battle front, into and through the first line trenches, from Ypres to Alsace. These chapters, except for their occasional graphic descriptions of the havoc wrought in French fields and villages and cities, pay slight attention to the horrors of the conflict. Everywhere Mrs. Wharton is more interested in the man behind the gun and the spirit that moves him than in the gun's achievement. Here is one of the things that her eyes, so well trained and so capable in the study of human beings, see in "fighting France"; "The French people no more think of a compromise than people would think of facing a flood or an earthquake with a white flag."

Checklist of Additional Reviews

Springfield [Massachusetts] *Republican*, 5 December 1915, Section II, p. 7.
Edwin Francis Edgett, "Edith Wharton in Fighting France," Boston *Evening Transcript*, 8 December 1915, p. 26.
Charles Hirsch, "Les Revues," *Mercure de France*, 115 (1916), 128–9.
George Le Cardonnel, "Ouvrages sur la Guerre Actuelle," *Mercure de France*, 117 (1916), 361–2.
"Les Livres de la Guerre," *L'Illustration* [France], 147 (24 June 1916), 574.
L.R., "Les Livres: Edith Wharton, *Voyages au front de Dunkerque à Belfort*," *Nouvelle Revue* [France], 26 (November 1916), 78.
Jacques de Bellaing, "Edith Wharton: Voyages au front de Dunkerque à Belfort," *Etudes* [France], 150 (January-March 1917), 531–32.

XINGU AND OTHER STORIES

XINGU

AND OTHER STORIES

BY

EDITH WHARTON

NEW YORK

CHARLES SCRIBNER'S SONS

MCMXVI

"Xingu,"
New York Times Book Review, 5 November 1916, pp. 465–6

Exceptionally rich in volumes of notable short stories as the present season has already become, its wealth is very greatly increased by the publication of this new collection of tales from the pen of Edith Wharton. Taken as an isolated book, it is one of extraordinary variety, the product of an accomplished artist; regarded in connection with its author's other work, it shows a deeper humanity, an effort, perhaps conscious, to escape from the hothouse atmosphere which permeated and limited the other volumes, an effort which, although it here results in one or two false steps, is nevertheless full of promise. For it proves that this skilled analyst of character and motive is still growing in artistic stature; much as she has accomplished in the past, it seems more than probable that she will do yet bigger work in the future.

Six of the eight stories in the volume are typical Mrs. Wharton tales, which might easily have fitted into one another of the earlier volumes. First comes that delightful bit of satiric comedy called "Xingu," the story of a little group of those ladies "who pursue culture in bands, as though it were dangerous to meet alone," and of their encounter with a distinguished novelist. Brilliant in its characterization and style, biting in its satire, this story is a model of its particular kind. "The Choice," apart from that beauty of phrasing never absent in Mrs. Wharton's writing, is interesting principally because of the deft portrayal of Cobham Stilling, the husband in this version of the familiar triangle situation, an egotist and bore

whose prototypes most of us have met. "Autre Temps . . ." and "The Long Run" are long short stories verging upon, if they do not cross, the borderline between the short story and the novelette, and both belong, like the tales already mentioned, to the society species of narrative. Of the two, "Autre Temps . . ." is the better. In its picture of the changes which have altered social judgments during the last few years, changes which meet and alter the present, yet have little influence on the "fait accompli" that has passed into a tradition, it is clever, penetrating, implying far more and touching inferentially on issues far broader than those bearing directly on the fortunes of Mrs. Lidcote and the daughter who followed in her footsteps, but reached a very different goal. "The Long Run" has more than a little of the gospel according to Ellen Key;[1] it is very modern, interesting in its climax and point of view, but rather drawn out.

The collection includes two notable ghost stories, "Kerfol" and "The Triumph of the Night." Of the two the former, whose scene is laid in Brittany, is the one we prefer, perhaps because "the most romantic house in Brittany," grim, desolate, with heavy walls and narrow, fateful stairway, is a better setting for a shiver-producing tale than a handsome modern residence. The descriptions of Kerfol, which suggested "a perspective of stern and cruel memories stretching away, like its own gray avenues, into a blur of darkness," is ample preparation for the tragic history which had given it its sinister reputation. The manner of its telling, the altered style which marks the shift from the direct narrative to the repetition of that found in the ancient "History of the Assizes of Brittany," the innumerable, skillful little touches which make person, situation or scene real and vivid to the reader, render this tale deserving of careful study on the part of those interested in the art of short-story writing, as well as one fascinating and absorbing to the casual reader.

But admirable, artistic, brilliant as are these tales, they are all representative of the sort of thing we have learned to expect from this remarkable writer. Hence the two that are from some aspects the most notable in the book have been reserved for comment until the last. One of these two is the only war story in the collection, "Coming Home." The young men of our American Relief Corps, says the author, "are beginning to come back from the front with stories." And it is into the mouth of one of these young men that she puts this account of what happened to a French Lieutenant and his family. Their home was by the Vosges in a little village, and they themselves were emphatically of the provinces—except the Lieutenant himself, who had traveled and lived in Paris. He was summoned to join his regiment as soon as war was declared, and before the others were fully aware of what had occurred the Germans came. It is a grim story, vivid, of a kind which we know to have been only too commonplace, and with a tragedy the more appalling because it is only suggested, never fully told. The descriptions are wonderful, biting deep into the memory. First we have a glimpse of the quiet, conservative, tradition-steeped little family, charming, distinguished people, living the narrowest, most upright of lives, in a peaceful smiling country. Then the "coming home" of the son, after the storm of war had swept back and forth over the land, leaving it a waste of stones: "Murder, outrage, torture; Scharlach's program seemed to be fairly comprehensive." Every detail of the picture stands clear, and it is full of such illuminating bits as the description of the old woman who drives the cart, and doesn't mind the shells any more. "She had only one boy—half-witted; he cocked a broom-

handle at them and they burnt him"; so she lives only to outwit Germans.

"Bunner Sisters," the last and longest story of the collection, is another departure from Mrs. Wharton's usual choice of themes. The story of the two spinsters who kept a tiny shop, it is pathetic to the point of painfulness. Ann Eliza's starved life is portrayed with wonderful sympathy and insight, but at the very end one feels that the author has added an unnecessary bit in Evelina's conversion; for this, nothing which has gone before has in the least prepared the reader, and it seems as though it were a needless heaping up of the agony to force upon poor Ann Eliza a conviction that the sister she so passionately loved is lost to her for all eternity. Another bit of over-emphasis is the companioned departure of Linda. It is as though in abandoning her accustomed environment the author had lost something of her sureness of touch; but the loss may well prove only temporary, while the gain in breadth of sympathy is very great.

1 Editors' note: a contemporary Swedish writer on feminist issues.

"New Novels," *Times Literary Supplement* [England], 30 November 1916, p. 572

Mrs. Wharton's clear, quick art is everywhere at home. In the eight stories of her new book (*Xingu and Other Stories*, . . .) she picks her cases out of almost as many contrasted climates, social and geographical, with a reach as easy and a discrimination as assured for one as for another. One could even feel that her wit is matched against some power which tries to baffle her by placing her appointed subjects in times and regions where she might possibly overlook them. If so it is, her antagonist shows some ingenuity; the thimble is hidden in a Breton castle, three centuries ago, or in a poor old milliner's shop in a back street of modern New York. But the issue is always the same; instantly the eye of the author lights on it, the article is appropriated, the thing is shown to be exactly suited to this particular distinguished art. There is ironic comedy, there is dramatic portraiture, there is romantic legend, each in its right place and right tone in these stories; and the versatile keenness of the imagination projected, always ready for fresh flights and desiring new difficulties, is remarkable in them all. It is this straining force that more and more strengthens Mrs. Wharton's handling of a tale, though that was always so neat and firm. But nothing tests a writer's method and style like the constant necessity of keeping pace with a strong imagination; and Mrs. Wharton's present skill of hand sufficiently proves it. In "Bunner Sisters," which is the tale of the old milliners, each small episode is seen and fashioned and placed with a lucidity of a very rare kind; each is an image round which the author's gaze has closed, if that could be, giving it all the value of an object. If the sentiment of this piece seems too easy for a writer like Mrs. Wharton—the pathetic effect of poor decayed milliners certainly needs no great art of evocation— the irony, which lies so lightly over it, demanded her. Irony of a darker kind is over the story (inadequately called "Coming Home") of a young Frenchman's sight of his home and his family in the Vosges after the passage of the Germans. There is no facility of sentiment here, and this grave and ominous little glimpse of provincial life, just revealed, immediately hidden, is unforgettable.

But above all, and after all, it is in the irony of the comedy of manners that Mrs. Wharton is at her best and freest. Her picture of some particular case or predicament is never so good as when it is set in the bigger light of a social scene; and somewhere in a set of stories by her one hopes for the scene of New York. "Autres Temps" is the story here—fifty pages of light sharp history, with fifty strokes of curious observation to the page. New York moves fast, no doubt, in its derangement of old standards. But Mrs. Wharton easily catches it out in a most pictorial inconsistency as it applies its new standards to new people and at the same time omits to reverse its old judgments on the old. The old person in the tale suffers so intelligently, and the new people triumph so densely, that the little drama is complete; and Mrs. Wharton has never done a better thing.

Gerald Gould, "New Novels," *New Statesman*, 8 (9 December 1916), 234

Mrs. Wharton's new collection of short stories contains all sorts, from the extremely good to the extremely bad: and the first two stories are among the worst, while the last is beyond any question the best. This disposition of forces seems unfortunate. But Mrs. Wharton's reputation as one of the most skilful and most important among contemporary writers of fiction will carry her readers forward over the bare patches to the delectable places. "*Xingu*" itself is merely an elaboration, sufficiently amusing in its way, though trivial, of the old joke to the effect that Botticelli is not a wine but a cheese. It satirises with excessive particularity the affectation of culture by the pompous uncultured, and its first sentence is typical of the contemptuous incisiveness of the whole: "Mrs. Ballinger is one of the ladies who pursue Culture in bands, as though it were dangerous to meet alone." "Coming Home," the only war-story in the collection, jumps to the opposite extreme: it is designed to move and thrill, and it uses to that end every available stage-property, but it fails—fails all the more noticeably because it *is* about the war, which, Heaven knows, is moving and thrilling enough for most people without any stage-properties whatever. We get a quite alarming adjustment of coincidences, fitted together like the pieces of a puzzle, only without the elements of surprise involved in a good puzzle. Everybody knows, naturally, of cases in which the rapid shifts of war have thrown old friends unexpectedly together, and provided other and stranger coincidences than that; but if Mrs. Wharton were to tell us that the pattern of her story was copied straight from real life, the fact that the life has gone out of it in the copying would remain. The triangular relationship here typified by the German officer, French officer, and French officer's *fiancée* was, even before the war, part of the familiar structure of melodrama: the arrangement of circumstances, to give the German officer the maximum power of wrong-doing and the French officer the maximum power of revenge, is equally artificial: the piling-up of atrocities includes the burning alive by the Germans of a half-witted, unarmed, and harmless youth. (Does Mrs. Wharton mean this case to be taken as authentic? If so, she would have done better to give her references: if not, she would have done better to omit the incident.) Even the tell-tale scar on the German officer's face (this particular brand of scoundrel always has this particular brand of scar) is provided. Mrs. Wharton's

well-known powers of significant detail are employed to cover the crude outline of the plot very much as "patter" is employed by a drawing-room prestidigitator to cover the crudities of his manipulation. With "Autres Temps . . ." we are back in an atmosphere where Mrs. Wharton is more at home—the gradations and implications of American Society's judgments and standards. Here the delicacy and irony of her mind have full play: the little tale is perfect of its kind. "Kerfol" is something new in ghost-stories, and "The Triumph of Night" is even more successful in the same gloomy vein: "The Long Run" is a study of a theme rather like Browning's in The Statue and the Bust, set in the fastidious modern world of a wealthy and sophisticated "set": "The Choice" relapses into some of the crudities of melodrama; but with "Bunner Sisters," the long concluding part of the volume, we get back to the Mrs. Wharton from whom we expect the perfection and restraint of quiet art. Here are no coincidence, no startling effect, no disconcerting violence, no dejecting strain—only the grey accumulations of sorrow and effort that make up the life of the shabby genteel. The Bunner sisters keep a little shop in a melancholy quarter of New York, and to them enters a suitor in the melancholy shape—romantic and exciting to them!—of an amiable but shiftless man addicted to the use of drugs. The excursions he takes them, the tiredness of the elder sister's feet, the congestion of the street-cars on which they go, are all put down: how the suitor transfers his wooing from one sister to the other is told as quietly as are the *minutiæ* of the excursions—and so are the failure of the marriage, the growth and triumph of disease, the heart-breaking little sacrifices and aspirations that end in threadbare tragedy and undignified despair. Excellences of style can scarcely be illustrated from such a narrative—everything is in the quietness, n the low tones, in the faint shadows. And anyway the reading public knows well by this time how right, how vivid, how delicately accentuated and controlled is Mrs. Wharton's style at its best. . . . The completeness of effect is carried by such a style into the intimacies and intricacies of psychological reaction as into the clear lines of scenery.

Edward E. Hale, "Recent Fiction," *Dial*, 61 (28 December 1916), 586–7

American writers have always done well with short-stories. Irving, Hawthorne, and Poe wrote famous short-stories at a time when few in our country were successful in their effort to write long ones, and since then the short-story has been one of the established forms of fiction. It is certainly one of the most popular forms, if we may judge from the great number of periodicals which seem to depend mainly on the magnet of brief fiction. Supplying the demand has become a trade which anyone can learn, according to the advertisements of the trade schools of the craft. Not many of the innumerable short-stories written, however, are preserved to posterity, indeed few ever appear in the solid form of the bound volume. There is no comparison between the number of novels published and the number of collections of short-stories. Publishers are likely to decline the latter without thanks. People hesitate before picking up a collection unless it is by somebody well known. There seems to be a feeling that they are well enough in magazines or newspapers, but that they are rather ephemeral. Mr. Bliss Perry some time ago said,

"Here is a form of literature easy to write and easy to read." However it may be with the writing of really good short-stories, it is generally easier to read a short-story than a part of a long one, which is probably the reason for the great number of story-magazines.

In spite of all this, there are still many fine short-stories, and great reputations have been founded on them. Kipling and Conan Doyle would stand much where they stand now had they never written novels. The talent of O. Henry found ample scope in the briefer form, and the great reputation of the late Jack London was made chiefly by his short-stories. Most of our writers of fiction at the present day, however, are best known by their novels. Such is the case with Mrs. Edith Wharton. Following the realistic tradition,—if we have in mind Henry James and Guy de Maupassant, who were, I suppose, the chief influences of the nineties in the particular form of art which interested her,—she often puts her impressions of life into short-stories or even sketches of character. But she is at her best in her novels. She has the grasp of fact and the power of imagination and the sense of art that sometimes contrive to make the reading of a novel a memorable experience. We have in "Xingu" a number of stories which were mostly written, it would seem, before her work in France; at least they show little effect of what has been a remarkable period in her life. Two of the stories—one of them the best of the collection—are French in subject, but the others are views of the world which Mrs. Wharton's readers already know. Situations in the individual life, developments or contrast of character, ironic phases, are recounted in a slow natural way, with all the implications and suggestions of life itself. "Xingu," the story that gives its name to the collection, is a lighter bit and very amusing, though on a subject hardly worth Mrs. Wharton's attention. The false culture of the ladies' library club is to our generation one of the conventional sources of humor, somewhat as the goat who ate tomato-cans and the man who put up stove-pipes used to be in the last generation. There are undoubtedly women who run after literary notabilities, who carry around volumes of "Appropriate Allusions," who quote literary opinions or catchwords without much idea of their meaning, who really care more for social amusement than for literature; but even if there are, it seems hardly worth while to say so again unless one says it exceedingly well. Aside from this (somewhat priggish) consideration, "Xingu" is certainly most amusing. The best in the collection, however, is "Coming Home," a story of the war where Mrs. Wharton uses her skill in something she clearly thought (and rightly) well worth doing.

"Short Stories from Life" comes in conveniently for one who is interested in getting an idea of what short-story writers nowadays are trying to do. If our other collection offered fair examples of literature, this collection might show the general run of the short-story as it appears in the periodical of to-day. It does not do exactly that because the stories in the collection are all pretty short. "Life," it appears, was interested in knowing how short a story could be, and therefore opened a competition with terms which should encourage the extreme of brevity. This was managed by the ingenious device of paying for the stories that were published at the rate of ten cents for every word less than fifteen hundred—paying, one might say, for what was left out instead of for what was there. That, of course, set a standard of extreme shortness; none of Mrs. Wharton's stories would have brought a cent in the competition.

It would be hard to say offhand just how good or bad these stories are. To read the book through is like trying to dine on nine cocktails, eighteen *hors d'oeuvres*, eighteen pieces of cheese, eighteen liqueurs, nine *demitasses*, and nine cigarettes, making eighty-one courses in all, which is too long even for a Chinese banquet. Or if not too long, it is long enough to spoil any delicacy of taste. It would take eighty-one hours to criticize it fairly. Fortunately the Introduction by the managing editor of "Life" suggests some sort of criterion. Mr. Masson says that "a short-story must be a picture out of real life which gives the reader a definite sensation." One may doubt this very seriously; many good stories are really stories and not pictures at all. In writing of the technique of the short-story, however, Mr. Masson says that its words should not suggest "the fatal thought that the author is dependent upon others for his phrasing. When, for example, we read 'With a glad cry she threw her arms about him' 'A hoarse shout went up from the vast throng' 'He flicked the ashes,' we know at once that the author is dealing only in echoes." This is interesting, partly because one of these test-phrases occurs (in a slightly different form, "flicking the ash") in the story which gained the second prize. It would be a foolish attempt at smartness to ask what must be the case with the others when the next to the best was at fault in so fatal a manner. Perhaps one would not agree that the test-phrases are perfectly reliable. Whether they are or not, the general idea is of course right, as well as that about the short-story coming out of real life. We feel that originality of seeing and writing is more likely to result in something good than the use of old, even well-tried material; we want something that a man sees for himself and tells for himself, not something that is but an echo of what may be read better elsewhere. These stories from "Life" do not stand that test so well as Mrs. Wharton's. I must confess that the story about the ladies' club talking about Xingu has some echoes in it, but in the main Mrs. Wharton is interested in things she has observed for herself, or heard of, in the great procession of life as it goes by.

The authors of the stories from "Life" often tell us of matters which I do not believe came direct from real life. Take the story which gained the first prize. It is the tale of a German commander of a submarine engaged to an American girl, who, after he has been highly praised for sinking a great ocean liner, finds that his fiancée was on board. Possibly that is a "picture out of real life"; it may not be "dealing in echoes"; but I have my doubts. It seems to me rather, a case constructed to illustrate the somewhat commonplace idea of a certain irony in life or a certain poetic justice or something of the sort. Many of the tales are more like the real thing. The story which seems to me to smack most of real life is one called "The Old Grove Crossing," in which a judge on the bench and a leader of the bar amuse themselves in court one day in rivalry in a conventional piece of sentimental rhodomontade. One good thing about the story is that the author austerely hides from us the fact (if it be one) that they both knew the whole thing was conventional. That seems very like life indeed; perhaps they thought they were genuine, perhaps not. Who can say? I presume I have rather a prejudiced view on this question because I sent a story to this competition which really was a transcript of a piece of life I found in a seventeenth century town-record. Perhaps (beside being poor in other ways), it did not seem to the judges to be a picture out of real life, although it was. If it had echoes in it (and it certainly did), they were echoes of the record. The fact is that we do not always recognize real life when we see it. These stories offer one a

good opportunity for amusement in testing the matter. Is Mrs. Wharton really like life? Are the seventy-two authors of the eighty-one stories? If one can answer that question, one will have a test that will enable one to enjoy much and reject more in the fiction of our day.

"Fiction," *Spectator* [England], 117 (30 December 1916), 836–7

We confess to approaching the novels and stories of Mrs. Wharton with mingled emotions, in which a reverent admiration for her ability, her subtlety, and her artistic skill is tempered by the apprehensions—quite old-fashioned, we admit—that we must put away all expectations of happy endings or even Indian summers of long-deferred contentment. We must resign ourselves to the somewhat depressing influences of a writer of whom it certainly cannot be said, as a rule, in the words of the laconic Latin epitaph, *neminem tristem fecit*. The events of the last two years and a half have not been calculated to raise the spirits of any one who, like Mrs. Wharton, has had personal experience of the ravages of war—and, let us add, has shown a generous sympathy with the Allies—yet by a happy inconsistency she has placed in the forefront of her new volume a story not merely detached from all European convulsions but conceived and carried out in a spirit of satirical comedy. "Xingu" is a highly diverting sketch of a small set of would-be literary ladies—the *précieuses ridicules* of fashionable modern America—who meet periodically at one another's houses to discuss books which they have not always read and movements which they are unable to understand. The activities of Mrs. Ballinger's Lunch Club culminated in their inviting the formidable problem novelist Osric Dane to one of their meetings, in the hope that she would enlighten them on the subject of her books and their perplexing lessons. But Osric Dane would not talk about herself or her books. She preferred to ask the Lunch Club about their literary preferences and tastes; she put awkward questions—e.g., asking them to define "objective"—and reduced them to such a condition of mental paralysis that the situation was only saved by Mrs. Roby, the prettiest and most frivolous member of the club, declaring that the subject in which they were most absorbed was Xingu. Osric Dane was puzzled, but the other members fell into the trap, and one and all professed a knowledge which they did not possess, floundering deeper and deeper into the mire of fictitious enthusiasm until Mrs. Roby beat a hasty retreat, followed immediately, to the general dismay, by Osric Dane. The sequel describes how by a process of humiliating mutual admissions the club realized that they had been hoaxed, the climax being reached when reference to an encyclopædia showed that Xingu was a river in Brazil where Mrs. Roby had once travelled. This rough outline gives no idea of the delicate irony with which the various members of the club are sketched by Mrs. Wharton, or of her ruthless exposure of that form of snobbish sciolism which thrives in an atmosphere of mutual admiration and invites and justifies the methods of the practical joker. Mrs. Roby was really a sensible as well as an attractive woman, and was not afraid to mention that she had been reading Trollope. We gather that she was expelled from the club, but we cannot imagine that it long survived the fiasco. Our only regret is that Mrs. Wharton did not reveal the conversation between Mrs. Roby and Osric Dane after they left. We have dealt with this story at length because it is the only one in which Mrs. Wharton makes any concession to the spirit of frivolity. In all the remaining stories we are, in her own phrase, moving among the grim edges of reality. "Coming Home" is a painfully vivid story—all the more vivid for its suppressions and omissions—of a young French officer whose family were cut off in the battle zone for months. When he was at last able to rejoin them, it was to find that they had escaped through the splendid coolness and courage of his *fiancée*. She had rescued house and inmates but his love was poisoned with a dreadful surmise as to the cost she had paid, and the act of vengeance in which the narrative closes wipes out the score but does not clear up the mystery. Then we have in "Kerfol" a *macabre* story of a haunted house in Brittany, and in "The Long Run" the tragedy of a lover who, at the supreme moment, only succeeded in convincing the woman who loved him that he was self-protective when he wished to save her from herself, and was tormented by the memory of his half-heartedness ever after. "The Choice" is another tale of an ill-assorted marriage, where the drunken husband is saved and the lover is drowned: and "Bunner Sisters" is a long and heartbreaking story of the struggles of two poor women who kept a small shop in New York, of the marriage, desertion, and death of the younger and the poverty and ruin of the elder.

In face of such distinguished talent and its generally depressing use, the plain person must feel very much like the members of the Lunch Club in the presence of Osric Dane. Mr. James Huneker, the most plain-spoken of American critics, speaks of the "glacial cruelty" of Mrs. Wharton's picture of the vulgar American woman of fashion in *The Custom of the*

Country. That is perhaps an extravagant way of putting it, but there is a certain truth in the saying. Mrs. Wharton is not glacial or cruel, but there *is* something inhuman in the detachment of her method and in her absolute self-effacement. And there is no doubt that she has a peculiar talent for the dissection of disillusioned, unhappy, uncomfortable, or disagreeable natures. "Triumphant democracy," with its exuberances and excesses and self-confidence, finds no panegyrist in this fastidious critical writer, whose outlook is eminently eclectic, cosmopolitan, and aristocratic.

F[rancis] H[ackett], "Mrs. Wharton's Art," *New Republic*, 10 (10 February 1917), 50–2

Mrs. Wharton comes very near affording complete gratification with this volume of short stories. She takes her subjects as only an artist can take them, for the values, the reasonances, they happen to have for her; and the fact that she writes mainly of a restricted class seems at the moment irrelevant. It would be really irrelevant if Mrs. Wharton didn't, in a subtle enough way, become condescending to persons, who live on, and off, the fringe. Sometimes as between a perfectly initiated pet and a bounding newcomer one gets a whiff of sublimated sensibilities. Of such assaulted class consciousness as this sort of thing implies, Mrs. Wharton occasionally gives signs. Among the petty bourgeoisie she moves with comparative sympathy. Among more formidable representatives of the same ilk she moves with something not unlike a sniff. She is difficult to please, but the difficulty is not always due to

intrinsic considerations. For a person of such lancing intelligence she is strangely deficient in comedy. It is not that one wants her to have a richer palette or a more dashing line. It is not that one wishes her to burst on the world exuberantly, with a barbaric yawp. It is merely that with a higher sense of comedy other realities would emerge in her landscape which, under the light that is habitual with her, is somewhat acid, cold and bleak.

But astringent as one may deem Mrs. Wharton's mood, it would be absurd to miss her deep excellences on that account. There are many manifestations of America for which she has not the faculty, but those that peculiarly arrest her, those that depend on being of the feminine gender among well-off people in a given time and sphere, extract from her the sort of appreciation that amounts to genius. The fate that she has most absorbingly contemplated and most handsomely represented is perhaps that of persons whose lot is enhanced by money or family or taste, and whose impulses pay reluctant toll to an order in whose establishment their happiness and their honor are involved. It is, if you like, worldly wisdom that here occupies Mrs. Wharton; it happens, however, to be wisdom. Congruous as she is with *Scribner's Magazine*, incongruous with the Walt Whitmans, she is still the intent observer of nature adaptive and assertive, of pliancies and subjections, desertions and rebellions. In some respects she is a pharmacist in her handling of vital forces. She deals in essences and double distillations. She uses a delicate measure to weigh out what is precious or deadly. She dispenses little that she regards as lethal or valuable outside what would fit in an apothecary scales. She is grave, minute, scrupulous, analytic. She is dramatic hypodermically. But to such fine uses does she put the sympathies and perceptions with which she is endowed, that a reader would be strangely callous who was not lost in admiration among the merits of her art.

Take as perhaps the best example in this volume the tale called, "The Long Run." It is a favorite theme of Mrs. Wharton's the drama of a love that is not coincident with marriage. In this case, as indeed in most of the stories in *Xingu*, Mrs. Wharton is seeing these things in retrospect, not as matters of palpitation so much as matters of eventual chemistry. The man in this instance harks back to his hour of decision, the hour when everything depended on the driving force of his impulse. . . . And what that decision came to . . . is the story Mrs. Wharton beautifully and sympathetically contrives. They are not people seen in the various successive attitudes of a morality, registering this and that. They are people whose morality is in solution, never labeled for that particular brand of interest by Mrs. Wharton herself. She has no intention for them save to reveal them, to give them in their own "flood of joy that comes of heightened emotion," their own persuasions as to life, and the price it cost them to have had him incapable of crossing a stream that had no bridge. A story like this is the flower of a career.

Permeated with equal sympathy, rather a dejected and vengeful sympathy, is "Bunner Sisters," a fascinating novelette of two middle-aged tradeswomen in old New York. The odor of condescension does not, for me, cling to this example of Mrs. Wharton's studies in a sphere not excitingly fashionable. There are inflections she catches with sharp exactness. There is no attempt to make Ann Eliza and Evelina seem less like morons than they really were. But the story has an almost affectionate completeness of detail and a totally affectionate occupation with both Ann Eliza and Evelina in the bittersweet of their intimacy with the fated Mr. Ramy.

The Bunners do not come off very well, defenseless in a fight so manifold and so complicated as life; but they are not exceptional. In not one of Mrs. Wharton's eight stories does any one come off particularly well, except of course the potential murderer in "Triumph of Night" and the brute-husband in "The Choice."

"Xingu" is perhaps the cleverest of these stories. It also the least valuably perceptive. A satire on the excessive seriousness, the pretentiousness, the false zealotry of a small American "culture" club, it goes rather too far in an acrimonious caricature of the women as human beings. Mrs. Wharton's acid bites fairly into their idiocy as the pursuers of culture, it scarifies them too deeply in their social character. The Laura Glyde and Mrs. Plinth and Mrs. Leveret of real life would be equally insufferable about books, but Mrs. Wharton's cold dislike for their natures is quite unjustified. It is in dealing with such women as these, women who if anything would err on the side of amiability and whose main mistake is to take too seriously the obligations imposed on them by a culture not native, that Mrs. Wharton becomes frigidly conventional. Her Mrs. Plinths and Mrs. Leverets are misjudged from the vantage point of Lenox or Tuxedo, or wherever it is that women do not allow even their illiteracy to detract from their self-confidence.

Despite "Bunner Sisters," it would be egregious loyalty to Mrs. Wharton as an artist not to admit that she is primarily a person interested in a restricted world. She has an ear for the clash and chime of life outside Lenox and those other places where ministers of grace draw your bath and steal about, exaggerating your wardrobe, while you pretend to be asleep. Her story of wartime in the Vosges and the German intrusion on a château there indicates that. But it is not too much to say that she tends to start with men of means and women who use those means to their ends. One has only to glance at her personae—. . . . These are not the kind of people with whom you share cracker-jack in a day-coach. These are not the lads and lasses who put skids under William H. Taft in 1912, abandoned themselves to "Onward Christian Soldiers" at Chicago, and helped Mr. Roosevelt to be a traitor to his class. Rather the contrary. But on the Atlantic seaboard, using the Alleghenies as a sort of privet hedge, Mrs. Wharton holds these persons in preference—out of proportion to their constituency in society as a whole though not by any means out of proportion to their interest. For their interest, as Mrs. Wharton considers them, is not fatuous fashionableness. It is the chance they offer for intensive human relations, those relations that include love but also so often preclude it, and always pivoting on marriage. Marriage and love are the great factors in the drama Mrs. Wharton concentrates upon. Of these the greater in the frankly middle-aged stories in *Xingu* is neither one nor the other automatically; she is cool enough to say that the cost of love may be too heavy, and warm enough to have its balance sheet her main preoccu-

pation. It is this absorption in the delicate processes, the feminized processes, which decide where the bemedaled warriors shall dine, and whom sit next to, and whom take to wife and whom to bed, that has kept her up-town and socially excited. The quality of that excitement is the principal charm of *Xingu*, an achievement that no other American is emulating.

Checklist of Additional Reviews

Edwin Francis Edgett, "Edith Wharton and the Short Story," Boston *Evening Transcript*, 28 October 1916, p. 8.

Athenæum [England], 4612 (December 1916), 598.

"Novels and Short Stories," *Review of Reviews*, 54 (December 1916), 679

Independent, 88 (25 December 1916), 552.

"Some Recent Short Stories," *Nation*, 104 (4 January 1917), 20.

"'*Xingu*' by Mrs. Wharton," Springfield [Massachusetts] *Republican*, 14 January 1917, Section II, p. 15.

THE BOOK OF THE HOMELESS

THE
BOOK OF THE HOMELESS

(*LE LIVRE DES SANS-FOYER*)

EDITED BY EDITH WHARTON

Original Articles in Verse and Prose
Illustrations reproduced from Original Paintings & Drawings

THE BOOK IS SOLD
FOR THE BENEFIT OF THE AMERICAN HOSTELS FOR REFUGEES
(WITH THE FOYER FRANCO-BELGE)
AND OF THE CHILDREN OF FLANDERS RESCUE COMMITTEE

LONDON
MACMILLAN & CO., LIMITED
MDCCCCXVI

A very remarkable and a very beautiful book is this which Mrs. Wharton has put together for the benefit of a specially deserving branch of the work in Paris to which she has devoted herself ever since the beginning of the war. Its beneficiaries will be the American Hostels for Refugees and the Children of Flanders Rescue Committee. In the preface Mrs. Wharton tells briefly how the work of these two organizations started, how dire was the need that called them into existence, what they have done, and what are their present necessities. "Moved by the urgency of the need for money with which to carry on the work through the coming year the idea of such a book as this came to me." And so, she says, "I appealed to my friends who write and paint and compose, and they to other friends of theirs—writers, painters, composers, statesmen, and dramatic artists—and so the book gradually built itself up, page by page, picture by picture."

Of poetry, prose, and music there are forty-two contributors, and fifteen of illustrations, the lists containing some of the most famous names of English, French, and American men and women. And the book is peculiarly distinguished by the fact that these famous contributors have given of their best. The need of the children, that most appealing of all human needs, has inspired each of them to distinctive, individual utterance, and while each of the written contributions has some kind of relation to the war and the purpose of the book, each one bears deeply the impress of its author. Mrs. Wharton's preface strikes the keynote of the book in its direct, simple, and graphic style, its personality, and its singleness of heart. Notwithstanding the few lines of statistics sandwiched between its sections, it is, as also is almost every contribution, a piece of real literature.

In half a dozen gallant lines Sarah Bernhardt voices her own unquenchable spirit in a promise to the children. Joseph Conrad writes twenty-five pages of descriptive narrative, as fine as can be found in any of his novels, telling of the trip which he made to Poland at the beginning of the war and of how narrowly he and his family escaped. When, at last, they reached Vienna, the American Ambassador, Mr. Penfield, was able to speed them on their way with safety, although barely in time. For, he says, soon after they left, the Austrian officials received orders to detain them until the end of the war.

Emile Verhæren's poem, "The New Spring," has three closing stanzas:

No flower shall bloom this year
But the wild flame of fear,
Wreathing the evil night
With burst of deadly light.

No splendor of portals red
But that which cannon shed.
Raining their death-bloom down
On farm and tower and town.

This is the scarlet doom
By the wild sea-winds hurled
Over a land of gloom,
Over a grave-strewn world.

Edmund Gosse, in the course of an account of a trip taken with Maarten Maartens some years ago into Germany, tells an amazing but illuminative story, from which he does not fail to draw its moral. Among the contributors of prose or verse are Thomas Hardy, William James, Edmond Rostand, W. D. Howells, Edith M. Thomas, Josephine Preston Peabody, Henri de Regnier, Francis Jammes, and many others. Igor Stravinsky and Vincent d'Indy are represented by musical compositions. More than a score of full-page illustrations, many in color, represent the work of famous artists, among whom are Leon Bakst, Dagnan-Bouveret, Edwin H. Blashfield, Claude Monet, C. D. Gibson, Rodin, John S. Sargent, and others. They include portraits, landscapes, interiors, sketches. Among the portraits are those of Thomas Hardy and George Moore by Jacques-Emile Blanche, of Henry James by Sargent, and of Emile Verhæren by Theo. Van Rysselberghe.

The book itself is a most satisfactory specimen of American book making, an achievement of which its printers, the Merrymount Press, Boston, can well be proud. The illustrations retain their artistic value, the binding has the workmanlike quality which makes the turning of the leaves a pleasure, while in type and printing each page is a work of art.

"The Book of the Homeless," Times Literary Supplement [England], 9 March 1916, p. 116

We hope that many purchasers, British as well as American, will be found for this beautiful quarto volume, which Mrs. Wharton has compiled, edited, and in great part written. Since the war began many books have been produced, singly or in cooperation, in aid of war relief and war charities, *The Queen's Gift Book* being a conspicuous instance, but none has had a worthier object than this *Book of the Homeless*, and probably none has equalled it from a literary point of view. To speak first of its object, as explained by Mrs. Wharton in her Preface, and by ex-President Roosevelt in his brief Introduction, it is to benefit the American Hostels for Refugees, and the Children of Flanders Relief Committee; two agencies by which, under Mrs. Wharton's guidance, America, aided by French friends and by the British Y.W.C.A of Paris, has saved thousands of Belgian refugees from starvation and housed, clothed, and taught many hundreds of their children. Horror succeeds horror so quickly in this war that we are apt to forget the misery of the first months, and the devastation caused by the invaders throughout the smiling land of Belgium. Mr. Roosevelt asks us to look back for a moment, and to recall

> the harrowing tragedies of the poor souls who were driven from their country on the verge of starvation, without food or shelter, without hope, and with the members of the family all separated from one another, none knowing where the

others were to be found and who had drifted into Paris and into other parts of France and across the Channel to England as a result of Belgium being trampled into bloody mire.

What has been done for these poor creatures in Paris since November, 1914, is briefly described by Mrs. Wharton; 9,300 refugees assisted, work found for 3,500 men, some 50,000 garments distributed, workrooms and nurseries provided, with schoolrooms for the elder children, who are taught English by Englishwomen, and a general clinic established for the free treatment of thousands of sick. The special work for the children is carried on at the Villa Béthanie, a few miles away to the north-west; a great house with park and fine old trees; here, at the request of the Belgian Government, the Committee is nourishing and teaching several hundred children, and finding a home for a number of Sisters and two hundred infirm old men and women.

Of course all this costs a great deal of money, and, though the two organizations are still solvent, thanks to the first year's subscriptions, the position is naturally becoming anxious. To help to relieve it, Mrs. Wharton has for the moment come back to literature, and has turned her organizing power to the production of this book. It may honestly be said that seldom has such a galaxy of first-rate authors, French, Belgian, British, and American, been brought together in one volume. Contributions in verse come from over twenty writers, among whom are Mr. Thomas Hardy, Mr. W. D. Howells, Mrs. Meynell, Mr. Laurence Binyon, Mrs. Woods, the Comtesse de Noailles, Henri de Régnier, Edmund Rostand, Emile Verhæren, and Mrs. Wharton herself, who not only sends a charming original poem, but provides admirable translations of all the French verses. In prose we have the work of Maurice Barrès, Paul Bourget, Paul Hervieu, and Maurice Maeterlinck, with two little words from Sarah Bernhardt, and Eleanora Duse; also contributions in English by John Galsworthy, Edmund Gosse, Henry James, Agnes Repplier, and Mrs. Humphry Ward. It is difficult in the space at our command to select among all this wealth of material; but among the verses we may perhaps call attention to the fiercely indignant little poem on "The Little Children" by W. D. Howells, who at 79 years of age writes with all the fervour of youth; to the equally passionate verses on "L'Exilé," by Henri de Régnier; to Edmund Rostand's fine sonnet in honour of King Albert and Cardinal Mercier; and to the noble lament of Verhæren for the spring of 1915 that was no spring:—

Hélas! plus n'est de floraison
Que celle des feux dans l'espace:
Bouquet de rage et de manace
S'eparpillant sur l'horizon.

Plus, n'est hélas! de splendeur rouge
Que celle, hélas! des boulets fous
Eclaboussant de larges coups
Clochers, hameaux, fermes et bouges.

Among the sixteen prose contributions, that of Henry James, almost the last work that came from his honoured hand, will be read with a special interest just now while Mr. Joseph Conrad's long account of "Poland Revisited" is particularly interesting as an account of that country and of Germany a week or two before the war. Mr. Galsworthy's single page called "Harvest" is a fine little poem in prose. Miss Repplier's defence of Russia, specially addressed to Americans, ought to have its effect upon a country where Russia till now has not been popular; and Mr. Gosse's anecdote headed "The

Arrogance and Servility of Germany" is an account of what he himself witnessed in 1911—a gross military outrage, and the shrinking humility with which it was received by the civilians—which would be extremely amusing if it were not so grimly significant. M. Barrès and M. Bourget send each a brief personal testimony to the devoted patriotism of the French population, while Mrs. Ward in her "Wordsworth's Valley in War-time" pays a like tribute to the fervour of devotion which, in the summer of last year, pervaded the most peaceful spot in England, the little town of Grasmere.

It should be added that there are original illustrations by Messrs. Sargent, J. E. Blanche, Claude Monet, Renoir, Rodin, and others; and that each of two composers, MM. d'Indy and Stravinsky, contributes a page of music.

"War Relief," *Independent*, 86 (3 April 1916), 29

The most beautiful of all the war relief publications is *The Book of the Homeless*, edited by Edith Wharton. It is a brilliant mosaic of story, verse, pictures and music, contributed by Joffre, Mæterlinck, Galsworthy, Bakst, Renoir, Henry James, Rupert Brooke, Rodin and other famous representatives of the arts of peace and of war in America and the Allied Nations.

Checklist of Additional Reviews

"*Book of the Homeless*," Springfield [Massachusetts] *Republican*, 30 January 1916, Section II, p. 15.
Dial, 60 (13 April 1916), 386.

SUMMER

SUMMER

A NOVEL

BY

EDITH WHARTON

AUTHOR OF

"THE REEF," "THE HOUSE OF MIRTH," ETC.

NEW YORK

D. APPLETON AND COMPANY

1917

"Mrs. Wharton's Story of New England: *Summer* a Pleasing Romance of Village Life," *New York Times Book Review*, 8 July 1917, p. 253

The announcement of a new novel by Edith Wharton is in itself quite enough to arouse the curiosity and pleasurable anticipation of those who care for what is best in contemporary fiction. Coming at the present time, however, when, as we all know, Mrs. Wharton has been so long in France, giving herself and her time to the splendid work of ameliorating some of the suffering brought about by the war, this curiosity and anticipation are greatly increased. For we cannot but wonder what type of story this most notable of present-day American authors will produce from the midst of the stress and turmoil with which she has been surrounded. And so the story which answers that question has a double psychological interest: in writing it, the author has gone as far as possible from the war and the questions raised by the war, choosing as the setting of her tale a little New England village untouched by railroad, telephone, or telegraph lines, sleepy, forgotten, almost moribund; for her plot one as old as civilization itself, one of those constantly recurring tragedies sung by balladists, related by storytellers of every country and in every age.

The characters, too, are not of the highly civilized extremely complex type we are accustomed to meet in Mrs. Wharton's novels. Charity Royall, the heroine and central figure of the book, has little in common with Lily Bart or with the heroine of *The Reef*. All her life, since her fifth year, had been spent in the little village of North Dormer, a "weather-beaten, sun-burnt village of the hills, abandoned of men." Once, and once only, had she had a glimpse of something different, when the clergyman who drove over from Hepburn every other Sunday "when the roads were not plowed up by hauling" took the dozen boys and girls who constitute the youthful population of North Dormer over to Nettleton, the nearest town, to an illustrated lecture on the Holy Land. For that once, and only for that once, Charity Royall "looked into shops with plate-glass fronts" and had other—to her—equally thrilling experiences. This exciting day taught her something of how small, insignificant and dull a place North Dormer was. Not in any way an intellectual person, without so much as a tinge of scholarship in her blood, the dusty volumes slowly mouldering on the shelves of the Hatchard Memorial Library appealed to her no more than they did to the rest of the inhabitants of the village. But if she "found it easier to take North Dormer as the norm of the universe than to go on reading," there were other things to which she was less insensible, and "to all that was light and air, perfume and color, every drop of blood in her responded." Sensitive, impressionable, ignorant, with a pride made all the more fiery and intense by her knowledge that she had been "brought down from the mountain," the little settlement of shiftless outlaws which was at once a menace and a shame to the frugality and respectability of North Dormer, that her very name was a reminder that she had been brought thence and cared for as a matter of charity, she found it difficult, if not altogether impossible, to be as thankful as old Miss Hatchard occasionally reminded her that she ought to be.

"She had never known how to adapt

herself," and she was spiritually an alien in the little village "with all its mean curiosities, its furtive malice, its sham unconsciousness of evil." And so one June afternoon she looked down the empty street, the only street in North Dormer, and murmured to herself, "How I hate everything!"

It is on this same June afternoon that the story begins, the story of Charity Royall's brief romance, that "Summer" of her life which was so quickly followed by a pain-filled Autumn. For on this June afternoon she first meets Lucius Harney, Miss Hatchard's cousin, an architect come to study the old houses in Eagle Country. He is an agreeable, well-bred young man with a pleasant manner and a charming smile, weak certainly, but not at all vicious; she an eager, glowing girl, longing to escape, not only from the dreariness of North Dormer, but from the house of her guardian, Mr. Royall, where one night a horrible thing had happened. From the very start much of what is to follow is entirely evident. Charity herself never blames Harney, feeling always that "she had needed him more than he had wanted her." But she is presently forced to realize that to her his life is an "inscrutable mystery," that of all the background of his existence, his opinions and his prejudices and his relations with other people she knows nothing—less than nothing, because were they explained to her she could not understand. Over her, and therefore over the book, the weight of fatality hangs more and more heavily, until at the last she does the one thing possible, no choice being left her. Always in moments of revolt she had declared she would go "back to the Mountain," but when on the night she did return she learned what "the Mountain" actually meant, she fled from it forever, fled to save that which was more precious to her than herself.

Never has Mrs. Wharton done anything more delicate, more exquisite, than the pen-pictures of the New England countryside with which this book abounds. We see it first in early June, when "the spring-like transparent sky shed a rain of silver sunshine over the roofs of the village," then in the heat of July and August.

> Behind the swarthy mountain the sun had gone down in the waveless gold. . . . For a few minutes, in the clear light that is all shadow, fields and woods were outlined with an unreal precision.

Follows the golden splendor of Autumn, and then and the last, after Charity had come to feel as one "to whom something irreparable and overwhelming had happened," all traces of richness and luxuriance gone, "the lines of the landscape were as finely penciled as in December." So the background blends with Charity's poor little romance, and the bleakness that follows seems to symbolize the bleakness of her coming years.

For despite the chivalrous consideration Mr. Royall presently shows toward her, the reader finds it difficult to echo Charity's final "I guess you're good, too." But this may be because he, like all the other people in the book, is seen only through Charity's eyes and to her he was for a long time only a drunken old man, living a life "debauched and degraded," although she did get one glimpse of another and very different Mr. Royall during the exercises at the Town Hall with which North Dormer celebrated its "Old Home Week," when he spoke in a way both unexpected and impressive. To the reader, as to Charity, he is a somewhat blurred figure, but she herself is vivid and real, so real that one finds one's self questioning her actions, wondering whether even her consciousness of the gulf between Lucius and herself, even her knowledge of

248

the usual fate of the girl married in order "to make things right"—there had been many such girls in North Dormer—would have sufficed to outweigh her consciousness of her supreme claim upon him. For she had no feeling of guilt at any time; only in the world as she knew it "she saw no place for her individual adventure."

The book is slighter in texture and far less complex than are the majority of Mrs. Wharton's novels. And it is also much shorter. In one or two places, indeed, the reader is a little surprised at the slight way in which certain important episodes are touched on. Perhaps the most impressive scene in the book is that of Charity's visit to the mountain, that mountain which all her life had loomed up behind her, at once a menace and a refuge. At last the hour comes when she returns to it, a grim hour in which she comes face to face with a poverty and a degradation beyond her imagining, comes too, face to face with death in a form which is devoid of dignity, devoid almost of anything human; neither in life nor in death does there seem to be any hope whatever for Mary Hyatt or her kin. There is, in this episode, just a trace of the compelling quality of *Ethan Frome*. The village life is but slightly sketched; Charity stood more or less apart from it, just as she always kept herself "contemptuously aloof from the village love making," and this is as exclusively Charity's story as it is ever possible for any story to be that of one person only. Of the sure and delicate analysis of her changing and developing emotions, as of the chiseled beauty of the style, it is unnecessary to speak; these are things which in connection with Mrs. Wharton's work may be taken for granted. *Summer* is not in any way a big book; it ranks with its author's lesser tales, not with *Ethan Frome* or *The House of Mirth* and their fellows. But to say that it is artistic and well worth reading is merely to report something which all readers of modern fiction will accept as a matter of course.

F[rancis] H[ackett], "Loading the Dice," New Republic, 11 (14 July 1917), 311–12

No novelist so accomplished as Mrs. Wharton could fail to write a personable story, but there is an air of falsity about this new invention of hers that arouses a good deal of interest. The idiom, so far as an outsider may guess, is quite true to New England. At the proper moment the girl Charity says, "I want you should leave me," and one hears a human voice. The background is intimately observed, so that one keenly sees the structure of New England houses of many types, and is constantly aware of the dominant Mountain from whose lawlessness Charity was redeemed into North Dormer, to look forward to that sexual limbo which rewards New England virtue. The sweet airs of New England summer fields and woods give a crispness and charm to those pages over which Mrs. Wharton lingers most affectionately, and the contrast of a hot holiday throng in a fair-sized neighboring town is prosecuted with all of her lynx-like sharpness. It is certainly not in these respects that the story can be said to be false.

The theme to which Mrs. Wharton gives such circumstantialities is no more alien to her, so far as intelligent comprehension goes, than the idiom and the background themselves. It is one of those stories of the inexorable that seem perfectly to lend themselves to Mrs. Wharton's icy restraint. If you want to get a region in which inexorability of the moral order has a

249

whacking good time, you do not have to go to New England. George Eliot, as I seem to remember from terrified perusal at the age of fourteen, made the mills of the gods grind with the usual insufficiency of car-grease in the Italy of Romola and Tito.

When it came to the inexorable in the classics, Greece was its favorite locale. Before that time the land of Job was its eminent home—and, if one is going to be open-handed in this respect, what's the matter with Wessex as the scene of cursed spite? But while New England has no exclusive proprietorship in the grim inexorable, there is no doubt that the specific gravity of human conduct is deemed higher in that estimable region than in any other region habitable by the serious story-teller. Mrs. Katherine Fullerton Gerould goes one better than Mrs. Wharton when she wants inexorability. She also resorts to New Englanders but she transplants them to Mocha or Java or Guatemala and serves them up with a little Golden Bough-wow. This mixture of strange and familiar gods jags one's nerves in a delightful manner, but there is a certain incontrovertible safety and sanity about harsh moral laws as they operate in New England, and Mrs. Wharton's instinct is perfectly sound when she proceeds to exhibit the inexorable doing business at the same old stand.

The trouble with *Summer*, however, is that Mrs. Wharton rather forces her note. It is not that seduction as a scheme for literary *bouleversement* is a little out of date. There is no such thing as a catastrophe too trite to be worth reciting. It is only that Mrs. Wharton, always inclined to be sub-human, is much too callous in the uses to which she has put this seduction. She has seen with that frigid eye of hers what an excellent chance there would be against the background of an outlaw Mountain, to show a child adopted into the prim village violating the code of the village, being utterly incapable of enduring the squalor of the outlawry from which she sprang, and being ruthlessly mangled between the stark cliff that rejects her and the waves that fling her blindly against it. This scene of the pitiless, the inevitable, the inexorable, has special attractions for Mrs. Wharton's peculiar temperament. It is not that she is so full of pity, like Thomas Hardy, that she cannot remove her eyes from the spectacle of hapless shipwreck. It is not that she is so full of lifebuoy morality like George Eliot, that she cannot help taking a coastguard interest in these perilous situations. It is more that she cannot help realizing the grisly effectiveness of seeing a fair skiff riding in on the waves of those forces that dominate life, and wrecked for one's fascinated eyes. The wreck may be merely to a dream, the insubstantial fabric of a vision, but the authenticity of that wreck, the bedevilment of the vision, give a wintry glow to the specialist in frustration that occupies a part of Mrs. Wharton's soul.

A good shipwreck, moral or physical, is by no means the least satisfactory of fictional themes, but no author has a right to run up and down the shore line waving a harmless heroine to destruction. What one dislikes in *Summer* is the undoubted purpose of the author to dish the heroine for the sake of the sensation of dishing her. One really suffers on account of the pace at which Mrs. Wharton hurries over the poignancy of a human record to arrive at a cruel predicament. The feeling is certainly established before the end that as a human being Charity Royall is nothing to her author, is merely a creature to be substantiated in detail in order that a dramatic sensation can be properly pulled off, and the curtain rung down before a breathless audience. The scene itself is not just an ingredient in Mrs. Wharton's contrivance, and the youth, Lucius Harney, is

250

not dislocated for the purposes of the story. But the primitive mountaineers, Charity's guardian lawyer, Royall, who wants to marry her, the fierce pride of Charity, the vague "other girl" in the offing to whom the seducer is engaged are all factors in an arrangement, a scheme, which has none of that generous human preoccupation about it which is needed to win the credence of the reader. Mrs. Wharton wants the credence of the reader, but she proposes to earn it by authoritative manner, not by any simple method of humane contagion. The result is a falsity that is scarcely accountable in an artist so acute.

Where this is most evident is in the perfunctory treatment of those situations in the life of Charity Royall that most ask one to put oneself in her place. There is, for example, the occasion on which this girl, in love with the young architect who has come for the summer to North Dormer, overhears her guardian disclose to him the secret she has never guessed of her disgraceful parentage. "'My God, how ghastly,' Harney murmured; and Charity, choking with humiliation sprang to her feet and ran upstairs. She knew at last: knew that she was the child of a drunken convict and of a woman who wasn't 'half-human,' and was glad to have her go; and she had heard this history of her origin related to the one being in whose eyes she longed to appear superior to the people about her.... It was too bitter to picture him as the detached impartial listener to such a story. 'I wish he'd go away; I wish he'd go to-morrow, and never come back!' She moaned to her pillow; and far into the night she lay there in the disordered dress she had forgotten to take off, her whole soul a tossing misery on which her hopes and dreams spun about like drowning straws." This is a curiously superficial and mechanical account of a heroine's crisis. Girls do moan to their pillows, of

course, and lie disordered far into the night. But assassination of a hope would create a more bitter fever than this. Imagine Mr. Howells, restrained as he really is, offering these few hackneyed and jejune phrases as part of a spiritual history. The fact is, Mrs. Wharton needed Charity Royall's unfortunate ancestry in her business as a story-teller, but the effect of disclosing what in reality was nothing more than a literary *convenance*, she could not take too seriously.

Because of this and other failures in sympathy and plausibility, *Summer* cannot be set to the right side of Mrs. Wharton's account. The predicament of the girl who loves more than she is loved is intensely valid, the social situation of a girl whose child is to be born out of marriage is the most crucial and difficult in the world. But Mrs. Wharton has arranged for Charity's misfortune too deliberately, deprived her of aid too sweepingly, afforded her marriage with her guardian too simply, to be known as an artist in handling this great theme. It is true that Mrs. Wharton has made the shadows of the Mountain funeral quite terrible, and has brought lawyer Royall to the fore as a welcome relief to an unremitting strain. This kind of skill, however, is the only real gift that *Summer* illustrates. It is not a repellent story, but is essentially an empty one, and suggests too often the failings of a person who is capable of going slumming among souls.

251

Edwin Francis Edgett, "Edith Wharton's Tale of Thwarted Love," Boston *Evening Transcript*, 25 July 1917, Part 2, p. 6.

Where in New England did Mrs. Wharton unearth the scene and the people for her latest novel? Is it possible that she knows either by personal contact or by hearsay in what obscure corner of this section of America is placed the bare and sparsely populated hamlet of North Dormer? Can she have seen the country slum district that she calls "the Mountain," or is she drawing solely upon her imagination when she describes to us its bleak aspect, its filthy hovels and its more than degenerate inhabitants? Is it merely for dramatic purposes, to give a newness to a well-worn plot, to enliven conventional episodes by placing them in the midst of an unusual atmosphere, to add a romantic stimulus to a tale utterly lacking in originality, that she invites us to follow Charity Royall through the rapid progress of her infatuation for the young man from the city who arouses in her the sex instinct and then calmly leaves her to her fate?

No reader of *Summer* would for a moment imagine its scene to be New England did Mrs. Wharton not explicitly tell us so. "The place lies high and in the open," she says on her first page, "and lacks the lavish shade of the more protected New England villages." Aside from this, and from an occasional mention of one or more New England cities, the story contains nothing to suggest its scene. Its personages are so few that even the New England character, habits of thought and tricks of speech have little if any part in it. During many of its pages we hear much and see nothing of "the Mountain," that strange and almost inaccessible district whence Charity Royall was brought in babyhood to the lawyer's house in North Dormer which she has ever since called her home. But towards the close of the story "The Mountain" looms impassive if not impressive as Charity, her love-life with Lucius Harney at an end, ascends its slopes under the wild impulse of returning to the people whence she sprang. There she found a settlement in which "two or three low houses lay in stony fields, crouching among the rocks as if to brace themselves against the wind." They were "hardly more than sheds, built of logs and rough boards, with tin stove-pipes sticking out of their roofs." In one of them Charity found her mother lying dead, and over her body, laid coffinless in a hastily made grave, the service was read by the village clergyman who had fortuitously overtaken her on her way up to the mountain.

This may be New England, and a New England that Mrs. Wharton has ventured into, but we fear, however, that it is simply a New England to which she has given a local habitation and a name merely for the purpose of offering impetus to what would otherwise be a very sluggish and a very commonplace story. For *Summer* is simply a tale of seduction of the sort that has been popular on the stage and in the novel since the beginning of the art of storytelling and novel writing. Time was when a moral lesson or a moral tag was essential. Time was when *Charlotte Temple* was held up as a Bible of sex instructions for weak and errant young women and for evil and depraved young men. But that time vanished long ago, and such stories as *Summer,* such adventures as those of Charity Royall and Lucius Harney, may be narrated without thought of a "lesson" to reader of either sex or of any age. Indeed more than once Mrs. Wharton seems to spice her story in order to stimulate the jaded appetites of readers who have been overfed on fictional diet of the Robert Chambers sort.

In days past, Mrs. Wharton has given us many a keen and subtle analysis of mind and conduct through the medium of fiction. Some of her short stories are among the best in the English language. Ideas were then to her living things, but in recent years it appears to be difficult for her to keep them alive. To be sure, *Summer* is told with something of her earlier skill, with not a little of her former sense of character. It goes forward at times with a directness, and with a certain impelling force of tragedy, but on the whole it is ramblingly discursive. The fact that its subject is old is nothing against it, but does it add anything new to it? In brief outline it simply restates the inevitable fate of a country girl when a city man crosses her path, showing the growth of their passion, describing their meetings in a secluded camp in the woods, relating her visits to a quack doctor when she suspects approaching motherhood, and finally bringing her to superficial respectability by marrying her to the elderly man who rescued her from "the Mountain" and in whose house she has ever since lived.

All this, without Mrs. Wharton's name and without her manner of telling, would make a wholly negligible story. But reputation has its value, and *Summer* will undoubtedly be sought because it is her latest novel. And that there is something in it worth while because it is Mrs. Wharton's cannot be denied. Although its substance is commonplace, its style is not. . . .

None of the few characters in the story is more than casually sketched. They are all as inconclusive and indeterminate as her scene. They move across her stage like shadows. Once in a while, however, she gives us a bit of description out of their mouths. . . .

Any reader curious to see this latest development of Mrs. Wharton's story-telling skill, or to gain new enlightenment upon New England life and people, need not hesitate to read *Summer*. Its combination of newness and oldness will certainly prove stimulating, and possibly it may open a hitherto neglected vista into an obscure corner of Yankeedom.

"Plots and People," *Nation*, 105 (2 August 1917), 124–5

Summer reenters the field in which, with *Ethan Frome*, Mrs. Wharton produced her single masterpiece. If she does not here duplicate or rival that amazing feat, it is because the new matter falls short of the old in tragic force and conclusiveness. There is an element of surprise in this tale: until the very end we seem to be preparing for some irremediable catastrophe; and spectators may differ as to whether the actual outcome is the happy ending or mere bathos. Here once more is the New England village that has seen better days, peopled by remnants of old families and old traditions—a race which has long ceased to prosper and which now hardly takes the trouble to hand on the torch of life. The countryside is sprinkled with the husks of ancient dwellings which retain something of their Georgian state even in the ruin. To make a book of them, comes a young stranger from the city; and stumbles at once, after the manner of his kind, upon rustic Beauty. But Charity Royall of North Dormer is as far as possible from the giggling coquette of usage. She bears the name of a gone-to-seed lawyer of the old stock and rules his house, but she is of wilder blood, the daughter of a loose woman of "the Mountain," whom Royall has adopted as a child. Charity herself is of fine womanly stuff, and easily keeps the widowed Royall in his place on the single occasion when her youth and his loneliness tempt him. But she has no chance at all against the young lover from the city, who has his way with her and leaves her as such young lovers will. She herself is to pay the full penalty in shame and suffering, and turns for refuge to her own people, the wretched outlaws of "the Mountain," whom she has not visited since childhood. But she finds them unspeakable and unthinkable, and escapes from them: without hope or goal, but determined that her child shall not be born to make one more in that foul nest. And it is at this moment, when we are saying, "Now she will throw herself over a cliff," or "Now she is going to die of exposure," that old Royall comes in search of her and saves her and marries her; and (a marvel!) the disillusioned Mrs. Wharton permits, nay, encourages, us to hope a good measure of happiness for them both. Gladly we own that to us the situation rings true, we believe in Royall, and we believe in Charity. But we do not believe in the young Lothario or in the various tricks of coincidence with which the integrity of the action is vitiated. Co-incidences happen, and so do pearls, but it is the human hand that strings them on a wire; and what need, we ask somewhat impatiently, has Mrs. Wharton of that kind of industry?

Parts of *Summer* . . . tend to shake the reputation for coldness and lack of sympathy sometimes imputed to Mrs. Edith Wharton, its author. Mrs. Wharton is perhaps the most brilliant analyst among American women novelists. Truth, a necessary requisite in accurate analysis, is only sympathetic in an emotional as distinguished from a literary sense—when the object under treatment is sympathetic. This obviously has been Mrs. Wharton's guiding principle, with the result that patients coming under her scalpel have sometimes withered beneath the strong rays of truth turned upon them. For this she has, of course, been the true artist. If the roots of this charge that she is aloof and unfeeling go no deeper than this, no stigma—no literary stigma, that is—can be attached to her work.

The principal characters of this story are dissected minutely, but the analyses, conducted in the author's characteristic manner, reveal no chilly or unfriendly sentiments, although of sentimentality there is none. Indeed, the character of Charity Royall, despite her impulses and moral faults, is very appealing. And some vividly described scenes, in their drama and pathos, show that Mrs. Wharton can betray depth of sympathy and feeling without yielding to the sentimentality which the situation invites.

The scene of the story, as of *Ethan Frome*, is in a stagnant New England country village, apparently in northwestern Massachusetts, and at some distance from the railways. The heroine, Charity

254

Royall, is born one of a small lawless community resident in the neighboring hills. She is a sort of ward of Lawyer Royall, an enigmatic recluse, whose home she has kept in a haphazard way for the several years after his wife's death. Royall offers her an affront and then asks her to marry him. She sharply refuses. Mrs. Wharton touches on moral conditions in the back country villages, and then makes of Charity's clandestine love affair with a young architect from the outside world the main event of the narrative. In the background, however, the figure of Royall is always in evidence. An impression of the man's unusual mentality is created, but the mystery of his habits, his personality and the reason for his isolation are, for the time being, merely glimpsed, or kept in abeyance. But there he is, waiting, waiting! He seems to know by intuition the inevitable consequences of Charity's romance, and the instincts that are driving her on. And when disillusion comes Royall is at her side to offer the protection of his name and home and asking nothing for himself. The final scene is preceded by a vivid description of Charity's return to her own people, the funeral of her mother, and her quiet removal therefrom by Royall. The story is brilliantly conceived, with many tense passages and is striking in its portrayal of diverse human passions, but its conception of New England character is that of a "literary," even a romantic, visitor.

John Macy, "Edith Wharton," *Dial*, 63 (30 August 1917), 161–2

Within the memory of a not very aged reader of American fiction there have been a few wonderful moments, moments when one has realized, perhaps without clear, critical consciousness, that something important has happened. Such unforgettable moments are one's first reading of *Roderick Hudson*, and *A Modern Instance*, and *Huckleberry Finn*, and *A New England Nun*, and *The Red Badge of Courage*, and *Sister Carrie* (the promise of that book has not been fulfilled), and two books by Mrs. Wharton, *The Greater Inclination* and *The Touchstone*. In those days, the end of the Nineties, most of the established literature of the world was still unexplored, and a new arrival from New York had to compete with the world's inexhaustible masterpieces and also with contemporaneous English fiction, especially the two gods of the undergraduate, Stevenson and Kipling. Mrs. Wharton dawned upon our ignorant but eager appreciation, a little bewildering to our immaturity because she was so mature and sophisticated. Henry James and Meredith had educated us to read her intelligently (though we had only begun to read them), and if our admiration was boyish it was genuine. I remember distinctly the emotions of surprise and delight at the appearance of a new writer, an American writer, whose first work showed the competence and finish of a practiced hand.

Then followed, at intervals sufficiently long to indicate careful workmanship, now a novel, now a collection of short stories, all of unvarying excellence. But there was another sense in which the work was unvarying, another interpretation of the moderate rate of production. Though the plots were ingenious, original, not cast in one mold, the kind of life so acutely and deeply studied was a limited, even thin, upper layer of society. Was her material restricted? She saw far, she penetrated to the bottom of a soul, but could she see broadly? Was her knowledge of life at once cosmopolitan and class-provincial, like the outlook of Henry James? One of her contemporaries, Mrs. Atherton, I think, was reported to have expressed, apropos of *The House of Mirth*, a somewhat envious fear lest Mrs. Wharton's vein should be exhausted and to have suggested that her success was due, if not to her snobbery, to the snobbery of a public that liked to read about the high life. I doubt if snobbery can find an ounce of nourishment in the gray pathos of the story of Lily Bart. And as for her creator, a woman who is born to the social purple and to the intellectual purple, whose attitude toward her own class is tragic and ironic, who treats with a fine disdain just those qualities and privileges of the upper ten which the next four or five tens admire and emulate is the shrewdest possible foe of snobbery. The powerful final answer to these questions was that amazing masterpiece, *Ethan Frome*. And the answer is reiterated by *Summer*.

Before *Ethan Frome* New England fiction was virginal. The stork preceded the doctor, but nothing preceded the stork. A doubtful exception is *The Scarlet Letter*, in which the sorrow of illicit love is covered by a romantic veil. The exquisite stories of Miss Jewett and Miss Wilkins give delicate expression to as much as the shy New England characters would have wished to tell of themselves. These stories show the grace of narrow lives, the charm and humor that can flourish amid rural poverty. By not making the deeper passions articulate the authors are precisely true to New England character. There are two kinds of suppression; one is the suppression of life by the author's ignorance or reticence; the other is the suppression of feeling by life itself. Passion beats against obdurate facts and falls broken and bleeding. This contest must be studied objectively, for the characters do not understand what is happening to them. The author understands, and sitting omniscient and Olympian at the right hand side of Fate, contemplates their lives; at the same time he enters into each life with immense tenderness. This is the greatest achievement of that kind of imagination which creates fiction. The combined power of impartial contemplation and sympathy makes the genius of Thomas Hardy and it makes the genius of Mrs. Wharton as it is found in *Ethan Frome* and *Summer*. For she cannot play with these people, as she plays with her people in New York society, shooting her own ironic shafts at them or analyzing them in terms of their own sophisticated talk. Her New England people are elemental, victims of circumstance (so also, of course, was Lily Bart), and they must be left for the irony of life to deal with. At the same time there is no cold detachment. A woman who had been reared on a bleak New England farm could not have a more intimate comprehension than has Mrs. Wharton of its pitiful details and lonely aspirations. And the New England woman's knowledge would not be so wise or so wide, for it would not include so much of the rest of life as to give by comparison a full realization of bitterness and frustration.

For the tragedy of *Ethan Frome* and of *Summer* is not a shattered love affair. That experience is so common that everybody has known a case or two among his own friends. The tragedy is the defeat, the spiritual death, of natures that have not merely capacity for strong sexual passion but the capacity, which passion indicates, to grow and make something out of better circumstances than chance happens to permit.

The saddest thing in New England, and no doubt in some other parts of the world, is the contrast between the splendor of the landscape and the aridity of some of the life that mocks its loveliness. A distinguished painter who knows the New England scenery but not the New England people told me that he admired *Ethan Frome*, but he could not believe that such people lived—they would all be dead by murder or suicide. Well, the only answer is that though murder and suicide are not unknown in rustic New England, Judge Brack was on the whole right: "people don't do such things." They live along, like *Ethan Frome* and his two women, after an abortive attempt at murder and suicide; or like the girl in *Summer*, after the wreck of passion, they drop into a life of more or less comfortable resignation. For her, at the end of summer, there is an autumn of peace. The story, in its beautiful natural setting, is mellower and gentler than *Ethan Frome*, which might have been called *"Winter."*

In her feeling for nature Mrs. Wharton is a poet. My friend the painter tells me not to mix up the arts, and says that words cannot describe. Perhaps they cannot, but they do. I could prove it by many quotations from *Summer*, but it is better for you to read the book and see whether I am wrong in regarding it as a marvel of composition. The descriptions have the same continuity with the narrative that trees have with the road they shelter. Mrs. Wharton is at once direct and subtle. She unfolds with perfect lucidity the complexities of human nature. Her sentences are so beautifully sequential that sometimes a passage seems to straighten out, tense and flexible, like a taut wire; and the vibration is the sound of life.

Lawrence Gilman, "The Book of the Month: Mrs. Wharton Reverts to Shaw," *North American Review*, 206 (August 1917), 304–7

It is a good many years since Mr. Bernard Shaw complained, in a famous Dedicatory Epistle to Mr. A. B. Walkley, that "though we have plenty of dramas with heroes and heroines who are in love and most accordingly marry or perish at the end of the play, or about people whose relations with one another have been complicated by the marriage laws, not to mention the looser sort of plays which trade on the tradition that illicit love affairs are at once vicious and delightful, we have no modern English plays in which the natural attraction of the sexes for one another is made the mainspring of the action." Mr. Shaw's lament would scarcely implicate the English-speaking stage of today. It is true that when the conformist Briton or American (who can bring himself to discuss matters of sex only in the genteel jargon of journalese) uses the word "betrayed" in connection with the passional relations of men and women, he does not yet follow Mr. Shaw's example and enclose the term in derisively challenging quotation-marks. Nevertheless, in our contemporary Anglo-Saxon theatre, matters are not as they were in 1903. The discussions in *Man and Superman* are today a good deal more familiar to our provincial Drama Clubs than are those blameless farces of Mr. Howells upon which our amateur histrions used to wreak themselves in the innocent American 'nineties. But however it may be in the theatre, to the greater part of our commercially engendered fiction the substance of Mr. Shaw's complaint would still apply. Among those wonderful beings who produce the bulk of our nation's fictional provender, the delusions of a legendary sexual philosophy persistently endure,—as ubiquitous as ragweed, though far more beloved; and for ninety-nine million American readers, Man is still the Pursuer and Woman the Pursued, just as if Mr. Shaw had never been born.

At first blush, for the reader habituated to the conventional novelistic philosophy of sexual experience, Mrs. Wharton's *Summer* will probably suggest familiar satisfactions. But we deem it only fair to warn those moral policemen of American letters whose vigilance may for the moment be diverted by public excitements of another kind that Mrs. Wharton, wearing the most guileless and disarming expression in the world, has in this novel dared to portray an erotic interlude in which Girlhood is exhibited to the reading public as instinctively bent upon fulfilling what Mr. Shaw so long ago called "the woman's need of the man to enable her to carry on Nature's most urgent work," claiming him "by natural right for a purpose that far transcends their mortal personal purposes." Mr. Shaw, in those distant days of nascent theatrical emancipation, observed, you will remember, that men, to "protect themselves against a too aggressive prosecution of the woman's business, have set up a feeble romantic convention that the initiative in sex business must always come from the man"; but that "the pretence is so shallow that even in the theatre, that last sanctuary of unreality, it imposes only on the inexperienced." In that still more impregnable sanctuary of unreality, the Popular Novel,—and also in the sentimental amber of newspaper chronicles,—is preserved the degrading myth of woman's sexual imbecility—a tradition which would make of her (in the imperishable phrase of Dr. Middleton) merely "a fantastical planguncula." Now Mrs. Wharton, whatever her defects of sympathy and her spiritual *lacunæ*, is, as M. Emile Boutroux observed of Pascal, "a singular mixture of passion and geometry." A recognizably malicious fellow-craftswoman of Mrs. Wharton's once characterized her fiction as the product of "an unslaked voluptuary." We need not view Mrs. Wharton in exactly that light to perceive that she is at least extraordinarily sensitive to the vibrations of a passionate mood; and when we take into account her grasp of psychic geometry,—her exquisite perception of spatial relationships and impingements in the emotional field,—we shall understand why it is that she can give us so veracious and precise and living a picture as her study of Charity Royall's intercourse with Lucius Harney. We shall also understand why, in her notation of this experience, she has necessarily been incapable of recognizing that "feeble romantic convention" which Mr. Shaw so energetically turned out of doors in his classic treatise on Woman as Pursuer and Contriver. Charity Royall is separated by a thousand worlds of origin and impulse and spiritual process from John Tanner's conception of Ann Whitefield; but she is an equally definite refutation of the tradition that Woman is the helpless prey of Man.

The raw materials of this erotic history of Mrs. Wharton's are traditional enough to have produced, in the hands of almost any one of the hucksters of our fictional marketplace, a conventional romance of seduction and betrayal (minus the Shavian quotation-marks), with its inevitable aura of disgraced and heart-broken parents, secret parturition, "a little unwanted and unloved," and matrimony ultimately enforced to appease an outraged community. Mrs. Wharton has employed this antique mechanism with a bold and free hand, with a fine disdain of its sanctified implications. Charity Royall knew perfectly well what "going with a city fellow" meant—knew that "almost every village could show a victim of the perilous venture." Crouching on the steps of the verandah and looking into the window of Harney's room through the parted sprays of clematis, seeing him brooding there under the lamp, she was aware, "in every pulse of her rigid body, of the welcome his eyes and lips would give her" should she make known her presence. "She suddenly understood what would happen if she went in. It was the thing that *did* happen between young men and girls, and that North Dormer ignored in public and snickered over on the sly. It was what every girl of Charity's class knew about before she left school. It was what had happened to Ally Hawe's sister Julia. . . . Since the day before, she had known exactly what she would feel if Harney should take her in his arms: the melting of palm into palm and mouth on mouth, and the long flame burning her from head to foot." And, fully knowing, eagerly desiring, she invited freely her lover, later on in the little abandoned farmhouse on the mountainside, with its bleached gray walls, its sun-washed empty rooms, its broken dangling gate, its rose-bushes run wild, and the long shadows of the old environing apple trees stretching their cool fingers over the grass in the evening light. . . . Here she and Harney lived flaming and secret and dream-like hours, "when the only reality was the wondrous unfolding of her new self, the reaching out to the light of all her contracted tendrils. . . . She had always thought of love as something confused and furtive, and he made it as bright and open as the summer air."

Here, and to the end, Mrs. Wharton conducts her tragic chronicle with a grave contempt for the *clichés* of sexual romance. That she chooses to direct the culmination of the tale to an issue that would have enraged Mr. Shaw's John Tanner, constitutes, of course, no lapse on her part from artistic integrity. In an ideal civilization, no doubt,—one governed by intelligence and feeling rather than by conventional sanctions and formulas and taboos,—the gestatory outcome of Charity's passion would have made her a subject for felicitation. In such an ideal civilization, we like to fancy that we should hear John Tanner exhorting some atavistic pharisee . . . "Good Heavens, man, what are you complaining of? . . . Here is a woman who has turned to her highest purpose and greatest function—to increase, multiply and replenish the earth. And instead of admiring her courage and rejoicing in her instinct; instead of crowning the completed womanhood and raising the triumphal strain of 'Unto us a child is born: unto us a son is given,' here you are pulling a long face and looking as ashamed and disgraced as if the girl had committed the vilest of crimes. . . . She is doing the States a service. . . . The whole world really knows, though it dare not say so, . . . that vitality and bravery are the greatest qualities a woman can have, and motherhood her solemn initiation into womanhood; and that the fact of her not being legally married matters not one scrap to her worth."

But Mrs. Wharton, as she might graciously remind us, is not projecting a social Utopia: she is denoting a social condition. And so the history of Charity Royall—a history uttered with beauty and memorable honesty—ends grayly, resignedly, with long anonymous years of kindly and terrible amelioration stretching vacantly before her.

"New Novels: *Summer*," *Times Literary Supplement* [England], 27 September 1917, p. 464

In *Summer* ... Mrs. Wharton matches her *Ethan Frome* with another great little drama of New England landscape; and the second is almost as strong and compact as the first, and in a particular way more clearly and brilliantly figured. Summer it is, indeed as much as *Ethan Frome* was winter—blaze and swelter of heat in the "large unconscious scenery," as Whitman called it, from which the kindly and *mitigating density* of history and memory is all absent. In this glare of New England sunlight everything is helplessly visible, and in the remoter corners the thinly spread wisps of civilization make about the same effect against the big background as a dropped paper bag in an Alpine gorge; they are irrelevant and accidental and detachable. In Mrs. Wharton's little dusty village there is indeed a public library, founded by a literary celebrity, with a custodian appointed by the celebrity's great-niece; but this reproduction of the methods and manners of culture makes the general immensity only the more blank. There drifts onto the scene a still more impalpable fragment of the civilized world in the shape of an agreeable young man from New York, haunting these byways on a summer holiday. Nothing so light or so trivial as this chance scrap from an organized society could hope to appear substantial in such a light, nor even to avoid the obvious—the obvious being that the young man should first dazzle and then abandon a maiden of the village. The weight of Mrs. Wharton's story does not rest on him, and like a good artist she does not demand an ounce more of resistance from him than she needs. The only substance in the scene is that which alone really belongs to it and could not belong elsewhere, and so is part of the texture of the soil. Public libraries and easy young men may look unreal there; but intractable jumps and chunks of character—the words which seem to suit Mrs. Wharton's couple of central figures—hold their own and throw heavy shadows. They are remarkable beings indeed, a bitter girl and a tarnished old man; and they are reason enough with all the illustration they are capable of giving, for a writer like Mrs. Wharton to wish to measure her skill against their toughness. One of them, the old man, would have given her more than she takes of him; he is a really rich piece of creation, a masterful *louche*, obscurely battered and defeated derelict of his world; he does not, one feels, get all the display he should have had. But the picture of the girl, between the first line of the story and the last, is complete, without a missing or a superfluous stroke. Her rage of passion and pride is not at all a romantic idyll, but it is a fine drama.

In her treatment of this drama, in her figuration of it through its short series of episodes, Mrs. Wharton does what we expect: she shows a hand which constantly grows in freedom and certainty. Anyone who cares about the way in which a pen is handled should take this book and read, and read again, such pages as those which record the excursion to the country town for the Fourth of July celebrations, or the girl's visit to the insinuating lady-doctor, or the wild night-piece of the funeral on the mountain. After considering these only—though there are others which might be named—a critic may well ask whether anyone but Mrs. Wharton now shows just this feeling for an incident, this sense that an incident has not been described until it has been imagined as a rounded and independent object, something which stands in the midst and which a spectator may walk right round. It is a quality, ever since Flaubert was, in which Flaubert has been the supreme master; and Mrs. Wharton, if any novelist at all, has something of this kind of power over a fact—an excursion, or a funeral or whatever else. Nowhere in her work is this quality to be admired more unreservedly than in *Summer*.

"Novels Whose Scenes Are Laid in New England," *Review of Reviews*, 56 (September 1917), 333

Edith Wharton draws a grim picture of New England in her story *Summer*. Even the ordinary reader will question the uncompromising texture of life in the village of North Dormer. And if that is incomprehensible, what of the "Mountain," that community of outlaws, ne'er-do-wells, and drunken vagabonds set in the fastnesses of the hills fifteen miles from this sedate New England hamlet? The characters seem drawn in the flat; they are two-dimensional so far as their emotions go. All the joy and pleasantness and tenderness has been extracted from their lives with a hand so skilled in literary portraiture that the sentences bite like the acids of the etcher. Charity Royall, a girl of the "Mountain," rescued in infancy from degrading surroundings and brought up in North Dormer, reverts to old blood strains and flees the monotony and repression of her narrow life to seek one careless summer of rapture with the first young man who chances to happen her way. She has her summer and pays toll to heredity. Then the grip of engrafted conventions strangles her impulses to do the fine thing when the young man leaves her to follow his own path; the animal instinct of the wild creature asserts itself and she seeks safety in marriage with the elderly man who rescued her in childhood from the "Mountain."

It is a sordid story. Possibly Mrs. Wharton has a distinct object in dragging to the light the worst side of a disappearing rural life. Possibly her exquisite descriptive passages contrasted with the delineation of the clutching ugliness of these country districts point the way to necessary missionary work which shall restore equilibrium. It has been said since this novel was published that no community similar to the "Mountain" has been known to exist in New England. In justice to Mrs. Wharton, it is only fair to state that but one remove from New England, in New York, there were just such communities before transportation problems had been solved and the country opened up by the use of the cheap automobiles. She has portrayed the sullen wilderness and clannishness of the natives with extraordinary fidelity and she is correct in her statement that the only outside force that touched them at all was that of religion.

H. W. Boynton, "Some Stories of the Month," *Bookman*, 46 (September 1917), 93–4

[Mary Wilkins Freeman's] own New England, the scene of the early tales, is an affair of black and white, of strong crude forces and repressions. Such is the New England of Mrs. Wharton in *Ethan Frome* and *Summer*. But while Miss Wilkins's voice had always a certain raw tang of the native, altogether lacked grace and flexibility, it *was* the voice of rustic New England. Mrs. Wharton has had the task of subduing her rich and varied and worldly instrument to its provincial theme. She has succeeded: *Summer* shows all the virtue of her style and none of its weakness. Here is no routine elegance, no languor of disillusion, no bite of deliberate satire. As in *Ethan Frome*, this writer who has come perilously near being the idol of snobs shows herself as an interpreter of life in its elements, stripped of the habits and inhibitions of the polite world. The story lacks the tragic completeness of the earlier one, has indeed a species of happy ending—an ending, at worst, of pathos not without hope. The scene is the New England village of North Dormer, once as good as its neighbours, but now deserted and decaying in its corner among the hills. It is vignetted in a few sentences at the beginning: "A little wind moved among the round white clouds on the shoulders of the hills, driving their shadows across the fields and down the grassy road that takes the name of a street when it passes through North Dormer. The place lies high and in the open, and lacks the lavish shade of the more protected New England villages. The clump of weeping willows about the duck pond, and the Norway spruces in front of the Hatchard gate, cast almost the only roadside shadow between lawyer Royall's house and the point where, at the other end of the village, the road rises above the church and skirts the black hemlock wall enclosing the cemetery." The Hatchards are the great people of the place, with an elderly spinster still solvent and in residence, and a Memorial Library bearing musty witness to that distinguished and now extinguished author, Honorius Hatchard, who had hobnobbed with Irving and Halleck, back in the forties.

Another old family are the Royalls. Their present representative is the middle-aged lawyer who, after showing promise elsewhere, has returned to North Dormer while still a young man, for the apparent purpose of going to seed there at his leisure. Above the village, though at a distance—fastness of a strange community of outlaws and degenerates—towers the craggy mountain from which, years back, Lawyer Royall has rescued a child. As Charity Royall she grows up in his household, and after his wife's death becomes its unchallenged ruler. Her little liking for Royall himself he has destroyed by making, in his "lonesomeness," a single false step toward her. Her own lonely lot in unyouthful North Dormer is lightened only by the vague dreams of girlhood. Then the fairy prince comes in the person of a young architect from the city whom certain local relics of fine building have attracted to the neighbourhood, and whom a swift romance with the girl Charity holds there. She becomes his mistress, he deserts her in her "trouble," she turns desperately to the haunt of her people, "the Mountain"; and is rescued for a second time and finally by Lawyer Royall. In her marriage with the aging man whom she has scorned there is, we really believe, some chance of happiness, or at least content. Young love is dead, but old love is ready to creep into its place. Mrs. Wharton has often been accused of bitterness: let her critics note that the whole effect of this powerful story hangs upon our recognition of the power of simple human goodness—not "virtuousness," but faithful, unselfish devotion of one sort or another—to make life worth living.

Until the end itself, *Summer* has seemed to be moving, as *Ethan Frome* moved, toward some grim catastrophe.

[H. W. Boynton], "Outstanding Novels of the Year," *Nation*, 105 (29 November 1917), 600

Mrs. Wharton's *Summer* would be ranked among the books of predictable quality only as being by the author of *Ethan Frome*, which was in its day a sufficiently exciting departure from the expected. It is a moving tale, with its action that hovers so long between the neighboring verges of tragedy and squalor, and is in the end drawn back by force merely of the saving goodness in human nature, to a foothold of safety and of real if wintry sunshine.

"Wharton (Edith Newbold), née Jones. *Summer*," *Athenæum* [England], 4623 (November 1917), 597

In externals this is a simple variety of the common theme of the butterfly lover and the sterling though repellent character in whom the betrayed maiden at last finds a sure refuge. But it is a thoroughly individualized version of the old story, and a small masterpiece of refined and economical art. The three main characters, and their human and natural environment in the little New England town nestling under the shadow of the Mountain, are blended into a subdued harmony well suiting the restrained tragedy of the tale.

[T. S. Eliot], "*Summer*," *The Egoist* [England], January 1919, p. 10

Even Mrs. Wharton's parerga have importance, and this parergon,[1] a very brief novel, offers interest as a work in a curious kind of satire which Mrs. Wharton has made her own; and just the kind of satire, it may be remarked, that her literary training and sympathies might have made most difficult for her. The book is, in fact—or should be—the death-blow to a kind of novel which has flourished in New England, the novel in which the wind whistles through the stunted firs and over the granite boulders into the white farmhouses where pale gaunt women sew rag carpets. Mrs. Wharton does the trick by a deliberate and consistent realism, by refraining from the slightest touch of irony, by suppressing all evidence of European culture. She even allows herself to be detected in just the slight smile of an inhabitant of Boston (where the type of novel in question is read) at the name of the Honorius Hatchard Memorial Library, 1839, in the village of North Dormer. The young man comes up from the city (Springfield), Charity gives him all she has, and the young man returns to marry Annabel Balch of Springfield. The scene of the county fair at Nettleton is one of unrelieved horror. This novel will certainly be considered "disgusting" in America; it is certain that not one reader in a thousand will apprehend the author's point of view. But it should add to Mrs. Wharton's reputation as a novelist the distinction of being the satirist's satirist.

1 Parergon: an incidental, subordinate or subsidiary work.

Checklist of Additional Reviews

"The New Books," *Outlook*, 116 (1 August 1917), 522.

Catholic World, 106 (October 1917), 127–28.

Spectator, 119 (13 October 1917), 389.

"Fiction in Brief," *Saturday Review* [England], 124 (3 November 1917), 352.

Louis de Mondanon, "Edith Wharton: Plein Eté," *Etudes* [France], 157 (October-December 1918), 378.

THE MARNE

THE MARNE

BY

EDITH WHARTON

AUTHOR OF

"THE REEF," "SUMMER," "THE HOUSE OF MIRTH"

D. APPLETON AND COMPANY

NEW YORK   1918

"Mrs. Wharton's Story of the Marne: Remarkable Romance of the War, Picturing Certain American Types in France," New York *Times*, 8 December 1918, Section 7, p. 1.

Among many people of the ancient world there was a popular belief that certain words and phrases were words of power—words which could conjure up spirits good or evil. And in this, as in other of those old ideas we now call superstitions, there lurked a tiny grain of truth. Words there are which now and throughout many centuries, if not for all time, are words of power, and can evoke visions. To the not very numerous company of these, that war which to us who are alive today must always remain "the war" has added a goodly number. Ypres, Louvain, Château-Thierry, the Marne—greatest and most powerful of all this last, symbolizing that beginning of the end which came four years ago with the hurling back of the first German onslaught, as well as the beginning of that débâcle which was to turn the boche into a whining suppliant pleading for mercy, who had shown none. The use of *The Marne* as the name of a book would be for nearly any writer presumption unspeakable: no higher praise can be given to this volume of Mrs. Wharton's than to say that it justifies its author's choice of a title.

For within its few pages, less than 150 in all, is concentrated much, if not the whole, of the meaning of the Marne, both to France and to America. It holds the best description we have yet seen of the attitude of certain classes of Americans toward the war: it shows us American tourists and refugees from Belgium and Northern France; France at peace and at war; the destruction and the wreckage, the indomitable spirit that four years of horror could not quell. And through it all there breathes a passionate, almost devout love of France, France which is "the phoenix country, always rising from the ashes of her recognized mistakes." The book is, of course, not without faults: its principal character, Troy Belknap, through whose eyes we are supposed to see it all, never becomes entirely real to us. Moreover, we are in truth shown it, not as it would or could appear to a boy in his teens, no matter how sympathetic and highly gifted, but as it has been seen by an experienced woman of the world, possessed of a keen and finely cultivated intellect. But this matters very little. The thread of the story which holds the book together is of the slightest, and not in itself of any particular importance.

It does, however, fulfill its manifest mission of a useful framework. The volume opens with a description of how as a small boy, the only child of rich American parents, Troy Belknap visited France every summer. Then, when he is 15, comes the war. His dearly beloved friend and tutor, M. Gantier, goes at once to join his regiment, and there is a vivid sketch of Paris in the days of stress, and another of those wealthy Americans who were chiefly concerned with an anxiety to get home and showed "a general tendency to regard the war as a mere background to their personal grievances" even while they gave lavishly of the money they could so easily spare. Troy himself of course was not one of these; he loved France, and presently he was vouchsafed a glimpse of the historic battlefield of the Marne. There he saw much he never forgot, and found a

267

grave which became to him as a symbol of the whole. After a while, the scene shifts to America, and we have a sharply etched picture of the days which now seem so remote when war tableaux and charity dances and "propaganda lectures given by handsome French officers" were the fashion, and New York society kept up "a kind of perpetual picnic on the ruins of civilization." One of the best things in this book, which is so full of good things, is the description of the gradual change from this viewpoint to that of three years later, when at last "America tore the gag of neutrality from her lips" and all her people found themselves "not only happier but more sensible than when a perpetually thwarted indignation had had to expend itself in vague philanthropy." Though they still had—and have—much to learn, as witness Troy's steamer companions, who talked of France with "glowing condescension," and promised themselves that they would teach her "efficiency" and "home life," it being their duty "to set the example."

Then once again the scene shifts to France, to those dark and terrible days of the German advance, when refugees once more thronged the roads, and Troy in a flash of horror saw that "the bitter history of the war was re-enacting itself and the battle of the Marne was to be fought again." Again—but with a difference. For in the darkest hour of all there appeared a long string of "huge square olive-brown motor trucks stacked high with scores and scores of bronzed soldiers. It was an American regiment being rushed to the front!" And then Troy, who had been too young, though not too proud, to fight, was plunged into the thick of his first battle, which might also have been his last but for one of those strange, inexplicable happenings about which men whisper to one another with bated breath and much hesitation, not knowing whether they were real occurrences or the fancies of delirium, yet which hold within them a truth of the spirit which transcends material fact.

The story, it is scarcely necessary to say, is beautifully written. Never, perhaps, has Mrs. Wharton's style been of a more pellucid clearness than it is in this, the latest and in some ways one of the most interesting books she has written. Yet the reader's first sensation on closing the volume is one of sheer wonder at its richness, for if ever the phrase "much in little" applied to any book it surely applies to this one. Always a critic of life, Mrs. Wharton has never written a broader, keener criticism than this, her first long story of the war.

"New Novels: *The Marne*," *Times Literary Supplement* [England], 19 December 1918, p. 642

Mrs. Edith Wharton's new story, *The Marne: A Tale of the War* . . . is a quarter the usual length of a novel. It is possible to point to no other quality in which the book can be said to have "suffered" from the strenuous practical work which its author has been doing in Paris through the war. On the other hand, it is possible to point to qualities in which, through that work, it has gained. The love and understanding of France, which are the spirit of the story, are born of intimacy with France at her greatest in the greatest trial of her history. Mrs. Wharton puts her passion for France into the breast of an American boy who had loved France from childhood and had learned to know France through his French tutor; and the story tells how too young to join the

American Army, he went to France as ambulance driver, slipped into the firing line in the 1918 battle of the Marne, and was wounded. It tells, also, how he was rescued. And, whatever doubts the reader may have about the cohesion of the rescue with the remainder of the story, Mrs. Wharton achieves her purpose in inventing it as a consummating symbol for her conviction of the immortality of the French spirit and the French civilization. In that aspect, at any rate, it makes a fitting close for a beautiful and enlarging tale.

One other "subject" Mrs. Wharton had, a subject which her acute social sense enables her to place with choice effect and delicate wit. That is the changing attitude of American opinion towards France as the war progressed. First, we have the wealthy Americans "held up" in Paris on the outbreak of the war, which was to them just a personal grievance. Then the playing at charity in New York and elsewhere, of people "keeping up a kind of continuous picnic on the ruins of civilization." Then comes the ardour of middle-class America to go and teach poor France the civic and domestic virtues, the meaning of "home," the love of parents and of children and other things in which poor France is, of course, notoriously deficient. And, last, we have the conversion of these well-meaning, ignorant folk brought face to face with France as she is. It is surprising to notice how much of France as she is—of her beauty, her great tradition, her homely simplicity, her restless intelligence, her unconquerable spirit—Mrs. Wharton has contrived to bring into this short tale. Her story is, like most of her stories, carved like a gem; but the gem glows with an inner light.

Frederic Taber Cooper, "A Clear-cut Gem of War Fiction," *Publisher's Weekly*, 94 (28 December 1918), 2033

In this comparatively short-length story, Mrs. Wharton has produced one of the very few clear-cut, pure-water, almost flawless gems of war fiction. And, like other gems of its class, it is surprisingly simple in its art and single-purposed in its theme.

It is built around an American boy, Troy Belknap, one of the countless scores of pampered only sons, annually taken abroad as part of the obvious course of their education. It happens that Troy has caught the spirit of the older civilization; he has a well-beloved young French tutor, who has taught him what French art and literature and music, French history and French life mean in the scheme of civilization. When only fifteen, he feels the aftermath of the first Battle of the Marne, in which this tutor was one of the first to fall; he comes back to America, to suffer miseries of shame and impotence thru nearly four years, while America talked futilely of neutrality, and the people tried to believe that raising subscriptions and knitting socks would wash off the stain of national indifference. Then comes the entrance of America into the fight; and with it what Troy finds almost as hard to bear as the former neutrality:—the monumental spirit of superiority in which thousands of eager young war-workers poured across to France, forsooth, to teach the French mothers to love children, to teach French sons to honor their mothers, to teach the French nation how to live clean lives!

Mrs. Wharton writes with a stinging frankness that will no doubt antagonize many a complacent reader who does not know the bigness and loftiness of French ideals as she does, nor the colossal, even the unconscious self-righteousness of these modern crusaders. They learn their lesson in proper humility, when brought face to face with the great leveling forces of actuality. And none are more ready than these same Americans to pay full tribute to the moral and spiritual greatness of France.

Cheklist of Additional Reviews

Edwin Francis Edgett, "The Indomitable Spirit of America," *Boston Evening Transcript*, 21 December 1918, Part 3, p. 8.

"Echoes and Shadows," *Nation*, 108 (11 January 1919), 56.

FRENCH WAYS AND THEIR MEANING

FRENCH WAYS
AND THEIR MEANING

BY

EDITH WHARTON

AUTHOR OF "THE REEF," "SUMMER," "THE MARNE" AND
"THE HOUSE OF MIRTH"

D. APPLETON AND COMPANY

NEW YORK   LONDON

1919

"French Ways and Their Meaning," New Republic, 20 (24 September 1919), 241

"Mrs. Wharton's Study of French Ways," New York Times Book Review, 28 September 1919, p. 497

Some American snobs adopt England; others adopt France. Mrs. Wharton has adopted France. Although her American horizon is bounded on the north by Bar Harbor, on the south by Aiken and has no westward extension, it seems to have been borne in upon her that certain untutored sections of the A.E.F. have come back with crude depreciations of France. This small book is apparently her attempt to set them right. She sets them right ethnologically. The difference between "Latin" and "Anglo-Saxon" is the difference between "those whose social polity dates from the Forum, and those who still feel and legislate in terms of the primæval forest." Thirty thousand years ago, according to Mrs. Wharton, the first Frenchmen scratched lovely pictures on their cliff-dwellings, and to the heirs of so venerable a culture how dare an infant nation raise the wall of criticism? If the French have faults, they are those inevitably contingent on an ancient civilization. They are not coarse pioneer faults. Americans, for instance, care for money-making as an end in itself (an observation presented as new by Mrs. Wharton), whereas the French, who admittedly also care for money, seek it only as a means of providing for their children and of enjoying life to the full. And so goes the apologia pro patria sua. Can it be possible that America will survive this apologist and France this defender?

Any writer who attempts to interpret in 149 pages the national characteristics of a people at once the most skeptical and the most religious in the world, the most romantic and the most realistic, the most unashamed of their instincts, and the most enslaved by social conventions, sets himself a task that must inevitably result in seeming contradictions and confusions. Such is the attempt Edith Wharton has made in her thoughtful book, *French Ways and Their Meaning*.

Mrs. Wharton sets out to prove that the dominant mental attributes of the French are the qualities of reverence, taste, and intellectual honesty. These salient qualities of the Gallic spirit, she believes, have made France the most "grown up" of all the nations and the torchbearer of civilization. Reverence she terms the life belt forced upon a nation whose geographical position has put her upon a raft. In the chapter on taste she says that French standards of education are higher than Anglo-Saxon ones. And to support her claim of the superior intellectual honesty of Frenchmen she scoffs with Mr. Howells at the American theatregoing public which "wants tragedy with a happy ending."

Mrs. Wharton has eyes for the faults of France as well. On various pages she characterizes the French as "not generous or trustful," "avaricious and lacking in compassion"; says that financial prudence approaches a vice with them, that they regard politeness as a coin, and that they do not respect the rights of others.

Despite these indictments, it is clear that the author has a deep love for "the flame that is French." "As long as enriching life is more than preserving it," she writes, "as long as culture is superior to business efficiency, as long as poetry and imagination and reverence are higher and more precious elements of civilization than telephones or plumbing, as long as truth is more bracing than hypocrisy, and wit more wholesome than dullness, so long will France remain greater than any nation that has not her ideals." For all the critics of France's weaknesses and shortcomings, Mrs. Wharton has the unanswerable retort, "Look about you, and you will see that the whole world is filled with her spilt glory."

There are many statements in the book that will give rise to debate. For example, Mrs. Wharton calls the French the most ascetic people of the Western world. It isn't until pages later that she modifies this attention-arresting declaration by defining ascetic as indifferent to creature comforts.

The most thought-provoking chapter in the book is one containing a discussion of the French and American conceptions of marriage. The French conception, she says, is built on parenthood, not passion—the "notion of love being tacitly excluded," because love is "not conceivably to be fitted into any stable association between man and woman."

Mrs. Wharton's attitude toward prohibition can be inferred from her remark that "a nation can have few more civilizing assets than the ability to produce good wine at home."

French Ways and Their Meaning, which was written in Paris during the last two years of the war and is confessedly somewhat desultory in scope, contains interesting chapters on the continuity of French culture and on "The New French Woman," in which she has incorporated the principal passages of two articles previously published in magazines.

"Books of the Fortnight," *Dial*, 67 (4 October 1919), 322

Not alone the welcomed-home doughboy and the repatriated Tommy, but nearly everybody else in the Anglo-Saxon world fails today as always to understand France. If curiosity were only as general as bafflement, Mrs. Wharton's new volume would perhaps be assured of the wide reading it deserves. Not that all the questions that puzzle Anglo-Saxondom find here a definitive answer; even if other conditions were altogether favorable, the pressure of war emotions would preclude finality. But the volume does transcend its self-confessed limitations; it offers more than one expects from a "desultory book, the result of intermittent observation, and often, no doubt, of rash assumption"; it does in fact discover the direction which any study of France should take, and goes some little distance along the road to understanding.

First and fundamentally, the society of France is "grown-up"—of all societies "the most completely detached from the lingering spell of the ancient shadowy world in which trees and animals talked to each other, and began the education of the fumbling beast that was to deviate into man." The outstanding qualities of this adult and worldly-wise society are taste, reverence, continuity, and intellectual honesty. Taste—the expression of "the mysterious demand of eye and mind for symmetry, harmony, and order"—is the natural inheritance of the heirs of a classical tradition refined again by centuries of living under conditions that made order and accommodation the prerequisites of existence. With the word "reverence" one is inclined to find fault—mainly because this word has an emotional quality that is foreign to the French mind, and would necessarily set limits to intellectual honesty. "Historical prudence" is perhaps a more accurate denominator for the quality the author has in mind; certainly it is more exactly descriptive of the type of intellect that raises no obstacles to investigation, but at the same time refuses to break the household gods until reason proves them false.

It is these adult qualities of proportion, poise, and intellectual fearlessness, rather than any over-emotionality, that make the French doubtful of excesses in vice and virtue, but nevertheless permit them to sample all that is new before they abandon anything time-tested of their fathers.

"Latin and Anglo-Saxon," *Times Literary Supplement* [England], 4 December 1919, p. 710

Mrs. Wharton's volume is deliciously entertaining and exquisitely salutary. She is down upon the poor Anglo-Saxon. But he has a tough skin, and we are not afraid that she will really hurt him; and then when she says Anglo-Saxon she does not as a rule mean Briton, so that, though, no doubt, we should be suing for mercy in two rounds if we were ourselves the object of her attack, we are, as it happens, merely called in to watch her at work upon her fellow-countrymen. She can hit hard when she chooses, and, shall we dare to say it, the weight of her blows is sometimes more remarkable than their direction? Here is the first; it is in her preface. She is defending her use of the labels Latin and Anglo-Saxon "for the purposes of easy antithesis." The terms are safe enough, she says, "if, for instance, they are used simply as a loose way of drawing a line between the peoples who drink spirits and those who drink wine, between those whose social polity dates from the Forum, and those who still feel and legislate in terms of the primeval forest." Of one thing we can be secure; Mrs. Wharton is innocent of statistics. What a shock it will be to her to discover that the first wine-growing country of the world is also the country in which alcoholism is acknowledged to be the gravest menace. Cæsar, too, did come to Britain, about the same time—was it not?—as his conquest of Gaul.

Mrs. Wharton's primary concern is to explain French civilization to America; and, as will have been inferred, she has not approached her task in the purely philosophic spirit, but with true moral zest, moved by the sense of a great urgency. French civilization is in her view the greatest present achievement of the breed of men; and she sees it—her book was written during the last two years of the war—exposed at one time to a double outrage, on the one side from the deadly enmity of the German, on the other from the deadly amity of the Anglo-Saxon. Every one knows that the first work of the Americans for France was what was called social or civil. During the first six months after their declaration of war, the Americans had no appreciable military force to throw into the scales; in the meantime they sent an army of doctors, nurses, and social workers in advance of the troops to do all they could to alleviate the sufferings of the civil population. American doctors and nurses had, naturally enough, not specialized in the study of French; many nevertheless found themselves assigned to independent work in a completely French *milieu*, Indeed all the American civil workers were required, one may say, to merge themselves temporarily in the current of the life of the French people, with only their abounding good will to be their guide. Comic situations frequently ensued, the more so that the average American does not want assurance. Mrs. Wharton must have witnessed many of these comedies, and some of them she has perhaps taken too much to heart. At any rate, the task to which she addresses herself is that of opening the eyes of the blind.

She divides her commentary into four main heads, exhibiting reverence, taste, intellectual honesty, and continuity as the leading qualities of the French race. No one would hesitate an instant in recognising the justice of her choice where taste and intellectual honesty were concerned; but that the French character is eminently reverent is more difficult to allow, and where continuity is concerned Mrs. Wharton seems to us to confuse the issue. Her book is so full of wisdom and experience, and, for all its underlying fervour, of wit and detachment too, that one is tempted to regard her as infallible. But already we have ventured one criticism, and now we are going to be so rash as to break a lance with her.

We were startled, in the course of a short lesson on the asceticism of the French, to be told that no moral idea attaches to that term, that it indicates "merely a natural indifference to material well-being." Mrs. Wharton speaks elsewhere very strongly on the importance of a sense of tradition in language; and we quote this almost unaccountable lapse on her part, because we believe it to be significant of a certain fundamental misplacement of emphasis in her book, a misplacement which indeed only here and there obtrudes itself through the correct and charming partizanship of its surfaces, but which does in a sense falsify her picture nevertheless.

It was our English forebears [she says, closing her chapter on Continuity] who taught us to flout tradition and break away from their own great inheritance; France may teach us that, side by side with the qualities of enterprise and innovation that English blood has put in us, we should cultivate the sense of continuity, that "sense of the past" which enriches the present and binds us up with the world's great stabilising traditions of art and poetry and knowledge.

and elsewhere—

It must never be forgotten that if the fashion of our notepaper and the cut of our dresses come from France, so do the conceptions of liberty and justice on which our republican institutions are based.

In her haste to scourge and belabour Anglo-Saxondom, Mrs. Wharton surely forgets here her loyalty to France or—would she not almost regard the two words as interchangeable?—to truth itself. A great love of France ought not to be inconsistent with a recognition in the French also of certain grave imperfections, which, just because the French are, as Mrs. Wharton says, more grown up than any other people, have for them particularly grave consequences; for the older we are the more difficult we always find it to correct our faults. And what is, after all, the chief danger to which they are exposed? This surely—and our experience of London streets during the war will explain the seeming paradox—that excess of light limits their vision. The French, including even their foremost thinkers, do really believe that France possesses and summarizes the secret of civilized existence. Read any of the articles now appearing in the French reviews on the Intellectual Crisis of the Time or the Problems of the Future and you will everywhere find that thought for them means French thought; and not by implication only: you will find Frenchmen summoned to remember that they are the custodians of truth and the world's rampart against invading darkness.

But truth is nobody's possession: she belongs, unseizable, to the vast circle of encompassing obscurity that those dimmed lights revealed. The Latin and the Anglo-Saxon civilizations approaching from a different side—or, shall we say, from a different centre—have each their vision, and what the world needs is that these two visions should be freely exchanged. And here we have an initial advantage; for, in spite of our supposed insularity, we are far more aware of them than they of us—we know their meaning far better than they know ours. We owe it to them, therefore, to do our best to make our own meaning clear. Just because we devote a larger proportion of our time to the enactment, the actualization, of our ideas than they do, we are too little concerned to give them a clear written expression, are less aware of them as ideas, less aware that they are our ideas. Perhaps we feel that the great and governing ideas, the ideas upon which the future of the world is now hanging, are not those which men are exchanging on paper, but those which nations have incorporated and are incorporating in their institutions and their lives. And perhaps it is in this way that it has come about that the French, who have certainly talked more about liberty and justice than any other nation, really believe themselves to be the true representatives of these ideas before the world and

can convince Mrs. Wharton that they are so. Whereas it should be common knowledge that France derived her conceptions of liberty and justice from England, and that she has not to this day succeeded in assimilating them. The practice of liberty and justice is essentially an achievement of our Anglo-Saxon civilization. Here, it seems to us, is a truth which every writer of English should make it a point of conscience to stand by, and to reiterate till it has penetrated the deafest and the most distant ears.

There is a further point, and to this, again, Mrs. Wharton's discussion of French manners naturally leads us. Suppose that we have to choose between two qualities of mind, clarity and—the other word is difficult to find, but the "integer vitæ" gives it to us, and we will say—integrity, which shall we prefer? In actual fact our preference has been given to the second of these qualities. And is not the Anglo-Saxon mind, as it feels along in what seems to be the right direction and formulates results only after obtaining them, is not such a mind, such a habit, more accurately responsive to the terms of the problem to be solved than that which precisely discerns and places the goal before reaching it? Is it not more necessary, is not *truer*, that your ideas should be "continuous" and, still more, susceptible of continuity, than that they should be precise? How beautifully clear and reasonable, to take a subject with which Mrs. Wharton also deals and up to a certain point deals so effectively, is the French attitude towards love and marriage! What a lamentable muddle our Anglo-Saxon civilization is in where the whole question of the relation of the sexes is concerned! Yes, indeed! But here, again, ought Mrs. Wharton to have said as much as she has— and almost all of it is admirable—without saying the last word? Above all, is it really true, as she maintains, that the word "love" itself is an emasculated word, that it will not bear a moment's comparison with "amour"? This is perhaps the most astonishing thesis that ever fell from the lips of a cultivated Anglo-Saxon. We cannot leave it unanswered; we must try to concentrate our reflections on it.

Roughly speaking, the same qualities of mind that produced the English constitution have produced the English language. It is in very many respects an inferior instrument to French; but it has one supreme merit, which more than makes up to us for all its defects. It has been the instrument of English poetry; it has made our poetry possible. We are not at variance with Mrs. Wharton when we claim for that poetry the leading place. But we would suggest that, if one word more than another can be called its corner stone, the word is love. Are we then who speak English absurd, childish and romantic, because we persist in associating love not only with poetry but with marriage also? and are we continually blinding our eyes when we think in the same terms of the love of woman and of the love of God? Mrs. Wharton tells us that it is so, and we believe that her error is profound. She is in error because she has failed to notice that our neighbors, with their gift of clear analysis, have spirited away out of life its very spring and key. How far better is it to be in a muddle, out of which you yet do not despair one day to emerge, than to have cleared matters up decisively, and at the same time to have blocked the door of egress and ascent! To the Anglo-Saxon mind, the central fact about love is one which it apprehends poetically, and the result is confusion if you will, but a confusion ever irradiated by hope, ever summoning to effort; to the Latin, the central fact is one which is placed scientifically and the result is serenity, *volupté*, and a railed park for romance, where among the most precious exhibits poetry herself is disclosed to the public view.

The gifts of Anglo-Saxondom to the world, government and poetry, are perhaps complementary gifts, each bearing witness in its way to a peculiar faculty for the practical recognition of truth. What is the function of the mind, if it is not this, and what is the last test of intellectual greatness, if it is not the capacity for loyalty to the significance in their totality of the facts which life puts before us? You are asked to divide seventeen into halves; which is better, to say "eight and nine," or to say "it won't go"? The method of the Anglo-Saxon is the second; he recognizes those margins of reality for which the most perfect explanation or ordering of the processes of life fails to account, and leaves the door open that life entering may continually check his bearings.

We suggest, then, to our great neighbours that the dull Anglo-Saxon mind has yet its hold, its superior hold, on certain essentials of salvation. But above all, shall we not have an exchange of vision? Let the Latin take from the Anglo-Saxon the lesson of continuity, which we might also call the lesson of reverence or of liberty or even of mere conduct. Fully to grasp it he would have to become a little less "grown up," he would have to sacrifice something of clarity itself to a more perfect rectitude of spirit, and to qualify his love of definition by an acknowledgment of the unfathomable mystery of life. And let the Anglo-Saxon take from the Latin the lesson of beauty, to value his passing life as it passes, to express its value in its daily ceremony, to eat food worth eating, to make thought itself a delight, to live without irretrievably soiling the land he lives in, to make that land itself, its cities and monuments, its rivers, hills and plains, a worthy expression and reminder of the purposes for which he lives and of the light which guides him.

"French Ways and Their Meaning," Catholic World, 110 (February 1920), 688

Here, in subject-matter at least, is an appropriate counterblast to *Madame de Treymes*, the brilliant novelette of French life with which Mrs. Wharton gratified some of her ardent readers and piqued other some, perhaps a dozen years ago. The earlier book presented an interpretation of the French moral and social code which was certainly anything but flattering. Even those who suspected that the sinister and all-devouring family depicted so tellingly in *Madame de Treymes* represented, in reality, a few instances erected into a generalization against whose darkness the simple Anglo-Saxon virtues of the hero might shine the more resplendently, could hardly have been indifferent to the result. Mrs. Wharton is so completely the master of her effects that one puts down the book, half convinced, at least imaginatively. In this present volume of studies, a totally different reading of the same society is presented—a reading which appeals to one as being probably much more faithful to reality. It leaves us in a mood which, if not always understanding, is, for the most part, profoundly respectful of a heroic, disciplined race, at once brilliantly homogeneous and brilliantly varied. Mrs. Wharton is particularly worth reading on the nature of French civilization.

Checklist of Additional Reviews

"Mrs. Wharton on the French," Springfield [Massachusetts] *Republican*, 14 September 1919, magazine section, p. 17-A.

"Travel and Description," *Outlook*, 123 (12 November 1919), 308–9.

Nation [England], 26 (6 December 1919), 368.

THE AGE OF INNOCENCE

The AGE of INNOCENCE

BY

EDITH WHARTON

AUTHOR OF "THE HOUSE OF MIRTH,"
"THE REEF," "SUMMER," ETC.

D. APPLETON AND COMPANY

NEW YORK :: MCMXX :: LONDON

Katherine Perry, "Were the Seventies Sinless?" *Publisher's Weekly*, 98 (16 October 1920), 1195–6

A new novel by Edith Wharton is by way of being an event in the literary calendar, and in this absorbing tale the almost metallic brilliance, which in the *House of Mirth* dazzled the reading public, hypnotizes the eager eye which would not lose one significant word. New York society in the '70s—the cynically christened "Age of Innocence"—is painted with Meissonier-like clarity of detail, beginning with vast Catherine Mingott, ruler of a great family of fashionables, down to her slim, pale grand-daughter, Countless Olenska, wife of a Polish roué, seeking sanctuary with her New York kin, who prove not always kind. From the opening opera night at the old red-hung Academy of Music, with Nilsson singing Marguerite in *Faust*, the scenes of luxury, black walnut, smug hypocrisy, formal festivities, and rampant family virtue continue in perfect sequence. Little help in such a *milieu* for young Newland Archer, who, having married a handsome white and gold débutante of regulation inexperience, finds himself appallingly and passionately in love with her cousin, the dark, seductive Countess. Again and again, the apparent artlessness of the young wife scores as if by accident; thru her, backed by the solid phalanx of family, respectability triumphs and the smooth surface of convention is never punctured, tho all New York relishingly infers that which never really came to pass. The plot is unobvious, delicately developed, with a fine finale that exquisitely satisfies one's sense of fitness, and as always with Mrs. Wharton, the drama of character is greater than that of event. One revels recognizingly in her clean-cut distinction of style, the inerrant aptness of adjectives, the vivisective phrase. No wonder that in the letters of Henry James his admiration for his dazzling disciple finds expression; she has a more human touch, a more vivacious humor. And in the closing scene her pen dwells lingeringly on the Paris she loves, rich in that warm atmosphere of beauty and art which New York of the '70s so crudely and coldly lacked.

William Lyon Phelps, "As Mrs. Wharton Sees Us," *New York Times Book Review*, 17 October 1920, pp. 1, 11

In this present year of emancipation it is pleasant to record that in the front rank of American living novelists we find four women, who shall be named in alphabetical order—the only order that makes the world safe for democracy; much appreciated by opera impresarios, managers of stock companies and other great diplomats. The big four are Dorothy Canfield, Zona Gale, Anne Sedgwick, Edith Wharton. From the first we have thus far had no new novel in 1920; but the year must be counted as a notable one in the history of American prose fiction when it has seen the appearance of three works of the distinction of *Miss Lulu Bett, The Third Window* and *The Age of Innocence*. Any modern British novelist might be proud to sign his name to each and all of these books.

283

Mrs. Wharton's admirable career is a progression from the external to the internal; she began as a decorator and is now an analyst. She has always been an expert in gardens and in furniture. Her first book was called *Decoration of Houses*, written in 1897 with O. Codman, and in 1904 she produced a work on Italian villas and their gardens. These studies of interior decorating and landscape gardening are much in evidence in her novels; I do not remember when I have read a work of fiction that gives the reader so vivid an idea of the furnishing and illuminating of rooms in fashionable houses as one will find in *The Age of Innocence*.

Those who are interested in good dinners—and who is not?—will find much to admire in these brilliant pages. Many years ago when reading about prehistoric banquets in Dickens, I determined that some day I would write an essay on novelists from the culinary point of view. I have never "got around to it"; but this story would loom large in such a disquisition. The formal and elaborate dinner parties in New York in the seventies are described here with a gusto that the steady undercurrent of irony quite fails to conceal; there were epicures in those days who sallied from their Fifth Avenue mausoleums not to talk, but to dine. They were professional diners-out, who noticed details—why does she allow her butler to cut the cucumbers with a steel knife?

It was *The House of Mirth* (1905) that gave Mrs. Wharton an international reputation; if one wishes to see how far her art has advanced since that popular book, one has merely to compare it with *The Age of Innocence*. By the side of the absolute mastery of plot, character and style displayed in her latest novel, *The House of Mirth* seems almost crude. That austere masterpiece, *Ethan Frome*, stands in a room all by itself; it is an illustration,

however, of the fact that our novelist, who knows Paris and Continental urban scenes so well, was equally at home in a barren American village.

I was not at all impressed by *The Custom of the Country* (1913); the satire became burlesque, and the writer's habitual irony—most impressive when most subdued—fell into cascades of feminine shrieks. Like her idol and master, Henry James, she is forever comparing America with Europe, to the latter's advantage. I have no quarrel with her on this score, for, after all, it is simply a matter of taste, so far as questions of art are concerned; but it is only occasionally in this latest book that the direct comparison is made. Describing a hot day in Boston:

> Archer found a cab and drove to the Somerset Club for breakfast. Even the fashionable quarters had the air of untidy domesticity to which no excess of heat ever degrades the European cities.

It is a matter of no importance, but I do not believe that statement to be true. I should not like to compare my knowledge of Europe with hers; Mrs. Wharton has either missed city scenes in Europe in the dog days, or has shut her eyes.

The two previous novels in her career which most clearly foreshadow the power and technique displayed in *The Age of Innocence* are *Madame de Treymes* (1907) and *The Reef* (1912). I think, with the exception of novel now before us, *The Reef* is her finest full-length story. In one of the many intimate letters written to her by Henry James, and now published in the already famous two-volumes, we find the following admirable remarks on *The Reef* and if one will read them immediately after finishing *The Age of Innocence*, one will see how perfectly they apply to Mrs. Wharton's style at its best:

In the key of this, with all your reality, you have yet kept the whole thing, and, to deepen the harmony and accentuate the literary pitch, have never surpassed yourself for certain exquisite *moments*, certain images, analogies, metaphors, certain silver correspondences in your *façon de dire*, examples of which I could pluck out and numerically almost confound you with, were I not stammering in this so handicapped a way. There used to be little notes in you that were like fine, benevolent finger marks of the good George Eliot—the echo of much reading of that excellent woman, here and there, that is, sounding through. But now you are like a lost and recovered "ancient" which *she* might have got a reading of (especially were he a Greek), and of whom in *her* texture some weaker reflection were to show. For, dearest Edith, you are stronger and firmer and finer than all of them put together; you go further and you say *mieux* and your only drawback is not having the homeliness and the inevitability and the happy limitation and the affluent poverty of a Country of your Own (*comme moi, par exemple!*).

The style of *The Age of Innocence* is filled with the "silver correspondence" spoken of by Henry James; and the book would be a solid satisfaction, as it is an exquisite delight, had the writer only possessed the homeliness, the rugged simplicity that is lost under the enamel of finished sophistication. The English critic, R. H. Hutton, said that Goethe was the wisest man of modern times that ever lacked the wisdom of a little child—this particular kind of wisdom is not to be found in the works of Mrs. Wharton, though we find everything but that.

Yet I am in no mood to complain. Edith Wharton is a writer who brings glory on the name America, and this is her best book. After reading so many slipshod diaries called "novels," what a pleasure it is to turn the pages of this consummate work of art. The common method today of writing a novel is to begin with the birth of the hero, shove in all experiences that the author can remember of his own childhood, most of which are of no interest to any one but himself, take him to school, throw in more experiences, introduce him to the heroine, more experiences, quit when the book seems long enough, and write the whole biography in colloquial jargon.

Here is a novel whose basis is a story. It begins on a night at the opera. The characters are introduced naturally—every action and every conversation advance the plot. The style is a thing of beauty from first page to last. One dwells with pleasure on the "exquisite moments" of passion and tragedy, and on the "silver correspondences" that rise from the style like the moon on a cloudless night.

New York society and customs in the seventies are described with an accuracy that is almost uncanny; to read these pages is to live again. The absolute imprisonment in which her characters stagnate, their artificial and false standards, the desperate monotony of trivial routine, the slow petrifaction of generous ardours, the paralysis of emotion, the accumulation of ice around the heart, the total loss of life in upholstered existence—are depicted with a high excellence that never falters. And in the last few pages the younger generation comes in like fresh air. Mrs. Wharton is all for the new and against the old; here, at all events, here sympathies are warm. She would never, like

285

Solness, fear youth knocking at the door.

The two young women of the story are contrasted in a manner that is of the essence of drama without being in the least artificial. The radiantly beautiful young wife might have had her way without a shadow on it, were it not for the appearance of the Countess Olenska, who is, what the other women are not, a personality. Newland Archer, between these two women, and loved by both, is not at all to be envied. The love scenes between him and Ellen are wonderful in their terrible, inarticulate passion; it is curious how much more real they are than the unrestrained detailed descriptions thought by so many writers to be "realism." Here is where Mrs. Wharton resembles Joseph Conrad and Henry James, for the love scenes in this book are fully worthy of those two men of genius. So little is said, so little is done, yet one feels the infinite passion in the finite hearts that burn. I wonder what old Browning would have thought of this frustration; for the story is not altogether unlike "The Statue and the Bust."

I do not believe I shall ever forget three scenes between Archer and Ellen—the "outing" at Boston, the night carriage drive from the ferry in New York, and the interview in the corner of the Museum of Art, with its setting of relics. These are scenes of passion that Conrad or Henry James, yes that Turgenev might have written.

I wonder if the horrible moment when Newland Archer, looking at his incomparably lovely and devoted young wife, suddenly has the diabolical wish that she were dead, is a reminiscence of Mrs. Wharton's early studies of Sudermann. In a powerful story by that writer, "The Wish," not only is that momentary impulse the root of the tragedy, but it is analyzed with such skill that no one is likely to forget it. It comes into this novel like a sudden chill—and is inexpressibly tragic. You remember what the doctor said in Sudermann's tale?

The harmony of Mrs. Wharton's management of English sentences is so seldom marred that I wish she would change the phrase, the only discord I found in the book (page 141): "varied by an occasional dance at the primitive inn when a man-of-war came in."

And is not Guy de Maupassant out of place in the early seventies? Archer is unpacking some new books (page 137): "a new volume of Herbert Spencer, another collection of Guy de Maupassant's incomparable tales, and a novel called 'Middlemarch,' as to which there had lately been interesting things said in the reviews." I suppose Mrs. Wharton knows her Maupassant thoroughly; but unless I am quite at fault, it was not in the early seventies, but in the early eighties, that his tales began to appear.

But these are flecks. The appearance of such a book as *The Age of Innocence* by an American is a matter for public rejoicing. It is one of the best novels of the twentieth century and looks like a permanent addition to literature.

[Carl Van Doren], "An Elder America," *Nation*, 111 (3 November 1920), 510–11

We can no more do without some notion or other of an age more golden than our own than we can do without bread. There must be, we assure ourselves, a more delectable day yet to come, or there must have been one once. The evidence of prophecy, however, is stronger than that of history, which, somehow, fails to find the perfect age. Mrs. Wharton has never ranged herself with the prophets, contented, apparently, with being the most intellectual of our novelists and surveying with level, satirical eyes the very visible world. By the "Age of Innocence" she means the seventies in New York during the past century; and the innocence she finds there is "the innocence that seals the mind against imagination and the heart against experience." To the hotter attacks which angrier critics have recently been making upon that age she does not lend herself. Her language is cool and suave. And yet the effect of her picture is an unsparing accusation of that genteel decade when the van der Luydens of Skuytercliff were the ultimate arbiters of "form" in Manhattan, and "form" was occupation and religion for the little aristocracy which still held its tight fortress in the shaggy city so soon about to overwhelm it. The imminence of the rising tide is never quite indicted. How could it be, when the characters of the action themselves do not see it, bound up as they are with walking their wintry paths and hugging their iron taboos? Newland Archer suspects a change, but that is because he is a victim of the tribal order which sentences him to a life without passion, without expression, without satisfaction. The Countess Olenska suspects it, but she too is a victim, too fine for the rougher give-and-take of her husband's careless European society and yet not conventional enough for the dull routine which in her native New York covers the fineness to which also she is native. The peculiar tragedy of their sacrifice is that it is for the sake of a person, Archer's wife, who is virtuous because she is incapable of temptation, competent because she is incapable of any deep perturbation, and willing to suit herself to the least decorum of their world because she is incapable of understanding that there is anywhere anything larger or

freer. The unimaginative not only miss the flower of life themselves but they shut others from it as well.

Mrs. Wharton's structure and methods show no influence of the impressionism now broadening the channel of fiction; she does not avoid one or two touches of the florid in her impassioned scenes; she rounds out her story with a reminiscent chapter which forces in the note of elegy where it only partially belongs. But *The Age of Innocence* is a masterly achievement. In lonely contrast to almost all the novelists who write about fashionable New York, she knows her world. In lonely contrast to the many who write about what they know without understanding it or interpreting it, she brings a superbly critical disposition to arrange her knowledge in significant forms. These characters who move with such precision and veracity through the ritual of a frozen caste are here as real as their actual lives would ever have let them be. They are stiff with ceremonial garments and heavy with the weight of imagined responsibilities. Mrs. Wharton's triumph is that she had described these rites and surfaces and burdens as familiarly as if she loved them and as lucidly as if she hated them.

Henry Seidel Canby, "Our America," New York *Evening Post,* 6 November 1920, p. 3

America is the land of cherished illusions. Americans prefer to believe that they are innocent, innocent of immorality after marriage, innocent of dishonesty in business, innocent of incompatibility between husbands and wives. Americans do not like to admit the existence (in the family) of passion, of unscrupulousness, of temperament. They have made a code for what is to be done, and what is not to be done, and whatever differs is un-American. If their right hands offend them they cut them off rather than admit possession. They believed in international morality when none existed, and when they were made to face the disagreeable fact of war, cast off the nations of the earth, and continued to believe in national morality.

In America prostitution is tolerated in practice, but forbidden in print. All homes are happy unless there is proof to the contrary, and then they are un-American. In its wilful idealism America is determined that at all costs we shall appear to be innocent. And a novel which began with the leaders in social conformity, who keep hard and clean the code, and swept through the great middle classes that relax its rigors themselves, but exact them of others, might present the pageant, the social history, the epic of America.

Of course, Mrs. Wharton's novel does nothing of the sort. This is how Tolstoy, or H. G. Wells, or Ernest Poole would have written The Age of Innocence. They would have been grandiose, epical; their stories would have been histories of culture. It would have been as easy to have called their books broad as it is to call Mrs. Wharton's fine novel narrow. Tendencies, philosophies, irrepressible outbursts served as their protagonists, where hers are dwellers in Fifth Avenue or Waverly Place—a cosmopolitan astray, a dowager, a clubman yearning for intellectual sympathy.

And yet in the long run it comes to much the same thing. They prefer the panorama: she the drawing room canvas. They deduce from vast philosophies and depict society. She gives us the Mingotts, the Mansons, the Van der Luydens—Society, in its little brownstone New York

of the seventies—and lets us formulate inductively the code of America. A little canvas is enough for a great picture if the painting is good.

The only objection I have ever heard urged against Mrs. Wharton's fine art of narrative is that it is narrow—an art of dress suit and sophistication. And this book is the answer. For, of course, her art is narrow—like Jane Austen's, like Sheridan's, like Pope's, like Maupassant's, like that of all writers who prefer to study human nature in its most articulate instead of its best or its broadest manifestations. It is narrow because it is focussed, but this does not mean that it is small. The story of The Age of Innocence could be set in a far broader background. It is the circumstances of the New York society which Mrs. Wharton knows so well that give it a piquancy, a reality that "epics" lack. They are like the accidents of voice, eye, gesture which determine individuality. But her subject is America.

This treating of large themes by highly personal symbols makes possible Mrs. Wharton's admirable perfection of technique. Hers is the technique of sculpture rather than the technique of architecture. It permits the fine play of a humor that has an eye of irony in it, but is more human than irony. It makes possible an approach to perfection. . . .

Her art is restrained, focussed upon those points where America, in its normality and its eccentricity, has become articulate. Therefore it is sharp and convincing. Who is the central figure in this story of the leaven of intellectual and emotional unrest, working in a society that has perfected its code and intends to live by it? Is it Newland Archer, who bears the uncomfortable ferment within him? Is it his wife, the lovely May, whose clear blue eyes will see only innocence? Is it the Countess Olenska, the American who has seen reality and suffered by it, and sacrifices her love for Newland in order to preserve his innocence? It is none of these, but rather the "family" moral according to its lights, provincial, narrow—but intensely determined that its world shall appear upright, faithful, courageous, in despite of facts and regardless of how poor reality must be tortured into conformity. And the "family" is just the bourgeois Puritanism of nineteenth century America.

Was May right when with the might of innocence she forced Newland to give up life for mere living? Was the Countess right when in spite of her love for him she aided and abetted her, making him live up to the self-restraint that belonged to his code? The story does not answer, being concerned with the qualities of the "family," not with didacticism.

It says that the insistent innocence of America had its rewards as well as its penalties. It says, in so far as it states any conclusion definitely, that the new and less trammelled generation must answer whether it was the discipline of the parents that saved it from anarchy, or the suppressions of its parents that made it rebellious. And the answer is not yet.

A fine novel, beautifully written, "big" in the best sense, which has nothing to do with size, a credit to American literature—for if its author is cosmopolitan, her novel, as much as *Ethan Frome*, is a fruit of our soil.

"The Age of Innocence," Times Literary Supplement [England], 25 November 1920, p. 775

Mrs. Wharton's new book, her first "full-length" novel for some years, is perhaps a

sign of the times. When the war broke in upon the settled, accepted "present day" of the novelists, it was easy to foresee the predicament in which they would find themselves before long. Since 1914 there has been no present day, in the old sense. Now we must know from the start whether we are dealing with the world before or during or since the war, and the action must be precisely timed; any and every novel, in other words, is bound to be now "historic." And since it is a hazardous venture to set about treating very recent times historically—it needs a great deal of information or a great deal of assurance to move upon that *cineri doloso*—it was probable that a writer like Mrs. Wharton, critical of the impressions of life, should hesitate to use the crude new material of 1920, while it is still daily shifting and cracking before our eyes. And so she goes back—back to the old world, and far enough into it to make the action of her story openly historic; she goes as far back as the early seventies, in fact, and to that New York of the early seventies which is now so much more remote, as it happens, than even our own past of that day, over here. Changes of the same general kind we too have seen, no doubt, but nothing to compare in extent with the change that has turned New York, socially speaking, from a trim and substantial old family mansion to a resounding, glittering, promiscuous monster hotel.

The old family mansion is more than a picturesque background for a story, though it is that too. But it is also a story in itself, or it very easily makes one, with the elaborately composed artificiality of the life that was led there. Nowhere, not among the most formal refinements of the *ancien régime*, has there been seen a society more carefully and consciously organized than that of New York a generation or so ago, when the tide of new money, bearing new people and new standards and new manners, was only just beginning to encroach upon the old, and when the family in possession—it was hardly more than a family, compactly knit together in one circle—was making its final and unsuccessful attempt to withstand it. This much is a familiar story, but Mrs. Wharton takes it at a different aspect. A young man, Newland Archer, belonging to the inner stock, the real right thing, finds himself in conflict with the traditions that have made him—in conflict, that is to say, with a very large part of himself. His traditions, working with the smoothness of long practice, draw him remorselessly into the discreet, distinguished, airless world of his kind, into a sound profession and a suitable marriage; while the strain of rebellion pulls on the other side towards freedom, pulls violently, but at last has to own itself beaten. It is easier for a stranger to get into the guarded enclosure, after all, than for a native to get out of it. For Archer freedom means Ellen Olenska, a member of the family party like himself, but one who has vividly (and also disastrously) succeeded in detaching herself, and who has returned to it for support and consolation after her wanderings. Ellen is exquisite, and she and Archer are both of them much too intelligent to underrate the virtue and the dignity of the forces opposed to them; the old order, in its way, is perfectly just and reasonable, its standards are honourable; two intelligent beings can only in the end respect them. And so the historic setting of the story has made the story—made it by being just what it is, strong and fine, ripely matured and absolutely sure of itself.

That is the plan of the book, and Mrs. Wharton covers it in a manner that hardly leaves an opening for criticism. It is admirably packed; the action is clear against its background, and at the same time the background, the good family party with its perfect manners, is never a mere decoration, it takes its proper place as an essential matter in the story. It does so, at any rate, very soon; for just at first Mrs. Wharton does not quite meet the besetting difficulty of these historic studies. If you are to present what is called a "picture of the times," how are you to keep the centre of interest in your drama? The interest, if you are not very careful, falls back into the romantic or the ironic evocation of the past, and the drama is overshadowed. Necessarily Mrs. Wharton's evocation is ironic—one *must* be ironic about the seventies, they are already too far and not yet far enough to be treated otherwise—and the balance of the tone, that amusing old New York on one side, this difficult drama on the other, is insecure for a time. But it rights itself, and the slight confusion is soon forgotten, and everything goes firmly and lightly, and altogether Mrs. Wharton has accomplished one of the best pieces of her work so far.

As for her picture of the times, how is any of us over here to criticize it, beyond saying that it is full of vivacity and of character and of colour, and that there is not a point in it which *seems* to be false? (A few small anachronisms of fact are of no consequence in such things; but we interject that even the most advanced young people could not have been reading books by Vernon Lee or Huysmans or M. Paul Bourget in the early seventies). From the despotic old matriarch, Catherine Manson, outward and downward through all the ramifications of the cousinhood, through the pre-Wagnerian opera and the "Grace Church weddings" and the liturgical dinner-parties, Mrs. Wharton takes her way with what we can only believe to be a thorough mastery of the whole situation. Certainly she makes it very convincing and very entertaining. And of her dealings with the drama, and especially with the sensitive, vibrating, po-

290

etic figure of Ellen, there is no shadow of doubt. These are matters of which we can all judge, and we can all see that Mrs. Wharton's hand upon them is more skilful and felicitous than ever.

"The Innocence of New York,"
Saturday Review [England], 130 (4 December 1920), 458

For many English readers this delightful novel will be a revelation of the depths which can be sounded by international ignorance. Gentlemen of unbounded leisure and a taste for commercial probity which amounts to a disease, ladies combining the angel and the bore in a measure beyond the dreams even of Thackeray, troops of obsequious and efficient white domestics! Not such are the inhabitants whom most of us have mentally assigned to New York—at any stage of that city's existence. But Mrs. Wharton abundantly demonstrates that this state of things obtained only in a very limited circle, to a degree inconceivable by older and more corrupt civilizations. A happy circle it cannot well be called, since to assert that happiness may be compatible with dullness is to state a contradiction in terms; by rights it should not be attractive any more than happy, but the author contrives to make it so, partly no doubt through the easy laughter called forth by its patently ludicrous standards, but partly also from admiration for the finer element contained in them.

The heroine, a daughter of this secluded aristocracy, ventures in defiance of its conventions on an exogamic alliance with a wealthy Polish nobleman, who transports her to a cosmopolitan atmosphere, where art, literature, and brilliant conversation are among the commonplaces of life. On the other hand, she is unfortunate in her husband, and the sympathy consequently bestowed upon her is of a different quality from that which under like conditions would have fallen to her share in New York. Returning, rather under a cloud, to the old home, she is received by her relations with a splendid loyalty, which she genuinely appreciates. But naturally she finds the former things insipid, and—with no evil intentions—drifts into hazardous intimacy with a young man yearning for "European culture," and for the society of women competent to discuss it. His wedded peace is gravely endangered, and only the traditional ideas intervene to hinder a tragedy from reaching its climax.

From a literary point of view, this story is on a level with Mrs. Wharton's best work. As a retrospect of the early 'seventies, it is less satisfactory, being marred by numerous historical lapses.

K[atherine] M[ansfield], "Family Portraits,"
Athenæum [England], 4728 (10 December 1920), 810–11

In The Age of Innocence, a novel of the early seventies in New York, we receive the same impression that here is the element in which the author delights to breathe. The time and the scene together suit Mrs. Wharton's talent to a nicety. To evoke the seventies is to evoke irony and romance at once, and to keep these two balanced by all manner of delicate adjustments is so much a matter for her skilful hand that it seems more like play than work. Like Mr. Galsworthy's novel it is a family piece, but in *The Age of Innocence* the family comprises the whole of New York society. This remote, exclusive small world in itself is disturbed one day by the return of one of its prodigal daughters who begs to be taken back as though nothing had happened. What has happened is never quite clear, but it includes a fabulously rich villain of a Polish Count who is her husband and his secretary, who, rumour whispers, was all too ready to aid her escape. But the real problem which the family has to face is that Ellen Olenska has become that most mysterious creature—a European. She is dangerous, fascinating, foreign; Europe clings to her like a troubling perfume; her very fan beats "Venice! Venice!" every diamond is a drop of Paris. Dare they accept her? The question is answered by a dignified compromise, and Ellen's farewell dinner-party before she leaves for Paris is as distinguished as she or the family could wish. These are what one might call the outer leaves of the story. Part them, and there is within another flower, warmer, deeper, and more delicate. It is the love-story of Newland Archer, a young man who belongs deeply to the family tradition, and yet at the same time finds himself wishing to rebel. The charm of Ellen is his temptation, and hard indeed he finds it not to yield. But that very quality in her which so allures him—what one might call her highly civilized appreciation of the exquisite difficulty of their position—saves them from themselves. Not a feather of dignity is ruffled; their parting is positively stately.

But what about us? What about her readers? Does Mrs. Wharton expect us to grow warm in a gallery where the temperature is so sparkingly cool? We are looking at portraits—are we not? These are human beings arranged for exhibition

purposes, framed, glazed and hung in the perfect light. They pale, they grow paler, they flush, they raise their "clearest eyes," they hold out their arms to each other, "extended, but not rigid," and the voice is the voice of the portrait:

"'What's the use—when you will go back?' he broke out, a great hopeless *How on earth can I keep you?* crying out to her beneath his words."

Is it—in this world—vulgar to ask for more? To ask that the feeling shall be greater than the cause that excites it, to beg to be allowed to share the moment of exposition (is not that the very moment that all our writing leads to?), to entreat a little wildness, a dark place or two in the soul?

We appreciate fully Mrs. Wharton's skill and delicate workmanship; she has the situation in hand from the first page to the last; we realize how savage must sound our cry of protest, and yet we cannot help but make it; that after all we are not above suspicion—even the "finest" of us!

Frederick Watson, "The Assurance of Art," *Bookman* [England], 59 (January 1921), 170, 172

The Age of Innocence is beyond everything else a triumph of the artistic freedom of Mrs. Wharton. It may be as good or less good than its predecessors—it is enough that it is Mrs. Wharton's and that no other living author handles with such fine ease the changing but authentic portraiture of the social aspect. She is in that respect inimitable. In this country the art of comedy flavoured by satire, never very cordial to the English palate, has fallen into neglect and disrepute.

Jane Austen is alone in her kingdom. Thackeray, in whose austere immobility is the redemption and perfection of humour, has no successor. The acceptance of the writer of great satirical comedy might almost be regarded as a proof of genius since its reception is so timorous and tardy. The capacity, moreover, to desert a familiar but never in her case down-trodden road is an example of the instinctive assurance of Art. When a novelist has scored a triumph—even a very small one—in one particular vein he is warned (should he have ideas) by his publisher that people who like stories about vicars in the country will resent vintners in the town.

The tendency, the road of the highest applause, is towards repetition until if you like a blue lagoon you know the author without any further mental strain, and if you care about the monkey house your way is clear.

So when Mrs. Wharton writes of New York in 1875 she asks for trouble. The reviewer works up a paragraph or two on the necessity of novelists to avoid the war, the public feel vaguely as though they were asked to wear bombazine (whatever that was), and those eager readers who want to know just what America is thinking about everything in these critical days are a little surprised and chilled by Mrs. Wharton.

She, unlike so many of her English contemporaries, has no religion to teach, no grievance to air, no political betrayal to reveal. Her subjects are people, of a period perhaps, but people whose characteristics of snobbery, isolation, conservatism and humbug are not peculiar to the year '75.

Into the serene, exclusive atmosphere of the miniature Dresden china New York society passes the Countess Olenska, as the leaven enters the dough. With her comes the breath of the greater world, the world on the threshold. "All the old ladies had got out their faded sables and yellowing ermines, and the smell of camphor from the front pews almost smothered the faint Spring scent of the lilies banking the altar." That was the old world waiting for the knock at the door. But no extract, no deliberate choice of all the words relegated to sounds of praise can give anything but a second-hand, musty conception of the Van der Luydens, who must be studied not in extracts but in chapters if you would possess for all time their unforgettable savour.

It is the highest compliment to an artist to say that one never questions a word or action of her characters as unnatural or frankly beyond belief. When any writer can step back half a century and write as though her people lived next door there is no more to be said.

Vernon L. Parrington, Jr., "Our Literary Aristocrat," *Pacific Review*, 2 (June 1921), 157–60

The note of distinction is as natural to Edith Wharton as it is rare in our present day literature. She belongs to the "quality," and the grand manner is hers by right of birth. She is as finished as a Sheraton sideboard, and with her poise, grace, high standards, and perfect breeding, she suggests as inevitably old wine and slender decanters. The severe ethical code which Puritanism has bequeathed to her, and the keen intellect which has made her a critical analyst, increase her native distinction; and the irony that plays lambently over her commentary, adds piquancy to her art. She belongs to an earlier age, before a strident generation

293

had come to deny the excellence of standards. No situation which she has conceived in her novels is so ironical as the situation in which she herself is placed; shaken out of an unquestioned acceptance of the aristocratic world to which she belongs, she turns her keen analysis upon her environment, and satirizes what in her heart she loves most.

The Age of Innocence is perfect Whartonian. It is historical satire done with immaculate art, but though she laughs at the deification of "form" by the van der Luydens of Skuytercliff, and the tyranny of their rigid social taboos, she loves them too well to suffer them to be forgotten by a careless generation. She has painted them at full length, to hang upon our walls, where they lend historical dignity to the background of the present and utter a silent reproof to our scrambling vulgarities. New York society of the eighteen seventies, with its little clan of first families that gently simmers in its own dulness —it would be inelegant to say stews— provides a theme that exactly suits Mrs. Wharton's talent. She delights in the make-believe of the clan, in "the Pharisaic voice of a society wholly absorbed in barricading itself against the unpleasant," and she half regrets an age whose innocence "seals the mind against imagination and the heart against experience." She herself, of course, will not defend herself against reality by a decorous denial, but she likes too well many things in that world to be harsh or angry with it. Against this background of the clan she projects three figures who come perilously near to realizing a quite vulgar situation. Between May Welland, physically magnificent but mentally equipped with no more than the clan negations, and Ellen Olenska, a clan member who has freed herself from its provincialisms by a European experience that ends in separation from her Polish husband, and whose "disgrace" rocks New York society till the clan rallies to her defense, stands Newland Archer, a third member of the clan, who has played with books and ideas without liberating his mind, who is shocked into naturalness by the more vital Ellen, endeavours to break the ties of clan convention, but is held fast and ends his rebellions in a mood of ironic abnegation. There are no scenes, no vulgar jealousies or accusations, nothing to offend the finest sensibility. A few frank phrases sound almost startling in their context of reticent pretense, but they do not really startle. The book unwinds slowly, somewhat meagerly, with much analysis and little vivacity of conversation. In an environment of dull and selfish respectability, how could there be vivacity; with no ideas, no spontaneity, no intellectual sincerity, it is idle to expect vivacity. The formal routine and hinting gossip wrap themselves like a boa constrictor about the characters and squeeze the naturalness out of them. Nevertheless the story never lags and is never dull. The skill with which dulness is made interesting is a triumph of art.

But when one has said that the craftsmanship is a very great success, why not go further and add that it doesn't make the slightest difference whether one reads the book or not, unless one is a literary epicure who lives for the savor of things. What do the van der Luydens matter to us; or what did they or their kind matter a generation ago? Why waste such skill upon such insignificant material? There were vibrant realities in the New York of the seventies, Commodore Vanderbilt, for example, or even Jay Gould or Jim Fiske. If Mrs. Wharton had only chosen to throw such figures upon her canvas, brutal, cynical, dominating, what a document of American history—but the suggestion is foolish. Mrs. Wharton could not do it. Her distinction is her limitation. She loathes the world of Jim Fiske too much to understand it. She is too well bred to be a snob, but she escapes it only by sheer intelligence. The background of her mind, the furniture of her habits, are packed with potential snobbery, and it is only by scrupulous care that it is held in leash. She is unconsciously shut in behind plate glass, where butlers serve formal dinners, and white shoulders go up at the mere suggestion of everyday gingham. She belongs in spite of herself to the caste which she satirizes, and she cannot make herself at home in households where the mother washes the dishes and the father tends the furnace. If she had lived less easily, if she had been forced to skimp and save and plan, she would have been a greater and richer artist, more significant because more native, more continental. But unfortunately her doors open only to the smart set; the windows from which she surveys life open only to the east, to London, Paris, Rome. She is one of our cosmopolitans, flitting lightly about and at ease with all who bear titles. And this the stay-at-home American secretly resents. What are titles to him, and for that matter, what are the vulgar rich of New York? Let the newspapers exploit them, for that becomes their vulgarity. But for Mrs. Wharton to spend her talents upon rich nobodies is no less than sheer waste.

Since we are quarreling with Mrs. Wharton let us go through with it and suggest another irritation that arises from less creditable, but quite human sources. She unconsciously irritates because she reveals so unobtrusively how much she knows and how perfect is her breeding. She pricks one's complacency with such devastating certainty; reveals so cruelly one's plebeian limitations. Her readers are always on pins and needles not to appear out of her class. It is impossible to be easy and slouchy in presence of her poise, and it is hard on us not to let down occasionally. We cannot always be mentally on the alert. It was inevitable, to fall back upon an illustration, that her dilettante hero should have gone in for Eastlake furniture, as Mrs. Wharton assures us that he did. But the easy way in which she assumes that the reader will understand her casual reference to Sir Charles's endeavour to revive a "sincere" furniture, puts one to scrambling to recall that Eastlakeism was the polite counterpart, in the seventies, of the robust rebellions of William Morris against a dowdy Victorianism. If Mrs. Wharton had only let slip the fact that she once wrote a book on household decoration, and "got up" on the Eastlake movement, it would have reassured us, and made us feel that she is a common mortal like the rest of us who have to "get up" on things. Which criticism, of course, arises from mere petulancy and self-conceit.

With her ripe culture, her clear and clean intelligence, her classical spirit, her severe standards and austere ethics, Mrs. Wharton is our outstanding literary aristocrat. She has done notable things, but she has paid a great price in aloofness from her own America. There is more hope for our literature in the honest crudities of the younger naturalists, than in her classic irony; they at least are trying to understand America as it is. "You'll never amount to anything, any of you, till you roll up your sleeves and get right down into the muck," commented the one plebeian in the book to Newland Archer, who "mentally shrugged his shoulders and turned the conversation to books." Mrs. Wharton too often mentally shrugs her shoulders over America. That she should ever roll up her sleeves and get down into the muck is unthinkable.

Checklist of Additional Reviews

Edwin Francis Edgett, "The Strange Case of Edith Wharton," Boston *Evening Transcript*, 23 October 1920, Part 4, p. 4.

Francis Hackett, "The Age of Innocence," *New Republic*, 24 (17 November 1920), 301–2.

A. E. W. Mason, Review of *The Age of Innocence*, *Bookman* 52 (December 1920), 360–61.

Lilian Whiting, "Novels on the Season's List," Springfield [Massachussetts] *Republican*, 5 December 1920, magazine section, p. 9–A.

R. D. Townsend, "Novels Not for a Day," *Outlook*, 126 (8 December 1920), 653.

Pierre Loving, "When Old New York Was Young and Innocent," New York *Call*, 12 December 1920, p. 10.

M. R. L., "Shorter Notices," *Freeman*, 2 (22 December 1920), 358.

Spectator [England], 126 (8 January 1921), 55–56.

"Mrs. Wharton's Novel of Old New York," *Literary Digest*, 68 (5 February 1921), 52.

André Bellesort, "Les littératures étrangères: le dernier roman de Edith Wharton," *Revue Bleue* [France], 59 (20 August 1921), 524–28.

F. C. Danchin, "Revue annuelle: Le Roman anglais," *Revue Germanique* [France], 13 (1922), 155–59.

IN MOROCCO

IN MOROCCO

BY

EDITH WHARTON

ILLUSTRATED

NEW YORK

CHARLES SCRIBNER'S SONS

1920

"*In Morocco,*"
Times Literary
Supplement [England],
7 October 1920, p. 649

There are certain impressions that remain clear in the memory when others of the same period have long gone dim and blurred. The mind is confined by numberless concentric mountainous barriers; once stumble on a pass in the nearest, and the mind's eye ranges freely for ever to a vaster horizon with mountains of its own—peaks of Darien—in the distance. The first sight of a slave is an illuminating experience, for the Western man groups slaves with giants, fairies, and witches; they contradict his fundamental conceptions. Mrs. Wharton does not mention Tetuan, but a few years ago one need go no farther than that from the mess at Gibraltar to be waited on by slaves. It was far enough; the wild-looking escort sitting huddled on his little horse, the scrub bushes which might conceal one knew not what, the tower-flanked walls, the pale, dignified Jews, so unlike the Jews of modern cities, the turning in through the narrow door in the street wall—all that was a preparation for the slave girls staidly bringing fruit at the host's bidding; one was at the top of the pass; below and beyond Africa, stable in instability, stretched illimitably back through time and space.

Mrs. Wharton has been to the top of that pass. She visited Morocco during the autumn of 1917; and though, thanks to the good offices of General Lyautey, Resident Governor of France in Morocco, she traversed the country from the Mediterranean to the High Atlas and from the Atlantic to Fez, the duration of her visit—one month—was fortunately too short for her to carry out her intention of writing a guide-book. One writes "fortunately," for her book would have lost in broad suggestiveness far more than it would have gained from precision in detail. A guide-book would have been useful to the few who can go to Morocco and see it for themselves; the book she has written has a much wider appeal, for, with her knowledge of other countries and peoples, her sensitiveness, her gift of vivid description, and her unobtruded skill in ordered presentation, she does more than one would have thought possible to convey what was suddenly revealed to her eyes to those who will never see it with their own. She has been vouchsafed a Pisgah sight of a forbidden land, and, with sensibility intensified by the knowledge that her experience must be brief, she has grasped the broad masses of its colouring and the main outline of its form.

Mrs. Wharton devotes a useful chapter of reference to the history of Morocco, but whatever historical knowledge is required to understand her account of persons, buildings, and institutions is imparted more dramatically in connexion with them. For the general reader it is enough that the story of Morocco from the dark backward and abysm of time has run in a recurring cycle; the scenes are repeated with a slight variation in costume. Fierce, hardy races break in through the mountains on the north, they conquer and rob and kill, their rulers build lordly pleasure houses; they adopt foreign arts and refinements and stamp them with an impress of their own; they give themselves to sensuality— "sensuality without seduction"; and they fall to the new invader disgorged by the mountains. We may take Mulai-Ismail of Meknez, contemporary of Louis XIV.—with whom he exchanged gifts—as a typical Sultan. His stables were three miles long; his chariot was drawn by women and eunuchs. When he set

299

himself to enlarge his palace he had all the houses near by demolished and compelled the inhabitants to carry away the ruins of their own dwellings. To build on the scale he proposed he needed labourers. Of such there was no lack in Africa for the man who could assert his authority. He asserted it by means of an army, and he raised the army in this way. He had all the negroes within his control collected in a certain district "till not one was left in the whole of Moghreb, slave or free." There they were bidden make themselves houses and gardens, and remain till their children were ten years old. Then the Sultan had all the children brought to him, boys and girls. Both were taught what was useful, and in due course the men were married to the women. All the children of these couples were destined for domestic service in the palace or for his Black Army. With that army he could command labour. He could keep order. "A Jew or a woman might travel from Oudjda to the Oued Noun without anyone's asking their business." In standardization he forestalled the American manufacturer: all his masons were obliged to make each stroke in time with their neighbours, and were bastinadoed if they broke the rhythm; if they presumed to die at their work their bodies were built into the wall. The story goes that at word of the tyrant's death every worker on the walls flung down his trowel and his hod, every slave fled; "at that very instant life ceased to circulate in the huge house he had built, and in all its members it became a carcass for his carcass."

That is the past of Morocco. Mrs. Wharton shows us how it is connected with the present. She saw, in addition to the ordinary "sights," many that until recently no foreigner—certainly no foreign woman—would have been allowed to see; for instance, the ritual dance of the Hamadchas and the great religious rite of the Aïd-el-

Kebir—the Sacrifice of the Sheep. She was admitted to more than one harem, and we learn from her all that the harem implies; but the most interesting reading in her book consists of her own comments and inferences—suggested by a first encounter with a veiled woman, by pilgrims, by architecture, by scenery, by the thousand and one things that are to be seen by anyone with a seeing eye.

Irita Van Doren, "A Country Without a Guidebook," *Nation*, 111 (27 October 1920), 479–80

In 1918 Mrs. Wharton, under the guidance of a French military mission, in a French army motor, spent a month travelling in Morocco. Her account of her travels in a country without a guide book is for the benefit of the travelers who she feels sure will flood the land when the war is over. All the properties of an Arabian Nights tale are here—camels and donkeys, white-draped riders, palmetto deserts, camel's hair tents, and veiled women; and in the midst of blazing sands such incongruities as the rescue of the French official motor, stuck fast in the desert, by a passing army of turbaned white figures on pilgrimage under many-colored banners to pray at some holy tomb. Towns are few, in scattered oases or fertile valleys marked from afar by minarets rising from olive gardens and inclosed in red earthen walls overhung by fig and stunted cork trees. An odor of spices rises from the bazaars. Within the walls are turquoise-blue and white buildings, strange gardens, irises and blue aloes around secret pools to which childless women are brought to bathe; mosques with inlaid ivory, ebony, and sandalwood, and inscrutable cedar doors; bazaars where men of all tribes and nationalities offer their wares; ghettos, filthy and dark, in which babies are nursed on date brandy, and fat grandmothers still in their thirties shuffle along by the side of "incalculably aged ancestors"; and close by the jasmine and the rose.

There are fascinating pictures of Salé, where Robinson Crusoe was held prisoner; of Volubilis, the ruin of a Roman city; of Moulay Idress (Mrs. Wharton uses the French spelling of proper names), the sacred white city of Morocco, forced only as late as 1916 to admit the Christian tourist and the French uniform; of the crumbling ruins of imperial Meknez, built in the seventeenth century by Moulay Ismael with his Black Army of 150,000 men all trained and brought up by his orders from the age of ten, and by 25,000 Christian captives. It was here that "any prisoner who died at his task was built into the wall he was building." From Marrakech come the beautiful "pomegranate red" book bindings made by the guild of Morocco workers. Under the reed-roofed streets of Fez the song of the blind beggars, "Dust and ashes, dust and ashes," constantly symbolizes the life of this land where there is no merry-making in the Occidental sense of the word, where even the dances are all static or ritualistic, and where dreams and realities are inextricably intermingled by the all-pervading spirit of languor.

Under the guidance of the French Ministry of Fine Arts and as the guest of Madame Lyautey, Mrs. Wharton found herself admitted to many ceremonials from which she as a foreigner and as a woman would under ordinary circumstances have been doubly barred. She was entertained by the ladies of various harems, and in all

found the same lassitude and dulness, relieved only by the passionate fondness of the women for their children, who if girls are married at eight or nine and if boys are "given their first negress" at twelve.

Mrs. Wharton, who has long loved France, has unqualified admiration for the way in which the French Ministry of Fine Arts has gone about its task, and the tact shown by General Lyautey in dealing with the native problems. She accepts without question the general theory of imperialism—"and the European powers were attempting, in the confusion of an ungoverned country, to assert their respective ascendencies. The demoralised condition of the country justified these attempts and made European interference inevitable." In the light of this premise it is easy to see how she regards General Lyautey's "pacification" of Morocco as an act of accommodation to the Moroccans and the French occupation as a benevolent institution. Caillaux's complacent revelations throw a somewhat different light on the matter.

Dorothy Lawrence Mann, "*In Morocco,*" Boston *Evening Transcript*, 22 December 1920, Part 3, p. 4

Until very recent days Morocco has been one of the few strongholds of the past. It has still no guide book in English which conveys magic to one type of traveller, terror and confusion to another. One may sail from Spain and land in Tangier, as many travellers have done for decades, but beyond Tangier lies mystery. Only within the last few years has it been possible for an American or European to push his way into the hinterland with safety or even with reasonable comfort. But all this is in the process of being changed.

Only too soon there will be many guide books of Morocco and an influx of tourists will have banished that atmosphere of strangeness which is so binding today. Only recently Christians were still massacred in the streets of Robinson Crusoe's Salé, that old renowned breeder of pirates. Under the present enlightened and appreciative French administration good roads and light railways are connecting the cities and towns of Morocco, and what is even more important, the French governor has revealed a sense of beauty all too rare in colonial governors and has insisted on the saving and restoration of the native art and building. In cities where government quarters have been necessary he has had them erected far enough outside the city so that the European colony has become a thing by itself, not an ugly excrescence on the native town. Some of Morocco was ruined before his day, but Governor Lyautey's policy has saved much of it.

Mrs. Wharton had the good fortune to visit Morocco just in the transition stage. It was in war time, and she hastened to assure us that General Lyautey won as great a victory for France when he saved Morocco, enlarged the boundaries of French power there, and increased the exports of the country, as Marshal Foch won when he turned the tide at the Marne. Had Morocco been allowed to fall into the hands of the Germans in the early days of the war, as it might easily have done when he was ordered to send to France every available soldier, a rich hostile colony on the southern shores of the Mediterranean might have worked incalculable harm to the Allies. Moreover, France needed vitally the wheat and meat which Morocco could export. General Lyautey's conquest, though more quiet than those which were achieved on the fields of France, is nevertheless, one of the important conquests of the war.

When Mrs. Wharton visited Morocco the lure of romance still lay heavily on the land. They passed from Tangier straight into a land of mystery. It had been arranged, when the plan of the trip was laid out, that there would be definite periods when the party would arrive at European hotels for meals and a "tub," with just enough picnicking in between to provide pleasure. On the very first day, however, the plan went quite wrong, for the chauffeur of the military motor in which she rode lost his way in the desert country. On top of this something went wrong with the motor, and the heat of the day descended at its torridest, so that the visitors had an immediate taste of the unpleasantness of travel in Morocco. It is a landscape of great emptiness and sameness, a brilliant sky, blazing sun, and barren land.

Morocco is Moslem and Near East, but General Lyautey's work has made an opening to Europeans unknown before. More than once Mrs. Wharton was invited to meet and talk with the ladies of a harem, and found them curious and critical of our Western ways. The most interesting of these visits was the one to the harem of the Sultan at Rabat. . . . [W]ord was received that the ladies of the imperial harem would receive the wife of the resident general and her friends, and the ladies were taken through the palace, received by the chief eunuch, passed from negress to negress through winding corridors until they met the first houri from the Arabian Nights. At each stairway one of these beautifully dressed, radiant favorites met them and accompanied them till they reached the inner apartments, where they sat surrounded by a dozen houris, all eager and chatting fast, asking questions and anxious to entertain the Westerners. They were interrupted again and again as the group was enlarged. Once there came a paler, more soberly dressed girl, who proved to be the legitimate daughter of the Sultan. Then the Sultan's mother, also soberly dressed, but a figure of power in the palace. Finally the Sultan himself with one of his little boys. Then indeed they discovered that these apartments, which except for the views they commanded were far less luxurious than many apartments in Western houses, were equipped with a telephone.

Apparently Mrs. Wharton feels that she cannot too frequently call attention to the achievements of Gen. Lyautey. Toward the close of the book she devotes a chapter to a detailed account first of his saving of Morocco in 1912, and then again in 1914, when France demanded every available soldier and ordered the abandoning of all but the coast cities. Then Gen. Lyautey made one of the famous replies of a great general and great patriot. "I will give you all the troops you ask, but instead of abandoning the interior of the country I will hold what we have already taken and fortify and enlarge our bounda-ries." Two years later the visitor in Morocco felt that he was returning to normal conditions, so well did General Lyautey fulfil his promise.

Checklist of Additional Reviews

Spectator [England], 125 (23 October 1920), 541.
"A New Touring Ground," *Saturday Review* [England], 130 (23 October 1920), 339.
Ben Ray Redman, "Mrs. Wharton Visits Morocco," *New York Times Book Review*, 31 October 1920, p. 9.
Independent, 104 (13 November 1920), 242.
"Travel," New York *Evening Post, The Literary Review*, 13 November 1920, p. 18.
Paul-Louis Hervier, "Courrier des lettres anglo-américains," *Nouvelle Revue* [France], 51-52 (January-April 1921), 92.
"Briefer Mention," *Dial*, 70 (February 1921), 231.

THE GLIMPSES OF THE MOON

THE
GLIMPSES OF
THE MOON

BY

EDITH WHARTON

AUTHOR OF "THE AGE OF INNOCENCE," "THE HOUSE
OF MIRTH," "ETHAN FROME," "THE REEF," ETC.

D. APPLETON AND COMPANY
NEW YORK :: LONDON :: MCMXXII

Katherine Fullerton Gerould, "Mrs. Wharton's New House of Mirth," New York Times Book Review, 23 July 1922, pp. 1, 3

The publication of a full-length novel by Edith Wharton is probably the most important thing that can happen in any current year of American fiction. For there is no doubt that, soberly speaking, she is the best of living American novelists. There are times when she disappoints high hopes—as in *Summer*—but she is never inconsiderable, and never abates the clear, close-packed distinction of her prose style. You may cavil at her presentment of this or that human being, at this or that not quite "inevitable" incident; but her superb gift of narrative, her well-nigh faultless building of a plot, none can question. Architectonicé, as Matthew Arnold calls it, is not usually the gift of the female artist; and perhaps the appearance of Mrs. Wharton's name on nearly all the submitted lists of the "twelve greatest women" is attributed to her masculine power of handling events. Whatever you may feel, in any given novel of hers, about the characters and situations chosen, the emotions selected for display, you have always to recognize her as a master-builder. She knows, infallibly, how to tell a story.

The Age of Innocence has had, recently, its due meed of praise. I incline to think *The Glimpses of the Moon* a much better book; it is more interesting, more memorable and closer to the heart of things. Part of the charm of *The Age of Inno-cence* lay in the picture of a vanished day in our own America. *The Glimpses of the Moon* is rigidly contemporary. There are no "crapy Cornelias" wandering about that cosmopolitan scene. I used to hear people say that *The House of Mirth* was a best-seller because it told all the people who did not live in New York "society" what New York "society" was really like; because Mrs. Wharton was capable of giving inside information to outsiders. *Pace* the cynics, I have never believed it. It was a best-seller because it was such a ripping good novel, and so extremely well made. Be that as it may, *The Glimpses of the Moon* is full of people even more frivolous and more unpleasant to the strait-laced than the characters of *The House of Mirth*. It is an age of anything but inno-cence. Let us admit at once that we sel-dom get into such bad company!

It is no part of a reviewer's business to give away the plot of a novel. That is a scurvy trick both to author and to pro-spective reader. I shall not give away the plot of *The Glimpses of the Moon*. Suffice it to say that it deals with a shifting group of the very rich and the largely immoral, and that it is the story of a hero and heroine who belonged to that group, yet belonged, spiritually, elsewhere. Most of the action takes place in Europe, for these Americans live as much in Europe as at home. A great deal of visual beauty is thrown in for good measure. Is it not the very moral of all these people that they can afford beauty in every form, not only clothes and jewels and exqui-site food and drink, but Italian lakes, Venetian palaces and blue Aegean seas ("the long golden days and the nights of silver fire") and that romance, none the less, remains for most of them as crudely conceived a business as though their back-ground were Greenwich Village or Coney Island? American plutocracy, British or Italian aristocracy—it matters not—they all swim together, denizens of the same deeps. There is more money, more immorality, more fever than in any of the author's earlier studies of similar groups. Discretion, poise, judgment, hardly exist among them. Inhibitions are very nearly gone.

To estimate that world Mrs. Wharton has chosen the device of two people who are in it up to the neck, who depend upon it for the framework of their days, yet who in their respective fashions revolt from its philosophy. They are poor, these two, and their very poverty compels them to be more comprehending, more charitable than they would instinctively be. They cannot afford to hold aloof. They cannot get the beauty they legitimately crave except from the possessors and purveyors of beauty—the swine guard the pearl. How much do they want the pearl? How far will they go with the swine to get it?

This is a pretty problem that Mrs. Wharton has set her pair of lovers. Nor, of course, has she done anything so crude as to tar all her people with the same brush. Violet Melrose wants different things from Ursula Gillow. There are gradations in degradation. We have Nat Fulmer and the Hickses as well as the Gillows and the Vanderlyns. Grace Fulmer hardly belongs, morally, in the group at all; and the creator of Ellie Vanderlyn herself has had the wit to make her kind and sweet-tempered—a very gentle Messalina. The only thing the Lansings, Hickses, Vanderlyns, even Fulmers, can be said to have in common is a realization of the importance of money.

Oh, the blessed moral freedom that wealth conferred! She recalled Mrs. Fulmer's uncontrollable cry: "The most wonderful thing of all is not having to contrive and skimp and give up something every single minute!" Yes; it was only on such terms that one could call one's soul one's own.

The question d'argent is as tightly woven into *The Glimpses of the Moon* as into any novel of Balzac's.

Yet, as a study of the question d'argent alone, this book could hardly stand with any of the members of the "Comédie Humaine." If, for Balzac, everything comes back in the end to money, he has proved his point more exhaustively than Mrs. Wharton has tried to. He illustrates more conclusively than she the all-importance of riches, since he shows the principle of greed, the sense of the purchasing power, at work in so great a variety of human types. Parisian, provincial, peasant, are all drawn into his picture. You cannot confront Balzac with any sort of victim that he has forgotten. Whereas these people in *The Glimpses of the Moon* are a special case. Not the worst hater of America or of modernity would pronounce them typical, though they may be symptomatic. The question d'argent, though it enters crudely or subtly into every situation of the book, is not the final interest. It is an assumption rather than the point at issue.

A good many people have considered *Ethan Frome* Mrs. Wharton's masterpiece. Taking it all in all, I believe that—until *The Glimpses of the Moon*—it has been. Ironically enough, it is also the production of hers which is most awkward in form. No one can say that *Ethan Frome* is a technical triumph. The secret of its greatness is the stark human drama of it; the social crudity and human delicacy intermingled; the defiant, over-riding passion, and the long drawn-out logic of the paid penalty. It has no contexts, no mitigations; it is plain, raw, first-hand human stuff. Compared with Ethan and Mattie, the lovers in her other books have seemed to be adoring each other in a vacuum. In no other way comparable with *Ethan*

Frome, The Glimpses of the Moon links itself to the earlier book at just one point: Susy and Nick are really in love with each other. They have an equal strength of passion with Ethan and Mattie, and the richness of their problem gives them even greater significance. If one criticism were to be made that would strike across the whole range of Mrs. Wharton's work, I think it would be a criticism of her more or less inveterate young man. As she pulled off Lily Bart, long ago, but did not pull off Selden, so she has gone on failing to pull Selden off. In most of her novels, Selden manqué has appeared as a hero. Nick Lansing comes perilously near being the same young man; yet he is not, quite. If Nick himself is not, his relation to Susy is, completely real; if Mrs. Wharton has not quite pulled him off, Susy has. These two people love each other; not as her heroes and heroines loved each other in the old days when sometimes a tired mind confused Mme. de Treymes with Mme. de Mauves.

And by just so much—the superior reality of Nick and Susy as a pair of lovers to all her preceding pairs—*The Glimpses of the Moon*, in spite of the unpleasant people it forces you to live among for a time, is a better book than *The Age of Innocence*, even than *The House of Mirth*. It is not sentimental cant to say that an author must somehow lay hold on essential human facts in order to do first-rate work. No amount of cleverness will take the place of real contact with permanent problems of the race. Mrs. Wharton is no John Knox, and no Dean Swift; she is neither preaching nor, in the technical sense, satirizing. She is offering an honest transcription of a "slice of life"—serious fiction, in other words. Slowly, inevitably, she pulls Nick and Susy out of the slough. The slough would hardly be worth our while if she did not, for it is a slough, believe me. And the fact that remains, in

the end, is not the question d'argent, but the fact of a fundamental human relation. It is one of Mrs. Wharton's great distinctions that she escapes, totally, one of the worst vices of the age—you can absolutely count on her, that is, not to be sentimental. It was great art not to rest her tribute to marriage on the single passion of Nick and Susy, but to add the sane and disillusioned comment of Grace Fulmer, even the suspicions of Nelson Vanderlyn's bewildered brain, and the faint apprehensions of Streffy. No; Mrs. Wharton is not sentimental; that particular falsification of facts she will never indulge in. Irony has always been one of her endowments; but humor (in the wide humanistic sense) has been a much less conspicuous gift. I can think of no instance of it in her work more outstanding than the presence of the Fulmer children at the end of *The Glimpses of the Moon*. It is not the humor, needless to say, that makes you laugh; rather, the humor that makes you say, half-tenderly, half-ruefully, "Yes, life is like that." Humor, in this sense, like architectonicé, is rather a masculine than a feminine gift. There were no humorists—in the Shakespearean sense—among the "twelve greatest women." But the Fulmer children, in the last two chapters of *The Glimpses of the Moon*, come very near that profounder wit.

Some of the things that people say are true. But Grace doesn't mind. She says she and Nat belong to each other. They can't help it, she thinks, after having been through such a lot together.

The point is that we're married. . . . Married. . . . Doesn't it mean something to you, something—inexorable? It does to me. I didn't dream it would in just that way. But all I can say is that I suppose the people who don't feel it aren't really married—and they'd better separate; much better. As for us—

There is the real centre of the labyrinth, which, at the beginning, we were not so sure of finding. Mrs. Wharton is too much of the modern world to make her modern folk take an ecclesiastical point of view about marriage. These are the people who announce their new engagements before they have actually got their divorces. Fortunately or unfortunately, the ecclesiastical theory of the indissolubility of marriage is a dead issue in most of the groups of which society today is made. This goes back to something more essential still than any law of the church; to the fundamental feeling of a certain type of human being concerning the marriage relation. You either feel it or you don't, as the quotation says. If you do feel it, you are as archaic as you are modern, and the Cave is rebuilt in the depths of the Ritz.

Whether *The Glimpses of the Moon* will take the Pulitzer Prize is another matter. It pays no particular tribute to America, and *The Age of Innocence*, in a sense, did. I can imagine critics whose personal disgust with most of the characters would take the form of depreciating the novel. All the same, it is a bigger book than *The Age of Innocence*, which did get the Pulitzer Prize. I can think of no American novel, written within the last few years, and dealing with contemporary life, to compare with it. And not only does Mrs. Wharton write better than any one else, but she knows how to unfold a more exciting tale.

Burton Rascoe, "An Entomologist of Society," New York *Tribune*, 23 July 1922, Section V, p. 5

This is the story of the triumph of true love over the forces of evil. Mrs. Wharton, doubtless, would expire of shock at so cheap and common a description of her novel; but that is, precisely, what, from one point of view, it is. It is perhaps a little quaint to find a moral in a book by a novelist who is conspicuously lacking in moral fervor; and yet by so observing the moral quality of this story, we hit, strangely enough, upon Mrs. Wharton's chiefest quality as a writer—her detachment. No one, not even Flaubert, has ever withdrawn himself so completely from the pages of his book, and no one has, for this reason, so completely let his story tell itself. When Mrs. Wharton's lovers proceed through certain hazards to a happy and moral ending, there is the same sort of inevitability about it as there is when, set in motion upon a given track, a locomotive arrives eventually at a given terminus. Mrs. Wharton sees that the valves are set, the bunkers stoked and the engine oiled; but we are no more conscious of her personal contribution to the story's progress than we are of the engineer's personal contribution to the progress of an express train we see flitting by at a distance on a summer evening. There is something trim and neat and graceful about the train and about her novel; we may speculate about the passengers aboard the train and between the covers of her book; we may thank our stars we are not bound for Pittsburgh in a stuffy Pullman or going to Fontainebleau by the uneasy route of debased self-respect and sponging, or we may think how nice it would be to be going somewhere, just to be going. But the odd thing about it is that we are likely to be as little concerned, personally, with Mrs. Wharton's characters as she is herself. We are likely to think they are vague and distant people going somewhere on a train, instead of flesh and blood persons having real tragedies of their emotions.

That is the fault with Mrs. Wharton's method. Flaubert, we know, felt very strongly about Emma Bovary; Mrs. Wharton's emotions are not at all engaged by Nick and Susy Lansing. A veritable J. Henry Fabre of the social apiary, she watches the movements of the insects and records them minutely, accurately and dispassionately, with a sort of scientific interest. There is no irony in her record, for irony is a method of comment and Mrs. Wharton never comments. (It is as much a mistake to call Mrs. Wharton an ironist as it is to call her a satirist, both designations implying an interpretation of things seen.) There is about her work, indeed, a rather chill, serene factuality which, in essence, is only a superior sort of reporting. The drones, she says, in effect, do so and so; there are certain parasites which have such and such characteristics, and on a certain day I saw this and that take place. Not once, or at least almost never, does she take up a specimen and say, "Now, this is a jolly little bug. I have a real fondness for the scamp. Something I observed him doing the other day endeared him to me. He is a little wild, a little foolish, a braggart and an egotist, and entirely devoid of a moral sense; but he has a heart of gold. Certain instincts make him very human and likeable." Indeed, Mrs. Wharton has less sentiment toward her insects than Fabre had toward his. Fabre's bugs often take on qualities we recognize as human because of his sympathy toward them, while Mrs. Wharton's human beings seldom seem more than slugs and parasites, moths and butterflies.

And so, when she takes a young married couple such as Nick and Susy Lansing, with a well polarized love for each other, and sees them through a definite course of events, the moral conclusion, the happy ending, the adjustment of difficulties—all is conclusive and not factitious. You know that, so loving, such a couple would inevitably weather the storms of their own weaknesses and of the disintegrating forces about them. The difficulty is that you, as a reader, are not overwhelmingly interested in whether they do weather the storms or not, and you rather wish, at moments, that Mrs. Wharton would, in the interest of drama, if not of art, whip up a terrific, unexpected gale and set Nick and Susy awash on the high seas of real tragedy, if only that she might save them in a burst of heroism and thus, by her act, show at least that she cared enough for them as human beings to risk her (artistic) life for them.

As it is, the only character in the book for whom one can work up any conceivable regard is the amiable bounder, Strefford. Mrs. Wharton grants him the attention of a discreet wink, and we love her for it. For Susy and Nick we can, after 200 pages, only wonder how Mrs. Wharton is going to contrive to find another rent-free house for them on the face of Europe. After so many pages of sponging incidents, after so many sacrifices of scruples in the interest of expediency, after so many acceptances of material favors in return for debasing acts, the story becomes frightfully repetitious. Only the intimate picture it gives of life as it is lived among the leisured and sophisticated class of cosmopolitans saves the story toward the end. The picture is neither pretty nor edifying; but neither is it particularly disgraceful in

311

its implications. It is very much the same sort of picture of human hates, envies, banalities, duplicities and weaknesses as one might get from a camera study of any other stratum of life.

The story, briefly, is that of a well-bred, popular young couple, favorites of society and living on their wits as their only resource. They sponge through a remarkable series of adventures, making sacrifices to personal honor with each acceptance of new favors. They see where such conduct might lead, but they are both—and especially Susy—unwilling to give up the life of leisure, comfort and luxury which is so readily thrust upon them by wives who require their assistance in deceiving their husbands and such drab little activities. They get fed up on this in time and, having been brought to their senses about their mutual need for each other, they forswear, when a propitious opportunity arises, the life which has galled them all along. There is, possibly, to some a serious flaw in Mrs. Wharton's conclusion that now that Nick has begun to break into the highbrow magazines as a literary freelance with some travel articles on Crete the harried couple can live the life to which they have been accustomed on the checks Nick will receive. The earnings from such articles for a year would not buy Susy's hats for a single season.

"A Page of Fiction," *New Republic*, 31 (23 August 1922), 365

In *The Glimpses of the Moon* Mrs. Wharton has done no more, in fact rather less, than she has done before. She has established what her publishers call "the rich background of American 'society'" in Europe, and patterned against it the marriage adventure of two attractive parasites who propose to live on their countrymen for a year. As in *The House of Mirth*, the woman reveals herself on a lower plane in respect to standards and scruples than the man; but he comes wisely to see that as a parasite he has no business with standards and scruples at all, and in the end they agree to take their little cash and let their credit go. The book conforms to the classic type of American novel in which the hero and heroine love each other at the beginning, want each other throughout, and are in possession of each other at the end. They stand out in their purity in the midst of a notably wicked and adulterous generation, and should win for their adept creator the Pulitzer Prize for "the American novel published during the year which best presents the wholesome atmosphere of American life and the highest standard of American manners and manhood."

Rebecca West, "Notes on Novels," *New Statesmen*, 19 (2 September 1922), 588

Every now and then some writer—either critic or novelist—announces that the novel is an art-form that is played out. The statement is, of course, not true. Art is the world of permanent things; and a form that is once inhabited by the spirit, though it may sleep, does not die. Mr. Gosse once said that all things that one may tell in verse had been told, and he said it at a time when the ink was not dry on *The Dynasts* and Mr. Robert Bridges was still writing, and Mr. De la Mare had hardly begun to write. In the first half of the nineteenth century the play seemed dead as mutton; there has grown up a generation in our time whose youth was shaped by the plays of Ibsen and Shaw and Barker. Even the little things of art do not perish; the rhymed epigram, that might reasonably have been supposed to be a flower that dropped all its petals when Herrick died, came to life again not so long in the hands of Father Tabb. There can be no fear that the novel will ever die. With Mr. De la Mare guiding the novel on to a new and starry plane in *The Memoirs of a Midget*, with Mr. Sherwood Anderson clinging on to the mane of Pegasus as it bumps him around and round an ugly little town in the Middle West and gasping out things that have not before been discerned, there need be no fear that it is even entering on a phase of suspended animation. But one can understand the mood of despair that makes people declare that all is up with the novel when one reads Mrs. Wharton's *The Glimpses of the Moon*.

Nothing more competent than this book could possibly be imagined. Mrs. Wharton has left undone nothing which she ought to have done; and on the other count, of doing nothing that she ought not to have done, her score is even higher. It has flashes of insight, as in that scene at the end of the book where the husband and wife after a separation that has nearly terminated in their divorce, are sitting quietly together, and the husband's mind ranges back to the partners whom they had tentatively selected for consolation and remarriage. He thinks of the girl who had been willing to marry him, who will be cruelly disappointed by his return to his wife, with compunction and tenderness; and he is shocked by his certainty that his wife has utterly banished from her mind all thoughts of her dismissed suitor, whose goodness and affection deserved respect. But he remembers the next moment that

whereas he had treated the girl very nearly like a cad, his wife treated her suitor with sincerity and courage. It is the neatest possible exhibition of the essential differences between Nick and Susy Lansing. Yet, for all those occasional reminders that the hand that wrote this wrote *Ethan Frome*, and for all its perpetual, vigilant competence, the book is a dead thing. It is as well done as it possibly could be; but it is not worth doing. There is a very great temptation to say that since here is a novel which is written with supreme accomplishment and which is as dust in the mouth, there must be something wrong with the novel as an art-form. But if one examines the case more closely the failure of *The Glimpses of the Moon* may be seen to proceed, not from any inadequacy of the novel, but from two circumstances attending on the development of Mrs. Wharton's talent, which act on it as adversely as if they were innate defects.

The first of these is that Mrs. Wharton was born in America at exactly the wrong time. One does not mean that it was unfortunate that Mrs. Wharton was able to win (as she did with *The Age of Innocence*) the thousand-dollar Pulitzer prize, which is awarded by Columbia University for "the American novel published during the year which best presented the wholesome atmosphere of American life and the highest standard of American manners and manhood." Though indeed this is unfortunate, for that there is something within Mrs. Wharton which responds to this note is demonstrated by her choice of a title, for with a certain lack of sympathy with Dr. Donne she uses the line as a metaphor for the fleeting vision of the moral good which two persons pursue through the obscurities of a murky environment. But the real misfortune of Mrs. Wharton's uprising is that it happened at a time when fastidious spirits of the kind to which she markedly belonged were obsessed by a particular literary method, and in a place where every day revealed situations which were bound to attract an eager intelligence of the kind she undoubtedly possessed but which could not appropriately be treated by that favoured method. The method was that of William Dean Howells and Henry James. The situations were those arising out of the establishment of the American plutocracy; and they were large, bold situations, blatancies in a marble setting, that could not be dealt with by the method that in Mr. Howells' hands was adjusted to the nice balancing of integrities in a little town, and in Mr. James' to the æsthetic consideration of conduct in a society where the gross is simply put out of mind. The moral problem in *The Glimpses of the Moon* is as coarse as one can imagine anything self-consciously concerned with morality possibly being. Nick and Susy are two penniless persons of charm who find it easy to pick up a good living by sponging on their millionaire friends. They fall in love and marry, and then their way of living suddenly fails them, for it involves them in actions which people in love cannot bear to see each other performing. They sulk over it. They separate. Each meditates divorce and a mercenary marriage. They are drawn together and towards independence by a certain fundamental worthiness in both of them. About this situation of crude primary colours Mrs. Wharton writes with an air of discussing fine shades in neutral tints. It is as disconcerting as if, say, Mrs. Gaskell had written *Mary Barton* in exactly the same style as *Cranford*.

The second circumstance of Mrs. Wharton's uprising which has been adverse to her development was the unfashionability at that moment of the truth that novelty is a test of the authenticity of art. Tradition is a necessity to the artist; he must realise that he is only a bud on the tree. The America into which Mrs. Wharton was born was almost extravagantly conscious of that necessity, destitute as it was of traditions, terrified lest ill-advised patriotism should hinder it from affiliation to European tradition. But he must also realise that no bud is exactly like another bud. Imitation has its place in life; it is of considerable service in enabling people who have beautiful things in their minds, but who are not possessed of the necessary initiative to find the shape for them.

Here is Mr. Bærlein, who is probably not a heaven-born novelist, but who has a love of Mexico, an interest in its history, and a sense of the crazy charm of its life, which it would have been a pity to waste. Mr. Bærlein has solved his problem through his admiration for M. Anatole France; for he has taken *La Rôtisserie de la Reine Pédauque* and has imitated its tale of the pastrycook's son and the Abbé Coignard in terms of Mexico, with a result that makes it well worth a place on anybody's library list. But the authentic artist is in a different case. His work must be as individual as his soul. If one heard that an actress was playing *La Gioconda* exactly as Duse played it, one would know that it was inconceivable that she should be as great as Duse; she would certainly be only an imitator and not a creative artist at all. An artist can be anything he likes except an echo. That is why Mr. Geoffrey Dennis's *Mary Lee* strikes one as a work of great promise. It is the study of a religious temperament; the story of a little girl brought up in a fierce and narrow Dissenting sect in the West Country in the 'fifties and 'sixties of last century. There emerges before one the portrait of a pallid woman with neat hair and eyes wild with the brave unguided spiritual adventure that is Protestantism; and a possessing realist force within her which twisted her religion till it served her real needs, and in the days of her loneliness sent her a saintly visionary lover, who,

314

when her flesh-and-blood lover comes, breathes ghostly words sanctifying earthly love. The tale is a shade too circumstantial and too squalidly so; but it is entirely individual in its accent and in its subject. The author has extended the frontiers of humanity's knowledge about itself, and that is exactly the aspect of creative work which has always escaped Mrs. Wharton. She would be content to write books that are exactly like the books of Henry James. She wants to be able to achieve just exactly the beauty he did; she wants to express just exactly the wisdom he expressed; and she succeeds astonishingly. Thus she feels she is in touch with a rich and worthy tradition. But then, also, she withholds the treasures of discovery which should have been made by such an unusual talent; and thus her readers are left with that curious mingled sense of satisfaction, disappointment at the extremest accomplishment, and the most deadly sterility.

Alice Sessums Leovy, "The Glimpses of the Moon," *Double Dealer*, 4 (September 1922), 157–8

It would, of course, be impossible for Mrs. Wharton to write a book totally devoid of interest, but she comes perilously close to it in her *Glimpses of the Moon*. If a less distinguished novelist had consulted her note-books and achieved this improbable jambalaya one would simply take it for granted that she was an inferior cook and let it go at that. It would be irritating, but unimportant. But in Mrs. Wharton's case

it is important because her ability to give us the best has been proved so often that it is unquestioned, and to find her also capable of giving us such poor fare—to find her *willing* to give it to us—is a distinct and unpleasant shock. It is rather a sad spectacle always to watch a fine artist becoming an indifferent one, and one fervently hopes that it is but a temporary metamorphosis.

The Glimpses of the Moon is concerned more or less with the marital difficulties of a group of well-dressed morons, principally American. Americans of the type who are forever on the wing in search of pleasure—or, if not pleasure, a new sensation of any kind—and who carry on their feverish, monotonously incessant, rather messy intrigues against a background of Como, Venice, and Paris. All the usual stock characters are here, even a poor little rich girl and a swarm of superior little poor children, and one of Mrs. Wharton's peculiar families, an unconvincing one, from Apex City. And then there is Susy, the little social parasite, with her sudden and extraordinary change of heart at the last possible moment, who might have stepped, complete in every detail, from the pages of some highly moral and uplifting tract. One mentions the fact with sorrow, but it is regrettably and undeniably true that there is a slight but unmistakable air of tract and uplift about the whole affair. One didn't think it of Mrs. Wharton. And one is left with the impression that, egged on by the "new" Susy, Nick's descent into a fine, upstanding, 100 percent American will be rapid. Mrs. Wharton doesn't actually say so, of course, but what else is one to infer? It is all most depressing.

While Mrs. Wharton refrains from telling us in so many words that

"Dawn harbours surely
East of the shadows"

315

she is constantly intimating it, and at times is even edifying; and she points her morals with a heavy hand.

There are a few flashes of the keen wit and almost uncanny penetration that one is accustomed to find in her novels, and the actual writing is—in spots—suave and full of dignity; but on the whole the book is very tedious. It is disjointed, badly put together, uncoordinated. One feels while reading that it has all been culled from half-forgotten note-books: a situation here, a likely character or two there, bits of description, an apt phrase, innumerable little details and odds and ends of ideas, all taken bodily from the note-books, stirred hastily into the jambalaya and the result presented to us with great éclat. But we are not amused. Nor interested. Nor tolerant. Merely bored. For of necessity one becomes infected with the author's apparent and quite justifiable lack of interest in her own creations. Like marionettes the characters move through the requisite number of chapters—like marionettes controlled and animated by someone who is thinking of other things—and they leave one cold.

Gilbert Seldes, "The Altar of the Dead," *Dial*, 73 (September 1922), 343–5

It has not been exactly roses, roses all the way for Mrs. Wharton's new novel, but it has been subject, subject. Mrs. Wharton has written a new book about the upper set. (*Cheers!*) Mrs. Wharton again exposes the vices of the rich. (*Excitement!*) Mrs. Wharton's hero says Men are different. (*Cries of* Take him out!) Mrs.

Wharton re-establishes marriage. (*Sensation in Heaven!*)

If I suggest with some asperity that these things are in the second order of importance it is not only to make again a plea for the kind of criticism which will concern itself, at least for a while, with the elements of form. It is because *The Glimpses of the Moon* is a peculiarly affecting example of nearly all the dangers which the novelist who cares for his form is likely to encounter; and that so conscientious and so intelligent an artist as Mrs. Wharton has failed to overcome them is exceedingly instructive. In a word I feel that even the enthusiasts for this new work are a little bewildered by it because they lack the fulfillment of satisfaction; and I am convinced that this failure is due not to Mrs. Wharton's preoccupation with any given social set nor to the domestic ideals which she gives to her hero nor to the celebrated coldness of her treatment of love; it can be explained only by the structural fault in the work itself.

What that fault is she has made exceptionally clear. The book deals with two young people, Susy and Nick Lansing, married in spite of their poverty and in spite of their loose association with the rich. They hope to live as long as possible on the bounty of their friends, then each is to give the other a helping hand to a more prosperous affiliation. In securing this bounty Susy is more or less against her will forced to do something she holds dishonourable; when Nick hears of it, hears from her that such compromises are likely to be the essence of their compact, he leaves her. Each then comes close to another marriage; but meeting again they return to each other. Giving thus the plot-subject of the book I have given enough for the reader who knows Mrs. Wharton's extraordinary skill in working-in backgrounds, in foreshortening the past, in dramatizing the present, to reconstruct the method of the book. For this plot the structure is perfect; if there were nothing more in *The Glimpses of the Moon* it would be faultless—and null.

The more in it is the theme: that those who have had glimpses of the moon are as those who have drunk the milk of Paradise, the circle woven round them not be transgressed. "In the balance. . . the balance of one's memories" says another character, small things are small indeed; that you cannot separate two who have been through many things together ("it's not the things, you see, it's the togetherness" adds Susy). And this is the very thing which Mrs. Wharton has failed to give us. For Susy and Nick go through virtually nothing in this book except the few episodes which sunder and separate. To give herself ample time and proportion with a plot requiring the treatment of an episode for Susy with Strefford and one for Nick with Carol, she has thinned the previous life of both almost out of existence; and in the chapters of their first married months she has had to work in the whole range of her characters and several threads of her plot. So that when we are informed that Susy

> "saw how much it had given her besides the golden flush of her happiness, the sudden flowering of sensuous joy in heart and body. Yes—there had been the flowering too, in pain like birth-pangs, of something graver, stronger, fuller of future power . . . something that Nick and love had taught her, but that reached out even beyond love and beyond Nick."

we want to cry out But that is exactly what *we* ought to have seen and haven't; we feel, for once in Mrs. Wharton's work,

cheated and unhappy. It is, of course, why she has not rendered the lives of Susy and Nick—since they did live them fully under other names and in another book. They do not resemble, they *are* Lily Bart and Lawrence Selden; and it is on the altar of her dead that Mrs. Wharton has sacrificed these living two.

In her failure to suggest the richness of life, and in the refusal to render the passion of love, Mrs. Wharton has left her work empty. The bowl is chastely proportioned and cunningly wrought; but it brims over with no rich liquor. Instead there is the watered wine of her plot. The distillation and watering are admirable. (By watering I mean the employment, instance by instance, of the material of her earlier work.) Among good things I note only the high dramatic sense which, after the two have parted, conveys to us through Nick, and not through Susy, the vital information that Streff has surprisingly inherited and is therefore the natural upward step for her; the reader unconsciously supplies and savours the drama which is never related of Susy's response to the news. Or the superb *dénouement*, prepared for with a masterly certainty and delicacy, of Susy's discovery that the hostess for whom she made her great false step was the unknown adulteress who dispossessed her at Como. One remembers with a positive thrill that Strefford, the owner of the villa, had with embarrassment given a jewel to Mrs. Vanderlyn's little girl; one sees brilliantly that the money came from Mrs. Vanderlyn's paramour; one sees why the discovery makes it impossible for Susy to marry Strefford. It is the magic of technique. It is not quite enough.

The strange thing is that the theme is worthy of Mrs. Wharton; it isn't in any sense cheap, or sentimental, or thin. Isn't it, essentially, the theme, too, of the *The House of Mirth* where, though Lily is dead, the word passes between them which makes all things irrevocably right? Why then the extraordinary sensation of Mrs. Wharton's own scepticism concerning the whole affair? Why does one feel so sure that she was unsure, believe that she did not at all believe? Why didn't the demands of her theme make themselves clear to an artist who has always shown so responsive a mind to the requirements of form? I can only suspect that she sets small store by the felicity which her protagonists have and lose and win again; and being unwilling to treat the subject with irony she treats it (in another sense of the word) with contempt. Or is this, possibly, Mrs. Wharton's final comment on the happy ends of men's lives?

Ruth Hale, "Two Lady Authors," *Bookman*, 56 (September 1922), 98–9

The next distinguished lady author on our list, Edith Wharton, presents us with *The Glimpses of the Moon,* a gaudy thing with no sincerity whatever, unless Mrs. Wharton has a more meagre capacity for honest writing than appeared in *Ethan Frome. The Glimpses of the Moon* is a puppet show. Every little figure in it is jerked about with visible wires. Their attitudes are necessarily limited, and it seems to us that they are also quite unnecessarily stale. Mrs. Wharton is entitled to her choice of methods, of course, and we cannot complain if she wishes to tell her story with a dashing flavor of unreality. Neither have we just cause against her for writing of absurdly impossible people. Probably almost anybody is possible. But there is a stereotyping in this book which is inex-cusable in an author who can do any better. We can give just one example on which, we think, we can rest our case. Two young persons have married who have spent their separate lives sponging on rich friends, and who believe they can make a go of it together for perhaps a year or so, by borrowing villas and banking the checks they get for wedding presents. The enterprise gets as far as Venice before it breaks up, with some violence. The departing husband, looking to find his wife in tears, catches sight of her instead arriving in a gondola at a festive party with four men for escorts.

As luck will have it, he, bound for his train, sees no gondola in sight but the one she has just so merrily left, whereupon he takes it. Then follows: "The cushions, as he leaned back, gave out a breath of her scent; and in the glare of electric light at the station he saw at his feet a rose which had fallen from her dress. He ground his heel into it as he got out." We might spot Mrs. Wharton to the heel grinding, but the scent in the gondola pillows is simply too much. Scents began to accumulate in the gondolas once upon a time, of course, but they reached the saturation point at about the time the last Doge wed the Adriatic. Edith Wharton has no business to be writing such trash.

"The Current of Opinion," *Current Opinion*, 73 (September 1922), 304

Elsewhere in the pages of this magazine is reviewed Mrs. Wharton's new book, *Glimpses of the Moon*. It is the general policy of this magazine to present no book to its readers that is not worth buying and reading. To this policy this book of Mrs. Wharton's is the exception. We would recommend nobody to buy it or to read it.

It is difficult to understand how this sort of writing can be any value to any human being. It may have good artistic technique, but the kind of people written about are of no value to the world either in or out of the pages of fiction.

We agree with Heywood Broun: "Even Mrs. Wharton has not sufficient skill in writing to make the doings of so dowdy a cast of characters enthralling."

J. Middleton Murry, "Books and Real Books," *Nation and Athenæum* [England], 32 (28 October 1922), 164–5

Here are two psychological novels [*Lucienne* by Jules Romains and *The Glimpses of the Moon* by Edith Wharton]. Both are interesting. And yet—shall we ever desire to read either of them again?

The answer is in the negative. Of course, the test is a severe one; perhaps unnecessary also. After all, the novel which has interested us once has done all that we have a right to require of it. There are not so many of them that we can afford to wag our heads over a couple. We ought rather to be grateful.

Professionally, we are. Any book which does not demand sheer, unmitigated effort; which, having begun, we desire, however languidly, to finish, is a book to be grateful for: with a sober and restrained gratitude. Hours that might have been "a heaviness and a weariness" have passed not unpleasantly.

And yet, hours are precious things. They seem to become fewer and fewer, to grow smaller and smaller, to pass swifter and swifter. The train begins to gather speed and rush us through the landscape of life; we want to be looking out of the window all the while. Time—we do not want to kill it, we have no need to pass it. It passes us; it kills us; every hour takes from us irrevocably something we might have seen, or known, or been. To sit with our eyes glued to a book to which we shall never desire to return is to know that we have lost the chance of wonders—a forest, a river, an apple-woman on the station platform, even our own thoughts, the thoughts which could have been then, and then alone, the thoughts we shall never have the chance to think again.

Books, devourers of time, cheats of life! No wonder we are angry with you. Had you been bad, we should have thrown you out of the window. But, alas! you were good—good enough to steal our priceless hours; good enough to persuade us that you might give back something even more precious than you stole; good enough to compel us publicly to call you good (though in our hearts we call you the wickedest of all); good enough to set us cudgelling our brains to discover why you are not better, why you do not belong to that other glorious company——

Books, creators of time, multipliers of life! Books which give us in an hour what we should not have seen or known in a century; books which, with a single word, a sudden phrase, light up the landscape of life, throw sunbeams into the dark forest of our thoughts, lift us up as Keats was lifted up, like Cortez on Darien, on the wings of a wild surmise that life is intimate and one, comprehensible and beautiful, if we could only see. Books that reveal, that dazzle or enchant, that whisper secrets or thunder oracles, that show a soul in a gesture, a mind in a word, a life in an incident, a universe in a story:

319

that make hours of our minutes, and lifetimes of our hours.

You "good" books, respectable books, decorous, intelligent, unoffending books—why are you not like these? Why is it so easy for us to see that you ought to be real books, and so hard to explain why you are not? Why is it that you have all the trappings and the outward show of life, yet do not live? Your appearance is immaculate, your manners irreproachable, the level of your conversation of the highest, the themes you deal with serious—you are perfect little gentlemen: and yet you are not *books*. You look like books, you behave like books, you want to be books; really, you know, you ought to be books.

You are full of ideas. If we take *The Glimpses of the Moon*, which Mrs. Wharton now revisits, we find it is built on a true and excellent idea:—

> "He had fallen in love with her because she was, like himself, amused, unprejudiced and disenchanted; and he could not go on loving her unless she ceased to be all these things. From that circle there was no issue, and in it he desperately revolved."

Surely, the idea of a little masterpiece: even, we are tempted to say, the language of a little masterpiece. Is it not, almost as it stands, the typical end of a Tchehov story? Mrs. Wharton is too kind to leave us with anything so depressing. They escape from the closed circle—escape fairly and humanly enough, indeed, if once we can be persuaded that they were ever in it. But Mrs. Wharton, with all her skill, cannot persuade us of that. At the critical moment we rebel, and protest that Nick is a silly young fool; and, unfortunately, if Nick is a silly young fool, he becomes straightway incredible. He was not built

for one; he is not made to look like one, and yet he acts like one.

It is not a mistake of this kind that M. Romains has made. If he has less vividness than Mrs. Wharton, he has more accuracy....

We are asking too much? From one point of view, yes; from another, no. One cannot be a writer of the capacity of Mrs. Wharton or M. Romains for nothing. What can it matter to them that their books are better than ninety-nine out of a hundred? If, by chance, it does matter, they may be satisfied. But we imagine them striving for more excellent things; some small immorality gained by giving to the world a fragment of the truth that is theirs, and theirs alone, to give. That is the standard by which a true writer elects to be judged; that is the standard we have judged them by.

S. P., "Edith Wharton's Latest," *Forum*, 68 (October 1922), 905–6

Edith Wharton's latest novel is not her best, nor is her best among those which preceded. Her best will not be performed until she has found the particular field in which she can do herself justice. Her successive novels reveal increasing powers. Her technique—we hate the word, but there is no other—is perfect. As for her choice in subjects, there is less to be said. If, therefore, *Glimpses of the Moon* proves less popular than *The Age of Innocence* (her publishers insist on the comparison) it will be due not to a weakening of narrative powers but to the difference in the lines along which they are exerted.

Glimpses of the Moon is a story of the conflict between a him and a her on the matter of honor. We insist on the pronouns, for in spite of names she has given the pair, they continue to be much less real than some of the minor characters of the book.

They are a pair of social pirates. She, a girl without family, moves about in the set which composes the social register, with no other means of support, visible or invisible, than her popularity. Trips to Europe and the Orient, one week-end party after another, places to eat and sleep in luxury for the balance of the week, and even her clothes, are supplied her by female friends because they like her company.

He earns an indifferent living as a hack writer, but also has his taste of luxury because he is a nice sort of chap to have around. They fall in love and marry, agreeing to pool their practical, social booty, but also agreeing to separate when and if it becomes apparent that two cannot sponge on their friends as cheaply as one. By insisting that all wedding presents be in the form of checks and by planning to live successively in one friend's house after another, they figure that they can make a go of it for a year at least.

Before the second month of the honeymoon is over, they discover that the use of friends' houses and servants must be paid for by favours which honorable people cannot give. She is inclined to wink an eye, but he will not. It were not fair to reveal the plot, which from this point on is concerned with the struggle between conflicting standards of honor. Whether the lack of plausibility of such a story can spoil the reading of it each reader must judge for himself.

The scene of the story is Europe's centre of gayety—the various houses which the pair plans to occupy are the baubles of rich Americans over there. The minor characters, with very few exceptions, are that type of American to whom houses full of servants, evening dress six times a week, flittings from Venice to Paris to London, and never a trip to Main Street, are as natural as lightning bugs in June. Not a single character is introduced but is not carefully and perfectly drawn. Edith Wharton can still sit a dozen characters down to a dinner and keep the conversation of all twelve going with remarkable realism. And she has increased her skill in the use of that very necessary appliance— the fluency which makes one eager to turn the page.

Checklist of Additional Reviews

Heywood Hale Broun, "It Seems to Me," New York *World*, 27 July 1922, p. 13.

Carl Van Doren, "Unsuccessful Parasites," *Nation*, 115 (2 August 1922), 128.

Lilian Whiting, "Mrs. Wharton Portrays Smart Life of Europe," Springfield [Massachusetts] *Republican*, 6 August 1922, magazine section, p. 7–A.

Edwin Francis Edgett, "Edith Wharton's Latest Novel," Boston *Evening Transcript*, 9 August 1922, Part 2, p. 6.

H. W. Boynton, "Mrs. Wharton on Character," *Independent*, 109 (19 August 1922), 79–81.

Henry Seidel Canby, "Out of Vanity Fair," *New York Evening Post Literary Review*, 19 August 1922, p. 883.

"Star-Laden Skies and Great Orange Moons," *Current Opinion*, 73 (September 1922), 391–93.

Wilfrid L. Randell, "Misunderstandings," *Bookman* [England], 62 (September 1922), 256.

Gerald Gould, "New Fiction," *Saturday Review* [England], 134 (2 September 1922), 355.

"A New Divorçons," *Times Literary Supplement* [England], 7 September 1922, p. 566.

Spectator [England], 129 (16 September 1922), 373–5.

R. D. Townsend, "The Book Table," *Outlook*, 122 (20 September 1922), 119.

"Can Social Parasites Reform?" *Literary Digest*, 74 (23 September 1922), 53.

Wilson Follett, "The Atlantic's Bookshelf," *Atlantic Monthly*, 130 (October 1922), 10.

F. C. Danchin, "Le Roman Américain," *Revue Germanique* [France], 14 (1923), 193–5.

A SON AT THE FRONT

A SON AT THE FRONT

BY

EDITH WHARTON

Something veil'd and abstracted is often a part of the manners of these beings.—WALT WHITMAN

NEW YORK
CHARLES SCRIBNER'S SONS
MCMXXIII

Maurice Francis Egan, "Sons and Parents at the Front," *New York Times Book Review*, 9 September 1923, p. 1, 19, 24

In one of Richard Watson Gilder's poems there is a little poet who complains that he has no theme and cannot do his part. To which the critic replies, "You do not lack a theme, you lack a heart." This is only a paraphrase, but it serves to point the truth that no novelist can ever lack a theme so long as men and women and social relations exist; but that many novelists do lack the source of the quality that moves us in literature—a heart.

Mrs. Wharton has been accused at times of being both heartless and artificial; but those who made these accusations had not taken seriously either *The Valley of Decision* or *Ethan Frome*. But it is true enough that she is uneven, that she sometimes takes the easiest way of solving a problem and that she has been known to slur her work rather than to throw off that engaging languor which prevents her from making arduous researches. In *The Age of Innocence*, for instance, she seems to have preferred to follow her memory or the memories of others rather than to verify her facts; none of these charges can be made against her latest book, *A Son at the Front*.

So far she has done nothing that equals it. She sounds the finest depths of sentiment without becoming sentimental for a moment. In choosing her time and her atmosphere, she was rather audacious. There are many reasons why most of us should dislike a novel dealing with the war: many reasons why the suggestions of such a book should prejudice us against it: and these reasons are obvious. Only the production of a masterpiece could reconcile us to the treatment of that terrible epoch by a writer of fiction. And even a masterpiece which was coldly correct and artistically done could only have gained from us a conventional approval. Mrs. Wharton, then, was greatly daring in choosing her theme: but even more daring in presenting four very modern people, brought up under conditions which did not make for the highest morality and in making them at once interesting and appealing without exaggerating the facts of life and without extenuation or apology.

The centre of the action is the artist, John Campton, divorced from his wife, who had been Julia Ambrose and had become the wife of Mr. Anderson Brant, an American millionaire living in Paris because she preferred it. George, the son of the first marriage, is deeply loved by all three, each according to his capacity of loving, and the delicacy of Mrs. Wharton's method in differentiating the capacities of these three for loving is as exquisite as it is poignant.

The war breaks, and the efforts of these three people are all turned to save George from going to the front; he has just returned from Harvard, handsome, charming, generous, unmoral and full of the joyousness of life. John Campton, when he was a poor and struggling artist, permitted his son to be brought up by his wife and her second husband. Now that he had become a fashionable painter, he wishes, above all things, to have his son, who had hitherto given an apparently impartial affection to his father and mother and Mr. Anderson Brant. Campton had staked all his hopes and happiness on this charming son. He had planned a tour in the South of Europe, and perhaps in Africa, for the sake of the vivid color and sunlight, with this darling boy; but he found that all his security had been dashed away in a few hours; George, by accident, was a French citizen, and his danger was suddenly revealed to his father when the young man carelessly emptied his pockets on the dressing table in the room adjoining:

Campton welling with a new tenderness on everything that belonged to his son, noticed a smart antelope cardcase (George had his mother's weakness for Bond Street novelties), a wrist watch, his studs, a bundle of banknotes; and besides these a thumbed and dirty red book, the size of a large pocket diary.

The father wondered what it was; then of a sudden he knew. He had once seen Mme. Lebel's grandson pull just such a red book from his pocket as he was leaving for his "twenty-eight days" of military service; it was the livret militaire that every French citizen under 48 carries about with him.

And in that book George's father read that when France should mobilize, his son would be forced to go to the front. George had been cured of tuberculosis. This cure made the three who loved him very happy; but, as he read, Campton found in it a source of new unhappiness. The plea of ill-health would not save the boy; it could only be done through "influence":

He still refused to admit that France had any claim on George, any right to his time, to his suffering or to his life. He had argued it out a hundred times with Adele Anthony. "You say Julia and I were to blame for, not going home before the boy was born,— and God knows I agree with you! But suppose we'd meant to go? Suppose we'd made every arrangement, taken every precaution, as my parents did in my own case, got to Havre or Cherbourg, say, and been told the steamer had broken her screw, or been prevented ourselves, at the last moment, by illness or accident, or any sudden grab of the hand of God? You'll admit we shouldn't have been to blame for that; yet the law would have recognized no difference. George would still have found himself a French soldier on the 2d of last August because, by the same kind of unlucky accident, he and I were born on the wrong side of the Atlantic. And I say that's enough to prove it's an iniquitous law, a travesty of justice. Nobody's going to convince me that, because a steamer may happen to break a flange of her screw at the wrong time, or a poor woman be frightened by a thunderstorm, France has the right to force an American boy to go and rot in the trenches.

The three intrigue with all their power. A clerical job was secured for George, and then followed feverish anxiety, the fear that "influence" might not keep him from the trenches. "Influence" does its worst from George's point of view. He will not stand aside, for he sees what the struggle really means. He cuts through all sophistries and timidities with his brave honesty; this the anguished three do not at first realize.

The treatment of this situation alone would put Mrs. Wharton in the first rank of modern novelists. There is, perhaps, no living writer today who could have satisfactorily pictured the character of the light, the frivolous, the unsatisfying, the tire-

326

some mother of the boy. She had bored Campton, but she neither bores the reader nor her second husband; and not by the slightest of ridicule does Mrs. Wharton suggest how really stupid she is. She does not step out of a frame, she is real. Educated in a fashionable Parisian convent she is still absolutely Protestant. George has been wounded. His father and Mr. Brant have reached his bedside in the hospital, and then his mother arrives:

> They thought the wound mortal; but the orderly and a stretcher-bearer had managed to get the young man into the shelter of a little wood. The stretcher-bearer, it turned out, was a priest. He had at once applied the consecrated oil, and George, still conscious, had received it "with a beautiful smile"; then the orderly, thinking all was over, had hurried back to the fighting and been wounded. The next day he, too, had been carried to Doullens: and there, after many inquiries, he had found his Lieutenant in the same hospital, alive, but too ill to see him.

Mr. Brant determines to leave for Paris on his wife's arrival at the hospital. Campton, who is not troubling himself much about conventionality, wonders why he has gone. He looks with horror at the prospect of a long succession of days spent in the society of his former wife. She explains. The nuns might consider it odd if George appeared to have two fathers. She wishes the sisters were out of the hospital. Campton asks, "What's wrong? They seem to be perfect." To which Mrs. Brant answers:

> It's all so dreadful—and this extreme unction, too! What is it exactly, do you know? A sort of baptism? Will the Roman Church try to get hold of him on the strength of it?

This amuses Campton, but his heart is pierced when he discovers that this lad had kept a secret from him. He had been making love in New York, and had continued it in Paris, to Mrs. Talkett, who had an unappreciated husband, a diaphanous soul and the morals of her circle. George is impregnated with what he calls "new ideas"; after his serious illness he does not take them too seriously. Mr. Talkett is an inveterate and tiresome talker, but he possesses as much intelligence as his wife. George, knowing the psychology of the lady, insists that he cannot be her lover; of this she complains loudly to his father. She must get a divorce or he will have nothing to do with her. Neither his father nor mother can complain of this. Their example has always been before him. He knows his Mrs. Talkett, and coolly explains that he has taken this way of letting the lady down easy—for, although she has no morals, she is afraid of getting out of a rut.

This situation baldly stated here would have been absurd or farcically humorous in the hands of a less skilled writer. Here it is part of the atmosphere, as are the characters and temperaments of even the most unimportant characters in the book, though the consummate art of the author prevents any of her characters from being entirely unimportant. Mme de Dolmetsch, Harvey Mayhew, the American delegate to a Peace Conference at The Hague; the fashionable physician, Fortin-Descluse, even Beausite, the fashionable artist become unfashionable; his wife, his mother, seen only in glimpses, are figures that cannot be forgotten.

The graphic power of Mrs. Wharton is worth all the pains she has evidently spent in acquiring it, and yet it could not be acquired unless her great talent was inspired by the keenest observation directed by the qualities of the heart. And Mme. Lebel, the humble mother of sorrows and typically French to the core! And the young Americans taken from life and shown with all the vivacity of life!

It is seldom of late that such vivid contrasts as those offered by the French and American temperaments have been so lucidly drawn in any picture of our modern life. Miss Anthony, the American old maid who is obsessed by her maternal love for George, we have met before. She is a type. But Mrs. Wharton saves her from triteness by making her typical.

It is difficult, even after a second reading, to find lapses in Mrs. Wharton's style. Her instrument is never out of tune. She uses similes infrequently; you can count them easily, and admire them greatly. By the use of them she raises or lowers the tone of her color scheme which is the use to which all similes and metaphors should be put. There is one paragraph however, spoiled by an exaggerated simile. It is the one in which Campton is described as entering the hospital where his son lies:

> On a landing Campton heard a babble and scream; a nauseating scream in a queer bleached voice that might have been man, woman, or monkey's. Perhaps that was what the French meant by "a white voice", this voice; this voice which *was as featureless as some of the poor men's obliterated faces*! Campton shot an anguished look at his companion, and she understood and shook her head. "Oh, no; that's in the big ward. It's the way they scream after a dressing. . . ."

The firm belief that existed before the war that money could do everything is one of the illusions which the war dissipated. When two dying men brought in from the battle field are put into the same room with the stepson of the millionaire, Mr. Anderson Brant is incredulous and horrified. It could not be possible that two mere unknown soldiers, even in an overcrowded hospital should be permitted to share a room with George!

"Yes—bad cases; dying," Campton drew a deep breath. "You see there are times when your money and your influence and your knowing everybody are no more use than so much sawdust." It is a short speech; the episode lasts scarcely a minute, but what could confirm more thoroughly our knowledge that, in the shambles of war, with the impartiality of mercy, there was no favor for the rich or the great.

"You're talking too loudly," the nurse merely said as she closed the door on the all-powerful millionaire and the great artist.

When the clairvoyant, Mme. Olida, enters, one recognizes a common phase of the effect of war on restless and darkened souls. Spiritism and black magic and white magic, crystal globes and all manner of esoteric divinations were resorted to. Benvenuto Cellini and his incantations were imitated by the incredulous who had become infinitely credulous in their attempts to break open the portals of the life after death. Great ladies of fashion had crowned her séances. She was as revered as the Delphic oracle. But her own son Pepito is taken. She believes that Campton has "influence." Campton must save him from death at the front! She heard nothing from this beloved child for whom she has made a fortune by her "gift" Campton asks her why she cannot use her "gift," her powers, for herself? She wants news, real news, of her son, and her "gift," which has brought crowds to her, is useless. This Spanish purveyor of black or white magic is made as clear in the picture as if she had been painted by Fortuny or Madrazo.

After George's recovery a comfortable staff appointment is found for him in Paris.

His people are serene. The crime of the Lusitania changes all this and George has a double reason for fighting again. We are made to feel the change that has taken place in his soul; and the end comes—a most moving picture. If a man should find his eyes moist, if he should be touched to the heart by the truth and the beauty of Mrs. Wharton's last pages, it would teach him what the effect of reality is when interpreted in the terms of life by a great artist.

At last, there is a novel by an American artist which is subtle as it is perfect in its simplicity; and one which can be read many times with an increasing feeling of reverence for the essential truths of life. It is not that Mrs. Wharton tells all or wears a heart upon her sleeve, it is that she knows the human heart; and in spite, or rather perhaps because of her knowledge of an artificial world, she pierces easily to the very depths of human joy and sorrow.

Burton Rascoe
"*A Son at the Front,*"
New York *Tribune,*
9 September 1923,
pp. 17–18

One wonders, after reading *A Son at the Front*, where in the world Mrs. Wharton has been all this time. Certainly she cannot have been remotely in touch with French, English and American fiction since 1914. Even to allow that she had limited her acquaintance with war novels to such reviews of them as to have come to her notice would lead one to the untenable inference that Mrs. Wharton considers herself so superior to her novel writing contemporaries that she may treat of precisely the same matters which engaged their faculties from five to eight years ago and beat them all to a frazzle.

That won't do, because it would impute to Mrs. Wharton both arrogance and bad manners—the very last qualities even a hopeless noodle would attribute to Mrs. Wharton. No, it must be conceded at once that Mrs. Wharton has been wholly oblivious of the war inspired fiction of the Messrs. Wells, Bennett, George, Cannan, Hankey, Hay, Mackenzie, McKenna, Barbusse, Latzko, Duhamel, Geraldy, Dos Passos, Cummings and Boyd, to say nothing of the work of the Misses Sinclair, West, Stern, Macaulay and Cather. It is notorious that novelists rarely read novels, least of all the novels of their coevals; and it is charitable to suppose that, in happy ignorance that the war had hitherto been used as a theme of fiction, it gradually came over Mrs. Wharton that here was a lot of good material going to waste.

This is rather a pity, for, as we reviewers are in a habit of saying, this novel is hardly likely to add anything to her reputation. It is rather late in the day, to be assured, even by so gifted a prosateuse as Mrs. Wharton, that the war occasioned a great deal of anguish and discomfort among the lower as well as among the upper classes in Europe; that poor charwomen no less than matrons among the best people grieved to see their only sons go off to the front and that mothers, whatever their station in life, bore the news of their sons' death with similar anguish and the same helpless fortitude of resignation; that among the noncombatants in Paris there were a great number of people who conducted themselves very much as their natures dictated in peace times, which is to say selfishly and discreditably; that the usual social and moral conventions were somewhat in abeyance owing to the general excitement;

that human imperfection was noticeable here and there among those who directed affairs during the war; and that the brave youngsters who did the fighting had a way of saying and doing things which surprised and mystified their elders—a way based upon a different attitude toward life from the attitude cherished by these elders.

All this tardy information is little likely to sweep many of us off our feet: We were already pretty familiar with it as long ago as *Mr. Britling [Sees It Through]*. And Mrs. Wharton has not, I think, touched upon a single point which Mr. Wells and Mr. Bennett did not go over thoroughly in novels which they have long since outgrown. Here is the same anxiety of parents over the possibility of their sons being killed and the same certainty that the war ought to be fought so long as the sons of other parents do the fighting; here is the same depiction of human greed and chicanery among profiteers and organizers of war charities; here is the same observation that many women, married and unmarried, looked upon the war as a sort of protracted Mardi Gras wherein they might indulge in certain liberties which discretion in other times would forbid; and here is the same conclusion that whatever the extent of the death toll, it is more than recompensed by the affecting democratic spectacle of a cobbler's exchanging condolences with an aristocrat of the Faubourg Saint-Germain and that of a Deauville duchess's abandonment of bridge long enough to share the sisterhood of tears with a Paris midinette who has also lost a lover at the front.

Indeed, one would almost fancy that Mrs. Wharton is under the impression that the war is still going on and that she wrote her little book to the end that America might help France and Britain see it through. She clings to the notion that war is an ennobling experience, and if her novel may be said to work up to anything at all

it is to the conversion to the cause of a highly caricatured cuckold of a pacifist and the decision of his wife that her place is at her husband's side now that her young lover had been killed, "I've never in my life been happy enough to be so happy!" is her enigmatic cry, which keeps ringing in the ears of Campton, who has lost his son. That phrase "associated itself suddenly with a phrase of Boyton's that he had brushed away unheeding: 'You've had your son—you have him still; but those others have never had anything.' Yes; Campton saw now that it was true of poor Madge Talkett, as it was of Adele Anthony and Mr. Brant, and even in a measure of Julia. They had never—no, not even George's mother—had anything, in the close, inextricable sense in which Campton in his own hour of destitution, that he understood how much greater the depth of their poverty had been."

This is a curious conclusion, seeing that until a short time before the boy's death Campton had never had his son at all, and that Campton's concentration of his affection upon his son had been brought about by the fact that he had wearied in turn of his wife, of other women, of society and of his art, and in the late autumn of his life had suddenly begun to demonstrate his devotion to his son by bungling his son's affairs every time he meddled with them, thereby incurring the son's benevolent estimate of his male parent as a well-intentioned damned nuisance. Having assured himself that Boylston is right, that he has "had his son and has him still" (although that son is among the slain), "while those others have never had anything," Campton considers himself blessed by heaven with extreme good fortune and turns again to his painting.

If there is an ironic intention in this muddled wind-up Mrs. Wharton has most deftly concealed it. She has tried, within the limits of her peculiar capacities, to make Campton a sympathetic figure throughout the novel, and has succeeded, with me, in making him only a petty-minded prig. The other characters are limned with such haste and unoriginality that they seem like stock figures out of the high comedy repertory. Even George, the boy, who, if any one should have been realized with touches of sympathy and understanding, is the fine, careless rapture out of Oxford war fiction, and nothing else: he has an airy cynicism about the war, but gets himself shot in it with as much expedition as possible; he is as old in wisdom and experience as he is young in freshness and vitality; he is in love and on terms of intimacy with the wife of a chap whom he twits at tea, and the war brings him to the momentous decision that Madge must divorce her silly, rich husband and marry him or hereafter they can be nothing but friends, because he "sees everything differently now" and they "must be first of all above board."

It seems amazing that Mrs. Wharton should still persist in the delusion that the personal relationships she depicts are peculiar to war. In war or peace, in whatever age, youth and senility are accustomed to look at life from somewhat different angles, and it is only because war brings the common interest of parents and sons into closer focus that this disparity between their points of view clash or is ever taken serious notice of. Human nature, not the so-called realities of war, frequently induces a young man who is deeply in love, to seek the sole proprietorship advertised by marriage over the woman he loves. And human nature, not the moral laxity of war times, often brings about those relationships anteceding the decision that from now on everything must be open and above board. . . .

It is a story that is a long time getting under way and one which, once it does get under way, has only a few scenes upon which one may look back with pleasure. If this were the year 1915 or even 1917 instead of the year 1923, Mrs. Wharton's novel might not seem so profitless an endeavor; and to any one who has not yet read a war novel it may be recommended whole-heartedly, for Mrs. Wharton has not lost her gift for anatomizing people she dislikes, which is to say the majority of those who compose the human race. But this very gift makes one suspect that with her chill temperament, she ought to be the last person in the world to write a war novel—and possibly she is.

Robert Morss Lovett, "A Son at the Front," New Republic, 36 (19 September 1932), 105

Like a soul belated comes Mrs. Whaton with her novel of the War. The only justification for such tardiness is to be found in a more elevated point of view and a broader understanding than were possible during the mêlée, conscience cleansed by pity and fear, a spirit moved to sympathy and compassion by the memory of the great conflict. These attributes Mrs. Wharton does not bring to her task. She sees the War as she saw it at Paris, with myopic vision, keenly observant of its humor and tragedy in detail, artistically conscious of the contrast between the tarnished idyl of the Parisian scene and the nameless horrors of the front, patriotically possessed by the love of an adopted country, and snobbishly blind to every point of view but that of her class. Thus after five years she still writes of the German officer who fractures the skull of a little girl, and the French father who declares: "If I live long enough I shall run the swine down. If not I'll kill as many of his kind as God lets me." She is able to build her climax to the arrival of the American troops in Paris, with a confidence undisturbed by any suggestion of the aftermath. The peace of Versailles and the invasion of the Ruhr cast no shadows upon her bright spirit. Her horizon is that of the War.

Mrs. Wharton's story is the simple one of John Campton, the great American painter, whose only son, born in France, is subject to military service. The father, his divorced wife, and her banking husband all interest themselves to keep the boy out of danger, but he eludes their care and while ostensibly on staff work he is really with his regiment at the front. He is wounded, recovers, goes back, is wounded again and returns to die. The theme of the novel is American participation in the war, dramatized by the conversation of John Campton from a position of indifferent neutrality at the outset to a conviction that no "civilized man could afford to stand aside from such a conflict." Its substance is the goings and comings of Campton among all sorts of people, his humble French servants, his distinguished Parisian friends, his nondescript fellow countrymen, each of whom represents some attitude towards the War. This is the usual method of propagandist fiction. In Zola's *Fecondité*, for example, the hero is kept so constantly on the move by his propaganda of propagation that he seems to have no opportunity for his own work of fatherhood; and Romain Rolland's hero, Clérambault, who must be Mrs. Wharton's antichrist, suffers from the same sort of unreality. John Campton is more sufferable because he is being converted, not preaching a gospel of his own. Moreover, since the War had stopped his painting, he really had nothing to do but drift about and Mrs. Wharton shows much adroitness in giving plausibility to

his relations. It is true, when we find him accompanying his divorced wife to a clairvoyant and discovering in that lady the Spanish girl—enlarged and remodeled but identical—on whose account he had suffered divorce twenty-five years before, we think of the art of Madame Humbert rather than of Mrs. Wharton.

Another way in which the propagandist in fiction weights the scales of his arguments is through his characters. The utterer of the protest: "That some senile old beast of a diplomatist should decree, after a good dinner, that all we love best must be offered up," is Madame Dolmetsch who intrigues to keep her lover safe at the war office, but in vain. Campton remembers "the fat middle aged philanderer with his Jewish eyes, his Slav eloquence, his Levantine gift for getting on and for getting out from under." There is an argument in the very name—Ladislas Isidor. Mrs. Wharton will meet with general approval for sending this caterpillar to his death at the front after he has played his part, by mere loathsome association, in persuading Campton that he was wrong in trying to make his son an embusqué. Again, the proponent of resistance to the herd instinct who repudiates "the idea of giving in now just because of all this deafening noise about America's danger and America's duties" is Mr. Talkett, whose husbandly honor is at the mercy of young George Campton. At times Mrs. Wharton takes the special pleading into her own hands as when she rhapsodizes: "Preparedness! . . . from a little group of discerning spirits the contagion had spread like a prairie fire, sweeping away all the other catchwords of the hour, devouring them in one great blaze of wrath and enthusiasm." Or when she gloats: "Now indeed America was 'in it;' the gross tangible proof for which her government had forced her to wait was there in all its unimagined horror." Or when she mourns:

"Before many days it became apparent that the proud nation which had flamed up over night at the unproved outrage of the Maine was lying supine under the flagrant provocation of the Lusitania." If Mrs. Wharton had written in the flaming emotion of the time, this would be natural enough, but five years after we expect a more mature reaction, some admission that the discernment of the little group of discerning spirits had its limits, or that we need not be so proud of remembering the Maine either.

But Mrs. Wharton is not writing in the flaming emotion of the time, and that emotion is beyond her power to recall or perhaps to represent. She has described the manners of Paris at war. She has satirized the busy philanthropists of her own American upper class, who so early appropriated the conflict, but these types are presented in a mechanical fashion. Henry Mayhew, Delegate to the Peace Conference at the Hague, who is caught in the jam at the outbreak and imprisoned for eight days by the Germans, is the best. There is a smile even on Mrs. Wharton's serried countenance when Mrs. Mayhew plans to sell the war to his countrymen— "to rouse public opinion in America against a nation of savages who ought to be hunted off the face of the globe like vermin—like the vermin in their own prison cells." But even this backstairs picture of war is not so brilliant as Miss Delafield's War Workers, or Mr. George's Blind Alley.

Beyond this Mrs. Wharton has isolated a human situation, and presented it with an oily sauce of fiction, but she has not penetrated it. And unfortunately the spurious quality of Mrs. Wharton's art does violence to her theme. It suggests that America's entrance into the war had something meretricious about it. Mrs. Wharton's own sincerity is beyond question. Her book is a tribute from America to France. It is a memorial of American boys who died at the front for France. But with all its richness of intention it somehow suggests the automobile excursions of American Red Cross girls in Paris to visit the graves.

"New Novels: *A Son at the Front*," *Times Literary Supplement* [England], 20 September 1923, p. 618

It would seem inopportune for most writers to bring out a war book at this date. But opportunity does not concern the artist. He is an artist largely for that reason. It does not concern Mrs. Wharton, or she would not have chosen this time to bring out her novel *A Son At The Front*; ... but no one can regret that she has done so.

Her canvas is the familiar one of Paris at the outbreak of the war, and after; but the French side is subordinated to the activities of the American colony in Paris. The American occupation, so overwhelming to themselves and other foreigners finding themselves there in these days, so immaterial to the majority of Parisians, is conveyed with the sharp precision, the undertone of irony of Mrs. Wharton's best work. We see again America "presenting" the war in the manner of a theatrical impresario to whom expense is nothing. The story centres in George Campton, a young man of twenty-five, the object of his divorced parents' jealousy and anxiety, and of the humble, hovering devotion of Mr. Brant, his mother's husband. Divorced Americans are quite unable to leave each other alone. Divorce, indeed, seems to unite those who would ordinarily see but little of each other in marriage. Mrs. Brant can never leave her former husband, the eminent portrait-painter, John Campton, alone, nor can she manage his affairs without Mr. Brant. This odd triangle is always consulting and manoeuvring about George, who is a French subject and has joined up at once. He is ostensibly safely ambushed at the base, but has had himself transferred to the fighting line without letting the anxious elders know it. "Something veiled and abstracted is often a part of the manners of these beings," Mrs. Wharton quotes from Walt Whitman as the motto of her book; and she insisted a little too much on the veiled brightness of all the fighting young men that she portrays. George remains a golden-haired puppet throughout; but his smile and his safety are enough for his adoring relatives and friends, who require no return for the devotion they lavish on him. This is true to life. He is wounded; and the Brants and his father, learning of his deception, rush to the hospital determined that if they can save his life he will never return to the front. Again George frustrates them. He discloses himself as the lover of a married woman, one of the most superficial and posing members of their group, but at the same time reveals the ennobling effect of the war by refusing to carry on the intrigue. When he sees that Mrs. Talkett will not face a divorce, he goes back to the front, is wounded, and dies.

The story is unusual, dealing as it does with three elderly people inspired almost entirely by fear and selfishness, and not ashamed to show it, never becoming heroic, meanly dependent on each other, driven to small sacrifices only to avoid great ones. Campton is fussy and unimaginative, Mrs. Brant "an ageing doll" with a fierce maternal resentment of the war as a domestic danger, Brant, touching and alive, is not once lovable. These figures are solid realities drawn with detachment and high skill, without the slightest sentimental wavering. The minor study of Adele Anthony is equally brilliant, a combative, lonely, fiercely partisan creature, going restlessly into society and "exhilarated by the nearness of people she did not know or wish to know, but with whose names and private histories she was minutely and passionately familiar." Admirable are the incidental sketches of character, the impressions of place, the glimpses into other minds, half a dozen views of a dark, benumbed city, a river empty of traffic.

All the characteristic qualities of Mrs. Wharton's style, her pliancy and penetration, her leisured, serious beauty are here. Accomplishment and certainty have gone to the making of her story. A war novel may be thought dull, unnecessary, at this time; but the pendulum swings back; and when the world is better adjusted this book will be seen to have its permanent value among the minor documents of the war.

H. W. Boynton, "The Incidence of War," New York *Evening Post: Literary Review*, 22 September 1923, p. 61

There are moments when the seasoned reviewer rubs his eyes and wonders whether "jaded reviewer" would not be the right ticket for him. In view of the enthusiastic reception being given Mrs. Wharton's latest novel in many quarters, I rather distrust my impression of it; without, however, in the least doubting what that impression is. The book gives me an odd sense of belatedness, both as to matter and manner. Why go back to all this business of the war, so painful to experience, so wearisome to remember? It was an unpleasant and even harrowing affair for most sons at the front and most parents back home; but merciful time has already dimmed that unhappiness. This humble reviewer had a number of sons at the front or thereabouts and most uncomfortable they and he were for a number of years. Forget it! That is all he or they ask to do and they can honestly applaud nobody who tries to bring back to them even a little of the old torment and the old tedium.

This may not be as it should be. There are earnest writers who are terribly afraid we are all going to forget the horror of that war and so to blunder presently into an even more dreadful hell of butchery and insanity. They are quite right, from their point of view, to keep the wound raw. But there is nothing of this motive in Mrs. Wharton's story. She has, as usual, a tale to tell of character and manners. For the rest, I believe the book is chiefly of cathartic value for its author. Every creative writer who felt deeply those war years has sooner or later to get them out of his system. Miss Cather has just done it—thoroughly, we may hope. I believe Mrs. Wharton has done it once for all in *A Son at the Front*. . . .

All of this in Mrs. Wharton's well-known flowing, cultivated, and slightly Henry-Jamesish style. Manner is the word I have used above, intimating that it here wears a somewhat belated, almost antiquated air. Somehow the style that one found so effective in *The Valley of Decision* and even in *The Age of Innocence* seems a bit quaint in this narrative. As for the substance of the story, I cannot rid myself of the feeling that the quivering parental sensibility of old Campton, his total surrender to emotional torments about his son's physical well being or even

survival, is untrue to "life" in so far as life is identified with the normal or average experience of even devoted fathers and mothers in war-time. He nowhere achieves that shifting of plane, that automatic adjustment of nerve and mental attitude to inevitable conditions, which kept most of us sane and tolerably calm with our sons at the front.

"Two Sides of the War Novel,"
Literary Digest, 79 (6 October 1923), 30–1

The first war novels were naturally written by the younger generation. They were on the field of battle and saw things first hand. But the war was not wholly won by the armies; those back of the line, even those so far back as to know it only in their nerves, their emotions and affections, may feel that they also played a part. Mrs. Wharton's novel, *A Son at the Front*, seems to make this assumption, and it has waited a discreet time before putting forward any claim. The mere fact that there is another word to say causes something like astonishment in younger minds. "One wonders . . . where in the world Mrs. Wharton has been all this time," writes Mr. Burton Rascoe in the New York *Tribune*. Doesn't she know, he says in effect, that the war novels have been written by Wells, Bennett, George, Cannan, Hankey, Hay, Mackenzie, Mckenna, Barbusse, Latzko, Duhamel, Geraldy, Dos Passos, Cummings, and Boyd; to say nothing of the ladies, Misses Sinclair, West, Stern, Macaulay, and Cather? And she dares to write something different! "This is rather a pity," observes this young man, "for, as we reviewers are in the habit of saying, 'this novel is hardly likely to add anything to her reputation.'" Fortunately for the book the task of reviewing it was not altogether left in young hands. Maurice Francis Egan does it for the New York *Times*, Dorothea Lawrence Mann for the Boston *Transcript*, and they do not miss the importance of the subject; the latter writer, indeed, speaks of "this important and penetrating study of what many have called the deepest tragedy of the war." Mrs. Wharton, she says, "makes startlingly real the tragedy of the helplessness of parents before the fact of war, when their arms have no longer strength to protect." In choosing her time and her atmosphere, says Mr. Egan, Mrs. Wharton was "rather audacious." But for a different reason from that with which Mr. Rascoe reproaches her. Thus Mr. Egan:

"There are many reasons why most of us should dislike a novel dealing with the war; many reasons why the suggestions of such a book should prejudice us against it; and these reasons are obvious. Only the production of a masterpiece could reconcile us to the treatment of that terrible epoch by a writer of fiction. And even a masterpiece which was coldly correct and artistically done could only have gained from us a conventional approval. Mrs. Wharton, then, was greatly daring in choosing her theme; but even more daring in presenting four very modern people, brought up under conditions which did not make for the highest morality, and in making them at once interesting and appealing without exaggerating the facts of life and without extenuation or apology."

Not to give too much of the story to discourage prospective readers, we let Mr. Egan present the theme:

"The center of the action is the artist, *John Campton*, divorced from his wife, who had been *Julia Ambrose*, and had become the wife of *Mr. Anderson Brant*, an American millionaire living in Paris because she preferred it. *George*, the son of the first marriage, is deeply loved by all three, each according to his capacity of loving and the delicacy of Mrs. Wharton's method in differentiating the capacities of these three for loving is as exquisite as it is poignant.

"The war breaks, and the efforts of these three people are all turned to save George from going to the front; he has just returned from Harvard, handsome, charming, generous, unmoral and full of the joyousness of life. *John Campton* when he was a poor and struggling artist, permitted his son to be brought up by his wife and her second husband. Now that he has become a fashionable painter, he wishes, above all things, to have his son, who had hitherto given an apparently impartial affection to his father and mother and *Mr. Anderson Brant*. *Campton* had staked all his hopes and happiness on this charming son. He had planned a tour in the South of Europe, and perhaps in Africa, for the sake of the vivid color and sunlight, with this darling boy; but he found that all his security had been dashed away in a few hours; *George*, by accident, was a French citizen and his danger was suddenly revealed to his father when the young man carelessly emptied his pockets on the dressing table in the room adjoining:

"'*Campton*, welling with a new tenderness on everything that belonged to his son, noticed a smart antelope cardcase (*George* had his mother's weakness for Bond Street novelties), a wrist-watch, his studs, a bundle of bank notes; and besides these a thumbed and dirty red book, the size of a large pocket diary.

"'The father wondered what it was; then of a sudden he knew. He had once seen Madame Lebel's grandson pull just such a red book from his pocket as he was leaving for his "twenty-eight days" of military service; it was the *livret militaire* that every French citizen under forty-eight carries about with him.

"'And in that book *George*'s father read that when France should mobilize, his son would be forced to go to the front. *George* had been cured of tuberculosis. This cure had made the three who loved him very happy; but, as he read, *Campton* found in it a source of new unhappiness. The plea of ill-health would not save the boy; it could only be done through "influence."

"'He still refused to admit that France had any claim on *George*, any right to his time, to his suffering, or to his life. He had argued it out a hundred times with *Adele Anthony*. "You say Julia and I were to blame for not going home before the boy was born—and God knows I agree with you! But suppose we'd meant to go? Suppose we'd made every arrangement, taken every precaution, as my parents did in my own case, got to Havre or Cherbourg, say, and been told the steamer had broken her screw, or been prevented ourselves, at the last moment, by illness or accident, or any sudden grab of the hand of God? You'll admit we shouldn't have been to blame for that; yet the law would have recognized no difference. George would still have found himself a French soldier on the 2d of last August, because, by the same kind of unlucky accident, he and I were born on the wrong side of the Atlantic. And I say that's enough to prove it's an iniquitous law, a travesty of justice. Nobody's going to convince me that, because a steamer may happen to break a flange of her screw at the wrong time, or a poor woman be frightened by a thunderstorm, France has the right to force an American boy to go and rot in the trenches.'

"The three intrigue with all their power. A clerical job was secured for George, and then followed feverish anxiety, the fear that 'influence' might not keep him from the trenches. 'Influence' does its worst from *George's* point of view. He will not stand aside, for he sees what the struggle really means. He cuts through all sophistries and timidities with his brave honesty; this the anguished three do not at first realize.

"The treatment of this situation alone would put Mrs. Wharton in the first rank of modern novelists."

It is easy to understand, says Mrs. Mann, "that these people are typical of a great many parents when war was declared." And again, "we can not help feeling that Mrs. Wharton has chosen just such a complicated situation as would delight her for the working out of this epic of the war." But Mr. Rascoe will have it that Mrs. Wharton "has not touched upon a single point which Mr. Wells and Mr. Bennett did not go over thoroughly in novels which they have long since outgrown." He can even be satirical:

> "Here is the same anxiety of parents over the possibility of their sons being killed and the same certainty that the war ought to be fought so long as the sons of other parents do the fighting; here is the same depiction of human greed and chicanery among profiteers and organizers of war charities; here is the same observation that many women, married and unmarried, looked upon the war as a sort of protracted Mardi Gras wherein they might indulge in certain liberties which discretion in other times would forbid; and here is the same conclusion that whatever the extent of the death toll it is more than recompensed by the affecting democratic spectacle of a cobbler exchanging condolences with an aristocrat of the Faubourg Saint-Germain and that of a Deauville duchess's abandonment of bridge long enough to share the sisterhood of tears with a Paris midinette who has also lost a lover at the front.
>
> "Indeed one would almost fancy that Mrs. Wharton is under the impression that the war is still going on and that she wrote her little book to the end that America might help France and Britain see it through."

Then, finally, Mr. Rascoe shows the hurt petulance over the discovery that some outsider has tried to play on our side:

> "If this were year 1915 or even 1917 instead of the year 1923, Mrs. Wharton's novel might not seem so profitless an endeavor; and to any one who has not yet read a war

novel it may be recommended whole-heartedly, for Mrs. Wharton has not lost her gift for anatomizing people she dislikes, which is to say the majority of those who compose the human race. But this very gift makes one suspect that, with her chill temperament, she ought to be the last person in the world to write a war novel—and possibly she is."

Gerald Gould, "New Fiction," *Saturday Review* [England], 136 (6 October 1923), 390

Last week I quoted Mr. Barry Pain's parody of *If Winter Comes* for the sake of its engaging flippancy: this week I find myself bound to quote from its prefatory note for the sake of its high seriousness. For Mr. Barry Pain, whom the reading public insists on regarding as a sort of society entertainer, is in fact not merely one of the best living writers of fiction but also one of the acutest and profoundest of living critics: his parodies are as deadly in their indication of his victims' weak places as the caricatures of Mr. Beerbohm. And, in the critical preface of which I am speaking, he gives me the perfect text for the discussion of Mrs. Wharton's book. He writes:

> I detest the utilization of the Great War at the present day for the purpose of fiction. It is altogether too easy. It buys the emotional situation ready-made. It asks the

reader's memory to supplement the writer's imagination. And this is not my sole objection to its use.

That other, unnamed, objection is the stronger of the two. When one reads *A Son at the Front*, one feels it so overpoweringly that one can feel little else. The book jars. Its points are not merely easy, but cheap. It labours, with an effect of almost incredible obtuseness, the emotions that are still fresh and dreadful in the living hearts of men. Only the other day—less than five years ago, in actual time, and scarcely any distance at all away in that other more vivid time which is reckoned in suffering and fidelity—that sword of terror was turning and turning in men's and women's waking and sleeping thoughts. A son at the front!—surely there is something sacred in the theme—something which ought not to be handled in fiction at all unless it can be handled with a greatness, unless it can be bathed in the light of a beauty, that shall at least attempt to "justify the ways of God." Mrs. Wharton, of course, has an incisive pen; she has mastered the tricks of her trade; she has even, in the past, when her subjects were kept within her compass, written books that might without offensive exaggeration be called great. But here she adds nothing to the recent lesson of reality. Indeed, she detracts from it. The contrast between the simple generous heroism of the young men who took it for granted, without any hesitation, that it was their job to kill and be killed, and the people who, in safety, either devoted themselves to bridge and bazaars in order to "keep civilization alive," or concentrated on the necessity of other people's going to the slaughter—that contrast, which occupies the majority of Mrs. Wharton's pages, was the inspiration of much bitter and indeed magnificent satire when it was with

us, less than those five short years ago. We are all utterly and sadly familiar with it. To revive it now is, æsthetically, worse than useless—unless some grandeur can be given it by new and deeper understanding. There is the question. All experience must lie open to the artist: one cannot shut him out from the war or from anything else: but he, on his side, must *be* an artist. It is all one asks of him—admittedly it is a good deal.

John Macy, "The American Spirit," *Nation*, 117 (10 October 1923), 398–9

... Mr. D. H. Lawrence [in *Studies in Classic American Literature*] deals only with American classics, with the "old people," and does not mention the living by name, except Sherwood Anderson, "who is so Russian"! But it would be interesting, if we could, to turn upon an important living American writer one or two reflections from Mr. Lawrence's glancing and erratic lights. Mrs. Edith Wharton was born in New York. Her father's name was Jones and her mother's name was Rhinelander. She is as authentically American as anybody can be. Like some other Americans she is cosmopolitan in her experience. The knowledge of eighteenth-century Italy which she shows in *The Valley of Decision* is somewhat deeper than that of the American tourists who arouse Mr. Lawrence's wrath, who "have done more to kill the sacredness of old European beauty and aspiration than multitudes of bombs." She is sufficiently familiar with French literature and American history to recognize the irrelevance of this from Mr. Lawrence: "America was not taught by France—by Baudelaire, for example. Baudelaire learned his lesson from America." Why pick out Baudelaire for an example, the most untranslatable poet, who did not learn "his lesson" from America, but did find a kindred spirit in Poe? Mrs. Wharton has studied American people intimately, presumably white people, the moderately aristocratic society of New York, with its tragedies, as in the story of Lily Bart, and in *Ethan Frome* the tragedy of the little New Englander of our time, a tragedy as terrible as that of Hester Prynne.

Mrs. Wharton's latest book, *A Son at the Front*, is not her best. It is the story of an American painter in Paris whose French-born son is killed in the war. The boy's mother is divorced from the father and is married to an American banker. Lawrence would love the banker as an occasion to swear about American gold. But what difference is there between American gold and other gold, between a French banker and an American banker? Between a French painter and an American painter? Is the American boy, who must have had an "essential American soul," "hard, isolate, stoic, and a killer"— in a time when all Europe was bent on the business of killing? Is not the period after the war, when the whole world went into a bigger and hotter melting-pot than America, precisely the time for philosophers like Mr. Lawrence to distrust generalizations about national characteristics, or at least keep them safely in the past— as for the most part he does—and not extend them into the doubtful indicative present?

There is one phrase of Mr. Lawrence's which applies to Mrs. Wharton's book in a way quite different from anything he intended. Her story is out of date. She evidently began it five years ago and laid its aside until last year. It need never have been finished. The war story with little love intrigues and personal sorrows plotted against that disaster is dead. Perhaps many years from now one greater than Hardy or Tolstoi will make an epic of it. For the present the love story with "news from the front" is staler than the Kaiser's memoirs. And that is why, much as I admire Mrs. Wharton's skill in character-drawing and her impeccable style, I find her book, as probably Mr. Lawrence would: "Post-mortem effects. Ghosts."

H. De W. F., "Mrs. Wharton Struggles with Masculinity," *Independent*, 111 (13 October 1923), 157–8

The "literature of the war," we are told by librarians, has swamped their shelves. Before the war it was the "literature of factory management" which made their shelves groan. It is right of course that "literature" should be used in no snobbish sense. What vitally concerns mankind is always fit subject for books. Yet it is convenient at *times* to remember the old-fashioned term "belles lettres," as well as the outworn distinction between the author and the book-maker—ability to create, signifying something more than recording the facts of life or ingenuity in plotting a story. In the higher sense Flanders poppies were made to flame the world over. Rupert Brooke, Allan Seeger, and other poets, mostly soldiers, made poignant moments continue to live.

The novelists have not been so fortunate. Without running through the long list, one recalls that Dos Passos received the lion's share of comment by virtue of a story which more than anything else turned out to be pacifist propaganda. It was the horror of war which lived in the reader's mind; not the personages who experienced it. Neither this tale nor any of its contemporaries could possibly be called a great novel of the war; raw material had not been refashioned to the needs of great art.

Mrs. Wharton now comes forward with *A Son at the Front*. The reception which the book has thus far received has at least this element of agreement—the critics cannot conceal their surprise that Mrs. Wharton should have attempted to revive details of the war at this late date. If she had waited longer before making the attempt, her action would have been understandable; novelists for years and years to come are sure to find treasure in the World War. But to revert to it just now, when publishers' lists had at length begun to find room for something besides the war, seemed like lugging in an old nightmare or else carrying on a rather futile bit of propaganda for France.

These guesses are beside the mark. What Mrs. Wharton has really done is to try to use the war for art's sake, and in so doing she becomes a pioneer. Her book will live or die not because of any light it throws on the great conflict, but because of a small group of personages placed in a war setting. The book is a study in sensibilities, with a son at the front as the irritant.

The central situation is one that would have exactly suited the taste and the capacity of Henry James. Besides the son, George Campton, who though clearly enough drawn is but a part of the machinery, the group consists of the father, *John Campton*, an American portrait painter living in Paris, who has suddenly become fashionable; the mother, *Mrs. Anderson Brant*, divorced from Campton early in their married life; and Brant

himself, a wealthy American banker in Paris. As the story opens, the scene is Paris and the date June 30, 1914—admirable choice for Mrs. Wharton's purposes. For Campton senior, whose circumstances until recently have been very modest, is all aglow at thought of the arrival of his son from America the next evening. Campton has planned to journey with the youth to some of the choice spots of Europe—places which he himself has loved. The prospect is all the more pleasing because until now George's rearing and education have been dependent upon the wealth of the second husband, who, it must be said, really loves the boy and who throughout shows admirable restraint in the face of trying conditions.

Follows the threat of a European upheaval, which comes with terrific force to *John Campton*, since George, by the accident of having been born in Paris, is a French reservist and eligible for service with the colors. There is just the hope that George, because of former lung trouble, will not be found fit. Then it may be that France will not declare war. The father struggles against destiny, continues to fuss over the proposed itinerary, and comforts himself with pretense. But war comes and the time is at hand when George must join his regiment. The father fumes about the injustice of French law; the mother, though a shallow woman, is possessed of the strongest maternal instincts and will stop at nothing in order to save her boy from danger; Brant relies upon his customary weapon, "influence." Dire necessity draws these three together, a situation in which the author glories, just as Henry James would have gloried in it. Influence does avail, and a sheltered staff job is found for George. There the trepidation might have ended for a spell except for the constant fear that the son might be transferred to the front. Contrast stalks in the foreground in the picture of

341

other parents who are enduring the loss of only sons with great fortitude. The three also have the perilous game of trying to read between the lines of George's censored letters. Does this sentence mean that he is soon to be shifted? Temperamental father, dolorous mother, and the self-confident Brant are kept in a continual flutter.

Meanwhile George himself has had something to say about his own destiny. He has been transferred to the front without the knowledge of his parents and is reported wounded and in line for decoration. The scene has been carefully laid for what follows. The mother being in Italy at the moment, Campton and Brant make the long ride to the hospital in the latter's motor car. The thought of these two—the highly sensitive, fastidious, and, on the whole, disagreeable artist and the smug but good-intentioned banker, husband number one and husband number two—sitting side by side for so long a time would have given Henry James food for an entire novel, and Mrs. Wharton herself finds it difficult to let go of the theme. Arrived at the hospital to discover George lapsing frequently into delirium, the two elders are seen in typical operation—Brant deferring to Campton and devising "influence" by which George may be taken to a hospital at the rear; the father jealous of every word his son utters in delirium lest it strengthen the position of mother and stepfather in the boy's affections, or perchance reveal some new affection not yet guessed. Poor boy! one wonders what terrible lot would have been his if he had lived. For George, be it known, dies as the result of a wound after having returned to the front. There remains for the father but one task—which he accomplishes to his satisfaction, even though it transpires that George has all the time been enjoying an affair with a married woman—to convince himself that

of the three he had meant most to George.

If this were in any sense a story of the war, Americans must needs blush at the way in which three of their fellow citizens failed to stand the test of war. But, as indicated at the outset of this notice, the book is the study of specimens, and in particular of one specimen, for Mr. and Mrs. Brant are in a manner merely accomplices of Campton's ingrowing disposition. The success of Mrs. Wharton's experiment depends upon your understanding of him, who, by all the gods, is most peculiar.

In *The House of Mirth* Mrs. Wharton pursued the study of a most complex, even if shallow, girl, and so well succeeded that one was reminded at a distance of such a subtle being as Meredith's Diana. Campton offered her a chance to depict similar subtlety in a man. But is Campton a man? Unfortunately the task of creating anything more than a male type has always appeared to be beyond Mrs. Wharton's powers. To the creating of Campton she very evidently came with the greatest zest. To prepare for the following expression of intricate contradictions (half way through the book) must have given her delight:

> He laboured with the need of self-expression, and the opposing instinct of concealing feelings too complex for Miss Anthony's simple gaze. How could he say: "I'm satisfied; but I wish to God that George were not"? And was he satisfied, after all? And how could he define, or even be sure that he was actually experiencing, a feeling so contradictory that it seemed to be made up of anxiety for his son's safety, shame at that anxiety, shame at George's own complacent acceptance of his lot, and terror of a possible change in that lot?

The trouble with Campton is not his subtlety—he might have been developed into a perfectly credible æsthete—but his inability to rise even to the height of simple, direct manliness. For that reason it is impossible to believe that he ever had the affair with the Spanish girl (lightly referred to in the early chapters) which wrecked his marriage. The inner recesses of his mind and feeling are disclosed by Mrs. Wharton with skillful discernment, but when they are laid open they can hardly prove interesting—at least to men.

"Behind the Line," *Spectator* [England] (Literary Supplement), 131 (13 October 1923), 514

Mrs. Wharton's new novel, which is dated "Paris, 1918—Saint Brice-sous-Forêt, 1922," presents a vivid picture of a section of American and French society in Paris during the War. That, at least, is the background to the story. The story itself is a lament for the men killed in the War. John Campton, the famous American portrait-painter, lives in Paris. His son George, a youth in the early twenties and the apple of his father's eye, is on the point of arriving in Paris and the two going off south together on a long, delightful holiday. At last, Campton feels, he will get the son whom he so much adores to himself. Hitherto, he has shared him with Mrs. Brant, the boy's mother, and her wealthy husband, for Campton's wife had divorced him and married a banker. Campton, till his sudden and recent accession to fame, has been poor; the Brants are rich and generously disposed towards the boy George. This has been a

continual source of jealousy to Campton; but, now that he is rapidly making money, it will obviously be possible for him to provide handsomely for his son. George arrives in Paris, but just when they were to set off on their holiday, war breaks out. George was born in France and is, therefore, liable for service, but Campton is determined to pull strings to get him released. What, after all, have Americans to do with a European quarrel? But George's young French friends are all called up and George himself joins his regiment. In the emergency Campton co-operates with the Brants to get George a staff appointment. The appointment is obtained, but they have reckoned without George himself. Without letting his parents know, he gets himself transferred to an infantry battalion. Mrs. Wharton shows very convincingly the gradual development of Campton's attitude towards the War. We see him slowly becoming secretly—so secretly that he hardly admits it to himself—ashamed of the fact that his boy has a safe job. Then comes the news that George is wounded, and Campton, despite his terrible anxiety and his pain at the fact that George did not confide in him, feels proud of the boy and almost relieved. And throughout the novel we see George, direct, simple, heroic, following the course which he instinctively knows to be right; Campton, tortured by his selflsh love for his son, gradually transcending his selfishness and rising to George's level; and Mrs. Brant, the mother, selfish, scheming and uncomprehending in her attempts to save George at all costs. The rest of the story is soon told. George, recovered from his wound, returns to the front, is wounded again and dies.

The character of George is exquisitely presented by Mrs. Wharton. He is the embodiment of youth, gaiety, gentleness and true heroism; a charming and lovable creature, shown to us always through the eyes of his father. Campton, too, is vivid and convincing, a subtle study of the artistic temperament in its strength and weaknesses; and each of the other characters receive the precise amount of definition which their position in the picture demands. The novel, in fact, is a fine one, in some ways the finest of a very fine writer. The emotion is genuine and profound, without the smallest taint of sentimentality or mock heroics; the characters and the scene are fully and vividly presented with an ease and certainty of touch that few living novelists can command. The book is, in fact, a deeply affecting one, almost, indeed, too painful for those who have not yet forgotten the War; and for those who *have*, we can imagine no more salutary reminder.

"A Son at the Front," Bookman [England] 65 (October 1923), 46

Not even Mrs. Wharton's great talent can make this story seem other than a belated essay in propaganda. Some day the war will fall into place and be a proper subject for artistic treatment; but it is not there yet, at any rate not to Mrs. Wharton. She is still too angry—angry at the attitude of Americans in Paris, angry at German atrocities, angry at the waste and horror of the war; and in spite of some beautiful passages, and some excellent humour and satire, *A Son at the Front* must be reckoned a failure. The son is George Campton, son of the great American painter who lives at Paris, whose wife has divorced him and married the millionaire banker Brant. There is much of Mrs. Wharton's old skill in her depicting of the relations between Campton and Brant, between George and his parents, between George and Brant. The introduction of the war, however, makes these personal issues seem trifling—and Mrs. Wharton is unable to decide about which she really wants to write. So the story rather falls to pieces—while George's love affair with Mrs. Talkett never gets real at all. It is for its incidental humours and its incomparably vivid accounts of Paris in wartime that this novel will be read.

[John Farrar], "Behind the Lines," *Bookman*, 58 (October 1923), 202

Mrs. Wharton has added another fine and true war book to the list which includes *Three Soldiers, Through the Wheat, The Odyssey of a Torpedoed Transport*, and one or two others. She has written as realistic a picture as any, yet she writes only of what she knew, felt, saw. *A Son at the Front* is a great piece of interpretative reporting. It is a story of the intricate events and emotions which made the social background of the war. Mrs. Wharton has taken a fresh, brave, thoroughly admirable American youth, around which to gather her people. It is the people who love George Campton that makes this book, and they are various. Not only has Mrs. Wharton succeeded in her portrait of the war fabric, but she has written a powerful study of the artistic temperament, and of divorce. She has used her superb technique, her clear understanding, for a picture worth painting. In the face of this heartrending but beautiful book we can forgive even the vapidities of *The Glimpses of the Moon*.

William Lyon Phelps, "Doctor Edith Wharton Makes a Diagnosis," *Literary Digest International Book Review*, 1 (October 1923), 15–16, 90

Edith Wharton, like Henry James, Anne Sedgwick, and Dorothy Canfield, has lived many years in France. She lives there now. Why? As the correct answer to this question might not be flattering to our national pride, suppose we consider the question unasked.

On page 366 of her latest novel, *A Son at the Front*, the elderly artist-hero is wondering what France will be if all the best of her men vanish in the war, and a bereaved French father tells him the Idea will remain:

> An Idea: they must cling to that. If Dastrey, from the depths of his destitution, could still feel it and live by it, why did it not help Campton more? An Idea: that was what France, ever since she had existed, had always been in the story of civilization; a luminous point about which striving visions and purposes could rally. And in that sense she had been as much Campton's spiritual home as Dastrey's; to thinkers, artists, to all creators, she had always been a second country. If France went, western civilization went with her; and then all they had believed in and been guided by would perish.

Thus, while Edith Wharton belongs to us by virtue of her parentage and birth in the city of New York, France is her *second country*. Dorothy Canfield, Willa Cather, and Zona Gale are products of our State universities, tho the former spent years in France in her childhood. Edith Wharton and Anne Sedgwick were educated "at home." There's no place like home for an education, if it is the right sort of home; illustrative cases are Robert Browning, John Stuart Mill, Henry James, and the two women I have just named.

After one grows up, one chooses a home for oneself, provided one is fortunate enough to be free. Whether or not Edith Wharton has any spiritual home is problematical; her intellectual home is France. Her chief characteristic is a serene, unclouded intelligence. Now, among cultivated French people the human quality most respected is intelligence; emotion is kept in its place, which is always subordinate. Among Normans and Bretons, even religion is secondary to prudence; their religion is often perhaps a form of prudence.

With the one exception of Booth Tarkington, Edith Wharton seems to have won her way to the foremost place among living American writers; the two are so different they can not be compared; one so native, the other so largely exotic. To boys and girls, whose ambition is equaled only by their impatience, let us recall the fact that Mrs. Wharton's reputation began when she was forty years old; she served a long apprenticeship.

In view of her European training, her linguistic accomplishments—her translation of Sudermann's *Es Lebe das Leben* is a work of art—her aloofness from the American point of view, it is rather surprizing that her best books have dealt exclusively with the American scene. In classifying *The House of Mirth* (1905) among these, I do so here in deference to the general opinion; personally, altho it was her first best seller and gave her a large public, it seems to me among her less important creations. But there can be no doubt that *Ethan Frome* (1911) and *The Age of Innocence* (1920) are masterpieces. If I could have only one of her works, I would take *The Age of Innocence*. Two of her novels seem to me quite unworthy of her; these are *The Fruit of the Tree* (1907) and *The Glimpses of the Moon* (1922). Were it not for their display of mere language, they would be negligible.

The acidity that often accompanies intelligence usually gives to her compositions just sufficient alloy to make them perfectly malleable; it is only occasionally that bitterness becomes a potent poison, and quite o'ercrows the spirit of the work. A clear illustration of that is *The Custom of the Country* (1913), which, instead of being a picture of America, is a vitriolic satire. If is worth reading for the spectacle of a woman of genius in a state of exasperation. Like all truly intelligent people, she dislikes with especial fervor brutality, stupidity, affectation, and silliness; those who wish to see a novelist in a mood of disdain will enjoy rereading that book.

In her latest novel, *A Son at the Front*, we have "another book about the war." Why not? The war is still in every one's mind, and will stay there until death. Evil begets evil; the bigger the sin, the more appalling the retribution.

The four novels about the war which have most imprest me are *A Son at the Front*, which gives a picture of the life in Paris from August, 1914, till the entry of America; *Adrienne Toner*, by Anne Sedgwick, which gives a picture of the life in England during the same period; *A Soldier of Life*, by Hugh de Sélincourt, which gives the state of mind of an English soldier who is sent home wounded, and becomes a pacifist; *Through the Wheat*, by Thomas Boyd, which takes us among the Americans actually in the trenches. Tho I know nothing about it by personal experience, *Through the Wheat* is the story dealing with actual fighting which seems to me closer to what must be the truth. These four books are works of art, written with honesty, sincerity, and intelligence.

A Son at the Front is an enormous improvement over *The Glimpses of the Moon*, which even its author's gifts could not save from triviality. Here there is nothing trivial; the subject has all the dignity of tragedy, and the style rises to the level of the theme. It must certainly rank high among our novelist's achievements.

The author is on familiar ground. She is an American, and France is her "second country." She was in France during the war, and, as every one knows, rendered notable aid to a cause which has probably been closer to her heart than anything in her life. The middle-aged artist, Campton, whose meditations take up much of the work, is an American living in France; his son at the front, altho a Harvard graduate, was born in France, and therefore subject to the first mobilization. Campton's divorced wife, having more beauty than brains, and more money than either, plays, together with her second husband, an American banker living in Paris, a prominent part; and the relations of the three are portrayed with a series of *nuances* that should awaken the most callous reader's enthusiasm.

Campton was so terribly bored by his former wife that he is glad enough to have nothing more to do with her; he quite unfairly despises her husband, and would hold himself gladly apart from that hateful household were it not for his son, a cheerful, healthy, unprejudiced and wholly natural young American. Young George, whose duplicate I have seen at least a thousand times, is the indissoluble

346

link uniting these three totally different adults. This boy loves his father and understands him much better than he is understood; his love for his mother is a compound of affection and pity; for his mother's second husband he has a cordial liking, is perfectly at ease in his company, and calls him "Uncle Andy."

There is, as might be expected by those who know her previous work, no sentimentalism here, not even the sentimentalism of patriotism; sentimentality, like any emotional excess, is abhorrent to Mrs. Wharton. Her walking so circumspectly and yet so surely on the very edge of it without slipping, is one of her most conspicuous accomplishments. Certainly such a feat could never have been more difficult than in this instance, because to her France represented everything good and Germany everything evil. No virageous virgin, engaged in war work at home, could have had more uncompromising certainty of conviction. During the war, I asked one of these if she wanted peace without victory; and the answer made me fear for her health.

For my part, I never can hate any nation as a nation, because I always in imagination see the *individuals* on the other side feeling and doing precisely as we. I am glad America whipt England in the eighteenth century; I am glad the Yankees whipt the Southerners in the war of the rebellion; I am glad Germany was beaten in the World War. But I do not hate Englishmen, Southerners, or Germans, because their convictions were the same in strength as our own. Did we believe in the holiness of our cause? So did they. Did we make sacrifices of our youth? So did they. Did we fast and pray? So did they. It is the accident of birth, not superiority of character, that determines one's attitude in war.

Mrs. Wharton puts on her extensive canvas persons in Paris representing many shades of ability, attitude, and opinion. No one is quite so fully revealed as the famous artist, John Campton, both because he is the most worth revealing, and because we actually live inside of his mind. The story opens with him in solitary reflection in his Montmartre studio, on July 30, 1914. His son is to arrive from America, and the next day they are to start on a holiday journey together to Sicily. A touch of irony is given at the start, for the father is so eager for to-morrow that he tears the present date off the calendar, forgetting that sufficient unto the day is the evil thereof. He did not believe in the possibility of war; in the twentieth century, such folly was inconceivable. Then he views the growing probability of it with a selfishness not uncommon; it would interfere with his plans. Later comes the deeper selfishness of his passion for his son, whom his conscious mind tries to save from danger, while his unconscious mind approves of his playing his part. He asks a shrewd old French woman how she would regard the outbreak of war, and receives a typical answer:

"Why, I should say we don't want it, sir—I'd have four in it if it came— *but that this sort of thing has got to stop.*"

Now that is exactly the way I heard people in Germany talk in 1911 and again in 1913. They believed, mistakenly, I think, but positively, that they were being "hemmed in," and that "this sort of thing had got to stop." The significant difference was that while England and France did not want war, Germany emphatically did. She longed for it. I suppose never in human history has a nation gone into a war with more united enthusiasm than Germany entered into it in 1914. There came a wave over the whole country like one vast ejaculation—"At last!

thank God, it has come!" This was the climax of years of organized nationalism.

His former wife's second husband is sent as an envoy to Campton, for to her and now to Campton the war means only one thing—*my son*. This is the natural, the inevitable first emotion. Our feelings are not altogether under the control of our reason, and what is nearest to us impresses our heart most deeply. A man actually feels worse about the death of his pet dog than about the decease of a foreign statesman, or the news of a railroad accident. The description of the banker is in Mrs. Wharton's best manner:

> Mr. Brant was a compact little man of about sixty. His sandy hair, just turning gray, was brushed forward over a baldness which was ivory-white at the crown and became brick-pink above the temples, before merging into the tanned and freckled surface of his face. He was always drest in carefully cut clothes of a discreet gray, with a tie to match, in which even the plump pearl was gray, so that he reminded Campton of a dry perpendicular insect in protective tints; and the fancy was encouraged by his cautious manner, and the way he had of peering over his glasses as if they were part of his armor. His feet were small and pointed, and seemed to be made of patent leather; and shaking hands with him was like clasping a bunch of twigs.

Yet he is not a satirical figure; the reader respects him long before Campton does, but Campton comes to it at last.

Like many enlightened people, Campton, his son, and perhaps their creator, had become by the year 1914 international in feeling; they were interested in art, in ideas, and were unaware of their own capacity for passionate patriotism; thus the boy shows no particular excitement at the thought of war, and merely assures his father that nothing of the kind will happen. The world is too advanced. We remember remarks like this in July, 1914; the Harvard graduate is talking to his father:

> "I know French chaps who feel as I do—Louis Dastrey, Paul's nephew, for one; and lots of English ones. They don't believe the world will ever stand for another war. It's too stupidly uneconomic, to begin with: I suppose you've read Angell? Then life's worth too much and now-adays too many millions of people know it. That's the way we all feel. Think of everything that counts— art and science and poetry, and all the rest—going to smash at the nod of some doddering diplomatist! It was different in old times, when the best of life, for the immense majority, was never anything but plague, pestilence, and famine. People are too healthy and well-fed now; they're not going off to die in a ditch to oblige anybody."

What Mrs. Wharton wishes the reader to see, and what he does see, is, that altho this kind of talk is all well enough before the declaration of war, the moment war breaks out, this boy will instantly take his place in it. He will not foam at the mouth either with love of a cause or hatred for its enemies; he will make no theatrical gesture; he will simply try to get to the front as quickly as possible. Those lads left the heroics, the cheers and the tears, to their elders and to women; they simply went. It is an absolutely typical case.

This matter-of-courseness, so characteristic of youth in college athletic contests and in war, so difficult to understand by

348

older people, who are forced to substitute excitement in speech for physical capacity, is portrayed by Mrs. Wharton with consummate art. In her war-work, she saw many of these undemonstrative young men, and George is a triumph of portraiture. His tact and consideration are perhaps somewhat above the average. Every one knows how eagerly the average boy entered the war; how he lied about his age, his health, and his nationality, in order to enter; but the maneuvers of George are more subtle. Knowing that his father and his mother are using every possible influence to get him a safe desk-job, he pretends to be satisfied with that; and for months after he is in the trenches, his parents suppose him to be safe and sound in his swivel-chair.

What is particularly interesting about this is the vacillation in the father's mind. He is pleased with deceitful letters sent home by his son, who writes calmly of his "office work"; but gradually the thought, "Thank God! he is safe," ceases to be quite satisfactory. He is at once glad and sorry for his son. Glad he is safe, and sorry that he is content to be. Sorry for himself, too; the pride of other fathers can not be his. For the average father, altho sleepless with heart-rending anxiety for his son's safety, was really proud to have him at the front.

It seems rather inconsistent for modern public opinion to condemn Abraham for his willingness to sacrifice Isaac at the command of Almighty God, when hundreds of thousands of devoted fathers during the years 1914–1918 were proud to offer up their sons. If Abraham had declined to obey the "higher call," with what curiously mixed feelings he would have regarded Isaac in the days and years that followed! He would have him safe, yes; but his satisfaction would not have been unalloyed. Now it is exactly that curious mixing of emotions in the paternal mind which to me is the most signal triumph of this novel. The analysis is made as deliberately, as leisurely, as Campton's own masterpieces; there is no sudden moment of revulsion of feeling, no dynamic conversion. The beauty of the thing is that altho Campton did not know his own mind, his son not only knew his but his father's as well. "This is what you all along really wanted me to do, father?" And Campton, tho he had moved heaven and earth to bring about the opposite result, knew that his son was right. That *was* exactly what he had wanted.

Paris in war-time, apart from the darkening of the streets and houses, seems much like any American city in 1917–1918. The feverish "war-work," the charities and philanthropies, the "business as usual," the resumption of social activities by those who were determined to "forget the war," the competent and the incompetent, the sincere and the hypocritical—Mrs. Wharton has given us representatives of every familiar class. The American Boylston is an efficient and sympathetic character, while the pacifist, unfortunately called Mr. Talkett, is faintly drawn, and does not remain a pacifist long. With her love of irony, Mrs. Wharton could not forbear giving us the picture of one noisy and preposterous ass, Mr. Mayhew, and the reader's attitude toward this man is what she presumably meant it to be. There are conventional scenes, as there are conventional people; but they are portrayed in a manner that is not conventional at all. Mrs. Wharton has never written with more mastery of subject and style than in some of these episodes, which one does not have to visit Paris to understand.

Apart from the extraordinary power and beauty of the story, I feel a special interest is observing what I guess to be the constant struggle between the author's emotions and her art. It is a book of rigidly supprest feeling; feeling held in check both by an aristocratic mind and by a conscientious artist. The composition of the story extended over four years; and I suspect many pages have been many times rewritten. Whenever, in writing at her desk, the thing "got away from her"—and I think this must have happened more than once—she was forced to call into play all the resources of her intelligence and of her craftsmanship. Somehow between the lines I can plainly see this struggle; tho it could end in only one way.

Elizabeth Shepley Sergeant, "The Atlantic Bookshelf," *Atlantic Monthly*, 132 (November 1923), 14

This novel, like a mirror, holds reflections of Mrs. Wharton's war-time consciousness. The frame of the mirror is France, 1914–1917, designed with conventional precision. The central image in the glass is that of a young American soldier of France, seen with a kind of wondering tenderness. About him move the ambiguous shades of the smart American colonists of Paris, observed with ironical detachment. It is inevitable that such images should haunt Mrs. Wharton in the postwar years, but was it not a little too soon, more too late, to transpose them into fiction? One misses the tragic immediacy of *Ethan Frome*, the evocative reminiscence of *The Age of Innocence*. There is something muted and devitalized about *A Son at the Front* that partakes, atmospherically, of the depression that followed the Peace Conference rather than of the tense-strung action in which the scene is laid.

The chief protagonists, who belong, of course, to the sophisticated, denational-ized American world where Mrs. Wharton is most at home, are a father, mother, and son. Campton, a long unsuccessful, if gifted, painter, divorced by an empty and frivolous wife who has remarried a rich Paris banker, has grown to fame through a portrait of his son, in whom all his hope is centred. The boy, materially his mother's, spiritually his father's, happens to have been born on French soil, and has therefore been called to the colors as a Frenchman in August 1914. The parents come together, joined by a common determination, in which they are abetted by the banker, to keep their treasure safe, back of the lines. Wires are pulled and George in theory occupies a comfortable embusqué berth, but in fact gets himself transferred to the front, where he is seriously wounded. But there is in the lad that irresistible dedication to death, that desire for immolation, that moved the best of the youth of all countries at this period. Nothing can save George; he goes back to his men, is wounded again and dies.

In the background war charities turn to intrigue and speculation in the hands of pleasure-seekers who cannot long be altruists, while good Americans work humbly on and suffer over America's tardy entry into the war. There is also a feeble "love interest" in the shape of Mrs. Talkett, a sort of denatured Lily Bart. What we are concerned with, however, is the psychological interplay of the central characters around that of George. The quality of youth is somehow essentially conveyed, though the features are blurred, and he is much of the time a remote symbol: "war had sucked him back into his awful whirlpool—once more he was that dark enigma, a son at the front." When he dies, Campton finds his solace in the young Americans who come to France to fight. "Sometimes to talk with them was like being on the floor in George's nursery, among the blocks and tin soldiers; some-times like watching with young archan-gels in a cold and empty heaven; but wherever he was, he always had a sense of being among his own." This sense, conveyed again and again through the father, is the salvation of a rather too well-made novel, least final where it is ex-pressive and most where it is baffled by the unknown and poignant face of Youth at War.

"A Son at the Front," English Review, 37 (November 1923), 664

The American colony in Wartime Paris is the field, and the central interest the son of a divorced couple who, in the Ameri-can manner, still preserve relations whilst competing for the boy's future interests. Technically French, the son is called to the colours just as his father, a painter with fame and fortune knocking late at his door, plans to get his son away from the wealthy banker who has married the mother and educated the boy. This com-petition turns to a combination to keep the boy out of danger, and whilst giving a wonderful picture of true and sham war activities, Mrs. Wharton develops this extraordinarily delicate relationship of the husbands, and gradually converts their anxieties and wire-pullings to a no-bler acceptance of the son's enthusiasm. This bare suggestion will indicate some-thing of the scope and scheme of this re-markably fine book. Mrs. Wharton is one of a school of American writers, of which Henry James is the best known example here. We have nothing quite like it on this side so instinct with the politeness of European letters, dispassionately ironic in

tone and masterly in its suggestive com-pleteness.

[J. B. Priestley], "Fiction," London Mercury, 9 (November 1923), 102–3

Mrs. Wharton, unlike Mr. Lawrence, is an admirable craftsman, who takes time and builds up her work solidly. This much we knew, and there is nothing in her latest book to make us change our opinion. It is well-planned and well-constructed and quietly and effectively written. Neverthe-less, it is very disappointing. It is a study, touched with delicate satire in the begin-ning but gathering emotion on its way, of the effect of the War upon certain mem-bers of the American colony in Paris. The leading figure, Campton, a distinguished portrait painter and doting father of a young French-born American who is mobilised with the French army, is very well done indeed, and there are scenes here and there of unusual dramatic inter-est; nevertheless it is disappointing. Per-haps it has arrived at the wrong moment, and has been produced either too late in the day or too early; certainly the distinctly "war" pathos, the fatal telegrams, the railway station and bedside scenes, for all the writer's reserve, are distasteful rather than truly moving; pathos of this kind still seems a somewhat cheap trick. And apart from such scenes, the novel is rather dull. It does not reach out to universality; it is always the story of a set, and not an interesting set. The war and the American colony in Paris might have made good journalistic fiction a few years ago, and might make good social historical fiction some years hence; but to most of us at the moment it seems a blighting subject. In spite of Henry James, the cosmopolitan American, who seems to promise so much in fiction, always contrives to be a most uninteresting figure. There is, of course, more in *A Son at the Front* than the War, but even then the central situation—which is brought about by the fact that not only the father but also his divorced wife and her husband live in Paris and are absorbed, not without mutual jealousies, in the soldier son—even this situation seems too topical, too local, to arouse more than a faint interest. It is, however, much too early to pass a confident judgment on such a story as this, and if ten or twenty years of this peace leave any of us alive, it will be interesting to see how it reads after that interval.

"New Books Revisited," *North American Review*, 219 (January 1924), 139–41

It seems as though a novel dealing even indirectly with the World War might be extraordinarily thrilling and deeply true. If a writer desires a theme of vast human significance, surely the war in some of its phases can provide it. Novels deal with character and with emotions, and they are the better for a background of events. The World War was the greatest of events; it strained every emotion to the breaking point; it was the most searching test of human character that has ever been made upon a great scale. Moreover, the war sifted ideas, caused a questioning of faiths, produced a tremendous effort toward fundamental thinking, an attempt to grasp larger meanings if perchance they might

be found. It has been quite natural, therefore, to expect that the after-war period would produce literature of a new and powerful kind. Instead of this, we have begun about where we left off.

It would be quite unfair to find fault with Mrs. Wharton's *A Son at the Front* on the ground that it is not great and moving in proportion as the war itself was violent and impressive. It could not be. The mere truth is, that this long, incredibly cruel and horrifying struggle had, and still has, a benumbing effect upon men's minds. The vast significance of it all has not yet been fully grasped: there is no reconciling of the mind to the thing, no real possibility of transforming it by art.

What a novelist can represent in such a novel as *A Son at the Front* is chiefly the benumbed war-mentality. This psychological task Mrs. Wharton has performed with her usual clearness and subtlety; yet it is almost inevitable that the result should partake of a certain dreariness pertaining to most war books; and if the reader has no right to complain of the author for not having achieved something nearly impossible, he is not to be blamed for preferring other stories of hers to this one.

The soul of the soldier, the secret of his heroism—that is something that cannot, in this instance, be convincingly portrayed. One has not the materials in his imagination wherewith to construct the picture. The sensitive soul who has been in the trenches will not and perhaps cannot give a clear account of his motives and feelings. Something like a blank mystery confronts us here; we have only a vague sense of something too big and too shocking for any but the most matter-of-fact speech. With all her art of suggestion and of understatement, Mrs. Wharton succeeds in depicting her young soldier, in his reserve and quiet heroism, only as a being mysteriously apart, "sealed to the thing," beyond ordinary motives of purely personal affection, removed as if already dead, yet with affections such as an angel might have. All this we must read into a youth whose behaviour is natural and commonplace enough so far as it is expressive at all. The dominant impression is that of the hopeless inadequacy of our imaginations and our emotions. We are perpetually under the strain of knowing that we should feel more than we do.

But what of the emotions of the father? These perhaps are more within our grasp. His state of mind is that of bewilderment, a perplexed reaching out after the personality of his son, which continually escapes him, because that son is no longer really his; a distressing alternation of hope and fear, of distraction and of obsessing dread. Here, too, what one principally feels is the inadequacy of the emotions. Superimposed upon the feeling that one ought to feel tremendously, is the disquieting thought that in such circumstances it is perfectly futile to feel at all. The paternal emotions are acute, but are suspected of a kind of irrelevance. The patriotic motive is an unknown quantity. There is no point of emotional rest—only doubt and dread, an attempt to be normal, and shame at the success of the effort.

It was, perhaps, a mistake on the part of Mrs. Wharton to make the father in the story an artist and something of an eccentric as well. The artistic temperament and all the vagaries of a somewhat jealous, hot-headed and wrong-headed man do not help to develop the essential theme; they merely complicate the situation to no particular purpose. Campton is not a person who thinks much or clearly. Whatever significance the story holds is with difficulty expressed through his somewhat twisted personality. Campton fumbles with his own impressions; a great variety of people come and go and express their rather futile ideas; sentiments and poses

are indulged in, for every one "carries on" in his own peculiar way; and at intervals come shocks in the form of news from the front. In such a story one is not carried on by the force of any clearly conceived theme or fully realized personality.

The book is a human document, in atmosphere like the war books, truthful in its delineation of character, veracious in its account of war psychology; admirable because of the sincerity with which it treats of a situation deeply interesting, but—not a great novel.

A Checklist of Additional Reviews

E. W. Osborn, "A Son at the Front," New York World, 9 September 1923 p. 8–E.

Dorothea Lawrence, "Edith Wharton Writes a War Novel," Boston Evening Transcript, 15 September 1923 book, section, p. 4.

R. D. Townsend, "The New Fiction," Outlook, 135 (26 September 1923), 149.

Henry de la Chaise, "Edith Wharton: Un Fils au front," Etudes [France], 4 (October-December 1924), 374.

Forrest Reid, "New Novels," Nation and Athenæum [England], 34 (6 October 1923), 20.

Raymond Mortimer, "New Novels," New Statesman, 22 (13 October 1923), 18.

"Mrs. Wharton's Novel," Springfield [Massachusetts] Republican, (15 October 1923), p. 6.

"A Father's Heart Is Bared in Mrs. Wharton's New Novel," Current Opinion, 75 (November 1923), 561–2.

Joseph Aynard, "*Un Fils au front*, par Mrs. Edith Wharton," *Journal des Débats* [France], 29 February 1924, pp. 348–50.

Gabriel Marcel, "*Un Fils au front*, par Edith Wharton," *Nouvelle Revue Française* [France], 23 (1 August 1924), 249–50.

A. Brulé, "Edith Wharton: *Un Fils au front*," *Revue Anglo-Américaine* [France], 2 (February 1925), 274–5.

OLD NEW YORK

OLD NEW YORK

FALSE DAWN

(*The 'Forties*)

BY

EDITH WHARTON

AUTHOR OF "THE AGE OF INNOCENCE," ETC.

DECORATIONS BY E. C. CASWELL

D. APPLETON AND COMPANY

NEW YORK :: LONDON :: MCMXXIV

Lloyd Morris, "Mrs. Wharton Looks at Society," *New York Times Book Review*, 18 May 1924, pp. 1, 24–5

In the dusty arena of contemporary American fiction Edith Wharton long ago achieved the cool isolation of distinction. Few of our living writers equal her in speculative interest; in *Ethan Frome* she wrote what is perhaps the most distinguished work of fiction produced in this century by an American writer, yet she has not infrequently produced books that, at best, may charitably be dismissed as unworthy of her proved capacity. Her admirable equipment and her occasional high accomplishment have set an exacting standard for her work. Her best is so far superior to mere adequacy as to make a merely competent performance by Mrs. Wharton seem little more than negligible. More than any other of her contemporaries, Mrs. Wharton is taxed by the discipline which she herself has imposed upon the expectations of her readers.

These expectations she has once again amply fulfilled. In *The Old Maid* she has written a story as universally significant and as enduringly beautiful as *Ethan Frome*, a story which exercises the inevitable authority of great art. Mrs. Wharton's lucid intelligence, sensitive perception and delicate irony have been admirably tempered by the passing years. In this story she has brought them to bear upon material in every way worthy of their subtle precision. *The Old Maid* affirms Mrs. Wharton's absolute command over the elements of her art, and again reveals that capacity to achieve flawless beauty which she has too often been content to deny.

The theme of the four stories of old New York which she has brought together in sequence is the theme with which she has principally concerned herself in her previous works: namely, a conflict between individual purpose or desire and a compact society which seeks to control it. She has always excelled in portraying the conditions under which such a society circumscribes and ultimately defeats the errant individual, whether the caprice is held to be sin, or stupidity, or mere unprecedented innovation. In the communities to which she has devoted her attention, a rigorous decorum establishes the pattern of life, and to deviate, however briefly, from strict conformity is to invite a disproportionate expiation. The old New York of the four stories is represented in four successive decades of its progress, yet its life reveals no qualitative expansion under the flow of time, and its social organism suffers no least modification. Of the society of all four decades Mrs. Wharton might truthfully have said, as she says of that of the fifties, that it "lived in a genteel monotony of which the surface was never stirred by the dumb drama now and then enacted underground." Four such dramas constitute her stories, and the protagonists are four individuals who violate the established pattern. "Sensitive souls," observes Mrs. Wharton, "in those days were like muted keyboards on which Fate played without a sound."

It may be that these four stories owe their inception to *The Age of Innocence*. In any event, readers who, like the present reviewer, hold that novel to be the most finely achieved of Mrs. Wharton's later work will welcome this group of stories in which an archaic and faded background of a bygone day only intensifies the emotional mood and dramatic action.

357

Against this background of an obsolete and vanished society the human conflict projects with the sharpened relief of absolute contrast. Irony seldom deserts Mrs. Wharton's pen, but too often she has blunted its edge with satire. In two of the four new stories, *The Old Maid* and *New Year's Day*, the fine thrust of her irony is unhampered by complications of mood; in one of them, *The Old Maid*, irony is the vehicle of concentrated tragic passion which lifts the story high above the circumstances of narrow convention in which it arises, and makes an austere and potent reading of life.

In the two remaining stories, *False Dawn* and *The Spark*, Mrs. Wharton writes as a satirist, and although irony and lucidity are not wholly absent from them, they have neither the significance nor the beauty of their companions. *False Dawn*, dealing with the New York of the forties, that New York which lived below Canal Street and had its country estates on the East River, tells of the disaster involved by a collection of paintings. In it, individual caprice, viewed by a compact society as stupidity, suffers a heavy penalty cruel expiation. Lewis Raycie, the sensitive son of a socially ambitious merchant, is commissioned by his father to collect a gallery of Italian paintings during the grand tour which is to prepare him for his future as a cultivated gentleman and man of fortune. Old Mr. Raycie views the members of his family as pallid reflections of his own tyrannical ego: they exist merely to translate into conduct the course of action which he has planned and willed for them. And so, with regard to his gallery of paintings, he has selected the artists approved by the conventional opinion of the society of which he is a respected member. But Lewis, pathetically sensitive and spiritually malleable, permits himself to drift into unprecedented innovation. Under the influence of the young John Ruskin and Dante Rossetti he makes the egregious error of substituting paintings by the Italian Primitives for the Raphæls and Carlo Dolcis and Guercinos socially approved by the conservative New York bankers of the 'forties and ordered by his father. His cruel expiation of his brief deviation from conformity and decorum constitutes the plot of the story. Mrs. Wharton deals with the affair of the pictures with a shrewdly satiric touch; they bring only tragedy into the lives of all who possess them, until three-quarters of a century later their chance discovery by a mercenary and meretricious descendant of the Raycies precipitates a fortune into the lap of an unworthy and stupid woman.

The Spark professes to deal with the New York of the sixties, but the action passes almost exclusively in the very late years of the last century. It concerns the domestic difficulties of Hayley Delane, a man of wealth whose stupidity and conventionality and preoccupation with the trivial amusements common to his circle conceal deep currents of unacknowledged idealism and instinctive chivalry. His tradition has made him essentially a respecter of convention, decorum and inherited preconceptions, yet a single event in his life has undermined the conservative foundations of tradition and driven him into sporadic rebellion. The event in question occurred in a hospital in Washington during the Civil War. Delane had run away from school to enlist in the Union forces, was wounded at Bull Run, and in hospital came in contact with a "queer fellow—a sort of backwoodsman," who spent his time caring for the wounded, and whose ideas left an indelible impression upon Delane. At moments of decision throughout Delane's life the figure of this uncouth, vigorous thinker kept returning to him in memory, forcing him into courses of conduct in absolute variance with the habitual decorum of his environment and with all the principles cherished by the tradition which he inherited. Delane never knew the name of the man who so profoundly affected his subsequent life, and only by chance at the end of his career picked up a book of incomprehensible verse in which he saw the portrait of his old friend. And Mrs. Wharton closes the story with a touch of delicate irony:

"Yes; that's it. Old Walt—that was what all the fellows used to call him. He was a great chap; I'll never forget him. I rather wish, though," he added, in his mildest tone of reproach, "you hadn't told me that he wrote all that rubbish!"

The Old Maid, which reasserts the theme previously outlined, does so in a mood far removed from the intellectual detachment and subtle cynicism of Mrs. Wharton's satiric vein. The story is one which lends itself to pure irony, and to that profound irony from which the accent of tragedy is seldom absent. It is a story which demands precisely the treatment given it by Mrs. Wharton. As she has told it, the story has the austere and uncompromising beauty of classic art. It is an illustration of Mrs. Wharton's solicitude for perfection of expression that the form of this story impresses the reader as being not only appropriate, but inevitable to its content. Seldom, indeed, does a writer achieve such absolute and flawless beauty as Mrs. Wharton has achieved in *The Old Maid*. The incident upon which the story is based is meagerly simple, as simple as that which supports *The Scarlet Letter*. An impoverished member of the tight little society of old New York has had a concealed love affair with a man too poor to marry her. Somewhat later she falls in love with and becomes engaged to a young and wealthy member of that society. But, unknown to her friends and to society in general, the earlier episode has had the consequence of making her the mother of a child, and the child has been farmed out as a foundling. The question which confronts her is the future of the child. Shall she part herself from it, or shall she reject marriage and happiness to continue her furtive care of her baby? Her heart is torn by the divided interest of her desire for personal happiness and her love of her child. In her dilemma she goes to a married cousin, the jilted flame of her earlier lover, the woman who, had circumstances been propitious, might have been the child's mother. To this woman she tells her story, putting her destiny in her cousin's hands. The cousin, eminently respectable but thoroughly tender, determines that Charlotte may retain her child by making herself responsible for its support, but exacts as the price of this solution the cancellation of Charlotte's engagement.

Somewhat later Charlotte and her child are taken in by the cousin, now a widow, and the ties of affection between the child and her benefactress become poignantly close. To conceal her relationship to the child Charlotte trains herself to an exaggerated prudishness and conventionality, but the little girl, inheriting the impulsive character of her father and mother, has nothing but amused tolerance for the severely constrained woman who is always forced to suppress and deny her passionate maternal soul. Ultimately Charlotte's misadventure threatens to repeat itself in the life of her child, and the child is saved only by a second intervention on the part of the benefactress, who now legally adopts her as her own, and spiritually assumes the burden of motherhood. The tragedy in the life of Charlotte centres in the ironical and terrible expiation involved by the relationship of herself and her cousin to her child, now a girl about to be married.

Only a superbly accomplished artist could dredge so deeply into the secret places of the human spirit on so narrow a canvas, and only a great writer could transmute such recalcitrant material into noble imaginative beauty. Mrs. Wharton achieves this with the greatest economy of means, but each stroke, each line, each word tells profoundly. She achieves complete characterization in two sentences: "The Ralstons were of middle-class English stock. They had not come to the Colonies to die for a creed but to live for a bank account." She implies the meaning of her story in scarcely more words:

> As the truth stole upon Delia her heart melted with the old compassion for Charlotte. She saw that it was a terrible, a sacrilegious thing to interfere with another's destiny, to lay the tenderest touch upon any human being's right to love and suffer after his own fashion. Delia had twice intervened in Charlotte Lovell's life; it was natural that Charlotte should be her enemy. If only she did not revenge herself by wounding Time!

And, within the limits of four slight episodes, Mrs. Wharton has revealed the complete character and experience of three people in all the conflicting and complicated threads of their relationship to one another. It is true that the essential theme of the story is the conflict between individual impulses and the inflexible decorum of established convention. But as Mrs. Wharton has written it, her story transcends the significance of her theme. In the opinion of the present reviewer *The Old Maid* is assured of literary immortality. It stands as one of the most imperishably beautiful and perfect stories in the whole range of American literature.

After *The Old Maid*, *New Year's Day*,

which tells of the tragic consequences involved for a woman by her superb sacrifice of her virtue in order that she may save the life of the husband whom she passionately loves—after *The Old Maid* this story seems lightly facile and effective only as melodrama. It is not that Mrs. Wharton's intelligence and her irony have deserted her. The irony is implicit from the opening lines, which constitute one of the most brilliant beginnings of a story ever achieved by Mrs. Wharton:

> "She was bad . . . always. They used to meet at the Fifth Avenue Hotel," said my mother, as if the scene of the offense added to the guilt of the couple whose past she was revealing.

No, it is not absence of irony which makes *New Year's Day* seem the lesser achievement. It is, perhaps, the effect of conscious artifice, of plot too painstakingly contrived, of character too obviously whittled down to type. A good story, and by any other hand an excellent story is *New Year's Day*. But adequate fiction— a merely competent, well-articulated story, is beneath Mrs. Wharton's capacities.

The four stories which constitute *Old New York* deserve wide popularity. Of them, one, *The Old Maid*, deserves and should acquire enduring fame. Not to read this story is to deliberately deny one's self an acquaintance with the finest contribution to our fiction made by any other in many years.

360

Louise Maunsell Field, "Edith Wharton Shows Us Old New York," *Literary Digest International Book Review*, 2 (June 1924), 538–9

Mrs. Wharton has tried an interesting experiment—that of publishing four new historical novels of New York life all at the same time. The novels are very short, but each is complete in itself, has its own plot, its own set of characters and situations, untouched by any contact with the others, save perhaps that of environment; yet each is part of a series which, taken as a whole, forms a progressive picture of social New York from the 'forties to the 'seventies. This is the scheme, at least, of the four volumes, and if the third—that story professedly of the 'sixties called *The Spark*—is in its general setting rather a tale of the 'nineties than of some thirty years earlier, it is nevertheless the influence of a great man of the 'sixties which is felt through and inspires it all.

First of the four books is *False Dawn*. This tells how young Lewis Raycie went from his father's handsome country house on the Sound, "a convenient driving distance from his town house on Canal Street," and only a very little way from the cottage where poor young Mrs. Edgar Allan Poe lay dying, to make that "grand tour" which was to complete his education. He was not merely to complete his education, but to buy pictures, for his father had dreams of a "Raycie Gallery" and wanted to own a few Old Masters—originals, not copies of "the Italian genius." For during this "False Dawn" of the 'forties, Mr. Raycie could feel that a taste for what he called "Art and Letters" was a desirable part of a gentleman's equipment. The irony of the result, influenced by a certain John Ruskin, is of the kind Mrs. Wharton delights to present, and does present inimitably. Atmosphere, characterization, situation, all are perfectly of the period; never dogmatized about, but always deftly implied.

Aspiration for culture and the possession of "Old Masters" have no part, it would seem, in the New York of the 'fifties, altho the story of *The Old Maid*" is one of those ever-recurring dramas which have small connection with time or place. It simply happens that Mrs. Wharton has chosen the New York of nearly three-quarters of a century ago for the setting of her version; with but little change, it could be transferred to the present day. Little change, either in incident or in the psychology of the two women who are its protagonists, a psychology so clearly and so subtly reproduced, that one knows them both, and lives and suffers with them. Delia, who "had once learned that one can do almost anything (perhaps even murder) if one does not attempt to explain it," is a fine and generous-hearted woman; yet one can easily understand how her very beneficence turned to venom as it touched poor Charlotte's torn soul. Charlotte we see only through Delia's eyes; with fine reticence, Mrs. Wharton indicates rather than expounds what went on in the heart of the woman whose tragedy it was to be a mother in fact but not in name.

Around these two there rises like a wall the combined spirit of the Ralstons, a family of a type known to all those whose connection with New York is not merely of yesterday. "Rich and respected citizens," scrupulously honest in business as well as in private affairs, keeping their unpopular personal opinions out of sight until they died for lack of air, taking their view of the life of the state and the community from the newspapers they "already despised," and themselves standing as far apart from it as possible. It was all but inevitable that the descendants of men and women such as these should become themselves the kind of men and women portrayed in the third novel, which, tho its merits are numerous, scarcely ranks with its three companions. Yet it is interesting, this sketch of a man of the 'sixties, as he appeared to a boy of the 'nineties, whose own father had stayed at home throughout the Civil War.

The leading character of this third book, *The Spark*, is Hayley Delane, who seemed to be nothing but "a card-playing, ball-giving, race-frequenting elderly gentleman," tho the young fellow who tells the story realizes that there is in him something "shut-up." For he could occasionally flare out in sudden rage, could on occasion take his own line, serenely regardless of other people's opinions. And he had fought in the Civil War, and in the hospital met a certain great man, a "Spark," whose spirit remained with him always. But of the New York of the 'sixties this book gives scarcely a glimpse.

New Year's Day is a New Year's Day of the 'seventies, a period which Mrs. Wharton has already christened "The Age of Innocence," and certain names from the earlier novel help to give atmosphere to this new one—among them, those of Mr. and Mrs. Henry van der Luyden and Sillerton Jackson. Moreover, the story it tells is essentially of this particular period, when even that "precarious beginning" of feminine independence indicated by "painting wild-roses on fans, ... manufacturing lamp-shades and trimming hats for more fortunate friends," was still a thing unheard of, and a dowerless girl must either marry or starve. Lizzie Hazeldean had all the "helpless incapacity"

of her time and her class; she was capable of one "great hour," but she did not know "how to create for herself any inner life in keeping with that one unprecedented impulse." And the irony of events thrust her into the positions for which she was least fitted. She loved greatly; and for that love she paid, not swiftly and at once, but in small sums exacted through the years, sums that grew larger as the years passed, and with their passing, made it more and more difficult for her to fill her days in the only ways she knew and understood.

Her story is developed with the sureness and skill Mrs. Wharton so well knows how to employ.

The motives which took her to the Fifth Avenue Hotel on that New Year's Day of the fire perplex the reader as much as they did Grandmamma Parret, and not until the tale approaches its end, in that tense, dramatic interview with the man in the case which took so surprizing a turn, does one discover the truth about this Lizzie Hazeldean, whom a good woman had denounced in the very first line of the novel. Lizzie had done one thing "heroically," but tho she could rise to the heights, she could not live upon them, and her New York, the New York where everybody who was "anybody" knew everybody else, and the etiquette of mourning was rigidly observed, forms as it were the inevitable background for her charming figure, her grace, her proficiency in that art of pleasing which was then regarded as a woman's only business.

From these four books arises a composite picture of the society of "Old New York"; very small, very closely connected in the first; little larger, almost as closely connected, and even more provincial, in the last. A society for the most part entirely materialistic. In religion, in politics, in social relations—in all that touches the intellectual or the artistic—dogmatic, self-satisfied, evasive, intolerant, and always and in everything small. Nothing of vision or of aspiration, nothing—magnificent. Atmosphere, not so much of the hot-house as of the dining-room, heavy with the fumes of one of those ten-course dinners so expressive of the 'seventies. One feels a longing to open all the windows, no matter how raw, cold, and generally unpleasant the air outside may prove.

Here and there, of course, some one individual rises above the general level, perhaps to suffer, like Lewis Raycie, from being born too soon, before his "true time's advent"; perhaps quietly to take his pleasure in the amusements and the books which were sealed to his contemporaries, as Charles Hazeldean did. But for the most part they are content with the life depicted, one lived entirely on the surface of things, pleasant, comfortable, complacent, unquestioning.

Mrs. Wharton denotes it all easily, with no straining after archeological effects, with no endeavor to be startling through topography. When in the course of any one of these novels there are allusions to customs, places, manners or costumes, it is because they are a necessary part of the narrative itself.

To dwell on Mrs. Wharton's style or technique has long since become superfluous. She has chosen here to present one small class as it existed in each of four decades—or seems to her to have existed. For some there are whose own ancestral tree is deeply rooted in the soil of New York, who may feel that she has looked through a diminishing glass, seeing it all as narrower, smaller, more bloodless, meaner in spirit than it actually was. But whether this is so or not, the series of *Old New York*, to which these four novels belong, compels respectful attention, as well as the deepest admiration for the author's exquisite craftsmanship and fine and subtle power of characterization.

"The New Books," *Outlook*, 137 (4 June 1924), 201–3

Curiosity and interest are excited at the outset by the scheme of Mrs. Wharton's group of stories called *Old New York*, related, so the sub-titles indicate, to the city's social life in the Forties, Fifties, Sixties, and Seventies. The plan's attractiveness is aided by delightful old-time drawings of scenes in those decades on the volumes' covers and lining papers.

This pleasing scheme, however, is an adventitious rather than vital element of value. It smacks of the publisher rather than of the author. The true interest is not one of period, but of eternal human nature. As a matter of fact, these four fine short stories were published in two different periodicals, and not, we believe, in their present order. Moreover, in their time-relation the stories of the Forties and Fifties might have been interchanged with a few touches, while that of the Sixties frankly has its action and talk in the Nineties, with only a backward glance at the Sixties, so that the reader who has not carefully perused his cover-blurb is mighty puzzled.

No; the worth of these stories is in their merciless, powerful depiction of human suffering under social bondage and the deadly pressure of convention. Mrs. Wharton has never gone deeper than here in showing how in "society" circles the individual who stumbles, or sins, or simply (as in *False Dawn*) is ahead of his time in recognition of genius, shrinks and shrivels under the iron necessity of keeping up appearances.

We seem to detect a new note in the author's writing, one of sympathy for the victim, stronger than the irony by which here, as elsewhere, she has lightly yet keenly flicked at society's dull and deadly tyranny. This is especially true of *The Old Maid*, which has rarely been surpassed as a study of inevitable tragedy in a woman's life. In this case the woman is unable either to show motherhood-feeling for her illegitimate daughter or to bear with fortitude the jealousy she feels when the daughter's life inclines to the woman who saves the girl socially by adopting her. Mrs. Wharton is far too great an artist in words to treat this situation emotionally or sentimentally, but one knows that for once her sympathy with distress is stronger than her ironical intent. *The Old Maid* and, but in a less degree, *New Year's Day* have situation and character in actuality enough to have been expanded easily into fuller and more complete works of fiction.

The Spark has an unexpected backward glance to Walt Whitman, who had by his chance talk influenced the life and ideas of a man who didn't know who Walt was. In *False Dawn* wise and self-sufficient New York regards Ruskin and Rossetti as art-quacks and lets an inestimably precious collection of Italian Primitives lie dust-covered in an attic long after their wistful collector had passed away—a laughing-stock and art-prophet without honor. These two tales are shorter and less well filled out than the other two, which might be called novelettes if that word had not a connotation not quite dignified enough.

It is a cause of congratulation that these four stories have been brought together in this pretty and fanciful format. They are collectively a substantial, although in a sense minor, addition to the author's literary production.

Edmund Wilson, "Old New York," New Republic, 39 (11 June 1924), 77

Mrs. Wharton's *Old New York* is a set of four novelettes dealing, respectively, with the 'forties, the 'fifties, the 'sixties and the 'seventies. In the first, a rich and complacent New Yorker sends his son on the Grand Tour with instructions to buy some Guido Rennis and Carlo Dolcis—with the result that the son, who on the trip has fallen in with the young Ruskin, buys Carpaccios and Mantegnas instead and when he returns is disinherited. In the second, two Victorian ladies, who have both been in love with the same man, carry on a ferocious life-long struggle under the outward semblance of calm respectability. In the third, a simple and chivalrous man who has fought as a boy at Bull Run, flares up for a moment in the polo-playing society of the 'nineties, which no longer has a place for him. And in the fourth, a woman whom a cultivated young lawyer has rescued, by marrying her, from dependence and humiliation, repays her debt, when he has developed tuberculosis, by carrying on an affair with another man and using the money he gives her to pay the doctor's bills; the husband dies and she is left to fade away in a twilight of social obloquy.

All these, as will be seen, have their point; they have something to say about American society. But there is not much in them which Mrs. Wharton had not already done more effectively in *The Age of Innocence*. Mrs. Wharton's short stories have always been, on the whole, more machine-like and less real than her novels; there is not usually much in them to admire beyond the expertness of the professional—the agreeable dexterity of a Sardou with not particularly significant situations. But in these stories, which are offered us as history, we demand significance or nothing—and what we get, along with some valuable observation of character and manner, is still a good deal of Sardou. The stories in *Old New York* do not, on the one hand, follow life quite faithfully enough to be impressive as social studies and, on the other, are not quite dramatically enough developed to be satisfactory as conventional short stories. The man in *The Spark*, for example—who has "been brought up on the best books—Scott and Washington Irving and old what's-his-name who wrote the Spectator," who has enlisted as a boy in the Civil War but who has "stopped living" at nineteen and with his kindliness, his dignity and his quotations from Byron and Gray, drifts on into the frivolous days of the end of the century—is a recognizable and significant American type; but Mrs. Wharton has executed this portrait with a little too much obviousness and slickness. She has always been the Sargent of American fiction and as time goes on seems to become more and more willing to deal facilely with her subjects.

Perhaps it is Mrs. Wharton's long residence abroad which makes her novels run a little thin nowadays. In *Summer*, her first novel published since she had been living in France, the American colors are already paling a little; *A Son at the Front*, which deals with Paris during the war, has perhaps more body than any of the others. *The Age of Innocence*, surely one of the best of her novels, succeeds through the intensity of the emotion it conveys rather than through the sort of vividness she once commanded; its settings and characters, admirable as they are, have some of the vagueness of memories. And the realities of *Old New York* are vaguer and

more remote still. Nonetheless, as details in Mrs. Wharton's extraordinary history of the New York civilization these stories are, of course, not negligible. The inferior boundary of that history is now marked by the first story in the collection, *False Dawn*; the superior boundary, I suppose, by *A Son at the Front*—though she leaves the New York scene itself with the elaborate and violent *Custom of the Country*, in which the city is already becoming too complicated and chaotic for the author of *The Age of Innocence* much to enjoy grappling with it any longer. Too chaotic and vulgar today; yesterday too correct and narrow. Mrs. Wharton has written the tragedy of the New York soul caught between the millstones of these two eras. She is probably the only absolutely first-rate literary artist, occupying himself predominantly with New York, that New York has ever produced. Henry James was born here and understood the city well, yet never treated it intensively. But the brick fronts of Washington Square, the brown monuments of Park Avenue, the glittering apartments of the upper westside—Madison Square, the Grand Central Station, the Weehawken Ferry and the downtown office-buildings seem still to burn with a sort of incandescence from having become the prisons of Mrs. Wharton's passion and the symbols of her indignation.

Gilbert Thomas, "New York and London Mixtures," *Nation and Athenæum* [England], 35 (28 June 1924), 416

In these four little novels of *Old New York*, Mrs. Wharton plays the double part of impressionist and story-teller, and succeeds in blending her two *rôles* with the perfection only attainable by a fine and subtle artist. Against a background rich in local and historical colour, she reveals those elemental human passions which, while they may superficially reflect their immediate setting, are perennially the same the world over. The New York to which she introduces us is the New York that accepted Thackeray, but declined to receive Charles Dickens—"the exclusive and impenetrable" New York of the middle decades of last century, with its self-sufficing little society of inter-marrying families, smugly Philistine and Pharisaical. Life, however, is life, and refuses to be dammed by any arbitrary social code. If it cannot flow naturally upon the surface, it will find its way into secret corners and subterranean channels, from which it will fitfully burst above ground to the shocked amazement of those who seek to repress it.

In each of Mrs. Wharton's four tales we see life defying the bounds prescribed for it by the complacent conventionality of Old New York. *False Dawn* describes how the comfortable and pompous Halston Raycie sends forth his son, Lewis, upon the Grand Tour, from which, having sown his wild oats in foreign fields, he is to return and marry into one of the best local families. Halston Raycie, moreover, has conceived the idea of founding a Raycie Collection, and to this end he commissions Lewis to bring back from Europe specimens of the "recognised" Old Masters—the lesser Raphaels—whose names he has painfully acquired. Lewis, however, is in love with Beatrice Kent, the ward of a poor relative, and his love for her, no less than a talk with a young Englishman, John Ruskin, whom he meets on Mont Blanc, has the effect of awakening in him a passion for the newer art. For in one of the Madonnas which Ruskin advises him to see, Lewis beholds the features of his own "plain" Beatrice—with the result that he carries back to New York, not Salvator Rosa and Carlo Dolci, but "Carpatcher" and "Piero della Francesca." These "worthless daubs" are received with frenzied scorn by his father, and Lewis's indiscretion costs him not only his inheritance, but eventually his life. After a vain effort to educate public taste, he and Beatrice die in poverty, martyrs to his artistic conscience. It is not until some decades later that an obscure descendant, changing residences, finds that a forgotten lumber of pictures in her attic can be turned into unlimited pearls and Rolls-Royces.

The Old Maid narrates the tragedy of Charlotte Lovell, who, having illicitly indulged her love for one outside her own circle, assumes the character of a benevolent spinster, and establishes a home for children, hoping by this means to retain her own baby, while avoiding social ostracism. *The Spark* turns upon the revolution—very disconcerting to respectability—which is wrought in Hayley Delane's heart by a chance meeting, in a Civil War hospital, with an "atheist" who has yet a strange capacity for inspiring Christian charity, and who is revealed to us at last as Walt Whitman. Finally, in *New Year's Day*, we are given a study of "that bad

366

woman," Lizzie Hazeldean, whose sin has in it a courage and nobility undreamt of in the philosophy of Old New York. Such bald summary, however, does scant justice to Mrs. Wharton's art, which, with its combination of ingenuity and fidelity to character, of irony and deep human compassion, of bold outline and exquisite delicacy of detail, adds, with this new achievement, a fresh lustre to American literature.

[John Farrar], "Authors Remember New York," *Bookman*, 59 (July 1924), 590

The four stories, separately bound, constituting Edith Wharton's *Old New York* (Appleton), are in a very different manner—Mrs. Wharton's best manner, as a matter of fact—and they are among the finest things she has ever written. They are human yet touched with an ironical note that is peculiarly satisfying. *False Dawn* (the Forties), while in workmanship it is flawless, is the most obvious of the four tales. Lewis Raycie and his wife are appealing. Here Mrs. Wharton strikes the note that links the four stories—the vulgarity of the rich and their blindness to the artistic. *The Old Maid* (the Fifties) is a masterpiece. It is a story of the warm human weaknesses and kindliness that lay under tight modes, codes, and manners, the story of two women and a girl bound by a stranger tie, and the delicate adjustments of character involved. Mrs. Wharton tells it with clarity and super-fine balancing of the emotions. *The Spark* (the Sixties) is the tale of what the Civil War

did to one young man, of his ill chosen wife, his patience with her, his quiet tolerance through life, and his final discovery of the man who greatly influenced his life. It is a piece of emotional writing bordered by most bitter cynicism. *New Year's Day* (the Seventies), while again obvious in outline, is superb in execution and in its handling of swerving emotion. Mrs. Wharton seems to let herself go on these novelettes; while she does not abandon her method, she lets shine through a warmth that is compelling. The tales certainly rank with her best work, and I suspect *The Old Maid* of being almost as good as—if not, for its kind, a little better than—*Ethan Frome*.

John Jay Chapman, "The Atlantic's Bookshelf," *Atlantic Monthly*, 134 (August 1924), 6

When I take up a short story of the day, I feel as an old stager might feel in watching a game of modern bridge. Most of the finesse is lost on me. The recent development of the short story in America resembles the progress of football: it has become a national sport, watched by thousands of erudite fans who have grown up with the rules and follow every point with passionate interest. The same thing is true of the movies. When I go to one of them I generally contrive to take with me a half-grown boy who knows the technique of the thing and shows me the high spots. Every now and then, he nudges me and whispers, "Do you get it, Uncle John?" and I pretend that I do.

The four sketches which Mrs. Wharton has woven together—or at least has put together in a box, shaking over them some handfuls of local reminiscence, old furniture, and chiffons somewhat too carefully described—belong to the modern game. They represent, as I guess, themes that had occurred to Mrs. Wharton at various times and which suit her genius. For she is a highly accomplished virtuoso who has arisen out of a particular school (the school of Stendhal, Balzac, Flaubert, Henry James, and others), and through sedulous training of her brilliant intellect has arrived at a cold mastership very valuable, very interesting. These sketches give no idea of her powers, for they are hastily turned off. I have to confess that I think my nephew nudged me, and all but convinced me, during *The Old Maid* story, which gives a powerful and accurate account of a lifelong duel between Charlotte and Delia as to who shall act as mother to the child whose father has been the seducer of one and the lost love of the other. But most of the characters in these tales are staged rather than studied and the historic coloring has been inaccurately splashed in. The causticity and pessimism which this branch of fiction affect have become with Mrs. Wharton almost a pose. One misses the masculine stomach and deliberateness of the greater writers of the school.

As for old New York it seems to me that Mrs. Wharton has given just such an account of it as must satisfy the imagination of the Middle West; but I doubt whether the place was ever quite so foolish as she would give us to think.

An odd fancy crosses my mind as I close the book. There have always been certain British novelists who were fascinated by the social distinctions, petty ambitions, and meannesses that come to blossom in an aristocracy. And when one of these novelists weaves melodrama into his plots and keeps the dark secrets of high-life still in the foreground, he is apt to become the favorite reading of housemaids. We have few housemaids in America, but we have millions of good citizens in our suburban towns who look with curiosity on any account of old New York—a city which their romanticism peoples with a race of degenerate provincial nobles, whom, perhaps, it is Mrs. Wharton's function to create.

Henry Seidel Canby, "Stories of Our Past," *Saturday Review of Literature*, 1 (16 August 1924), 43–4

Mrs. Wharton's four long short stories of old New York have been published for some time, but since two of them are of remarkable technical excellence, and the group a *tour de force* of historical re-creation, they must have notice, even if belated, in *The Saturday Review*. Admirers of the author of *The Age of Innocence* have by now read the first story *False Dawn*, and differed as to its merits. They have read that chronicle of a friendship between a sportsman and a genius, *The Spark*, where the fire flashes between two like characters, otherwise insulated, and this story they have not much approved, probably because, like some of Sherwood Anderson's themes, it is a difficult topic not finally grasped. They have agreed as to the high merits of *New Year's Day* and *The Old Maid*.

In a review of a book already much discussed, a reviewer may be allowed to talk pure technique. *New Year's Day*, as a piece of sheer virtuosity, equals *Ethan Frome* although it lacks the solemn power of that masterpiece of the American short story. The situation is of a faithless wife who deceives for cause a helpless husband. The problem is to make her faithless for his salvation—an old theme of melodrama—and yet conduct her story as in life—not melodrama—it might have happened and might have been revealed. The difficulty is a real one, a tempting one for a skilful artist, and Mrs. Wharton has bettered her opportunity. The story is touching, the heroine has the quality of one who has learned to be good by the cynical way. The skill displayed by the writer was essential to keep the values of the story subtly but unmistakably different from melodrama.

The Old Maid has been the most appreciated of this group of stories; and indeed its portrayal of fierce maternity is a contribution to psychological fiction, and its study of the suppressions of New York Victorianism, another claim for Mrs. Wharton as the best social historian of her native city. It, too, is technically difficult and technically excellent; but I prefer the milder *False Dawn*, as one who likes best a chef *d'oeuvre* of virtuosity or a simple chronicle simply told. *False Dawn* contains by implication the history of the timid æstheticism of æsthetic America amid bustle and brashness. The youth who acquires Italian primitives before they are fashionable is faced down by his mob, yet sticks by them, pathetically ineffective. His earnestness, his lack of self-confidence; the exploiters who profit by his heritage which has profited him nothing but resolution and pain: all this is an allegory, if you please, in the Hawthorne manner, of the taste for beauty in America. The story was easy to tell if you knew it, though not easy to tell as Mrs. Wharton has told it. I like *False Dawn* immensely. I admire *The Old Maid* and *New Year's Day*.

The dating of these stories in the 40's, 50's, 60's, and 70's seems a little adventitious, but their joint title *Old New York* is just. They are better read as a group

than read singly. An atmosphere accompanies them. We shall begrudge from now on Paris, Italy, London in Mrs. Wharton's stories. She can evoke our own past age of heroic innocence. She should be urged to send her imagination home more often; to keep it South of Forty-Second Street; unless indeed she has lurking another memory of the Berkshires, a second *Ethan Frome*.

"Mrs. Wharton,"
Times Literary Supplement [England], 11 September 1924, p. 553

The simultaneous publication of Mrs. Wharton's four long stories of *Old New York* and of an English edition of *Ethan Frome* enables us to measure more precisely the development of her talent during the thirteen years that separate them. During that time Mrs. Wharton's position in the world of letters has greatly changed. With *Ethan Frome* she impressed herself on the minds of that cultivated minority for which we have no more convenient name than the un-English one of the *intelligentsia*. There was a year in which everyone who knew what was what in contemporary literature had to have his opinion of *Ethan Frome*. Since those days Mrs. Wharton has achieved popularity. *The Age of Innocence* enjoyed a prodigious success in America and no small one in this country; and its author has finally enrolled in the blessed and somewhat mysterious company of American "best-sellers."

Progress of that kind is frequently lamented by the austere as a sort of rake's progress from artistic immaculacy. But if anyone were in search of a decisive proof of the reasonable contention that an increase of popularity is as often evidence of an increase in the skill and significance of the writer as of a diminution of his artistic conscience, no better instance than Mrs. Wharton could be found. Her popularity has been the reward of her maturity. Her later work shows a remarkable growth of strength and security. The ease of her narration, the certainty of her technical control over the art of storytelling, the elimination of preciousness from her language, the sense of the materiality of her backgrounds, are qualities which were hardly more than nascent in *Ethan Frome*; now they are in full flower. The ease of the natural writer, if the term will serve for one who has achieved spontaneity by right of conquest, is so marked in Mrs. Wharton's latest work, that it strikes one as a curious survival, like the persistence of some rudimentary and primitive elements in a highly civilized religion, that the crises of her plots should still be sometimes forced and melodramatic. Just as the attempted suicide in *Ethan Frome* seemed an event foreign to the temper of the narrative, an object which could not be assimilated into the surrounding atmosphere and showed like a property painted into the picture by another hand, so in the story called *New Year's Day* there is a similar discrepancy. It is more subtle, more deeply knit into the substance of the narrative, as befits a maturer art; but for all that it strikes us, and in fact more forcibly, as a downright psychological impossibility. That Lizzie Hazeldean should have become Henry Prest's mistress in order that her invalid husband should not lack necessary comforts, or be eaten up by the anxiety of poverty, is frankly incredible. That kind of some heroism—if indeed it be a real heroism and not some ancient invention of a romantic brain—is not possible for that kind of love. And, oddly enough, it is

not necessary to Mrs. Wharton's story. It is possible that Lizzie Hazeldean, out of the mere weariness of agony for her husband, might have succumbed to a lover as to a drug; but that she should have deliberately sought one as the only means within her power by which she could obtain the money that was necessary is the kind of thing which, as they say, happens only in books.

Another strain is put upon our sense of verisimilitude by the story *The Old Maid*. It is a tale of New York in the eighteen-fifties. Delia Ralston and Charlotte Lovell are cousins. But whereas Charlotte is impecunious, Delia, having properly suppressed a romantic inclination to young Clement Spender the artist, is comfortably married to Jim Ralston, a prosperous member of the prosperous tribe of Ralstons. And now, by a miracle, Charlotte the unmarriageable has set fire to the heart of his brother Joe. But there is a difficulty. The Ralstons (who think as a body corporate) object to Charlotte's continuing to devote herself to a day nursery for slum children which she started on her return from a long sojourn in the South, where she sought health after a mysterious illness, given out to be of the lungs. There is an impasse: Charlotte cannot give up her children, nor Joe Ralston his precaution against contagion to his children-to-be. So Charlotte goes with her trouble to Delia, to receive cold comfort. After all, she is being unreasonable. There is nothing for it; Charlotte confesses: one of the children is really her own, and Clem Spender is the father. She cannot give Tina up. So Delia, Ralston enough to take for granted that it is now out of the question for Charlotte to marry Joe, takes control of the situation. She will take to her bosom Clem's child, and arrange that Charlotte and Tina shall live together, and she will tell Joe that the engagement must be broken because Charlotte has had a re-

370

currence of her lung trouble. The scheme succeeds. Charlotte and her child live together in a remote farmhouse, and all the solid world knows that Charlotte is again recovering from her illness, and that her baffled maternal instinct needs the loved foundling to assuage it. To Tina Charlotte is her aunt.

Six years later Delia's husband dies, and Delia takes them both to her own house. Tina grows into a beauty, and into the habit of calling "Mamma" and Charlotte "Aunt"—an aunt who is very much of the precise old maid. According to her creator, Charlotte will have it so. It is an excellent situation, and the scene is set for a tense struggle between the two women for the soul of the girl. Mrs. Wharton has arranged it with extraordinary skill and economy: to have reached this point without impeding the flow of her narrative in a hundred tiny pages (not more than forty of an ordinary novel) is a triumph of exposition. Yet through all our admiration an obstinate misgiving persists. Is it not, we find ourselves asking, too beautifully contrived? Would Charlotte, could Charlotte, really have taken such an attitude? Could she have lived six years alone with Tina and been to her no more than a rather forbidding aunt? If such a situation can be made convincing, Mrs. Wharton has made it so. But in spite of ourselves (for the art is such that we are anxious to succumb to it) we are not convinced; and because of this doubt Charlotte herself becomes unreal and ghostly, and the silent struggle between the women, again most beautifully managed, a drama without real disputants.

Of the subtlety of Mrs. Wharton's narration there could be no better proof than the necessity of so long an account of but one-half of her story in order to show wherein the flaw consists. Mrs. Wharton cannot escape the defect of her quality: her handling of a plot is consummate, but

precisely because she has such skill in giving verisimilitude to her delicate contrivance she sharpens our keenness to detect its weakness. Her plots are not of the kind for which we are called to make that willing suspension of disbelief which constitutes poetic faith. No such initial act of faith is required of us. We glide into their intricacies as a realistic representation of life; and as we accept them naturally we criticize them naturally. We cannot suddenly make an act of faith when we have not been required to make one before. To a writer of a different kind we can give the benefit of the doubt over a hundred improbable coincidences, such as Mrs. Wharton would never dream of trying to impose upon us. But she, in tracing out the firm lines of her psychological pattern, suddenly makes a demand upon our sense of the probable in human character; and we cannot admit it. She requires her pattern perfect, and she makes a sacrifice to that perfection of something that cannot be sacrificed.

It is no accident therefore that the most truly satisfying of these four stories of *Old New York* are the two with the simplest structure: *False Dawn* and *The Spark*; nor is it an accident that there is a close relation between the two conceptions. *False Dawn* is a tale of the 'forties. A young man, only son of an opulent and slightly Pecksniffian Raycie, is sent to Europe to make the grand tour and given the supreme commission of buying enough rich brown, thoroughly guaranteed Old Masters to form a Raycie gallery. A Raphael is out of the question; but a Carlo Dolci, a Guido Reni, a Sassoferrato, a Salvator Rosa will do very well. Young Raycie goes on his mission; and somewhere in the Italian Alps meets a young man of his own age who opens his eyes to the beauty of the Italian primitives. The young man is John Ruskin. Raycie returns with a Piero della Francesca instead

371

of a Carlo Dolci for the *clou* of the collection. His father, indignant to the verge of apoplexy, cuts him out of his will except for the ironical legacy of the unestablished pictures, and dies. Young Raycie, with the fervour of an apostle, tries to reveal the loveliness of his pictures to an indifferent New York. He and his pictures are neglected and forgotten. Many years afterwards the pictures are turned out of an old lumber-room and sold for a few millions; even the survivors of the family can scarcely remember whence they came.

The Spark is even better. It turns on the chance encounter of a young volunteer in the Civil War with Walt Whitman in hospital. He does not know who Whitman is, but the great man makes his impression; and Hayley Delane has this remembered figure at his elbow through his life as a courageous conscience, driving him to do things which his New York society cannot comprehend. The story is beautifully told: it comes through the lips of a young man of a later generation who at once despises and serenely admires Hayley, and finally becomes his intimate. One day Hayley, in the midst of one of his lonely struggles for the good, drops in on his young friend and sees a portrait of his hero in a book. The young friend, enthusiastic at the discovery, reads some of Whitman's poems.

A little timidly, he spoke at length. "Did *he* write that?"

"Yes; just about the time you were seeing him, probably."

Delane still brooded; his expression grew more and more timid. "What do you ... er ... call it ... exactly?" he ventured.

I was puzzled for a moment; then: "Why, poetry ... rather a free form, of course. ... You see, he was an originator of new verse-forms."

"New verse-forms?" Delane ech-

oed forlornly. He stood up in his heavy way, but did not offer to take the book from me again. I saw in his face the symptoms of approaching departure.

"Well, I'm glad to have seen his picture after all these years," he said; and on the threshold he paused to ask: "What was his name, by the way?"

When I told him he repeated it with a smile of slow relish. "Yes; that's it. Old Walt—that was what all the fellows used to call him. He was a great chap. I'll never forget him—I rather wish, though," he added, in his mildest tone of reproach, "you hadn't told me that he wrote all that rubbish."

In its kind—and the kind is a distinguished one—*The Spark* is a masterpiece. It contains no trace of discrepancy; the intricate craft of the telling is wholly subdued to the perception of truth, and in unity and the depth of feeling and formal perfection it easily surpasses *False Dawn*, though that is an excellent story. But in both these tales, it is worth remarking, the assumptions we are called on to make —the meeting of young Raycie with Ruskin, the meeting of Delane with Whitman—we make with the utmost ease. An artist of Mrs. Wharton's eminence has full liberty to arrange events to suit her purposes, provided that they are merely events, dependent on whatever power it is that disposes the kaleidoscope of the world; but that she should arrange events that are not merely events, but the manifestations of human character, we cannot allow.

372

James L. Ford, "Maligning Old New York,"

Literature Digest International Book Review, 2 (October 1924), 785–6

To recreate in the printed page any period antedating the memory of the writer is a task that often baffles even those novelists who have shown skill in the portrayal of contemporary life. The usual procedure is to disinter from newspaper files and books of reference the more noteworthy happenings of the era, and by bunching them with the names of persons notorious at the time, endeavor to reproduce the atmosphere and spirit of days long gone by. But no bald recital of this sort can convey to the reader of to-day a trustworthy idea of life and conditions in a remote decade. Such information as lies within easy reach of any patient investigator is worthless unless vitalized by something that only the author's brain can supply. And in that something is contained the germ of the elusive quality called atmosphere, which should savor the whole.

Quite recently public attention has been drawn to the New York of the last century, and this interest has been fed by many volumes of personal reminiscence treating largely of the town in its social and artistic aspects. Coincidentally there have appeared books of a wider scope, and novels which aimed to give to past decades an air of verisimilitude. An interesting and it seemed to me a fairly accurate history by hearsay of a decade that lies beyond my own recollection was *The Fabulous Forties*, by Mr. Minnigerode,

native of the Southland, where national traditions are more carefully preserved than here. More recently we have had books by Mrs. Wharton and Mr. Thomas Beer which have entered the best-seller lists, and for that reason, if none other, are worthy of special consideration.

These writers have set for themselves a risky task, one that is certain to court merciless criticism should their efforts attract wide-spread attention. For New York contains in the midst of its many alien peoples a native element larger than is generally believed; among whom are many gray-haired persons with long and tenacious memories to whom the city's soil is sacred and her history and traditions objects of reverential worship. In their breasts survives the spirit of that devoted lover of the town, Washington Irving. When such as these assemble for social converse the talk is certain to relate to the city of their youthful days, and as they are diligent readers of everything printed on the subject the careless chronicle is apt to receive a sharp letter on his inaccuracy. These veterans read more newspaper than bound books, which is a fortunate thing for Mrs. Wharton, author of four thin volumes, termed *Old New York.*

In *False Dawn*, purporting to deal with New York of the fifth decade of the last century, there is a brief allusion to Edgar Poe and his wife living in extreme poverty in the "cottage down the lane," since removed to the Concourse as one of the city's show-places. There is also mention of one or two localities then fashionable, but otherwise there is no attempt at the local color readers might be led to expect. Instead we find a long-drawn-out and highly improbable tale of a young man of high social position sent abroad by his wealthy father to purchase the nucleus of a great picture gallery. But the youth fails to acquire the Raphaels and other "old

373

masters" desired by his sire and brings back a collection of paintings by unknown artists, the result being that he is cut off in the paternal will and inherits only a moderate income and the pictures on which he has wasted so much money.

But his faith in his own judgement does not waver, and after he has married and established himself in the then desirable neighborhood of Third Avenue and Tenth Street he displays his pictures in a gallery on the premises and hangs up a sign inviting the public to view them for the low price of a quarter of a dollar. Many people come, look scornfully at the exhibit and depart, believing the young man a fool for his pains. Many, many years later, the paintings are disinterred from the garret of an old New York house and subjected to the discriminating appraisal of more enlightened modern critics, who discover that the thirty are worth five million dollars.

The absurdity of this tale must be apparent to everybody at all familiar with the history of New York. The town of the 'forties was not entirely illiterate, but contained a cultivated society not blind to literary and artistic excellences. Mr. Samuel Ward had already established his gallery at the corner of Broadway and Bond Street, and other private collections were under way. Philip Hone, writing in 1839, describes the annual banquet of the National Academy of Design, then a well-known institution. Nearly coincident with the opening of the young connoisseur's exhibition on Third Avenue was the merging of the Sketch Club into the Century, which still ranks high among the clubs of the town. Washington Irving, William Cullen Bryant, Fitz-Greene Halleck, James K. Paulding, Guilian C. Verplanck, Henry K. Brown, N. P. Willis, and many artists of distinct talent, were all living in New York in the 'forties, and were quite as appreciative of paintings as

any of the steel-puddlers and copper-smelters whose homes line upper Fifth Avenue and whose collections have enriched the dealers who made their selections for them.

In the second volume of her series Mrs. Wharton tells the story of the *Old Maid*, and lays her scene in the 'fifties, tho what she relates might have happened in any other decade. She makes no attempt at local color save in her enumeration of a few of the works of art and decoration then in vogue, such as Cole's "Voyage of Life" and a statue by Harriet Hosmer. As in the case of her previous works, *The House of Mirth* and *The Age of Innocence*, she treats exclusively of a very small element in the city's social structure and does it, too, in a manner that suggests the non-existence of any other body. There is no mention in her pages of the many events that left their indelible impress on the town during the sixth decade.

A greater disappointment awaits the old-time citizen who enters upon the reading of *The Spark*, expecting to find in its pages a picture of New York during the momentous 'sixties. I was but a very small boy when that memorable decade began, but so deeply did its many stirring happenings impress themselves on my young mind that I took up *The Spark* in a spirit of delightful anticipation. A flood of memories crowded my brain as I turned the first page and recalled the visit of the Prince of Wales and the nearly contemporary one of the Japanese. Then came the firing on Fort Sumter, followed by Lincoln's call for troops, and soon I was surprised to note the appearance in our house of certain family friends clad in blue and with epaulets on their shoulders, a style of sartorial decoration entirely new to me. The fighting seemed very close to us, for regiments were hurriedly mustering and marching off to the front. The war fever raged to an extent unknown since then, and it affected us all, women as well as men, and even children, for we were set to work picking lint for surgical bandages, and everybody was singing "Rally Round the Flag, Boys," and "Tramp, Tramp, Tramp."

Of theatrical entertainment in those far-off days I recall Kate Bateman in "The Lady of Lyons" and the awe-inspiring feats of the Ravels, those matchless panto-mimists. Then the "Black Crook" stag-gered the town with its swarm of un-draped women, and the dust flew from pulpit cushions as the clergy denounced it. And Barnum's Museum was burnt—but enough of these futile maunderings! I have only mentioned certain happenings to show what I expected to find in a book dealing with the sixth decade of the last century under the title of *Old New York*. What I did find was a tale of recent times, in which one of the characters referred in conversation to the Civil War.

My hopes of local color revived as I turned to the volume dedicated to the 'seventies and saw that it was called *New Year's Day*, for I well remember my boy-ish enjoyment of that yearly holiday, when my brother and I made the rounds of the family friends for the sake of the refresh-ments provided at every house on our route. To this day the taste of that al-most obsolete delicacy, the pickled oyster, awakens memories of those well-spread tables. But of that hospitable old New York custom Mrs. Wharton's book con-veys only a meager impression, so intent is she in the telling of a tale that might be credited to any time and any place. The scandal on which the tale is founded rests on the very insecure foundation of a glimpse obtained by a New Year's party of a man and woman emerging from the Fifth Avenue Hotel. The pair might just as well have been caught in the act of leaving Central Park, for the lobby of that hotel was a thoroughfare and the house itself respectable in the highest degree.

Checklist of Additional Reviews

Edwin Francis Edgett, "Edith Wharton Depicts Old New York," Boston *Evening Transcript*, 24 May 1924, p. 4.

E. W. Osborn, review of *Old New York*, New York *World*, 25 May 1924, p. 7–E.

A. Donald Douglas, "Mrs. Wharton's Period Novels," New York *Herald Tribune*, 8 June 1924, book section, pp. 21–2.

Stanley Alden, "Edith Wharton, as Writer of Comedy," Springfield [Massachusetts] *Republican*, 31 August 1924, p. 7–A.

Régis Michaud, "Scénes de la vie New–Yorkaise," *Revue Anglo-Américaine* [France], (2 February 1925), 275–77.

THE WRITING OF FICTION

The Writing of Fiction

By

EDITH WHARTON

Order the beauty even of Beauty is.
—THOMAS TRAHERNE.

CHARLES SCRIBNER'S SONS

NEW YORK ▸ LONDON

1925

Brander Matthews, "A Story-Teller on the Art of Story-Telling," *Literary Digest International Book Review*, 3 (October 1925), 731–2

In this era of multitudinous anthologizing it is to be wondered at that no competent compiler has been moved to make a collection of the critical essays written by the novelists on the art of the novel. Howells and Henry James, Stevenson and Zola, were never tired of talking about story-telling and of declaring the laws of fiction, discussing its principles and setting forth its possibilities and its limitations. It may be doubted whether the result of the incursions of these practitioners of the art of fiction into the dangerous territory of theorizing has been altogether to their profit; and probably Hardy and Kipling have been wise in abstaining from the analysis of the craft in which they excel. Hawthorne stept outside the pages of his story only once when he insisted on the essential difference between the romance and the novel. Maupassant wrote only the preface to *Pierre et Jean* wherein he said his say about the scope of the novel; and Henry James thought scorn of this single attempt—probably because it exprest sharply opinions which he did not share. And now Mrs. Wharton, in the maturity of her power as a creator of character, has chosen to descend into the crucial arena.

It is immediately evident that she has thought clearly about the problems of her calling, and that what she says in this little volume—and says so well—was well worth saying. So, indeed, were many of the things which Howells, Henry James, Stevenson, Zola and Maupassant said. When the masters of a craft are willing to tell us what they think about it, what they think it ought to be, what its processes are, what its ultimate aim is—whenever this happens, we who are readers of fiction and not makers of it will do well to listen and to ponder, and to profit by what we hear. We do not have to ponder long before we perceive that these accomplished craftsmen are—all of them and all unwittingly, it may be—pleading for themselves. They are dwelling on the merits of the special kind of fiction they themselves are engaged in making; and they tend to be a little intolerant of all the other kinds.

They are inclined to be a little rigid, and sometimes more than a little. We can not help feeling an occasional deficiency in catholicity, as tho each of these devout worshipers at the shrine were convinced that the true faith was to be found only in his own chapel of the Cathedral and only at his own private altar. They are sometimes cruelly contemptuous toward those whom they hold to be heretics. Howells in America and Zola in France heaped high the faggots for the pyre to which they doomed the despised romanticists; and even Stevenson was, for once, a little lacking in geniality when he refused to be a pale martyr in a sheet of fire. It must be difficult (and it may be impossible) for a master of the craft to listen dispassionately to the empty futilities—as he can not but consider them—put forth pugnaciously by the adherents of another faith; and he is moved almost irresistibly to lay down the law and to declare a Draconian code to be obeyed of all men at their peril. And no two of them lay down the same laws.

A French critic (whom I can not now identify, altho I believe it was that stalwart historian of French literature, Ferdinand Brunetière) once asserted that the atrophy of French tragedy toward the end

379

of the eighteenth century was due to the fact that it was strangled by a multiplicity of indisputable rules, prescribing an imitation of the dead-and-gone masters and proscribing every innovation, whereas in those same years the novel, then dismissed as an inferior form, was despised by the theorists, who left it alone to expand of its own free will with no inexorable constraints, the result being that prose fiction went on its way, flourishing, expanding and developing a vigorous vitality in contrast to the puny ineffectiveness of tragedy. About the time that I noted this remark of Brunetière's—if it was his—I happened on the catalog of an autograph dealer, in which there was a letter of Sainte-Beuve's (even now not included in his correspondence). That modern "master of all who know" wrote to Champfleury in 1860 (when the earliest strivings of realism were becoming visible) a brief note from which I translate these sentences:

The novel has remained free—so much the better for it; and this has not prevented it from having masterpieces. The novel is a vast field of experiment open to all the forms of genius, to all methods. It is the future epic, probably the only one hereafter conformable to our modern manners. Let us refrain from restricting it. Let us avoid too much theorizing about it. Let every novelist on occasion set forth his ideas. So best! but let these expositions and apologies not cost us a single good novel that the author might have composed in the same time. The best explanation an artist can give is to produce continuously, to go forward and to keep on the march!

Could anything be more characteristically sensible than this? It is a warning that Howells and Zola might have heeded to advantage. It is a warning that Mrs. Wharton needs. She continues to produce—to the increase of our pleasure. She is going forward; and she keeps on the march. She is not intolerant or intransigent. Of course, like all her predecessors, she is tempted to codify her own practise into principles; or perhaps it would be fairer to say that what she has given us in this richly suggestive study is a statement of the principles which she has applied herself, because they have been approved by the modern masters at whose feet she has sat—Thackeray and Balzac, Turgenev and Tolstoy. She has a clear vision and she seizes the essential. She is not dogmatic nor domineering. In her theorizing about fiction, as in her own novels, she knows what she wants to say; she knows why she wants to say it; and she knows how to say it so that we can not help but hear. And what she has to say will be profitable even to the most accomplished of her fellow-craftsmen. Yet it is likely to be even more elucidating to the alert novel reader. There is a growing host who take their pleasure intelligently, and who joy in grasping the secrets of the art which enchants them.

Mrs. Wharton places herself by the side of Sainte-Beuve when she begins her book with the assertion that "to treat of the practise of fiction is to deal with the newest, most fluid and least formulated of the arts." And nothing could be less restrictive than the assertion in her final chapter that

There is no fixt rule about this or any other method; each, in the art of fiction, to justify itself has only to succeed. But to succeed, the method must first of all suit the subject, must find its account as best it can, with the difficulties peculiar to each situation.

Mrs. Wharton starts on her task with a general survey of the art of fiction, with a consideration of its slow development in the eighteenth century and of its superb outflowering in the nineteenth. Then she studies the short story with a discussion of its possibilities and of its limitations, seemingly unaware of the earlier, and in some respects ampler, analysis of Prof. Bliss Perry (who in his youth made more than one incursion into fiction, proving once more that the theorist is always more competent when he has himself been a practitioner of the art he is investigating). Then she devotes nearly half her space to the novel itself, and more especially to the technical problems of its construction, noting by the way the practical impossibility of drawing "a definite line between the technique of a work of art and its informing spirit."

She notes also that "the arts in their earlier stages are seldom theorized on by those engaged in creating them"— criticism here, as always, following after creation. She records that later writers, creators turned critics, are prone to lay down rules, "and in the search for new forms and more complex effects may even become the slaves of their too-fascinating theories"—as Henry James did, and after him Joseph Conrad. Then after sympathetically appreciating the vain efforts of the writers who are subdued to what they work in, she adds, "these are the true pioneers, who are never destined to see their own work fulfilled, but build intellectual houses for the next generation to live in." And she ends her all-too-short treatise—if that is not too severe a word— with a cordial study of Proust, explaining the apparent paradox of his seeming to be an innovator when he was really a renovator, a conserver of the noblest traditions.

I wish that space did not now fail me to make more copious quotation, since it is only by citing Mrs. Wharton's own words that I can show the clarity of her intelligence, the solidity of her judgement, and the delicacy of her style. In criticism as in creation she is a master-craftsman; and in this criticism she has supplied the standard by which she would desire to have her creation measured. But I can not deny myself the pleasure and the profit of excerpting here two sentences, perhaps no worthier of quotation than others that I might have chosen. She tells us that the great, the distinguishing gift of Henry Fielding "was a homely simplicity combined with an observation at once keen and indulgent; good humor was the atmosphere and irony the flavor of this great school of observers from Fielding to George Eliot." And a little later she remarks that

All the restraints of prudery which hampered the English novelists of the nineteenth century security have come down with a crash, and the "now-that-it-can-be-told-school" (as some one has wittily named it) has rushed to the opposite excess of dirt-for-dirt's-sake, from which no real work of art has ever sprung. Such a reaction was inevitable. No one who remembers that Butler's great novel, "The Way of All Flesh," remained unpublished for over twenty years because it dealt soberly but sincerely with the chief springs of human conduct can wonder that laborious monuments of schoolboy pornography are mistaken for works of genius by a public ignorant of Rabelais and unaware of Apuleius. The balance will right itself with the habit of freedom. The new novelists will learn that it is even more necessary to see life steadily than to recount it whole; and by that time a more thoughtful public may be ripe for the enjoyment of a riper age.

"This Week's Books," *Spectator* [England], 135 (7 November 1925), 836

There have been many books written lately on how to write, nearly all of them being either directions on how to supply what can be easily marketed or subterranean meditations by writers who were anxious to relieve themselves by analysing their own literary birth pangs. It is very refreshing to read Mrs. Wharton on *The Writing of Fiction.* . . . It is a direct and thoughtful piece of communication; a little book consisting of chapters on fiction and its development in general; on telling a short story; on character and situation in the novel; and on Marcel Proust. It would be difficult to summarize or take extracts from the book—it is so well knit—but here is one passage in which Mrs. Wharton is actually giving direct advice:—

> "The short story writer must not only know from what angle to present his anecdote if it is to give out all its fire, but must understand just *why* that particular angle and no other is the right one. He must have turned his subject over and over, walked around it, so to speak, and applied to it those laws of perspective which Paolo Uccello called 'so beautiful,' before it can be offered to the reader as a natural unembellished fragment of experience, detached like a ripe fruit from the tree. The moment the writer begins to grope in the tangle of his 'material,' to hesitate between one and another of the points that any actual happening thrusts up in such disorderly abundance, the reader feels a corresponding hesitancy, and the illusion of reality vanishes."

Lloyd Morris, "Mrs. Wharton Discusses the Art of Fiction," *New York Times Book Review*, 15 November 1925, p. 2

The criticism of art divides into two general kinds: that which attempts to define what an art ought to do; and that which attempts to determine what an art actually does. Plato, in his dialogues on poetic inspiration, illustrates the first kind; Aristotle, in his "Poetics," the second. The difference in intention is sharply reflected in difference in method. Plato set forth the ideal function of poetry; Aristotle, preoccupying himself with the drama that had flourished in Greece, studied its effect upon the audience and the means whereby that effect was accomplished. Criticism of the first kind conceives esthetic as a province of philosophy, like metaphysics, and produces general theories of beauty. Criticism of the second kind is concerned with art as the artist and his audience are concerned with it; it studies practice as the accomplishment of intention and seeks to clarify the processes by which intention is actually accomplished and predetermined effects are produced.

To fiction criticism of the first kind has accumulated with disquieting generosity. But in criticism of the second, more valuable kind, fiction is conspicuously deficient. Esthetic investigation has loitered behind practice with deplorable indolence. The insignificant elucidation of practice, despite a phenomenal production of textbooks on the short story and the novel, is all but restricted to Flaubert's letters, the prefaces of Henry James and Mr. Lubbock's admirable preliminary study for an esthetic of the novel.

Meanwhile, the contemporary condition of the art urgently invites the service of this special criticism. The efficacy of traditional conventions and methods, long employed but still imperfectly understood, is being questioned. An innovative technique has begun to offer new solutions to old problems. The practice of fiction is responding to the influence of intentions hitherto undefined. The novel, which in English literature has always been the most fluid and least formulated of media, appears to be becoming something other than it has ever been. In the circumstances, esthetic investigation might begin with the study of the medium of language, examine the psychology of rhetoric, never adequately explored, and pass on to an accurate analysis of the processes whereby, in the art of narrative, intended effects are brought to successful achievement. It is from the novelist rather than from the professional critic that this ministration is to be expected, for the affair is an inquiry into the economy of an art: in this the artist should be the most competent of experts. Ideas about an art derive their validity from the fundamental conditions to which the art is subject; the resources and limitations of its medium, the psychology of response by an audience to stimulation by that medium. Of these conditions the disciplined artist may be supposed to possess the most intimate knowledge: experience confers authority upon his conclusions.

Mrs. Wharton, writing of the practice of fiction, undertakes no such comprehensive inquiry. In four lucid essays—her prose is admirably clear—she sustains a number of familiar doctrines with contentions equally familiar. A fifth essay, devoted to the work of Marcel Proust, is appended apparently in illustration of what has gone before. Mrs. Wharton contributes no new ideas to our enlightenment; the notable excellence of her volume is its adequacy as a summary. Excellent as this service is, its limitation is a disappointment, for Mrs. Wharton is distinguished, among our novelists of established reputation, profound concentration upon the craft of her art, and her endowment of wisdom might have yielded more valuable gifts. That wisdom occasionally sheds a clear light upon perplexing problems in the course of parenthetical observations, as in the case of her discussion of the "descriptive passage." But more frequently its condensation results in inadequacy: her remarks upon the way in which a novelist may communicate the effect of the gradual passage of time, for example, compare disadvantageously with Mr. Lubbock's masterly analysis of methods available for the achievements of this effect.

Certain of the doctrines which Mrs. Wharton advances stimulate discussion. "A good subject," she states, "must contain in itself something that sheds a light on our moral experience." The remark appears innocent enough: from one point of view all experience is moral experience. Reflection suggests, however, that the illumination is not inherent to the subject, but is an effect of the treatment given that subject by the novelist. When Mrs. Wharton assures us that "any subject in itself must first of all respond in some way to that mysterious need of judgement on life of which the most detached human intellect, provided it be a normal one, cannot, apparently, rid itself"; when she further assures us that "in one form or another there must be some sort of rational response to the reader's unconscious but insistent inner question: 'What am I being told this story for?' 'What judgement on life does it contain for me?'"—she appears to be confusing significance with moral edification. The psychology of fiction-reading is probably more simple than her statements indicate. The reader usually reads a novel for enjoyment. Enjoyment is an effect of entering upon a vicarious experiences interesting in itself, and yielding a perception of meaning more intelligible than those yielded by the majority of experiences to which the reader submits in actual life. An extension of repertory in experience, and an extension of insight into life appear to be the real, if unconscious, satisfactions sought by the reader of fiction. They can scarcely be said to be equivalent with a "judgement on life" or moral verdict upon experience, though undiscriminating readers frequently assume an identity.

It is interesting, in view of Mrs. Wharton's position in contemporary fiction as an exponent of traditional technique, to consider her discussion of the more notable recent technical innovations in the novel. Chief of these, perhaps, is the method of psychological naturalism; what Mrs. Wharton terms the "stream of consciousness method." Mrs. Wharton does not name the writers whom she considers exponents of that method, but it may be assumed that she would include Joyce, Virginia Woolf, Dorothy Richardson, Valery Larbaud, and most of the "surrealistes." The method, Mrs. Wharton asserts, is similar to that employed by those early French realists who produced the "slice of life."

The stream of consciousness method differs from the slice of life in noting mental as well as visual reactions, but resembles it in setting them down just as they come, with a deliberate disregard of their relevance in the particular case, or rather with the assumption that their very unsorted abundance constitutes in itself the author's subject.

Mrs. Wharton's objection to the method is founded upon an assumption that it is essentially non-selective, hence, by definition, non-esthetic. Yet it seems difficult to deny the existence of a basal selective process in the work, let us say, of Joyce; a process necessarily the more discriminating by reason of the fact that its object is to produce an effect of indiscrimination. Critical objection to the method appears to require a more substantial foundation than the mere assertion that it rejects the process of selection. Nor does Mrs. Wharton materially improve her case by asserting that the method has, in the past, been employed by "most of the greatest novelists, not as an end in itself, but as it happened to serve their general design; as when their object was to portray a mind in one of those moments of acute mental stress when it records with meaningless precision a series of disconnected impressions."

All of the greatest of them, from Balzac and Thackeray onward [she later adds] have made use of the stammerings and murmurings of the half-conscious mind whenever—but only when—such a state of mental flux fitted into the whole picture of the person portrayed. Their observation showed them that in the world of normal men life is conducted, at least in its decisive moments, on fairly coherent and selective lines, and that only thus can the great fundamental affairs of bread-getting and home-and-tribe organizing be carried on. Drama, situation, is made out of conflicts thus produced between social order

384

and individual appetites, and the art of rendering life in fiction can never, in the last analysis, be anything, or need to be anything, but the disengaging of crucial moments from the welter of experience.

Mrs. Wharton supplements her discussion of the practice of fiction by an essay on Marcel Proust. Of Proust she says that "his endowment as a novelist—his range of presentation combined with mastery of his instrument—has probably never been surpassed." She deplores his occasional lapses from what she terms "moral sensibility," and asserts that in them his characters lose their vitality and become mere puppets. As an example she cites the famous episode in which the narrator of the cycle conceals himself to spy upon a scene between the Baron de Charlus and Julien. But French critics, although equally perplexed by the moral problem offered by this scene, have not, like Mrs. Wharton, solved it by denying power to the scene itself; her explanation is scarcely convincing, and the problem still remains to the reader. Her praise of Proust centres upon his power of evocation, his capacity for making his characters live. "Proust," she observes, "is in truth the aware and eager inheritor of two great formulas: that of Racine in his psychology, that of Saint Simon in its anecdotic and discursive illustration. In both respects he is deliberately traditional." In his psychology, although no other author has "carried as far the analysis of half-conscious states of mind, obscure associations of thought, and gelatinous fluctuations of mood," Proust's object is always "to report the conscious, purposive conduct of his characters." He believed that "the proper study of mankind is man's conscious and purposive behavior rather than its dim unfathomable sources." Mrs. Wharton does not, to our loss, analyze the difference between Proust's method of dealing with "half-conscious states of mind" and the method which she terms "the stream of consciousness method." Proust deals, not with the immediate content of consciousness, but with that content as reconstituted by memory; it is the selective process of memory which contributes the design. The psychological naturalists, however, deal with the immediate content of consciousness, before automatic selection has begun to operate upon it; in their work design is not inherent to the material, but imposed—as, for example, in *Ulysses*—by a formal esthetic structure. This fundamental difference in method probably explains a characteristic difference in effects; one wishes that Mrs. Wharton had enriched our knowledge by her discussion.

Her little book serves admirably as an introduction to the general problems of narrative art. It may be pondered profitably by readers of fiction, and writers will find it at least provocative. Perhaps it is not too much to hope that Mrs. Wharton, at some future time, may be disposed to produce, for the benefit of both, a more comprehensive discussion of the esthetic of fiction.

Osburt Burdett, "Contemporary American Authors, I: Edith Wharton," *London Mercury*, 13 (25 November 1925), 52–61

As I write, four essays on *The Writing of Fiction* are announced. They take the form of analysing the technique of the short story and the novel, and of constructing characters and situations. In this book we do not find an artist expressing opinions on his favourite masters, but a student classifying masterpieces and giving us the benefit of her experience with her tools. The book, in fact, is a text-book for beginners and critics, but it has more than a technical interest. It is a valuable piece of evidence of the mind that has gone to the creation of the novels, and I do not find in it anything to alter the judgement I have ventured on them. They possess more form than feeling. Hawthorne evokes where Mrs. Wharton describes, and he was often as poor in construction as she is capable. It so happens that they have one scene in common, where the two types of imagination may be compared. The difference is felt in the prose. The mind waits on Mrs. Wharton's style, attentive, alert, and interested. To Hawthorne's the ear answers as to music. It is rare to find writers as true to their respective types as these, and the art of prose narrative has room and need for both of them.

J. B. Priestley, "The Novelist's Art," *Spectator* [England], 135 (5 December 1925), 1047

As a subject for criticism, fiction is still a gigantic virgin continent, compared with which other forms of literature are overpopulated little islands, all mapped, measured and drained ages ago. Now and then an explorer sets out for this unknown territory, or a group of pioneers clear away some of the undergrowth. Thus, Henry James in his critical prefaces may be said to have made camps and trails right across the continent. Then came Mr. Percy Lubbock, with his *Craft of Fiction*, who succeeded in linking up all these camps

with a light railway. And in her new book, Mrs. Wharton may be said to take a trip on this railway, but occasionally she makes not unladylike excursions into the surrounding jungle. In her last chapter (there are only five in all), we hear a great crashing in the undergrowth, and we see her emerge in triumph leading a jungle monster she has discovered and captured, one Marcel Proust. Her little study, consisting of short chapters on the Short Story, Constructing a Novel, Character and Situation, is very sensible indeed, but not only is it rather slight, it is also rather scrappy. The text, though presented smoothly enough, suggests notes rather than an argument. It may be urged that this is no disadvantage, that the subject of technique in fiction is so vast that an approach to it by way of scattered notes instead of a closely-woven argument (like that of Mr. Lubbock) is more likely to be fruitful in results. But the business of presenting and proving a thesis, of developing an argument, demands more consistency and clarity of thought than the business of producing notes, random comments. And the richer the subject, the more extensive its ramifications, the more necessary it is to think clearly and consistently about it. For example, I do not think that if Mrs. Wharton had been developing an argument, she would have talked of "the novel of manners," as she does so frequently in these pages. She would have left such a crude category to the literary historians, who must, of necessity, work with the clumsiest tools. The fact that her study is slight and scrappy—a bundle of notes rather than a closely-woven argument— makes it disappointing, and we cannot accept it as a companion volume to Mr. Lubbock's *Craft of Fiction*. But Mrs. Wharton has practised and reflected upon her art too long and too scrupulously not to give us some really valuable comments on the novel. Thus, she puts forward a shrewd parallel between the "slice of life" fiction of the French realists of the 'eighties, afterwards imported into this country, and the ultra-subjective, the "stream of consciousness" novels that are so fashionable at the moment. Both of them are a departure from the vital tradition in novel-writing, a turning aside into blind alleys, "stunts" rather than genuine developments in the art. Mrs. Wharton's comment upon this "stream of consciousness" fiction is so good that it must be quoted:—

"This attempt to note down every half-aware stirring of thought and sensation, the automatic reactions to every passing impression, is not as new as its present exponents appear to think. It has been used by most of the greatest novelists, not as an end in itself, but as it happened to serve their general design: as when their object was to portray a mind in one of those moments of acute mental stress when it records with meaningless precision a series of disconnected impressions. The value of such "effects" in making vivid a tidal rush of emotion has never been unknown since fiction became psychological, and novelists grew aware of the intensity with which, at such times, irrelevant trifles impinge upon the brain; but they have never been deluded by the idea that the subconscious—that Mrs. Harris of the psychologists—could in itself furnish the materials for their art. All the greatest of them, from Balzac and Thackeray onward, have made use of the stammerings and murmurings of the half-conscious mind whenever—but only when—such a state of mental flux fitted into the whole picture of the person portrayed. Their observation

showed them that in the world of normal men life is conducted, at least in its decisive moments, on fairly coherent and selective lines, and that only thus can the great fundamental affairs of bread-getting and home-and-tribe organizing be carried on. Drama, situation, is made out of the conflicts thus produced between social order and individual appetites, and the art of rendering life in fiction can never, in the last analysis, be anything, or need to be anything, but the disengaging of crucial moments from the welter of existence. . . ."

This is well said, even if you do not agree, as I do not agree, that drama, situation, can only arise out of the conflict between social order and individual appetites.

She might have added, though she does not, that behind all these "stunts" in fiction, the dead "slice of life" of the 'eighties, the "stream of consciousness" trick of to-day that will be equally dead in ten or twenty years, there is the desire, on the part of inferior writers, to substitute for the exacting and wearing process of vital creation some more mechanical and far easier process. After all, it is comparatively easy to fill notebooks, as the old realists did, with descriptions of furniture and pots and pans, out of which they made novels. In the same way—as people will soon realize—it is comparatively easy to slap down, just as they come, someone's mental reactions, which cannot be challenged and must be accepted. Here is the opening passage from a recent wild specimen of this manner, an American one:—

"Ineffably cataclysmic he watched the swallows rippling in. Wave after wave. Would they engulf him? Detachedly he beheld the lapwings, lap, lap, lap, lay a ripple farthering

387

up the beach. Footprints on the sands of crime. No. Peck, peck, peccadilloes. Lapses of lapwings fluttering over the shore. He lay back on the beach, was it under the beech; memories of rumpled protesting petticoats swept aside the beech no beseeching he besought silence to break. No breach."

It is far easier to do this than to write a short report of a street accident. I will guarantee to teach any person over twelve years of age and possessing a fair vocabulary the trick of it in a morning. The writers who abuse this ultrasubjective manner imagine that they are beginning a new chapter in the history of fiction. As a matter of fact they are actually ending an old one. The more promising younger novelists are showing a desire to return to a more objective manner of presentation, having read their Tehekhov, and it is safe to prophesy that in twenty years the Joyce tradition will be as dead as the Zola tradition is now. There is something mechanical, pedantic at the heart of both that is powerless to save them from putrefaction.

"The Writing of Fiction," *New Statesman*, 26 (12 December 1925), supplement, xxii, xxiv

She shows that modern fiction began when "the action of the novel was transferred from the street to the soul." In the chapter on the short story she maintains that "situation is the main concern of the short story, character of the novel." The modern novel grew out of the French novel of psychology and the novel of manners in England, and it necessarily changes its character with its theme. These essays are well thought out and expressed with (if the adjective be not offensive in this connection) masculine brevity and clearness. The volume closes with an essay on Proust which might have been more thorough. A good book of criticism.

"The Writing of Fiction," *Times Literary Supplement* [England], 17 December 1925, p. 878

Mr. Percy Lubbock's book, *The Craft of Fiction*, was addressed rather to the reader and the critic of fiction than to the novelist. Mrs. Wharton's is addressed rather to the novelist than to the reader. It is very far from being the sort of book which play-making seems to induce people to write: the sort of book which lays down the rules and leaves it to be understood that any fool can write a good play if he will but follow them. But two of the sections in the book are headed:— "Telling a Short Story" and "Constructing a Novel"; and it seems to have been the first intention of this experienced and very skilled novelist to share her experience and her skill with beginners of her craft.

It remains doubtful whether any teacher can, in the end, teach anything except what not to do. He can say: "Don't hold on by the reins, don't use words unless you know what they mean, don't mistake a crotchet for a quaver, and so on up the scale of accomplishment"; but riding, writing prose, and playing the piano are not to be positively taught. We are not, therefore, either surprised or disappointed to find that a great deal of Mrs. Wharton's instruction is negative. A novelist of her achievement and her fine taste can make her negatives very far-reaching; and so thoughtful a woman of letters can give very good reasons for them. Her first chapter is headed, "In General," and after a short (and not very satisfactory) history of the modern novel, she comes to this: that in fiction, as in every other art, "any theory must begin by assuming the need of selection." A page or two later we read: "The art of rendering life in fiction can never, in the last analysis, be anything or need to be anything, but the disengaging of crucial moments from the welter of existence." It is not hard to guess what modern form of fiction lies between those two statements; but Mrs. Wharton's way of approach to it is distinctive. She begins with the "slice of life." A few of those who proposed this theory of fiction—Maupassant, Zola, the Goncourts, for instance—"are still readable in spite of their constricting theory, or in proportion as they forgot about it once they had closed with their subject." Her real object in discussing the "slice of life" at all is to lead up to "the stream of consciousness." This idea is, to Mrs. Wharton, merely the "slice of life" enlarged to include mental as well as visual reactions. And how old it all is!

This attempt to note down every half-aware stirring of thought and sensation, the automatic reactions to every passing impression, is not as new as its present exponents appear to think. It has been used by most of the greatest novelists, not as an end in itself, but as it happened to serve their general design: as when their object was to portray a mind in one of those moments of acute mental stress when it records with meaningless precision a series of disconnected impressions. The value such "effects" in making vivid a tidal rush of emotion has never been unknown since fiction became psychological, and novelists grew aware of the intensity with which, at such times, irrelevant trifles impinge upon the brain; but they have never been deluded by the idea that the subconscious—that Mrs. Harris of the psychologists—could in itself furnish the materials for their art.

The distinctive feature of the creative imagination, in Mrs. Wharton's view, is that it not only penetrates into other minds, but can stand far enough aloof from them to see beyond, and relate them to the whole stuff of life out of which they but partially emerge. Mere re-presenting is no more possible in fiction than in painting or statuary, although the novelist works not in paint or marble, but "in the very material out of which the object he is trying to render is made." The artistic vision of an object is not the same as its reality. We need, of course, some reason why a novel should be a work of art. Mrs. Wharton, finding guidance in Flaubert's "perfect formula"—"Plus la pensée est belle, plus la phrase est sonore," goes some way towards the old notion of "a criticism of life." The reader, she says, asks about a story: "What judgement on life does it contain for me?" and she sums up: "A good subject must contain in itself something that sheds a light on our moral experience." Perhaps she could have reached the same point without the use of so mistrusted a word as "moral." The object of making your story what Mr. Lubbock would call "a book," is merely the need for significance. Mere representation (were such a thing possible) could have no significance. But a book, a work of selection, construction, proportion, has a significance in addition to that of such of its parts as may excite the reader's brain or touch his feeling; and it is in the search for the means of achieving this significance

389

that Mrs. Wharton lays stress on the need of form, which, to her, is "the order, in time and importance, in which the incidents of the narrative are grouped," and style, which is "the way in which they are presented, not only in the narrower sense of language, but also, and rather, as they are grasped and coloured by their medium, the narrator's mind, and given back in his words."

Starting from this general view of the novel, and going on to classify novels under three types—not for examination purposes, but because "from the creator's point of view classification means the choice of a manner and of an angle of vision"—Mrs. Wharton makes her negatives—her "don't hurry," "don't sprawl," "don't be slipshod," and so forth—full of suggestions to the young writer of fiction. If her remarks upon the right use of dialogue and upon the choice and employment of the "illuminating incident" are well weighed, there will be more novels that are truly "books," and fewer of which the significance is hard to find. But nothing that serves the writer of fiction can fail to be of interest to the reader of fiction; and besides Mrs. Wharton's principles, there are her many and very shrewdly chosen illustrations to make the re-reading of well-known novels an exciting pleasure. Nothing that she says of Balzac, of Thackeray, of Henry James but will be borne in mind when their books are read again; and where the chance occurs it is amusing to compare what she says of particular novelists with what Mr. Percy Lubbock says of them. One element in the making of novels has roused them both to a sense of mystery; and that is the expression of the flight of time. Mr. Lubbock came to it by means of *War and Peace*; and few things in his book show more discernment than the pages which disentangle Tolstoy's success in expressing the flight of time from his failure in giving it full significance. The great secret seems incommunicable. But something may be hazarded:—

A study of the great novels—and especially of Balzac, Thackeray, and Tolstoy—will show that such changes are suggested, are arrived at, in the inconspicuous transitional pages of narrative that lead from climax to climax. One of the means by which the effect is produced is certainly that of not fearing to go slowly, to keep down the tone of the narrative, to be as colourless and quiet as life often is in the intervals between the high moments.

Besides the frequent illustrations from the works of other novelists, which at once help Mrs. Wharton's arguments and bring a delight of their own, we get a larger taste of her criticism in a final note on Marcel Proust. It is a very interesting study, and all the more valuable because Proust's fiction is so very different from Mrs. Wharton's own and because a good many readers have failed to find in Proust the qualities which Mrs. Wharton insists upon as proper to the novel. Her discernment of the true immorality of Proust's books, too (which she does not, in accordance with the common cry, find in his presenting such a character as M. de Charlus) is a subtle and just piece of criticism; and at least one cannot lightly reject her conclusion that in Proust it was fear which "formed the inexorable horizon of his universe and the hard delimitation of his artist's temperament." And perhaps the knowledge that she admires Proust will reassure anyone who may feel shy of this new book. "Fiction made easy" is not its subtitle.

Wilbur Cross, "Mrs. Wharton on Her Art," *Yale Review*, 15 (April 1926), 600–3

It is expected that novelists shall at some time write of the art they practise. Fielding, having no other place for the words he wished to say on "a new province of writing," put them directly into *Tom Jones*, where no reader of his novel could fail to see them. Had Fielding lived in an age of magazines he would doubtless have published his little essays in one of them, and afterwards collected them in a neat volume with gray covers and red back— much as Mrs. Wharton has done with her charming essays about the ways to write fiction, still "the most fluid and least formulated of the arts."

"Modern fiction," says Mrs. Wharton, "really began when the 'action' of the novel was transferred from the street to the soul: and this step was probably first taken when Madame de La Fayette, in the seventeenth century, wrote a little story called *La Princesse de Clèves*, a story of hopeless love and mute renunciation in which the stately tenor of the lives depicted is hardly ruffled by the exultations and agonies succeeding each other below the surface." Who among us, I wonder, now reads *The Princess of Clèves*, whose exquisite art and style were praised by Sainte-Beuve? The novel so admired (of which an excellent English version has recently been made for "Broadway Translations") takes its cue from the everlasting triangle which the mediæval romancers invested with a strange beauty in the story of Guinevere and Lancelot, with Arthur looking on and intruding disastrously in the end. But Madame de La Fayette saw the triangle from another point of view. At every step in her narrative her discernments are certain and sure. Given the situation and the characters as she conceives them, and renunciation, though not altogether "mute," is the only issue. *The Princess of Clèves* is a perfect transformation of the romance into the novel.

Of the many ways in which a novelist may present his subject, Mrs. Wharton comments upon two principally. Like Madame de La Fayette, the novelist may begin with a "situation" which must in large measure determine incident and character. The danger lurking in this form of presentation, as may be seen in thousands of contemporary short-stories, is that the characters are likely to become little more than marionettes cleverly manipulated by the wires that the author holds and plays with, whimsically if he so desires. Still, there are very great novels in which the "situation" is predominant. Mrs. Wharton cites Goethe's *Elective Affinities* and Hawthorne's *Scarlet Letter*, where the "situation," always kept before the reader, appears from the outset to involve terrible consequences.

More often, however, characters come first to a novelist's mind and are allowed, without the restraint of a fixed situation, to work out their destinies in accordance with a rather flexible plot or design. A "situation," of course, there must be, but it recedes to the background. As the author goes on, ambient and characters together expand, perhaps imperceptibly to him; not foreseen is the issue surely in many details. This is the kind of novel in which large groups of men and women live; in which, as we say, the characters develop, going downward or upward, like Becky Sharp and Rawdon Crawley or like men and women we see in the world about us, moulded by the stress of changing circumstance, over which they have at most but partial control. Only, art is

391

expected to do rather better than nature. Jane Austen's *Emma*, Mrs. Wharton remarks, "is perhaps the most perfect example in English fiction of a novel in which character shapes events quietly but irresistibly, as a stream nibbles away its banks." When Mrs. Wharton wrote this sentence, *Emma* must have been fresh in her memory, for the same thing might be said with equal truth of *Pride and Prejudice* or *Mansfield Park*. In a little company of men, so the story goes, each one was asked to write on a slip of paper the novel of Jane Austen's that he liked best. Each man, as it turned out, gave the title of the novel he had read last.

After Jane Austen came Balzac with a larger vision. Hitherto, says Mrs. Wharton, novelists with few exceptions had studied their people more or less as detached individuals, hanging them in the air, as it were, and as only casually conditioned by heredity and environment. She does not, I think, quite make out her case. There are perhaps few conditioning factors in *Clarissa Harlowe* or *Tristram Shandy* or *Pride and Prejudice*. This is, however, not so nearly true of *Tom Jones* or *Roderick Random*, nor is it at all true of any one of Scott's novels, whose romantic backgrounds always play a conspicuous part in the characterization. What appears to be true is that Balzac, more than any one of his predecessors, took into account inheritance and social habits, relating his men and women to their occupations and the towns and houses and streets they lived in. It was an application to fiction of a new psychology which held that personality is not circumscribed by a physical body but rather "flows imperceptibly into adjacent people and things." This new conception of personality has been of immense significance for the drama as well as for fiction. It would be interesting, were this an essay, to comment on Mrs. Wharton's remarks on

the great Victorians, whose characters are as real as Balzac's except in so far as they may be sacrificed to the exigencies of an artificial plot. How to make an end, she quotes Nietzsche as saying, requires genius, such, I may add, as Thackeray showed in the last scenes of *Vanity Fair*. It was a mistake, Mrs. Wharton thinks, for Henry James to cast *The Awkward* Age in dialogue throughout, instead of reserving his dialogue for "the culminating scenes." With this stricture on the extreme James method, most readers will doubtless agree, after futile attempts to construct the story out of "the look and the speech of the characters." It does not, however, follow that a simpler theme may not lend itself admirably to a purely dramatic form. Perhaps Mrs. Wharton has in mind H. G. Wells when she scores hard against the habit of jumping in and out of one's characters, and James Joyce when she shows that there is a lack of a sense for art in those writers who would set down all mental reactions just as they rise halfway into consciousness, "with a deliberate disregard of their relevance in the particular case," as if the bare record of a stream of consciousness constituted in itself a novel. "The art of rendering life in fiction," Mrs. Wharton says in summary, "can never, in the last analysis, be anything or need be anything, but the disengaging of crucial moments from the welter of existence." In this connection, Mrs. Wharton holds with Meredith and Hardy and with most of the great novelists backward to her Madame de La Fayette, who, according to Sainte-Beuve, wrote her novels on the principle that a sentence cut from a page is worth a louis of gold, and a single word no less than a franc.

Mrs. Wharton closes her book with a discriminating study of Marcel Proust, which originally appeared in *The Yale Review*. A point she makes for Proust is that, though this subtle novelist wanders through the jungle of half-conscious states, he always takes a lantern with him and eventually emerges into the light of day. Mrs. Wharton likewise carries a lantern with her through a multitude of perceptions that give us new insights into an art which she has happily made her own.

Checklist of Additional Reviews

"John Smith," "III. The Writer and His Readers," and "IV. Nothing New Under the Spotlight," *Literary Digest International Book Review*, 3 (November 1925), 784.

Helen Wallerstein, Review of *The Writing of Fiction, New York Evening Post Literary Review*, 28 November 1925, p. 11.

"New Books in Brief Review," *Independent*, 116 (2 January 1926), 23.

A. M., "Mrs. Wharton Discourses on the Novelist's Art," Springfield [Massachusetts] *Republican*, 3 January 1926, p. 7–A.

Joseph Aynard, "L'Art du roman d'après Mrs. Wharton," *Journal des Débats* [France], 3 (22 January 1926), 119–21.

Henri Peyre, "Edith Wharton: The Writing of Fiction," *Revue Anglo-Américaine* [France], 3 (April 1926), 366–8.

THE MOTHER'S RECOMPENSE

THE MOTHER'S RECOMPENSE

BY

EDITH WHARTON

AUTHOR OF
"OLD NEW YORK," "THE AGE OF INNOCENCE,"
"THE GLIMPSES OF THE MOON," ETC.

Desolation is a delicate thing.
SHELLEY.

D. APPLETON AND COMPANY
NEW YORK :: LONDON :: MCMXXV

Percy A. Hutchison, "Mrs. Wharton Brings *The House of Mirth* Up to Date," *New York Times Book Review*, 26 April 1925, pp. 7, 21

It may be recalled that not so very long ago George Moore, assisted by his two literary friends, John Freeman and Walter de la Mare, compiled what Mr. Moore insisted was to be an anthology of "pure poetry"; by which he meant poetry which achieved a complete detachment from the personality of the poet.

It was an interesting thesis, but somewhat strained. Reduced to ultimate terms, it resolved itself into the old formula of "art for art's sake"; and this formula, when in turn tracked down to its ultimates, ends in a reductio ad absurdum. Art solely for art's sake—"pure" poetry, "pure" painting—would be the babbling of the idiot or a colorless blur of colors. But when Moore's statement is cleared of its overstatement, when the term "pure" is dropped (it was probably intended mostly as a catchword), the English novelist and essayist will be found enunciating a truth which is of supreme importance as a test of art. And this truth, succinctly stated, is that the measure of detachment achieved by the artist will in no small degree be the measure of his artistic achievement.

What first and most strongly impresses itself on the reader of Edith Wharton's new novel, *The Mother's Recompense*, is precisely that detachment for which George Moore was arguing. True, from the very outset of her career as a novelist,

this detachment has been dominatingly a feature of Mrs. Wharton's work. But never before was it so completely attained, or so consistently maintained, as in the present narrative. Moreover, those who have recognized it as one of the cornerstones on which Mrs. Wharton's fame as an artist has hitherto been based, could not escape the fear that with one whose output is so fairly continuous as hers, there would, sooner or later, come a lapse from a standard so exclusively belonging to the world of art, so little a standard of that social comity which it is the novelist's business to reproduce. For the novelist, because he is primarily dealing with life, and only secondarily with ideas and emotions, detachment is more difficult to achieve than for the poet.

The story of *The Mother's Recompense* must not be told in advance; it is always the unalienable right of the novelist that the retelling of his story should be refrained from when to do so be to destroy the effect for which the novelist has planned. To retell this particular narrative would be to rob it of its planned effect. But something of the general drift of the "plot" may be given without infringing; and the dilemma posed may be stated, if kept to general terms and the solution withheld.

The chief personage of Mrs. Wharton's soul tragedy is the mother, Kate Clephane, who, after nearly eighteen shabby years in Europe, returns to the Fifth Avenue home of the daughter she had deserted before she was little more than out of the cradle. Subsequently shut off from her daughter, first by the outraged husband and father, and after his death by his mother, Kate Clephane comes back not to "Baby Anne" but to an imperious young woman, by law and by temperament the mistress of her own destinies. The dilemma which presently ensues, although on the surface a conflict of wills, in reality and in poignancy reaches far deeper, for it is the daughter's future in conflict with the mother's past. The two can never be happy; the happiness of one or the other is at stake. In *Lohengrin* the happiness of Elsa was destroyed by her insistence on the fatal question. Should Anne's happiness be destroyed by telling her the fatal truth? The tragedy is apparent; the depths of sorrow and suffering through which the mother must pass are clear. If, as novelist, Edith Wharton is detached on the side of her art, there is nothing of detachment in her perception of human values, in her appreciation of the call of human affections.

One sentence of Mrs. Wharton's although it is employed by the author to convey an impression of Anne, might fitly be used to convey the impression made by the book, "Anne's happiness," writes her biographer, "shone through her, making her opaque and guarded features luminous and transparent; and the mother could measure from her own experience, the amount of heat and force that fed that incandescence." The features of the narrative are "opaque and guarded" ever; *The Mother's Recompense* is no blustering tale, easily as it might have been (and surely would have been) turned into melodrama in unskillful hands. But likewise are those features ever made "luminous and transparent" by the incandescence of Mrs. Wharton's imagination, fed in turn by a heat and force, of what intensity one's own experience furnishes the thermal measure.

To say that Mrs. Wharton is to some degree an ironist would probably be true; but she is not primarily an ironist. In no sense is she a satirist; although she may appear as much to those who make the common mistake of confounding irony and satire. But she sets off the daughter, Anne, who is very much, although in a constrained sort of way, a modern—she sets the modern Anne off against the "tribe" of Clephanes, with all their traditions of family and social prestige, much as Galsworthy sets Fleur off against the background of the Forsytes. But ironic distinctions are in Mrs. Wharton's novel, less frequently the object of the author's interest than is the case in the "Saga" and in *The White Monkey* and more frequently they are generalized than kept to the particular, as for instance here:

> But the young people—what did they think? That would be the interesting thing to know. They had all, she (Kate) gathered, far more interest and ideas than had scantily furnished her own youth, but all so broken up, scattered, and perpetually interrupted by the endless labor of their endless forms of sport, that they reminded her of a band of young entomologists, equipped with the newest thing in nets, but in far too great a hurry ever to catch anything.

When Mrs. Wharton desires, she can hit off much in a few words; quite as much as John Galsworthy, or her own literary master, Henry James. Take, for example, the house which had been old Mrs. Clephane's wedding gift to one of her daughters, the house in which everything had "obviously been selected by some one whose first thought concerning any work of art had been to ask if it would chip or fade." Or, once again, "Poor Lila!", who "could not see a new room without wanting to fox-trot in it," and for whom life consisted "in going somewhere else to do exactly the same things."

But there is nothing of irony in the main theme of the story—except, of course, the gigantic, soul-searing and never ending irony of life of which every human being is the victim, and which is the underlying impulse to every novel other than the avowedly and unblushingly sentimental novel.

And here, again, the detachment, or, perhaps, more exactly the restraint which Mrs. Wharton imposes on herself and on her art, is supremely evidenced. Never did a novel scream so loudly for a sentimental ending as does *The Mother's Recompense*; the author must have laid violent hold on herself to keep from answering that cry. But she remained steadfast. That she could exercise such restraint in view of the temptation is due to some degree, at least, to the fact that although she has always written for the most part of America and Americans, and thus ever exposed herself to the sentimental virus, her art is rooted in the English tradition, which only now and again has been broken by sentimentalism.

But on one phase of the story many a reader is more than likely to raise a perplexing question. The "hero" of *The Mother's Recompense*—"hero" being here used in its conventional sense of labeling the chief male person—is decidedly a cad. There would be no story if he were not. But it is surely a legitimate question as to precisely how far a novelist can go in predicating a tragedy on caddishness and cowardice without so weakening the interest of the reader in the human side of the story that the effectiveness becomes weakened. It was laid down by Aristotle that tragedy must evoke both pity and horror; and all great tragedies, upon inspection, are found to substantiate this contention. In *The Mother's Recompense* Edith Wharton evokes horror, but she fails to arouse the corresponding degree of pity. When it devolves upon a man to renounce the woman he is pledged to marry, or else sacrifice another woman, as in the dilemma Mrs. Wharton presents, it can be done; there are regions about the North Pole

still to be explored; there are wars, even if petty wars, in which a Major, D. S. M., Chevalier of the Legion of Honor, can enlist; and the sources of the Amazon have not yet been discovered. These for spectacular methods of clearing the stage. The other method is to make the coward the centre of interest, as Lord Jim is the centre of interest in Conrad's story of the same title, in which case the novel becomes a study in cowardice. The weakling is not the central figure in *The Mother's Recompense*, but the victim of the weakling; and thus, while the horror, the mental horror, is increased and heightened, pity is not evoked, for the mother is but the sport of extraneous and senseless fate.

It may be objected that this is hypercriticism. No doubt it is. But the fact that Mrs. Wharton furnishes grounds for hypercriticism is but another proof of the heights to which her novel rises. With inferior work there is so much that not only is bad, but glaringly bad, it becomes an act of supererogation to pursue minor faults. Nor is the reason in this case far to find. Mrs. Wharton, as a general thing, has shown greater interest in her women than in her men; in this novel her interest in the mother, Kate Clephane, is so intense, so ever-present, that at times she is positively careless of every other character; in fact, Anne, althoughly sharply sketched whenever the moment is crucial, is at other times more or less shadowy. Kate Clephane is never for an instant shadowy. In fact, unless one is greatly deceived, Kate Clephane will stand beside Lily Bart as one of Edith Wharton's most lasting creations of women.

Always, as a final word, one comes back to Mrs. Wharton's art—to her consummate art. It can be said without casting reflection that on this score no other novelist in America today is Edith Wharton's peer. She can carry through a story without a break or lapse as only

John Galsworthy in England can do. She has the feeling for shade, the perception for gradations of value, that Galsworthy has. *The Mother's Recompense* is a study in the warfare between mind and emotion that stultifies criticism with the sheer naked grandeur of its living truth. The novel, whatever may be urged against it, is Mrs. Wharton's best since *The House of Mirth*.

"New Novels: *The Mother's Recompense,*" *Times Literary Supplement* [England], 14 May 1925, p. 332

Mrs. Wharton, with a word of apology to the print shade of Grace Aguilar, has borrowed one of her titles for her new novel, and *The Mother's Recompense*... reappears—with a difference! A mother, in Grace Aguilar's day, behaved better than Mrs. Wharton's heroine, one supposes, and was duly rewarded with the love and respect of an enormous family connexion, including many grandchildren. Not so Kate Clephane, who deserted her husband and child when the latter was but three years old, put herself beyond the pale of society by running off with another man, and thereafter, tiring of him and denied access to her small daughter, knocked about on the Continent in shabby and doubtful surroundings suffering all the loneliness and remorse of the involuntary exile. She was "good," among a set of frumps, hypocrites and doubtful characters; and only one other lover had succeeded the man she had run away with and lived with for a year. "At thirty-nine her real self had been born," thanks to Chris Fenno, who had loved her and

waked her, and had kept her excited and stimulated for years although in actual time he had lived with her only for a single week. But for some years before the story opens Chris had slipped out of her life, unresponsive to her hints; and we first meet her in her second-rate Riviera hotel bedroom tremblingly opening a telegram that she hopes will be from him. Instead it is to tell her that her mother-in-law, unforgiving old Mrs. Clephane, is dead; and it is followed immediately by a second message from America asking her to go out at once to make her home there with the sender—"your daughter Anne."

The stage is now set for the social re-establishment of Mrs. Clephane, the subject of such scandal nearly twenty years before; and the story is handled with the first-rate competence that Mrs. Wharton's readers count on. The New York scene, the particular social background, the various busy, rich, rushing people belonging to Anne's world, efficient Anne herself, the implication of changed standards, and Kate's reaction to these things are all remarkably real, without being novel in any sense. The book is a sympathetic study of people whom it is not easy to like or admire very much; and the relation between Anne and her mother, which is based on sincere attachment but subject to a good deal of strain, is affecting. Mrs. Wharton, in the second part of the book, uses a plot which has been presented on the stage and often discussed. Anne is in love, is engaged to Chris Fenno, and she suddenly breaks the news to her appalled mother. Shall Kate Clephane tell her daughter why she is so stricken by the news? She cannot, but she goes to Chris—who has got into the affair in good faith, unaware till recently that Kate had a daughter—and the result is a broken engagement and the half-estrangement of Anne. The reconciliation and marriage of the two which follows later, very cleverly and probably managed, foreshadows permanent estrangement. The mother's recompense (combined with the recompense of bitterness that comes to the woman who sees her lover gone from her for ever) is fresh exile. Mrs. Wharton's touch has never been more certain than in this swiftly moving, admirably finished story. Kate Clephane stands out in her gallery of feminine portraits as living, as typical, as Lily Bart.

Henry Seidel Canby, "Pathos Versus Tragedy," *Saturday Review of Literature*, 1 (23 May 1925), 771

Mrs. Wharton has chosen a Greek theme for her latest novel, but she has not chosen to be Greek in her handling of it. The theme is tragic but the book is not. That a woman who has fled from a stifling husband, leaving her baby daughter behind her, should, a score of years later, let this daughter marry her mother's lover without a word, is a situation so pregnant with disaster that only a search for Nemesis would seem to justify its choice. Mrs. Wharton has not been concerned with Nemesis, nor with the fate of Anne, the lovely daughter. It is the mother, such a penurious protégé of society as Lily Bart, who has caught her imagination. The pathos of a woman returning to the maternal relation and not daring to shatter its sweet renewals by asserting the past is her goal. Adroitly as ever, she depicts with a mingled irony and affection the social scene in those coasts of Europe where live the castaways, and the fatted New York to which the mother returns at the daughter's call. A European wanderer, a runaway from a husband and a lover, the mistress of Chris Fenno, an artist who deserts her only fatally to reappear, her blighted life flowers again in a sudden, passionate love for her Anne. She is afraid that her new love will be lost; she does not tell her daughter that she has been Fenno's mistress because her daughter loves him; she does penance by a rather futile sacrifice of a new marriage for herself—and drifts back to Europe of the castaways.

Mrs. Kate Clephane is pathetic. The tension of her mingled love and horror is great and Mrs. Wharton, in the scenes that spring from the situation, could not fail to be aroused to poignancy and force. But pathos is not enough for such a plot; it leaves us cold and a little scornful at the end of the novel, which is inevitably the beginning of double tragedy—the mother's and the daughter's. It is a Greek play minus the fifth act, and with a most un-Sophoclean willingness to be sorry for the protagonist because her will was weak. Kate Clephane was a moral coward, whose instincts, even, fail her at the moment when she sees her lover in her daughter's arms and cannot give voice to her jealousy. The pity one feels for Mrs. Clephane is clouded by distress and disbelief.

Mrs. Wharton has been led by her own sympathy for an unfortunate woman to mistake the true values of her theme. It is not a vehicle for sentiment; it strikes too violently upon the emotions of readers and of the actors in the story. It demands an inexorable working out. When Conrad was accused of deliberately making the end of "The Planter of Malatta" unhappy, he replied that to one who understood his characters a happy ending was inconceivable. Anything but tragedy is unbelievable in *The Mother's Recompense* as Mrs. Wharton has plotted it, yet while her conclusion is not happy, it gives

401

a makeshift illusion of permanence in compromise.

Many will be moved by the interest of the plot and the poignancy of certain scenes in this novel. As narrative it has its high merits. But as a novel it must disappoint Mrs. Wharton's admirers because she has chosen a subject beyond the powers of all but a few of our contemporaries, though not beyond her own, and has not wished to lift her story to meet its implications. Her imagination has been more tragic than her will.

"New Books in Brief," *Independent*, 114 (30 May 1925), 619

Competent, skillful work, adequately chiseled and polished like painting by a competent, but rather tired, artist. Mrs. Wharton seems to say, "About time for a new novel! This one will tell the story of a mother whose lover marries her daughter. A good plot, in three months I can do it." There is a sense of artificiality about the book. The emotional scenes are effective as a good emotional scene ought to be on the stage, but at heart the audience is cold. It knows the suffering isn't real. Mrs. Wharton, who has written stories of genuine passion and strength, will only injure her fame by this conventional gesture in novel form.

Louise Maunsell Field, "Mrs. Wharton Pictures New York Society of Today," *Literary Digest International Book Review*, 3 (June 1925), 463, 466

New York Society of to-day, with its cabaret parties, its dance-mania, and its matter-of-course attitude of taking things for granted, provides the background of Edith Wharton's new novel. This changed social attitude is important, in so far as its so-called tolerance makes Kate Clephane's return possible—a tolerance composed of about equal parts of indifference, moral laziness, and a general consciousness of living in houses which, if not entirely built of glass, have at least one or more of their walls constructed of that venerable material. But the book is far more than the study of a social set and its attitude; for the situation it unfolds is one which might have arisen at almost any period of the world's history, and one's attention is focused, not on the change in the social point of view toward divorce or the etiquette of mourning, but on the mental and moral torture of Kate Clephane, caught in the trap of a situation which could never have been sprung upon her had she not failed to fulfill her obligations.

Her attempt to battle with the situation, her deceptive, transient success, her desperate turnings, first in this direction, then in that, seeking a way out where no way out exists, have an emotional intensity which communicates itself the more fully to the reader because it is so evident that no matter what she does, the "sterile pain" she dreads imposing is bound to be inflicted sooner or later. It seems inevitable that some time the secret will be discovered; for even putting aside the strong possibilities of an accidental or malicious revelation, Anne is not a fool. Once at least she already approached dangerously near the truth; it is too much to expect that she will long remain contented with the kind of explanations which are all that can be offered. And then, too, there arises the question whether Kate's decision was not as much the result of cowardice as of love, her choice destined to result in even greater unhappiness than that she endeavored to prevent. It is partly because there is, so far as Kate is concerned, no way out of the situation—because it fills the reader's mind with questions—that the novel presents so much tempting material for discussion.

Eighteen years before the time at which the story opens, Kate Clephane had run away from her husband's grim old house on Fifth Avenue, leaving behind her three-year-old daughter, Anne. For two years she traveled with Hylton Davies, who to her was rather "the agent of her release" than her lover. Then they parted, and she went from one Continental watering-place to another, living a life of strictest propriety until she met Chris, the man eleven years younger than herself, with whom she fell violently in love. Their liaison was to a great extent screened by the outbreak of the World War; but presently he tired of her and left her, tho for long she hoped against hope that some day he would come back. One morning two telegrams came to the dingy little hotel where she was living; one announced the death of Mrs. Clephane, her dead husband's severe old mother; the other was from her daughter Anne, now a girl of twenty-one, asking her to return to New York. She went to Anne immediately; a few very happy months followed; then Chris reappeared, and her agony began.

The story is told exclusively from Kate's point of view; the reader sees and knows only what she sees and knows. She is absolutely, entirely real, both in the strength of her love and in her weaknesses, an ardent, impetuous, yet intelligent woman; and real, too, is Anne. The rest, except for Fred Landers, who arouses keenest pity, are all rather shadowy. Kate's whole being becomes centered in Anne; other people are to her comparatively unimportant, and for this reason they are unimportant to the reader. But it is unfortunate that Chris should be among the shadowy; if you could see him more clearly, it might be easier to understand his power over two very different women. But that he, the only one who could have done something to solve the situation, should find excuses for arranging matters as much as possible to suit himself, is entirely consistent with what is known of his character.

It is in the early part of the book that we get the more detailed pictures of social life of the kind that Mrs. Wharton so well knows how to draw. I would like, did space permit, to linger over her sketch of the expatriates at the small Riviera town, their efforts to fill their lives with "engagements," their clutchings at "respectability," the general dreariness and futility of their existences. No less admirable is the author's picture of modern New York and the modern young people Kate meets:

They had all, she gathered, far more interests and ideas than had scantily furnished her own youth, but all so broken up, scattered, and perpetually interrupted by the strenuous labor of their endless forms of sport, that they reminded her of a band of young entomologists, equipped with the newest thing in nets, but in far too great a hurry ever to catch anything.... Kate

403

wondered when there was ever time to enjoy anything, with that perpetual alarm-clock in one's breast.

That *The Mother's Recompense* is one of Mrs. Wharton's best novels, few will deny. I am inclined to place it above *The Age of Innocence*, because its central situation is one which transcends periods and classes; its tragedy is not one confined to any one rank of life, nor to any particular time. Yet it is always difficult to estimate fairly the value of a contemporary novel; how difficult, is clearly shown in Mr. Robert Morss Lovett's interesting if rather planless and not especially discerning little monograph on *Edith Wharton*. Mr. Lovett—whose volume necessarily ends with the publication of the four stories of *Old New York*, and does not include *The Mother's Recompense*—has some admiration, but no great sympathy or liking, for Mrs. Wharton. He regards her as "among the voices whispering the last enchantments of the Victorian age," and his attitude toward her is tinged with something of the polite condescension with which, a very little while ago, it was fashionable to regard the giants of those days. In his summing-up he declares that "Mrs. Wharton can stand outside of her own world to criticize—not to create." Certainly *Ethan Frome* is not a novel of Mrs. Wharton's "own world," yet it is admittedly "a little masterpiece."

Mr. Lovett traces Mrs. Wharton's artistic development, her inheritance of the George Eliot tradition, the influence of Henry James. He very justly appraises the limitations imposed on her by the fact that "the American upper class is not deeply rooted in the soil by the long feudal process, but grows rapidly, rankly, in the forcing-house of wealth." The statement, if a little sweeping, is yet accurate enough to account for certain obvious difficulties in the way of the American

"novel of manners," producing what I some time ago called "the hot-house atmosphere" which pervades so many of Mrs. Wharton's novels, and is to some extent perceptible in this ironically titled one of *The Mother's Recompense*.

Robert Morss Lovett, "New Novels by Old Hands," *New Republic*, 43 (10 June 1925), 79

In *The Mother's Recompense* Mrs. Wharton has returned to the field most her own, and to the material which is her best. That field is aristocratic New York, with its ancient mores giving way before new and urgent demands upon life by the younger generation. The narrative follows the return to America of Mrs. Clephane, long expatriated in Europe as the result of a post-marital elopement, and summoned back to rehabilitation by her daughter when the latter comes into the family inheritance. This is the situation which Mrs. Wharton has used in one of her best short stories, "Autres Temps," as well as in *The Age of Innocence*. It gives her an opportunity to develop the contrast between the old New York of Mrs. Clephane's young matronhood, and the New York of the present. The case of conscience which Mrs. Wharton uses as a test is one which was familiar in French and British problem novels and plays of a generation ago—in Maupassant's *Fort comme la Mort*, for example, and in Pinero's *The Second Mrs. Tanqueray*—the case on which Mrs. Wharton herself based *The Reef*, and from which Mrs. Anne Douglas Sedgwick rescues her *Little French Girl*. The question which Mrs. Clephane is obliged to answer—shall she allow a marriage between her daughter and the man who has been her own lover—is presented as an individual one. It searches her to the soul. But Mrs. Clephane with her laxity in respect to the Seventh Commandment, is genuinely Victorian, and as much shocked at condoning a breach within the boundaries of consanguinity as Aubrey Tanqueray. The test thus becomes a social one, marking the difference between two periods. The Reverend Mr. Arklow announces the verdict of both: "She must tell her daughter. Such a shocking situation must be avoided; avoided at all costs. . . . Unless," the Rector continued uncertainly, "she is absolutely convinced that less harm will come to all concerned if she has the courage to keep silence—always."

It would be a mistake to infer, because Mrs. Wharton has taken an instance as old as the Bible or as Greek Tragedy, that her novel lacks freshness and originality. The fact that she has treated the same theme herself, in *The Reef*, though there the relationship involved is less direct, affords an admirable opportunity for comparison of her later with her earlier art, by no means to the disadvantage of the former. *The Reef* was thought to be the most successful of Mrs. Wharton's novels, at least up to *The Age of Innocence*. It is done with an elaboration of natural background, a precision of dramatic structure, a penetration in the analysis of character that excited the admiration of Mr. Percy Lubbock. *The Mother's Recompense* is less elaborately wrought than *The Reef*. It moves more swiftly, with a cleaner stride. While toward its close the story in *The Reef* goes almost entirely into the minds of the characters, that in *The Mother's Recompense* remains in the open. When in the final chapter we see Mrs. Clephane back in her old habitat on the Riviera, entertaining Dr. Arklow, who has become a bishop, we realize that the story

has swung its full circle, and ends according to the logic of events, not the a priori logic of scruple and motivation. On the other hand, the similar case presented by earlier novels and plays, including *The Reef*, seemed distinctly more important, more worth the author's and the reader's pondering. This is because an issue seemed fraught with deepest consequence to a generation that considered its salvation menaced by marriage to a deceased wife's sister is now really a matter of social adjustment and taste.

Edwin Muir, "Fiction," *Nation and Athenæum* [England], 37 (13 June 1925), 328

The theme of *The Mother's Recompense* is very difficult, and in spite of her great talent, sincerity, and intrepidity of mind, Mrs. Wharton has not completely mastered it. The mother's former lover seeks the daughter's hand, and eventually secures it; and the story describes, first, the mother's struggle to prevent the marriage without antagonizing the daughter, and, secondly, her struggle with herself, torn between the necessity to "tell," and the necessity of avoiding the "sterile pain" which the avowal would cause. It is this inward struggle which chiefly occupies the author's attention; but while it culminates in one or two really beautiful scenes, it never reaches a single, supreme climax. The scenes do not develop in an ascending scale; they are more or less repetitions of one scene, and when we have read that we have in effect read them all. We feel that the author, as well as the suffering

405

mother, is entangled in the web, so that the book gives not merely a sense of monotonous suffering, but of monotony of treatment. In one or two scenes Mrs. Wharton does mount to the height of tragedy, but she tries to remain there without intermission, not allowing enough for the ebb and flow of pain. She fails to reach a katharsis because, one might almost think, she is determined by an act of the will not to reach it; to maintain, rather, the intensity of tragedy at all cost, when it is past its term and our endurance. Yet the qualities which have contributed to this failure are high ones; and there can be nothing but praise for Mrs. Wharton's beautiful style, her integrity of imagination in her great scenes, and the sincerity of her art.

J[ohn] F[arrar], "Society and the Fringe," *Bookman*, 61 (June 1925), 469–70

To group Edith Wharton and F. Scott Fitzgerald may seem, at first glance, ridiculous; but if you will read *The Mother's Recompense* and then *The Great Gatsby*, I think you will discover my reason. In one, we find a mature woman, with an amazing tolerance of life and an understanding of its smallest values, writing with force and clarity on a theme as tremendous as any she has ever touched. In the other, a brilliant young man, immensely puzzled by life and disturbed by shifting values in his own scheme, writes vividly but chaotically on a theme that is as tremendous but scarcely as clear. *The Mother's Recompense* ... is, it seems to me, the best story Mrs. Wharton has ever written. It is the same in theme as a rather

lame play which flared forth on Broadway recently for a week, *Ostriches*. A man falls in love with a former mistress's daughter. The plot is as simple as that; but in the character of Kate Clephane we have delicacy and complication of emotion that is dramatic and poignant. Mrs. Wharton tells this story swiftly, and with her usual command of masses of dialogue. She does not attempt to explain differences in the generations. She shifts from the Riviera to New York gracefully and with a complete understanding of both moods. I think she has achieved an even greater understanding of the mother-daughter relation than Edna Ferber evinced of that of mother and son in *So Big*. To be sure, *The Mother's Recompense* is not always pleasant reading. It is painful, exceedingly painful, and cruel. This author never spares heroines; with unflinching zeal she lets us see their souls. Kate Clephane is so human that she terrifies, and her tortures and psychological adventures hold the reader as do few mystery stories, for in this novel suspense plays a large part. Actually, we do not know the solution until the final page, and it is a solution in which we are vitally interested.

Checklist of Additional Reviews

Sherwin Lawrence Cook, "The Modern Mother's Recompense," Boston *Evening Transcript*, 2 May 1925, book section, p. 5.

Herbert S. Gorman, "Above Sentimentality," New York *World*, 3 May 1925, p. 7-M.

Louis Bromfield, "Mrs. Wharton Sticks to New York Life," *New York Evening Post Literary Review*, 9 May 1925, p. 3.

R. D. Townsend, "Six Important Novels," *Outlook*, 140 (13 May 1925), 69–70.

Stuart P. Sherman, "Costuming the Passions," New York *Herald Tribune*, 17 May 1925, Section V, pp. 1–2.

Gerald Bullett, "New Fiction," *Saturday Review* [England], 139 (30 May 1925), 588.

E. O. G. , "The Bookshelf," *Woman Citizen*, 10 (30 May 1925), 24.

P. C. Kennedy, "New Novels," *New Statesman*, 21 (6 June 1925), 230.

"Two American Novels," *Spectator* [England], 134 (6 June 1925), 940.

Joseph Aynard, "Le Nouveau Roman de Mrs. Wharton," *Journal des Débats* [France], (12 June 1925), pp. 986–8.

E. C., "Sterile Pain," *Forum*, 74 (July 1925), 154–5.

Ethel W. Hawkins, "The Atlantic's Bookshelf," *Atlantic Monthly*, 136 (July 1925), 8, 10.

H. C. Harwood, "Books Abroad," *Living Age*, 326 (11 July 1925), 123.

Francine de Martinoir, "Un Immense Continent Romanesque," *La Quinzaine Littéraire* [France], 398 (16 July, 1925), 8–9.

"Briefer Mention," *Dial*, 79 (November 1925), 431.

Régis Michaud, "Edith Wharton: *The Mother's Recompense* . . . Robert Morss Lovett: *Edith Wharton*," *Revue Anglo-Américaine* [France], 3 (February 1926), 276–8.

Ch.G., "Les Livres qu'il faut avoir lus: Le Bilan, par Edith Wharton," *Vient de Paraitre* [France], 8 (November 1928), 441.

TWELVE POEMS

TWELVE POEMS BY
EDITH WHARTON

"Twelve Poems,"
Times Literary Supplement, 17 March 1927, p. 183

Mrs. Wharton calls one of her poems "La Folle du Logis"; another name for it might have been, as we suppose, "The Poet's Address to his own Genius," to the spirit who has

> bared for me
> The heart of wonder in familiar things,
> Unroofed dull rooms, and hung above
>   my head
> The cloudy glimpses of a vernal moon,
> Or all the autumn heaven ripe with
>   stars.

The description is interesting, for although it is a poet who speaks, the genius spoken of is not a poet's but a novelist's. To "unroof dull rooms" is the business of a novelist, and it is not Mrs. Wharton the poet but Mrs. Wharton the novelist who can show us "the heart of wonder in familiar things." In these poems familiar things remain familiar, as they do not in the novels. We may take this elegy as an example:—

> Ah, how I pity the young dead who
>   gave
> All that they were, and might become,
>   that we
> With tired eyes should watch this
>   perfect sea
> Reweave its patterning of silver wave
> Round scented cliffs of arbutus and bay.
>
> No more shall any rose along the way,
> The myrtled way that wanders to the
>   shore,
> Nor jonquil-twinkling meadow any
>   more,

> Nor the warm lavender that takes the
>   spray,
> Smell only of the sea-salt and the sun,
>
> But, through recurring seasons, every
>   one
> Shall speak to us with lips the darkness
>   closes,
> Shall look at us with eyes that missed
>   the roses,
> Clutch us with hands whose work was
>   just begun,
> Laid idle now beneath the earth we
>   tread—
>
> And always we shall walk with the
>   young dead—
> Ah, how I pity the young dead, whose
>   eyes
> Strain through the sod to see these
>   perfect skies,
> Who feel the new wheat springing in
>   their stead,
> And the lark singing for them overhead!

We are reminded of a poem in a different manner whose thought is the same, Mr. Wilfrid Gibson's "Lament," which ends:—

> A bird among the rain-wet lilac sings—
> But we, how shall we turn to little
>   things
> And listen to the birds and winds and
>   streams
> Made holy by their dreams,
> Nor feel the heart-break in the heart of
>   things?

Here the old thought becomes new to us, and it is this rebirth which is not achieved in the elegy, for all its accomplishment. This absence of surprise, this failure to move us from our accustomed standpoint, is characteristic of these poems, and makes them perhaps rather deserve the name of verse. But verse has a

411

place of its own among the arts of writing; and, if we are content not to expect here the surprise of poetry, we shall find that we are not disappointed of the peculiar pleasure of verse. There is much music in this little organ and Mrs. Wharton is a skilful player; she can command it to the utterance of various subtle harmonies.

I lie among the thyme,
The sea is at my feet,
And all the air is sweet
With the capricious chime

Of interwoven notes
From those invisible and varying
    throats,
As though the blossomed trees,
The laden breeze
The springs within their caves,
And even the sleeping waves
Had all begun to sing.

This book has been printed at the Riccardi Press, and the fine arts of the printer and of the writer seem to be here in peculiar sympathy.

412

HERE AND BEYOND

Here and Beyond

Edith Wharton

Decorations by E. C. Caswell

D. Appleton & Company
New York ❧ London ❧ Mcmxxvi

"Edith Wharton's Finely Fashioned Tales in *Here and Beyond*," *New York Times Book Review*, 2 May 1926, p. 9

From the outset of Mrs. Wharton's career a book from her pen has been a literary event. Not in every instance, perhaps, has she reached the same high point of achievement: that would be too much to expect. There have been some lapses. At worst, however, these have been few, and as easily forgotten as forgiven. Edith Wharton has attained her place in American and English literature, a place which she will occupy securely in spite of changes in literary manner and in the face of changing critical standards. Her newest book, a volume of short stories, even should it add nothing to her fame, will not detract therefrom; and there is at least one sketch among the half-dozen which is as notable as anything she has done in the short-story field. Within its narrower compass, "Bewitched" has much of the same tragic power which was the commanding feature of *Ethan Frome*; and if the remaining pieces are not quite up to the same level, or of the same fine literary texture, only one, "Velvet Ear Pads," may be regarded as negligible, and when one is allowed to plead the humor of the tale then even this can be saved from the indictment.

One would like to know exactly what Mrs. Wharton herself thought of her first story, which she gives the title "Miss Mary Pask." It must be admitted it was an excellent story to place in the shop window; it should serve admirably in drawing custom. But it is like those coats which the ready-to-wear dealers so ostentatiously display—of too patent perfection. The reader will not be convinced that Mrs. Wharton was to any important degree compelled by her theme; she seems rather to have decided upon it in cold blood. And this is scarcely the mood in which to approach a story in which the finer shades of mental aberration are to be conveyed. Edith Wharton was never an imitator; yet "Miss Mary Pask" gives the impression of willful imitation. For our own part, we should consider such a verdict too drastic; the influence—the literary influence, that is—is Edgar Allan Poe, but Poe considered as a school rather than an individual. Mrs. Wharton, we believe, was in what might be termed the Poe mood; and "Miss Mary Pask" was the result.

And that is precisely why it was a fine story for the shop window, for who can draw custom better than Poe? Mrs. Wharton, it hardly need be said, is completely the mistress of every trick necessary to the theme: at the outset she makes a lively howdy-do in the first person, and for a time she has the reader hoodwinked into the belief that she is showing him a mystery even while he is convinced that no mystery exists. For a person either is dead or he is not dead; and when a "recent bout of fever" is admitted, any ghost an author has been at pains to conjure flies contumeliously out of the window. Yet for all the artificiality of the piece it gives a moment of pleasure. Closely analyzed, the pleasure doubtless is derived precisely from this artificiality. There is no such thing possible as a convincing story of a ghost—or of a near ghost, the theme, by its very nature, is an incitement to literary trickery, and the fun is in seeing how well the trickery succeeds. Mrs. Wharton is measurably behind Poe in this; but in another aspect of the game she as measurably exceeds him. Poe is just as artificial in the background of nature which he builds up as he is in the action he stages in front of the background. His oceans and his lakes are the product of the scene painter, and his horticultural accessories come from the factory. Not so with Mrs. Wharton. She may falter in conveying the nuances of a previously distraught mind brought suddenly into contact with a fact imperfectly comprehended, but she never errs in conveying the nuances of changing nature. Her "Baie des Tréspassés"—Bay of the Dead—is as real as it is sombre, and the mood she inspires by the name alone is an authentic mood.

In the second story of the book—it is as if there were an actual historical progression here, a story the title of which is "The Young Gentlemen," Mrs. Wharton exhibits genuine increase in power. In this tale, as in the one that follows it, "Bewitched," she goes to the New England of *Ethan Frome* not merely for her background but for her psychology as well. It is an aspect of life (not confined to New England probably) which is rarely touched on openly—the pride of family which counsels the concealment of anything which might be taken to reflect on the family name. Many a one is familiar with a case or two of this sort, or has at least heard vaguely of one—the family in which there is an insane person, or a cripple, who is incarcerated for life, tended carefully, even with affection, but shut off from the world. And the reason—and here is the point on which Edith Wharton has seized—is not that the unfortunate one would be the worse for discovery; the reason for the incarceration is that the pride, actually the false pride, of the members of the family who are whole may be saved.

The story will not be retold; a narrative such as "The Young Gentlemen" must be allowed to unfold itself, under the author's guiding hand. Mrs. Wharton has done a marvelously skillful piece of work, a piece of work that rings true at each step of its progress. She early establishes in the reader the same cognizance of mystery which the townsfolk of Harpledon felt; but in this case she also convinces the reader of the genuineness and the legitimacy of the mystery. And when the fact finally bursts through, the feeling of horror which is produced is likewise genuine; yet the horror is so skillfully mingled with pity that recoil stops half way. Entirely apart from the profound humanity of "The Young Gentlemen" the story merits more than passing study as an achievement in narrative.

Yet it is in the story "Bewitched" that Mrs. Wharton's method is seen in all its possibilities of power. Again this is a tale which should not be retold, but more may be hinted at than with the preceding narrative. As every one knows, there is a portion of New England in which once women believed to be bewitched were cruelly put to death. There were other superstitions in regard to persons suspected of spiritual defilement. Mrs. Wharton lays her scene in this region, among descendants of the witch-hunting community. Nevertheless, there is nothing recondite in the story; in fact, so nakedly simple is the plot when finally apprehended in its entirety that it will rouse chagrin in the breasts of writing folk, who will wonder why they did not themselves seize on anything so obvious.

The central figure of the story is a farmer's wife, and never before with so few strokes has Mrs. Wharton created a character of such visuality and psychological articulation. Angular, unprepossessing, nasally twangy, Mrs. Rutledge carries Yankee shrewdness to the point of virtuosity. She is the victim of a crime, a crime which the perpetrator believes he has concealed by pleading that he is "haunted." The astute descendant of the witch-burners feigns to acquiesce in the explanation, and, calling on three of her townsfolk, farmers all, to bear witness to events, she convinces them, with

Scriptural text, that there has actually been a recrudescence of witchcraft. The dénouement is as swift as it is dramatic.

For the next story Mrs. Wharton moves to Africa. But one gathers that her interest in writing "The Seed of the Faith" was less in the objective aspect than in the subjective. Whether she is entirely successful in keeping the two phases distinct is open to question, but the story is in the main successful. Such criticism as may be raised hinges on this point: to some it will seem that she indulges in too much explanation, she does not, as in "Bewitched," make the events reveal the psychology, she uses psychology to explain the events. The story is of a missionary, twenty-five years in the field, who perceives his failure, and who becomes obsessed with the conviction that if he were to insult the religion of those he seeks to convert to Christianity they would give heed to him as they had not done before.

It is a story of religious fanaticism, engendered by a sense of defeat, intolerable heat, dirt and flies. "The Seed of the Faith" is not without its capacity to move. The aged evangelist, driven on both by illusion and by disillusion, is stoned to death, and the futility of his labors becomes mournfully evident. Mrs. Wharton seems a little astray in Africa. Paris, Cannes, London—the haunts of the sophisticated cosmopolitan—these are her foreign demesne.

Two more stories remain, the title of one is "The Temperate Zone," and "The Velvet Ear Pads" the title of the other. There is nothing of tragedy in either tale, and the second is perfectly frank buffoonery, not a little in the manner of O. Henry, with his modern Bagdad. It is amusing, if slight; and admirably and deftly told.

The story "The Temperate Zone" is the one richly ironic, and at the same time completely suave, tale in the entire collection. The Edith Wharton who writes it is the pupil of Henry James, and it will give infinite delight to those readers whose sense of the artistic can be tickled by watching an author whip a none-too-sturdy idea—the mouse under the paw of the cat—until the last faint breath of life has been extracted from it. To be sure, one has to admit that the juggler is not greatest among performers, but there is a certain thrill derivable from his act that nothing else can give.

The story when brought down to simplest terms is that of a sentimental worshiper of two artists both of whom have died, one a woman poet of mark, the other an equally great portrait painter. The former husband of the poet and the widow of the painter have married, and the sentimentalist, compelled, quite by accident, to view his idols through their nonsentimental eyes, is to some degree disillusioned. Yet, here is the truly subtle thing about the story, the thing that raises it out of the region of mere literary preciosity; the dilettante, with all of his sentimentalism, indeed, because of his sentimentalism, gets nearer to the truth than those who have deluded themselves into thinking they saw so clearly.

Grace Frank,
"Grave Tales,"
*Saturday Review of
Literature*, 2 (29 May
1926), 822

In these two volumes of distinguished short stories [including Anne Douglas Sedgwick's *The Nest*] the authors are concerned with mental states and psychological subtleties rather than with the more dramatic aspects of man's adjustment to his physical environment, and yet drama is always implicit, often explicit, in them. Grave in pitch, suave and mellow in tone, self-assured in technique, they deal with themes made doubly poignant by the absence of the shrill stridency and flashy virtuosity that characterize the average magazine tale of the day.

To be sure both Mrs. Wharton and Miss Sedgwick reveal a gentility of spirit and manner that strictly delimits the action and *milieu* of their tales and that may well seem overnice and finical, old-fashioned, if not archaic, to the post-war generation. But the tales themselves, perhaps because they have so largely to do with themes that are ageless, do not "date" and the fact that their scenes are laid for the most part in a world of gracious ways need not dismay even the reader who likes his pease-porridge hot.

Mrs. Wharton's book begins and ends somewhat lamely. "Miss Mary Pask" for all its atmosphere—and anyone who knows the fogs of Brittany will shiver in the realities of the setting if not in the unrealities of the action—is a near-ghost story in which the main interest and intention seem a little out of perspective. "Velvet Ear-Pads" is merely an amusing and extravagant travesty of the kind of story Mrs. Wharton does *not* write. Was it concocted on a wager that she could if she would?

At least two of the other four tales, however, are superlatively well done and essentially significant. In "The Temperate Zone" a dead poet and a dead painter suffer a kind of second death at the hands of their living lovers, and the gossamer threads of intricate personal and spiritual relationships are woven into a design that suggests the eternal conflict between artist and Philistine. "The Seed of the Faith," perhaps the most dramatic of the stories, evokes not only the filth, smells, and moral lassitude of a small Moroccan town but convincingly mingles with them the religious questionings and doubts and the physical martyrdom of two American missionaries determined to put their faith to the test.

These two tales, as well as "The Young Gentlemen," are models of construction. Never a clue is wasted, never a hint too strongly stressed, and in every instance we follow the action through a narrator or participant perfectly calculated to make the conclusion seem inevitable without being obvious. Mrs. Wharton's scalpel has a keen edge and the hand directing it does not waver. Whether the carefully hidden sorrow of a shy New Englander or the ghostly wraith of a secret sin be laid upon the table, the surgeon remains detached, impersonal, a little unfeeling perhaps, but always understanding.

"New Books at a Glance," *Saturday Review* [England], 141 (29 May 1926), 653

In consequence of the strike there is still some disorganization in the publishing world, and the books we have received are hardly typical. Nevertheless, they include several with a measure of topical interest and one or two with serious literary claims.

In fiction we have *Here and Beyond* . . . by Mrs. Wharton; three stories, apparently, of a more or less mundane character, and three that may conveniently be described as psychic. New England, Morocco, France, and Monte Carlo provide the settings.

"Fiction," Nation and Athenæum [England], 39 (19 June 1926), 325

Undoubtedly Mrs. Wharton is old-fashioned. She has pity and sentiment; she studies real people rather than sequences of reaction stimuli, and complexes. The half-dozen stories in *Here and Beyond*, despite Henry James, are actually stories: they have a satisfying plot. The first story of a conventionally haunted Brittany deals tenderly with a ghostly visitation, but Mrs. Wharton brings us back at the end to our armchair with as sound an explanation as any invented by Wilkie Collins: whereas a more modern writer would think it sufficient to dump us in a mystical border world and walk off. "The Seed of the Faith," the story of an aged missionary in Morocco, who attempts to shock the East into interest after a life of failure by emulating the insulting zeal of the early evangelists faced by the riddle of pagan tolerance, is tender, powerful, ironic. In her last story, taking a conventional Monte Carlo and a conventionally absent-minded professor, she turns so human and humorous a plot that one finds oneself chuckling suddenly in the street a day or two later. But despite the vast fiction around the subject, can one really fling a hundred-franc note on the roulette table? We have only observed dull counters in use.

P. C. Kennedy, "New Novels," New Statesman, 27 (19 June 1926), 266

In Mrs. Wharton's new collection of short stories, there is only one that will bear any sort of comparison with her best work in the past, and that is the story of the mental decay and religious mania of two Baptist missionaries in Africa. "The Seed of Faith" is strongly conceived and skilfully elaborated; the atmosphere, both spiritual and physical, is made vivid and real; and the disgusting ugliness of the climax is neither slurred nor overdone. For the rest, there is some light social comedy, whose manner is too grand for its matter, and there are some half-ghost-stories.

L. P. Hartley, "New Fiction," Saturday Review [England], 141 (19 June 1926), 754

The six stories in *Here and Beyond* all have an architectural quality. They do not come up as flowers but as buildings, and their true lines are not revealed until the scaffolding is cleared away. In this they differ from much modern work, which is often uncertain and careless of its ultimate shape: it may or may not be a satisfactory specimen, according as its roots have been plentifully or scantily nourished by the author's mind. In much modern work, too, there is diversity of method but one compelling consciousness—the author's; story and presentation alike are subdued to the mind, sometimes to the mental processes, of the author. They are variations on the particular æsthetic credo which holds his mind at the moment, they are a chain of milestones marking his progress, and have the limited individuality of milestones.

Mrs. Wharton's stories are not like this. She has arrived at a technique which satisfies her, and when she makes an experiment it is in subject-matter, not in method. Her novels are not even semi-detached; they are as independent, as unlike each other, as she can make them. Each tale makes its own private effort to win a foothold in the imagination. It is true that the first three stories in the present collection are concerned with the supernatural, but in design and intention they are entirely distinct; while the last three are so dissimilar they might have been written by three different people. We honour Mrs. Wharton's determination to find fresh worlds to conquer. Her campaigns are not all equally successful, but the reader enjoys exploring, in her company, the new territory, some of which opens its arms to Henry James's most considerable marshal, and some of which does not. As to the story called "Bewitched," we simply could not tell what the issue had been. It is a tale so full of evasions, elisions, suggestions and half-tones that it left us utterly bewildered. "Mary Pask" and "The Young Gentlemen" are easier to follow. They are not "thrillers" and could not be, for in her anxiety to avoid crudity Mrs. Wharton has made us familiar with the abnormal: she works up to it by easy stages and insensible gradations. That people should be haunted, should have premonitions and psychic powers, seems to be the natural thing. New England is, of course, a happy hunting-ground for the ghost-monger. In two of her stories Mrs. Wharton makes

the most of this; to the Puritan conscience sin readily assumes a tangible shape. Obstinate, tenacious, superstitious, the New Englanders were at the mercy of their fears. Unlike Hawthorne, Mrs. Wharton does not use the supernatural as a literary device, or as the playful half-serious symbol of a theory of sin and punishment; she accepts the psychic world as an alternative to the real world and binds herself to obey its rules. And therefore, to the incredulous, it may appear that she is telling, quite seriously, a tale which neither she nor her readers can possibly believe. Of the other stories "Velvet Ear-Pads" is the best—a very broad farce founded upon a chance meeting between a Professor of Philosophy and a beautiful Russian refugee. Mrs. Wharton carries this off perfectly. All her many triumphs are won against odds; inspiration sometimes fails her; difficulties and improbabilities in the narrative obtrude themselves: and yet by keeping her eye unflinchingly on the main point of her theme, by always knowing what she is going to do if not how she is going to do it, by balance of judgment and force of intention she succeeds in turning a forlorn hope into a victory.

Louise Maunsell Field, "In This Month's Fiction Library: *Here and Beyond*," *Literary Digest International Review*, 6 (June 1926), 450–1

The publication of a new volume of short stories by Edith Wharton is always a cause for rejoicing—rejoicing enhanced when the book includes one of her rare returns to the New England of *Ethan Frome*. And in this collection of six short stories there are no less than two of these returns, altho "The Young Gentlemen" is perhaps less of a definite return than of a hovering on the outskirts.

It is the essentially New England story of "Bewitched" which is the most notable of a notable collection. In its superbly drawn portrait of the self-contained Mrs. Rutledge, in those of the three men she summoned, that snowy winter day, to the place which seemed "so far away from humanity," in theme and in the spirit pervading it all, the tale belongs absolutely to that one section of the United States. Mrs. Rutledge's way of using her husband's explanation to further her own purposes is as completely in character as are those last words of hers, spoken as she enters the cutter to drive away from the graveyard after the funeral. Tho on a smaller scale, the story is carved from the same material as *Ethan Frome*, and in the same manner of an austere and impressive simplicity, a wonderful example of the difficult art of short-story writing.

Only to such a perfect thing as "Bewitched" could the tale of "The Young Gentlemen" possibly come second. Here too the setting is New England, a once prosperous port "discovered" by a small summer colony of artists and writers. But the forebears of some of these had lived at Harpledon, and something of its essence was in their blood. Yet the concealment practised by Waldo Cranch was of a kind which has been known elsewhere, and not so completely of New England as the concealment of Aunt Cressidora Cheney, shut up for years to save her relatives' pride. The tale begins quietly; then comes the note of a vague uneasiness, a vague apprehension, quickening and intensifying into dread and fear, culminating in horror. There is more of detailed explanation, less of suggestion and of dependence on the reader's own imagination than in

"Bewitched," but the story is quite as skilfully handled.

"The Seed of the Faith" shows us the hot, crowded little town of Eloued in Morocco, thronged with "beggars, pilgrims, traders, slave-women, water-sellers, hawkers of dates and sweetmeats, leather-gaitered country-people carrying bunches of hens head-downward, jugglers' touts from the market-place, Jews in black caftans and greasy turbans, and scrofulous children reaching up to the high counters to fill their jars and baskets." Here in this alien place are two American missionaries, a young man, and an old. No one bothers them. No one pays any attention to them. And in that fact lies the measure of their failure. It is the sudden appreciation of this utter unimportance crashing through his dreams which rouses weak, unwieldy Mr. Blandhorn, "so ignorant, so defenseless, and so convinced," to a desperate attempt to answer the insistent, "What's the use?" which echoes pitilessly in his ears. The position of the missionary has been a not infrequent theme of recent fiction; seldom has it been presented and summed up so effectively and so clearly as in this one short story.

"The Temperate Zone" reveals the author in one of her ironic moods. The widow of a great painter marries the man who had been the lover, and would, had she lived, have become the husband of a great poet. To the newly married pair comes a young, enthusiastic admirer of the two geniuses, ready to hang on every word they have to tell him of the great dead whom they, he takes for granted, must worship as devoutly as he does. The situation is one deftly devised for the enjoyment of those who, like Mrs. Wharton, delight in irony.

The other two stories are those which begin and end the volume, "Miss Mary Pask," and "Velvet Ear-Pads." Different in every other way, they are alike in this, that they both seem the result of deliberate intention, rather than of spontaneous growth. The first is a ghost story of the explained type, where the apparently supernatural is eventually proved to be entirely natural. But the description of the uncanny effects of the fog, there on the Brittany coast, with the waters of the "Bay of the Dead" crying hungrily through the darkness, is a thing to make one shudder. "Velvet Ear-Pads" is farce, a somewhat labored tho amusing account of an absent-minded professor, who went to Monte Carlo and encountered a beautiful young Russian refugee.

Mrs. Wharton's style has been so often commented upon, that to write of its brilliance, its subtlety and deft sureness seems superfluous. Among these tales are several which show her artistry at its best, and show too the depth of her understanding of human beings, their actions and reactions. One does not often come across a volume of short stories as thoroughly worth while as this collection.

John T. Rodgers,
"An Age of Innocence,"
North American Review,
223 (June–August 1926),
375–6

At the moment we do not recall how far Mrs. Wharton has hitherto succumbed to the lure of the short story. But if the good lady harbors the intention of carrying on th' imperial theme, we can only implore her to cultivate her better manner. In brief:—

Of all the silly, inconsequential, irrelevant bits of flubdubbery, these "six exquisite gems," as they are called, stagger criticism. There is, so far as we can see, not one page from the opening line of *Here and Beyond*, the first "gem," to the final word of release in "Velvet Ear-Pads" which deserves five seconds consideration.

In complaining that the tales are irrelevant, it is not meant, of course, to imply that they should be hung upon a central theme, for each is designed to stand alone. We refer rather to the author's penchant for what she evidently considers gay repartee, wherein the party of the first part puts forth a remark to which the party of the second can only respond by saying something screamingly funny—to the unbounded delight of the fair creatix. This, as Mrs. Wharton should know, will not do. In a play such artifice is called padding; in a goose, stuffing; and Mrs. Wharton is obviously in love with the trick.

But a far graver offense from the point of view of one who has read and genuinely admired Mrs. Wharton's earlier stories, lies in the literary puerilities to which she here descends. Example:

> Hadn't she laid the cable before my eyes, her own streaming with tears while I read: "Sister died suddenly this morning requested burial in garden of house particulars by letter"—with the signature of the American Consul at Brest, a friend of Bridgeworth's I seemed to recall?

It needs no critical judgment to tear this travesty on grammar to pieces. Even the double possessive was not spared. The informal, thinking-aloud discursiveness apart, there is no excuse for such stuff in a writer who presumably has some acquaintance with the decencies of composition.

Again: "When he came back a frown still lingered on his handsome brows." [Complete sentence.] Is this Harold Bell Wr—? No, Edith Wharton.

Not all the sophomorics, however, can wholly obscure the great virtue which shines forth in all the works of Mrs. Wharton that have come under our notice. She has always had, preëminently, the gift of character-sketching; like Willa Cather, she can make one see and feel her people after half a dozen words of introduction. Her art does not desert her even now, and consequently it makes one the more impatient of the follies of style and literary technique which mark *Here and Beyond* from start to finish.

If Mrs. Wharton is determined to continue the inviting path of short story writing, we can offer no better advice than the suggestion that she take down the familiar, but still incomparable, O. Henry and read, read and read him again.

Dorothy Bacon Woolsey, "Short Stories," *New Republic*, 47 (21 July 1926), 262–3

It is almost a misfortune to win the favor of those exacting mentors the critics to such an extent as Mrs. Wharton did with *Ethan Frome* and *The Fruit of the Tree*—for nothing she has since done has been allowed to fall short of these admitted heights without the most vociferous remonstrance, which in the case of the present volume of excellent tales seem to the present reviewer unfair. One of the stories ("Miss Mary Pask") is undeniably futile and wambling, unredeemed by the finish of its style. Another ("The Young Gentlemen") is strained and far-fetched, and "Velvet Ear-Pads" is disappointingly brittle and ineffective. But "Bewitched" held for us all Mrs. Wharton's accustomed vigor and sharpness of contour and the stern

poise and purposive movement of her best work. "The Seed of the Faith" has power, sweep and dark passion, and "The Temperate Zone" reaffirms the Jamesian tradition with delicate psychological shadings and all the refinements of a rigid aesthetic code subtly conveyed to the reader. We feel sure that if this volume came to hand under an unknown name it would be received with praise if not general enthusiasm.

George D. Meadows, "*Here and Beyond*," *Catholic World*, 123 (August 1926), 715–16

This volume of six stories will be welcomed by all readers who seek relief from the jazz tempo of so much of our contemporary fiction. Mrs. Wharton's clear and unshrinking analysis of human character and motive is clothed in an English prose that is the work of a supreme artist in words. After reading book after book of hers, one is still amazed by her power of handling the most diverse material. In the present volume, for example, there are stories such as "The Young Gentlemen" whose setting recalls what many critics regard as her highest achievement, *Ethan Frome*; with it one may contrast "The Seed of the Faith," a poignant story of zeal without perspective and religious fervor without saving humor, wherein are conjured up for us the picturesqueness and the squalor of the Arab *souks* in North African towns with a truthfulness which no traveler can gainsay.

As the title of the collection suggests, some of the stories are of what is generally called a "psychic" kind. In this difficult medium Mrs. Wharton works with the sure touch of an Emily Brontë, although with more restraint.

"Here and Beyond," Times Literary Supplement [England], 2 September 1926, p. 578

Strictly speaking there is very little of the "beyond" in the six stories that make up Mrs. Edith Wharton's *Here and Beyond*. ... The only one which contains an unrationalized ghost is "Bewitched," where a deacon and two friends are summoned to a remote American farm to hear that the farmer is bewitched by the dead daughter of one of the friends. The success of this story is in its suggestion of bleakness, of wintry skies and temperaments, and in the figure of the farmer's wife, Mrs. Rutledge—a figure of extraordinary dourness. Its weakness, on the other hand, is in its somewhat arbitrary ending and its not too successful handling of the specific ghostly terror. Indeed, our criticism of all these stories is that their manner and technical accomplishment, which are distinguishing qualities of Mrs. Wharton, are more remarkable than their matter. In "Miss Mary Pask" an artist relates his supposed entertainment by the ghost of an old American lady in a lonely cottage on the coast of Brittany. The effect is very nearly attained, but not quite for even an over-worked man would hardly accept a ghost who lighted candles, presumably with real matches; and it is therefore no surprise to learn that the old lady was not dead after all. "The Young Gentlemen" is the kind of tale which, perhaps, more would have been made by Mr. Walter de la Mare. It turns on the discovery of an old man's long-hidden secret, which was the ex-

istence of two sons who had never grown out of childhood. Mrs. Wharton is admirable while she is working up the atmosphere of the old New England village and the position in it of old Mr. Cranch, its doyen; but when it comes to the discovery by the narrator and Mrs. Durant of the two poor middle-aged simpletons playing with toys in their concealed nursery, something of the uncanny that ought to be there leaks away.

The best story in the book is undoubtedly "The Seed of the Faith." The scene is Eloued, a village in Morocco, where Mr. Blandhorn has carried on an American Baptist mission for twenty-five years without making a single convert. The arrival in the stifling, seething bazaar of a young American commercial traveller, who had once been a lay brother of the mission, brings home to Willard Bent, Mr. Blandhorn's assistant, and to the old pastor himself the realization of their failure. This is admirably done; we realize the scent and squalor of the East, the dust, the flies, the intense heat, and the swarming population, indifferent to the harmless white strangers, who in their narrow but confident religion have remained entirely ignorant of the people they set out to convert. But the spirit of an Old Testament prophet is in Mr. Blandhorn, who, with a text upon his lips, proceeds to testify by insulting the religion of Eloued on a solemn day, and pays the penalty contentedly. Another story, "The Temperate Zone," is too reminiscent of Henry James. The last story in the book, however, shows Mrs. Wharton in a most unusual vein, that of light-hearted extravagance. "Velvet Ear-Pads" is a most absurd and diverting business in which a highly intellectual professor wins a fortune at Monte Carlo with the hundred franc note of a Russian adventuress, allows the winnings to be stolen by the lady's adventurous betrothed, who loses them again at the tables.

Which fact being satisfactorily established, all heartily embrace. It is neither here nor beyond, but certainly in the region of pure laughter.

Checklist of Additional Reviews

Edwin Francis Edgett, "Here and Beyond with Edith Wharton," Boston *Evening Transcript*, 8 May 1926, book section, p. 4.

Margaret Leech, "Edith Wharton's New Book of Short Stories," New York *World*, 9 May 1926, book section, p. 6–M.

Frances Newman, "Deserves Pulitzer Prize Every Year," *New York Evening Post Literary Review*, 22 May 1926, p. 2.

Edmund Pearson, "Fiction," *Outlook*, 143 (2 June 1926), 186.

"New Books in Brief," *Independent*, 117 (7 August 1926), 164.

TWILIGHT SLEEP

TWILIGHT SLEEP

Edith Wharton

FAUST. *Und du, wer bist du?*
SORGE. *Bin einmal da.*
FAUST. *Entferne dich!*
SORGE. *Ich bin am rechten Ort.*

Faust. Teil II. Akt V.

New York ✻ London
D. APPLETON AND COMPANY
Mcmxxvii

Isabel Paterson, "The New Sin," New York *Herald Tribune*, 22 May 1927, Section 7, pp. 1–2

When the Fathers of the Church included melancholy among the mortal sins they drew upon experience as well as inspiration. They had another word for it; accidie (acedia), which fell out of common use about the time America was discovered. The substitution is significant, for it is not an exact synonym. What we understand by melancholy is but a passing shadow compared to the "dark night of the soul" they had in mind. Life must have been hard indeed in those days; so comfortless and perilous for the majority of mankind that settled despair was a very real temptation. Had any one suggested that a too facile cheerfulness might come to be a spiritual danger in the future, the quaint notion might well have provoked a smile. It was understood that human nature could make a virtue of necessity; but there were not enough instances to give rise to any proverb about making a merit of good fortune. The nearest they got to it was when kings claimed their privileges by the grace of God. It remained for the New World to invent the new sin of excessive and habitual optimism.

Naturally, European eyes have been keenest to detect this complacent attitude of prosperous America; it is now a familiar rebuke. But only an American pen could have drawn that subtle synthesis of traits which constitutes a type to embody the accusation. No doubt her long residence abroad gave Edith Wharton a helpful perspective, Europe's well-justified pessimism serving as a camera obscura to define the outlines of the spectacle which so dazzles and irritates the Old World.

If American civilization is, as charged, the apotheosis of materialism, Pauline Manford is an appropriate figure to epitomize this cult of temporal well-being. She had everything. Though her past contained "a little cemetery of failures," it was "a very small one—planted over with quick-growing things, so that you might have walked all through her life and not noticed there were any graves in it," and still more effectively blocked out by her success in greater enterprises.

Her first husband, Arthur Wyant, was one of Pauline's failures, but she had disposed of him neatly and expeditiously by divorce, and even managed to keep on terms of distant cordiality with him, for the sake of their son, Jim Wyant. Moreover, Arthur Wyant had not been a dead loss; through him she had secured a firm foothold in the front ranks of New York society. Her second choice, Dexter Manford, was all that a husband should be; distinguished in his profession, the law, and devoted not only to Pauline and their daughter, Nona, but to his stepson, Jim. Nona was an attractive girl, not a vacuous trouble-hunting flapper. Jim's wife, Lita, was a little difficult, perhaps, but no doubt her baby would keep her steady. Pauline herself, in her early forties, was still handsome and healthy. And in her own right she was immensely rich, having inherited one of the vast new fortunes created by the motor industry—a neat symbolic touch.

For all these blessings Mrs. Manford gave thanks, not mere lip-service, but by an incessant round of benevolent, uplifting and hygienic activities. Not a minute of her day was unemployed. When Nona tried to see her mother out of turn, Mrs. Manford's harassed secretary, Maisie Bruss, showed the maternal tablets of the law, Mrs. Manford's engagement book.

"Just run your eye down that list—"

"7:30—Mental uplift. 7:45—Breakfast. 8—Psycho-analysis. 8:15—See cook. 8:30—Silent meditation. 8:45—Facial massage. 9—Man with Persian miniatures. 9:15—Correspondence. 9:30—Manicure. 9:45—Eurythmic exercises. 10—Hair waved. 10:15—Sit for bust. 10:30—Receive Mother's Day deputation. 11—Dancing lesson. 11:30—Birth control committee." And so on. If the family broke in at odd hours, the whole schedule would be disorganized beyond recovery.

It made no difference that Nona wanted to give her mother a hint of impending domestic disaster. Mrs. Manford simply refused to listen to unpleasant things. It was a matter of principle with her and her associates—"bright, elderly women . . . all inexorably earnest, aimlessly kind and fathomlessly pure," who "advocated with equal zeal birth control and unlimited maternity, free love or the return to the traditions of the American home." They stood for organized action in large affairs; and in personal matters they took refuge in "believing the best of every one, persuading themselves that to impute evil was to create it, and to disbelieve it was to prevent its coming into being."

To fortify this roseate philosophy Mrs. Manford had recourse to a variety of spiritual quacksalvers. For a time her pet Mahatma, with his School of Oriental Thought, held first place in her esteem. "The Mahatma certainly had reduced Mrs. Manford's hips—and made her less nervous, too; for Mrs. Manford sometimes was nervous, in spite of her breathless pursuit of repose." And when the Mahatma had to be dropped because of certain ugly rumors—which Mrs. Manford resolutely refused to credit—there was Alvah Loft, the Inspirational Healer, author of "Spiritual Vacuum Cleaning" and "Beyond God." Sacha Gobine, the Russian Scientific Initiate, came after the efficient Alvah; not to mention Mrs. Swoffer, and Orba Clapp: names to conjure with, indeed.

For this was Mrs. Manford's unconscious aim: to eliminate all first-hand emotion and thought by cramming her time and her mind with artificial substitutes. Her energy was spent in paying blackmail to reality, fending herself from any possible contact with the ancient, insoluble problem of pain and evil. Sorrow is the shadow of joy; and though only the truth can give substance and savor to life, it is bought by suffering.

Yet according to her lights, Mrs. Manford was a good woman. Illness and distress she met with an instant response in money; but visiting the sick she considered morbid, aside from the risk of infection. She certainly was not bigoted, for her highest ambition was gratified when she managed to assemble a visiting Cardinal, the Episcopal Bishop of New York, the Chief Rabbi and her Russian Initiate at one evening party. It was a pity she couldn't have the Mahatma, too, but that did not seem advisable, in view of the fact that her husband had come very near prosecuting the Oriental Thinker for something or other, which Mrs. Manford did not inquire into.

She never inquired into anything and declined to be told. If she did not know it was because she did not choose to know that Dexter Manford had long since ceased to care for her, that Nona was hopelessly in love with a married man, that Jim was helplessly miserable over Lita's frivolous coldness, and that Arthur Wyant was fuddling himself into the mood for murder on Jim's behalf. The delayed but inevitable explosion left Mrs. Manford's orderly, glittering world in moral ruins; but by a fluke the facade remained intact. And Mrs. Manford, with a very good imitation of heroism, instantly began to rebuild over the wreckage.

430

Mrs. Wharton's admirable craftsmanship has never been more evident than in *Twilight Sleep*. The title, by the way, is an ironic allusion to Mrs. Manford's creed: "Of course, there ought to be no pain. It ought to be one of the loveliest, most poetic things in the world to have a baby." It isn't of course; and though one may entertain a fleeting wonder whether Mrs. Wharton would insist on the penalty of Eve being left unmitigated by any interference of science, since science is material progress, the objection is easily met by recognition of the function of satire as a brief for the prosecution. The satirist is not required to state both sides of the case.

And Mrs. Wharton has always been preeminently a social satirist, not a creator of character for its own sake. It is manners rather than men and women that interest her, and manners almost in the drawing room sense, as local and ephemeral phenomena, not the *mores* which spring from fundamental instincts and necessities, and therefore are invested with supernatural sanctions. She does not examine the nature of human institutions, property, marriage, patriotism, piety, as the great satirists do. At moments she comes perilously near to invoking Mrs. Grundy instead of the divine Spirit of Comedy. For instance, when the Manfords and Wyants were horror-stricken at the idea of any of their clan "going on the screen," becoming film stars—, for of course they would be stars, from the first engagement; wouldn't they just! This delusion of grandeur is accepted at face value; why? Because although the Manfords and Wyants have been fully exposed as shallow, commonplace, dreary creatures, who would be perfectly at home in Hollywood except that they would fall short of the Hollywood standard of beauty and mimetic ability, they are still, to Mrs. Wharton, "the best people." There is a heightened asperity in her presentation of Lita, a faintly personal annoyance at this incomprehensible creature who cared nothing for a social position which entailed so much sheer boredom.

Mrs. Wharton's talent is confined to contemporary aspects of folly, therefore the texture of her prose is perishable. Yet it is flawless of its kind. Hers is the artistry of a first-class French modiste. In their season all her best novels are absolutely "right," combining elegance with smartness, *chic*. They must date in time precisely because of their up-to-dateness. Fiction lives through its characters, regardless of costumes. Mrs. Manford and her group are mannequins; but every feature, every gesture, every accessory is justly selected, keenly observed and appropriately graced with the jewelled phrases of Mrs. Wharton's witty comment.

Percy Hutchison, "Mrs. Wharton Tilts at 'Society,'" *New York Times Book Review*, 22 May 1927, pp. 1, 27

Despite the infelicity of the title *Twilight Sleep*, Mrs. Edith Wharton will receive the usual felicitations on the production of a new novel. Mrs. Wharton's achievements may vary from book to book; and it seems increasingly probable that she will never again quite equal *Ethan Frome* and *The House of Mirth*. But she maintains herself at so consistently high a level that any occasional faltering of the imagination may be charitably set down as nothing more serious than a change of pace, any lapse in artistry as a mere peccadillo of the pen.

In *Twilight Sleep* Mrs. Wharton has written a novel of present-day New York. At times one is aware of the fact that the author has done part of her work, if not all of it, out of immediate contact with place and people. There are turns of phrase which are English rather than American (for example, "cinema" has not yet become acclimated); and certain of her characters seem marionettes operated from a distance rather than persons actually at our side. On the other hand, Edith Wharton has perhaps never told a tale with equal refinement of method. The story is verily a startling one; but it is told with such reticence, with so many withholdings, with implication everywhere taking the place of direct statement, direct presentation, that not until the book has been finished and laid aside is the reader fully conscious of the tragedy which has been played out before him. And this is realism of a most subtle sort, for not until the catastrophe has come and passed do the persons of the story perceive the precipice along which they walked and over which they have all pitched, some of them to receive hurts from which they will never wholly recover. Hence the title; Mrs. Wharton's characters, lulled by the security which comes of wealth and social position, or from false ideas of freedom, are semi-somnambulists; they are in a sort of "twilight" sleep.

Mrs. Wharton has ever been capable of an irony far from dull; but seldom has she whetted it to such sharpness as in the present book. *Twilight Sleep* abounds in passages of infinite delight. The engagement-pad of Mrs. Pauline Manford (kept, of course, by her secretary) is by no means the least, although the first, of such passages; "7:30, Mental uplift. 7:45, Breakfast. 8, Psychoanalysis. 8:15, See cook. 8:30, Silent meditation. 8:45, Facial mas-

sage. 9, Man with Persian miniatures." And when Nona, Mrs. Manford's 19-year-old daughter, requesting an interview, suddenly appears, one quite understands the secretary's deprecating, "Your mother didn't *expect* to see you before lunch, now, did she?"

Neither Pauline nor Nona is, however, the centre of the story or the persons chiefly involved in the tragedy when it falls, although each is hurt irreparably and each in a different way. But Pauline is more in the forefront of the narrative than any one else, with Nona perhaps a few steps behind. And the story is generally told as seen through their eyes (especially Nona's, Pauline being highly myopic) and when not told as seen by them, told as reflects on them, as on a mirror.

Pauline Manford is a woman whose "altruistic energy" would exhaust her had she less than a superabundance of it. She is not precisely the older generation, although of the older generation. One will be struck by the fine gradations of period achieved by Mrs. Wharton. Pauline's ex-husband, Arthur Wyant—"Exhibit A" in the divorce proceedings and still on terms of acquaintanceship with his former wife—is of the high-hat and coaching days that were New York's in the '90s. Arthur, father of Jim Wyant, Nona's half-brother, who has married Lita Landish and been superseded, is the old versus the new: "Well, and your honor, man—what about your honor?" and he says, 'What's my honor got to do with it if my wife's sick of me?' and you say, 'God, what of the other man—aren't you going to break his bones for him?' and he sits and looks at you and says, 'Get up a prizefight for her?'—God, I give it up. My own son! We don't speak the same language, that's all."

Nona is of the new generation; but not so new as Lita. Nona takes her cabarets, her cocktails and her cigarettes, but all in

432

moderation. But then, Nona had more solidity behind her; not absolutely "family," but very near to it. Lita, an orphan, had been brought up by a somewhat questionable aunt. To be sure, there is also "post war" disillusionment; nevertheless, Mrs. Wharton must always have a little heredity in the account. Every one knows a Lita. "But that was all life ever meant for Lita—would ever mean. Good floors to practice new dance steps on; men—any men—to dance with and be flattered by; women—any women—to stare and envy one; dull people to startle, dull people to shock—but never any one, Nona questioned, whom one wanted neither to startle nor shock, neither to be envied nor flattered by, but just to lose one's self in for good and all. Lita lose herself? Why, all she wanted was to keep on finding herself, immeasurably magnified in every pair of eyes she met!"

And her portrait, with but just a suggestion of Meredith's "rogue in porcelain"—

> Lita's face was something so complete and accomplished that one could not imagine its being altered by any interior disturbance. It was like a delicate porcelain vase, or a smooth, heavy flower that a shifting of light might affect but nothing from within would alter. She smiled in her round-eyed, unseeing way, as a little gold-and-ivory goddess might smile down on her worshipers.

To be sure, this type of girl should never remain married to a Jim Wyant, who, it must be confessed, is something of a washout, despite Mrs. Wharton's best efforts. But then, to whom should the mollusk type be married? That a tragedy must ensue is inevitable, especially when there is also on the scene the self-made, coldly intellectual but, for all its intellectuality, blunderingly passionate type of which

Dexter Manford, Jim's stepfather, is the example. Mrs. Wharton has assembled a dramatis personae of "humors" that would delight Ben Jonson could he come back to earth with his psychological keenness educated to the present day.

And if fault is to be found with *Twilight Sleep* it would be on this score. Except for Pauline, whose importance the author has unconsciously magnified, although she is a marvelous vehicle for Mrs. Wharton's superb wit—"She dominated them all, a grave and glittering goddess of velocity"— there is a little too much psychology and not quite enough flesh and bone. It is true that the cunning watchmaker—who has no interest in the encircling case—articulates with baffling skill the innumerable parts of his complicated "movement." But novel writing is not watchmaking. And it is just a little too much as if Mrs. Wharton had assembled a collection of subtly differing psychological mechanisms and then had grasped at cases, appropriate ones, in which to install them.

Or is it, perhaps, that she has not gone quite far enough in this direction? It may very well be that in clamoring for a little more of differentiating personality among the characters of *Twilight Sleep* one is asking for something that would cheapen the book by bringing the story—which we have purposely refrained from telling, or even suggesting—into too bold relief. But this much may be said: Jim, Nona, Pauline and Dexter Manford, each in his or her blundering way, is striving to keep Lita in bonds which Lita is bent on breaking; and although the bonds actually hold, a world has been shattered. And perhaps one of the keenest of Mrs. Wharton's satiric thrusts is the frantic and successful manner in which is concealed from the universe at large that a lesser orb has been shattered, to be held together forever after only by mutual sufferance born of the need of protective coloring for those whose

433

social elevation places them above the common run of mankind. Those heavy window coverings along the streets where society reigns—Mrs. Wharton pulls them rudely aside for the moment, and then they are hastily snatched back into place by unseen hands within.

Taken all in all, therefore, *Twilight Sleep* is the most satirical of all of Mrs. Wharton's novels. Nona, "only winged," as she bravely puts it, by the catastrophe which has tumbled two houses built of cards, is the one who in reality is unalterably affected.

> "Married? Marry? I'd a thousand times rather go into a convent and have done with it!"
>
> Pauline got to her feet. "I never heard anything so horrible. I sometimes think you want to break my heart, Nona."
>
> The girl let her head drop back among the cushions.
>
> "Oh," she said. "I mean a convent where nobody believes in anything."

Mrs. Wharton has not, in *Twilight Sleep* written a colorful story. Rather it is a steely gray. She intended it to be. And it is a story told with a singular lack of emotion. This also was clearly intentional. For this reason the dénouement, when it is reached (and, another stroke of art, swiftly passed), is the more impressive in the single moment of revelation. The author makes her one high note sound higher by reason of the minor key which has been played throughout. Some ears may become slightly wearied of so much of the minor, but there is always the amusing Pauline —who never dreamed she was amusing— to help one through.

The present novel does not appear to be quite so vitally alive as *The Mother's Recompense*, but in artistry, at least, it is a superior piece of work in that it is sufficient unto itself; in the latter novel any one of several endings was possible, and the whole was weakened by the lack of inevitableness. In *Twilight Sleep* the end is a logical growth, inevitable, ordained.

Edmund Wilson, "*Twilight Sleep*," *New Republic*, 51 (8 June 1927), 78

As Mrs. Wharton grows older, her touch becomes lighter and her attitude more tolerant. *The House of Mirth* was a tragedy; *The Custom of the Country* a ferocious satire. *Twilight Sleep*, which deals with a later New York, the New York of today, but a society of which Mrs. Wharton seems to disapprove hardly less than of the New York of yesterday and of which her picture, in its implications, is by no means reassuring, remains a comedy. Mrs. Wharton's "twilight sleep" is the smoke-screen of "new psychology," Hindu theosophy and Russian mysticism which the too efficient mother of a New York family interposes between herself and the tragic problems of her own household. Her daughter-in-law, the bronze-and-ivory Lita, evades these problems in another way—through night-clubs, drinking and love-affairs—while the sensible, conscientious and disillusioned daughter bears the brunt and pays the price which the others shirk.

It is, from one point of view, so agreeable to find so old a friend as Mrs. Wharton coming at last to lose something of her old harshness, to contemplate the wrongheadedness of humanity with comparative equanimity, that we are hardly disposed to complain if her novels become proportionately less vivid. At most, perhaps, we may regret that she should have lived so long abroad that her pictures of life in America have a tendency to seem either shadowy or synthetic. Thus, the New York of *Twilight Sleep*, though it has been got up with perfect competence and interpreted with great intelligence, has nothing of the solidity, the poetic reality, of the New York of her earlier novels. The beautiful and irresponsible Lita, who dances at the "Cubist cabaret" and almost goes off to Hollywood under the auspices of a movie magnate named Klawhammer, is extremely well observed but somehow rather slighted. We feel that Mrs. Wharton has had to make an effort in order to compass Lita. We are mostly made to watch the action through the eyes of the self-deluding mother and the conscientious daughter, and we are continually being excited in expectation of the catastrophe which will upset the equilibrium of the household. But when the catastrophe finally occurs, it is not quite dramatic enough. The hushing up and glossing over of the scandal are, of course, of the essence of Mrs. Wharton's intention: her point and, as it were, her surprise, lie precisely in the capacity of her characters for continuing to evade the situation even when it has apparently brought the roof down on their heads. Yet the result, from the reader's point of view, is no less a little disappointing. Lita is hardly given her day in court: we have far too much of the mother and the daughter, who after all, are more or less inactive. We are also, at first, allowed to watch the action through the eyes of the self-made father, who falls in love with his stepson's wife (that is, with Lita); but as soon as it is certain that he has succumbed, our view of his consciousness is shut off and we are thereafter excluded from his company.

In any case, however, Mrs. Wharton has written a most entertaining novel and a distinguished piece of social criticism. It is a striking proof of Mrs. Wharton's insight that *Twilight Sleep* should be something other than (what with many novelists, even of high gifts, we have to be content) a mere paler repetition of the author's earlier characters and situations. She has really, to a surprising extent, renewed herself with the new age.

Charles R. Walker, "Mrs. Wharton Versus the Newer Novelists," *Independent*, 118 (11 June 1927), 615

Others have observed that Mrs. Wharton was one of the first American novelists to write about Americans unfavorably. She began to do so and to obtain a cultivated hearing when Sinclair Lewis was an infant, while Sherwood Anderson was a drummer in the Bible belt; Dreiser was writing, to be sure, but he still went unnoticed, even by the vice commission. But since those old days, American authors, goaded and encouraged by the pen of Mencken, have self-consciously held up the American soul to both analysis and ridicule. The average American novel today of reasonable intellectual stature will contain ironic dissection of some phase or other of American barbarism, just as the average novel of the early nineteen-hundreds contained both a "problem" and in the end a glorification of American womanhood.

It is impossible to read Mrs. Wharton's study of certain rich Americans who spend their lives applying the anæsthetics provided by comfort to crude reality and not contrast this novel with other fictional diagnoses of the American scene. To begin with, one does not feel in Mrs. Wharton's reporting of environment or even of speech that vivid sense of realistic recognition that comes, say, from the photographic pages of Sinclair Lewis. One has a certain sense that this or that scene, this or that dialogue are quite accurate in a general, a typical, but not in a particular sense. This is much more true in the earlier chapters while the characters are rounding out in the reader's mind, than in the latter ones where the sweep of the story compels them to act with acute sensitiveness to their own individuality. There is no point where an environment is false or a spoken sentence out of character, but there is lacking, one feels, that emotional immediacy which produces such a strange sense of reality in a Dreiser or an Anderson.

At the other pole, so to speak, of reporting, the setting down of what occurs in the mind, the probing of inner whim and impulse that make up the mental life of man, there is again a loss of immediacy and recognition as compared with the newer novelists. It is sometimes a refreshing and agreeable loss. Much of what the modern "stream of consciousness" novelist includes in his story is repetition or waste. It neither advances the story nor adds to an understanding of character. None of the mental processes which Mrs. Wharton records, are superfluous. Selected with economy like all other materials in her story, they win the reader's admiration for their pertinence. Nevertheless, anyone who, for example, is familiar with Virginia Woolf reads these pages with a certain lack of conviction. They are clearly translations, in terms of Mrs. Wharton's mind and the necessities of the plot, of what occurs in the minds of her characters. This is, of course, the actual process for any writer of fiction. But it ought not

to be apparent. They ought not to *appear* as translations.

It has been said by some that Mrs. Wharton writes with less energy and vitality than certain other novelists whose pages are said to glow with a more immediate warmth and vitality. My own sense in the matter is of a high energy nicely controlled to produce a given result: the well-rounded novel with emphasis on character and story. One has the sense in this novel, as in all of Mrs. Wharton's, of the beauty of the whole; of not too many characters, but plenty, and all carried without effort; of a nice balancing and contrasting of temperaments; of a masterful marshaling of fictional cohorts for the climax which is organic and immensely effective. Mrs. Wharton's artistic energy has successfully expressed itself in the architecture of the novel. And it is when we begin to get the perspective of the building that we begin to believe in the details. But not till then.

Twilight Sleep is the story of The Manfords and the double set in which they move as a result of Mrs. Manford's two marriages. Mrs. Manford is one of those American women of wealth and Puritan ancestry who drive themselves through a rigorous but essentially meaningless schedule of daily activity. She combines with a belief in industry the philosophy that "pain is a sin" and refuses consistently to admit its existence. There are, however, "frustrations" in her life; she has to admit *them*, and in order to put them out of mind employs a startling series of mental healers and quackish purveyors of serenity. On the first page of the novel, Mrs. Wharton records her engagement schedule for a day: "7·30, Mental uplift. 7·45, Breakfast. 8, Psychoanalysis. 8·15, See Cook. 8·30, Silent Meditation. 8·45, Facial massage. 9, Man with Persian miniatures. 9·15, Correspondence. 9·30,

Manicure. 9·45, Eurythmic exercises. 10, Hair waved. 10·15, Sit for bust. 10·30, Receive Mother's Day deputation. 11, Dancing lesson. 11·30, Birth Control committee at Mrs. . . . ." Is it necessary to describe her character further?

This lady's second husband, while yearning secretly for a simpler and more satisfying existence, yields to the demands of his wife's energy and social ambition. His attitude toward her is an odd mixture of resentment and admiration. In a sense all the characters gyrate about Mrs. Manford, who wills sternly and continuously that life and all its events return to her gaze a roseate and slightly altruistic glow. She controls not only her present husband but her divorced one, whom she treats with benevolent pity, and visits in a sisterly way at intervals. But it is in the attempt to control her son's wife that the story grows intensely emotional.

"Lita," who is Mrs. Wharton's representative of the younger generation, as "Nona" is the uncomfortable personal link between the two generations, is crude, beautiful, animal, and sincere. She announces that her husband no longer "amuses her" and that she "wants a new deal." Mr. and Mrs. Manford succeed in postponing the dreaded divorce by inducing Lita to spend a week at the country home of the Manfords. Mr. Manford, feeling at first a purely paternal and protective interest in his daughter-in-law, finds himself yielding in the end to a more intimate passion. Though many other volcanic scandals threaten eruption 'neath the smooth social surface of Mrs. Manford's set, she resolutely keeps them out of sight and, by "mental uplift," out of mind. Her former husband—never quite reconciled to the new order—appears unexpectedly and most untactfully at the Manfords'. Madame is alone. Mr. Manford is out "looking after Lita." It is hard to know just what he suspects or what he intends, but at any rate Mrs. Manford, by her characteristic resolution to avoid a scene and to "see only good in everybody," gets rid of him by aid of the weather before any harm is done.

Then comes the dramatic scene to which all of this leads. It is an act of shooting in which concealed and glozed-over jealousies and complexities have a momentary and dramatic exposure. But the exposure is only momentary. Nona lies ingeniously and bravely, the butler backs her up, Mrs. Manford readily believes, and the actors in the drama retire to their artificialities.

It is a full and a rich canvas, though in the first half of the book Mrs. Wharton is less successful than when the outlines are filled, and both story and characters sharpen in subtlety and in conviction.

"Twilight Sleep," Times Literary Supplement [England], 16 June 1927, p. 422

In her new book, *Twilight Sleep*, Mrs. Edith Wharton has once more produced, with supreme competence, a picture of New York luxury livers, men and women whose days are softly padded with many thicknesses of dollars, who command service and protection because they are so rich, and who assiduously avoid any contact with what is disagreeable and painful. We are taken into the household of Pauline and Dexter Manford, shown them as they live, meet their friends, discover much that they do not know about themselves or each other, and then the door is softly closed and we are left pondering the miracle of civilization. Mrs. Wharton exhibits with an amused irony the English butler, the orchids, the secretary who slaves at telephone and typewriter over Mrs. Manford's daily programme, the glorious Gainsborough over the dining-room mantelpiece ("which Pauline sometimes almost mistook for an ancestral portrait"), all the appointments of a perfectly run establishment—with the usual special mention of bathrooms which the bath-conscious American never omits—which serves as background for the self-cherishing owners.

The family ramifications include a former husband of Pauline's, Arthur Wyant, visited and petted by herself, her two children (one of them Wyant's son) and her present husband; poor Arthur is humorously known as "Exhibit A," a name which he does not appear to resent, and why he does not go to Manford's house and shine at Pauline's dinner parties is a mystery of the social code known only to those concerned. She looks upon him as a responsibility, although she has divorced him not only because he is a muddled and futile person but because, when she was having a rest-cure in California, he had had an "affair" with a cousin, and "immorality no high-minded woman could condone." Mrs. Wharton has added in Pauline Manford a notable portrait to her gallery of society women. She is moral and kind and cultured. Her outside is perfectly cared for, her mind fed with appropriate food, she relaxes, she withdraws, she visualizes the beauty that she hopes to radiate; she never has an idle moment. Contrasted with her elaborate artificiality is the fresh candour of her daughter Nona, and the animal naturalness of her daughter-in-law, Lita, a vivid sketch of the new youth alternating between luxurious idleness and a passion for something like professional skill in half a dozen games, ignoring any claims of husband or child the instant either becomes tiresome. Dexter Manford is half

in love with her, and she readily plays with fire. Scandal is averted by Nona, and Lita and her husband sail for Europe, the usual refuge of those in temporary social discomfort. Dexter and Pauline go to Egypt. Nona, the only person in the picture who has principle and feeling, is left bitterly disillusioned wishing she could retire into a convent "where nobody believed anything." Mrs. Wharton is exceedingly cruel in her satire, unsparing to the ageing woman, and not much kinder to the young. The world of self-delusion, of "twilight sleep," seems to her so horrible that at times she can scarcely laugh at it. She sets it brilliantly before her readers, writing with such certainty and vigour that their senses anyhow will not be lulled.

Edwin Clark, "Six Months' Fiction," *New York Times Book Review*, 26 June 1927, p. 18

This brings us to the performances of some of the established names in the novel. In *Twilight Sleep*, Mrs. Wharton has written one of her most technically perfect stories. A wealthy woman masks herself behind a complacently busy life of social interest in order that she may never come to close quarters with life. The inevitably tragic episode occurs and is detachedly observed. It is a gracefully written, hard, relentless, ironic study of "the best people" and their folly.

Edwin Muir, "Fiction," *Nation and Athenæum* [England], 41 (2 July 1927), 452

Like almost all Mrs. Wharton's novels, *Twilight Sleep* is well written, well constructed, full of understanding and good sense, and serious, but not too serious, in spirit. She is an admirable writer; she has recognized her limitations; she has set her standard; and in her excellence there is inevitably a touch of monotony. The present story will maintain her reputation.

L. P. Hartley, "New Fiction: *Twilight Sleep*," *Saturday Review* [England], 144 (2 July 1927), 24–6

Twilight Sleep is a grim, depressing book. Although the title is metaphorical there lingers about this tale—or should one say this diagnosis?—of modern New York a suggestion of the sickroom, a whiff of chloroform, mixed with the indefinable smell of something that has been artificially deodorized. Mrs. Wharton's world is a circle of old, rich families. Her heroine, Mrs. Manford, had married into this charmed milieu—"her own red corpuscles were tinged with a more plebeian dye... Not that other ingredients were lacking in her hereditary make-up: Mrs. Manford, in certain moods, spoke of 'The Pascals of Tallahassee' as though they accounted for

all that was noblest in her." This Pauline Manford had divorced her first husband, the amiable liquor-loving Arthur Wyant, to marry Dexter Manford the barrister, a younger and more vigorous man. The divorced families, however, were on very good terms, and criticized and interfered with each other just as if they had been one real family. Pauline represents the older generation. She is full of engagements and always dancing attendance upon Faith-Healers and purveyors of Eastern mysticism. To read of the money she spends on them makes one's mouth water, for no one knows better than Mrs. Wharton how to make the rich seem rich. Mrs. Manford was also devoted to good works and went about delivering speeches: "Personality-room to develop in: not only elbow-room but body-room and soul-room, and plenty of both. That's what every human being has a right to." Every minute of her day was accounted for, and if ever left to herself she had the sensation of slipping into a mental vacuum, and was terrified:

Her whole life (if one chose to look at it from a certain angle) had been a long uninterrupted struggle against the encroachment of every form of pain. The first step, always, was to conjure it, bribe it, away by every possible expenditure—except of one's self. Cheques, surgeons, nurses, private rooms in hospitals, X-rays, radium, whatever was most costly and up-to-date in the dreadful art of healing—that was her first and strongest line of protection; behind it came such lesser works as rest-cures, changes of air, a seaside holiday, a whole new set of teeth, pink silk bed-spreads, stacks of picture papers, and hot-house grapes and long-stemmed roses from Cedarledge...

She had indomitable energy, she looked on the bright side of everything, she was a female Robot. But, would she only have recognized it, all about her storms were brewing and threatening to destroy the Manford family ship which breasted so gallantly the waves of financial prosperity. Danger from her step-son's wife, from her daughter, from her husband. They had more nature in them than she had; they wanted mistresses and lovers. As for Dexter:

> The philanthropy was what he most hated. All those expensive plans for moral forcible feeding, for compelling everybody to be cleaner, stronger, healthier and happier than they would have been by the unaided light of nature. The longing to get away into a world where men and women sinned and begot, lived and died, as they chose, without the perpetual intervention of optimistic millionaires, had become so strong that he sometimes felt the chain of habit would snap with his first jerk.

It did snap with results that would have been tragic but for his wife's ingrained habit of looking on the bright side of a bedroom-scene which contained, or had contained, a daughter wounded in two places, a daughter-in-law in hysterics, a former husband a little drunk, with a revolver, and a contemporary husband whose presence needed a great deal of explaining. . . . Mrs. Manford triumphed; she sterilized everything, even the irregularities of her own family. She encountered the grasping insatiable Italian marchesa, Amalasuntha, and defeated her with no other weapons than a long purse and infinite charity. We do not grudge her her victory; but it is the victory of organization over impulse, of society over the individual. *Twilight Sleep* is not merely an indictment of the lives of a single group of rich people; it is a horrified forecast of what the world may be coming to. Mrs. Wharton has bestowed on this new novel all her gifts. It is marvellously organized, marvellously coherent: it moves in a rich deep stratum of thought, the colour and density of which never change, giving the story a magnificent unity of mood and conception. So opaque is this medium that the characters and the life they lead appear blurred; there are no sharp edges, few occasions when the raw taste of life asserts itself above the fine flavourings of literature. There is little spontaneity, perhaps too little. But any unfledged author can produce startling effects of verisimilitude; it is only Mrs. Wharton who can write a novel like *Twilight Sleep* in which are displayed an exacting craftsman's conscience, a method which combines almost equally the arts of statement and suggestion, and a complete knowledge and realization of the author's own intention. It is impossible to exaggerate the difficulties, technical and otherwise, which Mrs. Wharton faces and overcomes.

Naomi Royde-Smith, "New Novels," *New Statesman*, 29 (2 July 1927), 377

Reading Mrs. Wharton's new novel *Twilight Sleep* has reminded me of the criticism on an English novel, published some months ago, made by a chorus of the author's aunts. These good ladies were distressed, in the first place, that any relation of theirs should be capable of writing about human folly without pronounced condemnation: but the deepest source of their annoyance sprang from the fear lest this outspoken record of what was supposed to go on in the stately homes of England should be widely read in America.

And in the same way Mrs. Wharton's aunts, if she has any, may at this very moment possibly be shaking their heads over *Twilight Sleep* and saying: "Of course there are women very like Pauline Manford in New York Society in these days, but what a pity that dear Edith's book should be so widely read as it will be in London."

For Mrs. Manford, inexhaustibly rich, indiscriminately charitable, visiting her divorced husband once a week and completely failing to understand how horrid a mess she is making of her second marriage, is a thoroughly American type. And Mrs. Wharton has exposed her with a thoroughness that only just stops short of caricature. We see this exhausting woman, who finds time to attend to everybody's business but her own, going through a day which begins with mental uplift at 7·30, includes a Birth Control Committee, a meeting of the Mother's Day Association (the aim of which was to encourage rather than control American birth), a sitting with a Mental Healer and another to a new French sculptor for her bust, interviews with both her husbands (separately), a five minutes' visit to her daughter-in-law and the infant grandson, and ending with an enormous, and enormously successful, dinner dance-party given in her own house. She runs a town house and a country estate with the utmost efficiency, and wears out everybody in both households, including her desperate secretary, Maisie Bruss, and her nineteen-year-old daughter Nona. Pauline is an unflinchingly virtuous woman. She has divorced James Wyant, not because she had ceased to care about him, but because she owed it to her own virtue to proclaim against his solitary lapse, and, though she continues to see

the sinner, "the scent she used always reminded him of a superior disinfectant."

But it is not in her satire of Mrs. Manford's conjugal comprehensiveness, not even in the carefully prepared crash with its mixture of foolish tragedy and crazy farce, that the real exposure of Mrs. Wharton's book is to be found. The desert she makes in the lives of her husbands and their children, a boy by Arthur Wyant, a girl by Dexter Manford, is explored for us with the biting impartiality that reaches one last moment of real tenderness, as is Mrs. Wharton's own inimitable way with the characters she handles so masterfully. In *Twilight Sleep* the writer's second string plays the louder music. On it we hear alternate themes. One is the air of disillusioned boredom sung fretfully by Lita Wyant, Pauline's lovely unprincipled daughter-in-law, and in a more tragic key, by Nona Manford, a girl of the same age whose final sigh is for the peace of a convent. "Oh, but I mean a convent where nobody believes in anything." This, according to Mrs. Wharton, is the song of post-war American youth. The other air— the twilight sleep tune—is played by rich and hearty American middle-age. It is an amplification of the doctrines of Mrs. Eddy and all her disciples and imitators: "There is no such thing as Pain," they chant. "Poverty, Disease, Wrinkles, Fatigue, Misunderstanding are all False Claims. Illusions—you have only to *say* they don't exist and they are gone." But this attitude takes a great deal of keeping up. It has to be taught and re-taught:

The Mahatma certainly had reduced Mrs. Manford's hips—and made her less nervous too: for Mrs. Manford sometimes was nervous in spite of her breathless pursuit of repose. Not, of course, in the same querulous uncontrolled way as poor Arthur Wyant, who had never been taught poise, or mental uplift, or being in tune with the Infinite; but rather as one agitated by the incessant effort to be calm.

So the Mahatma is succeeded by Alvah Loft, "the Busy Man's Christ," who charged on a geometrically progressive scale for three, six or ten minutes of Inspirational Healing. But, in a week or so:

> She sometimes suspected that Alvah Loft's doctrine might be only for beginners. That was what Sacha Gobine, the new Russian Initiate, plainly intimated. Of course there were innumerable degrees in the spiritual life, and it might be that sometimes Alvah Loft's patients got beyond his level—got above it— without his being aware of this fact. Frankly, that was what Gobine thought must have happened in the case of Pauline.

The book, it will be seen, is full of good, acid reading. And its satire will not be lost on London or Paris, where Mrs. Manford and her Inspirational Healers and Initiates have their counterparts. Mrs. Wharton is not telling that uncomfortable thing the Truth exclusively about American millionaires.

S.F.H.,
"The Bookshelf,"
Woman Citizen, 12 (July 1927), 36

Again New York society lives and breathes through the pen of Edith Wharton—this time in *Twilight Sleep*, a novel of modern Manhattanites. Fearful of pain, whether mental or physical, avoiding reality, these moneyed men and women live in a little world of delusion all their own. For a moment life breaks through and leaves them staring at tragedy, but they soon stumble away, helpless, seeking only new realms of "twilight sleep."

Moved by the master Wharton hand the characters go convincingly on their appointed way, with only the reservation that Pauline Manford is perhaps overdrawn as chief vehicle for Mrs. Wharton's satire of the cult of pleasantness at any price. Pauline is devoted to improving the world, and incidentally her own figure, on a program of miscellaneous causes, manicures and mahatmas—a program so crowded that nothing distressing and real can find foothold. Her two husbands, Arthur Wyant, poor Exhibit A, whose old, do-nothing, New York blood exasperated his energetic wife to the point of divorce, and Dexter Manford, a country Babbitt, raised bewilderingly to the heights of city society, are more successful personalities. So, too, is Nona Manford, who serves in the rôle of "author's eye" in the approved Wharton manner, and her half-brother, Jim Wyant, whom she tries to shield from the inevitable tragedy of a beloved but utterly selfish doll-wife.

How Nona gives up her own chance at love and even risks her life to save the unseeing people about her makes an absorbing story, told as only Edith Wharton can tell it. There is all her typical style— the culminating moments when narrative breaks into dialogue, a room seen through different pairs of eyes, the skilled reticence, always the deft use of words, the pungent wit. But the brilliance that made *The Age of Innocence* and that never-to-be-forgotten *Ethan Frome* are not here. *Twilight Sleep* belongs with *Glimpses of the Moon* on the second shelf of the Wharton collection.

William Lyon Phelps, "Edith Wharton," *Forum*, 78 (August 1927), 315-16

Twilight Sleep . . . is not really a good title for this novel, however alluring it may be to the casual book buyer; for the whole story is in a positively painful glare of light, and it is as wakeful as a predatory bird of the night. This latest production of Edith Wharton's pen is marked by those qualities that have made her the foremost of our living American writers; keen intelligence, knowledge of the manners of fashionable society, mastery of literary style, and a coldly ironical view of those grown up children we call men and women. As Ibsen in Munich wrote about Norway and Browning in Italy wrote about England, so Mrs. Wharton from the security and isolation of her home on the Riviera writes about New York.

The last thing to call Mrs. Wharton would be preacher or moralist. None of our American writers has less evangelical fervor. But this novel, like some of her others, is in truth a tremendous Puritan sermon preached from the text, "For what is a man profited, if he shall gain the whole world, and lose his own soul?" If this is the way people live in the upper reaches of society, the expression "well off" is inaccurate. No Diogenes, regarding from his tub with cynical disdain the world of business and pleasure, could give a more unattractive representation of it than does Mrs. Wharton from her place in the sun. These people in the East Sixties, Seventies, and Eighties are too busy to live. *Est fuga, volvitur rota.* They are strivers in a strife that has no importance and no goal; they are as active as squirrels in cages, and make no more progress. They live lives of active uselessness.

Mrs. Wharton, with her incomparable literary art, has done for metropolitan society what Sinclair Lewis has done for Main Street and for Zenith. If one were forced to choose among unhappy alternatives, one would gladly take Main Street in preference to such febrile activity as this. But I ought to add, that although my acquaintance with the members of the fashionable set in metropolitan circles is extremely limited, those persons whom I *do* know seem happier and more worth knowing than these horrible puppets. But then, I always seem fortunate in my acquaintance; I must, indeed, be a lucky man, for in the wide circle of my intimate friends, those engaged in business are better than Babbitt, those living in small towns are better than the denizens of Gopher Prairie, and those who own boxes at the Opera are better than the insane dervishes of fashion represented here.

Who put that tincture of gall and copperas in Edith Wharton's inkstand? What makes her see the activities of her fellow creatures through the wrong end of the telescope? God knows there is plenty of sin and folly in the world, plenty of ignorance, affectation, and conceit. And there is this to be said for the mordancy of Mrs. Wharton. She does not, like so many of our would-be satirists, attack virtue and idealism and self-sacrifice; she attacks wickedness in high places, selfishness in its million manifestations, the follies and futilities of those who serve the Prince of the Power in the Air.

Furthermore, she shows that however skeptical this age may be in religion, it is gullible in everything else. Never was there a time more propitious for the Prophets of the Grand Bluff. Fortune-tellers, mind-healers, intellectual vacuum cleaners, psychological masseurs, are making hay in every sense of the words. "Just relax,—

443

yes, fifty dollars, and you have an appointment for Wednesday. This is the way out." Is it?

Mary Webb, "Irony and Mrs. Wharton," *Bookman* [England], 72 (September 1927), 303

Ironic genius is rare, though plenty of us have observed the generous helpings of irony, with or without tragedy, which Fate lades out to us. Nobody, one supposes, ever felt it as the Greeks did—a beautiful race in a lovely summer land, yet obsessed by this dark vision. But after all who is afraid of a dead leaf in winter? Only in the rose gardens of summer is it a threat. So the people of richest vitality and fullest experience are usually those whom irony haunts.

Mrs. Wharton is one of them.

This is what puts a fine point on her drama and gives a steeliness to her work, whether it depicts city or country life. The lover of nature, by the way, must deplore Mrs. Wharton's partiality for writing of cities, because she is so wonderful when she is expressing hills and gardens and the people of the wild who move before the purples and the rich mists of the landscape as emanations of it. Ethan Frome and the people in *Summer* are of these. Ethan is a marvellously restrained, still rocky personality. He has in his setting, a power he would lose in a town, just as the heroine of *Summer* has a wild-rose charm which would wither if Mrs. Wharton sent her to the city. Hence, one finds that whenever Mrs. Wharton deliberately waives her second great gift—the interpretation of nature—her people at once become stereotyped, especially when they are rich

people. It is the same with Thomas Hardy, with whom Mrs. Wharton has a decided kinship, for when he leaves the open country we are always conscious of a dimming of the lustre. So when Mrs. Wharton's millionaires sit around and drink cocktails—amazingly many cocktails!—it is impossible always to remember who said what, and who is who's husband and which of the characters are just bankrupt, divorced or dead. This is not altogether because Mrs. Wharton disapproves of the set she describes, nor because these spoilt children of wealth are necessarily dull, for one cannot help thinking that many rich men must be in their secret souls as wild, fascinating, relentless and ferocious as bandits. It is perhaps because in the hot, scented air of those languorous—often drug-soaked—rooms, where ennui prays for some new thing to prick its failing nerves, where life is one long sluggish dream of *Twilight Sleep*, she feels that there is something incurably effete, utterly at variance with the storm-beleaguered lives which are her true *métier*.

Twilight Sleep is of course a deliberate "showing-up" of all the absurdities of modern American "fast" life. That very fact weakens it, for the novelist is not a reformer. If it were not for the sudden exquisite touches of nature, and the solid pathos of Maisie, and the sudden development of Nona in her father's hour of need, one would be almost bored. In chapter after chapter they lounge on divans, ring bells, give orders, go—without interest—in cars like furnished houses, from places which bore them to other places which bore them rather more. If they would grow a potato, get in their own winter logs, do the household washing—how it would save them! Again, one cannot say, as in that wonderful book, *The Mother's Recompense*, with its sudden swift-hidden drama silently shattering a life, that the end (the ironic end)

444

crowns all. For somehow the end of *Twilight Sleep* is less tragic than sordid. One feels that here Mrs. Wharton has plagiarised her own earlier book unconsciously and unsuccessfully.

For whereas there is, in the story of a man who, unknowingly, falls in love with the daughter of his sometime mistress— she and the girl being ignorant of it also— the germ of an almost Oedipus-like tragedy, there is in the adultery of an effete young woman with her father-in-law nothing but a kind of squalor. There is no inevitability, there is nothing of the sense of helpless humanity struggling in a net set for it before time was. The power of *A Mother's Recompense* is that we know there is no help for these trapped ones. God himself cannot let them out.

Still, having achieved such works of genius as this and *Ethan Frome*, with its astounding ending of the sick wife nursing with lifelong devotion her husband and the girl with whom he attempted suicide, and *The Glimpses of the Moon*, and *The Age of Innocence*, and *Summer*, Mrs. Wharton can, without in the least disturbing our allegiance, write what she likes. Only one feels that it is not what she likes. And one greatly desires that she will return to the mood and the milieu of *Summer*.

Checklist of Additional Reviews

Dorothy Foster Gilman, "In New York with Edith Wharton," Boston *Evening Transcript*, 28 May 1927, book section, Part 6, p. 5.

"Evening Post Guide to Current Books," New York *Evening Post*, 4 June 1927, p. 9.

Rachel Annand Taylor, "Fiction," *Spectator* [England], 138 (11 June 1927), 1028.

"Fiction," *Outlook*, 146 (29 June 1927), 290.

"Among the Very Rich," Springfield [Massachusetts] *Republican*, 31 July 1927, p. 7-F.

Orlo Williams, "*Twilight Sleep*," The *Monthly Criterion*, 6 (November 1927), 440–5.

THE CHILDREN

THE CHILDREN

Edith Wharton

NEW YORK   LONDON
D. Appleton and Company
Mcmxxviii

Grace Frank, "Bittersweet," *Saturday Review of Literature*, 5 (1 September 1928), 8

Pitched in different keys, written in different tempi, the two themes of this novel alternate as melody and counterpoint to one another. The resultant harmony is curious, the rhythms strange, but there is considerable piquancy and humor in the contrast. Neither theme can quite qualify as major—in any sense—nor should one listen too intently for dominant chords in them. The effectiveness of the whole is dependent upon sharp shifts of tone, sudden modulations and resolution, jolly trills and grace-notes.

The Wheater children who give the book its title are the medium through which we judge most of their elders. Miscellaneous progeny of frequently remated parents, some are real Wheaters, some are "steps," but all are animated by the same desire to remain together. This desire seems a little grotesque when one remembers their various origins: Zinnie derives from Mr. Wheater's infatuation for a movie actress, and Beatrice and Astorre—alias Beechy and Bun—are the offspring of Mrs. Wheater's second husband, Prince Buondelmonte, by a previous wife of professionally acrobatic accomplishments. However, these youngsters feel bound to each other by the storms they have weathered together, by their common horror of being discarded in each new matrimonial deal of their assorted parents, above all by their devotion to their oldest sister, Judith.

Judith is one of Mrs. Wharton's most unusual and most delightful creations. Not yet quite sixteen, with most of her life spent in wandering from one Palace Hotel to another, Judy has never received any proper education—indeed only one of the small Wheaters, through the accident of a borrowed tutor, can spell—but hotel life and contact with her various parents' affairs—and "affairs"—have given her a disconcertingly improper acquaintance with facts no youngster should possess. Nevertheless, unconsciously sophisticated and disenchanted as she is, with quick eyes that detect new lovers and mistresses on the parental horizons almost as soon as they appear, she is an altogether lovable child in most of her ways and fancies. When it comes to the little Wheaters' chief preoccupation—the presents people are likely to give them—she is as much a normal youngster as any of them. It is when their great oath is in danger—their oath, solemnly sworn to on the "Cyclopædia of Nursery Remedies," never to be separated again, no matter what happens—that Judith becomes a shrewd and worldly-wise grown-up. All the children distrust penitent parents with sudden longings for their forgotten offspring. But Judy alone knows how to deal with them. "When there are seven children and a lot of parents, there's always somebody fighting about something," and Judith has learned to protect her flock by speaking of courts and lawyers to as good purpose as any of the new fathers and mothers she has encountered.

We soon meet most of these fathers and mothers appropriately enough at the Lido, where old, new, and potentially newer mates mill around in a mælstrom of steam-yachts, pearls, cocktails, jealousies, and imperturbably lifted faces. The reflections of their hectic existence in the impressionable surfaces of their children are as amusing as they are disturbing. Youngsters who can distinguish between the models of Chanel and Callot, who can narrow their glances to the best advantage, and whose appraisal of the genuineness of jewelry is as astute as their citations of Gallic witticisms, tweak one's conscience as well as one's sense of humor.

Except for Judith and one or two of the other small Wheaters, the people of this world of easy divorces and remarriages are pricked out with swiftly satiric strokes. Occasionally the holes are a little jagged, the needles too blunt, in want of emery. Not so, however, the contrasting world of Martin Boyne and Mrs. Sellars. Here the author draws her threads with deft delicacy, however intricate her pattern. Martin first sees Judith as, in the company of governess and nurses, she is transporting her unruly flock from Biskra to Venice. Martin himself is on the way to Cortina to meet the woman—recently widowed—whom he has long desired. An engineer, tired of wandering all over the earth, he is contentedly thinking of the beautifully ordered existence of Rose Sellars. The way in which, in the mind of this middle-aged man, the gaudy, wistful, uneasy figure of little Judy impinges upon that of the gracefully harmonious woman whom he hopes to marry is exquisitely indicated. And in Martin's subsequent relations with Rose and Judith there is ample opportunity to test the wisdom—or fatuity—of his own aphorism that when a man loves a woman she is always the age he wants her to be, whereas when he ceases to love her she is either too old for witchery or too young for technique.

The scenes shift back and forth from the cool quiet and simplicity of the Tirol and the lipstick feverishness of the Lido, and the mood of the book shifts with them. If the satire seems squeezed directly on to the canvas in thick raw blobs at times, nothing could be more suavely mixed or more lightly laid on than its tenderness and gaiety. And whether the author is mocking or mellow, her hand

is equally sure, her observation equally keen. Moreover, the very combination of mockery and mellowness, of something preposterous and something universal, gives to the story its peculiarly pleasant, bittersweet flavor.

Percy A. Hutchison, "Humor and Satire Enliven Mrs. Wharton's Novel: *The Children* Is a Moving Study of the Effects of Family Discord on Sons and Daughters," *New York Times Book Review*, 2 September 1928, p. 2

Long master of every resource open to the satirist and the ironist, possessed of wit as keen and as destructive as a Damascus blade, not until her present novel, *The Children*, has Edith Wharton demonstrated that she also is possessed of humor, of the power to move to tears while provoking laughter. And while humor may be somewhat lower in the scale than pure wit, further from the ultimate, something less than Olympian, it is more generally welcomed by men and women. Most persons toiling in the work-a-day world distrust the judgments of the wit; his sureness, the finality of his utterances, seem to them not always true to the reality of their experience. They find life as bristling with dilemmas as does the man of wit; but whereas he states dogmatically that one horn or the other must be embraced (and always the horn that pricks most sharply), they perceive the issue is not so easily

450

resolved, in fact, that generally it is not to be resolved. It is then that they find in humorous acceptance of the situation, in smiling though the lashes are wet, a saving solution in which the ingredients are suspended and, though ever present, rendered less venal.

In *The Children* Mrs. Wharton has turned the searching light of her imagination on the problem which arose with the first divorce of parents. Henry James, in one of the most brilliant of his novels, *What Maisie Knew*, attacked the same problem. Others of lesser fame have focused their attention on one aspect of it or another. The law, which has laid upon it the duty to finish one way or another any piece of business that comes before it, has its solution, awards to one or another, or parcels out between both the fruits of the one-time union, and moves on with unfeeling stride to other matters. But oh, how blind Justice! says Henry James in effect. Where it thinks to have made an end it has only made a beginning, a beginning of fresh, and perhaps even greater trouble. Mrs. Wharton never bothers with the law, for she is aware of its impotency. With the small person of Judith Wheater instead, she confounds the law and the prophets: "Judy," who combines the sophistication of the serpent with the benign wisdom of the angels.

When Martin Boyne first saw Judy she was carrying a heavy baby up the gangway of a liner touching at Algiers. Martin was on the deck, looking down; and he declared that such things should not be allowed—girls scarcely into their teens marrying and having to lug children about! But presently he finds that his premise had been an erroneous one. The girl is not the mother of the child; she is his eldest sister, and there are five other children in between—five, that is, including the "steps," for Judy's father and mother have been divorced, and each married to an-

other, and each divorced, after which they have remarried, and all seven offspring of these several unions are now hurtling about Europe in a troupe (as it were) shepherded by governesses and nurses, and 15-year-old Judy managing them all. For father and mother lead too agitated a life not merely to look after the children, but even, half the time, to know where they are.

Mrs. Wharton's gift of satirical intention, masked by the most innocent monologue or dialogue, was never better displayed than in the passages she puts into the mouth of the elder Wheater boy, a grave, frail lad of 11. Terry, whom chance has made a cabin-mate of Boyne, on learning that the latter had been in college with his father, begs Martin to intercede for him with his parent. . . .

It is a simple task for a review to exhibit the satire, the irony, the biting scorn of Mrs. Wharton's study, for quotations serve. To make clear the humor is not so simple, for it resides neither in sentences nor in paragraphs but in the general situation, in the episodes, in the individual situations that the episodes create. Boyne encountered the little Wheaters on the way to Venice to join the Wheater parents; but Venice proves no more lasting an abiding place than the then matrimonial status of the elders—i.e., husband and wife—was to prove a permanent state. For, not long after Boyne had translated himself from the city of canals and gondoliers to Cortina, he suddenly awakes to find the tribe at his heels, not sent thither but escaped; the younger ones and their nurses virtually abducted by the unreasoning but far-seeing Judy, whose experiences of matrimonial change have been so many she can sight one heaving into view while it is still hull-down on the horizon. It is this escape which precipitates all that follows in the book, for Boyne, solid, tender-hearted, an example of probity, is

451

so horrified that Judy should have pur-
loined $5,000 out of her father's millions
that he consents to become guardian for
the brood, at least for a time.

So far we have confined our attention
to the Wheaters—parents, offspring and
"steps"—and to Martin Boyne in his
contact with them. But the story covers
more than these; and to the thinking of
this reviewer, not always with success.
Indeed, it even seems as if Mrs. Wharton had two separate stories in contemplation, and had, for some inscrutable
reason, decided to combine the two.

Martin Boyne, engineer, man of forty
or thereabout, had once been in love with
a woman who had married another. Rose
Sellars's husband having died (at last),
Boyne is actually on his way to Cortina to
ask her to marry him at the time he falls
in with the Wheater troupe. The two
stories thus become intertwined; and although the contrast between the impulsive, sophisticated yet innocently child-like
Judy and the faintly radiant but virginally
self-contained Rose, presents precisely the
object for that kind of study in which
Edith Wharton can be at her best; the
change in tempo and atmosphere instantly
invoked dampens the enthusiasm which
the antics of the Wheaters had aroused in
the reader. One feels as if one had passed
from the boisterousness of a circus tent to
a cloister cell. Whether or not there were
at any time two stories under consideration by the author, or whether from the
first she saw The Children as it has
emerged in its entirety, Mrs. Wharton's
purpose is clear. Boyne's espousal of the
causes of the wandering youngsters, an
adventure which springs from his latent
but suppressed humanity, Rose cannot
share, and after a half-hearted trial, she
gives up both the children and Boyne. This
is part of the pathos, as it is part of the
ironic implication of the narrative. Mrs.
Wharton's sermon is: The plight of children of divorcees may become an insoluble problem—hence, see that it does not
arise.

Few, we imagine, will be satisfied with
the ending of the book. Yet how the author was to end it otherwise and avoid
the banal (because the obvious), one is at
a loss to say. It needs not the reviewer to
tell that, of course Martin falls in love
with Judy, rather, that all his being is
moved to love of her because she had so
little love. What Mrs. Wharton does with
this situation the reader shall discover for
himself. There is a study of repressions, of
inarticulateness, conducted with all the
keen zest, the exact analysis of the Wharton novels of the past. And the fact that
the author is led into such a study is
grounds for saying that two themes have
combined in the book, that it has not
followed a single theme. Nevertheless, we
venture to say that The Children is more
than likely to prove the most popular novel
Mrs. Wharton has ever penned. The portions of the book in which the little
Wheater clan plays a predominating part
are better than similar pages of The
Constant Nymph. There may be just a
taint of burlesque, but they are carried
through with éclat, general fidelity, revealing pathos, friendliness, and good-will. Ir-
respective of the esthetic volte face of the
second part, the youngsters can but carry
their assault of the reader's heart to a
devastating conclusion.

Rachel Annand Taylor,
"Children Errant,"
Spectator [England], 141
(8 September 1928), 309

Mrs. Edith Wharton's new novel is a deftly
satiric attack on that many-millioned

group of American men and women who, drifting from scene to scene of vanity and senseless pleasure, realize nothing of the most intimate human relationship but the impermanence with which they have invested it.

With smiling malice Mrs. Wharton exposes these folk, compact of luxury and greed, idling in their huge hotels, parading on the Lido the "standardized beauty" of the women, involved in passionless intrigues. She diagnoses such existence as a "lapse into savagery," in which nothing matters but "food, finery, and dancing." Indeed this savage crudeness under sophisticated fashions provides poor stuff for a novelist of Mrs. Wharton's quality; and the tragic power of her nobler books would be irrelevant here. But her chief concern in this story is with the children of these careless, changing people, distracted infants fought over by contending parents, poor casualties of the divorce courts with no fixed home. This very modern version of the "cry of the children" hesitates between mirth and pathos, comedy and serious expostulation; and, if the artistic unity is slightly imperilled, it is in the nature of the case that it should be. The Wheater pair have been divorced; each has married again; after farther divorce, they have been reunited. The family consists of four little Wheaters, and three "steps"—the daughter of Clive Wheater by the movie star he had wedded in the interlude, and two children belonging to a former marriage of Prince Buondelmonte, who had been Mrs. Clive Wheater's husband during that interval. (This is really so complicated that the situation is flavoured with a suggestion of improbability.) The pathetic tribe is governed by the eldest girl Judith, hardly sixteen, whose persuasions have remarried her parents, and whose consuming anxiety is to keep her charges together, since in their solidarity seems to lie their only hope of a regularized and decent existence. On the steamer between Algiers and Venice she finds an ally in Martin Boyne, who after long absence is returning to seek at Cortina Rose Sellars, a lady loved years before and now free to be his. She is still gracious and lovely; and Martin Boyne rests contentedly in the rare mountain air, till Judith, terrified by divination of more mutability in her elders' attitude, runs away with all her company to Cortina, and Martin, after some farcical conferences with an array of fantastic parents on the Lido, finds himself temporary guardian. Then his spirit gradually ceases to murmur praises of the "one autumnal face"; realizes that the wild spray from the fountain of youth that is the Wheater family is more invigorating, and that the immature and touching grace of Judith has shaken it into the true agony of love. The excitements of the Wheaters' daily life, the sorrowful conflict with Rose, the foredoomed struggle to preserve the integrity of the "army of babes," the surprising development of Mr. Dobree the lawyer, who appears to succeed where Boyne fails, and the humiliating moment that reveals Judith as all unripe for love, are matters related with supreme skill in the art of story-telling. The conclusion, when Boyne, long after, by mere chance learns that the children had been separated after all, and sees the wavering beauty of Judith in the distance, is bitterly but brilliantly contrived.

The charm of the book dwells chiefly in the girl Judith, so initiated into the follies of her world, and yet so completely innocent. There's a touch of Miss Kennedy's Tessa about her, though she is altogether unawakened. Rose Sellars, reticent and refusing, "made of light and reason," possesses the exquisiteness that is bought by limitations; yet some of her words and actions seem too obvious for her finesse. A certain dissatisfaction in the reader's mind hints that the central situation is too artificial, created as it is by the caprices of valueless people. Mrs. Wharton is best when she is more profound. But here is mirth, compassion, understanding, and many passages of admirable English. One remembers Judith asleep in the bracken, her sandalled feet crossed "like a resting Mercury's."

Tess Slesinger, "The Innocence of Age," *New York Evening Post Literary Review*, 15 September 1928, p. 5

Edith Wharton clearly belongs to an age which looks upon post-war happenings with continuous naive surprise and delighted horror. In her official capacity as a sophisticated New Yorker of pre-war vintage and as an ironic portrayer of other sophisticated New Yorkers, she feels herself called upon to assume a smirk of blasé superiority and fall suavely into what she conceives to be the spirit of the times. Consequently, she has shingled her intellectual hair and shortened her intellectual skirts with the obvious aplomb of one not accustomed to either. From writing of a small and decadent phase of old New York society, of which she had at least some knowledge and comprehension, she has turned with astounding self-importance to a subject with which she is fundamentally out of touch—

The Social Problems of the Present.

The marvelously overrated tenderness and irony are still with her. She has preserved that air of underlying gravity and concern which has excused in the eyes of thousands the flippancy with which she treats her ridiculous, posturing characters. She holds firmly to the pre-war delusion that a sad ending converts the worst book into a good and thoughtful one, a book which automatically recommends itself to discriminating readers. The last three sentences of *The Children* place Mrs. Wharton both chronologically and artistically: "Then he got up and walked away into the night. Two days afterward the ship which had brought him to Europe started on her voyage back to Brazil. On her deck stood Boyne, a lonely man." Walking away into the night simply isn't done anymore.

The jacket states that "Beneath the tender gayety of this story Mrs. Wharton has posed a question which we may not escape: What of the children of nonchalant divorce?" Mrs. Wharton poses this question with the pomp of a discoverer. To illustrate her discovery (that there are children of divorced parents) she concocts the Wheaters, two abominably cheap and fantastic persons who married each other, then married everybody else in Europe and finally remarried, only to get divorced again. Mrs. Wharton in a mood of tender gayety made them very fond of children, so that they not only had a number themselves, but adopted the offspring of all the people they married and divorced on the side. The story opens with a troop of seven, mothered by the oldest, a girl of fifteen, whose passionate desire is to keep them all together, regardless of the changing affairs of their various sets of parents.

The Children amazingly resembles, in form, spirit and detail, *The Constant Nymph*. The Wheater troop make every attempt to be as much as possible like the children in Sanger's Circus. Both groups are collected from various arrangements of matings: both are constantly reiterating shockingly frank words and thoughts to the excruciating mirth and disapproval of their hearers.

454

The resemblance continues. Martin Boyne stands in the same relation to *The Children* as did Louis in Sanger's Circus. Just as his prototype fell in love with Tessa, Boyne falls unwittingly in love with Judy, the fifteen-year-old leader of the children. Even as the other, he is overwhelmed by the delicacy of a fashionable lady who has spent her life in learning to do everything gracefully. Rose Sellars obligingly bears out the resemblance by following the pattern set by Florence, the gracious lady of *The Constant Nymph*. A slight variation follows: the young man in Margaret Kennedy's superior novel married the lady and then left her; young Boyne leaves her before marrying her. And it is here that Mrs. Wharton shows a fine streak of originality. It will be remembered that the appealing and unfortunate Tessa died before her marriage was consecrated. Judy Wheater, however, doesn't die. She merely misunderstands, until it is too late, that Boyne is making love to her, and mistakes his amatory advances for the kindness of an elderly man. So Boyne walks out into the night.

"New Novels: *The Children*," *Times Literary Supplement* [England], 20 September 1928, p. 664

Mrs. Edith Wharton now seems to find nothing in the world so pathetically entertaining as the vagaries and immoralities of ultra-rich Americans. One cannot help regretting that the talent of one who has the art of novel-writing so admirably can find no better theme upon which to spend itself. However, the worthless crew bulk largely in certain parts of the world, and their mode of existence gives rise to problems some of which are serious. *The Children* is concerned with one of these. Suppose that a fat and material money maker named Cliffe Wheater, devoted only to business and sensual enjoyment, marries one of his own kind; that, after having three children, they divorce, the husband to marry a film star, the wife a scoundrelly Italian prince; that another child is born to the film star and that two children of the prince, by a tight-rope walker, join the family of young; that the film star runs off with an English marquis and the prince turns out to be legally married to another; that Cliffe and his wife remarry and produce another baby, but remain what they are—sensual creatures haunting the Lido and Paris, and bound inevitably for more liaisons and more divorces: what is going to happen to the seven children?

This problem is bounced upon a middle-aged American engineer, Martin Boyne, as he travels by steamer to Venice *en route* for Cortina, where the love of his youth, now an exquisite but no longer young widow, is waiting for him to claim her. The peculiarity of the seven children—five American and two Italians irregularly adopted—is that they cling together. The whole tragedy of such a band is expressed by fifteen-year-old Judith, the eldest, the mother, and the champion of them all. They are sick of being sent about all over the world at their parents' whim in charge of a governess, of being claimed by one or the other parent, of being wrangled over, of not being educated. They have sworn on the gaunt governess's book of nursery remedies never to be separated again. And now they are on the way to meet their pleasure-loving parents at Venice, full of forebodings. Worst of all, while ignorant in the scholastic sense and unmannerly, they know far too much of the world.

Judith and Terry have an abysmal knowledge of such men and women as their parents: they judge them and predict their immoral actions with the uncensorious wisdom of rich experience, and by such standards they judge all men and women. Blanca, Terry's twin, and Zinnia, the film star's child, are corrupted beyond all redemption. The "wops," Bun and Beechy, are sheer barbarians, and the baby, Chip, alone is thriving in the care of Judith and Miss Scope. Martin's sympathies are aroused by Judith and Terry, by Judith in particular, who combines the wistfulness of a "Constant Nymph" and the twisted vision of Henry James's Maisie. She is half-child, half-old woman, changing disconcertingly from one to the other, a figure drawn by Mrs. Wharton with great skill and charm. We cannot wonder that Martin Boyne is compelled by her pathetic and ardent loyalty to become the children's ambassador to their unspeakable parents, at the cost of his own future. His embassy to the Lido, carried on amidst cocktails and frivolities, the disconcerting visit of the latest Princess Buondelmonte, an up-to-date graduate in education, and her entire defeat by the children, the growing hopelessness of Martin's task, the children's pathetic wedding present to him of a cradle on the day of his rupture with Mrs. Sellars, and the climax in Paris, where Martin is forced to turn tail, are things richly and beautifully done. All the same, there is here either an element of caricature or a fundamental want of decency in the situation that weakens artistic treatment. Either one must laugh without thinking or one becomes too angry to be amused.

R[obert] M[orss] L[ovett], "Recent Fiction," *New Republic*, 56 (26 September 1928), 160

In *The Children* Mrs. Wharton has developed an elementary theme, the conflicting appeal of woman, in the singular, and child, in the plural. Martin Boyne, crossing the Mediterranean to meet at Cortina the woman whom he has loved for years and who is now free to marry him, is overtaken by youth in the form of a family of children, the result of social miscegenation between certain old friends of his, the Cliffe Wheaters, and others, including an Italian prince and a movie actress. The case of the child, as victim of the domestic misadventures of parents, which Henry James explored in *What Maisie Knew*, is here elaborated, for there are seven children; and there is no question of what they know, for they know everything, and have bound themselves by an oath to stand together in their tottering world. Their appeal to Boyne's paternal chivalry is sharpened by Judy, the eldest, the mother *pro tem.*, for whom his feeling is perfectly that of the foster lover in Francis Thompson's "The Poppy."

Between the clasp of his hand and hers
Lay, felt not, twenty withered years.

All this and the attitude of Mrs. Sellars, fastidious and understanding, is rendered in Mrs. Wharton's best manner. The situation threatens at the close to topple over the verge of the preposterous, but Mrs. Wharton saves it—or almost—and the epilogue, which is all that life leaves to Martin and Mrs. Sellars, rings with the truth of the inevitable.

R. Ellis Roberts, "New Novels," *New Statesman*, 31 (29 September 1928), 761

In *The Children* Mrs. Wharton is not attempting to repeat the grand attack made in *The Custom of the Country*. This is a lighter book, and deals with a more serious subject. The fate of fools like Cliffe and courtesans like Joyce is not of much importance to the State—though it is a pity that the State cannot, by the removal of their monstrous fortunes, throw them into the obscurity they should never leave—but the fate of children under the care of these carnal half-wits is important. I must trust Mrs. Wharton to be right in matters of fact—that the children would have been left in the nominal charge of Mr. and Mrs. Wheater, and that there is no equivalent to our wards of chancery in the United States. The consequence, anyhow, is that Judith, sixteen years old, innocent in character and incredibly sophisticated in experience, devotes herself, with the aid of Miss Scope—an exquisite little etching—to her "brothers and sisters." Of course the burden is too heavy for her, and so Martin becomes involved, and it is through his kindly, distressed and loving interest in Judy that we see this pitiful little menagerie—Terry, Blanca, Zinnie, Beechy, Bun, and Chipstone. Yet *The Children* is a novel far more than competent. It is in Mrs. Wharton's easier, later manner, less dependent on Henry James (there are bits, even, which might have been written by "Elizabeth"); but it has a seriousness, a gravity of idea, a genuine indignation which we do not as a rule find in her work. And if there are some people and scenes which are not entirely necessary, there is none which is not significant—has not a relative value that prevents it seeming intensive. For instance, Rose Sellars, who is half engaged to Martin, helps us to understand Judith better just as she helps the unfortunate Martin to discover that he is falling in love with the child who regards him as an elderly friend, of an extremely helpful temperament. It is really a formidable book this—but I do not suppose those whom it leaves dead on the battlefields of the Lido will ever know they have been touched. To attack those whose main vice is insensitiveness is a heart-rending business—for how can you make feel those who cannot feel?

Francis Birrell, "New Novels," *Nation and Athenæum* [England], 44 (6 October 1928), 19

The novel is an art form. It is the province of the artist to make beautiful objects. Therefore all novelists should be judged by their success or failure in producing these objects of beauty. But while they generally fail in this attempt, they frequently provide very interesting information in the meantime and are in fact indispensable to the student of the age. A foreign novelist is generally more interesting than the home product, because he will provide more novel information. We therefore welcome the immense amount of American novels now published in England, mostly chock-full of brand-new knowledge.

Unfortunately, Mrs. Wharton has already told us everything she knows, and now has got to be judged on her merits. She is becoming an old-fashioned writer, with two plots, and everything handsome about her. *The Children* is as slick, efficient, and readable as any of her former books, though perhaps it is just a little tired. The publisher tries to do her as much harm as he can by stating on the "blurb," "Mrs. Wharton has posed a question which we may not escape: What of the children in a world of nonchalant divorce?" The book is much better than this, of course. The family of "steps" are all lifelike and vivid. The hero, torn between two women, one little more than a child, the second little less than middle-aged, and losing both through his doubting, is a well-drawn character. Mrs. Wharton's weakness lies in the fact that she is in too much of a temper. Millionaires have got on her nerves, and she can see nothing else all round her. This interferes with her sense of proportion. After all, American millionaires are comparatively few in number, live among themselves in special compounds, and announce their movements in all the newspapers; so that it only needs a very little to avoid seeing them altogether; that is, if one is not Mrs. Wharton.

Still here rage does add a certain venom to her pen, and on occasion makes her attain almost to eloquence:—

> "All about them, at other tables, exactly like theirs, sat other men exactly like Lord Wrench and Wheater, the Duke of Mendip and Gerald Ormerod, other women exactly like Joyce and Zinnia and Mrs. Lukmer. Boyne remembered Mrs. Sellars's wail at the approach of a standardized beauty. Here it was in all its mechanical terror—endless and meaningless as the repetitions of a nightmare. Every one of the women in the vast crowded

> restaurant seemed to be of the same age, dressed by the same dressmaker, loved by the same lovers, adorned by the same jewellers, and massaged and manipulated by the same beauty doctors."

Nevertheless, for all its merits, *The Children* falls half-way between being a book of information and a work of art.

Marie Luhrs, "*The Children* Is a Polished Novel," New York *World*, 7 October 1928, p. 11-M

In the good old days when divorce was a rare and daring novelty, every discussion of the subject was usually unanswerably concluded by the question: "But what will become of the Children?" Mrs. Wharton in her latest novel endeavors to show what does become of the children of the many-times-divorced. Her attitude is that of one who views with alarm the problem of the offspring of impermanent unions; she is a veritable Mother Grundy—lace mittens and all—in this book; her disapproval of the sophisticated scenes that she depicts with such sleek art is obvious.

To point her moral and adorn her tale Mrs. Wharton has chosen the numerous children and step-children of the Cliffe Wheaters, who are very rich in a bland American way. Dragged about from one European hostelry to another, subjected to periodic raids by one parent or another, the Wheater flock—half-sisters and brothers, step-sister and brothers—try to hold themselves together under the leadership of Judith, the oldest daughter, and with the sympathetic help of Martin Boyne, a middle-aged bachelor. Martin falls in love with Judith and fails to win her. The Wheater tribe, after the most gallant battle toward a unified home life, are scattered by the disintegrating forces of their various irresponsible parents. A gentle, pitying despair hangs over the book, for the social pattern that Mrs. Wharton loves is blurring and breaking.... The writing is, as always in a Wharton novel, fluent, with a brilliant surface of color and a shadowy depth of emotion. The characterization is as naked and revealing as that of a cartoonist—without any of a cartoonist's vulgarity. Elegance and ease, so rare in modern American literature and rarer still in modern American life, richly permeate the book. But for all its aristocracy of manner *The Children* is a slight book and thin. Partly is this thinness explained by the fact that most of the characters are children, and therefore the book is largely given up to the irrational and irrelevant pranks of children; partly is it explained by the fact that there is a very modern doubt as to whether children without conventional home life are so wretched after all. Parentage is often as suffocating as it is protective, and children at loose ends in the world are often more resourceful and winning than the hot-house variety. As a bitter comment on the cruelty and inherent unhappiness of the modern code of selfishness and self-indulgence, *Twilight Sleep* is a more perfectly convincing book. Its painful intensity and beautiful bitterness are replaced in *The Children* by so pale a pity as to be almost sentimental. Mrs. Wharton's latest book needs some hot rage.

Yet in its very conventionality of outlook is *The Children* refreshing and, in a certain sense, courageous. It is much more fashionable and popular to be in favor of the movie actress type of mother than against her and to recommend bread and milk instead of cocktails is, to say the least, unique. It is doubtful if any novelist save Edith Wharton could have achieved such smartly glittering results with such wholesome ingredients.

Clifton P. Fadiman, "Cable and Fine Wire," *Nation*, 127 (10 October 1928), 370–1

Neither of these books [Edith Wharton's *The Children* and Morley Callaghan's *Strange Fugitive*], taken individually, remains very long with the reader, and both, it is perhaps safe to state, represent minor efforts on the part of their authors; but read in conjunction with each other they furnish a double springboard from which to launch some interesting comparisons.

Mr. Callaghan is a pat example of a good, hard-boiled writer. He is typical of a rapidly growing school. One can trace quite clearly in his work the things the school has rejected: variability or beauty of style, complication of character, neatness of construction, the exposition of a thesis or a problem, the intrusion of the author's point of view, and—most important of all—the division of his personages into sympathetic and unsympathetic characters. In *Strange Fugitive* the world is the world of the tabloids, divested of romance. Jerry Trotter, the protagonist, is a primitive being with sufficient power of reflection to be uncertain about his desires, which are mainly reducible to money, power, and women. By a series of steps too rapid and schematic to be quite real, he rises from the position of unsuccessful foreman in a lumber yard to the estate of bootlegger king. The extension of his blind will-power to power is accomplished, as is usual in such cases, by a diffusion of his sex awareness. He leaves his wife but is sufficiently uneasy in his mind to be unhappy away from her. The denouement of the story is straight cinema: sawed-off shotguns, racketeers' battles, and the brutal abrupt murder of Jerry. The entire story is conceived in terms of incident and told in a cold, vernacular prose. As has probably been remarked before, it is Hemingway carried to the point of absurdity. The style is so expressionless that it is insufficient even to project the simple figures of Jerry and his wife and their universe of bootleggers, prostitutes, and gunmen. The characters are conceived as primitive and animal: but by a curious irony they turn out to be artificial, almost dreamlike. We cannot believe in them, even as we cannot believe in the murderers and gunmen served to us in the tabloids.

Turn to Mrs. Wharton's latest novel and you seem to step into another world. A minute ago there was nothing but blind pigs, onion sandwiches, smuggled whiskey, assault, brutality, murder, bestial lust. All this—signifying naught. Vicious energy in action, from which nothing is to be learned, no morals are to be drawn. Then, in a moment we are whisked into the Riviera with its cocktails, American millionaires, decadent heiresses, a deracinated and tired cosmopolitan society, chattering, twittering—and divorcing. Plenty of problems here: the problem of the children of divorce, the problem of the ageing woman, the problem of a rootless transplanted American society. These are not people merely coolly noted by a reportorial mind, as in *Strange Fugitive*, but a group carefully selected and elaborately maneuvered so as to bring into sharp focus a set of ultra-civilized social dilemmas.

There is a corresponding difference in style. Mrs. Wharton, ever mindful of the Master, still glitters, winds, and surprises. Her paragraphs are all shows of subtlety, whereas Mr. Callaghan works equally hard to show us he has nothing up his sleeve, and that he has whittled his prose down to the bone. In both cases the effect is unsatisfactory. There is a point at which directness transforms itself into banality and a point at which refinement becomes mere meticulousness.

Similarly with the question of point of view. Mr. Callaghan, the fashion-plate hard-boiled novelist of 1928, has none at all. His characters undergo no interpretation, no criticism. The corollary is that his characters are neither sympathetic nor unsympathetic. You neither like nor dislike Jerry. Indeed, this particular result of the objective method is in modern fiction becoming so significant a factor that an entirely new attitude toward novels is becoming established. The query, Did you like the book? no longer has any meaning in terms of our identification with any of the characters. This sweeping change becomes clearer still when reference is made to Mrs. Wharton's book, which, true again to the Henry James formula, is careful to build up a character (intelligent, sympathetic, and essentially colorless—the regulation Henry James hero) through whose eyes the story, or rather the problem, is seen and who is obviously at times the mouthpiece of the author. The function of such a character is to provide for the reader a resting place for his sympathies, to make the reader feel at home and comfortable and certain that he understands completely and judges sympathetically all that is going on (although, of course, it is the hero who is really doing this for him).

Curiously enough, however, the two books, apparently so dissimilar, are alike in their final emotional impact. Mr. Callaghan's world is so simplified and stripped that it becomes an abstraction and we believe in it no more than we believe in the crude truths which daily journalism offers us. On the other hand, the complexities of Mrs. Wharton's universe of enormous wealth and enormous decadence, are so foreign to most of us that they become merely farcical. (Parenthetically it may be remarked that the farcical possibilities implicit in the novel are not developed as fully as they could be: healthy absurdity is sacrificed to "thoughtfulness" and "the problem"). It is as impossible to believe in Mrs. Wharton's divorcées and precious hotel children and ex-movie-star marchionesses as it is to believe in Mr. Callaghan's steely-eyed gunman, lush-limbed kept women, and steak-eating truck drivers.

Beulah Amidon, "The Family Circus," *Survey*, 61 (1 November 1928), 180

Ever since *The Constant Nymph,* we have been running into the loosely knit, unconventional family, more or less irregular in constitution and behavior, half-rooted or not-rooted at all, and always with brilliant, sophisticated, uncared-for children suffering for the social sins of their parents. Well here they are again.

The seven confusedly related youngsters of Mrs. Wharton's book tumble pell mell from their zigzagged background into the brief story of fifteen-year-old Judith's final struggle to give them some basis for sane and normal life. There had been no time, what with quarrels, separations, intrigues, remarriage and constant travel, for their scrambled parents and guardians to arrange any sort of home or schooling for Judith or Terry or the "littler ones." Ju-

dith was educated only in the harsh sophistication of her environment. But out of her brooding passion to make a home for "the children" and her terrified certainty that her parents were on the verge of a fresh quarrel, she found the courage to pick up a roll of bills from her father's desk, to gather up the children and their two nurses and to fly to a remote village in the Alps. A casual detail in that summer's kaleidoscopic pattern was the shattering of Martin Boyne's coolly adequate romance by the stinging beauty of love for Judith, thirty years his junior. Perhaps Mrs. Wharton meant us to pity Martin, as he certainly pitied himself. But it is possible only to rejoice that once in his ordered life he broke through his conventional safeguards to the pulsing reality of great emotion.

It is an easy temptation, of course, to read this book as a tract on modern marriage and divorce. (Easy, too, to imagine the quiet scorn with which Edith Wharton would declaim a "message.") But it would be no more justifiable than to pin to the story of Lily Bart, Moral: give girls vocational training; or to base art criticism on *Old New York.*

Mrs. Wharton has a sincere artist's preoccupation with her canvas and brushes, with problems of drawing and color, of perspective and shadow and light. Perhaps that is why this picture comes to us lucid as a Zorn etching and unsparing as a Soviet cartoon. It is not muddled with efforts to raise sociological questions or to answer them with neat formulae. It has caught, somehow, the insistent, arresting rhythm of the modern scene it gives back again, even to the pale mauve of Martin's final pain and frustration touching faintly the jazzy planes and angles of these chaotic young lives.

461

[Gorham B. Munson], "*The Children*," *Bookman*, 68 (November 1928), 337

There can be no supposing this were a first-novel game about Edith Wharton's *The Children*. The book is too plainly by a hand kept steadily in practise for the last thirty years. Although *The Children* is not by the inspired Edith Wharton who wrote that finest of New England tragedies, *Ethan Frome*, it is a characteristically competent Wharton product, and the sun of Henry James, once refracted, still brings out the polish of the pages that regret the decline in manners and record the new vulgarities.

But her people of breeding, Martin Boyne and Rose Sellars are too tepid! Judith Wheater, the fifteen-year-old girl who leads the six children in their revolt against being separated by each fresh divorce, is better blooded and almost becomes a vivid portrait. She might have, were not Mrs. Wharton's interest elsewhere: it falls upon a social problem of the lighter sort, namely, what happens to the castabout children of parents rich enough to afford many divorces and re-marriages? No solution is presented for this problem: that would be "inartistic"—in this particular novel, at any rate.

But it is no wonder that *The Children* was serialized in a large woman's magazine. Here is an international divorce problem, which to the homekeeping readers of such publications is "spicy." Attacking it from the angle of the children adds the sentimental appeal. And the master stroke is to make the bachelor, Martin Boyne, so fatherly, such a dear guardian of the little Wheaters; for who appreciates the appearance of such improbable virtues in a man more than feminine readers who have missed the full measure of devout self-sacrificing paternalism in their husbands? Not in disparagement or praise, but merely for placement, let it be said that Mrs. Wharton has written a fine serial for a certain type of audience.

Arthur Maurice, "Scanning the New Books," *Mentor*, 17 (February 1929), 54

Mrs. Wharton's new book might be called *The Revolt of the Seven, or The Cry of the Unhappy Children*. In the course of her brilliant literary career Edith Wharton has seldom assumed the role of the preacher. She is conspicuously the preacher in *The Children*. The book is a scathing indictment of "American divorce." The present writer begs to call attention to the quotation marks. Mrs. Wharton holds no brief against the legal definite separation of American man and wife when life together has become for them intolerable, and where they have no one else to consider. Her arraignment is of "American divorce," which implies the giddy, reckless exchange of partners, the riotous license of great wealth, the pursuit of the monotonous rattle and glare of cosmopolitan pleasure, the easy recource to the courts of Reno and Paris of yesterday. She attacks "American divorce" at its most vulnerable point. She voices the cry of the children, hungry, not for material things, but for the warmth and the solidity of the home. In spirit she is in hot sympathy with her hero, Martin Boyne, in leading the revolt of the seven.

Like Martin Boyne in the story, the

reader is likely to be puzzled for a time finding the way through the tangled maze of relationship. The seven children vaguely ascribed to the Cliffe Wheater family are Judith the girl of fifteen who plays the little mother to the rest; the twins Blanca and Terry; Beatrice and Astorre, known as "Beechy" and "Bun;" Zinnie; and the baby, Chipstone. Judith is the oldest child of Cliffe and Joyce Mervin Wheater, his first wife. Then, as the governess, Miss Horatia Scope, flippantly called by the children "Horrorscope," explains, came Blanca and Terry, born after "the second serious quarrel." Mrs. Wheater, becoming infatuated with an Italian Prince, divorced Cliffe and married Buondelmonte. "Bun" and "Beechy" are his children by an earlier disreputable marriage. The deserted husband Cliffe consoled himself by contracting a matrimonial alliance with a film star, Zinnia Lacrosse. Disagreeing, they resorted to "American divorce." Zinnie is their child. Finally Joyce tired of her Italian, and the Wheaters were legally reunited. The baby Chipstone is their latest hostage to fortune.

Despite a continual atmosphere of the clash of infantile battle, the children adore one another; wish always to be together under the motherly wing of Judith; and revolt when the whim of a suddenly interested parent threatens them with separation. Martin Boyne, who had been a classmate of Cliffe Wheater at Harvard, and a suitor of Joyce Mervin before her marriage, encounters the strange group when starting by boat for a roundabout trip from Algiers to Venice. He is immediately adopted by them as their champion and protector, rôles he accepts with all his heart, despite the complicating fact that he is on his way to join a recent widow, Rose Sellars, to whom he has been devoted through long years of absence. Relying upon Martin Boyne's support, the children, under the direction of Judith,

run away from their various parents, collected in Venice for the gayeties of the Lido season, and hide themselves in the mountains.

The story is the story of the loves of Martin Boyne and of Rose Sellars, of Martin Boyne and the girl Judith, thirty years his junior; but above all it is the story of the children, their strange environment, and their hunger for parental affection. In their humorous moments the collection is as original and as interesting as "Sanger's Circus," of *The Constant Nymph* of a few years ago. Brought up to hearing daily of divorce and the conditions of divorce among the very rich, looming large in their minds is a material figure whom they call "Sally Money." "Why didn't the children go with their old fathers and mothers? asks one child of another. Because their old mother's friend, Sally Money, wasn't big enough ... enough ... for her to take them all with her" is the reply.

Poignant in theme, brilliant in portraiture, keen in its humor, rich in the cosmopolitan background that Mrs. Wharton knows so well and handles with so mature a grasp, *The Children* is one of the year's conspicuous and distinguished novels. The reader's last thought, as Martin Boyne, a lonely man, stands on the deck of the steamer that is bearing him from Europe to Brazil, is not of the children, but of the delicate romance of Martin and Judith. Should Martin have married her despite the disparity of years? Would it have been a happy and permanent marriage, or would there have been in the future another "American divorce"? What do you think?

463

Janet Flanner, "Dearest Edith," *New Yorker*, 2 March 1929, pp. 26-8

Her current success, *The Children*, has . . . been sold for a cinema, was the Book of the Month Club's selection for September past, and reached two hundred thousand copies within a month of publication. In thirty years of writing, Mrs. Wharton's enormous output, with one exception, has been published by two houses, Scribner and Appleton, she not being one to make changes hastily. Her publishers have always found her an enemy of publicity and her standard press photograph shows her in pearls and décolletage, dressed for her public as for a ball.

Mrs. Wharton's real excellencies are never marketed. Even those who love her most come by accident upon her golden qualities. She is regarded as cold. Yet a chord of Bach once recalled to her a moment passed half a century ago with a woman who was ever after to be her fondest companion. And to the same woman, she recently wrote, after clipping her garden's roses in the summer dawn, that the ripe sweetness of the flowers personified and brought their amity endearingly to mind. Mrs. Wharton has the tender and reserved sentiments of the truly literate. From many she has earned the title of Dearest Edith and for herself she has perfectly written what she hopes will finally be her epitaph—"She was a friend of Henry James."

Checklist of Additional Reviews

Sherwin Lawrence Cook, "Edith Wharton and Divorce Problems," Boston *Evening Transcript*, 1 September 1928, book section, p. 2.

Mary Ross, "The Children of Divorce," New York *Herald Tribune*, 2 September 1928, book section, pp. 1–2.

"New Books in Brief Review," *Independent*, 121 (22 September 1928), 285.

L. P. Hartley, "New Fiction," *Saturday Review* [England], 146 (29 September 1928), 397.

A. B. O., "Wealth and Divorce," Springfield [Massachusetts] *Republican*, 7 October 1928, p. 7-E.

HUDSON RIVER BRACKETED

HUDSON RIVER BRACKETED

BY

EDITH WHARTON

All things make me glad, and sorry too.
CHARLES AUCHESTER

D. APPLETON AND COMPANY
NEW YORK LONDON MCMXXIX

Percy Hutchison,
"Mrs. Wharton's Latest
Novel Has a Mellow
Beauty: In *Hudson River
Bracketed* There Is Less
Irony and a Greater Fund
of Human Sympathy,"
*New York Times Book
Review*, 17 November
1929, p. 4

Since a reader is almost certain to be puzzled by the title with which Edith Wharton has endowed her latest novel, *Hudson River Bracketed*, the explanation may be given at once. A writer on land-scape gardening in America had placed in brackets a style he designated as "Hudson River." Hence, since her story was to centre mainly about an old manse supposedly standing somewhere north of Manhattan Island, Mrs. Wharton chose the title that would indicate the period to which the estate belonged. The period of the novel, however, is the present, although a present which has been influenced, more than commonly, perhaps, by the past.

In *Hudson River Bracketed* Mrs. Wharton has turned from her favorite millieu of New York, and, especially, Fifth Avenue. But she deals with a world she should know quite as intimately—the world of authors and publishers. The latter may repudiate certain of her suggestions, and the book reviewers surely will. Nevertheless, since all is fair in war and fiction, nobody is likely to sue the distinguished writer for libel, especially since she has added another to her long list of excellent novels.

Not that *Hudson River Bracketed* is

Edith Wharton's best piece of work. It has not the flashing irony of many of her books; and her pages for the most part lack that luminous quality which has been such a striking characteristic of virtually all her novels. But there is compensation. Mrs. Wharton could not do bad work if she tried. Nor would she permit herself to publish bad work if such could come from her pen. There is body to the story; both body and breadth. And there is generally texture to her style. And how many novelists there are whose fiction lacks body and whose style is devoid of texture! And one thing else has Mrs. Wharton done, she has interwoven the pages with the story of a girl-wife that is more moving than almost anything else she has ever done. If, then, there is lacking something of the cutting edge of *The House of Mirth* and *The Age of Innocence*, there is, as we have said, compensation. The creator of the pathetically beautiful Laura Lou introduces a more mellow Mrs. Wharton.

Irony, nevertheless, is not entirely absent. Indeed, the portrait of the central character of the book, the struggling young author, Vance Weston, is essentially an ironic study. Unfortunately, Mrs. Wharton has drawn so extensively on her knowledge of the book-producing world as often to blunt the force of her irony with prolixity of detail. Warned, the reader will hurry through certain of the chapters and many of the pages, collecting all that is necessary to carry the story forward for him. Thus the narrative will acquire for him the movement which in the pages themselves is often lacking, and the portrait of Vance will become clearer in outline. It is to be regretted, however, that the author did not do the cutting herself, before entering on publication.

If the scene of *Hudson River Bracketed* is mainly New York City and its northern environs, Vance Weston is himself out of

467

the Middle West. Yet if Edith Wharton has started with what appears at first glance a hackneyed proposition, the genius from the prairies conquering with his literary power the Philistines of the great city, it is the proposition only that is hackneyed. It is not Vance's career in which she is interested, and in which she would interest the reader, but the bundle of thoughts and emotions which are Vance Weston. Who but Edith Wharton would have had her struggling young novelist seek from the woman, who offers an annual literary prize—the loan of $2,000, that he may properly care for his tuberculous-stricken wife? No one, probably. For no writer could venture so daring a stroke unless it were logically possible for the character she had created. Too few of the fictions of literary genius are convincing logically and psychologically. Mrs. Wharton's Vance Weston carries conviction, even though he elicits little sympathy. The egotism of the artist (generally unconscious with Vance), the poetry in the boy's soul, which renders so many of his acts, especially the motive of so many of his acts, unintelligible to those about him, Mrs. Wharton brings out with clearness. And so, though we do not thoroughly like him, he is understandable.

Hudson River Bracketed, unlike Mrs. Wharton's earlier novels, gets away to rather a poor start. Vance Weston, in his Illinois birthplace, Euphoria (where also he was graduated from college), the Weston family, and the grandparents, Mr. and Mrs. Scrimser, could have been done with far fewer strokes and more telling effect. Indeed, the grandparents could have been omitted entirely. Nor is one likely to be convinced, when one presently finds Vance who has come East, making acquaintance with the poetry of Marlowe and Coleridge, that he could not have heard of them (as is alleged he did not) in his college on the prairies. Mrs. Wharton, we fear, has slandered Western educational institutions! But after this unnecessarily clumsy beginning, and when Mrs. Wharton has got her protégé to Paul's Landing, somewhere up the Hudson River, the story picks up briskly.

Though we shall say little, if anything, of Laura Lou, since no reviewer has a right to mar the beauty of the unfolding of an idyl by cursory summation, we shall have something to say of "Halo," as Héloïse Spear had been nicknamed. Only a very few years older than Vance (and both are young), Mrs. Wharton finds in Halo, a more intellectual romantic than poor little Laura Lou, material for a study in antitheses. Halo it is who leads Vance into the rich poetic pastures denied him in Euphoria, and as she spends a rather lonely life with her out-at-heels but aristocratic family, it is not unnatural that the two should quickly form a strong attachment for each other. However, Halo marries Lewis Tarrant, partly because she loves luxury, but more especially because he will provide her aging parents with luxury; Vance marries Laura Lou.

More than once has Mrs. Wharton carried on such a double study of two loves in the life of one man, or in the life of one woman, as the case may be. Yet she has never moved with more discretion (and she is noted for her discretion in writing) than in the present novel. That the spring of affection between Halo and Vance is their intellectual companionship is always evident, although not dwelt upon. For Laura Lou, soft and warm and beautiful, little educated and very frail, Vance is both the protecting male and the male desired. His dual nature, that of artist and of human being, craves dual satisfaction. And this Mrs. Wharton so profoundly understands and so discerningly portrays that the imagined triple relationship will stand as an authentic reflection and revelation of life. More than this, which is the end of all art, no artist can achieve. And in the achievement Mrs. Wharton has renewed the laurels she has worn so long and so deservedly. Of Halo, looking back upon her life, she writes:

> She had been happy, after all, in that happy-go-lucky muddling household of her parents. They had a gypsy-like charm, and they were always affectionate and responsive. The life of the mind, even the life of the spirit, had been enthusiastically cultivated in spite of minor moral short comings. If she loved poetry, if she knew more than most girls about history and art, about all the accumulated wonders peopling her intelligence, she owed it to daily intercourse with minds like her own.

And Halo had married to restore the family fortunes. She is not a disillusioned young woman, one of those so-called and not convincing disillusioned young women with whom the pages of modern fiction are too often strewn. She is a sane American, handled by a novelist eminently sane.

And this is the dominant and enduring characteristic of the work of Edith Wharton—its sanity. In a bustling time of innovations and experiment, both in life and in fiction, she holds to human verities, moving with calm, unimpassioned tread. *Hudson River Bracketed* will not stand foremost among this novelist's works; but it will not stand last. It is three-dimensional; not two, and not four. As we have already said, the story has body and breadth. There may not be throughout the same sureness of touch that has characterized Mrs. Wharton's former work. But the story of little Laura Lou is deeply affecting, and beautiful in its pathos.

[Mary Shirley], "A Novel and Some Biographies," *Outlook*, 153 (20 November 1929), 465

When Mrs. Wharton writes about New York society, she has a subject which she, alone of important contemporary novelists, knows. Greenwich Village writes about Park Avenue, Park Avenue writes about Broadway, everybody writes about Harlem. But nobody, not the clever Jews from Poland nor the deep schoolmarms from Ioway, writes about the increasingly obscure group of people which lives and has long lived in New York, downtown, moving slowly up, caught in Murray Hill eddies, lost in brownstone backwaters; not always rich, not always prominent, not always virtuous; but always secure in the right of eminent domain. Perhaps nobody knows that such a group exists.

In *Hudson River Bracketed*, her new novel, Mrs. Wharton began to write about these people, and they are in it, proud and conciliatory and ridiculous. But they are not the story. Mrs. Wharton began with one story and was diverted into another because the first story was a romance but the second, a cause. She started out with an old family, run to seed in mesalliances, wayward sons and high-strung daughters; people rich in background and poor in cash, tied to an old house such as one sees lost in the trees above New Hamburg or Fishkill; the Hudson River, New York of fifty years ago, bracketed by the covers of her book. And then a young genius from the West came, stumbling from Euphoria, "cradle of all the advantages," into Paul's Landing, and he caught Mrs. Wharton's eye. And he became the past as well as the present, part of onswimming Time. He is a beautifully integrated figure, an unswerving compound of egoism, honesty and passion. His way is beset with pitfalls. He stumbles into all of them because he is not, like others, watching his step: his eyes are on the stars. He falls into the hands of the Philistines. The New York literary game, as it is now called, entices him, and he is beaten by those who play it skilfully. Mrs. Wharton spares him nothing, no petty success, no gross disillusion, no exquisite tragedy; because he is a genius and must stumble up the steep road to glory—or to silence. Which it is to be, we close the book without knowing.

No recent novel of Mrs. Wharton's has impressed us so much as this one. It is beautifully written. Long ago Mrs. Wharton knew what her hero receives for the first time when he is turned loose in the library at the Willows, "the mighty shock of English prose." She has never forgotten it, nor the lessons in human psychology which she learned from her great master. In plot structure her book is perfect. Through the development of each character and each event, through the interplay of characters and events, the ends of poetic justice are served. Mrs. Wharton's books are always read, and this one will be. It will be found to compare favorably with the finest work she has ever done.

Catherine Gilbertson, "In the Willow Pattern," *Saturday Review of Literature*, 6 (7 December 1929), 509

Into her first complete study of a writer and a writer's background and problems, Mrs. Wharton has gathered up enough of what Mr. Percy Lubbock called "the adventure of her rare and distinguished critical intelligence," to give it, intellectually at least, the flavor of autobiography—delectable for genuine lovers of her work, despite the fact that its very fulness robs it of something of the clear-cut definiteness of design that has distinguished the rest.

"Hudson River Bracketed" is the architectural style of "The Willows," an old house on the Hudson, "impregnated with memories . . . thick with tangible tokens of the past." To Young Vance Weston, whose "own recollections could only travel back through a succession of new houses, . . . all without any traces of accumulated living and dying," it is not only a revelation of his own poverty of spiritual background, but also a soil in which his mind may strike root "deep down in accumulated layers of experience." Through its influence—its treasure of books, its vista of generations of gracious living—the boy, who, at nineteen, has invented a new religion, at twenty-four is moved to exclaim to his grandmother that "the greatest proof of the validity of a religion is its age, its duration. . . . Who wants a new religion, when the old one is there, so little exhausted or even understood in all its agelong beauty?"

This young writer, "the raw product of a middle-western town . . . trying to tell the world about things he isn't really familiar with," and his heart-breaking child wife, married in romantic heedlessness, and "Halo," sympathetic friend—symbol, like "The Willows," which is hers, of the quiet wisdom, the emotional control, the ordered beauty, of a well-treasured inheritance from the past—, are all near and dear to Mrs. Wharton. Indeed, nothing more comprehending, more compassionately just, has come from her pen than her account of the struggle of the soul of Vance Weston to use its wings, in brief Icarian flights, its cry for freedom, its hunger for warm, human understanding, its passionate need of a sustaining faith.

Frank commercialism that would tie him up to real estate, is against him; and a more insidious commercialism in the world of letters, that would turn him into a clerk. Poverty and Laura Lou cut him off from leisure and the more gracious living that charms his imagination and draws his senses. The age in which he lives, "this after-war welter, with its new recipe for immortality every morning," has shaken his faith in himself. But these are trifles compared with his own sense of inner destitution. Not ignorance of books merely, but "the meagerness of his inherited experience, the way it has been torn off violently from everything which has gone before, strikes him with a pang of impoverishment." Like Lily Bart and Ralph Marvell and the little Wheaters, if in a different way, he is a victim of the national love of tearing up roots, forsaking "the old house stored with memories," moving on, getting ahead,—of what, or where, or why, few know or care.

His artistic salvation, however, lies in the very realization that ignorance of the past accounts for the sense of unrelatedness in the present; that insensibility to those mysterious forces continually at work beneath the appearance of things, is responsible for the shallow brilliance, the merely superficial accuracy of our literary photography; that there can be no great books unless writers have felt "the beauty of continuity in the spiritual world," have heard "that footfall of Destiny" that rings out "in the first pages of all great novels, as compelling as the knock on Macbeth's gates, as secret as the opening measures of the Fifth Symphony."

Those of us who have browsed among Mrs. Wharton's books, for twenty years and more, will find much here that is happily reminiscent.

But we would not leave the impression that *Hudson River Bracketed* is merely a treatise on the dilemma of the writer. It is an absorbing story. Vance and Halo and Laura Lou catch hold of the heart strings. And the book has, besides, a fair share of significant background portraits, done in the best manner of the "Comic Spirit."

Herschel Brickell, "Fiction," *Bookman*, 70 (January 1930), 559

In *Hudson River Bracketed* Mrs. Wharton tells how an Illinois boy came to New York, saw, and was very nearly conquered. At the age of twenty-three Vance Weston is a promising writer, with one well-received novel to his credit; his fresh point of view meets with favor in the literary circles of Manhattan and he has a regular job with a recently established review. Unfortunately this review, although recently established, is endowed with the cunning of the ages, and has most devilishly got poor Vance to sign a contract which forbids him to write for any other publication for four years. Affairs are complicated by the fact that he has married and is quite unable to support his wife on his meagre salary. In spite of his growing fame, they are forced to live from hand to mouth, in cheap boarding houses, without enough money for decent food.

One would not expect Mrs. Wharton to stay in this atmosphere for the five hundred odd pages which comprise her book, and indeed she does not. Her hero's wife is a pretty country girl who cannot understand any of her husband's thoughts or ambitions; he loves her but cannot talk about anything with her, which leaves the field open for the Other Woman. Her name is Halo Tarrant; unhappily married to the man who runs the review which employs Vance, she stands for sympathy, intellect, wealth and social position. She shows Vance a world which he never dreamed of; he is lionized in circles where his wife would never be more than tolerated, and which would, moreover, bore her to the bone. This contrast in social conditions, which runs through the book, is fairly effective, but one prefers the author's earlier books, where one could enter the houses of the wealthy without having servants, softly shaded lamps, pictures and luxurious furniture thrown at one in such obvious profusion.

Mrs. Wharton, as usual, writes fluently and with distinction; but her characters, with one exception, are shallow. Her portrayal of Mrs. Tarrant is not sufficient to account for the charm, intelligence and sympathy with which this person is supposed to be endowed. She seems rather smug and limited, however well meaning; and one cannot understand Vance's respect for her mind after reading the hesitating and superficial criticism which she accords his work when he brings it to her for judgment. Vance himself is unconvincing in that he never grows up; responsibility, achievement and social experience do nothing to make him seem less boyish—indeed, childish. He behaves throughout like a schoolboy. His wife, Laura Lou, is the only real person in the book; the account of her short married life, with a husband whom she knows has outgrown her and death staring her in the face, has genuine pathos.

"Fiction Briefs," *Nation*, 130 (15 January 1930), 76

Mrs. Wharton, like all writers great and small, has her failures; *Hudson River Bracketed* is one of them. No one belittles an author's attempt to extend his scope, but Mid-Westerners have shown themselves so able to express their neighbors' frustrations that Mrs. Wharton's unsuccessful foray into their field adds nothing to her laurels. Her ambitious young genius from Illinois is only the husk of a character because his creator, scorning to exaggerate his potentialities or to allow him to become melodramatic about himself, fails equally to plumb the depths of his character, to show the internal play between his dawning self-consciousness and the pathetic experience of his career. As is to be expected, the description of the uninhabited house on the Hudson filled with the personality of the dead, the projection of the past into the present, the brief sketch of the Spears, are the best parts of the book—an observation which forces the repetition that Mrs. Wharton is still the one fine novelist of that small but tenacious class of Americans with a social and cultural tradition.

"New Novels: *Hudson River Bracketed*," *Times Literary Supplement* [England], 16 January 1930, p. 42

The hero of Miss Edith Wharton's novel *Hudson River Bracketed* . . . is a novelist, and her theme is the old theme of the creative artist's reaction to the hard facts of life, into which he does not fit and which, nevertheless, by the suffering it imposes on him, wrings out of him his masterpieces. There are two passages towards the end of this very spacious book which sum up Vance Weston and his relation to other human beings. He is living in great poverty in a little village near New York, his pathetic young wife Laura Lou is dying of consumption, and he should be writing "blurbs" for an advertising firm whose director, from whom he had snatched Laura Lou some years before, had advanced him five hundred dollars. The money is nearly gone, there is no hope for Laura Lou; yet, as he sits down to fix his mind on the writing of model advertisements, he is overwhelmed by an uncontrollable longing to plunge again into his novel.

> He clenched his fists and sat brooding over the model "ads." till it was time to carry in the iced milk to Laura Lou. But he had not measured the strength of the force that had propelled him... Words sang to him like the sirens of Ulysses; sometimes the remembering of a single phrase was like entering into a mighty temple. He knew, as never before, the rapture of great comet-flights of thought, across the heaven of human conjecture, and the bracing contact of subjects minutely studied, without so much as a glance beyond their borders. Now and then he would stop writing, and let his visions sweep him away; then he would return with renewed fervour to the minute scrutiny of his imaginary characters.

Oblivious of all material considerations, he surrenders himself, as he had surrendered himself before in moments of an-guish, to the rescuing sweep of his own imagination. A week after his wife's death, as he is about to go home to the town in Illinois where his father, a real estate agent, and his family represent the modern commercial standard of American life, he is visited by the woman who had first opened his eyes to that other standard of life for which her family and the old house on the Hudson River stood. Héloïse Tarrant, when she found him reading "Kubla Khan" in the deserted library of "The Willows," had unlocked for him, then an unhappy boy of nineteen, the door to a many-vista'd life. He had not loved her then, and he had cared little when, for her family's sake, she had married the rich and clever amateur, Lewis Tarrant. He had loved her later, with that fierce greed for essentials that characterized him, and, in an admirably written scene, had made to her his confession, forgetting every obstacle, even the existence of his own wife. They had parted then in dumb agony, and now, Héloïse Tarrant, freed from her husband, finds Vance again. Not knowing that his wife is dead, she pleads that their old friendship should be resumed, and he, in triumph, responds, only realizing, as he blurts out that Laura Lou is dead, Héloïse's horror at having been allowed to speak in ignorance of it. He does not understand her feeling: the past seems to him unimportant.

> And when at last he drew her arm through his and walked beside her in the darkness to the corner where she had left her motor, he wondered if at crucial moments the same veil of unreality would always fall between himself and the soul nearest him; if the creator of imaginary beings must always feel alone among the real ones.

These are the final words of the book,

473

and we may take them as expressing its essence; and in them, too, is implied the criticism that this particular theme invariably calls forth—namely, that the tragic solitude of creative people is realized in life with a thousand times the force that the writer of fiction can give it. So that here, while the career of Vance Weston simply appears as a series of sudden swoops punctuated by long failures, the figures of Laura Lou—a very sympathetic portrait of utter simplicity—of Héloïse, of Bunty Hayes, the vulgar but truly loyal heart, and even of old Grandmother Scrimser, with her passion for religion and her lectures on "meeting God," have a greater roundness and continuity. Miss Wharton's art is equal to all the demands which so large a canvass makes on it; as the reflection of modern American life and its contradictions in the mirror of a mind nourished on tradition this novel takes a worthy place in Miss Wharton's work.

V. S. Pritchett, "Warnings," *Spectator* [England], 144 (18 January 1930), 99

Edith Wharton is the Court painter of the old order, and of Mr. [Edward] Dahlberg's vernacular world [in *Bottom Dogs*] she is unaware. She has two Americas which she depicts with the wisdom, serenity and irony of one whose values are established; the vast clearing-house for success, new religions, and new talent; and the America of old families where everything but a vital sense of continuity is declining. *Hudson River Bracketed* is a good old-fashioned novel of huge proportions. The central figure, Vance Weston, is a raw young man from the Middle West who, brought into contact for the first time in his life with the past, discovers his own genius. After a flashing literary success, he finds himself caught in an intricately woven net of troubles. Although miserably poor and with a frail child-wife to support, he must for his art's sake resist the forcing house of the New York literary world; and this difficulty is complicated by the impulsiveness of his temperament, and the fact that, ceasing to find understanding in his wife, he has gone to the wife of his publisher for comfort, inspiration and love. These are the main threads of an almost too wide and ingenious tangle of relationships which bear upon the main problem without greatly elucidating it. The portrait of Vance Weston's ailing wife is beautifully done, particularly at the time of her marriage and of her death. That death scene in the miserable bungalow outside New York is unforgettable, but Miss Wharton's ingenuity spoils the end of it by rushing in an earlier lover to witness the last moments. Vance Weston is perhaps more of a problem than a man. He is, nevertheless, far more satisfactorily portrayed than geniuses usually are in fiction. The host of subsidiary characters have been drawn and shaded with satirical care. The merciless description of the New York literary world and the intrigues for literary prizes is too generalized to be alive, as the wholesale tying up of loose strands at the end of the book is comforting but arbitrary.

Gilbert Seldes,
"Notes on Novels,"
New Republic, 61 (29
January 1930), 283

L. P. Hartley,
"New Fiction,"
Saturday Review [England],
149 (1 February 1930),
144–5

It is evidence of the respect in which Mrs. Wharton is held that the recurrence of one of her "off-year" novels still dismays us. The present one is less interesting than most of her other failures because it restates a theme she has used too often, and often with success, and whatever might give freshness and vitality is spoiled by Mrs. Wharton's obvious unfamiliarity with the setting. The young man of fine perceptions (in this case a writer) married to an attractive and stupid child, trapped by business, and supported by the friendship of a noble, but married, woman repeats bits of half a dozen other novels by Mrs. Wharton; and when this young man enters the literary life of New York (as represented by artistic magazines, drinking authors and rapacious publishers) he ceases altogether to have substantial reality. Another theme is vaguely suggested. The young man comes out of the Middle West, where prosperity and social distinction are measured by "*confort moderne*," and discovers an older America which he knows to be finer than anything he has experienced; yet this older America seems not to care for money and telephones. Even its degenerate members, when they steal, steal first editions. One can see an entirely different novel in birth. By the law of Mrs. Wharton's alternating books, it should be a good one.

Hudson River Bracketed also concludes with the promise of a home-coming—though "The Willows" was not Vance Weston's actual but his spiritual home. It attracted him because its architecture, and its library, were a complete change from the Middle West; and all through his painful initiation into manhood—his literary beginnings, first encouraging, then disappointing, his marriage, first a source of irritation then a source of anguish—the memory of "The Willows," its graciousness and tranquillity, was balm to his mind. He was thrown into life without experience, he was unlucky, he made many mistakes. In one sense he has a great deal of temperament; but it is artistic temperament, sensibility, a different thing from character. Before his marriage, and even after his marriage, he was so busy taking in the American scene which Mrs. Wharton spreads so brilliantly and generously before him that he acted automatically, as in a dream and with disastrous consequences. His nature craved the sympathy *and* understanding which Halo Spear could offer him and which his wife, poor soul, could not. He was not made for an uphill fight, but when it was unavoidable he acquitted himself well and emerges from the ordeal a more considerable figure. As a man, he is less vivid than, say, Lewis Tarrant, Halo's husband, less vivid than several of minor characters. But this is not to be wondered at, for he is the sensitive plate on which Mrs. Wharton imprints her vision of modern America, a vision far more inclusive than the partial glimpse of New York society afforded by *Twilight Sleep*. Inclusiveness is the note of *Hudson River Bracketed*; it shows what, in Mrs. Wharton's opinion, America is like to-day. A tremendous undertaking, for which we owe her all our thanks. For though there are moments when we could wish the canvas smaller, we never wish that it was being painted by another hand. Dreiser's panorama presents more striking features, men like sky-scrapers, for instance, but it lacks the perspective which Mrs. Wharton, from her European vantage-point, knows so well how to give. Belonging to an older school of novelists, she can see men and women apart from their occupations and functions; she does not regard man and business-man, or man and he-man, as identical. Her book is a contribution to our knowledge of America.

Checklist of Additional Reviews

Fanny Butcher, "New Book by Edith Wharton Full of Skill," Chicago *Daily Tribune*, 16 November 1929, p. 11.

Mary Ross, "Babbitt's Son," *New York Herald Tribune Books*, 17 November 1929, p. 3.

Harry Hansen, "The First Reader," New York *World*, 19 November 1929, p. 13.

Sherwin Lawrence Cook, "The Era of *Hudson River Bracketed*," Boston *Evening Transcript*, 30 November 1929, book section, p. 5.

"The Bookshelf," *Woman's Journal*, 14 (December 1929), 32.

Lilian Whiting, "Mrs. Wharton's Work," Springfield [Massachusetts] *Republican*, 22 December 1929, p. 7–E.

Lyn Irvine, "New Novels," *Nation and Athenæum* [England], 46 (25 January 1930), 582.

Proteus, "New Novels," *New Statesman*, 34 (1 March 1930), 669.

CERTAIN PEOPLE

CERTAIN PEOPLE

BY

EDITH WHARTON

D. APPLETON AND COMPANY
NEW YORK   MCMXXX   LONDON

Dorothy Foster Gilman, "Some Distinguished Stories," New York *Herald Tribune*, 2 November 1930, book section, p. 5

A collection of short stories is never easy to estimate, because the literary balance is invariably delicate. In the case of Mrs. Wharton's latest book the proportion between tragedy and satirical comedy is judiciously blended, and the quality of sameness, so characteristic of lesser writers, is entirely absent. We find in *Certain People* a fastidiousness of phrase, a warm recognition of emotion and an emphasis on the drama of life which evoke our deep and warm appreciation. Yet these stories are emphatically the product of a novelist rather than of an author of tales. And with two exceptions all six narratives have a quality more reminiscent of the sketch book than the framed product of an accomplished artist.

The first story, "Atrophy," is decidedly Mrs. Wharton at her worst. It has that well bred lifeless quality which has marked certain of her books these latter years. Its title suffices as an adequate description. With the tale called "A Bottle of Perrier" we find ourselves in Africa. Several errors of fact may be observed in her character drawing, but the background and atmosphere of mystery are portrayed with distinguished beauty. Like the final story in this volume, "Mr. Jones," "Bottle of Perrier" is an attempt to cajole readers into finishing an account of something diabolically mysterious and weird which turns out ultimately to be a matter of second rate importance. The author of *Ethan Frome* and *The House of Mirth* ought never again to attempt such a tedious reckoning with the supernatural. "After Holbein" is beyond question, the most remarkable story in the book. In some aspects it might be described as the best American short story of the last decade. "After Holbein" is indescribably tragic and magnificently written. Even in this indecorous age we are moved by the pathos with which Mrs. Wharton relates this drama of senile futility. We see the entire social game lying before us like a backgammon board with two elderly, wrinkled figures bending over it. The second story particularly worthy of mention is not "Dieu d'Amour," but that gay, ironic account of life in London early in the month of September, 1914. In simple truth has the author named it "The Refugees." Something in the description of these eager British rescuers is reminiscent of ironic paragraphs in that famous tale "Xingu," which was brought out by Mrs. Wharton's publishers in 1916 with other short stories. Giving ourselves eagerly to the author's mood we sympathize with the bewildered American professor. How diverting are the witty descriptions of Lingerfield, of the Duchess and Lady Ivy Trantham ("the most successful refugee raiders of the district") and the determined Miss Rushworth, who finally becomes engaged to the Bishop of the Macaroon Islands.

Despite the ability shown in the other four stories the two best examples of Mrs. Wharton's art remain "After Holbein" and "The Refugees." They are totally different in style, but genius glows behind them both. With characteristic restraint she pictures what happens to hundreds of men and women like poor Anson Warley and Evelina Jaspar, obsessed even in old age by the desire for social accomplishment. When Mrs. Wharton leaves her legitimate generation her pen is not so steady.

Despite a practiced stirring of bobbed hair, synthetic gin cocktails and modern ideas into a 100 per cent American background, Mrs. Wharton must remain forever of that generation that saw *The Age of Innocence*. She is the best social historian America has ever produced.

Percy Hutchison, "Mrs. Wharton's Mastery of the Short Story Revealed in Six New Tales," *New York Times Book Review*, 9 November 1930, p. 7

Despite the fact that Edith Wharton has for the most part devoted her talents to the novel, it would not have been possible for one so markedly of the school of Henry James to eschew utterly the short story. With authors for whom the circumscribed moment, the fleeting mood, is so heavily freighted with consequences, the short story becomes a necessity since it affords the only outlet for the moment or the mood not sufficiently freighted to sustain the complete novel. Those who used to have the pleasure of meeting Henry James, on the rare occasions when he visited his brother William, well remember how, sitting with hands extended upward and fingertips touching, he would murmur, as the talk veered to this or that, "Ah, there is a story." No doubt a vast percentage of such mental notes would be rejected, but the remainder would be brought to fruition. And probably it has been the same with Mrs. Wharton. The stories in *Certain People* are very likely but a fraction of the subjects that in their immediacy

have appeared promising. But with a single exception she has selected well. Of the six tales that go to make up the collection, four are above the average in importance, and one is a triumph in short-story writing. This is "After Holbein."

Mrs. Wharton has in the past made fashionable New York her major field of operation. When necessary, she has made an occasional excursion into London or to the Riviera. Her people have, for the most part, been born and have lived and died within a certain social group—the group for whom the word "Society" is set always with a capital letter. But she has been no slave to her group other than a literary slave, and it has gained little comfort from the ministrations of her pen. The reverse, rather. And seldom has that pen been sharper than when it was used to set down "Atrophy," a study in futility, the debasement and frustration of a woman who thought she had dared and really did not know the meaning of the word daring. Nora Frenway had a lover, yet "her life had been so carefully guarded, so inwardly conventional in a world where all the outer conventions were tottering, that no one had ever known she had a lover."

Nora Frenway's lover is dying at his home in Connecticut and the story opens with Nora cowering in a Pullman on her way to see him before death comes. She arrives at the house—and goes away again, frustrated in her errand by Christopher Aldis's sister. But it is really not Jane Aldis that defeats Nora; it is convention which defeats her. The façades of society's houses may have changed, people may drink cocktails instead of sherry before dinner, and in other outward respects be more lax than before. But there change ends.

What nonsense to pretend that now-adays, even in big cities, in the world's greatest social centres (so ruminates Nora), the severe old-fashioned standards had given place to tolerance, laxity and ease! * * * You turned your eyes on to your own daily life and found yourself as cribbed and cabined, as beset by vigilant family eyes, observant friends, all sorts of embodied standards, as any white-muslin novel heroine of the '60s!

It was another Nora who blustered out through the door of a *Doll's House*. Well, it can't be done, says Mrs. Wharton, rather savagely. And who is right? Crestfallen, spiritually bedraggled Nora Frenway's clattering back to the Connecticut railway station in the antiquated taxicab may become quite as important a literary figure as Ibsen's Nora, from whose eruption cataclysmic social changes were predicted. If Mrs. Wharton is right, then those changes were not so cataclysmic after all, and it is pretty much the same old world. "Atrophy" is a story to be read and pondered.

Two stories, "A Bottle of Perrier" and "Mr. Jones," because so delicate a matter is the suspense on which the reader is carried forward, will not be more than touched upon. Suffice it to say that when Mrs. Wharton elects to handle a story of this type she can do it quite as well as many of the writers who have made the gradual unfolding of a mystery the major literary work of a lifetime.

It is the piece called "The Refugees" which we find negligible. When Mrs. Wharton elects to pass from irony, the humor of which is by definition tinged with something of sourness, to full-throated humor, she is lost. Humor of the sort that is attempted in "The Refugees" is not in her, and in consequence the story, except for some adroitness in handling, scarcely rises above amateur attainment. But the failure is more than compensated

for in the miniature masterpiece, "After Holbein," a story in which the author returns to the New York of her many longer triumphs, to the Fifth Avenue of *The House of Mirth* and *The Age of Innocence*. There are but two characters, other figures being but stage supernumeraries. The two are Anson Warley and Mrs. Jaspar, each a ruin and a relic of the old régime—Warley the absolutely correct man-about-town of his generation and Evelina Jaspar the leading hostess. The latter is slowly dying of softening of the brain, but, in imagination, she still gives her vast dinners, sitting at a guestless table set with common china, instead of gold plates, and decorated with artificial orchids. And as for Warley, "he could not tell people that that very morning he had arrived at the turn in the path from which mountains look as transient as flowers—and that one after another they would all arrive there, too." It is Anson's heart, an old man's heart. And if Edith Wharton had never written another line in all her life this would stand for as delicate a foreboding of approaching dissolution as ever penned. If Mrs. Wharton had not given evidence again and again in her writings that a playwright had been with great difficulty suppressed by the novelist, one would call attention to the drama in "After Holbein." But to do this is superfluous. Yet there is a difference, for it is the novelist describing the drama at the same time that the drama is being played out. Anson Warley, by some freak of senile remembrance, decides to call on old Mrs. Jaspar, though in his livelier days her heavy functions had somewhat bored him. It happens to be a "dinner" night, and Anson is shown in just as Evelina, in purple wig and diamond tiara, is descending the stairs. With antique gallantry Warley offers his arm.

The couple continued to advance staring straight ahead. All their attention was concentrated on the immense, the almost unachievable effort of reaching that point, half way down the long dinner table, opposite the big Dubarry dish, where George was drawing back a gilt armchair for Mrs. Jaspar. At last they reached it, and Mrs. Jaspar seated herself and waved a stony hand to Mr. Warley. "On my right."

In lesser hands the mockery of the scene would escape and appall, for if Anson Warley sits at the old lady's right it is death sits on her left. But over it all Mrs. Wharton spreads such a mantle of pity, the pity of one who closes sightless eyes, that the scene is not a mockery so much as it is a consecration. But it is a consecration of the past only less futile than the moment. And it is in this that Mrs. Wharton's art reaches as supreme a moment as art may hope to reach. In "After Holbein" pity softens irony—but the very pity is itself ironic. Vanitas vanitatum! For all is vanity.

The sixth story, "Dieu d'Amour," while not without charm, is out of key with Mrs. Wharton's work as a whole, and for this reason need not be dwelt upon.

V. S. Pritchett, "Clashes—Mental and Physical," *Spectator* [England], 145 (22 November 1930), 804

To Kipling again in Miss [*sic*] Edith Wharton's *Certain People*. It is full of entertaining ideas. The first story, describing how a distraught married woman hurries to see her lover who is seriously ill, and is

prevented from seeing him by a sister who puts her off with cruel trivialities, has Mr. Kipling's sardonic realism. The murder of an English recluse in the Egyptian desert by his Cockney servant, who has been maddened by loneliness, is another theme of the same order. One cannot press the comparison: Miss Wharton is not summary, and her caustic satire is written from some rock of belief and not from the tragic spleen of a divided soul. The short story, indeed, seems too mechanical, too reticent for her talent, and one is left over and over again with the sensation that, though expert in inventing ingenious situations, she has brought them off with ingenuity and not with art. She has a satirical study of the grotesque old age of two "diners out" which one would have liked to see in the accomplished hands of Mr. Osbert Sitwell.

Maxim Lièber, "Edith Wharton and Zona Gale," New York *World*, 23 November 1930, p. 3E

It is interesting to compare these collections of short stories by two such dissimilar authors as Edith Wharton and Zona Gale. The first is not unlike the work of a virtuoso who appears on the platform, bows correctly, and promptly sets to playing a varied program of difficult, almost acrobatic numbers, each rendered with a meticulous precision. . . .

Mrs. Wharton's stories are composed with a flawless technique, so that one must agree with the opinion of Henry James with regard to her "diabolical little cleverness." One cannot deny, when one has read the excellent story, "After Holbein," that Mrs. Wharton knows that social stratum she deals with. Neither can one escape the fact that most of her present stories are "composed." For instance, "A Bottle of Perrier" or "Mr. Jones" are deft little mystery stories. Nevertheless, they leave one untouched. And they certainly do not add to the stature of the artist who created that little masterpiece, *Ethan Frome*. For good measure we have the mildly humorous sort of comedy of errors, "The Refugees" and the somewhat dull tale, "Dieu d'Amour." . . .

"New Novels: *Certain People*," *Times Literary Supplement* [England], 27 November 1930, p. 1010

Mrs. Edith Wharton's collection of short stories, *Certain People* . . ., is a happy indication of her unfailing vitality, the quality without which the school of fiction to which she belongs is apt to seem wilfully remote from modern minds. There is no remoteness in Mrs. Wharton's work, and yet she makes no obvious sacrifices of that integrity which her great master prized above all. Of the six stories here included two are comedies, one is an essay in the modern macabre, two are definitely grisly and shuddery and another is pure romance with a very pretty setting in Cyprus.

In some respects, the two comedies, "Atrophy" and "The Refugees," are the most successful; for Mrs. Wharton has an inimitable touch in depicting without overemphasis such a scene as that where a married woman, on hearing that her secret lover is sick to death, throws the prudent concealment of many years to the winds, takes the train, drives to the country house where he lies, and is bleakly met by the dying man's sister who, by no more than her polite insistence that this is but a friendly call, fences her brother's bedside with steel and repels the intruder. Nor can anybody better describe a situation such as that of Mr. Charles Durand when, having become involved in the stream of Belgian refugees coming to England in 1914, he finds himself eagerly snapped up as a refugee by an elderly spinster of good family to whom "nothing had ever happened," while he was busy making up his mind to rescue her. Perhaps, however, the latter story is carried a thought too far: we do not see the wistful Miss Clio Rushworth of 1914 as a stern commandant of a canteen in 1918. Possibly there is a slight stiffness in the process by which in "After Holbein" old Anson Warley, the New York man-about-town, is brought in to the nightly mummery that old Mrs. Jaspar, once a great hostess in New York, went through nightly under the mocking eyes of her nurse and the pitying eyes of her old maid; but the mummery itself is powerfully described. Nightly, Mrs. Jaspar performed the scene of her last dinner partly before she had a stroke. The gown was put on, the jewels taken out of the safe, the guests announced by the footman, a whole dinner-table laid with partial make-believe, and the semblance of a banquet proceeded with. On the last night of his life, Anson Warley, who had long since dined away his soul, drifts in at Mrs. Jaspar's front door on an icy night suffering from a lapse of memory. He only knew that he was dining somewhere. A real guest, under the eyes of the astonished household, hands the old lady into the dining-room, and the ghastly banquet of two old mummies proceeds. This is brilliantly rendered, and its macabre comedy more than atones for any preliminary weakness. One of the grim stories, "Mr. Jones," is of a baleful presence in an old house, in a village of memorable name, Thudeney-Blazes. Here the suggestion of the hidden influence is very cleverly done; but perhaps it needs a more determined revelling in the sinister to justify its violent ending. The story innocently called "A Bottle of Perrier," with a still more horrible climax, is placed in the desert, where a certain Mr. Medford has come to stay in the old castle where his eccentric host buries himself. When Medford arrives he is told that his host, Mr. Almodham, is away on some antiquarian investigation, and his entertainment devolves upon the English valet, Gosling. It is from Gosling that the growing uneasiness emanates, until, in a moonlit courtyard, it comes admirably to its explosion in tragedy. Mrs. Wharton's neatness and ease, besides her keen enjoyment of natural beauty, distinguish every page of this book, which is both a pleasure to read and a lesson to analyse.

"Certain People," New Statesman, 36 (29 November 1930), 250

Mrs. Wharton is only at her best once in this book of stories—in the dreadful and fascinating variation on The Dance of Death, which she calls "After Holbein": it is a great little story, probably too true and uncomfortable to be greeted at all loudly in this self-cosseting age. "A Bottle of Perrier" is good—but a little too like a pastiche of a Hichens story; and in "Mr. Jones," a study in the supernatural, Mrs. Wharton's grip is slackened. But what mastery there is, even in her weakest work,

compared with most of the work done by her juniors!

"New Novels," Saturday Review [England], 150 (6 December 1930), 747

Presumably there really existed, at some point in the world's history, an aged gourmet who died in action over the nuts and wine. There must be some foundation in actuality for a character to whom such frequent tribute is paid in fiction, not only by old English writers but by modern American ones as well. That elderly epicure is positively a hall-mark of a certain standard of slick, near-intelligent authorship and, bore though he has now become, you will find him grimly taking his place somewhere in the collected works of every successful contributor to the "class" magazines.

Mrs. Wharton's Man of the World makes his appearance in "After Holbein," one of the six short stories contained in *Certain People*. Wanly he eats his last dinner before crossing the Bar; he has no palate left and hardly any sight, he does not realize that the "Perrier-Jouet, 'ninety-five" is only Apollinaris, or that the orchids upon the table are merely bunched-up pieces of newspaper. Finally he says good-bye to his hostess and her phantom guests and stumbles out to meet death on the pavement. The quality aimed at here, one feels, was the pathetic-macabre, but something has gone agley. Perhaps the subject seems too easy and familiar and Mrs. Wharton over-generous with her effects.

She is much more successfully grim in "A Bottle of Perrier," a tale of murder in an African desert and an ingenious exercise in sustained suspense. In "The Refugees" her rather acid wit finds a vulnerable subject in the excesses, at the beginning of the war, of an English county family with refugee-adopting mania. A duchess, for example, is planning a garden-party in aid of the Relief Fund and looking for someone to do a lecture on Atrocities. It is explained:

> The committee has given us a prima donna from the Brussels Opera to sing the Marseillaise, and the what-d'ye-call-it Belgian anthem, but there are lots of people coming just for the Atrocities.

Mrs. Wharton is very much at her ease with this sort of straightforward satire, and, of course, whether she is being witty or grisly or just understanding, she is never at a loss for an effective phrase.

[Florence Codman], "Short Stories by Novelists," *Nation*, 131 (10 December 1930), 654

In general what may be said for these authors [Edith Wharton, Elmer Davis, May Sinclair] as novelists may be said for them as short-story writers. None of them is a novice or an initiator. They each transfer a well-formed, facile style, which by long practice has become a convention with them, to another medium without any serious results to either style or medium. Of the three Miss Sinclair is the ablest, treating the short story as an independent form, a distinct æsthetic expression capable within its brief and brittle outline of manifold variety and richness. Mrs. Wharton's book, with a single noteworthy exception, is shockingly third rate, and "Morals for Moderns" is a lesson and a warning to all students of fiction writing. . . .

There is no excuse for *Certain People* except what resides in the quality of "After Holbein." The two mystery stories are incredibly naive and maladroit, the medieval romance is little more than a literary exercise, and "Atrophy" suffers from the success of "After Holbein." The latter story preserves in miniature all the essentials of Mrs. Wharton's talent. It deals with death and decay among New York society leaders of the older generation. It is a prism—delicate, transparent, colorful—containing a whole social order, a perfect imprint of a vanishing race. From behind its worn-out forms, its self-imposed seriousness, importance, and virtue Mrs. Wharton draws whatever humanity it has. She draws it conventionally so far as style goes and painlessly so far as ideas are concerned, but she draws with mature grace and rich understanding.

[John Chamberlain], "The Short Story Muddles On," *New Republic*, 65 (7 January 1931), 225

By reading Edith Wharton's latest volume, we discover that the behaviorist-Freudian split is not the full measure of the story writer's failure; it is mainly the measure of the experimentalist's failure.

Edith Wharton is neither behaviorist nor Freudian. Indeed, she is not at all concerned with world views, or total human views; but she has her prejudices, and these cause an orientation toward a dead life. More often than not she seems to be practising a dexterous but perfunctory technique upon anything that comes to hand out of the past. She is like a pitcher who, confident of his lead and his ultimate ability to control the situation, lets a ball go with perfect coordination—but down the fatal groove.

Checklist of Additional Reviews

Dorothy Foster Gilman, "*Certain People*," Boston *Evening Transcript*, 13 December 1930, book section, p. 2.

"Short Stories of Varying Themes by Edith Wharton," Springfield [Massachusetts] *Republican*, 28 December 1930, p. 7-E.

THE GODS ARRIVE

THE GODS ARRIVE

BY

EDITH WHARTON

The gods approve
The depth and not the tumult of the soul.

D. APPLETON AND COMPANY
NEW YORK : LONDON : MCMXXXII

Isabel Paterson, "Egeria on the Left Bank," *New York Herald Tribune Books*, 18 September 1932, p. 3

As a literary expatriate of the generation of Henry James, Mrs. Wharton must have been equally astonished and amused by the arrival, during the last decade, of the barbarian frontier legions, bringing up the rear of the long procession. Doubtless she had the present volume in mind while writing *Hudson River Bracketed*. In that novel she showed the Middle Western novelist capturing New York. Paris was the next stopping place; and her hero, Vance Weston, proceeds thither inevitably in *The Gods Arrive*. The title probably refers to the love story which supplies the thread of plot; but it might be an ironical salute to the standard bearers of all the Little Magazines of the Left Bank.

The names alone must have been irresistible to her as one committed to the craft of words. Wouldn't Gratz Blemer, Jane Meggs, Imp Pevensey, Brank Heff, Andros Nevsky and Yves Tourment look thoroughly plausible in the list of contributors to "This Quarter" or "transition"? Along with Bravig Imbs, Hector Rella, Karlton Kelm, Franz Blei, Anais Nin, Vladimir Sirin and Philippe Soupplate. The former group are the inventions of Mrs. Wharton's fancy; and she must have exercised considerable ingenuity to avoid the trap of unconscious memory. She slyly insinuates that maybe the others aren't real either. Jane Meggs was actually christened Violet Southernwood, and abandoned the sentimental syllables because her lover, Lorry Spear, "declared himself unable to endure the sound of so nauseatingly pretty a name." Why he didn't ditch his Whartonesque cognomen in favor of something more cacophonous, such as Ed Blimp, is not quite clear. But it doesn't need to be; maybe he had gone so far ahead of the crowd that he had got back to the plush and haircloth period.

Vance Weston himself is faintly reminiscent of the moon-calves of Floyd Dell. It will be remembered that in his previous adventures he wandered through New York's Bohemia and on its upper borders met Héloïse Spear, a heroine from a moated grange on the Hudson, the last of a line of Old New Yorkers, whose social importance had faded as their money disappeared. Héloïse, nicknamed Halo, married Lewis Tarrant, a moneyed young man of equally genteel extraction, with aspirations which Halo hoped to share. Lewis was editor of a magazine of parlor radicalism in New York. But Halo "had left out of account the uneasy vanity which exacted more, always more ... her complete belief, the uncritical surrender of her will and judgment. ... To be 'understood,' for Lewis Tarrant, was an active, a perpetually functioning state. The persons nearest him must devote all their days and nights, thoughts, impulses, inclinations, to the arduous business of understanding him."

The great danger of demanding to be understood is that finally the yearner gets his wish. And the next step is divorce. Lewis beat Halo to it, asking for his freedom. Halo was entirely willing; which must have been another jolt to Lewis.

However, Halo had got the habit of understanding unappreciated genius. Like a drug addict, she could not resist the appeal of Vance Weston for an immediate understanding. So the story opens with the pair eloping, bound for Paris.

Halo must have been the last woman to elope in the classic manner. How she

489

managed about passports is not mentioned; perhaps Mrs. Wharton overlooked that detail. To further the equally traditional plot, Lewis changed his mind about the divorce. So Halo wandered about Europe with Vance in a natural bewilderment, between two worlds. In Montparnasse she was rather at a loss because living in sin was in itself a convention. She was reassured when the wealthy Mrs. Glaisher, a patroness of the arts but also a member of Halo's own social group, cut her dead; on the other hand, she was annoyed when a chance acquaintance in Spain omitted to introduce her, with Vance, to a Spanish marquess. There didn't seem to be any definite rules, and Halo needed rules. Vance's middle class origin gave him no clue to Halo's feelings as an errant lady. And his temperamental touchiness was the egotism of the writer, not the vanity of an intellectual snob of the type of Lewis Tarrant. In her simplicity she had imagined that the writer wanted constructive criticism of his work, and to be urged forward in this task. It was a fresh disillusionment to discover that Vance demanded her to fortify his excuses for idleness, and cheer him on, when he did not work, with unqualified praise.

Whether or not by her creator's intention, Halo is a complete embodiment of the sentimental nineteenth century ideal of a woman as the inspiration of genius, mistress and school mistress in one. If such a being ever existed, her function vanished with the passing of the century. What survived, and saved Halo from a second failure, was Vance's small-town morality, which springs from immutable elements in human nature. Vance was naturally a married man. He might stray but he always came back to the woman he thought of as his wife.

Mrs. Wharton satirizes the modernists in her own leisurely way, conceding not the fraction of an inch in either theory or

practice to their literary claims. So the issue is fairly drawn, and the decision is left to the reader.

Percy Hutchison, "Mrs. Wharton Probes a Social Period: Her New Novel Is a Searching Study in the Patrician Caste," *New York Times Book Review*, 18 September 1932, pp. 6, 20

When Edith Wharton elected to take the title of her latest novel from Emerson's lines,

When half-gods go
The gods arrive,

it was unquestionably for the purpose of directing attention away from the characters in the story to the theme that lay behind, a request in advance, as it were, that the reader be prepared to interest himself less in Halo Tarrant and Vance Weston than in the emotional problem confronting them, and in that problem's working out. Mrs. Wharton has more than once in her long and distinguished career as a novelist similarly turned from the persons in her story—however intense her engrossment in them—to a preoccupation with the relationships she has established for them; but seldom has she done so with the aggressiveness here shown. It is as if this novelist, confronted by changes in the world about her not even imaginable in the social era of Lily Bart and *The House of Mirth*, had fiercely set herself to work to penetrate that new world in the hope of finding for it standards under which it might attain to something of the orderliness it seems so conspicuously to lack. That no writer is better qualified than Mrs. Wharton to carry through such a literary task in a manner to bring conviction goes without saying.

In *The Gods Arrive* the author deals with an extramarital relation, established before the beginning of the book. Halo Tarrant is the wife of a scion of what might be termed Manhattan's old nobility, a child of the period when Society was the tail that wagged the dog. A little less of that nobility, but still not so lowborn that she might not be grafted on the more aristocratic stem, was Halo Spear, whom he had married. Into the life of Mrs. Tarrant, unhappy in her elevation, came Vance Weston, an increasingly successful author of novels somewhat second-rate, who finds in Halo's brilliant presence stimulation and the critical help he needs. The story opens with these two on board the steamship, Europe-bound, which will carry them, as Mr. and Mrs. Weston, to a life together. How will this alliance work out? This is the problem Edith Wharton has set for herself, by no means a problem entirely new to novelists, but one that has become increasingly interesting since a war reduced stability to fluidity.

At this point in the story it may be well to turn for a moment from the narrative itself to considerations more literary in their nature, for, in a sense at least, *The Gods Arrive* comes under the classification of what used to be termed "problem" novels. Mrs. Wharton has brought together these two characters—with Tarrant hovering in the background—in precisely the same way a scientist might bring together two or more elements, namely, to see how they will act. And how will this couple act? What will be the resulting parallelogram of forces? But in a scientific investigation everything that would be interfering or diverting in its influence must be disposed of at the outset. The problem must be what might be termed "purely" posed. And it is in getting her problem purely posed that the literary sagacity of Mrs. Wharton demonstrates itself. Whether Weston be a bachelor or a widower is unimportant; Mrs. Wharton chooses for him the former status. But what of Mrs. Tarrant? To preserve sympathy for her it is necessary that the reader be convinced of her right to divorce, and, having that right, for some reason to have been deprived of it, while, at the same time, the husband must be kept from the rôle of dog-in-the-manger, from the part of mere brute. Mrs. Wharton attains this by indicating that Lewis Tarrant has that antipathy to divorce which the generations preceding him had made one of the principal tenets of their social code. Suffer in loneliness he will—for he was in love with his wife; but set her legally free he will not. Thus has Edith Wharton got Halo and Vance together to work out their destinies; the problem has been set with scientific purity.

Should the reviewer have written it in the singular—destiny? For of course that is what these two lovers, idealizing the future, are taking for granted it will be—a single destiny of happiness. But there are flaws in the compound which they have mixed, as Mrs. Wharton knows there must be. And the principal flaw is just that very thing, happiness. "Marriage is a frame," one of the lesser characters in the book is made somewhere to observe; and Halo and Vance, not married, are to find presently that what they lack is a frame for their lives. Hence, when they go away together, with nothing to hold them to each other but such happiness as they may mutually secure, such happiness as they have already caught up to themselves, they are consorting only with the half-gods;

491

the time is still far off, and much must happen in between before the gods may arrive.

The reader may find himself a little annoyed at some of the conversations on art, especially the literary art, which are introduced from time to time. Nevertheless, since it must be conceded that the author is in a position to understand the caprices of the literary worker, it must also be conceded that when her Vance Weston begins to yearn for companions other than Halo she knows what she is about. Vance does not yearn for other women, but he must take up with every dilettante writer who happens along, and with every halfbaked expounder of literary platitudes. Later on there is a woman, but she is one who has read scarcely a book in all her life and never one of Weston's books! Of course the point is that Weston has not found himself. First attracted to Halo because of her interest in his work—a wholly intellectual contact—when something more personal between them asserts itself, as Mrs. Wharton demonstrates, the intellectual contact weakens, and he must seek, unconsciously perhaps, to establish new ones. Alders is the first of these, a young man in whom Halo "recognized the roving American with a thin glaze of culture over an unlettered origin." Yet in some ways Alders was good for Vance.

His talk was a blurred window; but through it Vance caught glimpses of the summits. Halo could have given him a clearer sight of them; but she recognized that the distance was yet too great between her traditional culture and Vance's untutored curiosities. This dawdling Autolycus, with his bag of bright-colored scraps, might serve as a guide when she was useless.

So poor Halo effaces herself more and more from that part of her lover's existence which, with increasing fame, becomes more and more his complete existence; and, that hold upon him weakened, there comes a day, the other woman having entered on the scene, when Weston deserts her who had so bravely come away with him. Halo sitting "alone among the ruins" is as poignant a bit of drawing as has ever come from the magic pen of Edith Wharton. Nevertheless there is not at first a complete break. The reader may feel that any Vance Weston in real life would be deserving of having his neck wrung, as at best an unstable weakling, and at worst something of a cad. But it must be granted that Edith Wharton has pictured her hero's vacillating nature with extreme subtlety. And that he should be vacillating is necessary to the study. Vance returns to Halo, and for a time there is some semblance of happiness; the half-gods do as well as may be expected of them. Eventually the break seems final, and Halo accepts it as such. It is then that Tarrant comes back upon the scene.

In this sketch, light as it is, of Lewis Tarrant, Mrs. Wharton will be seen upon reflection to have drawn more lastingly than at first appears. Beneath coldness, and the vanity of one belonging to the socially patrician caste, there is an emotional intensity which at last breaks its restraining leash. There is nobleness as well as pathos in Tarrant's plea to the deserted Halo to return to him:

"What stands between us? Some idea that things can't be as they were before? Perhaps they can't—entirely. But if I assure you of my friendship—my devotion—God, Halo, what I'm proposing shows how I feel—there's no use talking."

Unless the reader up to this point has found himself in agreement with the present writer, that Mrs. Wharton has conducted a study rather than told a tale merely for the sake of the telling, then Halo's reply to her husband's proposal may seem a descent into a lower literary stratum than Edith Wharton has been accustomed to move upon. Halo will not return to Tarrant, because she is to bear Vance a child. This is a dangerous device, but it is used not for the usual purpose when employed by the writer of fiction. Halo is to "find herself" through the medium of the child. We shall presently discover that Vance has found himself through his failure as a novelist, though the precise ending of the narrative the reader must discover. But it may not be wholly amiss to wonder here whether Tarrant's insistence that the child's future would be better served by its bearing the name Tarrant rather than by bearing no name, as seems probable, is not, considering civilization's present stage of advancement, more cogent than Halo's outburst, "I've no right to give your name to another man's child! Can't you understand that a woman should want to be free, and alone with her child?" Did Mrs. Wharton fail to notice the subtle shifting of possession here? And what would the majority of women, asked to consider hypothetically the dilemma of another's name for an offspring of flaunted illegitimacy, give for an answer?

But let us not cavil. *The Gods Arrive* is not likely to take its place as one of Edith Wharton's most masterly achievements. But she has done nothing more sincerely dictated by the desire to probe a period to its depths. In those novels with which her name is most illustriously associated, such stories as *The House of Mirth* and *The Age of Innocence*, she mirrored an era, she did not probe into it. Hence, coming as it does from the pen of an author so distinguished as Mrs. Wharton, the impeccability of whose style no change can

dim, *The Gods Arrive* is a novel far transcending the general run of books.

Elmer Davis, "History of an Artist," *Saturday Review of Literature*, 9 (1 October 1932), 145

This is a sequel to *Hudson River Bracketed*, whose events are so skilfully recalled in the opening chapters that *The Gods Arrive* can be read itself. But for full effect the two books should be read together, for in structure if not in viewpoint they are one piece—the first three hundred thousand words of a history not yet concluded. For despite the title, the gods have not yet arrived at the end of the book; neither the artistic development of Vance Weston nor his emotional relation to Halo Spear has reached a point that satisfies the reader, and it is hardly to be supposed that so scrupulous an artist as Mrs. Wharton would be more easily satisfied than her customers.

Hudson River Bracketed was essentially the early history of an artist—of Vance Weston of Euphoria, Illinois, who came to New York, married the devoted but hopelessly unintelligent Laura Lou, found his intellectual and eventually his emotional inspiration in Halo Spear, the impoverished New York patrician who married Lewis Tarrant; and finally, after his wife's death and Halo's break with her husband, could look forward to the companionship of a woman who understood him. It was a long book, and much of it was the sort of thing that Mrs. Wharton simply cannot do; she understands gentlefolk, artists, and servants; but if she knows the lesser breeds without the law she is unable to transfer her comprehension to the reader. Especially she writes of the Middle West and its inhabitants as if she had never been west of the Metropolitan Opera House, and had learned about Middle Westerners from a careful study of *Main Street* and *Martin Chuzzlewit*. But one thing she can do—and there are not more than half a dozen Americans who could attempt it with any pretence of knowing what they are talking about—and that is the nature of the artist.

It may be hard to believe that anyone so utterly innocent and incompetent as Vance Weston could have been thrown up by twentieth-century America; but there have been artists like that—Shelley, for instance—and as a picture of an intellectual angel in New York of the nineteen twenties *Hudson River Bracketed* was just about as good as possible. Mrs. Wharton not only knows but can convey the essential perceptions and psychological processes of the artist; methodical worker that she is herself, she understands why other artists cannot be methodological; and perhaps a more astounding insight than any, she understands the feeling and the dreadful consequences of a type of poverty that she herself can never have known. Whatever Vance Weston did or did not do, you felt that he was authentically alight with the divine fire and that some day he would prove it.

The Gods Arrive puts both Vance Weston and Halo to a much severer test. Vance has money now—an allowance from his father, presently supplemented by the royalties of a successful book (what became of that bad contract that played so large a part in *Hudson River Bracketed?*), and he and Halo can travel about Europe in passably decent style without financial worries. Vance is still learning, still assimilating; his relation to Alders, the "half-cultured" American he met in

Spain, from whom he could take what he needed better than from Halo's far deeper culture, is an admirable piece of insight and of depiction. But when he falls in with the literary sets of London and Paris he becomes, all of a sudden, only another small-town boy who made good. He borrows the mannerisms of those around him, he becomes insufferably inflated, and at the end of *The Gods Arrive* he has not yet written anything that justifies his promise.

Now this has happened to a thousand young men and women of late years—people who had a spark of genuine artistic instinct, but not enough to survive the systematic exploitation of the literature industry (or racket) as at present organized. But the Vance Weston of *Hudson River Bracketed* was not the ordinary small-town boy with enough talent for two or three pretty good books; he was presented as something authentic. In *The Gods Arrive* he has little of the artist but the characteristic vices; and after all it was not an avidity for other men's money and other men's women that made Richard Wagner an artist. If there was stuff in Vance Weston, the stuff that his beginnings promised, it will have to come out in the third volume of the trilogy.

But the emphasis in *The Gods Arrive* is on Halo. When Vance wanted her she went to him, though her precipitance annoyed her husband into refusing her the divorce he had promised; and thereafter she devoted herself to the congenial task of "serving the genius while she adored the man." Completely devoted, she made no effort to become anything in her own right; and eventually she learned that such a gift as Cosima Wagner's is perhaps even rarer than her husband's. It had been Halo, years before, who first opened the world of the mind to Vance Weston; later, when they were both unhappily married but as yet unaware of their love, her consciousness "seemed an extension of his own, in which every inspiration as it came, instantly rooted and flowered, and every mistake withered and dropped out of sight." She was, in short, his best pal and his severest critic; "she was the woman his arms longed for, but she was also the goddess, the miracle, the unattainable being who haunted the peaks of his imagination." But when the unattainable being was attained, when his arms that longed for her had only to reach out and take her, when the force that had translated itself to their innocent minds as a spiritual sympathy had found its direct and natural outlet—then, in due course, she presently became the woman he wanted to get away from.

The thing has happened several billion times in the history of the human race, and it is a measure of Mrs. Wharton's skill that she keeps you interested in this familiar fable, even though neither of the leading characters is as respectable, intellectually, as in *Hudson River Bracketed*. Granted that Halo was madly in love, it might be supposed that a woman of her background and experience would have handled herself and her artist a little more shrewdly. Yet even after she knew him, even after the tie between them was strained, she fatally tried to go on being his intellectual inspiration; she told him what she really thought about a bad book he had written, and his response to criticism was that of every artist, good or bad, authentic or spurious. So presently he was back home in Euphoria, enjoying a new harmony with his sister Mae because "for want of an intelligent ear he had to turn to a merely sympathetic one." By that time he would have preferred sympathy, even if intelligence could have been had.

The Gods Arrive suggests what the married life of Agnes Wickfield might have been, if the last chapters of *David Copperfield* had been written some eighty

years later. Granted that an artist such as Vance Weston needed the stable framework of marriage—a permanent woman, to get away from and to come back to—on the basis of the record so far Laura Lou, who could never understand him and never tried, would have been a better wife for him than Halo, who had much to give him and tried to give him all of it. At the end he comes back to her, but it is hard to believe that this is more than another of his impulses, that he will not leave her again the next time she imprudently says what she thinks about his writing, if another comet like Floss Delaney flames across the sky. If Vance Weston is to become the real artist that he once promised to be, if Halo is to learn how to manage him, it will have to be done in the next book.

"New Novels: *The Gods Arrive*," *Times Literary Supplement* [England], 6 October 1932, p. 708

Mrs. Edith Wharton treads familiar ground when she takes us into the highways of Europe frequented by exiled and uprooted Americans, fabulously rich or fabulously silly and continually amazed by the miracle that has got them there. Much of her new novel, *The Gods Arrive* . . . , deals with these almost stock figures repeating their crude antics under the mild satiric beam she turns upon them; but they are there to provide the background for Halo Tarrant and, more particularly, Vance Weston, and in this relation they are freshly amusing.

With a leisurely air and the precision of

art and experience Mrs. Wharton builds up the pattern of her book, amplifying the detail and decorating the structure till it stands complete as one of her most solid achievements. Halo and Vance have been met before by the reader, in that old house on the Hudson River, where the boy was permitted to browse among the books left by Halo's romantic maiden relative. In the pathetic and musty drawing-room of "The Willows" Halo had come upon the attractive and ambitious youth, and that sympathy had been born between them that finds its full expression in this novel. Vance's futile little wife is dead, and Halo is thoroughly disillusioned with her married life. To force Tarrant to the Divorce Court, she and Vance go off openly together to Europe. Spain, Paris, a small Riviera port appropriately called Oubli-sur-Mer, the fashionable French resorts. London and America, once more complete the circle of their wanderings. Halo is a temperate creature deeply in love and wise enough to be patient with the unstable Vance, who has a disconcerting habit of going out for a stroll and taking a train to some distant spot, where he remains, communicating nothing, for weeks at a time. She fights against tradition and the conventions that she has been bred in; and constantly she is exposed to the slights and mortifications of her ambiguous position. Vance has to struggle with his weaker self, an idle and second-rate self inclined to indulgence and infatuated with a shop-soiled siren now masquerading as a young woman of fashion. On the whole Halo has a very great deal to endure before the half-gods go and the gods arrive. But the happy ending, marriage and infant included, is provided by the management with a lavish hand; and an added touch of romance is added by staging the reunion of the two—who have been definitely separated for some time—in the old Hudson house with the brackets. Mrs.

Wharton's rich and ample picture is filled in with many subsidiary characters, clear and faithful portraits in little. The sad English colony among the wind-bitten olives of a cheap and dismal French townlet will not readily be forgotten, and the social scenes are presented with her customary brilliance and finish.

R. Ellis Roberts, "The Woman Novelist," *New Statesman and Nation*, n.s., 4 (22 October 1932), 488, 490

. . . Mrs. Wharton is not disillusioned. *The Gods Arrive* is not one of her best books. It is extremely workmanlike. It has passages of insight, of wit and of a robust intolerance with pretentious modernity that make it extremely good reading. It continues the story of Halo Tarrant and Vance Weston which began in *Hudson River Bracketed*. Many men will object to it—and they will often make the same objection in reading other novels by women, that the chief male character is disgusting. Vance is not only more selfish, more inconsiderate, more stupid and less attractive than one's noble self: he is lower than any except the most vulgar nit-wits of one's acquaintance. That is why a man should study women's novels: he will get an idea of what a woman thinks women have to, and can, tolerate, and he may revise his own naturally high opinion of himself. Halo displays unending patience to this evidently third-rate author who ignores, teases, and mortifies her: and the "happy ending" surely preludes a long life of boredom for Halo in her ministering to Vance's vanity.

Ethel Wallace Hawkins, "The Bookshelf," *Atlantic Monthly*, 150 (October 1932), 14, 16

The half-quotation that is the title of Edith Wharton's new novel indicates plainly enough that the conflict in this book is resolved by a clarifying of ideals and purposes. *The Gods Arrive* ..., the further history of Vance Weston, the young writer in *Hudson River Bracketed*, shows once more Mrs. Wharton's definiteness in artistic and spiritual standards.

The Gods Arrive has a triple interest. It is a study of the life of Vance Weston and Halo Tarrant after they have entered openly into an irregular relation in the expectation that Halo's husband will divorce her. It is a study of an unformed and rather weak nature struggling between a true devotion and an aberration of the sense. And it is an expert and ironic picture of the affliction that must be endured by a successful writer, and incidentally a crisp expression of the author's opinion of the stream-of-consciousness fiction as practised by the many.

Once more in this novel one recognizes Mrs. Wharton's command of the significant detail that makes clear a whole situation or state of emotion. All of Vance's misery of mingled grief and distaste at Grandma Scrimser's funeral is in "the readings from Isaiah and James Whitcomb Riley, intermingled by a practised hand." All of the callousness of Floss Delaney's common soul is in her triumphant recounting of her cleverness in blackmailing the wealthy Shunts family by means of the desperate love letters of young Honoré Shunts: "He wouldn't listen to reason; but he had to. I never saw anybody cry

so. ... It was horrid of him, not being willing to see how I was placed." And all the physical and spiritual healing that Vance finds in the Northern woods is forecast in the moment when he gets out of the train: "The icy air caught him by the throat and suddenly swung him up on wings."

If anyone in the novel may be said to sum up, it is the egregious Grandma Scrimser, so truly pious, so canny in her acquisition of funds for her creed, so robust in her negation of whatever might dampen the spirit of mortals, who whispers on her deathbed: "Maybe we haven't made enough of pain—been afraid of it. Don't be afraid of it." *The Gods Arrive* is an effective study of growth through pain.

Dorothea Brande, "Four Novels of the Month," *Bookman*, 75 (October 1932), 673–8

The two central characters of Edith Wharton's earlier *Hudson River Bracketed*, Halo Tarrant and Vance Weston, come together in *The Gods Arrive* ... as lovers barred from marriage by the selfish obduracy of Halo's husband. The whole novel is the record of Halo's attempt to make an enduring relation between her lover and herself against the odds of social disapproval, the novelist's temperament of Weston, and the insecurity which, she comes at last reluctantly to recognize, must always be present when there is not the actual, legal tie of marriage to hold the man and woman together through the ordeals of loss of rapture, outbursts of individualism, and crises of pride. In the process of bringing her lovers to the realization that marriage is a vital and necessary bond, Mrs. Wharton carries them through the literary worlds and half-worlds of Spain, France, and Italy; and Weston gets his fill of literary London and America as well.

It goes without saying that *The Gods Arrive* is one of the important books of the year. Mrs. Wharton has never, in the deepest sense, evaded the responsibilities of her gift. It would be impossible for her to turn out a novel on a superficial theme, or have superficial convictions on her subject. She is firmly established in the public regard and in critical esteem, so I approach with some trepidation the thankless task of setting down a heterodox opinion.

It was disturbingly noticeable in *Hudson River Bracketed*, and even more uncomfortably obtrusive in the present book, that when Mrs. Wharton turns from her central figures to the secondary characters, when she is writing of the literary and social Bohemia which she loathes, she is frequently content to put her artistry aside and to write as a journalist. These Parisian studio parties, and the sketches of figures for them—is there not something distressingly like Sunday-supplement comment and observation about them? This American sculptor, Brank Heff, who says to a dancer whom he wants to use as model: "I guess you'd do first rate"—did he ever have his being outside a London hack-writer's imagination? Do the Mrs. Glaishers of this world think and talk about themselves as "society women"? I am unable to believe it, and my incredulity, spreading and deepening, begins to flow over and obliterate the impressions of the central characters themselves. I remember withholding judgement when I found Mrs. Wharton making her hero say, of the Duke of Spartivento, "I wonder what's become of Alder's duke—you remember, the one with the name like the clanging of shields," and retroactively en-lightened by the unbelievable talk put into the mouths of the Paris group, I return and say flatly that such a phrase as "the name like the clanging of shields" never issued from a human throat in a sober moment.

And so this almost frivolous sketching of the secondary characters as subhuman caricatures undermines the importance of *The Gods Arrive*. One admits the gravity and interest of the theme, the dramatic effectiveness of many of the dilemmas which Halo and Vance are forced to meet; but, made wary by the Mrs. Glaishers and Brank Heffs, one looks for—and finds, alas—evidence that not even the figures of Halo and Vance have been spared the touch of the manipulating hand. That this discovery is not fatal, that one does not lay aside the book at the moment when suspicion becomes certainty, means that Mrs. Wharton is still Mrs. Wharton and that her second rate is better than many another author's best.

Margaret Chaney Dawson, "False Gods," *New Republic*, 73 (23 November 1932), 33

In *Hudson River Bracketed* Mrs. Wharton surveyed New York's Bohemia and was annoyed. And as she guides Vance Weston, the author whose progress from the Middle West to the Atlantic seaboard she has already traced, into the midst of the left-wing American literati in Paris, her irritation deepens. Here, she admits, there is a brilliance, a closeness of argument, lacking in the Greenwich Village groups. But the speciousness, the basic frivolity, above all the lack of mental order! Not that she does not understand, even pride herself on understanding the tortuous irregularities of the creative process—this is, in fact, the old story of the artist's struggle to fit the mysterious eruptions of inspiration into a humanly livable existence—but that, nevertheless, one feels behind her sympathy a relentless belief in the final goodness of her own creative process and her own form of discipline.

With Vance is Halo Tarrant, the wife of the Review editor who, it will be remembered, found her not sufficiently tireless at the full-time job of "understanding" him. Halo is unmistakably a heroine—not one of the feeble and forlorn human beings who double on their tracks and do unaccountable violence to their own feelings—but a steadfast, womanly creature with a sure instinct for what Mrs. Wharton, despite her fair-mindedness, obviously thinks of as The Right. As Vance's mistress, Halo finds herself subject to a number of unexpected confusions and maladjustments. Tarrant's sudden decision not to permit divorce proceedings destroys her whole plan of living, leaving her with no agreeable alternative. For a temporary challenge to the conventions, in the traditionally gallant and high-minded manner, she had been prepared. But to find herself forced either to build up a life with people who outrage her deep sense of social forms or to drag her lover into a succession of solitudes, is more than she had bargained for.

The villainess who further complicates Halo's problem is cut to a pattern as conventional as her own. Floss Delaney, an old love of Vance's youth, albeit one who had brought him a bitter disillusionment, turns up at Monte Carlo with a newly acquired fortune and an international male following. The affair between these two, or rather Vance's attempt to have an affair with Floss, desperately injures the relation between Vance and Halo and finally brings about his departure for America. But there is the reunion of true lovers at the end which the title calls for. And there is an implication of that other homecoming which Mrs. Wharton may have had in mind when she suggested the departure of the half-gods; for after publication of a Paris-inspired novel called *Colossus*, Vance begins to draw away from the "microcosmic" school of writing and to seek a more personal revelation.

Mrs. Wharton is not an author whom one thinks of as being controversial. Yet if ever issue was squarely drawn and sides unbudgingly taken, it is in this novel. Except for its excellent craftsmanship, in which the author never fails, this passionate intellectual partisanship is perhaps the most distinctive thing that it has to offer.

Louise Maunsell Field, "The Modest Novelist," *North American Review*, 235 (January 1933), 65–6

The relations of men and women in the holy but difficult married and in the less holy but quite as difficult semi-married state were once almost as provocative of panaceas as those of capital and labor. But look at the way Edith Wharton deals with those of the semi-married in her new novel, *The Gods Arrive*. Her heroine, Halo Tarrant, whom readers of *Hudson River Bracketed* will remember, leaves her husband and goes abroad with Vance Weston, the young writer in whose genius she believes. The resulting situation is developed with all Mrs. Wharton's well-known skill and understanding, developed logically and with a sureness one does not even question, until Halo Tarrant, separated from her lover, returns to her old home on the Hudson, and there prepares for the birth of her illegitimate child. This is the point where interest grows tense. What is to become of Halo and her baby? How will she behave, how will others behave towards her, when she is in a position which, despite all present-day talk of freedom and the woman's right to complete sexual liberty, still remains distinctly unconventional, at least in the class to which Halo belongs? And what about the child? How is it to be brought up? Dozens of questions arise. But having brought her heroine thus far, Mrs. Wharton evades every issue. The only solution she can offer is to make "an honest woman" of Halo in true Eighteenth Century fashion. She presents her problems; then disposes of them by means of a reconciliation in which, it may be incidentally remarked, the reader does not believe for a moment.

Checklist of Additional Reviews

Fanny Butcher, "Skill of New Wharton Book Thrills Critic," Chicago *Daily Tribune*, 17 September 1932, p. 10.

Lilian Whiting, "Mrs. Wharton's Upper Class," Springfield [Massachusetts] *Republican*, 9 October 1932, p. 7-E.

Dorothea Lawrence Mann, "Mrs. Wharton Sees the Gods Arrive," Boston *Evening Transcript*, 11 October 1932, Part 4: "Literary World," p. 3.

"Books in Brief," *Forum*, 88 (November 1932), viii.

W.K.R., Review of *The Gods Arrive, Christian Science Monitor*, 26 November 1932, p. 12.

Helen MacAfee, "Outstanding Novels," *Yale Review* n.s. 22 (Winter 1933), xxii.

HUMAN NATURE

HUMAN NATURE

BY

EDITH WHARTON

D. APPLETON AND COMPANY

NEW YORK LONDON MCMXXXIII

Florence Haxton Britten,
"The Perfection of
Technique: Edith Wharton's
New Stories Reveal Her
Old Mastery in Studies of
Personal Relations,"
*New York Herald
Tribune Books*, 9 (26
March 1933), 6

Mrs. Wharton, if we may judge by these five fine stories—four of them short, one a novelette—which comprise *Human Nature*, has grown complete master of herself and her materials with the passing years. She writes with an assurance which, in a less painstaking workman, would be an annoying nonchalance. Obviously, there is nothing that she wants to say which she cannot express with utmost adeptness. Her stories are as neatly contrived and executed as a complicated architectural design.

But, curiously, the theme's not the thing; nor yet the characters and events which clothe it. The technique—the slow, smooth modulation of persons and incidents, the maintaining of a high pitch of suspense, half-revealing, half-concealing the underlying motive of the story—this is the cunning business which has engaged Mrs. Wharton's creative faculty and turned it into something perilously like finesse.

Toward both them and characters she is selfless and aloofly cool: as unsentimental as one fancies a scientist should be; and just as precise of vision. But though her heart may be cool, it is not bleak. Hers is the coolness of a vantage point well above the battle and, perhaps, of fatigue. She is capable at rare intervals of a distilled intensity of emotion. But it is white heat and none of those foolish, cheerful, leaping flames.

All of these stories are suffused with humor—sometimes radiant and light-hearted, more often ironic. Yet all but one touches closely that dramatic cæsura, death. Not that death itself, or sorrow over it, is at all their theme. Mrs. Wharton seems to have chosen death to bulk large in them not so much because it is an inevitable finale to life as because in the period round death, both the dying and those about him seem to be more intensely themselves than usual. It's "Human Nature."

The most striking story in the group is called "The Day of the Funeral."

The story is set in a small, conventional college town and deals with the swift, strange changes in feeling of the guiltily bereaved husband—a member of the faculty—on the day of the funeral, by which he arrives in the course of a few hours, at passionate desire for the girl who was the indirect cause of his wife's death. His gradually shifting mood, together with the slow seeping in of knew knowledge, makes this story seem an extraordinarily impressive tour de force. It is much more than that.

"A Glimpse" is the jolliest story of the lot. A man on shipboard en route for Venice watches the progress of what appears to be a violent lovers' quarrel. He is just out of earshot, and infectiously moved by what he imagines the middle-aged, intense couple are saying to each other. The rest of the story is devoted to his pursuit of the facts, which make, when he roots them out, a deliciously humorous, but perfectly credible surprise.

"Her Son" is a novelette, very much in the genre of *Ethan Frome*. But the mounting suspense which in *Ethan Frome* becomes almost unbearable before the secret is out, is in "Her Son" cheated of its effect because, to the average worldly reader, the outcome is too easy to guess. When an innocent, not too keen, very rich elderly woman undertakes to search the resorts of southern Europe, baby picture in hand, for a lost son who by now must be twenty-seven years old, the chances are a thousand to one that what will happen is just what does happen in "Her Son." The pathetic story of gentle Mrs. Glenn in the hands of an expatriate adventuress and her lover is as carefully built up as the tragedy of Ethan Frome, but the illusion does not survive for long. After its collapse one reads on in enjoyment of the skill with which Mrs. Wharton scatters her clews, and for undiminished interest in her conception of character and conduct. But "Her Son" would have been more successful had it been compressed to the length of the other four stories in the volume.

And what Mrs. Wharton can accomplish in the space of six to eight thousand words is astonishing. Her characters reveal themselves fully, there is amplitude of event, and under and through all is a steadily marching plot.

"New Short Stories by Edith Wharton," *New York Times Book Review*, 2 April 1933, p. 7

This new volume by Edith Wharton consists of one story running to something less than half the pages of the book, and four shorter stories. To say that all exhibit in a uniformly high degree the many excellences which have given Mrs. Wharton her high rank among American and English novelists and practitioners of the short story would be to give the book considerably less than its due. Edith Wharton remains almost the last of those elder craftsmen whose motto was: If a story is worth writing at all, it is worth writing in as nearly perfect a manner as is humanly and artistically possible.

In *Human Nature* the predominating note is that of irony. How supreme an ironist Mrs. Wharton can be when she so desires has been demonstrated again and again; but even when irony has been the major characteristic of her work there has usually been the relief of either romance or mild humor. Such relief is conspicuously absent in this book. One would not say that the author has written with a corroded pen; but she has, in the main, chosen to confine herself to a quill sharply pointed.

The two most bitterly ironic stories are "Her Son" and "The Day of the Funeral"; but, whereas the latter lacks the compensation of that humanizing pity which is the attribute of the gods, and is, for that reason, one of the few consistently hard stories Edith Wharton has done, the first, through the abundance of that pity, becomes an ameliorating and comforting document.

"Her Son" is the story of a woman most grievously tricked by three scoundrels who divert a somewhat too doting mother-love to their own debased ends. Perhaps the author draws a trifle too heavily on our credulity in asking us to believe that Mrs. Glenn, searching the world over for her lost boy, Steve, would not have demanded more positive proof of identity; but Catherine Glenn's will to believe was so powerful she left herself all but defenseless against deceit. Obviously, it is not a pretty tale as Mrs. Wharton has devised it; and it would be unendurable but for the solvent of pity to which we have referred. Mrs. Wharton conveys it all in one deft line—a line which by its extreme deftness suddenly raises the story from the mire in which it has been wallowing to heights fanned by refreshing and revitalizing winds. It is the arch-conspirator of the three, at least the most cruel conspirator of the three, who writhingly jerks out the words of contrition: "Before I knew her I thought I could pull it off—but, you see, her sweetness—" Technically, "Her Son" may not be one of Mrs. Wharton's best pieces of short-story work (it is not another "After Holbein"); but it is one of her most penetrating glances into human nature, of which she is too understandingly aware always for one's complacency. Let not the complacent read Edith Wharton at any time; especially, let them beware this book!

We shall not go beyond the opening paragraph of "The Day of the Funeral," which is a story that must unfold itself. But this paragraph is really an entire story in miniature, the sort of compressed drama which only those who are masters of their craft can achieve, and even they but rarely. This is the passage:

> His wife had said: "If you don't give her up, I'll throw myself from the roof." He had not given her up, and his wife had thrown herself from the roof.

"The Day of the Funeral" is a story of egotism, as, indeed, all four of the shorter pieces are studies in egotism. But in this tale both the man and the girl are egotists; more usually in such studies novelists confine themselves to the male, permitting his female partner to shine a bit by contrast. Tersely written, with rigid exclusion of color, this story artistically is one of the very finest in the author's varied repertory. As the reader will discover, it is also one of her most severe indictments.

"A Glimpse," decidedly a light piece, views also two egotists, a man and a woman; but the two are artists, and as forgivable as children. One but laughs at them, as the author intended. One will laugh, at least chuckle, over "Diagnosis" also, and the killing fear of a man who, coming accidentally upon a scribbled note dropped by his consulting physicians, believes he has been sentenced to death, and is not so supremely happy as one would expect when he learns he is not. The tale is one of many subtle twists and turns. And with what candor does Mrs. Wharton in this piece expose the wiles to which the most well-bred of her sex can resort to gain and hold a man! "Joy in the House" is the one piece bordering on ineptness; but it is also the one piece in which is allowed most sharply to extrude the fundamental crudeness of human nature which is the foundation of this salutary collection. And we commend "Human Nature" not only for its art but also for its salutariness.

Theodore Purdy, Jr., "Character Studies," *Saturday Review of Literature*, 9 (22 April 1933), 549

This latest in the long canon of Mrs. Wharton's books is called *Human Nature*, but in spite of a spacious and all-inclusive title it is actually devoted to the presentation in five short stories of a limited and familiar Whartonian gallery of character studies. Nearly half the volume is given up to the most detailed of them, "Her Son." In it, one of those New York dowagers existing at present only in the pages of this author's fiction, seeks and apparently finds her illegitimate son, who has been brought up in Europe by foster parents. The depressing tale of her victimization by a group of adventurers is admirably told, with all of Mrs. Wharton's facile mastery and technique. The description of the rivalry between the two "mothers" is superbly ironical, and as always the author is at home in her handling of the European scene, and the expatriate character. Yet the story as a whole lacks variety and is excessively long drawn out.

The four shorter stories which make up the rest of the book are more effective, often showing glimpses of the author's old penetration into the mysteries of personality, as well as a narrative quality rare nowadays in this sort of work. "The Day of the Funeral" is sombre, "A Glimpse" an interesting study in artistic temperament, "Joy in the House" and "Diagnosis" satiric tragedies of modern married life. All are highly artificial in their choice of subject and setting, bearing the unmistakable stamp of their authorship. Mrs. Wharton has, in fact, perfected with the years an unreal but useful apparatus into which any situation or problem can be forced for fictional purposes. The loss in vitality is great, but it is also true that an increased clarity results. Those who are willing to accept the conventions of this world in which Mrs. Wharton's characters live and move will find her stories excellent, and the more critical few who feel that she has in some ways lost contact with life since the days of *Ethan Frome* and *The House of Mirth* may at least appreciate the immense competence with which she still carries out her chosen formula.

Raymond Mortimer, "New Novels," *New Statesman and Nation*, n.s. 5 (22 April 1933), 507

In the future the drearier sort of don will no doubt write textbooks in which the effects of the slump on literature will be neatly tabulated for the benefit of the more industrious sort of female student. Already some of these effects are apparent. The first ten years of the peace, at any rate in England and France, were a period in which our relief, our hopes and our prosperity were reflected by vigour and enterprise in all the arts. The rebels of before the war found a public eager to appreciate the works of their maturity....

The most enjoyable book of this bunch is *Human Nature*, partly, perhaps, because it is pre-slump, but chiefly because Mrs. Wharton is an enormously accomplished novelist. In comparison with Herr [Hans] Fallada's cumulation of naturalistic detail and E. M. Forster's use of the interior monologue, the stories in *Human Nature* appear in a sense unreal. Often the situations are improbable, the patterns of human behaviour neater than they would be in actuality: Mrs. Wharton, in fact, is intent on shaping her stories into objects. At the same time, the conventions of her form—a form surely as justifiable as that of a sonnet or a French classical drama—positively help her to display an uncanny knowledge of the human heart. She imposes on her characters just the actions that will show their paces. *Human Nature* is a treat for the reviewer because he never has to make allowances, the execution is always as good as the intention. Mrs. Wharton knows her *métier* backwards, and though I don't suggest that young writers should imitate her technique, they could learn a helluva lot from carefully studying it.

"New Novels," Times Literary Supplement [England], 27 April 1933, p. 292

Human nature as Mrs. Wharton perceives it in her new book of short stories *Human Nature* . . . is a series of ironic disillusionments. Viewed objectively, they show the comic spirit at work in its most revealing mood. From the point of view of the actors in them, the skull is for ever grinning behind the laughing face, in humourless mockery.

"Joy in the House" may serve as an example of her mood. Christine Ansley, happily and wealthily married, with a delightful little boy, has a violent love affair with a worthless artist, Jeff Lithgow. Her husband, on the authority of Mrs. Wharton and Mr. Sinclair Lewis, to be natural to American husbands, allows her to go abroad and have her fling, with the proviso that if she does not return by the end of six months he will divorce her. Before the six months are over she has broken with Jeff, and in spite of his entreaties sails from Havre for New York. On the last day out she is welcomed by a cable from her husband, Devons, with the words, "In two days there will be joy in the house." When she gets home the words "Joy in the house" are hung in flowers on the landing to greet her. Her husband and mother-in-law are all affection and tact. As she breakfasts in bed on the following morning she hears Devons dealing kindly and firmly with reporters in the hall, and realizes gratefully that she need expect no emotional reconciliation scene from him. All he wishes is to ignore and deny unhappiness and suffering in his own house. When she comes downstairs she finds Jeff Lithgow's wife waiting to see her, to accuse her of his death. Jeff, unable to face life without Christine, had killed himself two days after she left. Joy in the House was not only a loving greeting to a returned mother and wife, but also Devons's expression of triumph over his dead rival, of whose death he had learned on the day that he sent the cable. On this thought Christine will have to live in the future.

In this story the material for a full-length novel is compressed into thirty pages, and it is our tribute to Mrs. Wharton's skill that in no place is the compression felt. With the same distinction and economy she tells three other short stories, and one longer one, "Her Son." This tale of heartless deception and pitiful self-deception has the elemental cruelty of such earlier work as *Ethan Frome*. It moves in a world where all kindness is doomed to abuse, all beauty to neglect or annihilation. We read it with mute impotent protest against its injustice, from the tragic concealment of Catherine's seduction to the moment at which, heart and courage broken, her mercifully clouded mind spares her the final anguish of knowing who Stephen really was, and her tormentor is silenced by the gentle words, "My dear—your hat's crooked."

A.B.,
"New Novels,"
Saturday Review
[England], 155 (29 April
1933), 414

Graham Greene,
"Fiction,"
Spectator [England],
150 (5 May 1933), 654

Mrs. Wharton's first book of short stories was published in 1899, and for many years before that she was, in the strict sense of the phrase, practising her craft. She belonged to a time when only people of marked gifts dared to write, and only those who had subdued their gift cared to publish. Whereas to-day you earn while you learn, in those days, during a long apprenticeship, you learnt then you burnt. The idea of approaching authorship as a high emprise would be thought too perfectly priceless now; but old-fashioned reverence did bring results.

These short stories have a commanding maturity; they are as sound as well-seasoned timber and subtle as a vintage (though I am not sure Mrs. Wharton would approve this metaphor-making); and the writing has an art and ease which delight. Just as some hats are too exacting for the faces below, so *Human Nature* would be too rigorous for most authors; but this artist understands and portrays it; above all, she profoundly and disquietingly knows the selfishness of men. Mrs. Wharton has that precious gift of confidentially opening the motives and minds of characters, let them say what they will; and yet there is always the incident, the twist, the climax which the reader has not foreseen. One cannot do anything in summary of these five tales beyond hinting that they tend towards the ironic and the tragic; but one can promise that everybody who likes that elusive feat, the short story, will read with admiration.

Mrs. Wharton and Herr Plivier make an amusing contrast, possibly a significant one. Mrs. Wharton writes in the tradition of Henry James; from that superb portraitist she has borrowed a trick or two of style, the use of alliteration for example, the habit of introducing her minor characters in an ironic vignette and her general scene—the more "visited" of Continental cities. Human nature, exemplified in particular by wealthy Americans, is her study, and her attitude, admirably maintained, is cool, aloof, a little withering. Human nature, in fact, does not come well out of the ordeal of being closely regarded by so shrewd and unsympathetic a critic. A widow, whose son has been killed in the War, combs Europe to find her illegitimate child, born before her marriage, who had been adopted by a pair of Americans called Brown. She is deceived and ruined by a trio of adventurers, a terrible middle-aged flapper "with layers and layers of hard-headed feminine craft under her romping ways," her young consumptive lover Stephen, and her elderly husband, "Boy" Brown, full of "jocular allusions and arid anecdotes." The widow herself is admirably described in her sentimentality, her weakness, her absurd beauty. "When she sat on the beach beside the dozing Stephen, in her flowing white dress, her large white umbrella tilted to shelter him, she reminded me of a carven angel spreading broad wings above a tomb (I could never look at her without being reminded of statuary)." Deception, which was Henry James' prevailing theme, is Mrs. Wharton's also in these stories: a wife returns to her husband in America, after living for six months with a painter in France, and is greeted with a pulverizing Rotarian generosity. "Joy in the House" is written above the door in flowers. Next day the wife discovered the meaning behind the "Joy in the House": her lover, when she left him at Boulogne, had killed himself.

The surface of Mrs. Wharton's stories have an ingenuity and a wit almost equal to her master's; but one wonders how far her attitude to human nature has been borrowed, for it is broken occasionally by sentimentalities: "You're a lovely buried lady that I've stumbled on in a desert tomb, shrouded in your golden hair," the painter tells Christine. This is certainly not Henry James; one has an uneasy feeling that it may be Mrs. Wharton.

Checklist of Additional Reviews

"Les Lettres et le théâtre," *Le Mois* [France], 29 (May 1933), 167.
Charles Cestre, "Edith Wharton: Human Nature," *Revue Anglo-Américaine* [France], 11 (April 1934), 378.

A BACKWARD GLANCE

A
BACKWARD
GLANCE

by

EDITH WHARTON

Je veux remonter le penchant de mes belles
années . . .
    Châteaubriand: *Mémoires d'Outre Tombe*

Kein Genuss ist vorübergehend.
        Goethe: *Wilhelm Meister*

D. APPLETON-CENTURY COMPANY
INCORPORATED
NEW YORK   LONDON
        1934

Amy Loveman, "The Life and Art of Edith Wharton," *Saturday Review of Literature*, 10 (28 April 1934), 662

Mrs. Wharton's remembered yesterdays, despite the long agony of war which interrupted their even tenor, and for all that of recent years death has been levying its toll upon her friendships, are by and large the recollections of a singularly happy life. Born to wealth and position in the New York of the sixties, her existence was from the beginning laid in pleasant places. New York, Newport, Rome, parents who entertained and were entertained constantly and who upheld the standards of good manners, good education, and good speech insistently, friends blessed like herself by kind fortune, books, the country, and foreign travel: these filled her early years. At a tender age Edith Wharton might have been observed assiduously reading aloud—but reading aloud from a book held upside down and illegible to her ignorance the while she fluently made up stories never written on its pages. Only a few years more, and, in all the maturity of eleven, she embarked upon her first novel, and had discovered the delights of her father's library. Already the future writer was born, and that passion for reading as well as writing which runs all through her book like a refrain was to the fore.

From out the pages of her volume start a host of sharply drawn figures, her parents and grandparents, her childhood playmates, the companions of her youth and her young married life, the friends and acquaintances of the last years.

A goodly galaxy of the great and prominent it is that sheds lustre on her chronicle. Here are the aged Thomas Hardy with little interest in any of the literary movements of his day, "entirely enclosed in his own creative dream," Henry James, in the earlier days of a long and intimate friendship, "the bearded Penseroso of Sargent's delicate drawing," and in the later grown to voluminous proportions, exchanging spruceness of appearance for comfort, and only spasmodically interested in dress; George Moore, "who hated and envied James and missed no chance to belittle and sneer at him"; Meredith, white-haired, deaf, and covering up his deafness by pouring out a stream of conversation, the Comtesse de Fitz-James, who cared little for literature and knew less of it and had the most brilliant salon in Paris; Howard Sturgis, Geoffrey Scott, Jusserand, Theodore Roosevelt, and many others. It is Henry James, however, who holds the center of the stage. Henry James, welcoming his friend to his house, and going each time on her arrival through the ritual of kissing her twice when they reached a certain rug in the hall. Henry James on a visit to America and the country home of Mrs. Wharton in the Berkshires, so desperately uncomfortable because of the heat that the entire house party had perforce to motor without ceasing from morning to night, Henry James discoursing on literature and life, and finally Henry James dying a slow and harrowing death.

Though personalities take up the greater part of her chronicle, inevitably much stress goes on the craft of writing and Mrs. Wharton's own relation to her work and her art. Woven into the very warp and woof of her reminiscences is the passion for creation. In one of the most interesting, as it is from the literary point of view, one of the most illuminating chapters in her book, "The Secret Garden," Mrs. Wharton sets forth the

513

processes of her art, "the growth and unfolding of the plants in my secret garden from the seed to the shrub-top." A fascinating record it is—this of the characters which spring full-panoplied to her mind clamoring for a story to bring them to life. It is these sidelights on her art which give to a volume of picturesque recollections a significance beyond the memories they unfold.

Percy Hutchison, "Mrs. Wharton Recalls an Era: Brownstone New York and Europe Share in Her *Backward Glance*," *New York Times Book Review*, 6 May 1934, pp. 1, 13

The New York into which Edith Wharton was born as Edith Jones no longer exists. The war dealt it a stinging blow, and in the helter skelter days which supervened on the war's close there was no time to attempt resuscitation. Very likely old New York, when society insisted on its capital S and had strict mathematical limits, would eventually have gone down before the encroachment of apartment houses, however luxurious, and the exigencies of ever further-flung business rendering impossible the maintaining of caste. But the demise would have been lingering and dignified.

It is a life intimately of this old New York that Mrs. Wharton now looks back upon, from the storehouse of her memory bringing forth picture after picture, until the whole is a mosaic of many hues and lively, if restricted, pattern. This is the world into which the débutante Edith Jones stepped at her coming-out:

> Some of the hostesses had drawing rooms big enough for informal dances, and to be invited to these was the privilege of a half-dozen of the younger girls. A season of opera at the old Academy of Music was now an established event of the Winter, and on Mondays and Fridays we met each other there, Wednesday being, for some obscure tribal reason, the night on which the boxes were sent to dull relations and visitors from out of town, while the inner circle disported itself elsewhere.

Edith Jones was of Dutch descent on her father's side; there were Schermerhorn and Stevens and Gallatin and Rhinelander relatives. Her grandmother Rhinelander's country house at Hell Gate had been one of the finest places of earlier decades. Her father had his own country estate at Newport—Pencraig—and his city residence. But for a period when Edith was small he closed both his town house and Pencraig and the family lived in Europe. "When I was 4 years old," Mrs. Wharton writes, "I was playing in the Roman forum instead of on the lawns of Rhinecliff." Eventually back in New York the little girl read "every book" in her father's library. But what she liked better than reading was "making up," and at the age of 11 she put one of her stories down on paper. Here is what Mrs. Wharton tells of her juvenile effort:

> I wanted to write, not improvise. My first attempt was a novel which began, "'Oh, how do you do, Mrs. Brown?' said Mrs. Tomkins. 'If only I had known you were going to call I should have tidied up the drawing

room.'" Timorously I submitted this to my mother, and never shall I forget the sudden drop of my creative frenzy when she returned it with the icy comment, "Drawing rooms are always tidy."

The Whartons lived in Boston, and when Edith Jones was married she and her husband went occasionally to stay with his family. And she writes that she recalls saying once that she was a failure in Boston because people "thought I was too fashionable to be intelligent, and a failure in New York because they were afraid I was too intelligent to be fashionable."

But the desire to travel was deep-seated with this pair, and soon they were on their way to Europe; and Mrs. Wharton also on her way to the distinguished literary career which has been hers ever since. Some short stories written in New York, and accepted by Scribner's, which, in turn, had been preceded by *The Decoration of Houses*, done in collaboration with Ogden Codman Jr., and then, in 1902, her first adult novel, *The Valley of Decision*, and she was established. Three years later came *The House of Mirth*, and in 1911 *Ethan Frome*.

A Backward Glance is, perhaps above all else, the vivid record of deep and abiding friendships, for Mrs. Wharton's genius for friendships has been scarcely less than her talent as a literary artist. And none among these engaging reminiscences is more entertaining than her recollections of Henry James. How much the expatriated American novelist meant to this younger artist, quivering with her ambitions, almost frightened by her successes, is discernible in her opening paragraph on James:

What is one's personality [writes Mrs. Wharton] detached from that of the friends with whom fate happens to have linked one? I cannot think of myself apart from the influence of the two or three greatest friendships of my life, and any account of my growth must be that of their stimulating and enlightening influence. From a childhood and youth of complete intellectual isolation, I passed in my early thirties into an atmosphere of the rarest understanding, the richest and most varied mental companionship.

If Mrs. Wharton's autobiography, therefore, seems to lack dramatic episodes, let the reader remember that she is attempting a far more difficult recording—the transference to the printed pages of these nuances of reciprocal understanding and mental companionship.

Many a one has probably wondered if Henry James talked as he wrote, with parentheses and convolutions. And we have it from Mrs. Wharton that he did. But she adds:

To James's intimates, however, these elaborate hesitancies, far from being an obstacle, were like a cobweb bridge flung from his mind to theirs, an invisible passage over which one knew that silver-footed ironies, veiled jokes, tiptoe malices, were stealing to explode a huge laugh at one's feet.

And Mrs. Wharton, although this was not her primary purpose perhaps—and yet again it may have been, a "tiptoe malice"—gives us the picture of a motor drive with James to Windsor, where they wished to be directed to the King's Road.

My good man [James would like to inquire of an aged countryman] if you will be good enough to come here, please; a little nearer—so. My friend, to put it to you in two words, this lady and I have just arrived here from Slough; that is to say, to be more strictly accurate, we have recently passed through Slough on our way here, having actually motored to Windsor from Rye, which was our point of departure; and the darkness having overtaken us, we should be much obliged if you would tell us where we are now.

And so on, gradually, after alarums and retreats, arriving at the fact that what he would like to know is—just how to get on the King's Road. To which the aged man at the window of the car, disgustedly: "Ye're in it!"

James, in America, guest of Mrs. Wharton at her house at Lenox, The Mount, sincerely as his hostess admired and loved him, must, for all of his unwillingness to be a trial, nevertheless have tried her patience more than once with his sensitiveness and perturbations. But Henry James was one of those great souls who are forgiven all trifling matters.

Although Mrs. Wharton has treated of the writing of fiction in a book devoted to that subject, her chapter in the autobiography with the title "The Secret Garden" doubtless adds to that book, and is more intimately personal. She is of the opinion that few English and American novelists are interested greatly in the deeper processes of their art.

Their conscious investigations of method seldom seem to go much deeper than syntax [she writes], and it is immeasurably deeper that the vital interest begins.

She lays down two essential rules, first, that the novelist should deal only with what is within his reach; and the second, that the value of a subject depends on what the author sees in it and how deeply he is able to see *into* it. But she adds an "almost," for there seem to be subjects too shallow, she says, to yield anything to the most searching gaze.

I had always felt this [she continued] and now my problem was how to make use of a subject—fashionable New York—which, of all others, seemed most completely of all to fall within the condemned category.

Fashionable New York was nearest at hand—she had been "steeped" in it from infancy. But its flatness! Its futility! What could even so expert a novelist as Mrs. Wharton had already become do against futility and flatness? The passage which follows should be committed to memory by all beginners (and some not beginners), and every critic should keep it hanging before his eyes as a measuring rod for the value of results:

The problem was how to extract from such a subject the typical human significance which is the story-teller's reason for telling one story rather than another. In what aspect could a story of irresponsible pleasure seekers be said to have, on "the old woe of the world," any deeper bearing than the people composing such a society could guess? The answer was that a frivolous society can acquire dramatic significance only through what its frivolity destroys. Its tragic implication lies in its power of debasing people and ideals.

And how terribly this power could do its work, how tragically, Mrs. Wharton was to prove in Lily Bart and *The House of Mirth*. It is what John Galsworthy proved in *The Man of Property* the year following.

It is very probable that in no other book can one find the social difference of three of the world's social capitals—New York, London and Paris—so skillfully differentiated as in *A Backward Glance*. As, for instance, when Mrs. Wharton observes that

> The whole raison d'être of the French salon is based on the national taste for general conversation. The two-and-two talks which cut up Anglo-Saxon dinners and isolate guests at table and in the drawing room would be considered not only stupid but ill bred in a society where social intercourse is a perpetual exchange, a market to which every one is expected to bring his best for barter.

We have not even scratched the surface of the varied riches of Mrs. Wharton's pages. If Henry James was of all her intimate friends perhaps the most distinguished, at least in the literary world, there are hosts of others equally distinguished, only less her close friends. There is, for one, Mrs. Meynell. There are Ambassadors. There was George Meredith, whom, however, she met but once. We have not spoken at any length of her travels or of the distinguished services which Mrs. Wharton rendered to the Allies during the war.

A Backward Glance—in view of the book's authorship, one does not have to comment on the quality of composition— is a record which will be read and stored away by all who wish to view a pageant of a period which can never, in the nature of things, be revived. Mrs. Wharton not only had painted New York as none other had done, but she had made that New York wince. No slight feat! *A Backward Glance*, a book to be mulled over and enjoyed, reveals something of her secret.

"A Backward Glance," *Times Literary Supplement* [England], 17 May 1934, p. 359

"I am born happy every morning"—this rare and delightful confession comes late in Mrs. Wharton's book, but it is implicit in every page. Her revivifying interest in people, in books, in places, her two absorbing passions—writing and gardening—have kept burning in her the glow and eagerness of youth in spite of her ample share in the common lot of illness and loss. "Unafraid of change, insatiable in intellectual curiosity, interested in big things, and happy in small ways," is the expression of part of her secret, which also includes an inability to remember long to be angry and a refusal to admit that she has ever known sensational grievances or met with real enmity.

As her friends and readers would expect, this is a wise and gracious book, with a golden twist of wit running through it and a curiously restful charm. It begins with a glance back at the three or four generations of forebears closely identified with colonial New York whose stories and characters have served Mrs. Wharton well. Her ancestors were mainly merchant ship-owners, bankers and lawyers, prosperous and cultivated people, who maintained a high standard of living and good manners, and who had good looks and excellent minds, kindness and a pleasant gaiety as well. Edith Wharton was born in New York, but at four years old she was playing in the Roman Forum and beginning to be a cosmopolitan. A

517

visit to Spain followed, "and as the off-spring of born travellers I was expected even in infancy to know how to travel." An incurable passion was born in her, the lucky child who was to have many enchanting journeys in her life and to explore romantic cities and countries before they were spoiled by progress. After Spain came residence in Paris and the beginnings of formal education; and these pages contain some charming glimpses of the small girl with her red hair rolled into sausages and her sleeves looped back with coral, miming, dancing, playing with other children and above all "making up" endless dramas and tales.

At seventeen the young girl was launched in New York society to correct the habit of reading too much; and after the first "cold agony of shyness" her natural social gifts and her still unrealized gifts of literary perception made contact with men and women—preferably older than herself—immensely exciting and pleasant. More foreign travel and her father's death in France interrupted the routine of entertainment; and at the end of a second winter in New York she was married to Edward Wharton, a member of a Virginian family living in Boston. Thereafter her time was spent between Newport, New York and Europe, her husband sharing her joy in travel and long foreign adventure which once gave them four perfect months in the Aegean. Oddly, as it seems, Mrs. Wharton's first published book was on interior decoration, written in collaboration with a young architect, Ogden Codman. It struggled for a publisher, but after forty years it is still bringing in royalties. Short stories that attracted the attention of discerning critics began to appear in the American magazines; and a volume of these, *The Greater Inclination,* was Edith Wharton's first effort in fiction. *The Valley of Decision, Crucial Instances* and the celebrated *House of Mirth* fol-lowed in quick succession, together with a number of studies of seventeenth and eighteenth-century Italian architecture, on which the young woman was becoming an expert.

"I am far from thinking 'Ethan Frome' my best novel, and am bored and even exasperated when I am told that it is," says Mrs. Wharton, admitting that of all her books it is the one "to the making of which I brought the greatest joy and the fullest ease." She had long wanted to draw life as it was in the derelict mountain villages of New England, not as sentimental predecessors thought it was, and she had a close knowledge of the district and the people for more than ten years. She began the tale as a French exercise, wishing to bring her idioms up to date because Paul Bourget laughed at her for using "the purest Louis Quatorze." This much-criticized story, now held to be an American masterpiece, had a slow success, and its accuracy was questioned by blithe readers who asserted that the writer knew nothing of New England.

A Backward Glance is, however, concerned very much less with her literary work than with her friends and the general business of living fully, wisely and vividly. Mrs. Wharton was fortunate in her friends, and pays loving and appreciative tribute to them—Egerton Winthrop, the Paul Bourgets, Walter Berry, Professor Norton, Eugene Lee-Hamilton and Vernon Lee, Robert Minturn, Clyde Fitch, Howard Sturgis—the subject of some most amusing pages—and a great number of other social and literary international figures. There are chapters on Henry James, a lifelong and intimate friend; and Mrs. Wharton's picture is rich in new detail and a brilliant contribution to the gallery in which so many portraits—most of them so heavy—of Henry James are hung. In her hands he is simpler and more natural, with endearing foibles of economy and domestic eccentricities, but the truly great man none the less, singularly lovable.

Pre-War Paris, pre-War England come to life again in these engrossing recollections, which contain no spite or littleness and only one outburst of indignation against an eminent writer who was not above these failings when he spoke of his contemporaries. Mrs. Wharton sketches quickly the War years and her work in France, of which she has written fully elsewhere, touches on personal losses, and comments on the new and difficult world, but still finds "a thousand little daily wonders to marvel at and rejoice in." She dedicates her book "to the friends who every year on All Souls' Night come and sit with me by the fire." Another and larger company will sit by that fire and walk in her garden and thank her for the privilege.

William Troy, "Flower of Manhattan," *Nation*, 138 (23 May 1934), 598

Among the many crisp utterances on her craft which Mrs. Wharton sprinkles throughout this volume is the following: "There could be no greater critical ineptitude than to judge a novel according to *what it ought to have been about.*" For the reader of these reminiscences desirous of extracting their very special quality of charm and interest this remark is an excellent one to keep in mind. Nothing could be more foolish than to throw down this book with the objection that its backgrounds, its people, and its events seem lacking in vital significance to the harried and very much preoccupied reader of

today. It is beside the point to make uncomplimentary comparisons between the author of *The House Mirth* and the man with the dinner pail—that latter-nineteenth-century specter whom Mrs. Wharton quaintly invokes in one passage. The point is rather that Mrs. Wharton was the flower, the exquisite and certainly altogether undeserved flower, of a social group in America whose always tenuous existence has for some time now shaded off into oblivion. Daughter of Rhinelanders and Stevenses, debutante of the age of innocence, intimate of those frail and neurasthenic lovers of culture who flitted back and forth between Europe and America in the eighties, Mrs. Wharton was unquestionably affected by the moral and social values of the period and milieu into which she happened to be born. She would have been something of a monster not to have been so affected—up to a certain point. For like every authentic novelist, Mrs. Wharton was at once the product of a very particular set of conditions and the observer and critic of those conditions. What made Mrs. Wharton a novelist rather than just another occupant of a box at the Metropolitan was of course a very early perception of what she herself calls the "flatness and futility" of the society of her time. But what was in the first place responsible for this perception on the part of a young woman who had every reason to be admirably conditioned, as one says nowadays, remains something of a mystery. Heredity, in her case, offers no clue: her mother seems to have been a perfect model of her class; and her father, except for a slightly adventurous taste for Spanish travel, was apparently undistinguished by any special sensibility or intelligence. Yet sensibility and intelligence were both gifts which Edith Wharton possessed and which set her apart automatically from her family and her class. The weaknesses of her writing—the thinness of her most characteristic material, the increasing fragility of her point of view, and the still insuperable aura of gentility—can all be laid to her time and her class. But her strength is her own—the strength which enabled her, in her very best work, to pass so far beyond that conditioning process which is regarded as so inevitable today. This is the mystery which will not be found revealed in either the handbooks of American cultural history or in the gospel according to Marx.

If there is any continuous dramatic interest in these pages, it consists in the unbroken persistency of Mrs. Wharton's effort at emancipation—the old battle of the artist with the world. Contrary to what might have been expected, reconstruction of old New York, its manners and its people, occupy rather little of the book. Most of it is concerned with Mrs. Wharton's personal friendships with people who, like Walter Berry and Henry James, had made the same renunciations as herself or who, like the Bourgets and the Comtesse de Fitz-James, belonged by right of birth to the "richer soil" of Europe. For Mrs. Wharton's life, once she had decided to commit herself to perspective rather than participation, was necessarily cast on the more intensely personal plane of friends, books, gardening, and travel. But even these compensations were not tolerated when they encroached too much on the practice of her craft. Unlike Gertrude Stein, she found in war work less a romance than a distraction. And there is something half-apologetic in her account of the brilliant salons in Paris attended in the pre-war epoch. What emerges throughout is an insistence on the priority for the novelist of the claims of his craft over all other claims that might be made.

The question will occur, of course, how well this attitude is sustained by the evidence of so much of Mrs. Wharton's actual practice of her craft—especially in recent years. It is not an exaggeration to say that it is almost impossible to believe that *Ethan Frome* and *Twilight Sleep* could have been written by the same hand. Speaking of Balzac and Thackeray and Proust, all novelists of manners like herself, Mrs. Wharton remarks on the tendency of such novelists "to be dazzled by contact with the very society they satirize." But she goes on to justify them with the suggestion that *pour comprendre il faut aimer*, and perhaps this is the best justification that can be offered for Mrs. Wharton herself. Because in all her later fiction love takes precedence over understanding, the ambiguity that has always marked her writing is less productive of those qualities which we look for in the true satirist. But there is in the present work a kind of recrudescence of that old ambiguity which gives it a much more interesting quality than will be found in many works by authors who have more definitely made up their minds about things.

Christopher Morley, "Granules from an Hour-Glass," *Saturday Review of Literature*, 10 (2 June 1934), 727

There are many pleasures waiting for the reader of Edith Wharton's volume of reminiscences, *A Backward Glance*. I was prejudiced in favor of Mrs. Wharton's delightful book from the very start, for I noticed that in her brief preface she quoted Madame Swetchine, an admirable writer of whom one rarely hears. I encountered Mme. Swetchine's *Letters* years ago, doing some college reading in the history of the French Republic of '48, and I always experience a special pleasure in meeting anyone who has even heard of her. She (I refer still to Mme. Swetchine) is one of those felicitously unfamous writers who have been divinely shielded from being read by the wrong people.—Incidentally Mrs. Wharton's parents, during a trip to Europe in their early married days, saw the flight of old Louis Philippe across the Tuileries gardens.

And Edith Wharton herself—how easily she might never have been a writer at all. She was reared under handicap, as a member of the dress circle of New York's provincial and complacent little bourgeoisie sixty years ago. I had always been a trifle alarmed by repeated allusions in print to Mrs. Wharton's background of social azure, so it was a relief to learn that it was nothing more serious than the Rhinelanders and Joneses (of West 23rd Street and Hell Gate). For one has never been able to be wholly solemn about the tradition of New York "society" unless by that term you mean such people as Irving, Bryant, Whitman, Melville, Poe. And, as Mrs. Wharton points out with most urbane humor, bohemians like those were scarcely recognized in the fashionable world of her youth. The worthies of that time, who were proud of not being in retail trade, all had "libraries" of calf-bound books regarded as "standard," but would be painfully agitated if called upon to meet an actual author. This, Mrs. Wharton very shrewdly suggests, was not from any sense of snobbish superiority, but rather a genuine shyness or embarrassment, "an awe-struck dread of the intellectual effort that might be required." And what has been so much and so foolishly hallooed as New York "society" was probably only a swath of kind, simple, innocent, and rather self-indulgent people, intensely timid and conventional at heart.

If one pauses to reflect upon the dullness, architectural misery, parochial naivete, and self-satisfaction of New York in the '70s and '80s, one must realize that our bewildering and pinnacled uncertainty of today has its merits.

I didn't mean to get into argument; merely to say that Mrs. Wharton, with extraordinary patience and courage, overcame the most serious obstacles, obstacles perhaps more deadening to the soul than poverty or mean birth. The happy accident of living abroad several years as a child gave her a valuable disgust for the banality of New York's architecture; the somewhat prudish Anglophilia of her parents implanted a sensitive gusto for English undefiled. In the American children's books of the day, her mother said, the children spoke bad English *without the author's knowing it.* (Which was perfectly true; it is not until much later that one learns bad English has its uses too.)

I can scarcely imagine the youngest generation, hotfoot upon its own desperations, taking time to read Mrs. Wharton's very wise and moving book; yet it might start some interesting thoughts if they did. Among many charming things her glimpses of Henry James are particularly interesting. We see Mrs. Wharton as a young person, putting on a new hat and a pretty dress to meet the great Henry, but so appalled by her shyness that she could not speak—and the new hat was not even noticed. We see James suffering grotesquely from a heat wave in Lenox and finding his only relief in constant motoring; how one would have loved to see that party pausing in roadside shade to read Swinburne aloud while Mr. James perspired. We hear James talking about "the Emmetry" (so he called his vast and labyrinthine cousinship) and in lengthy soliloquy bringing them alive to a group of hearers on a summer evening. "They glimmered at us," Mrs. Wharton says, "through a series of disconnected ejaculations, epithets, allusions, parenthetical rectifications and restatements . . . and then suddenly, by some miracle of shifted lights and accumulated strokes, there they stood before us, sharp as an Ingres, dense as a Rembrandt."—Or James at Lamb House in Rye, welcoming his visitors at the front door; James's firm and visible belief that he knew best how to direct the chauffeur to find the destination yet always missing the way—and only succeeding to confuse the yokel whom he asked for direction. This is surely of excellent purport. James, under the stroke that killed him, in the very act of falling, hearing a voice that seemed to say, "So here it is at last, the distinguished thing." Always terrified of death (and of much of living too) yet he could meet it with his own absolute word. There is a very distinguished thing to be found and honored in Mrs. Wharton's book. I hope many will discover it. Her description of James's conversation—and humor—are exquisitely happy. Peter Dunne, she tells us, was perturbed by the Jacobite circumlocutions and felt like saying "Just spit it right up in Poppa's hand," but

> to James's intimates, these elaborate hesitancies, far from being an obstacle, were like a cobweb bridge flung from his mind to theirs, an invisible passage over which one knew that silver-footed ironies, veiled jokes, tiptoed malices, were stealing to explode a huge laugh at one's feet. The moment of suspense in which there was time to watch the forces of malice and merriment assembling over the mobile landscape of his face, was perhaps the rarest of all in the unique experience of a talk with Henry James.

And surely I shall long remember her description of James sitting by the moat at Bodiam Castle, watching the reflection of the towers and the hovering dragonflies. "For a long time no one spoke; then James turned to me and said solemnly: 'Summer afternoon—summer afternoon; to me those have always been the two most beautiful words in the English language.'"

Newton Arvin, "The Age of Innocence," *New Republic*, 79 (6 June 1934), 107

Protean are the obstacles that may rear themselves in the path of a young and aspiring writer, and not all of them are of the sort with which Hamlin Garland, say, or Theodore Dreiser had to contend. Mrs. Wharton reminds the readers of the thirties that even if you didn't grow up on a bleak Dakota farm or in a sultry little town in Indiana—even if you grew up within a short walk of Washington Square and began your European travels at the age of four—you might still, if you chose to be an artist, find a hobgoblin or two to put to rout. You might find that New York good society in the seventies and eighties—not the society of the newly rich, but that of the old mercantile families, the city's leisure class—was, in its way, as hostile to the vocation of letters as many another. "In the eyes of our provincial society," says Mrs. Wharton, "authorship was still regarded as something between a black art and a form of manual labor." Even Washington Irving, in an earlier age, had been tolerated because of his unimpeachable status as a gentleman, and Herman Melville, despite his high connections, had placed himself outside the reach of polite consideration. Presentability and the pen were held to be virtually incompatible; and "on the whole, my mother doubtless thought, it would be simpler if people one might be exposed to meeting would refrain from meddling with literature."

Only an unmistakable call could have made itself audible through such a fog as this, and clearly Mrs. Wharton, as a young woman, heard the call. It is evident from her story that she was not a person to be deterred from her purpose by a few whispers and a look or two of courteous incredulity. Her gifts were too genuine to be suppressed, and the need of overcoming a good deal of intangible opposition was a positive advantage: it forced her to step aside a little from the life of her group, and to see it in some other light than that of its own kindling. Only Edith Wharton could have written *The House of Mirth* and *The Custom of the Country* at the time when she wrote them—only a child of that society who was willing to question a few of its assumptions; and the fact makes it tempting to agree with her conclusion that the drawbacks involved in growing up as she did were outweighed by the advantages.

Tempting, but not irresistible. Mrs. Wharton's talents it is impossible not to respect, but her reminiscences are too full and too frank to leave one under any illusions about the social climate in which she has always moved, and its effect upon her vision. She has been a serious enough writer to look critically at the foibles of her set, but it would be obvious from her novels that she has never looked any farther inward than that, and her autobiography confirms the judgment. She says, to be sure, that though she has always lived among the worldly she has never been "much impressed" by them, but the remark leads one to wonder whom she means by the "worldly." From some points of view, the great mercantile swells of the days before the Civil War would have seemed to be a fairly mundane lot; but Mrs. Wharton, like any romantic, declares that their leading qualities were "social amenity" and "financial incorruptibility." And the nearer she approaches our own time, the more her voice tends to take on the conventional overtones of the society page. "The inauguration by King Edward VII of the beautiful hall . . . Etonians who fell in the Boer War . . . the simple and dignified ceremony . . . private grief and national pride . . . in whose house one met most of the worth while in Paris . . . the wise and witty Jules Cambon . . . the Argentine Ambassador . . . the Embassy . . . the celebrated archeologist . . . charitable work . . . the Embassy . . . France had never wanted war . . . France's North African subjects . . . Sainte Clotilde . . . Algeria . . . the Embassy. . . ."

"Worldly" may not be the word for the leisured pre-war society of notables, of cosmopolitan sophisticates, of "wise and witty" rulers, which Mrs. Wharton thus evokes; but certainly she was never unimpressed by it, and her record of it, especially in the lively passages on her master Henry James, has a great deal of documentary value. What she never hints is that, for a writer who would really see his age without delusions, the fogs engendered by such a society are quite as thick as those engendered by the old New York families in the age of innocence. She would have towered higher in American letters than she does if she made some effort to overcome these obstacles too.

Edward Sackville-West, "War and Peace," *Spectator* [England], 152 (15 June 1934), 929

It is difficult to say much about Mrs. Wharton's book except to recommend people to read it. Over these admirably written and exquisitely well-mannered pages hovers the peace of riches that are not only material. The opulent, but unvulgar, New-York of the 'seventies and 'eighties furnishes the background of the early part of the book, and for those who know the place and the period, this is probably the most interesting. Others will enjoy it, too, because of the wisdom and the acute but kindly intelligence with which it is informed. But the European will probably prefer the full and intensely interesting account of Henry James, whom Mrs. Wharton knew intimately; of Rome in the days when it was not so very different from the Rome of Nathaniel Hawthorne; of Paris during the War. Friendship has been the leading theme of Mrs. Wharton's life, as told in these pages—friendship and good conversation; and on this subject she says a true, but often unregarded, word: "Our society was, in short, a little 'set' with its private catchwords, observances and amusements, and its indifference to anything outside of its charmed circle; and no really entertaining social group has ever been anything else." The chapter in which the authoress gives an account of herself as a novelist is distinguished for its candour and modesty, and the acuteness of its analysis of the creative process.

E. M. Forster, "Good Society," *New Statesman and Nation*, 7 (23 June 1934), 950, 952

Goethe made a rather bitter epigram on Good Society: It is "good," he said, if it offers no opportunity whatever to poetry. Mrs. Wharton applies this epigram without bitterness; she would certainly prefer poetry to society, and a performance of *Bérénice* to a polo match, but she is not emphatic, and more inclined to chaff her worldlings than to excommunicate them. For this reason her career (or such of it as she has chosen to describe) has few moments of high tension; the dominant impression is comfort—comfort honestly enjoyed and generously shared, but extending uninterruptedly from a New York childhood through Continental trips down to a residence in France. The author of *The House of Mirth* and *The Reef* was well connected and well educated, she always had enough money and was often rich; cars, shaven lawns, servants are in unostentatious attendance, important officials helping when they can, editors accessible, salons open. Because of her intelligence and self-control, this constant prosperity does not spoil her work, but it does make for autobiographical monotony. The change which has signified so much to her, personally—the change from fashionable circles where literature is ignored to ample retreats where it can be practised—cannot be presented dramatically on the great stage of this world, where extremes contend, and a post-war generation will feel a certain tameness in the road she has trodden, and in the "interesting" people who have hedged it

524

on each side. They might contrast it with the path taken by Gauguin. Gauguin also felt that society offered no chance to poetry, so he went off at a tangent, gave up comfort, helped no one, died in filth.

Mrs. Wharton belongs to a tradition which is ending. She realises this, and surveys without asperity the succeeding chaos. It is essentially an American tradition, though not one which has been able to flourish in America. Rooted in Puritanism and financial stability, it has put forth in Europe the flowers of a conscientious and distinguished art—an art which would not bloom until it had been transplanted. Paris, London, and Rome were the chief conservatories, Henry James the outstanding exhibitor; Proust looks in through the window panes, Joyce and D. H. Lawrence do not.

The atmosphere, though artificial, is not exotic. And the art, though cosmopolitan, is never international. It is connected with great cities and with the country houses dependent on them, and takes no stock of a new social order.

Though Mrs. Wharton is an excellent gossip and well-informed *diseuse* she is at her best when she talks about this beloved art. The chapters on her own work and on Henry James', and the references to that neglected novelist Howard Sturgis, are all illuminating. She tells us, for instance, that her characters come into her mind with their names attached, that she is still seeking a fictional home for a lady called Laura Testvalley. If Miss Testvalley gets as well suited as was another homeless character, the Princess Estradina, who finally arrived into *The Custom of the Country*, she will not have waited in vain. But, as her creator realises, she may take some suiting. All this discussion about books and the ways they are created and worked up is stimulating for readers as well as writers. And Henry James! She knew James well and was de-

voted to him, and her patience with his fussifications and affectations will strike the outsider as miraculous. But she is detached enough when she comes to his work, for the reason that she is serious about literature. She passes some very shrewd remarks about his later novels and she sees that his very conscientiousness as an artist led him to be a narrow critic, because he required all writers to be conscientious in exactly the same way.

She was also a friend of Howard Sturgis, her account of whom made me take down *Belchamber* again. *Belchamber* was published in 1907, by Constable (can it still be in print?), and it seems to me now, as it did then, brilliant, amusing, unsparing, poised, full of incident and characters, indeed, well on the way to a masterpiece. The public ignored it, Henry James deplored it because it did not conform to his rules, and for the latter, rather than for the former, reason Howard Sturgis abandoned literature for embroidery. Perhaps he was before his time. The public was not yet ready for that wide yet careful canvas of aristocratic life. But now that Henry James is coming into his own again, and young men in their twenties are reading and admiring him, Sturgis may have his revival also. If he does, Mrs. Wharton will have prompted it by her amusing and sympathetic tribute. He wrote two other novels—*Tim*, and *All That Was Possible*. But, as she says, his triumph is *Belchamber*.

How much did the war destroy? It destroyed "good society" though the butler still brings the tea out under the cedar on occasion. Did it damage poetry too? And will writers ever recover that peculiar blend of security and alertness which characterises Mrs. Wharton and her tradition, and which has served her art so well?

Wilbur Cross, "A Happy Chronicle," *Yale Review*, 23 (June 1934), 817–20

Mrs. Wharton's reminiscences show a mind and temper very feminine, very charming. She has lived, as it were, two lives—one with her family and friends and one apart with her imagination, with the books she has read, and with the men and women she has created in her novels. Both lives coalesce in long talks by the fireside with intimate companions. Without aid of journal or diary, she tells the story so far as it returns to memory, in this regard reminding one of the method of Proust, whom Mrs. Wharton admired but never knew. Here and there in the happy chronicle comes in a note of sadness for the loss of friends through the years. "Life is the saddest thing there is, next to death; yet there are always new countries to see, new books to read (and, I hope, to write), a thousand little daily wonders to marvel at and rejoice in, and those magical moments when the mere discovery that 'the woodspurge has a cup of three' brings not despair but delight."

The story Mrs. Wharton tells of herself is delicately psychological, relating less to her first than to her second life. Her earliest recollection is of a little girl who on a bright Sunday morning was put into "a new and very pretty bonnet." She looked into the glass and thought the face and bonnet beautiful. Her father took her by the hand, and they walked up Fifth Avenue, where they met her little cousin Henry, who lifted her soft woollen veil and planted a kiss on her cheek. The incidents of that morning were the first faint premonitions of the tremendous passions of vanity and love! From them Mrs. Wharton dates the consciousness of being herself and not another. Just after so memorable a day, the gift of a white Spitz puppy was destined to awaken "love and pity for all inarticulate beings."

With this auspicious beginning was built up a most distinctive personality through friendships, through books, and through travels and life abroad. France and Italy she loved. Spain and Germany she knew. In the background were always old New York and Newport and the hills of western Massachusetts. She was a cosmopolitan child. She belonged to a New York family of merchants and bankers, of good colonial stock, whose members made comfortable fortunes. Outside of business their interests were confined to social visits, dinners, and dances under rather strict codes of behavior. As a rule, they kept aloof from public affairs, regarding government and politics as beneath their dignity. Their well-furnished houses always had a library, but the books were little read. No poet or novelist as such was a part of their exclusive world. The first break came with the little girl. Her father explained to her the alphabet, and she quickly learned to read without much assistance. By herself she went through the family libraries, reading at random. A few years later, someone gave her little volumes of Keats and Shelley. After that she was never alone.

Even before she could read, the girl of a lively imagination was an incipient novelist, just as Pope in childhood "lisp'd in numbers, for the numbers came." She loved words and the sound *and* rhythm of great phrases, as she read them aloud from the poets, the Prayer Book, and the Bible. Fairy tales perplexed her, for they seemed to have no relation to the men and women she knew. She used to watch people whom she saw at her father's house and elsewhere on her travels, and then she would go off by herself and "make up" stories about them. After she learned to write, she began to put the stories on paper. Mrs. Wharton was thus a born realist. Most fiction dealing with contemporary life begins like this, in the practice of "making up." It is a natural art. A novelist meets, perhaps casually, a man or a woman whose looks and behavior interest him. He lets his mind play upon the acquaintance or the stranger until he has created in his imagination a past and a future for his victim and given the character a proper place in some pattern or design, more or less complicated.

In time, Mrs. Wharton discovered that the transition from real life to art meant hard labor, requiring the close study of her predecessors, long meditation, and the personal advice of friends of wide knowledge. How a particular story can be best told has always been her problem. She started with the short story and with fear and hesitancy passed into the art of the long novel. It will be news to many readers that Mrs. Wharton was for a time uncertain whether she was destined to become a novelist or a poet. She wrote verse in childhood, some of it getting into a newspaper, and not long afterward she was publishing poems in *The Atlantic Monthly*.

Several of her novels she passes in review in order to explain her art or her purpose against current criticism. Theodore Roosevelt rebuked her because she admitted an unlawful passion in *The Valley of Decision*, and she had to explain to him why it must be there. On reading *The House of Mirth*, her dear friend Charles Eliot Norton reminded her that "no great work of the imagination has ever been based on illicit passion." Had the famous translator of Dante forgotten the Francesca episode in *The Divine Comedy*? In the mind of Mrs. Wharton there would have been no "tragic significance" in the career of Lily Bart of *The House of Mirth* had it not been shown in that girl how a frivolous society debases people and ideals and at last destroys. There is no answer to Mrs. Wharton's contention. Such protest against *The Age of Innocence* fifteen years later was less loud, for a franker and more sincere age was upon us.

On *Ethan Frome* Mrs. Wharton says much that is new. This tragic tale and its companion piece, *Summer*, represent her art in its most extreme realistic aspects. They were very painful reading to a generation that had been brought up on the rose-colored New England stories. Mrs. Wharton, who knew well the grim life in the mountain districts of western Massachusetts, described its tragedies as they actually were. By many readers *Ethan Frome* is now put at the top of all her novels. It was begun, very curiously, in French as an exercise in French composition. Soon Mrs. Wharton saw what fine material there was in the story and wrote it out in English. Though she is still annoyed when people tell her that it is her best novel, she admits that she brought to the making of *Ethan Frome* "the greatest joy and the fullest ease."

Were I to go on, I should tell of Mrs. Wharton's great and enduring friendships and their bearing on the development of her art. The most perfect and the most influential was the friendship of Henry James, on whose character, whims, and intimacies much is related. She cannot quite free herself from her admiration of *The Portrait of a Lady* to accept without reserve the novels of his full maturity, wherein the real life of men and women seems to be sacrificed to experiment and intricate pattern. And his act in renouncing his American citizenship seemed to her "rather puerile and altogether unlike him."

527

"Reminiscences," *Saturday Review* [England], 157 (21 July 1934), 863

Mrs. Wharton has had a literary career going back to the nineties. She has been a prolific writer, but in everything she has written there has been a charm of style that was at once arresting.

This distinctive feature is not absent from her reminiscences just published. . . .

They introduce us to her early years as well as to that more spacious existence which came to her with her fame.

It is perhaps surprising that she ever took to writing novels in face of her mother's disapproval of that class of literature. But family discouragement was perhaps not wholly a disadvantage, since it turned the youthful Edith Jones' tastes into more classic channels and thus served to create a style which, with the qualities noted below, has won for Mrs. Wharton her literary reputation.

Henry James was of course, one of Mrs. Wharton's closest friends, and in her reminiscences she tells us much about him. There is one entertaining anecdote illustrating his inability to come down to the mind of a simple rustic whom he had asked in a most circumlocutory manner to direct him on his way. The ancient yokel he addressed was in danger of being drowned with his torrent of words when Mrs. Wharton eventually intervened. . . .

Here is what Theodore Roosevelt said to her after his accession to the American Presidency:

"Well, I *am* glad to welcome to the White House someone to whom I can quote 'The Hunting of the Snark' without being asked what I mean. Would you believe it," he added, "no one in the Administration has ever heard of Alice, much less of the Snark, and the other day, when I said to the Secretary of the Navy: 'Mr. Secretary, *What I say three times is true,*' he did not recognise the allusion and answered with an aggrieved air: 'Mr. President, it would never for a moment have occurred to me to impugn your veracity?'"

Mrs. Wharton has always written about life exactly as it has appeared to her. Eminently sane in her own outlook, she has resolutely declined to fall into the grooves sometimes suggested to her. As she says:

I think it was Edwin Godkin, then the masterly Editor of the New York "Evening Post," who said that the choice of articles in American magazines was entirely determined by the fear of scandalising a non-existent clergyman in the Mississippi Valley; and I made up my mind from the first that I would never sacrifice my literary conscience to this ghostly censor.

Add to this determination a true sense of proportion and understanding, a sympathetic mind and a distinctive style and we have the foundations on which Mrs. Wharton's literary fame rests.

L.H.M.,
"Reviews,"
America, 51 (28 July 1934), 378

No one would expect an intimate or revealing autobiography of Edith Wharton. Her position as our most distinguished contemporary writer of fiction has been achieved without notable concessions to the spirit of the time; and when she writes of herself, of her travels and friendships, she brings to her task something of the same aloofness that we have come to associate with her novels and short stories. There is much small talk, inconsequential enough but pleasant reading for those who would cultivate the alert repose of the old aristocracy. Chapters on Mrs. Wharton's ancestry and early life are significant in suggesting the influences that formed her later philosophy of life and paved the way for that accomplished distinction of style that characterizes her best work as well as her best sellers. Mrs. Wharton's debt to Henry James is once more acknowledged and emphasized. The old master is seen as critic and as friend, as one who stood with her in the attitude of "high seriousness" toward the art of fiction, of resistance to the extremes of realism as well as the emptiness of sentimentalism. There is much talk of New York and points east, of notable figures in Europe and America, moving comments on the War and its effects, and pleasantly ironic observations on the passing of the genteel tradition and the emergence of a more nervous civilization.

E. K. Brown,
"*A Backward Glance*,"
American Literature, 6 (January 1935), 474–5

This book of memories is dedicated to "the friends who every year on All Souls' Night come and sit with me by the fire"; no dedication could be more Fitting, for Mrs. Wharton's has been "a life bound up in a few close personal ties" (p. 375), and, with the lonely exception of Paul Bourget, all those who have been her intimates are dead. In this book, in vivid anecdotes and phrases, they live again: Edward Burlingame and W. C. Brownell, who welcomed her as a Scribner author; Walter Berry, who, in her early thirties, revealed to her what an intellectual and spiritual companionship might mean and who for almost thirty years was her *alter ego*; Paul Bourget's wife and the Comtesse de Fitzjames, who made her free of Paris; and, dear beyond the others, her master Henry James. With the death of each of them a part of the author herself perished, for "what is one's personality, detached from that of the friends with whom fate happens to have linked one?" (p. 169).

Precious as a memorial to a few exquisitely civilized beings who have left a deep impress upon Mrs. Wharton, the book is disappointing as an account of her creative activity. Only one chapter is devoted to this; and this chapter opens with an apology for its presence, digresses at length from its true theme, and loses itself in speculation. There are indeed, here and there throughout the book, *obiter dicta* upon her own works, the circumstances under which they were written (*Ethan Frome* was begun as a French exercise, p. 295), and the way in which they were received (the popularity of *The Age of Innocence* took Mrs. Wharton completely by surprise, p. 369). The curious error of calling the heroine of *The Valley of Decision* "a humble bookseller's daughter" (p. 127), when she was in fact the daughter of a professor and man of letters, strengthens one's impression that the center of Mrs. Wharton's interest has been not in her books but in her friends. Still more curious is the conflict between her account of the renaming of *The Touchstone* and that given by the person responsible, Mr. John Murray. In a prefatory note to the English edition Mr. Murray asserts that while *The Touchstone* was passing through the press in England he "was informed that a novel of this name was already in circulation." He at once proposed to Mrs. Wharton to call the novelette *The Touch of a Vanished Hand*; this proposal Mrs. Wharton rejected in favor of a title which Mr. Murray does not record and which had also been preëmpted; and Mr. Murray was at this point informed that there was already in existence a novel entitled *The Touch of a Vanished Hand*. Unable to communicate further with Mrs. Wharton, who was traveling in Italy, he adopted the title *A Gift from the Grave*. Rather ungenerously, Mrs. Wharton declares that Mr. Murray (whom in error she calls Mr. John Lane) took "care not to consult me" (p. 123), and she ascribes the change in title to the English publisher's belief that the American title was "too colorless" (*loc. cit.*).

The early chapters in which Mrs. Wharton evokes the New York of her childhood and youth give the background of *The Age of Innocence* and *Old New York*. Some traits and incidents developed in these works are here recorded in their original form. Her own mother's account of the pyramid of New York society (p. 10) closely resembles Mrs. Archer's in *The Age of Innocence*; the account of Egerton

Winthrop and his circle (pp. 94–96) discloses the model of Newland Archer; the reference to William Astor's boldness in hanging a Bouguereau Venus (p. 61) recalls one of Julius Beaufort's audacities in the same novel; the stratagem employed by Mrs. Wharton's father to visit his fiancée (p. 18) is utilized in *False Dawn*. There are other less palpable examples of Mrs. Wharton's use of her milieu in her fiction.

Checklist of Additional Reviews

Fanny Butcher, "Edith Wharton Is Herself in Memoir Book," Chicago *Daily Tribune*, 28 April 1934, p. 15.

Edwin Francis Edgett, "Edith Wharton Takes a Backward Glance," Boston *Evening Transcript*, 28 April 1934, book section, p. 1.

L. A. Sloper, "Mrs. Wharton Recalls," *Christian Science Monitor*, "Book of the Day," 28 April 1934, p. 14.

Isabel Paterson, "Edith Wharton Recalls the Age of Innocence," *New York Herald Tribune Books*, 29 April 1934, p. 7.

"The Last Survivor," *Time*, 83 (5 June 1934), 101–4.

Lilian Whiting, "Mrs. Wharton's Life on Two Continents," Springfield [Massachusetts] *Republican*, 17 June 1934, p. 7–E.

Edith H. Walton, "The Book Parade," *Forum*, 92 (July 1934), iv.

R.T., "Two Literary Lives," *Current History*, 40 (September 1934), vii, xii.

"Les Lettres et le théâtre," *Le Mois* [France], 49 (January 1935), 171–2.

Aldo Sorani, "Edith Wharton: A Backward Glance," *PAN* [Italy], 3 (January 1935), 147–50.

THE WORLD OVER

THE
WORLD OVER

by

EDITH WHARTON

D. APPLETON-CENTURY COMPANY
INCORPORATED
NEW YORK   **LONDON**
1936

"Mrs. Wharton: *The World Over*,"
Times Literary Supplement
[England], 25 April 1936,
p. 353

What a pleasure it is to observe mastery of a craft! Mrs. Wharton learned her craft in the days when mastery was still generally appreciated, and now, an unsuppressed survivor of a tradition temporarily obscured, she continues by her example to show to a raw world what ease, finish and lightness mean in fiction. Here are seven short stories, none of them, for Mrs. Wharton, exceptionally brilliant but all, even the slightest, admirable examples of an art.

To a generation obsessed by the flux of ideas and the flux of personality, by revolts, complexes and cravings, she once more exhibits the short story as the treatment of a situation. A New York business man, by marrying a Russian wife, finds himself deeply involved in providing for a growing host of her charming but unstable relations; the wife of a celebrated economist, having her hair waved on the eve of elopement with a dashing young airman, for a while believes that she is a day too late: a business man convalescing in Switzerland falls in love with a woman who turns out to have been the notorious heroine of a murder trial: two middle-aged American widows, sitting on the terrace of a restaurant overlooking Rome, discuss their daughters and remember their own youth in Rome: or, for a touch of the ghostly, a second wife observes her husband's agony of mind when, periodically, letters arrive in a faint handwriting. Some people may say that stories about the wealthy and well-connected of the United States are no longer interesting: then this is not a book for them. Others may say that these situations are dead bones compared with the vital issues raised by So-and-So, their favourite writer of to-day: then they are wrong, for they will see how a master brings dead bones to life. The conversation in Rome, for instance, between Mrs. Slade and Mrs. Ansley, punctuated by their private reflections about each other, never seems other than natural between two women who had been girls together, yet it is directed with subtle skill towards the surprise of its close, where Mrs. Slade confesses a secret to Mrs. Ansley and gets another secret fired at her in return. Again, the first story, "Charm Incorporated," is, in its way, an absurdity, for Mr. Targatt's happy thoughts for Boris, Katinka, Paul Dimitri and the other Kouradjines owe their success to Mrs. Wharton's delightfully satirical invention: one laughs and goes on till, with a stroke, she introduces a touch of real feeling that, without spoiling the soufflé, gives it a finer flavour. The maintenance of suspense in "Pomegranate Seed" without a touch of sensationalism, and the maintenance of the narrator's urbanity when faced by sensationalism in "Confession"—these also are lessons in craftsmanship and, like all supremely well conducted lessons, a pleasure to an intelligent audience. And, above all, there is that gaiety of mind which never becomes jocular or trivial—another virtue of masters, but hardly won.

Percy Hutchison, "Mrs. Wharton's New Stories and Other Recent Works of Fiction," *New York Times Book Review*, 26 April 1936, p. 6

In the seven short stories collected under the group-title *The World Over* Edith Wharton, in spite of some minor lapses, proves that her reputation as a master of this form of literary art remains for the most part unimpaired. There may be certain authors of the present generation who conceive situations and relationships generally more striking, perhaps even more valuable as problems to be considered; and who write with greater pungency. But few can equal her in getting under the skin of a character or in getting under the skin of a reader. And in purity of style Mrs. Wharton is still unsurpassed.

We bar the first story, "Charm Incorporated" (originally published under the caption "Bread Upon the Waters"), as not her best. But the story is so vastly amusing, coming nearer to hilarity than Mrs. Wharton usually comes, that it serves admirably as the lead-story for a book. "Charm Incorporated" is the comedy of an increasingly prosperous New Yorker who marries a Russian refugee, and who presently finds himself supporting a small host of his wife's relatives. The adroit way in which Nadeja places one after another in a position of opulence (usually by engineering a wealthy marriage!) to the complete bewilderment of her husband is productive of much justifiable laughter. We are not sure, either, that the last story, "Duration," is fully up to Mrs. Wharton's

highest standards. But this piece also justifies itself to the reader by reason of its humor.

We now have left five stories, each of which can withstand any critical light, however intense, which may be turned on it; with one, "Roman Fever," as notable a piece, within its brief compass, as one is likely to find. It is, indeed, as memorable a short story as Mrs. Wharton has ever done. The titles of the remaining four are: "Pomegranate Seed," "Permanent Wave," "Confession" and "The Looking Glass."

The first is a definite excursion into the realm of the occult, where Mrs. Wharton is unaccustomed to stray. Were she more at home in that misty field she would have been more at pains to make plausible the manner in which the letters from the spirit world come into Kenneth Ashby's letter box. But this failure in planning her story may be passed over in view of the deeper significance of the tale. Mrs. Wharton is not striving to be an Edgar Allan Poe. The point of the story is that Kenneth Ashby has committed what might be called moral bigamy in that he has married a second, and deeply devoted, wife without dismissing his dead first wife actively from his life. He would fain have done so; supposed he had. But actually he could not. Hence, a double pathos dominates the history. Because Elsie still stretches her dead hand across Kenneth's life he cannot be all-in-all to Charlotte. And Charlotte cannot find her all-in-all in him. In one of those initial paragraphs, heavy with foreboding, for which Mrs. Wharton is justly famous, we have premonition of the spiritual tragedy which is to ensue. A tragedy which will remain in doubt to the last line.

> Charlotte Ashby paused on her doorstep. . . . The contrast between the soulless roar of New York, its devouring blaze of lights, the op-

534

pression of its congested traffic, congested houses, congested minds, and this veiled sanctuary she called home, stirred her profoundly. In the very heart of the hurricane she had found her tiny islet—or thought she had. And now, in the last months, everything was changed, and she always wavered on the doorstep and had to force herself to enter.

Seldom has the key to a story been more accurately struck at the outset. A reader is sure to go on avidly.

We scarcely know what to say about "Confession," it raises so many unanswerable questions. It is a theme which must have stirred many an author to speculation, although none, so far as this reviewer is aware, has attempted to carry the problem through. On the surface the problem is simple enough. What of a woman tried for murder and acquitted? What would her after-life be? Her attitude toward the world? The world's attitude toward her; and her meeting of the world's attitude? Mrs. Wharton's story may bristle with inconsistencies. We fear that it does. On the purely technical side we feel that Mrs. Wharton has confessed a weakness in putting her narrative into the first person. But she is so undeniably the supreme craftsman that she undoubtedly explored every possible method before making her decision. Hence, what impresses is the field for thought this unusual story opens up rather than the story itself.

"Permanent Wave" is a short, sharp piece; apparently hard, but in its dénouement surprisingly and reassuringly human. "The Looking Glass" is not only deep but is also engagingly witty.

And this brings us, in conclusion, to "Roman Fever," a superlative bit of work. As sharp-cut as a diamond, and as hard of surface, "Roman Fever" is the culminating encounter of two women who have been lifelong enemies, but superficially lifelong friends. On the deaths of their husbands they made "an appropriate exchange of wreaths and condolences." Which won in the end? The answer is likely to depend on the individual reader's point of view; the point of view on life which he brings to the story in advance of reading. But never did Mrs. Wharton (or Henry James) push social satire to a more demolishing conclusion. If all the other tales in *The World Over* were negligible the book would still be outstanding in the short-story field for "Roman Fever" alone.

Peter Quennell, "New Novels," *New Statesman and Nation*, n.s. 11 (2 May 1936), 670

Mr. Spender's stories are stimulating but unsatisfactory; Mrs. Wharton's by comparison refreshingly competent; yet not quite up to the standard of the novels that have established her claim to be remembered as a minor master of early twentieth-century fiction. Here again, as in *The House of Mirth*, *The Custom of the Country*, *The Glimpses of the Moon* and *Twilight Sleep*, is the tone of dry worldliness—the cynical appreciation of mundane values—that makes everything Mrs. Wharton writes so insidiously readable. Thus, "Charm Incorporated" describes one of those amiable leech-like Russian refugee families who bully, blackmail or imperceptibly edge their way into English or American upper or upper-middle class life. "Pomegranate Seed" is an ingenious ghost story; "Permanent Wave," the brilliant and brutal portrait of a woman whose vagueness is only equalled by her fatuity, and whose plans of elopement are held up because she cannot distinguish between to-day and to-morrow. But "Roman Fever," I think, is the best story in the book. Two middle-aged American ladies sit on the terrace of a restaurant overlooking the Roman Forum. They review their youth. They go back to a time when Rome was a very different place. They recapture a period when they were both in love with the same fascinating young man. One of them discovers an unsuspected relationship.

Mrs. Wharton belongs to a tradition of American life that has now almost disappeared; both Mr. Farrell and Mr. Steinbeck reflect the Americanism of to-day and are the products of a world at once more interesting—because it is less Europeanised—and far more disturbing. . . .

G.S., "New Books," *Saturday Review of Literature*, 14 (2 May 1936), 19

One gets much the same pleasure from Mrs. Wharton's stories as from W. Somerset Maugham's. They are told with a precision and intelligence which are a pleasure to encounter. They are not deep—in this book, at least—but they are dramatic; if occasionally melodramatic, none the less entertaining. Her elderly society ladies from New York and Boston are familiar characters: so much the better, as this focuses the attention on the story ideas. And the ideas are good ones: a perpetual poor relation becomes the most

important person in the family by virtue of living to be a hundred; a young man traveling in Europe falls in love with a girl who had once been tried for murder; an Irish masseuse brightens the life of a client by pretending to bring spirit messages. A younger generation of story-writers has turned to plotlessness and often to pointlessness. Mrs. Wharton's new book reminds us that there is much to be said for construction, and good story-telling even when they do not produce an *Ethan Frome*.

"Cultivated Garden," *Time* (4 May 1936), 80

Like so many neat flower-beds, the 43 books of Edith Wharton stand in polite rows that many a ruder gardener of words might envy. Few society women have gone in for such a messy job as professional writing, but even in working dress Edith Wharton is patently *grande-dame*. To the eyes of the younger generation, her polite and cultivated formality might well seem quaintly behind the times, but for survivors of the pre-War garden age she still has a nostalgic charm. If the stories in her latest book are not quite so cosmopolitan as the title suggests, nor her characters quite so lifelike as they proclaim themselves, they show that Author Wharton's eye for formal effect has lost none of its cultivated keenness.

An ant-like Manhattan broker finds his Russian wife's family a strangely charming incubus; upset and then educated by their grasshopper example, he discovers how much he loves his wife.

A young wife, lately married to a widower, finds that the dead hand of her predecessor will not let him alone, even writes him threatening letters.

Two widows, staying with their grown daughters in Rome, indulge in reminiscent chat. The brilliant, condescending one is left speechless at the news that the quiet one's envied daughter is also her husband's.

An unconsidered poor relation attains family importance by outliving all her generation, and on her 100th birthday behaves like nobody's business.

Graham Greene, "Short Stories," *Spectator* [England], 156 (22 May 1936), 950

It is a humble, amiable trait in human nature to seek authority, and perhaps the last remnant of a religious impulse is working in the attention some of us pay to the committees of the Prix Goncourt, of the Book Society, the Hawthornden, the Femina-Vie Heureuse and the O. Henry Memorial. But the divine should remain the inscrutable, and it is with rather mistaken frankness that the last-named committee publish not only the stories from which they have made their final choice but their reports as well. There is something pleasantly naïve in the action, something reminiscent of the American hick face the films have made familiar, something incredibly frank, open, high-cheekboned and a little shiny. This committee at any rate, we feel, has nothing in common with the visiting cards, the intrigue, the lobbying which are said to precede the Goncourt award. Yet the innocence in the American nature upsets the cart every time, and the shady Gallic decisions of the Old World produce the better results.

The American first prize has been awarded on points to Miss Kay Boyle for a glossy and arty little piece about Austrian politics which should be treated less superficially or not at all: the second prize goes to a long, worthy tale of the depression, tiring in its lack of selection. Among the dozen or so other stories there is none by Mr. Faulkner or Miss Katherine Anne Porter, none by the other American authors on this list, by Mr. Caldwell, Miss Gellhorn or even by Mrs. Wharton, whose suave, well-bred tales in her latest volume are technically very expert, though in the essential triviality of her anecdotes it is hard to recognise the author of *The Children* or that superb horror story, "A Bottle of Perrier." Perhaps the O. Henry judges were not allowed a very interesting range of choice, but their remarks on the stories they have dealt with seem sometimes a little curious: remarks like that of Mr. Jackson, a San Francisco literary editor, who praises the original material of a tough tale by Mr. Upton Terrell: "William Wister Haines's stuff is high tension lines, and this is telephone work."

"The World Over," *Nation*, 142 (27 June 1936), 852

Why Mrs. Wharton should ever have allowed these slick little bits to be exhumed from the files of the ladies' magazines is difficult to determine. Probably they read very nicely between the advertisements, but here they seem a very ordinary vintage. Nor do they tend to lessen the suspicion that our memories of her accepted works have been tinted somewhat rosily by time. Mrs. Wharton's style, of course, is still impeccable: crisp, succinct, and above all, taut. But the best to be said of the best piece here, "Charm Incorporated," is that it would make a sprightly skit for some revue. As for the other tales—they can charitably be ignored. It is far more satisfying to remember *Ethan Frome* with gratitude.

Joseph Reilley, "*The World Over,*" *Catholic World*, 144 (December 1936), 367–8

Nobody can read Edith Wharton's fiction, long or short, without admiration for her artistic conscience and unfailing artistry. For nearly forty years (*The Greater Inclination* appeared in 1899) she has written steadily and those qualities together with striking talent, have appeared on every page of her large output. More than once Mrs. Wharton's work came close to genius; once, in *Ethan Frome*, it reached it so decisively that some of us place that novelette on the plane of *The Scarlet Letter* and *Huckleberry Finn*.

No story in the collection under review can, of course, challenge *Ethan Frome*; neither Mrs. Wharton nor anyone else writing in English to-day is likely to do that. But all these tales take high rank and three, "Charm Incorporated," "Confession" and "Roman Fever" belong among the best short stories she has ever done. "Charm Incorporated" is a study of those scions of Russian aristocracy, let loose upon us since the Great War, who offer real charm and unreal titles in return for wealth and are willing to endure marriage, at least temporarily, to consummate the bargain. Somehow Nadeja has captured Jim Targatt, hard-headed New York business man, whereupon she devotes her days to "placing" the rest of her family. The success of Nadeja, aided and abetted by Targatt in self-defense, is told with a delicate and penetrating irony unique in current American fiction. "Confession," the most gripping of these tales, concerns the love of a young American for a woman once tried for the murder of her father. Before marrying him she puts into his hands the document that will reveal everything. They live five perilously happy years until her death. "On my desk lies the paper I have never read, and beside it the candle with which I shall presently burn it." The story most adroitly handled is "Roman Fever," which reminds us beyond anything else in the book that Mrs. Wharton began her career as a disciple of Henry James. But long ago she developed an art of her own for which she is indebted to no one else and of which *The World Over* is a fresh and convincing revelation.

Checklist of Additional Reviews

Fanny Butcher, review of *The World Over*, Chicago *Daily Tribune*, 25 April 1936, p. 10.

Katherine Simonds, "Edith Wharton's Evocative Stories," *New York Herald Tribune Books*, 26 April 1936, p. 5.

W.K.R., "Bittersweet," *Christian Science Monitor*, 27 April 1936, "Book News of the Day," p. 16.

F.R., "Mrs. Wharton," *Manchester Guardian*, 15 May 1936, p. 7.

GHOSTS

GHOSTS

by

EDITH WHARTON

D. APPLETON-CENTURY COMPANY

INCORPORATED

NEW YORK   LONDON

1937

"Briefer Mention," *Commonweal*, 27 (5 November 1937), 55

This book gives us the ghosts of Brittany, New England, New York, England and the Arabian desert. The author's outstanding qualities in the use of different methods of short story writing make this a fascinating selection to browse through in nocturnal hours.

"Ghosts and Ghost Stories," *Times Literary Supplement* [England], 6 November 1937, p. 823

[. . .]

But in Mrs. Wharton's book, which consists entirely of eleven fictitious stories, at least three are so well fogged that, although the reader may be thrilled, he is likely to be very uncertain what happened. The three are "The Eyes," "The Lady's Maid's Bell" and "The Triumph of Night." Though the title of the book is *Ghosts*, the three best stories are ghostless. "All Souls" shows witches in New England going to a coven, but the troubles resulting to an invalid left at home are not at all occult. "Mary Pask" only thought she was a ghost. And in the most striking story, "Bewitched," it is left uncertain whether Rutledge met the ghost of Ora Brand or her live young sister Venny. Brand shot at the ghost, but whom did he hit? Mrs. Wharton in her excellent prefatory essay on the needs of ghosts in fiction claims that "reading should be a creative act as

well as writing," and so justifies herself for leaving the reader to invent several endings and choose for himself.

Desmond Shawe-Taylor, "New Novels," *New Statesman and Nation*, n.s. 14 (6 November 1937), 758

The gentle, leisurely tales of Miss Edith Wharton make a pleasant contrast; their air of leisure is due, not to the accumulation of dead detail, but to the fact that she is a story-teller whose speech is naturally quiet and unhurried. Her new volume is a collection of ghost stories; and while I cannot say I found them hair-raising, they have a half-eerie, half-cosy charm of their own. You begin to feel the silence around your chair; she is a past mistress of that curious art which makes you put the book down for an instant, poke the fire, and settle comfortably back with the thought: "Well, here I am, reading a ghost story; what could be more agreeable?"

W.R.B., "The New Books," *Saturday Review*, 17 (6 November 1937), 19

Some years ago, of an evening when a group of friends got into the mood for ghost stories, the reviewer heard a now well known American novelist give, as his contribution, Edith Wharton's tale of the ghostly dogs in "Kerfol." The narrator recaptured its atmosphere acceptably, afterward acknowledging the author. More recently Alexander Woollcott has chosen Mrs. Wharton's "The Lady's Maid's Bell" for inclusion in his forthcoming *Second Reader*. Both are good stories, indeed, and both are in this volume: though the present reviewer thinks that "The Eyes," owing to its psychological significance, and "A Bottle of Perrier," because of its Arabian atmosphere, and perhaps also because of its perfectly reasonable and excessively grim explanation, are superior to the lady's tales of mere "fetches" and witches and letters from the dead.

If you like good ghost stories then, this is the book for you. Edith Wharton knew her craft. There is a short preface which discusses the art charmingly. Maybe you will like best poor young Rainer in "The Triumph of Night." The setting is excellent. And what is that peculiar green face looking over your shoulder?

Mrs. Wharton seems a little tame compared with M. R. James, a less accomplished writer who never failed at the lineaments of horror.

Checklist of Additional Reviews

Thomas Moult, "Short Stories," *Manchester Guardian*, 19 November 1937, p. 7.

Graham Greene, "Short Stories," *Spectator* [England], 154 (24 December 1937), 1155

Ghosts: what gives a ghost story its thrill? First I think its *physical* sense, and here Mrs. Wharton fails (except in "A Bottle of Perrier"—to drink water from a well in which a friend's body is rotting, aware only of an odd smell, an unpleasant taste, is an idea which certainly graduates in horror); secondly, a moral twist. Mrs. Wharton, following her master Henry James, is good at this, but he could convey the physical as well (who can forget the appearance of Peter Quint?). And so

THE BUCCANEERS

THE
BUCCANEERS

By

EDITH WHARTON

D. APPLETON-CENTURY COMPANY
INCORPORATED

NEW YORK   1938   LONDON

Percy Hutchison, "Edith Wharton's Unfinished Novel and Other Recent Fiction," *New York Times Book Review*, 18 September 1938, p. 6

The first thing that a possible reader will wish to know about a novel left unfinished by its author is whether the story has been completed sufficiently to form a substantial and interesting book. Not only did Edith Wharton all but finish *The Buccaneers* but she also left so full an outline, a portion of which is appended to the novel by her literary executor, Gaillard Lapsley, that the story, as distinguished from the book, is brought to her intended conclusion. Hence, this posthumously published tale of three American heiresses who storm the citadel of British aristocracy with varying success, except that its dramatic finale lacks the visualized vitality it would have received from Mrs. Wharton's pen, is almost completely her own.

Mr. Lapsley speaks of *The Buccaneers* as if planned not so long ago, and this is probably true. But any reader familiar with the bulk of Mrs. Wharton's work will find it difficult to escape the conviction that the story was conceived some decades back, for it assuredly belongs to the period of *The House of Mirth* and *The Age of Innocence*. This is nothing against the novel; quite the contrary. There have been few novelists with Edith Wharton's power accurately to parade a definite phase of American social life, and always with an impeccable style. But the book as we have it is unsatisfactory in respect to precisely these two points. Often the characters seem mere sketches and the scene highly nebulous, also much of the writing is hasty and far from firm. The reason is, of course, obvious. We have in the published pages many, indeed a majority, with which Mrs. Wharton had finished.

Others are stop-gaps, or bridges hurriedly constructed to carry the tale forward, and destined for the revision and the rewriting Mrs. Wharton was never to bestow. Moreover, there is a lesser character who completely runs away with the first part of the book. I cannot believe that Mrs. Wharton intended the governess, Laura Testvalley, an English substitution for her own Italian name, to take the spotlight from her young charge, Nan St. George, who was to be the Duchess Annabel. Much as Edith Wharton must have reveled in many of the tart observations she ascribed to her adventuring instructress, her perception of novel values was so great there can be little doubt that at the end she would have relentlessly blue-penciled the obstreperous Laura. Thus, as it stands, the tale is out of focus. The story belongs to the Duchess of Tintagel, not to Miss Testvalley.

The date of the action is about 1875, and the Closson, St. George and Elmsworth families, having become wealthy, aspire to New York and Newport society for their several daughters. But Newport and New York reject them, and it is then that the crafty Testvalley suggests London; if the girls are successful during a London season, they can return triumphant to America. They are only too successful; it sounds more like a lesser novelist than one with the unerring discrimination of Mrs. Wharton that four of the girls should marry each a peer, and in revision I believe she would have reduced at least one of these husbands to a mere knight. Had she done this the result would have been that Ushant, whose Duchess Annabel St. George is to become, would

545

have stood out more individually than he does. In fact all of the men in the piece remain a bit too close to "pattern"; even Guy Thwarte, who at the end is to be the principal male actor in the drama, is not fully drawn. But Annabel is. It is on Nan, who has not yet "come out" at the beginning of the tale, on whom Edith Wharton lavishes her abundant powers of artistry. She will occupy a high place in the Wharton gallery of feminine portraits.

Is "artistry" the right word, however? As in her drawing of Lily Bart, Mrs. Wharton is dealing with the moral and psychological factors which in their sum are Annabel St. George and the Duchess of Tintagel; for the child, she is little more, does not really know which she is. In her relations with Ushant it is American psychology in conflict with the psychology of aristocracy entrenched in tradition, spiritual imponderables fluttering uncertain wings against turrets and battlements. Not for nothing did Mrs. Wharton marry her forthright little American girl, the least good looking of the invaders in ancient Cornwall, where tradition would hold even more strongly than anywhere else in the British Isles. The triangle of Ushant, his Duchess and Guy Thwarte, as the solution nears, holds the reader tautly suspended.

The Buccaneers, then, since Edith Wharton is a past master at telling a story, is never less than interesting, even in its hasty and unrevised parts. And when the final writing has been done these portions take their place among her best work, cynical, witty, tender and understanding by turns. The bewilderment of the American mothers, leading their trailing children in the wake of Laura Testvalley, is delicious and a little pathetic. The reader is likely to question now and then as to whether the novelist did not intend a faintly shadowed moral to her tale. The title suggests it. They came, they saw, they made more or less successful forays. But did they really conquer? The irony is unmistakable.

May Lamberton Becker, "Last of Edith Wharton: Wherein She Reverted to the Secure Mood and Period of Her Greatest Books," *New York Herald Tribune Books*, 18 September 1938, p. 6

To the last, Mrs. Wharton kept faith with her public, even in the novel for whose completion she could not stay. *The Buccaneers* is complete as far as the story goes, and may be read without the sense of final frustration that attends so many unfinished novels. By far the greater part, all indeed but the climax, the conclusion and the scenes by which these were to be directly approached, are not only in print, but in what amounts to final form. What was to happen in these unwritten chapters her own synopsis—unusually rich in detail and in emotional undercurrent—leaves in no manner of doubt.

Furthermore, there can be no reasonable doubt that these unwritten chapters would have been great. Not all her novels could have claimed place among our major works of fiction, it is true. Mrs. Wharton worked at her best only in security. The nearer she came to an America of today and the conditions and problems of its contemporary society, the more a sense of insecurity made itself evident in her treatment of these themes. She had long since lost touch with America as it is. But in an

America that had ceased to be, in the Gilded Age, in the Age of Innocence, in Lily Bart's New York, she was serenely, firmly secure. Whatever she wrote of that world came to us not from one who had read a great deal about it, but from the inside; she knew it as a man knows that he is himself and no other. The period of which she wrote influenced for this reason even the details of her craftsmanship; her art was lapidary and gem-cutting calls for a steady hand.

It was never steadier than in this book about social buccaneers of the American '80s, not only the lovely daughters with whom the story is chiefly concerned, but the cheerful predatory papas who made money all the week in Wall Street and the mammas who wore their best gowns in hotel parlors because they had no better place to wear them, mammas listless but anxious, conscious that their girls must dance too often with one another because eligible young men were flocking to that Newport from which bands of invisible iron barred them and their beautiful daughters. This is the story of the first American invasion of England; it opens at the Grand Union Hotel in Saratoga, when crinolines had capitulated to tight perpendicular polonaises bunched up in the back, in the days of afternoon naps, iced lemonade and palm-leaf fans. Here are the politics of the piazza, the rocking-chair coalitions into which wives must enter because business ambitions of husbands require it. Here above all are social ambitions of mothers for daughters cheerfully tolerant of parental care because they know how well they are able to take care of themselves. Here is a world where wealth may crumble at a touch, a society without background, beauty sprung from nowhere—and among all these insecurities the story moves securely and serene.

At the center of all this is the St. George family; the Colonel with his easy money

and handsome ironic eyebrows; Mrs. St. George fanning her way through vacant hours; Virginia, the beauty; young Nan, still theoretically in the schoolroom, but enjoying the sort of halfway liberty that, according to Jane Austen, never prospers. The governess, to whom her "finishing" is entrusted, had interrupted a career in the households of the English aristocracy only because there was no money in it there and a great deal for one of her gifts to earn overseas. This Laura Testvalley was of Italian stock, her cousin the "decried and illustrious" Rossetti. "If I'd been a man," she sometimes thought, "Dante Gabriel might not have been the only cross in the family." Her ironic humor, clear-eyed Latin practicality, and basic good feeling are invaluable to the St. George social campaign. It is she, indeed, who may be said to push them into it, convinced that England must first be stormed and after that the citadels of Fifth Avenue would go down at a touch. Laura knows the field; the marriage of a South American stepdaughter of the Colonel's business ally, their admired Conchita Closson, to the prodigal son of a great family, gives the girls a foothold. Their lovely lines advance, not in battle formation, but in groups swiftly forming and dissolving like alliances of young girls, like melting clusters in a *corps de ballet*.

They were soon lost to us in real life, those American beauties; their sons, their grandsons, became bulwarks of Britain; once married, they settled into English life as comfortably and as competently as Victoria Woodhull. How this assimilation came about so rapidly and completely, it is easy to see from what goes on in the career of the St. Georges and the Emsworths. The highest alliance is that of Nan St. George, who becomes the wife of one of England's wealthiest Dukes. Not so long after, her friend, Lizzy Emsworth, now married to a member of Parliament on his way higher, is telling a husband often made breathless by her swift social intuitions that "Nan's dying of boredom and longing for a change." At this point the manuscript breaks off. It is already clear that a crisis in Nan's life approaches. Mrs. Wharton's statement makes it plain that this will involve a resounding international scandal.

But meanwhile something has been taking place that lends far greater significance to these unwritten chapters. Laura Testvalley's character, seemingly submerged in the action, has been gradually revealed as a prime force in controlling it. It is Laura who will come secretly to the aid of the first deep love in which she has ever believed, and cheerfully sacrifice to it her own last chances of affection and security. In what has gone before there is every evidence of the sweep with which these scenes would have risen to this opportunity.

The Buccaneers places one more "unfinished window in Aladdin's tower" that, like the first, defies succeeding craftsmen to complete it. We know what gems she had at her disposal; we know what shape the finished work was to take. What remains for magnificent conjecture—and Gaillard Lapsley, her literary executor, leaves it to conjecture in his admirable opening and closing notes—is the way in which these lights and colors would have been combined to bring out the full richness of the design.

Christopher Morley, "Edith Wharton's Unfinished Novel," *Saturday Review*, 24 September 1938, p. 10

The critics, mostly a low-class lot, used to lay stress on the steep social reredos that lay behind Mrs. Edith Wharton. (Her name, as Pearsall Smith has lately reminded us, was Mrs. Edward Wharton; the other was a solecism she rightly abhorred, even when uttered by the London *Times*). But Mrs. Wharton herself was not able to take Society very seriously, either here or in London; she took care to live her most intelligent years in France, enjoying such quaint or humorous outcasts as Henry James and Pearsall Smith. And in the last (unfinished) novel she was amusing herself by one final spoof in which she made impartial hay both of English and American fashionable fetiches.

Mr. Gaillard Lapsley, her literary executor, makes eloquent but surely unnecessary apology for the publication of this incomplete novel. It is surely among her most interesting and shrewdest studies. Parts of it are obviously still in plan, and it breaks off just at the point where she is tightening the threads for important and rebellious emotions. Briefly the theme is the importation into England of a group of American Beauties who have been socially unsuccessful at home. An interesting contrast, if anyone cared to mediate it, is the wholly different treatment of a not dissimilar situation in Daphne du Maurier's *Rebecca*. There also we have a young female outsider marrying into a great English house; the younger treatment of the theme is to melodramatize and romanticize; Mrs. Wharton keeps to the mood of crisp and tart sardonics. So, excepting one scene which Mr. Lapsley admires but which I find impossibly Boucicault in tone, she manages some credibility for an otherwise fantastic plot.

But this is a novel in which the defects are precisely as fascinating (to the sophister) as the merits. All of it, even in passages Mrs. Wharton would undoubtedly have given some revision, is done in the agreeable suavity of the fin de siècle. But be not deceived; the great old lady knew precisely and well what she was doing; her plot structure was as formal and as obvious as the seating of a dinner-party, but she had a merciless eye for character. She could portray the high life because she had lived it. How pleasing it is that our subtlest observers of British social comedy were (not Henry James, who was terrorized by Society) the Americans Smith and Jones. For don't forget that Mrs. Wharton was née Jones. She remains worth keeping up with.

"Last Novel," *Time*, 26 September 1938, pp. 67–8

Death last year ended Edith Wharton's work on a novel which might have been her masterpiece. She had written 29 chapters of a book apparently planned to run about 35 chapters. The story had reached its climax; the characters were at a moment in their careers when they were compelled to make irrevocable decisions. While Mrs. Wharton left notes suggesting how she intended to end the novel, she gave no hint of how she intended to solve its moral and esthetic problems. Last week her literary executor, Gaillard Lapsley, offered *The Buccaneers* as a novel complete as far

as it went but with its conclusion a puzzle which readers might work out themselves. Because it contains two first-rate characterizations, some sharp social satire, and a tantalizing dilemma at the end, *The Buccaneers* makes far better reading than most novels, finished or unfinished.

The Buccaneers begins in Saratoga in the 1870s, where Mrs. St. George and her husband are watching over their two handsome daughters. Because Colonel St. George, a shady Wall Street speculator, needs the financial assistance of a still shadier Mr. Closson, Mrs. St. George agrees to entertain Mrs. Closson. This brings their girls into friendship with the Clossons' wild daughter, and gets ambitious Mrs. St. George in wrong with the Manhattan dowagers.

Until this point in *The Buccaneers*, 16-year-old Nan St. George has been its heroine. Thereafter she shares the limelight with her governess, a cool, prim, middle-aged Englishwoman named Laura Testvalley. Laura decides that since the girls have no chance in Manhattan, they may succeed in London. Their London triumph is so complete it almost destroys them. Nan becomes the Duchess of Tintagel, discovers that she does not love her husband, falls in love with a young widower, calls her former governess for help. But in the heady sequence of brilliant marriages, Miss Testvalley has also recovered her youth, is making a brilliant marriage herself. At this point *The Buccaneers* breaks off. Mrs. Wharton's notes suggest that the governess was to sacrifice her own future to help Nan escape. That ending, however, would create almost as many difficulties as it would solve.

The best parts of *The Buccaneers* are its glimpses of raucous and pretentious Gilded Age society in New York, where social maneuvers interweave with Wall Street plots and humble wives of new millionaires squat uneasily on upholstered fortunes. Although Editor Gaillard Lapsley compares scenes in *The Buccaneers* to passages in Proust, the comparison only calls attention to Mrs. Wharton's limitations; brilliant chapters like those laid in Saratoga fade out quickly, to be followed by weary passages scarcely superior to the average fiction in women's magazines.

"*The Buccaneers*," *Times Literary Supplement* [England], 8 October 1938, p. 641

This novel, which was during the last few years of Mrs. Wharton's life "the centre of her creative interest and activity," remained at her death unfinished in more than the obvious sense of lacking all but the barest preliminary synopsis to acquaint us with its intended climax. It was her habit as a writer to "move on an irregular front," declares her literary executor, Mr. Gaillard Lapsley, who contributes both prefatory and postscriptive notes, and also includes Mrs. Wharton's own brief (three-page) outline of her story; and so we find some scenes seemingly polished to the last degree, while other episodes or characters are little more than lightly sketched to form a bridge between, or a motive for, this or that other part. One even finds oneself wondering a little who would ultimately have won the undecided race for position as heroine—attractive young Nan St. George, by all worldly standards the most brilliantly successful of her group of American raiders upon the English aristocracy of the 1870's, or Laura Testvalley, her clever, tactful, middle-aged governess.

However, enough was done—some 350 pages—to give one the solid body of this story in which, returning to a familiar Henry Jamesian model and her own earlier backgrounds, Mrs. Wharton depicted the clash of raw American vitality upon an excessively stuffy corner of Victorian high society, the demands of youth and dazzling beauty for a recognition and acceptance denied them in their own country. Both her material and her style—suave, gracious, formal—may savour today of the "old-fashioned," but she could bring her characters singularly alive, make one *care* what came of and to them, and the gentle malice of her observation, the lightness of her treatment, saved her from more than a glancing charge of taking too seriously the social snobberies which formed so much of her material.

Louise Bogan, "The Decoration of Houses," *Nation*, 147 (22 October 1938), 418–19

Mrs. Wharton has told how she was haunted, before the books in which they ultimately appeared were written, by her characters, or, even, by their disembodied names. In her autobiography, *A Backward Glance*, she mentioned a name then in her mind: Laura Testvalley. *The Buccaneers*, Mrs. Wharton's last and unfinished novel, gives Laura Testvalley her scene and character. She is a governess, granddaughter of a hero of the Risorgimento (Gennaro Testvaglia), cousin to Dante Gabriel Rossetti, once employed by a duchess, and later governess in an "old" New York family. She goes on to the higher wages offered by a "new" family (whose money is based on "deals" and financial manipulation); takes the fortunes of the younger daughter in hand and pilots her, over the heads of the disapproving Newport and New York sets, to London, and into a titled marriage. The manuscript breaks off before the novel's denouement: Laura's sacrifice of personal happiness in order that her former pupil, now the ranking duchess of England, may escape from her dull duties and her dull duke into "deep and abiding love" with a lover. The outline left by Mrs. Wharton describes the entire plot very clearly.

It is interesting to see how Henry James's insistence on "form" in the novel was simplified by his friend and follower, Mrs. Wharton, into mere adherence to plot. The plot must proceed, through all its ramifications, even though characters be wrenched out of shape to serve it. Minor figures, put in purely to prop up the plan, soon are shuffled away, and are featureless from the beginning. The long arm of coincidence snaps up the roving actors and places them down neatly in surroundings cleverly arranged to suit their situation. The background is filled in with great color and accuracy; there is continual movement and interest in the action; the details of life in drawing-room, ducal seat, and dower-house, on Saratoga verandas, in a ruined Cornish castle, on American railway platforms, all suitably lighted by the atmosphere of the '70's, are written down by a mistress of genre. But The Buccaneers, for all Mrs. Wharton's cleverness and skill, is dead at the heart. The book brings out, however, the way in which Mrs. Wharton's work formed a bridge from the nineteenth-century novel to the magazine fiction of the present, where in a superficially arranged scene manners, clothes, food and interior decorations are described carefully and at length; how she was, in herself as it were, the whole transitional period of American fiction, beginning in the bibelot and imported-European-culture era of the late nineties, and ending in the woman's-magazine dream of suburban smartness.

The essential numbness in her novels—with the exception of Ethan Frome, where her talent for local color and her insight into the simpler ingredients of human character succeeded, because she did not attempt too much—goes back to the fact that she based her values not upon a free and rich feeling for life but on a feeling for decorum and pre-Wall Street merchant respectability. James praised early in her career "her diabolical little cleverness, the quality of intention and intelligence in her style, and her sharp eye for an interesting kind of subject." Added to these gifts was a highly trained taste, a thorough acquaintance with the "great world" of her time, and a passion for artistic people, provided, of course, that their background and manners conformed to the rather stuffy standards of the late-nineteenth-century upper bourgeoisie. She admired, it should be remembered, not only Henry James but also Paul Bourget. An example of her fundamental bias against the disordered life of the artist is her astonishment when she discovered that George Sand's home, Nohant, showed no sign of the wild life which had streamed through it; it did not look déclassée, but on the contrary traditional and respectable. (The sympathetic attitude expressed in James's two essays on Sand is in strong contrast to Mrs. Wharton's surprise.) And Mrs. Wharton's mildly ironic description of life in great English houses should be put against the true dissection apparent in James's approach to the same subject. For the difference between a subject treated with ingenuity and one treated with imagination, Nan St. George, the "new" rich girl in The Buccaneers, and her family can be set beside Daisy Miller and hers. We love the living people and merely watch the puppets.

Edmund Wilson, "The Revolutionary Governess," *New Republic*, 96 (26 October 1938), 342–3

Edith Wharton had been working on this novel during the last four or five years of her life, but died before she was able to finish it. The first section has a certain brilliance. It is concerned with the children of the *nouveaux riches* at Saratoga during the seventies, when the post–Civil War fortunes were rolling up, and it makes a counterpart to the picture in *The Age of Innocence* of the older well-to-do New Yorkers of this period. It all comes back rather diminished in memory but in lively and charming colors, like a slide in one of those magic lanterns which are mentioned as a contemporary form of entertainment: the pretty girls who are not in society but who get so much attention from the young men, while their parents try to prevent them from running wild, in the atmosphere of the Saratoga race track and the old Grand Union Hotel.

Later, she takes her Americans to London and has the girls make what are regarded by their parents as highly successful marriages with men of the aristocracy and of the rich industrial middle class. But Edith Wharton was never anything like so good when she was dealing with French or English society as she was with the United States; and this part of *The Buccaneers*, even allowing for the fact that a good deal of it was left in the form of an unworked-over first draft, seems banal and perhaps a shade trashy. Also, the mellowness of Mrs. Wharton's later years here as elsewhere dulled the sharpness of her fiction. There are passages in *The Bucca-neers* which read like an old-fashioned story for girls.

Something more interesting appears in her scenario for the unfinished part of the tale. In this last novel, Edith Wharton has more or less reversed the values of her embittered *Custom of the Country*: instead of playing off the culture and tradition of Europe against the vulgar rich Americans, who are insensible to them, she dramatizes the climbing young ladies as a revivifying and air-clearing force. But in the last pages she wrote, she made it plain that the hard-boiled commercial elements which were on the rise in both civilizations, representing fundamentally the same thing, were to understand each other perfectly. In what was to follow, the English governess, who had helped to engineer the success of the Americans and who is the child of Italian revolutionaries and a cousin of Dante Gabriel Rossetti, was to have sacrificed her own hopes of capturing an amateur esthete of the older generation of the nobility by aiding his son to elope with the most interesting of the American girls. Nan St. George has sensibility and generous instincts, but she is married to a dreary English duke, who has confined her in the routine of his castle but who does not understand her interest in trying to improve the living conditions of the tenantry. Her elopement with the only one of the young Englishmen who has any imagination and enterprise was evidently to have represented a triumph of all that was most vital in human feeling and culture, as Mrs. Wharton understood them, over the coldness and decadence of the aristocratic past and the crassness of the commercial present. In order to secure this triumph, Miss Testvalley, the governess, was to have let herself in for spending the rest of her days amid the poverty and dullness of her home, where the old revolution had died.

Miss Testvalley is much the best thing

in the book; and there is a peculiar appropriateness and felicity in the fact that Edith Wharton should have left as the last human symbol of her fiction this figure who embodies the revolutionary principle implicit in all her work. As the light of her art grows dim and goes out before she has finished this last novel, the image still lingers on our retina of the large dark eyes of the clever spinster, who, like her creator, in trading in worldly values, has given a rebuff to the values of the world; in following a destiny solitary and disciplined, has fought a campaign for what, in that generation, would have been called the rights of the heart.

Seán O'Faoláin, "Edith Wharton's Last Novel," *London Mercury*, 39 (November 1938), 88–9

We do not, let us say, know anything about Mrs. Wharton. We pick up a novel called *The Buccaneers*, with a little note saying that it is the last, and not quite finished, novel of a woman who wrote many: there is also an appendix giving her summary of the novel she wished to write. The first paragraph is concisely synoptic: "This novel deals with the adventures of three American families with beautiful daughters who attempt the London social adventure in the 'seventies—the first time the social invasion had ever been tried in England on such a scale." The girls are of parvenu stock, and, as even New York considers them a little loud, Mrs. St. George, one of the three mothers, engages an English governess, Laura Testvalley, who has known some of the best families, to train them. It is she who suggests the daring gamble of the London season. "The three families embark together on the adventure, and, though furiously jealous of each other, are clever enough to see the advantage of backing each other up; and Miss Testvalley leads them like a general."

All goes unexpectedly well in London, where the unaccustomed "naturalness" of the girls proves a great attraction, but Nan St. George, the youngest of all the girls, rebels against the offered prizes. "She is as ambitious as the others, or thinks she is, but it is for more interesting reasons, intellectual, political, and artistic. She is the least beautiful but most seductive of them all." This complication of psychology at once captures our interest; we see that this is not going to be a mere satirical social comedy but something in which spiritual and moral values are involved. Nan is dazzled for the moment, weds a Duke but really loves a poor Officer of the Guards, Guy Thwarte. At this point Guy's father, Sir Helmsley, a widower, is captivated by Miss Testvalley, now referred to in the summary as "the great old adventuress"; in a marginal note on Mrs. Wharton's MS. she is better named "*eine Intrigantin*, but with a great soul"; and the possibilities of the general turning traitor, on finding her October love, is exciting. But Laura Testvalley has too great a soul for her ambitions: she helps the young Duchess of Tintagel to elope with Guy Thwarte—the scandal of the season; enrages his father, who breaks with her; and "goes back alone to old age and poverty."

Nobody who reads such a summary can hesitate a moment in acknowledging that it is a theme which only a real novelist could conceive; it has depth and variety and leaves the stage to the characters; even in summary it peoples the imagination: one can foresee the drama. The idea of beginning to write a novel with several obvious heroines, and then permitting a lesser character to steal the play—"the little brown governess with eyes like torches"—is the mark of a master. One thinks at once of Becky Sharp; and Mrs. Wharton's executor reminds us of the similar case of Gina in *The Charterhouse of Parma*; possibly Jeanie Deans did the same thing with Scott. Only I am certain that Mrs. Wharton knew what was going to happen.

It is a very great pity that she did not live to finish her novel, not merely as to the conclusion but as to a number of bridge-passages, and roughed-out scenes. Four times she wrote the *scène à faire* where the "buccaneers" come face to face with the enemy—Virginia St. George versus Lady Churt, with Lord Seadown as the prize. I do not think it comes off. It is much too explicit, and overt. The mere mechanical business of transferring the Americans to England is done without that minimum of concession to the reader, the absence of which makes for hiatus. And the veracity, the visibility, the penetration of the obviously finished parts is so admirable that the lacunæ are painfully noticeable. Finished or unfinished, *The Buccaneers* is, nevertheless, so real and sincere as to be worth an indeterminable number of completed novels from the generations which ousted Mrs. Wharton from public adoration.

The Age of Innocence came in 1920 as a peak to the long series of successes that began with *The House of Mirth* in 1905. Mrs. Wharton's style reads to-day, in places, almost Ouida-ish; e.g.—"Swans sailed majestically on the silver flood (of the Thames), and boats manned by beautiful bare-armed athletes sped back and forth between the flat, grass banks." I could quote other examples. But what does it matter? Style is a convention, and conventions pass—even realistic conventions will pass. What matters is that her style is always decorous, and suitable, and her feelings are refreshingly positive. Because of that decorum, and decency, and positiveness, is it not more than probable that she will, in time, prove the realists, who are rarely positive and whose best decency is their anger, not to have been so realistic after all?

Checklist of Additional Reviews

Arthur Bernon Tourtellot, "Buccaneers and Snobs," Boston *Evening Transcript*, 24 September 1938, Part 3, p. 1.

L.W., "Mrs. Wharton's Unfinished Novel of Society," Springfield [Massachusetts] *Republican*, 2 October 1938, p. 7-E.

Harold Brighouse, "Two Novels," *Manchester Guardian*, 11 October 1938, p. 7.

"Mrs. Wharton's Unfinished Novel," *Christian Science Monitor*, 26 October 1938, weekly magazine section, p. 12.

"Shorter Notices," *Catholic World*, 148 (December 1938), 369–70.

Index